Total Facilities Management

Third Edition

Brian Atkin PhD, MPhil, BSc, FRICS, FCIOB

Adrian Brooks BSc (Hons), MBA, MRICS

A John Wiley & Sons, Ltd., Publication

First edition published 2000 by Blackwell Science Ltd
Second edition published 2005 by Blackwell
Publishing Ltd
Third edition published 2009 by Blackwell Publishing
Ltd

Library of Congress Cataloging-in-Publication Data

Atkin, Brian.
   Total facilities management / Brian Atkin, Adrian
Brooks. — 3rd ed.
      p. cm.
   Includes bibliographical references and index.
   ISBN 978-1-4051-8659-9 (pbk. : alk. paper)   1. Real
estate management.   2. Facility management.
3. Building management.   I. Brooks, Adrian.   II.
Title.
   HD1394.A86 2009
   658.2—dc22

2009005450

A catalogue record for this book is available from the
British Library.

Set in 10/12 Palatino by Graphicraft Limited,
Hong Kong
Printed in Singapore by Ho Printing Singapore Pte Ltd

5   2013

Contents

Preface to the Third Edition

The rate of facilities management development since the publication of the second edition in 2005 has been such that we felt it necessary to expand our coverage of the subject. New chapters have, therefore, been added and new material has been contributed to other chapters.

As facilities management develops to embrace still wider interests, so too have we brought new topics into the structure of this edition. Social and environmental interests have continued to challenge those with responsibility for our buildings and facilities and these are reflected in this update. Specialist services and information systems have their own chapters, allowing us to examine the diversity of service provision falling under the umbrella of facilities management, and the information and communication technology (ICT) infrastructure required to support it. The connection between facilities management and facilities planning, and related issues of space management, design briefing and real estate management complete our expansion of the subject.

In the course of our professional work, we have been encouraged by the extent to which practitioners have used our work and by the valuable feedback they have provided from their own experiences. Knowing that our advice and information is being put to effective use in the routine practice of facilities management reconfirms our original intention – to make our work accessible to the widest possible readership. Finally, our special thanks go to Dr Robert Wing for his contribution in the area of smart sensors and controls and to Gunnlaugur B. Hjartarson for his work in briefing and information systems.

Brian Atkin   *Adrian Brooks*
Reading   London

Preface to the Second Edition

The first edition of *Total Facilities Management* was, at the time of its publication, the latest phase in a collaboration that had begun five years earlier. This collaboration was illustrative of how serious research into an ill-defined problem can yield not only improved and even new insights, but also how it can provide answers for practitioners who need guidance based on tested theory. The original work was 'a study of value for money in facilities management' in a key area within the public sector in the UK. The study helped us understand how real organisations were coping with issues such as best value, customer satisfaction and the development of the professional discipline of facilities management. From this work, we were able to set out practical guidance which we were pleased to see published by the UK government through the Stationery Office (formerly known as HMSO). The guidance was written for practitioners, not an academic readership, and was well received by the public sector and, to our delight, by many organisations and individuals in the private sector. This reaction was instrumental in taking the decision to draft *Total Facilities Management* as a means for others to access our research findings and practical guidance.

The success of the first edition encouraged us to update and expand the treatment of the subject and to draw in a broader appreciation of how facilities management is practised in parts of the world other than the UK and North America. In this connection, we are especially grateful to Dr Keith Futcher, Managing Director of EastPoint Management Services Limited[1], and his colleagues for providing access to so many examples of best practice facilities management. The location of EastPoint – in Hong Kong – has added a further dimension, one of managing a different organisational culture and context to that found in the UK and North America. What is also interesting about EastPoint is that it has taken and applied, tested and refined, many model practices and procedures. This has allowed us, as authors, to establish this broader international appreciation and to enable readers to access material from a market leader.

We are also grateful to several organisations in the UK that have helped us deepen our treatment of a number of issues which we introduced into the first edition. Important changes have taken place in the UK during the past five years and these are reflected in an expansion of our concern for human resources management, change management, workplace productivity

---

[1] Now ISS EastPoint Facility Services Limited.

and the dramatic growth in public–private partnerships. Particular thanks go to Karen Gunther of Sun Life of Canada (UK) Limited, a prominent life assurance and pensions provider, and Ruth Saunders of Diageo plc, one of the world's leading premium drinks businesses, for allowing us to incorporate case studies of their in-house activities. Finally, we should like to thank Dr Roine Leiringer for his input on public–private partnerships, drawing as it does from his doctoral research in this area.

We trust this second edition of *Total Facilities Management* will go some way towards satisfying a market need for balanced guidance based on best practice underpinned by robust theory. If it does, it will demonstrate the important connection between research and practice, as well as offering something for everyone with a professional interest in facilities management.

Brian Atkin   *Adrian Brooks*
Reading   London

Introduction

Managing non-core business services enables an organisation to function at its most efficient and effective level. Implicit in this management role are the issues of customer satisfaction and best value. The focus for these issues is facilities management, which has traditionally been seen as the poor relation of the main real estate and construction disciplines. The significance of facilities management is now recognised and this book offers a progressive look at how facilities management applies to organisations of all kinds. The book contains many examples of how facilities can be better managed; these are largely derived from practices known to work well, although the approach is not intended to be prescriptive.

The organisation

This book is directed at organisations within both the public and private sectors. The types of organisation addressed might therefore range from colleges to entertainment companies, from manufacturers to airport operators. The structure, management and accommodation of these organisations will vary widely; nevertheless, the information contained in this book is intended to have a correspondingly wide application. It is necessary, of course, for each organisation to consider the relevance to itself, its sector and its country of each of the points raised. Thus, where specific public sector regulations, or UK and European legislation, are referred to, it is the principles embodied within that legislation that should be noted if the legislation itself is not directly applicable.

The customer

In the broadest sense, the customer is the client organisation acting as a purchaser of services. These will sometimes be procured in-house and sometimes from external providers. Although the distinction between purchaser and provider is more obvious in the case of external provision, it is important that the same distinction is recognised within in-house provision. The customer in this instance might be an internal department being served by the organisation's facilities management team, with a financial exchange between the two different cost centres. The relationship between the two parties therefore remains a formal one requiring guidelines and procedures for its formulation and implementation.

In most organisations, customers will therefore be the organisation's employees and constituent departments, as the principal facility users. In some, such as leisure centres or department stores, the external user of the organisation's facilities becomes an additional type of customer whose needs must be considered within facilities planning and operations. This book generally refers to the former type of customer (internal user), with these users typically providing the interface between the external user and facilities management service providers.

Abbreviations

AEC	architecture, engineering and construction
ANSI	American National Standards Institute
ASHRAE	American Society of Heating, Refrigerating and Air-Conditioning Engineers
B2B	business to business
B2C	business to consumer
BIFM	British Institute of Facilities Management
BIM	building information model or modelling
BOT	build-operate-transfer
BPR	business process re-engineering
BREEAM	Building Research Establishment Environmental Assessment Method
CAFM	computer-aided facilities management
CCT	compulsory competitive tendering
CCTV	closed circuit television
CDM	Construction (Design and Management) Regulations 2007
CIOB	Chartered Institute of Building
CIPS	Chartered Institute of Purchasing and Supply
COSHH	Control of Substances Hazardous to Health Regulations 2002
CPD	continuing (or continuous) professional development
CSF	critical success factor
CSR	corporate social responsibility
DBFO	design, build, finance and operate
EBITDA	earnings before interest, taxes, depreciation and amortisation
EC	European Commission
EDI	electronic data interchange
EU	European Union
EVA	earned value added
FM	facilities management
GIS	geographic information system
GPS	global positioning system
HRM	human resources management
HSE	Health and Safety Executive
HVAC	heating, ventilating and air-conditioning
IAI	International Alliance for Interoperability
ICF	informed (or intelligent) client function
ICT	information and communication technology
IFC	industry foundation class or classes

IFMA	International Facility Management Association
ISO	International Organization for Standardization
JCT	Joint Contracts Tribunal
KPI	key performance indicator
LAN	local area network
M&E	mechanical and electrical
NEBOSH	National Examinations Board in Occupational Safety and Health
OJEU	Official Journal of the European Union
PACE	Property Advisers to the Civil Estate
PDA	personal digital assistant
PES	project execution strategy
PEST	political, economic, social and technological
PFI	private finance initiative
PPE	personal protective equipment
PPM	planned preventive maintenance
PPP	public–private partnership
QA	quality assurance
RFID	radio frequency identification
RIDDOR	Reporting of Injuries, Diseases and Dangerous Occurrences Regulations 1995
SBS	sick building syndrome
SLA	service level agreement
SME	small and medium sized enterprises
SQL	structured query language
SWOT	strengths, weaknesses, opportunities and threats
TFM	total facilities management
TUPE	Transfer of Undertakings (Protection of Employment) Regulations 2006
VR	virtual reality

1 Background to Facilities Management

Key issues

The following issues are covered in this chapter.

- There are a number of definitions of facilities management. One that is commonly used is 'an integrated approach to operating, maintaining, improving and adapting the buildings and infrastructure of an organisation in order to create an environment that strongly supports the primary objectives of that organisation'.

- In any discussion of facilities management it is, however, necessary to stress the importance of integrative, interdependent disciplines whose overall purpose is to support an organisation in the pursuit of its (business) objectives.

- The proper application of facilities management techniques enables organisations to provide the right environment for conducting their core business on a cost-effective and best value basis.

- If buildings and other facilities are not managed, they can begin to impact upon an organisation's performance. Conversely, buildings and facilities have the potential to enhance performance by contributing towards the provision of the optimum working and business environment.

- In practice, facilities management can cover a wide range of services including real estate management, financial management, change management, human resources management, health and safety and contract management, in addition to building maintenance, domestic services (such as cleaning and catering) and utilities supplies.

- There is no universal approach to managing facilities. Each organisation – even within the same sector – will have different needs. Understanding those needs is the key to effective facilities management measured in terms of providing best value.

- Quality of service or performance is a critical factor in any definition of value, and the relationship between quality and cost or price has to be properly understood in this respect.

- Cost savings cannot be looked at in isolation from value. Organisations must be able to demonstrate what they are getting for their money and should not assume that paying less today is proof of better value for money.

- The many risks involved in the search for best value should be recognised and transferred to those who are able to manage them effectively. This means that organisations should examine all options carefully and adopt those that are most likely to achieve best value.

Origin

As recently as forty years ago there was only fleeting mention of facilities management. Buildings were maintained, serviced and cleaned: that was largely it. A united concept was far from broad acceptance in the real estate (or property management) sector. Few common procedures were in circulation and it was left to innovative organisations – many of them in the fast-growing banking, telecommunications and media sectors – to devise ways of effectively managing their buildings and burgeoning portfolios. Since then facilities management has not only emerged as a service sector in its own right, it has helped to establish a new professional discipline with its own codes, standards and technical vocabulary.

Rationale for facilities management

This introductory chapter sets the scene, by discussing the importance of facilities to an organisation (acting as client) and how approaches to facilities management can differ between organisations, even within the same sector. There is no single formulation of facilities management that will fit all situations. Nonetheless, the concept of the informed client function is common to all situations and is described and discussed in this chapter. It is a theme that runs throughout this book, reflecting a deliberate focus on the client organisation, its values, culture and needs. The reader is introduced to the necessity of securing best value in the provision of services and is acquainted with some of the attendant risks – more are to be found listed in the appendices. The context for facilities management is first described and an overview follows in the form of a simple functional model. This is developed in the text to show the distinction between core and non-core business – something that is essential to understanding the correct focus for facilities management.

Most buildings represent substantial investments for organisations and usually have to accommodate and support a range of activities, taking into account competing needs. Within those activities is the organisation's core business, for which an appropriate environment must be created in buildings that may not have been designed for the purposes for which they are now used. Yet, no matter how well focused an organisation might be on its core business, it cannot lose sight of the supporting services – the non-core business. The relationship between the two is shown in Fig. 1.1.

Organisations may have already considered the distinction between their core business and non-core business (such as security, payroll or cleaning) as part of the drive to deliver customer satisfaction and achieve best value.

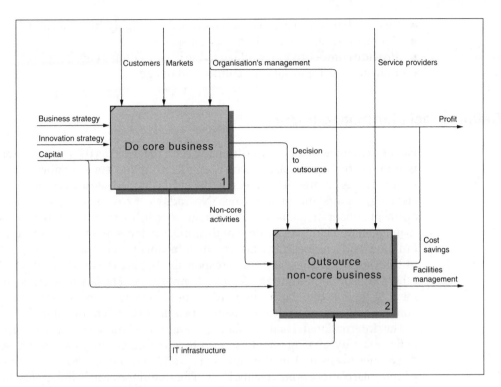

Fig. 1.1   Basic relationship between core and non-core business.

Since running costs account for a significant part of annual expenditure, there is bound to be pressure to look for savings in non-core business areas. Cutting operating budgets can be financially expedient, but may not favour the organisation's long-term development. Since the running of an organisation involves complex, coordinated processes and activities, it is necessary to take an integrated view. A piecemeal approach to cutting costs is unlikely to produce the required savings and may impair the organisation's ability to deliver high-quality services. For this and other reasons, we can begin to see why facilities management is a more powerful concept than real estate (or property) management, because it takes a holistic view of the dynamics of the workplace – between people and processes and between people and their environment.

Facilities management can therefore be summarised as creating an environment that is conducive to carrying out the organisation's primary operations, taking an integrated view of the services infrastructure, and using this to deliver customer satisfaction and best value through support for and enhancement of the core business. We can develop this definition to describe facilities management as something that will:

- Support people in their work and in other activities.
- Enhance individual well-being.
- Enable the organisation to deliver effective and responsive services.

- Sweat the physical assets, that is, make them highly cost-effective.
- Allow for future change in the use of space.
- Provide competitive advantage to the organisation's core business.
- Enhance the organisation's culture and image.

Defining facilities management

Facilities management has traditionally been regarded as the poor relation within the real estate, architecture, engineering and construction (AEC) sector. This is because it was seen in the old-fashioned sense of caretaking, cleaning, repairs and maintenance. Nowadays, it covers real estate management, financial management, change management, human resources management, health and safety and contract management, in addition to building and engineering services maintenance, domestic services and utilities supplies. These last three responsibilities are the most visible. The others are subtler, although of no less importance. For facilities management to be effective, both the 'hard' issues, such as financial regulation, and the 'soft' issues, such as managing people, have to be considered.

The International Facility Management Association (www.ifma.org) defines facility[1] management as 'a profession that encompasses multiple disciplines to ensure functionality of the built environment by integrating people, place, process and technology'. This definition clearly illustrates the holistic nature of the discipline and interdependence of multiple factors in its success. Elsewhere, the British Institute of Facilities Management (www.bifm.org.uk) promotes the development of facilities management as a critical, professional and strategic business discipline.

An oft-cited definition of facilities management is provided by Barrett and Baldry (2003) who see it as 'an integrated approach to operating, maintaining, improving and adapting the buildings and infrastructure of an organisation in order to create an environment that strongly supports the primary objectives of that organisation'. They continue by reminding us that 'the breadth and scope of facilities management are not constrained by the physical characteristics of buildings. For many organisations the effectiveness and behaviour patterns of the workforce and the effectiveness of their information technology and communication systems are of considerable importance and the profession of facilities management continues to evolve to reflect this.' Whatever is adopted as a definition, either in this book or by practitioners communicating with their clients and customers, it should stress the importance of integrative, interdependent disciplines whose overall purpose is to support an organisation in the pursuit of its (business) objectives.

---

[1] The word 'facility' is used instead of 'facilities' in some parts of the world. Whilst the authors appreciate the distinction that other authors and authorities might attach to the former, we consider such distinction largely a matter of individual preference.

Approaches to facilities management

Organisations may not be aware of the extent to which value for money in facilities management can be improved – the search for best value. This suggests that it is not the outcome that needs to be scrutinised, but the decision-making that leads to it and the assumptions upon which it is based – see Fig. 1.2.

There are common themes and approaches to facilities management, regardless of the size and location of buildings, although these may not necessarily result in common solutions to problems. In some cases, estates-related and facilities services are contracted out – a form of outsourcing – and in others retained in-house for good reasons in each case. There are also many organisations that operate what might be described as a mixed economy, where some services, even the same services, are partially outsourced as well as being retained in-house. Whichever course of action has been taken, the primary concern is the basis for the decision. Where the organisation's decision has been arrived at for entirely proper reasons, such as demonstrating better value for money from one approach as opposed to the other, facilities management can be regarded as working effectively.

Informed client function

Organisations need to act as informed or 'intelligent' clients if they are to be sure of delivering customer satisfaction and achieving best value. The informed (or intelligent) client function (ICF) is a requisite irrespective of how facilities are procured. The following outlines the scope of the ICF.

- Understanding the organisation, its culture, its customers and needs.
- Understanding and specifying service requirements and targets.
- Brokering the service amongst stakeholders.
- Managing the implementation of outsourcing.
- Minimising risk to the organisation's future – risk management.
- Agreeing monitoring standards.
- Managing contractors and monitoring their performance.
- Benchmarking performance of service(s).
- Surveying users for satisfaction with the service.
- Providing relevant management reports to users.
- Reviewing service levels/requirements to ensure they still meet user needs.
- Developing, with service providers, delivery strategies for services.
- Agreeing, with service providers, changes to service requirements.
- Maintaining the ability to re-tender, as and when required.
- Understanding the facilities management market and how it is developing.
- Undertaking strategic planning.
- Safeguarding public funds, where relevant.
- Developing in-house skills through education, training and continuing professional development (CPD).

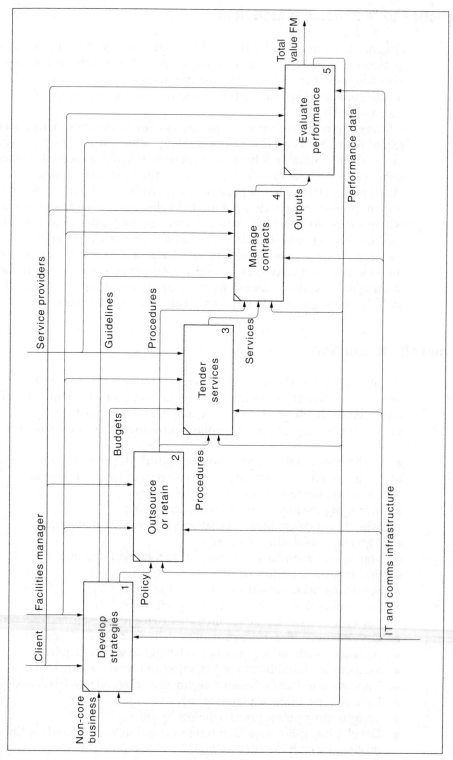

Fig. 1.2   Overview of the top-level functions within facilities management.

Concept of best value

Value for money is a term long used to express satisfaction with the cost of a good or service of given quality. The term 'best value' extends the concept of value for money to imply a need to strive continually for something superior at the lowest practicable cost.

The 'best value decision' is generally cited as the determinant of whether to outsource a service or to retain it in-house. Despite this, many organisations are likely to be unaware of the extent to which they can improve value for money. Value is about the relationship between cost or price, and quality or performance. However, value for money is often simply equated with achieving a reduction in cost. Organisations may believe they are achieving value for money if they are paying less for a given service this year compared with the previous year. Whereas cost is easier to measure, value for money is concerned with quality of a service and the economy, efficiency and effectiveness with which it is delivered. Organisations should therefore set themselves cost and quality objectives for the management of their facilities, the cost objective only taking priority where financial constraints are severe.

When choosing options for service provision and service providers, organisations therefore need to include an assessment not only of cost implications but also of quality (see Chapter 7 for cost and quality evaluation and the cost/quality mechanism). They should choose the approach and service provision that offer best value, not simply lowest cost, and measure performance against both cost and quality. Benchmarking can help in checking performance (see Chapter 18).

Normally, the achievement of best value is demonstrated by acceptance of the lowest tender price in a competition where all other criteria (quality, performance, terms and conditions) are equal. Best value can also be achieved through collaborative arrangements with suppliers and service providers. Economies of scale offered by bulk purchasing of utility supplies – see below and Chapter 14 – are an obvious example. An additional benefit from collaboration is that risks are also shared.

Supplier relationships

There are a number of options open to organisations beyond simply entering into a price competition each time a new supply or service is required or a contract is renewed. For instance, collaboration with other organisations can often enable more favourable terms to be leveraged from suppliers, because negotiation and procurement powers are improved. In fact, there is a wide range of possible relationships from which to choose the one(s) that fit the requirements of the (client) organisation.

At one end of the scale, both client organisation and supplier may be concerned primarily with optimising their immediate interests without making long-term commitments. Such relationships are typical of many commodity markets. At the other end, both parties may look for a long-term, cooperative partnership. The type of relationship that will produce the greatest benefits will depend upon circumstances such as the nature of the market and the demands of the service to be provided. Choosing the right relationship with suppliers and managing it well requires skill, judgement and experience.

The best contribution that organisations can make to the raising of supplier competitiveness is to manage their own procurement intelligently. An important element of this will be to combine competition and cooperation to optimal effect. Mutually satisfactory relationships between buyers and sellers are fundamental to successful procurement activity. Yet, whatever the chosen relationship with suppliers, organisations should avoid taking an adversarial or unaccommodating approach. Relationships should be as open and supportive as possible – given the need to maintain competition and to treat suppliers even-handedly – and should be based on mutual respect. Organisations should recognise that it is in their interests to help suppliers develop in ways that make them better able to provide what is required by the organisation and to do so to the desired quality and at a competitive price. The relationship should be one that encourages continual improvement.

Sourcing services based on partnering or partnership has become a popular (even established) basis for relationships with suppliers. Partnering is another type of arrangement for procuring services that offers the chance to develop a strong relationship with a service provider who can ensure that best value is achieved whilst risks are better managed at the same time. Customers and suppliers decide to collaborate closely in order to deliver requirements such as cost reduction, improved quality or innovative solutions, rather than to conduct their business at arm's length. Essentially, partnering is acceptable in terms of accountability – particularly important in the public sector – if the following apply:

1. There is competition at the outset in the choice of partners and periodic re-competition.
2. The partnering arrangement is established on the basis of clearly defined needs and objectives over a specified period.
3. There are specific and measurable milestones for improved performance as part of the contract in order to demonstrate, through the use of benchmarking (see Chapter 18), that best value is being achieved.

Partnering is likely to bring greater benefits than other approaches in certain circumstances, for example, where there is a poorly developed or highly specialised market or where the requirements of the purchaser are complex and continuously developing. Purchasing (or procurement) managers should consider carefully whether or not a partnering arrangement would best suit the needs of their organisation in each particular case – see Chapter 14 for further discussion of partnering.

Matters of risk

In managing any organisation, there are innumerable risks involved in meeting business objectives. These risks have the potential to hinder, even negate, attempts at achieving best value. Table 1.1 indicates some risks that

Table 1.1   Risks faced by organisations in their facilities management.

1. Inadequately resourced or inexperienced client function (Chapters 1, 2, 17, 19 and Appendix B).

2. Inadequate planning of the implementation – no analysis of implementation or allocation of related responsibilities (Chapters 2, 4, 6, 7, 8, 17 and Appendix D).

3. Misapplication of Transfer of Undertakings (Protection of Employment) Regulations 2006 (TUPE) (Chapter 6).

4. Poor relationship between service provider and contract manager (especially if the latter was once involved with preparing an in-house tender) (Chapters 7 and 17).

5. Conflicts of interest when dealing with in-house tenders, arising from inadequate split between purchaser and provider personnel (Chapters 7 and 8).

6. Unclear or imprecise roles, responsibilities and targets for effective teamworking (Chapters 4, 6, 7, 8 and 17).

7. Possible loss of control over the facilities management function and ownership of, and access to, documents and knowledge (Chapter 7).

8. Lack of standard forms of facilities management contracts or inadequate conditions of contract (Chapter 7).

9. Inappropriate allocation of risks and rewards between the client organisation and service providers (Chapters 7, 8 and 19).

10. Inadequate definition of the scope and content of services (Chapter 9).

11. Lack of consideration of all stakeholders in the facilities management sphere (Chapter 9).

12. Specifications that are overprescriptive and/or concentrate on procedures not outputs (Chapter 9).

13. Stakeholders 'gold plating' their requirements (Chapter 9).

14. Poorly controlled changes to user requirements (Chapters 9 and 17).

15. Excessive monitoring of contractor performance (Chapter 9).

16. Absence of, or poor system for, providing incentives for performance (Chapter 9).

17. Inflexible contracts unable to accommodate changes in user requirements during the contract and work outside specification (Chapter 9).

18. Failure to take account of relevant health and safety legislation at the correct time, leading to excessive cost later (Chapter 10).

19. Redundancy in the supply chain where cost is added without necessarily adding value (Chapter 14).

20. Poor bundling/grouping of activities to be outsourced (Chapter 13).

21. Absence of shared ownership of outcomes (Chapter 14).

Table 1.1   Cont'd.

22. Poor cashflow position for client organisation and for service providers (Chapter 17).
23. Financial failure of chosen service provider during contract period (Chapter 17).
24. Absence of benchmarks of cost and quality against which to measure performance and improvement (Chapter 18).
25. Lack of education and training in facilities management (Chapter 20).
26. Fraud or irregularities in the award and management of contracts (Appendix B).

organisations face in their facilities management. The relevant chapters of this book, in which the underlying issues are considered, are indicated in the table. Some of these risks may be easier to address than others. In certain cases, organisations will need to acquire new skills or insights into how problems can be tackled.

In pursuing more efficient and effective facilities management, organisations should also be aware of the opportunities that stem from a greater awareness of potential risks. To a large extent, the opportunities mirror the risks and counter their influence, as Table 1.2 shows.

Table 1.2   Opportunities arising from a greater awareness of potential risks.

1.   Enhancing client capability and quality of provision, and proper assessment of requirements for the scope and content of services (Chapters 4 and 6).
2.   Identification and allocation of risks on a rational basis to help clarify relationships between contractors and facilities managers (Chapters 4, 7 and 13).
3.   Proper separation of duties between purchasers and providers (Chapters 4, 7 and 8).
4.   Clear responsibilities and targets for effective teamworking (Chapter 6).
5.   Proper contract documentation with appropriate conditions of contract for both in-house and outsourced services (Chapters 7 and 17).
6.   Proper allocation of risks and rewards (Chapter 4).
7.   Improved response to customer and market requirements (Chapters 2 and 4).
8.   Improved performance with proper incentivisation (Chapters 7, 8, 14 and 17).
9.   Health and safety legislation incorporated into facilities management policies at the appropriate time (Chapter 10).
10. Shared ownership of outcomes (Chapters 7 and 8).
11. Proper monitoring of contract performance (Chapters 7, 8 and 17).
12. Improved cashflow forecasting and budgeting (Chapters 2 and 4).
13. Opportunity to build up quality and cost benchmarks against which to measure performance and improvements (Chapter 18).
14. Properly focused education and training for in-house personnel in facilities management matters (Chapters 6, 8 and 20).
15. Proper assessment of activities to be grouped/bundled for outsourcing (Chapters 7 and 9).
16. Efficiency gains enabling resources to be released for the improvement or expansion of core-business provision (Chapter 2).

Conclusions

Facilities management is about providing support to an organisation's core business. To benefit most, organisations need to understand that they must be informed clients in managing their facilities. This requires a focus on service delivery that provides customer satisfaction and best value in an environment in which risks abound. Effective facilities management comes from being able to devise and implement practices that reduce or eliminate the risks and that add value to the core business.

CHECKLIST

This checklist is intended to assist with the review and action planning process.

		Yes	No	Action required
1.	Does facilities management have a sufficiently high profile in the organisation, i.e. is it connected to the business objectives of the organisation?	☐	☐	☐
2.	Has senior management articulated a workable definition of facilities management?	☐	☐	☐
3.	Could the organisation be considered an informed client?	☐	☐	☐
4.	Is the organisation able to determine whether or not it is achieving best value in relation to its facilities management services, however provided?	☐	☐	☐
5.	Are relationships with suppliers considered on a needs basis or is a blanket approach to procurement adopted?	☐	☐	☐
6.	Has the organisation undertaken a formal risk assessment of its facilities management and then implemented a risk response method?	☐	☐	☐

2 Developing a Strategy for Facilities Management

Key issues

The following issues are covered in this chapter.

- The development of a facilities management strategy is a project in its own right and must be undertaken rigorously using appropriate techniques and tools. The organisation should follow three stages – analysis, solution and implementation – to produce an effective strategy for the management of its facilities:
  - o *Analysis* – all relevant facts are assembled, including the organisation's objectives, needs and policies, a review of resources, processes, systems and the physical assets, together with their attributes in terms of space, function and utilisation.
  - o *Solution* – criteria for judging options are defined and evaluated against the objectives of the organisation to produce the facilities management strategy.
  - o *Implementation* – this completes the strategic planning and development process through the establishment of an implementation plan that incorporates the key elements of procurement, mobilisation, training, communication, review and feedback.

- On completion, the facilities management strategy should become an integral part of the organisation's strategic and operating plans. The facilities management strategy document should incorporate:
  - o Financial objectives
  - o Goals and critical success factors (in terms of quality, cost and time objectives)
  - o Targets for potential efficiency gains and quality improvements
  - o Customer requirement
  - o Technical issues
  - o In-house/outsourcing strategy
  - o Procurement strategy
  - o Human resources plan
  - o Business processes
  - o Methodology for managing change
  - o Information and communication technology (ICT) strategy.

- The organisation needs to see its facilities management strategy as the cornerstone of its accommodation (or space) strategy, not as an adjunct to it.

- Facilities management needs to encompass a diverse range of issues that impinge on the success of the organisation's core business. As such it will have to base much of its decision-making on the expectation that change is a constant feature of the workplace today and into the future.

- The rise in the use of ICT and the integration of other forms of technology into buildings – especially 'smart' sensors and controls – imply that facilities management strategies must be tied directly to the organisation's ICT strategy, as well as its business strategy.

Introduction

There are basically two ways of looking at the management of facilities. The first is to consider what must be done to maintain current services or even to improve upon them – a largely short-term perspective. The second adopts a longer-term view that takes into account the potential changes likely to be faced by the organisation into the future and how these will impact upon the services required. Clearly, a desire to improve current service provision is not wrong, but does overlook the inevitability of change occurring and perhaps invalidating earlier decisions. Facilities and the demands placed upon them are unlikely to remain static in all but the most stable of organisations, which is why an approach must be devised to manage the process of moving from where the organisation is today to where it wishes to be at some point in the future. In other words, a strategy is employed to deal with a dynamic situation in which major business decisions – perhaps affecting the very viability of the organisation – are connected with the organisation's existing facilities provision and forecast requirements. The approach is implicitly top-down, otherwise current operations would be effectively dictating the organisation's business development – a sure route to failure.

The starting point for managing the facilities is, therefore, the organisation's business plan together with its accommodation (or space) strategy. Combined, they embody the goals of the organisation and make clear what is needed to support the organisation's development. Naturally, these key documents should be kept up to date so they are always available for assessing the nature and level of services support required by the organisation. This chapter reviews the approach to developing a strategy for facilities management that will reflect the organisation's business objectives, needs and policies, as well as the practicalities imposed by its accommodation (or space). It will consider the successive stages in the process and reveal that a wide range of techniques and tools are at the disposal of managers to help them in their work. In this respect, the approach is one of applying accepted theories of strategic business planning and development to the facilities management 'problem'.

Developing a facilities management strategy

In order to manage facilities efficiently and effectively, robust strategies must be developed within the context of the organisation's strategic business plan and accommodation (or space) strategy. These should include development of strategic objectives and a business plan for the facilities management function, with proper reference to the organisation's business plan and accommodation strategy in which it might be contained. A business plan for facilities management should have the following goals.

- Consider the needs of the organisation, differentiating between core and non-core business activities.
- Identify and establish effective and manageable processes for meeting those needs.
- Establish the appropriate resource needs for providing services, whether obtained internally or externally.
- Identify the source of funds to finance the strategy and its implications.
- Establish a budget, not only for the short term, but also to achieve best value over the longer term.
- Recognise that management of information is the key to providing a basis for effective control of facilities management.

This process of developing a facilities management strategy is illustrated in Fig. 2.1 and shows three main stages with their contributory elements. The three main stages in the development of a strategy are:

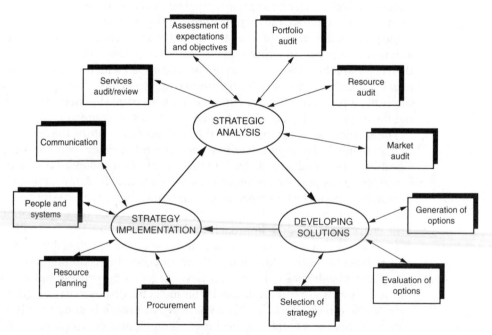

Fig. 2.1   Process of developing a facilities management strategy.

1. Strategic analysis
2. Developing solutions
3. Strategy implementation.

Table 2.1 presents possible management techniques and tools that are available.

Strategic analysis of facilities requirements

The aim of the analysis is to establish a thorough understanding of the present state of the organisation's real estate and its approach to facilities management. This means assembling all relevant facts including:

- Organisational objectives, needs and policies (from the organisation's business plan).
- Physical assets and space utilisation achieved (from the organisation's accommodation (or space) strategy).
- Review of resources, processes and systems to provide a broad picture of the current provision of services.
- Detailed breakdown of costs involved in the form of a cost analysis.

Services audit and review

The organisation should be in the position of having already identified and differentiated between its core and non-core business activities. This differentiation is necessary to ensure that effort can be concentrated where it is needed most, that is in developing the best working and business environment. General examples of non-core business activities, in addition to those mentioned in Chapter 1, are catering, printing, vehicle maintenance and conference facilities. Important in this respect is to appreciate that since no two organisations are the same, there is the likelihood of some organisations (of an apparently similar nature) regarding certain activities as core business, whilst others would class the same activities as non-core. It is not for the authors to say which activities are core and which are non-core business. These are matters for the senior management of the organisation and, in most instances, are likely to be decisions upon which the future of the organisation is predicated.

The organisation should critically review the operation of services provided by considering:

- *Policy* – examining existing policies in terms of corporate guidelines and standards, performance standards, quality assurance, health and safety and other statutory requirements, human resources, financial and other approvals.
- *Processes and procedures* – defining business processes, including budgeting, procurement, purchasing approvals and payments.

Table 2.1   Techniques and tools to support development of a facilities management strategy.

Development stage	Phase	Technique or tool
Strategic analysis	Services audit/review	Benchmarking
	Assessment of expectations and objectives	Political, economic, social and technological (PEST) analysis Strengths, weaknesses, opportunities and threats (SWOT) analysis If . . . then analysis Mega trends Quantitative analysis Scenario analysis
	Portfolio audit	Space analysis Real estate register Maintenance plan Risk assessment
	Resource audit	People and skills profiling Service provider audit (existing internal arrangements) Business process analysis
	Market audit	Service providers (external) Real estate availability Market trends
Developing solutions	Generating options	Outsource modelling Business process re-engineering (BPR)
	Evaluating options	Maintenance plan Risk analysis Stakeholder analysis Cost–benefit analysis Life-cycle cost appraisal Feasibility analysis
	Selecting option	Optimisation model Sensitivity analysis
Strategy implementation	People and systems	Change management Training and personnel development Business process re-engineering (BPR)
	Communication	Organisation's intranet Newsletters, noticeboards and memoranda Workshops and seminars
	Resource planning	Project planning, scheduling and control Resource levelling/optimisation
	Procurement/purchasing	Service provider selection Market testing Benchmarking

- *Service delivery* – auditing all aspects of the real estate and facilities management strategy and service delivery, including relationships with customers (especially quality, cost and time objectives).

In carrying out a review of the above aspects, the organisation should make use of benchmarking (see Chapter 18) as a method or tool for measuring current levels of performance and achievement. Measuring a process is also an aid to understanding it, as well as offering valuable insights into how it might be improved.

Assessment of expectations and objectives

The organisation should be able to define its expectations and objectives for its facilities with relative ease. For instance, it might aspire to expand its core business into areas for which different kinds of facilities and services will be required to those currently provided. It would be useful, therefore, to broaden discussion to identify potential extensions and additions, as well as noting where closure of business operations is necessary or likely. These objectives should be embodied in a formal statement as part of the organisation's overall mission statement, or linked to it, and should relate to needs identified in the business plan.

Portfolio audit

Implicit in an audit of real estate and related assets is consideration of the necessity for and provision of support services, maintenance plan(s) and an assessment of risks. The organisation also needs to consider its space utilisation and procedures for charging for the use of space. In itself, this kind of auditing can succeed in raising awareness of how space is being used and how economical that use is. However, there is the danger that perceptions of space utilisation will vary within the organisation and across regions, with the result that what is regarded in one location as the norm is seen either as extravagant or inadequate by those elsewhere.

Organisations operating across regions – for example Scandinavia and the UK – are bound to notice differences in the allocation of space per worker. The same company operating in Stockholm and London would likely record quite different figures for space allocation. British workers, because of their acceptance of higher densities, would see their Swedish counterparts as having generous, even too much, space; the Swedes would disagree. Climate and culture can have a significant influence on the amount and quality of space expected by workers. Attempts to normalise standards across regions is likely to prove counterproductive. With the emergence of large regional markets – even global markets – problems can so easily arise from cultural differences, and local customs and practice. Understanding that there are going to be differences – and that such a situation is normal – is a way to avoid problems.

Space is rarely provided freely, even if present use suggests otherwise. An evaluation of the true cost of providing space, that is, the cost of providing support services, must always form part of any assessment. This will help to establish which spaces are providing best value and which are not. In this connection, it is necessary to look at the value (to the organisation) of activities against the cost of locating them. For example, it would make little economic sense to house a printing press – no matter how convenient it is – in prime real estate that attracts a premium rent. In such a case, relocation should be actively considered. See Chapter 3 for a discussion of space management.

Practice Point 2.1   Spaced out.

Key point: the organisation must have an up-to-date picture of its use of space and the extent to which it is satisfying customer needs.

When a health care facility decided to audit its use of space and establish a basis for charging, some departments expressed concern. In one case, a department felt that it was paying far too much for the space it had and was determined to seek a reduction. In another case, the department was complaining that its rooms were overcrowded and lacked certain amenities. Worse, it might have to restrict the number of patients it could see, which would lead to longer waiting lists. The case was strengthened by the department's threat to go public on the length of its waiting list and the associated risks to proper medical care and attention. These matters were resolved only after management was able to make an informed decision based on an up-to-date statement of the use of space, the need for space and the availability and cost of space elsewhere. The subsequent circulation of a space plan and analysis helped to make everyone aware of who had what, as well as helping to pinpoint priority needs for changes to space allocation.

Resource audit

Part of this top-level analysis should include a review of personnel employed in the provision of facilities and support services. This will, of necessity, cover both in-house and contracted out (outsourced) arrangements. The organisation should also review the extent of available human resources, information about which should be available from its human resources planning (see Chapter 6). Additionally, the organisation must analyse the processes that are contained within its facilities to determine, amongst other things, patterns of use, areas of intensive use and areas of under-use. Methods for determining these factors are increasingly supported by ICT, but should always be based on *good* science and ethical practice. Many organisations now routinely survey their facilities using CCTV for reasons of security, and general health and safety. When used for the right motives, this kind of technology can provide proof of a particular need or the lack of it.

The resource audit should concentrate on:

- *People* – determine skills profiles and identify gaps.
- *Providers* – assess capability, scope and terms of engagement.
- *Systems* – establish the status of all procedures and technology by process analysis and systems audit.

Market audit

The organisation should consider undertaking periodic audits to establish the state of the real estate market (should acquisition or disposal become an option) and the position regarding service providers (see Chapter 13) in all the categories affected. It is possible this kind of information will be available from market audits carried out when preparing the accommodation (or space) strategy and from the valuation of assets for financial accounting purposes.

Developing solutions

Once information from the analysis stage has been assembled, a robust and structured approach to the interpretation of the information must be adopted. It is essential that the interpretation of information derived from the analysis is open, without bias and allows new ideas and innovative solutions to flow. The recommended approach is:

- Generation of options
- Assembly of criteria for evaluating options
- Evaluation of options
- Selection of preferred option, that is, the organisation's actual facilities management strategy.

Generation of options

There are many ways in which organisations can establish options, for example, consultation with stakeholders and invitations to external experts. The strategic analysis stage should have highlighted precisely how well the organisation's accommodation or space and other attributes of its facilities match up to its needs. This means that options should be considered for bridging identified gaps as well as for aligning innovative solutions with present and future needs. Creativity is a useful commodity to have at this stage and should even extend to 'thinking the unthinkable'. Important also is the need to avoid prejudging the merits of any option as this runs the risk of corrupting the process: evaluation should be left until later. If an option proves unworthy then that will become evident later, so little purpose is served here in trying to complicate matters.

Criteria for evaluating options

Before any attempt is made to consider the relative merits of options, it is essential to identify and agree the criteria for judging them. Moreover, there needs to be a very clear separation between the assembly of criteria and their application to options to ensure objectivity. All criteria must, however, include assessments of best value and likely customer satisfaction. Options should be evaluated consistently against the set criteria to ensure objectivity, parity and accountability. Criteria should therefore be explicit and open to review. Sometimes the options will not be mutually exclusive and, on occasion, senior managers may find that a combination of two or more, or a variation in one, provides a better way forward. If this does happen, it may be evidence of a failure in the 'generation of options' stage and worth noting for future occasions.

Selection of the preferred option(s)

In many respects, this is a fairly straightforward matter. If the tasks in the preceding stages have been undertaken rigorously the preferred option or options will be clear enough. Should the position be otherwise, it is likely that a failure either in identifying relevant criteria or in applying them correctly is to blame. At the conclusion of this stage, a facilities management strategy can be reflected both in the organisation's overall strategic plan and in its accommodation (or space) strategy. The strategy should contain the following elements:

- Financial objectives
- Goals and critical success factors (in terms of quality, cost and time objectives)
- Targets for potential efficiency gains and quality improvements
- Customer requirements
- Technical issues
- Risks and areas of uncertainty
- In-house and outsourcing strategy (see Chapter 4)
- Methodology for managing change (see Chapter 5)
- Human resources plan (see Chapter 6)
- Procurement strategy (see Chapter 7)
- Business processes
- Supporting ICT strategy.

Strategy implementation

Once established, broad policy statements should be developed into operational plans and implemented through a process that is capable of managing change. A change management process should therefore be instigated (see Chapter 5), incorporating best practice in human resources management (see Chapter 6). The implementation plan should include timetables, milestones and details of the organisation's risk management as it relates to its facilities. The risks to successful implementation should be identified and responsibilities for managing them assigned (see below for an approach). The plan should encompass people and systems, communication, resource planning and procurement, each of which is discussed below. Senior management must be committed to the successful implementation of the resultant strategy. Where this involves the decision to outsource, attention should be paid to the demands of the informed client function – discussed in Chapter 1.

A risk assessment should be performed to identify risks arising from the implementation of outsourcing, particularly the impact on core operations, and how to address them. Responsibilities for dealing with them should then be assigned on the basis of a full understanding of the ability of the party (or individual) to handle the risk(s) in question. Assignment of risk without regard to the capacity of a party or individual to handle it can lead to increased exposure for the organisation, when the objective is to mitigate or eliminate risk.

Typical of the risks that can occur are the following:

- Unclear definition of roles and responsibilities
- A timetable that is too demanding
- Insufficient time allowed for contract negotiation
- Insufficient expertise in the negotiation of contracts and drafting of service level agreements (SLAs)
- Lack of definition of requirements before contract award
- Too short a transition period between the award and start of contract.

Whilst we have yet to consider the position regarding outsourced services, there are some issues that need to be addressed. For example, the effect of a major breakdown in a key service area could threaten continuity of operations for the organisation and should be examined at this point. Contingency plans must be drawn up and validated. In some cases, it may be necessary to introduce trials or another kind of 'run through' to test the efficacy of the proposed arrangements and their ability to cope with various eventualities.

The organisation should also plan and run through the arrangements for managing the transition period. For example, it should plan the handover of information to any newly appointed service providers and other contractors. Sufficient time must be allowed for this activity – two to three months – as this will generally set the tone of the relationship between the organisation and its service providers. The accuracy and completeness of information to be handed over must also be verified.

In the transition period before any new contract starts, the service provider (as contractor) should visit users (the customers) and discuss the new arrangements and what might be expected from them; for example, changed goals and new procedures must be communicated.

People and systems

The most important aspect of an implementation strategy, when bringing about any change, is to carry it through in a controlled way. In order to achieve this, organisations need to develop employees' skills and understanding so that they are fully conversant with the meaning and practice of facilities management. Education and training, together with the mentoring of individuals, will achieve these aims and enhance competence. Close monitoring and control of systems and procedures will help to ensure that these, too, develop in the ways intended. This is not a one-off exercise; there has to be a culture of continual improvement with periodic checks on performance.

Communication

Effective communication between the organisation (acting as an informed client) and service providers is essential to ensure that the implementation of a strategy is both understood and acted upon (see Chapters 1 and 5–7). It is important to involve all stakeholders in the discussion about organisation and structure. Failure to do so is bound to lead to complications later.

A stakeholder is anyone who has a legitimate interest in a business or process; this includes, but is not limited to, customers, employees, statutory authorities, neighbours and the public, to varying extents. Employees need to recognise that facilities management is an especially active process and not one of simply reacting to problems as and when they arise. In organisational terms, this demands a structure that is flat, so that employees with decision-making powers are in close contact with other internal and external users to head off problems before they have the chance to develop. Cultivating relationships is really only possible by communicating clearly and often.

Resources planning

Planning and controlling the use of resources in an efficient and effective manner is a job in its own right. Where organisations are large employers (of either in-house personnel or external service providers), it makes good sense to plan for the optimal use of resources. When management teams are small and the demands on them appear modest, it is still necessary to take formal steps to plan resources. Even the best managers cannot keep everything in their heads, besides which there will be absences when others have to assume responsibility. ICT can help here through the use of low-cost project planning and scheduling software to allocate resources to individual tasks and provide a means for measuring progress and performance. Important in this respect is to avoid unnecessary levels of detail that serve to do little more than show off the features of the software in use.

Procurement

Finally, the point is reached where procurement of services can be considered and, as appropriate, partners can be selected (see Chapters 4, 7, 8, 13 and 14 for a detailed treatment of this subject). Procurement may seem a rather inflated term for what might be seen by some as largely a purchasing decision. The purpose in using the word procurement is to make it clear that we are dealing with a broader set of considerations than the act of obtaining quotations and placing orders. A wide range of issues must be taken into account that, more often than not, requires technical knowledge of the area in question.

Relationships between client organisations and service providers

There will be changes of personnel and other aspects of an organisation's management over time. Arrangements and agreements, with respect to facilities management, may well outlast the terms of employment of key personnel. It is important, therefore, that organisations recognise the need for:

- The purchaser – i.e. the organisation – to be an informed client
- A purchaser–provider relationship to develop between those commissioning the service and service providers (both in-house and outsourced).

In coming to terms with these needs, organisations might benefit from a better understanding of the new tasks that this role as an informed client represents (see Chapter 1). This function will need a significant degree of operational knowledge and experience, not only of the client organisation's own business, but also of the services being provided.

The success of any change initiative in the delivery of services will depend on two main parties:

1. The (client) organisation's representative (facilities manager, estates manager or other senior manager).
2. Service providers, whether internal or external to the client organisation.

Both parties need to share the common objective of delivering best value. To be successful in achieving this goal, the potentially divergent interests of individuals within the two parties also need to be recognised. A cooperative approach, which recognises individuals' interests and aligns efforts with the goals of the organisation, has the potential to deliver the greatest benefit. A cooperative approach (for example, partnering) is also one of the recommended arrangements for managing external service providers (see earlier note in Chapter 1 and Chapter 14; also see Chapter 6 on human resources management).

Case study – Developing a strategy

This case study considers how a facilities management consultant worked with a client to increase awareness of the benefits of facilities management and to develop a robust facilities management strategy for the present and the future. The approach involved raising the profile of facilities management within the client organisation and working in partnership to re-engineer and support business processes to enable the client to operate in a strategic and effective way. The case study also considers the need for the facilities management consultant to protect its own business interests, not least to ensure that it is fit to provide the most appropriate service to the client organisation.

External factors leading to a significant drop in the air travel market fuelled the need for a well-known airline to reduce its fixed cost base. The company decided to outsource its maintenance activities, for the majority of its operational portfolio, to a single provider. In so doing, the property function within the airline changed from a large in-house resource of engineers and supervisors to a small number of contract managers. This in turn led to the need for a clear definition of the retained roles, significant changes to the supporting business processes and the replacement of legacy systems with up-to-date ICT that could provide meaningful management information.

Recognising that it was in an entirely new position, both functionally and managerially, the airline decided to enlist the help of an external facilities management consultant. The newly appointed head of facilities was instrumental in this decision. Being new to the organisation, the head of facilities was unfamiliar, as yet, with the resources at his disposal and the precise nature of the task ahead of him. As the projected consultancy work could not be specified in detail, being of an unknown quantity and composition, the company chose to approach four organisations with which it was familiar. There was, therefore, a competitive element, although only among organisations identified by the airline as prequalified for the role. The four consultants were asked to tender for a three-year period of consultancy aimed at helping the airline to manage the transitional period within its property function. The successful consultant was selected to manage 10 million sq ft (900 000 m²) of buildings and, as part of the restructuring of the airline's property department, it was required to provide a breadth of support services through an expert team of facilities managers, project managers, procurement specialists, contracts managers, electrical and mechanical engineers, building and quantity surveyors, administrative personnel and health and safety specialists.

Facilities management had scarcely been a recognised discipline within the organisation, being considered more as a maintenance function. The nomenclature attached to posts, such as 'head of maintenance', reflected the fact that the requirement to manage facilities, particularly within the wider context of the organisation's overall business needs, was not fully recognised. Similarly, the type of reactive approach that dominated maintenance activities was evidence of a lack of strategic thinking and of a failure to recognise facilities as something more than a cost; that is, to appreciate their ability to add value to the core business.

The profile of facilities management within the organisation was therefore very low and it was this that the consultant set out to address, by educating the client as to the full role of the discipline, what it required of the organisation and what it could offer in return. Part of this education involved the development of the informed client function (ICF), vital if the airline were to stand on its own after the three-year period of support. As things stood, there was essentially no recognition of a client role within services provision. Work was requested and performed on a reactive basis, with no element of strategy or evidence of an overall facilities plan related to wider organisational needs. The property department was used to managing its own labour under this sort of regime, but now line managers were required to be contract managers and had no existing framework for this kind of management.

The airline and the consultant formed a partnership through a framework agreement based on an open-book approach. Remuneration was not linked to output, because it was not clear at the outset what that output should be. Instead, the consultancy and operational services were reimbursed at base costs plus an agreed markup. The airline was free to draw on the expertise of the consultant as it found necessary. As we shall see below, although the venture proved to be a success for both parties, the consultant was obliged to protect its own wider business interests as the airline's demands threatened to draw too heavily on the former's resources. The partnership did not involve the sharing of risk and reward, both of these accruing to the airline, but the monitoring and measurement of performance and benefits played a key part in the agreement and the pursuance of common goals was central to its structure. Openness and trust, which are an essential element of partnering, also played a part in this less formal, temporary business partnership.

Outlining what those common goals were was an early challenge. As noted above, neither established personnel at the airline nor the new head of facilities knew what would ultimately be required or desired. It was therefore necessary for the consultant's personnel to work alongside the airline's management to ensure a complete understanding of its business objectives, changing needs and organisational culture. From this it could develop a comprehensive facilities management strategy to suit the company's particular requirements in the specific context of its current and future core business needs.

Current reality also played a part in providing the guidance and impetus for change. When the airline realised that it simply did not have the ability within its current set-up to manage the input of a major contractor, it became obvious that a re-engineering programme would have to be undertaken. In order to allow forward movement, therefore, the consultant adopted a re-engineering approach to the property department's business processes, which had already proved to be unwieldy and based upon a model which had supported a large in-house resource of more than 400 employees. Initially, existing business processes needed to be re-engineered, but subsequently the development of a new process model was required and the design and procurement of a new property management information system.

In the ICT field, therefore, re-engineering involved establishing a central and accessible information system, capable of coordinating the disparate information sources and systems into an intelligible format which could make visible the connections between different elements not only of the facilities management function but also of the overall business. In the human resources management (HRM) field, clarity of role, responsibility and accountability were required, particularly for newly created, or re-designated, positions. Contract managers became senior facilities managers and ultimately property managers, each step involving more than simply a change of title. It was the consultant's role to help the airline perform this initial step in such a way as would ensure that the change was not only sustainable but also incorporated a system capable of continuous adaptation to changing business and economic circumstances.

In parallel with this project, and with other corporate initiatives aimed at restructuring the organisation, was the further definition of the property and facilities function, a facilities management strategy for the airline and, as part of that strategy, the identification of service levels and appropriate service delivery mechanisms. As discussed above, the department's operational managers had found themselves operating in a reactive way, which in turn left them little time to plan strategically with their customers within the airline the direction of their own business and the optimal support for their customers. The consultant quickly adopted a role as a business partner that gave the senior managers some initial 'breathing space' in which the property department's business plan could be developed. This plan reflected their aspirations for the new business. This was a fundamental step, as the facilities management function wanted to bring about significant change in a way that caused the least disruption to the airline's core business. This required the secondment of a number of the consultant's personnel into operational roles while the airline spent time recruiting a number of suitably qualified permanent employees to take over from them. With these front line roles occupied, time was then made available to shape the future business strategy.

A series of collaborative senior management workshops took place, involving personnel from both sides' management teams, through which the open exchange of knowledge and information was enabled and coordinated. By this means, a re-engineering project was initiated and an execution plan prepared. Initially, the project sought to identify goals and objectives together with tangible measures following *The Balanced Scorecard* (Kaplan and Norton, 1996) approach. Once this had been completed, key processes were identified linked to the goals and objectives by these measures. The four key processes were identified as follows:

1. Customer-relationship management
2. Estates-related and facilities management planning
3. Service delivery
4. Service and organisational development.

Work progressed through a number of small teams, each led by a senior airline manager, to redesign these processes. Once completed, a clear set of deliverables was defined related to each of these processes:

- Customer property plans
- Customer profiles
- Customer feedback
- Service level agreements
- Service delivery feedback
- Cost and charging
- Property portfolio details
- Property guidance
- Project management framework
- Master schedule
- Low-value catalogue items.

Through the development of appropriate key processes and their core deliverables, work was started on the specification of a management information system, the first phase of which was focused on the management and maintenance of the airline's corporate assets.

As noted above, the whole period of change, both prior to and during the consultant's involvement, raised HRM issues. When the new head of facilities came in, personnel were required to reapply for their redefined jobs, where those existed. This action and the general atmosphere of change inevitably made personnel unsettled and anxious about the future. One of the consultant's roles was to use its expertise to manage the process of change within the HRM context on behalf of the airline. In order to do this, the consultant used an input–output model, devoid of references to names or existing mechanisms, in order to analyse the revised personnel requirements, both in terms of roles and numbers, without any threat of bias from vested interests. The consultant also became involved in TUPE issues within contracts being procured on the airline's behalf.

Performance was judged annually on the basis of the consultant's costs and the savings that it had delivered to the airline. Each project or initiative was scoped in order to make its success measurable. The incorporation of targets or milestones over the three-year period was considered important as a defence against the complacency which can develop within a long-term relationship founded on trust, and which may lead the consultant to feel too much at home in the client organisation. The division between operational and consulting divisions within the consultant also guarded against this. Although quality is difficult to measure, it was deemed to have improved and, more tangibly, during this period the partnership identified and achieved annually recurring savings in excess of £2.5 million.

As shown above, the form of the partnership agreement was such that the airline could draw on the resources of the consultant as it saw fit, with reimbursement being made accordingly on an open-book basis. As a result, from an initial six people from the consultant being involved with the project, the numbers rose at one point to 70; this was potentially detrimental to the consultant's wider business interests. It therefore set up a separate company to safeguard the interests of the parent company and to cope more appropriately with the changing demands being made by the airline in response to its developing situation.

Over the initial three-year period the task set for the consultant was subject to continual change. One response, as discussed above, was to establish a separate business, which reflected its origins and purpose by drawing in two employees from the airline. After three years, the period of the initial contract, the emphasis had moved from facilities management to project management. The shape of support required therefore differed, and to accommodate and reflect this change, as well as to protect the primary business interests of the consultant, a separate project management organisation was established. This enabled the consultant to recruit more project management personnel to fit the redefined task. Meanwhile, the facilities management function set up by the consultant was handed over to the airline's own in-house team, incorporating not only the latter's employees but also several former employees of the consultant.

In retrospect, those involved at the consultant's end of the partnership felt that the biggest problem faced was encouraging the airline's personnel to spend the time and make an effort in areas the consultant saw as important. It was felt necessary to work against the given reactive approach and to replace it with the reality of strategic thought and a fuller understanding of its significance within the facilities management role.

Overall, the project enabled the airline to initiate change in a controlled and systematic way with a clear set of deliverables and has subsequently delivered a support function that is customer-focused and responsive to the support needs of the airline. Operating on the basis of a partnering relationship meant that personnel from both organisations worked collaboratively in an open and trusting way, which enabled rapid progress to be made towards common goals. Subsequent changes within the airline have occurred with increasing frequency; however, the fundamental changes begun by the partnership, and the strategy set out, have stood the test of time, allowing the property department to adapt more readily to these frequent changes.

Conclusions

Organisations need to see their facilities management strategy as the cornerstone of their accommodation (or space) strategy, not as an adjunct to

it. By identifying the kind of accommodation and facilities currently provided and required in the future, an organisation will be able to quantify
the gap that has to be bridged. There are, however, other aspects relating to
facilities management that have to be considered carefully if the most
appropriate strategy is to be developed. Various tools and techniques are
available to support a rigorous process of analysis, solution development
and implementation, success in which will lead to a workable strategy for
effective facilities management.

CHECKLIST

This checklist is intended to assist with the review and action planning
process.

	Yes	No	Action required
1. Does the organisation accept the importance of a proper facilities management strategy within the context of the strategic plan and accommodation strategy?	☐	☐	☐
2. Has the organisation completed a strategic analysis of its facilities requirements?	☐	☐	☐
3. Have new ideas and innovative solutions been considered in the context of the facilities management strategy?	☐	☐	☐
4. Has the organisation's senior management avoided the temptation to prejudge options before they have been systematically evaluated?	☐	☐	☐
5. Have criteria for judging options generated in the strategic analysis been prepared objectively?	☐	☐	☐
6. Has the broad strategy been developed into an operational plan addressing the issues of managing change?	☐	☐	☐
7. Has the organisation considered its relationship with service providers in all areas and at all levels?	☐	☐	☐

3 Facilities Planning

Key issues

The following issues are covered in this chapter.

- Traditionally, real estate management took responsibility for estate-related services including those recognised today as the core of facilities management. The emergence of the latter has meant that responsibility for real estate – in organisations without a prior interest in it – has become part of the facilities management function. Where the organisation has a defined real estate management function it must clarify the relationship between real estate and facilities management including roles and responsibilities.

- Space efficiency can be a key factor in the success of an organisation. The drivers for space and demand into the future have to be understood. A balance has to be struck between what the organisation needs and what it can afford, and this is referred to as its 'sustainable estate provision'.

- Planning the use of a new facility can arise from the ongoing management of an existing facility; it may otherwise arise from a business decision that has identified a need that is best satisfied by a new building or refurbished facility.

- Design briefing is a process for engaging the client organisation (i.e. building owner) in structured discussion about the functions and other characteristics of the new building. There are defined steps which should be followed to ensure that the right solution is being designed.

- Two important aspects of briefing are defining operational requirements for the building and planning for a smooth commissioning and handover phase. In some cases, a separate facilities management brief will be prepared with input from the operations team (or facilities manager); other specialist briefs may be required.

- The proof of a building or facility is in how it measures up to expectations. Post-occupancy evaluations should be designed to reveal any gaps between original expectations and delivery, but need to be conducted shortly after handover and repeated periodically.

- Organisations today enjoy many options for their real estate. These range from the highly formalised, such as the acquisition of a new building, through to renting temporary space (furnished or unfurnished).

- For organisations that are in the early stages of business growth, totally serviced workplaces have much to offer in the way of convenience and economy. For more established organisations, there could be need for readily available workplaces to help mobilise a new operation, relocate an existing one or recover from an incident.

Introduction

Facilities management is generally regarded as having ongoing responsibility for the continuous operation of services in support of the organisation's core business. Whilst we have already stressed the importance of facilities management in a more strategic role – see Chapter 2 – we need to understand how it can make a more complete contribution to the success of the organisation. If we adopt a life-cycle perspective then it is clear that planning for, and of, a facility precedes its realisation and operation; however, we have to consider how the need for that facility arises. It could be seen as a 'chicken and egg' situation; which comes first: facilities planning or facilities management? Much depends on where the organisation is in the business cycle and how present arrangements satisfy needs. Whichever, the organisation must adopt this holistic approach because planning for a new facility may be based to a great extent on what is currently being managed and experienced. This chapter deals collectively with the issues that enable us to complete the cycle and in so doing realise that the output from one process, e.g. facilities management, is the input to another, i.e. facilities planning. Of course, some would argue that planning is part of management and so it is, but we need to have a way of linking facilities to the strategic goals of the organisation and vice versa. Understanding how a facility is measuring up to expectations about its performance provides valuable feedback to planners, designers and corporate decision makers, and how information needed to drive the planning and design process forward can be best utilised. We also consider the options that are available to the organisation in terms of how space can be provided from, at one extreme, commissioning a new building that could take several years to complete through to the relocation of employees in a totally serviced workplace overnight.

Real estate management

The relationships between real estate management and facilities management and their link to business strategy are often debated. For certain organisations – perhaps those with a short history and a rapid rate of growth – facilities management may be where responsibility rests for all matters of real estate. In other cases, there may be a long history of real estate acquisition and disposal. Moreover, the discipline of facilities management may have emerged from building maintenance management, domestic services or a combination of the two. Given that background, it would be easy to accept real estate management as the natural home for facilities management. Without that background, however, the organisation may see real estate as a part of facilities management. Buildings are acquired and disposed of according to the need for space as defined in the facilities management strategy. This would make sense in a market where there are options other than taking a long lease on a building. Yet acquiring and disposing of buildings may take the facilities management function outside its core competence. If this extends to commissioning the design and construction of a new office building, for example, we are in a new situation altogether and one for which even real estate managers will need to bring in other expertise.

When the organisation has a view of real estate as an asset to be traded and profited from, the facilities management function will likely fall outside its remit and would, therefore, report separately to senior management. Corporate real estate management (CREM), as a discipline and practice, has the objective of making a return from real estate without changing the organisation's core business. CREM should be handled in such a way that it helps to secure and strengthen the competitiveness of the organisation. The intention is that strategies for, and methods of, CREM should contribute to the attainment of the organisation's business objectives. The gains for the organisation are that its resources can be better utilised, costs can be reduced and potential synergies realised to add value to the core business.

Space management

An important function of facilities management is to ensure the efficient and cost-effective use of space. This purpose presumes that the space provided will satisfy all requirements – often it does not. Organisations can spend considerable time and resources redefining their use of space only to find they are little better off. Chapter 5 on change management discusses a number of issues concerning the management of people during periods of change within the organisation. For now, we will concentrate more on ways in which the organisation can be sure it has the right space for its needs and if it does not, how it intends to make good that shortfall. Consideration of owned space includes operating, maintenance and depreciation costs.

The Space Management Group (SMG) at the University of Westminster in the UK has developed a reputation for its research in the higher education field where estates are generally large and many. Its particular research into space management (SMG, 2006) had the aim of developing guidelines and tools to help deliver effective space management. An objective was to identify key drivers for the size of the estate and then, by studying practices in a number of other institutions, assess the size of estate that was affordable.

Output from SMG's studies into the cost of space and drivers for the size of the estate were analysed and a model was developed for use by higher education institutions. Energy management data and certain other parameters are given as default settings in the model, which users can override with their own data. The cost part of the model enables users to calculate both the provision needed to maintain a sustainable estate and the total provision taking into account the opportunity cost of the funds tied up in the estate. This 'sustainable estate provision' can then be used to determine affordable estate size. The approach seems to have much to offer other kinds of organisation, not least those in the public sector, with similarly large estates and a finite level of resources and funding.

In terms of the impact of changes in higher education, the project found that academic drivers meant that institutions were unlikely to experience a significant contraction in their overall space needs, since reduction in one area was likely to be offset by new demand elsewhere (SMG, 2006). Several examples were cited:

- More space for learning will be required, particularly student-led and blended learning activities.
- Online distance learning will have a limited impact on institutions' overall space needs.
- Research activities will result in a small net increase in space, but will not affect all institutions in the sector.
- Work-based and itinerant learning will lead to some reduction.
- New central administrative functions will likely generate demand for more space.
- Space will be increasingly remodelled to meet new needs, higher standards and to provide for a multiplicity of use – a matter of *sweating* the assets.

SMG uncovered practices in other organisations for ensuring space efficiency in the design of new buildings:

- Maximise space on the footprint of new buildings.
- Match new uses to refurbished buildings.
- Increase the ratio of usable to gross floor area.
- Incorporate design features to support different activities at different times.
- Provide space, furniture and fittings that can be adapted for different activities.
- Create office and research space that mixes open-plan, meeting and quiet spaces.

- Provide wireless data access to enable maximum use of common space.

Good practice in promoting space efficiency was also identified:

1. Appoint a champion for space management and operating costs.
2. Systematically collect and update space utilisation and cost information.
3. Agree targets and monitor their achievement.
4. Incorporate space efficiency concepts into the facilities management strategy.
5. Incorporate the need for space efficiency into project design briefs, feasibility studies, option appraisals and design reviews.
6. Develop and maintain a clear decision and communication structure for building projects, including stakeholders.
7. Promote the benefits of adaptable spaces and furniture.
8. Assess space efficiency through post-occupancy evaluations.

Design briefing

As alluded to above, the need for space efficiency should be incorporated into the design brief of new building projects. As such, it constitutes one of a large number of considerations in the design of a new building or facility, and a significant one. A design brief is a comprehensive written document developed jointly by the building owner (as client) or client's representative and appointed designer(s) based on the business case for the new building. The brief articulates the case for the building in terms of its functions, performance requirements, and possibly overall design concept; however, aesthetic treatment is normally beyond the scope of the brief.

The aim of briefing[1] is to have an objective assessment of needs so that feasibility studies can be carried out, leading to a scheme design supported by cost and schedule information. The steps involved should follow the sequence below in which the first and second are the primary inputs to brief development and the remainder are the outputs to be critically examined and refined:

1. Business case
2. Statement of need
3. Brief development
4. Functional brief
5. Feasibility studies
6. Scheme design.

---

[1] In some countries, briefing is referred to by such terms as planning and programming, where the former is about planning for the design and the latter is a programme for developing the design.

There may not be, however, a single brief or briefing document: several may be needed depending on the scale, complexity and special requirements of the client or demands of the project including, for example:

- Financial arrangements
- Procurement and contracts
- Stakeholder engagement and communication
- Design
- Construction management
- Commissioning and handover
- Facilities management.

As we see, one of the briefing documents covers facilities management and this provides input to the design process in terms of what has to be managed and the performance (i.e. service levels) expected. The general idea is that multiple briefs should interlock to provide adequate coverage of the arrangements for the project. Increasingly, owners are preparing project execution strategies (PES) to incorporate these arrangements. The intention is to create a coordinating document that can be used as a reference by project team members, consultants and specialists, as well as providing a link to more detailed information.

Facilities management brief

The positioning of facilities management in the life-cycle of a building or other structure is such that it can be regarded as a bridge between the end of construction (or more precisely, commissioning and handover) and the beginning of design (for a change of use or the building of new facilities). In practice, it is likely to mean that the facilities management brief is the result of an iterative process in which facilities managers analyse the owner's statement of need to provide advice during development of the design brief on a strategy for managing the facilities. The results are then embodied in a set of performance requirements, either as a part of the design brief or as a separate document.

This process could become quite complicated as some conception of the emerging design will be needed to confirm any original hypotheses about how the facility will be managed. This will mean retaining some flexibility over the likely management of the facility until at least a scheme design has emerged. The purpose here is to establish a strategy or framework to guide scheme design – followed by outline design and detailed design – rather than being prescriptive and, thus, putting an unnecessary restraint on the designer or the design. Even so, to work properly design must take account of how the facility will be managed, but, equally, facilities managers must respond positively to owner and designer wants and help turn them into reality. In short, the facilities manager has a pivotal role in preparing a brief and then retaining a role during feasibility and subsequent design stages. A similar approach applies to other consultants and specialists who must be able to engage with the (lead) designer and be prepared to look for the most workable outcome. A potential weakness in this approach is that it needs both the building owner and designer to recognise the value of the operations team's (or facilities manager's) input.

Another issue to address here is the growing importance of extracting the correct information from the design process to verify or evaluate design decisions from an operational perspective. An example is the case of build-operate-transfer (BOT) projects under a public–private partnership (PPP), where the operator has a fixed budget for the operations over the term of the concession and is, therefore, attempting to optimise operational costs over the lifetime of the facility (see also Chapter 19 on public–private partnerships). Put another way, the operator is taking a calculated risk that has to be based on an objective assessment. If this need is denied there is the likelihood of an ill-informed commercial decision that serves no one's interests. Operators not only have to carry risks, they do so based on the decisions of others. Being locked out of decision-making raises the prospect of a later failure when it could so easily have been avoided.

Information for briefing in the facilities management area can be classified under three headings:

1. Description of operations and activities to be performed in the building or facility – this information is needed to plan the layout and arrangement of spaces and functions.
2. Definition of information required from the design process and deemed critical for the operations team to evaluate design solutions, taking into account long-term operational costs.
3. As-built information – records of how the facility was built are vital for its successful operation and must be kept from the earliest point then embodied in a facility handbook for handing over to the owner.

Below are examples of the kind of information required under these headings.

Description of operations and activities

Most information under this heading will be generated by the designer in discussion with the owner. The information should reveal how different stakeholders expect to see and experience the facility. The following details are not meant to be exhaustive, but are illustrative of what has to be considered.

Overall concept

- Vision and image of the organisation (i.e. the extent to which these are reflected in the appearance and general design).

- Impressions of different stakeholders as they approach, enter and circulate in the facility.
- Extent of design for sustainability, including rationale for selection of materials.

Internal operations

- Descriptions of the functions and activities to be supported in the facility.
- Zoning, internal circulation and transportation (e.g. offices, service cores, lift/elevator lobbies and stairways).
- Security, safety and resilience (e.g. response in the event of a failure or incident and arrangements for business continuity).
- Energy use, water management, waste disposal and pollution control (i.e. the facility's environmental management).
- Organisational structure (i.e. departments, divisions and other units), as well as types of employees and the anticipated number.
- Communication between departments and divisions, and with customers and other stakeholders.
- Demands for space supporting different working environments (e.g. creative areas, private space for reflection, meetings and conferences, safety areas, social areas and lunch rooms).
- Flexibility in the internal design to allow for growth and change, e.g. reconfigurable space and expansion (and reduction) possibility.
- Support services (i.e. estate-related services and supplies).

External operations

- Zoning of external areas and security (landscaping, parking, fencing, lighting and surveillance).
- Employee and visitor entry to, and exit from, the facility including emergency access and 'means of escape' routes.

Information for evaluating design solutions

This kind of information has become especially critical for operators who have entered into long-term contracts for a concession based on a fixed monthly or yearly rate. In these cases understanding operational costs is paramount. In the same way that the quantity surveyor (or cost manager) needs to be kept informed of changes to the design as it evolves, so must the operations team (or facilities manager) be aware of anything that could materially affect operational costs. Normally, a change control system would be implemented so that any proposed changes are evaluated and their full implications known before anything is committed. The purpose is primarily to ensure that the operator can determine the effects of various design solutions on the building's operational parameters. The designer should be requested to present specific information in due time as indicated below.

- The designer should indicate when alternative solutions (designs, materials, products and systems) are available so that the owner can determine which offers the lowest whole-life cost.
- The designer should obtain information from manufacturers on the cost of operation, maintenance, breakdown frequency and lifetime of system components and parts.
- All information should be provided in sufficient time to determine whether or not operational parameters are acceptable, with the option to visit manufacturers to verify their assertions.
- The designer must make assumptions explicit when deciding on any matter that could affect operations.

As-built information

Strictly speaking, as-built information is not part of briefing, but it is necessary to ensure that at the start of the project there is a clear understanding of what must be provided at the point of handover: it is too late to think about it once the design is complete. During commissioning and prior to handover, detailed information about the facility, including operation and maintenance of systems, should be made available to the owner and facilities manager, if appointed. Information should be supplied digitally wherever possible, with paper copies. Requiring information in this format should be a condition of every contract with designers so that there can be no chance of a later claim for additional costs. In most cases, the information is generated routinely in the course of design and construction and should not present extra work; it is a matter of good practice in design management. Details should be forwarded to designers at the outset about the information required and its format. Typical of this information are:

- Drawings – architectural, structural and building engineering services drawings, including those for operational purposes.
- Specifications – materials and finishes used in spaces and rooms, and on the exterior of the building.
- Inventory – using a recognised hierarchical classification system (e.g. CI/SfB[2]) to itemise all plant and equipment, fixtures and fittings.

Post-occupancy evaluations

Surveying the opinions of users in a new facility provides a means for evaluating the extent to which the facility is providing what was expected. A post-occupancy evaluation determines how well facilities match users' needs and identifies ways of improving facility design and functionality,

---

[2] CI/SfB stands for Construction Index/*Samarbetskommittén för Byggnadsfrågor*, a Scandinavian system of classification established in 1959 and specifically designed for the construction sector. The system is used worldwide for construction technical and trade literature.

performance and 'fitness for purpose'. A post-occupancy evaluation differs from many conventional surveys because it seeks the opinions of those directly affected. Naturally, the worth of any evaluation will depend on how well it has been designed and conducted, not least the extent to which it aligns with the organisation's facilities management strategy.

Interviews with users are one way of eliciting opinions, but these need to be properly structured if the data gathered in them are to be compared. Moreover, individuals may be reluctant to discuss issues and the whole process could take a long time if a representative sample of users is to be assured. Questionnaires are the most common tool for eliciting opinions and care needs to be exercised when drafting one. Doing the job properly is more than a few hours of work. The golden rules are that the more time spent on designing the questionnaire the greater will be its usefulness and that no questionnaire should ever be distributed unless it has been piloted first and found to be fit for purpose. When preparing questions it is better to adopt an approach where respondents (i.e. users) can indicate the extent to which they agree or disagree with a statement about their situation or the extent to which they are satisfied or dissatisfied with aspects of the facilities. Questions that require a simple 'yes' or 'no' may not provide meaningful information and also risk leaving respondents feeling frustrated that their opinions are not being properly canvassed. The best advice is to allow respondents to express their feelings about those matters they believe are important and about which the organisation has a genuine concern.

Post-occupancy evaluations have a purpose beyond directly measuring user satisfaction. Other uses include:

- Obtaining feedback to help in fine-tuning new facilities and optimising building engineering services installations.
- Informing planners and designers of needs in regard to new facilities.
- Resolving persistent or recurrent problems in facilities that might otherwise go unchallenged.

Evaluations can also help to draw out suggestions from employees about how to improve their own well-being and that of the organisation. Means for reducing waste, pollution and energy can be found when employees are motivated to make suggestions in the belief that they will be taken seriously. Finally, it is important to stress that a post-occupancy evaluation should not be seen as a one-off exercise. For it to be of real benefit, it has to be repeated and, in between times, employees need to be made aware of the results and how the organisation intends to deal with any issues arising.

Real estate options

The options available to the organisation in terms of its needs in real estate and facilities cover a broad spectrum, from commissioning the design and construction of a major new facility to employees' hot-desking in an

Table 3.1   Real estate and space provision options and occupancy periods

Option		Occupancy period
New building	(purpose built)	25 years or more
Leased building	(long lease)	between 7 and 25 years
	(short lease)	up to 7 years
Rented space	(tenant fitted-out)	between 5 and 15 years
	(furnished)	between 1 and 5 years
	(totally serviced workplace)	up to 1 year

externally provided, totally serviced workplace. In terms of new building, the organisation has the option of commissioning the services of a designer and then awarding a contract to a construction company. This traditional approach may suit some, but for others a management style of contract or a single point of responsibility, such as design and build, may be better. Whilst important considerations, there is insufficient space here to discuss the advantages and disadvantages of the different approaches; there are many texts that deal adequately with the subject.

More important is that the organisation recognises the periods of occupancy that are appropriate for each of the options and, thus, the nature of the commitment that is being made. Table 3.1 illustrates the periods that might apply to the options available. Actual periods will, however, vary according to location and prevailing market conditions, but they should help focus the organisation on the kind of real estate solution that best fits its needs.

It is also important to recognise that several different life cycles may be imposed on a single building or facility and that the organisation will have to plan for refurbishment at intervals to maintain an optimal working environment, as well as to fulfil any leasehold or other conditions imposed by a landlord or owner. In the example of office buildings, it is accepted that the design life of the structure will exceed 60 years, major items of plant and equipment (building engineering services) may last no longer than 15 years, internal partitioning can last between 5 and 10 years, whilst individual workstations and sets may need replacing, upgrading or redecorating every 3 to 5 years. No hard and fast rules apply so the organisation would be wise to examine the likely refurbishment and renewal cycles for any building or facility that it has a responsibility to maintain. Furthermore, returning a building to an as-new condition upon expiry of a lease could result in unforeseen cost and disruption if not taken into account.

Totally serviced workplaces

Increasingly, the marketplace is offering novel solutions for organisations wishing either to outsource all or part of their facilities' requirements, or to support new business development. Common amongst these solutions is

what is termed the totally serviced workplace. The idea is that an organisation looking for a temporary solution to an accommodation problem can
rent fully serviced office space for as little as one month up to a few years.
In some cases, the serviced workplace may be intended as a permanent
solution or at least one that does not have a specified time horizon. For
organisations looking to expand their business internationally, the availability – at short notice – of this kind of solution can be very attractive,
albeit obtained at a premium.

In one case, a major telecommunications company has secured several
thousands of workplaces for its international operations. Moreover, it has
an arrangement that is simplified to the point of its paying a lump sum fee
based on the number of workplaces multiplied by a unit rate per month.
Reducing transaction costs for the organisation is another benefit from the
arrangement, alongside low risk exposure and a high level of flexibility. Of
course, the client organisation in this case has to be absolutely certain of the
financial standing of the service provider and the status of the underlying
property title.

High-quality, fully serviced space can be available in a variety of forms
to suit different organisational demands. The broad categories are:

- Office space – serving a full-time, part-time, branch, project, start-up,
  team or hot-desking need.
- Virtual office – offering call handling, business address, messaging and
  mail forwarding, space when required for meetings and private office
  work – see also Chapter 11.
- Disaster recovery – providing workplace recovery to support business
  continuity in the event of an incident.

Conclusions

Organisations need to be clear about the relationship between real estate
management and facilities management where this could risk becoming a
distraction. In all cases, organisations need to know what space they have
and what they can afford, otherwise they will not achieve a 'sustainable
estate provision'. Planning for, and planning of, the space required by an
organisation is affected by drivers for that space, trends in those drivers
and the cost of providing space. Understanding how to provide space, and
of which type, falls to the client organisation and its designers. A rigorous
design brief must be prepared for any new building or facility and this
may involve the preparation of a separate facilities management brief. The
brief is the cornerstone of a process for ensuring that identified needs are
delivered in the completed building or facility. Determining whether or
not the facility measures up to expectations can be determined by the
results of a post-occupancy evaluation conducted with users shortly after
handover, and should be repeated periodically to see if the facility is still
delivering. Organisations have many options for their real estate and may

not even have to embark upon a process of acquisition. They may also benefit from the totally serviced workplace, which offers a set of options for organisations that need some flexibility in their space management, perhaps in response to the rapid deployment or redeployment of resources. For businesses in the early stages of the growth cycle, totally serviced workplaces may provide the ideal solution, allowing them to concentrate on growing their business without concern over support services: they are, in effect, outsourcing their facilities and facilities management.

CHECKLIST

This checklist is intended to assist with the review and action planning process.

	Yes	No	Action required
1. Has the organisation classified the relationship between real estate management and facilities management, including roles and responsibilities?	☐	☐	☐
2. Has the organisation determined if the size of its estate and facilities are affordable, i.e. is there sustainable estate provision?	☐	☐	☐
3. Is information readily to hand on space efficiency?	☐	☐	☐
4. Does the organisation have an explicit plan of how it deals with design briefing?	☐	☐	☐
5. In the event of a requirement for new facilities, does the organisation have a procedure for preparing a facilities management brief?	☐	☐	☐
6. Is post-occupancy evaluation conducted shortly after handover of a facility?	☐	☐	☐
7. Is post-occupancy evaluation repeated periodically?	☐	☐	☐
8. Is the organisation aware of the options available in the marketplace for space?	☐	☐	☐

4 Retaining Services In-House vs Outsourcing

Key issues

The following issues are covered in this chapter.

- The organisation must identify the key attributes of the services it requires so that a balanced view of needs is established as the basis for evaluating available options within the decision to retain in-house or to outsource.

- The organisation should define its own evaluation criteria with respect to these attributes of service so that the importance or weight given to options is truly reflective of the organisation's accommodation and facilities management strategy and policies.

- Consideration must be given to direct and indirect costs of both in-house and outsourced service provision so that a complete financial picture is gained, with comparison made on a like-for-like basis to enable a decision to be taken on best value.

- Support services should represent best value on the grounds of afford-ability for the organisation in the implementation of the objectives of its strategic plan, irrespective of the cost of those services.

- Evaluation criteria for the sourcing decision must embrace 'hard' and 'soft' measures and compare all costs with the required quality.

- Roles and skills must be derived from the services to be provided, with specialist skills highlighted.

- Since the factors affecting the choice of in-house or outsourced facilities management may change, the route by which services are procured should be reviewed at appropriate intervals by market testing.

Introduction

This chapter considers the issue of whether to retain services in-house or to outsource them. There can be many possibilities open to organisations and each has to be considered carefully if the route that leads to best value is to be followed. It is not a simple choice between retention in-house or outsourcing. The choice between in-house and outsourced services is not always clear-cut, which is why there has to be a proper understanding of requirements. If the procedure advocated in Chapter 2 has been followed, the organisation will have not prejudged the situation; instead, it will have determined its requirements precisely. The first step is to consider the attributes of each service that are seen as important. Realism has to prevail so that attributes are stated in terms that are 'within range' and not so demanding of service providers that they are unlikely ever to be fulfilled. Many of the attributes will seem obvious; others will be less so. The issue of cost is bound to be a prominent factor for many organisations – it may have been the main motivation for considering outsourcing as an option. However, as we shall see, it is important to understand how cost is generated. Finally in this chapter, the organisation is presented with the means by which it is able to determine the arrangements through which service provision can take place. This step is a significant one and has many implications for the quality of service as well as cost. Even so, it is not a 'once and for all time' situation, but one that has to be revisited periodically as conditions change in the market for services and supplies.

Attributes of service

The organisation is free to determine those features of a given service that are important to it: to do otherwise would not make sense. Even so, the organisation must be realistic, both in terms of the features demanded and the ability of others to deliver them. For any given service, there will be a number of features (referred to as attributes) that can be considered significant and/or important to the organisation. They can include, but are certainly not limited to:

- Customer service
- Uniqueness of service
- Priority, flexibility and speed of response
- Management implications and indirect cost
- Direct cost
- Control.

Customer service

The organisation will have established the scope and standard of services it requires. In addition to the many 'hard' measures that are usually associated with them (for example, responding correctly to a need) a number of 'soft' measures must also be considered (for example, the level of customer service provided). These become particularly important when dealing with people who are external to the organisation, although are still important when dealing with people within it. Soft measures might include:

- A courteous and responsive helpdesk in preference to a logbook in which faults are simply noted.
- Call-back to the customer to verify that the work has been carried out.
- Adoption of performance measures for courtesy, response, presentation and tidiness.

Practice Point 4.1   A helping hand.

Key point: the organisation needs to have a helpdesk or central coordination point if it is to deal effectively with customer enquiries about facilities and related services.

The organisation in question did not believe that, given its relatively small size, it warranted a helpdesk. After all, the facilities manager appeared to know what was going on and he always seemed to be receiving calls from various people to tell him if there were problems. In fact, over a six-week period, the facilities manager was so overwhelmed with the number of calls and visits he received that he managed to do little other work. Furthermore, there were complaints that some problems were not being resolved. In the end, he discussed the matter with his senior management and obtained permission to set up a helpdesk on a three-month trial basis. Its scope was to cover security, transport, catering, cleaning, porterage, maintenance, mail services and room bookings. In the first two weeks, the helpdesk attracted 500 enquiries most of which were dealt with promptly and to the satisfaction of the individual enquirer. In establishing the helpdesk, the organisation had created a focal point for dealing with problems. This meant that personnel were generally able to resolve matters immediately, rather than allowing them to escalate.

Uniqueness of service

When contemplating different ways of providing a service, the special demands of that service must also be considered. While most tasks will not represent an undue challenge to providers within the facilities management sector, the organisation might, for example, possess specialist plant and equipment unfamiliar to maintenance operatives. This may restrict the potential choice of the provider of maintenance and supplier of spares. In some cases, legislation will ensure that only certain qualified persons and firms are authorised to perform maintenance. The maintenance of lifts (or elevators) is an obvious example. Generally, issues can include:

- The number of external providers that can potentially offer the service.
- Location of the service provider and its distance from the organisation's facility in question.
- Cost of, or premium charged for, the service.
- Average delivery time, i.e. waiting time and time for undertaking the service.
- Level of specification needed to place orders.

Priority, flexibility and speed of response

The priority of services to be provided must be expressed clearly, so that critical services can be highlighted and the required level of response taken into account. A risk assessment should be undertaken for high-priority services, so that the consequence of failures is made clear and the appropriate level and speed of response can be planned. This can be undertaken as follows:

- Identify all sources of risk that might affect service provision.
- Undertake a preliminary analysis to establish the probable high-priority risks for further investigation.
- Examine these high-priority risks to assess the severity of their impact and probability of occurrence.
- Analyse all risks to predict the most likely outcome.
- Investigate alternative courses of action.
- Choose the course of action deemed necessary to hold, avoid, reduce, transfer or share risks, as appropriate.
- Allocate responsibility for managing risks – these should be placed with those best able to manage them.

High-priority services and their related risks must be identified and assessment made of the probability and consequences of such risks. The management team can use questionnaires and checklists to identify risks. These could then be scored as shown in Table 4.1.

Risks scoring a total of 5 or more would be unacceptable and consideration would need to be given to how such risks might be avoided, reduced or transferred. Thus, risks can be recognised and assessed so that appropriate action can be taken. In the process of doing this, risks impacting on services provision may be ranked to allow the organisation to look objectively at how they can best be managed.

For example, the occurrence of a significant failure in the heating system during the winter months might be improbable (score 1), but the consequences could be serious (score 3). The full impact of this risk is rated as 4 and is something that the organisation might be prepared to accept (hold). This can be contrasted with the 'as likely as not' event that fuel will not be delivered on time (score 3). If this were so, the consequences

Table 4.1 Risk scores.

Probability	Chance of occurrence (%)	Score	Consequence	Score
Improbable	10	1	Insignificant	1
Unlikely	25	2	Marginal	2
As likely as not	50	3	Serious	3
Probable	75	4	Critical	4
Highly probable	90	5	Catastrophic	5

for heating the buildings could be serious (score 3). This gives a total score of 6. In other words, fuel deliveries are a high-priority service and, as such, must be made at the required time. The organisation should take steps to reduce the chance of non-delivery on specified dates or to hold a reserve fuel supply, whichever is more appropriate in terms of cost and practicality.

The organisation should also consider the level of flexibility required for each of the services provided. Variable demand for some services, such as porterage[1] and transport, which may peak at certain times of the year, can cause difficulties in maintaining a constant resource level. In such instances, the ability to call off labour from an external provider at short notice can help and is also likely to provide a cost-effective way of delivering those services.

The speed with which a service provider can, under each service approach, respond to orders or requests is a factor for further consideration. For example, the response time of an external provider in the case of an emergency call-out, may or may not be longer than that of an in-house resource. In the case of a remote site, the response time for a maintenance contractor may be significant and a premium to reduce this time might prove prohibitive. Alternatively, if an emergency were to escalate, a large external provider may be preferred to the in-house alternative, because of ready access, out of hours, to necessary equipment and labour.

Management implications and indirect cost

The decision to outsource or provide services in-house must take into account both the capability of service providers and the effort required to manage them. An organisation that takes the decision to outsource can delegate the direct supervision of work and service operatives to the provider. The role for the organisation's representative then becomes the management of the output from the service provider. The representative should act as an informed client (see Chapter 1) managing performance against specifications and service level agreements (see Chapter 9). Organisations need to consider their approach to this new management role carefully.

When contemplating a mix of support services such as cleaning, security, building and mechanical and electrical maintenance, it is easy to see the diversity of tasks involved. This may mean that a manager or supervisor who is trying to cope with such a range of services may not be proficient in all. This could prove to be a problem for smaller organisations where, although the tasks are not extensive individually, their diversity is great, requiring the manager or supervisor to be multi-skilled. For larger organisations, specialist management and supervision may be cost-effective and efficient, because more of it is required.

---

[1] The word portering is also commonly used.

A further consideration is that of the expertise available within the organisation for the management of these services if retained in-house. Whilst accommodation services such as cleaning and porterage do not require high levels of expertise, statutory equipment testing and maintenance of major appliances do. For a manager whose remit includes the management of such services on a part-time basis, the initial learning and the continuing professional development (CPD), to keep abreast of legislation and industry practice, represent a significant investment in time and effort. Consequently, in-house service provision may not be the most cost-effective choice.

In choosing the approach to service provision, total cost is frequently misreported. In evaluating the comparative cost between an in-house or outsourced service provision, organisations should identify all costs, both direct and indirect. A common mistake is for direct costs only to be reported. Indirect costs include those incurred in the internal management of external contracts and the ongoing training and development of in-house personnel. Furthermore, the full administration of the services such as permit-to-work procedures, competent and approved person regimes, together with the technology to operate them, all attract a cost that must be recorded.

The organisation also needs to consider the cost of financial administration. For instance, a small number of labour and material contracts means that invoices can be processed more cost-effectively than in situations where invoices are many and frequent. Clearly, the method of procurement has an implication for the accounting function.

Direct cost

By way of contrast, direct cost is easier to ascertain than indirect cost. In the case of an outsourced service, the contract sum is a clear figure that is readily available. For in-house provision, the direct cost calculation would include employees' salaries and benefits. As noted above, these more obvious costs should not be looked at in isolation from the associated indirect costs.

Control

Linked closely to the management variable is the issue of control. For many organisations considering outsourcing, the greatest concern is that of a perceived loss of control. The level of control that can be achieved is closely correlated with the method of procurement and the contractual relationship established between the organisation and the service provider. Through a more traditional contract the level of control is limited. For greater control, a partnering arrangement may be appropriate (see Chapter 14).

Table 4.2 Illustration of options and their implications.

Attributes of service of importance to the organisation	In-house	Special company/ business unit	Managing agent	Managing contractor	Managed budget	Total FM	Off-the-shelf/ agency
Customer service	+	+	++	+	++	+	−
Uniqueness of service	−	+	+	+	+	+	−
Priority, flexibility, speed of response	++	+	++	++	++	+	++
Management implications / indirect cost	−	+	+	+	++	++	−
Direct cost	+	−	−	−	−	−	−
Control	++	++	++	+	++	−	+

+ + = an attribute is most likely to be satisfied; + = may be satisfied; and − = unlikely to be satisfied.

Whatever arrangement is put in place, ICT has a part to play in the delivery of reliable management information. It is through accessible management information that many of the control issues can be resolved. Value can also be added if management information is delivered as a consequence of service provision and is, therefore, available without cost or, at least, for a nominal sum.

Overview of options and implications

Choice is not limited to in-house provision or outsourcing. Table 4.2 shows seven options (defined subsequently in Table 4.3) that an organisation might consider and how the different attributes of service of importance to the organisation can be scored against each option. The particular interpretation represented by this model is hypothetical and based on the authors' experience. Moreover, it should be used only at the early stages when determining an approach to the overall provision of services. Many of the attributes listed will, at a later stage, be used in the assessment of tenders.

The organisation should always consider its own evaluation criteria to determine the importance or weight that might be given to an option in terms of its potential to add value to the core business. Although plus and minus signs are used in the example based on the authors' perceptions and experience, a numerical system could have been used to arrive at similar,

Table 4.3   Definition of options.

In-house – The retention of the organisation's employees for the delivery of estates-related and facilities services.
Special company/business unit – The reconstitution of the in-house team into an independent company, with the objective of expanding its business by gaining contracts from other clients.
Managing agent – The appointment of a specialist to act as client representative. This person (or organisation) is then responsible for arranging the appointment of service providers.
Managing contractor – The appointment of an organisation to manage all service providers as though part of one large contracting organisation. The contractor is paid a fee for providing this service, usually as a percentage of the value of the expenditure managed.
Managed budget – A variation on the *managing contractor*, where a contractor takes responsibility for the payment of all suppliers and provides a consolidated invoice at the end of each month. The fee is related to the contractor's own resources as deployed.
Total facilities management (total FM) – The responsibility for providing services and for generally managing the facilities is placed in the hands of a single organisation.
Off-the-shelf/agency – The contractual employment of personnel through a specialist or general recruitment agency. Agencies provide variable standards of selection expertise, personnel support and training, and customer support.

if not the same, results. Whichever approach is adopted, the basis for each score must be made explicit so that there can be no misunderstanding of the relative weighting of attributes. Furthermore, the exact interpretation of options will differ from one organisation to another, but the adoption of such an approach should enable objective comparison to be made and for it to be transparent to all stakeholders.

Market testing

Going to the market should be an honest attempt at establishing the attraction or otherwise of outsourcing. This does not, however, imply frequent tendering exercises, where in-house providers compete for work alongside external contractors. It is preferable for clear-cut choices to be made between internal restructuring and outsourcing, wherever possible. This avoids the counterproductive effects that the anxiety caused by market testing, or the demoralisation caused by an unsuccessful tender, may have on the in-house team and its subsequent dealings with its new, external employers.

Appropriate use of the market would include regular comparisons of current prices and rates for services using published data, participation in a benchmarking club (see Chapter 18) or indicative quotations from potential service providers. An awareness of the state of the market for services means that at any time a judgement can be made as to whether or not a preferred option is the most appropriate. Some of the requisite information, however, may already be contained within market audits carried out during the strategic analysis stage (Chapter 2).

It is the performance of the service provider that should be reviewed on an annual basis, rather than the decision to outsource or retain services in-house. Once that decision has been taken it should not be subject to continuous review. The organisation should try to avoid letting contracts on less than an annual basis. Longer-term contracts for three or more years can be let with break clauses. Annual reviews should, in any case, be incorporated into contracts running for two or more years. In some countries, legislation may still force re-tendering on an annual basis for public sector contracts. This can add to cost, as well as limiting the performance of the service provider. In such cases, it can only be hoped that the institutions concerned eventually recognise the short-sightedness of their approach and move to an arrangement that is capable of achieving best value. It is surely not beyond the ability of those institutions in question to draft contracts that incorporate annual reviews and break clauses to cover the eventuality of poor performance by the service provider. The mechanisms for reviewing performance are dealt with in Chapters 9 and 17.

Other implications of outsourcing

Should an organisation decide to outsource, it is then faced with a further decision as to how the outsourcing will be organised and structured. How will the contracts be let? Will there be separate or bundled individual contracts, a total facilities management package or a management contract (see Chapter 13)? What might make sense for the organisation might not prove attractive to service providers – much can depend on the market at a given time. If the option of a management contract is exercised, the organisation will need to consider whether this should be undertaken for a fee or on the basis of service performance.

Conclusions

The decision to outsource can be made rationally and objectively, based on attributes of service that are realistic. At any time, organisations can apply the evaluation model shown in Table 4.2 to help determine whether or not to outsource a service. They should do so having regard to those attributes of service that are meaningful and relevant to them. The benefit in using a model of this kind is that specific options can be evaluated with sensitivity and the correct decision for the organisation at any point can be made. Time is an important factor, since needs change and sometimes the most appropriate option is the one that can be adapted over time to suit new circumstances. Limited and periodic market reviews are useful for information gathering, but habitual market testing is not considered best practice and may be counterproductive. There will be advantages and disadvantages to providing services either in-house or by outsourcing. The organisation must decide the route that provides the best value for itself in the long term. This is achieved by taking full account of the implications, especially the true cost of all options.

CHECKLIST

This checklist is intended to assist with the review and action planning process.

	Yes	No	Action required
1. Has the organisation established the scope and standard of customer services required and compared it to its current provision of facilities management services?	☐	☐	☐
2. Do the current facilities management arrangements properly address priorities and provide flexibility and speed of response?	☐	☐	☐
3. Have the management implications of outsourcing services as opposed to retaining them in-house been considered?	☐	☐	☐

	Yes	**No**	**Action required**
4. Have both the direct and indirect costs of service provision been properly identified?	☐	☐	☐
5. Has the level of control required been properly integrated with the methods of procurement and the contractual relationships that might be established between the client organisation and the service provider?	☐	☐	☐
6. Do contracts run for more than one year, with the provision of annual reviews and break clauses to enable poorly performing service providers to be removed?	☐	☐	☐
7. Is market testing undertaken periodically irrespective of the route taken to the provision of services?	☐	☐	☐

5 Change Management

Key issues

The following issues are covered in this chapter.

- Change is normal, but its consequences can be abnormal for the people affected by it.

- Organisations need to adopt an intelligent approach to planning, co-ordinating and controlling a process of change that ensures continuity of operations, whilst injecting new energy and impetus into the 'business' and its social infrastructure.

- A recognised methodology exists for guiding organisations and individuals towards implementing a change management process – something that can be defined, detailed and determined.

- Change management is rarely, if ever, a linear process; instead it is likely to involve some degree of iteration and/or reworking.

- Planning is key to success and, in many respects, there cannot be too much of it. Organisations should not underestimate the time required to plan (and then implement) a change management project.

- Facilities management provides a mechanism for handling routine change, but it cannot deal with wholesale change – other approaches must be taken, perhaps drawing on key project management skills.

- Consultation with all stakeholders is essential, otherwise just one disaffected party could ruin the chance of success.

- Targeted change management can lead to results that dramatically improve the viability of the organisation and its competitiveness, where the latter is a relevant factor.

Introduction

The idea that *things* – and this includes organisations – must change has become abundantly clear over the last few decades. From a world in which stability was the norm, we have come to a time where normality itself is a state of change. This apparent paradox serves to make us realise that in order to progress we have to do things better – we have to do them differently. The point is that change has always been present: it is simply that the rate of change nowadays is so great as to be visible to all. Change management can be defined as a set of techniques that aid in evolution, composition and policy management of the design and implementation of an object or system. However, this starkly abstract view overlooks the human dimension that is a fundamental condition of facilities management. Another view is that it is an organised, systematic application of the knowledge, tools and resources of change that provides organisations with a key process to achieve their business strategy. Clearly, the introduction of a focus on business strategy helps to contextualise the definition, but in order to humanise it we must go further. By incorporating the 'people side' of business and coupling it to the workplace, we can offer the following definition for the purpose of this work: 'the process, tools and techniques to manage the people side of business change to achieve a required outcome and to realise that change effectively within the social infrastructure of the workplace'. This sharper focus on the problem with which we are faced helps when exploring the approach that organisations must take. This chapter therefore examines change management in an organisational setting, where the objects of change are the facilities to serve the core business and the subjects are the people who will deliver this new order.

Change in an organisational setting

As we have seen from earlier chapters, facilities management is about, *inter alia*, helping organisations to manage change. Facilities management moves an organisation from where it is today to where it needs to be in the future to meet its business objectives. In practice, this may mean the requirement for more or better accommodation and pressure on the organisation to adapt what it has already. Such are the symptoms of a rapidly changing business world. Organisations can be sure of one thing – the nature of work and business will be different tomorrow. The difficulty is in predicting how and in what ways things will be different. For some organisations, the need to change may be one of extreme urgency and a consequence of events past or in anticipation of those to come. Organisational change can thus be the result of the need to:

- *Refocus* – reduce diversification of activities
- *Re-engineer* – redesign business processes
- *Downsize* – concentrate on core business
- *De-layer* – remove redundant levels of management.

Organisations face other pressures for change and these can stem from a variety of causes:

- Organisational structure/relationships – as mentioned above
- ICT
- Productivity demands

- Human skills and resources
- Time pressures
- Health, safety and environment.

Change can therefore occur in various ways and at various levels, and is often influenced by decisions and behaviour that are people-oriented. Change management is about where an organisation aims to be, how it will get there and how it will involve people.

Managing change in practice

Later in this chapter – through the means of a case study – we shall introduce the notion of an organisation venturing towards a project management style of operation for its facilities management. As we shall see, some actions can be translated into projects, enabling them to be subject to an established discipline with a proven methodology, techniques, tools and metrics. The attraction is in the control that can be exercised over delivery to quality, time and cost objectives. This thinking does, however, fall short of advocating a project-managed approach to facilities management and it is important to avoid mixing concepts. Even so, there is the possibility of gaining benefit from looking at different approaches from which, hopefully, one can find better ways of achieving objectives. Any new insights that might be provided would justify the time expended.

Bringing about change in a controlled way will draw on many skills, not least social skills in dealing with the people affected by alterations in some aspect of their work. The potential for failure, or a less than satisfactory outcome, looms large and demands attention to be directed to those factors that might threaten success. A later case study – see Chapter 6 – shows how it is possible to help people make the transition from an established and, therefore, familiar situation to one that is unfamiliar and potentially threatening. The need for early involvement of all stakeholders cannot be overemphasised. These are the people upon whom the outcome rests.

Change as a process

First and foremost, change management should be seen in terms of a process – something that is eminently capable of being 'defined, detailed and determined'. Fig. 5.1 shows the essential form of the change management process.

By using the device of an explicit, shared model of the process, it is possible to obtain feedback and, importantly, 'buy-in' from stakeholders. Used as the starting point for the redesign or re-engineering of an organisation's business processes, the model avoids drawing people into descriptions where reading between the lines is one of many drawbacks. A process model, as an abstraction of the real world, can be used to focus attention on the sequence

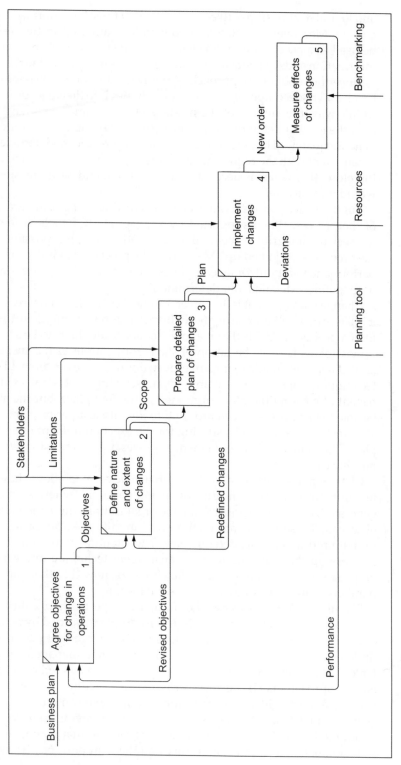

Fig. 5.1   The change management process.

and logical relationship between activities that must be performed to deliver change. Moreover, the standard conventions adopted in the model can be used as a checklist of 'who shall be involved', 'where' and 'with what information and/or control'? The protocol thus helps to define the process.

Since the modelling approach is implicitly top-down, it is possible to break down (decompose) higher level activities into their constituent tasks. In this way, the authors of the model – change managers – have control over the level of detail that is required to portray the process (or any part of it) adequately. The golden rule is to decompose the model to a level that is consistent with the requirements of the job in hand. The level of detail is, therefore, that which is necessary and sufficient and no more, since more would mean waste.

Building such a model is an exercise in creating a single, integrated view of the process. When supported by appropriate ICT tools, it is possible to check the integrity of the model. Put another way, it is possible to see if the process is 'all joined up'. Measuring the process, that is determining its performance and outcome, completes the exercise. The process has now been 'defined, detailed and determined'.

Change management is, however, rarely, if ever, a linear process; instead it is likely to involve some degree of iteration or reworking. A further benefit of a process model is that it allows sequence and logic to be scrutinised – most of which can be accomplished from simple visual inspection – and adjustments made to improve, even optimise, the outcome. Like other techniques, such as project planning and scheduling, it is not so much the benefit of creating the plan (or model) in the first place, but the ability to be able to test different scenarios and to identify a superior plan. Without such techniques, one risks striving for the exact attainment of an inferior plan. This outcome is likely when processes are described in words and not shown as deeds.

Change management, and the approach advocated above, have much in common with the principles of 'action research', where scenarios are generated, tested and fed back into the organisation where their effects are observed. These results are then used to modify the approach or model until it produces the desired outcome. The intention here is not, however, to dress up the application of a management technique into some kind of quasi-scientific theory; rather the aim is to show that there are always parallels from which one can gain useful insights.

Planning is key to success and, in many respects, there cannot be too much of it. Time spent 'up front' is usually amply rewarded by certainty of delivery; in other words, there are no surprises. Organisations should not underestimate the time required to plan a change management project. Unless it is taken seriously it will not produce the desired effect and the entire approach may be needlessly discredited. Facilities management can provide a mechanism for organisations to manage routine change; however, it cannot deal with wholesale change – other ways must be found such as outlined above. Whatever approach is taken it is vital to consult with all stakeholders: their input is necessary and their support may be too. Since implementing change generally involves alterations to the organisation's structure and tasks of the employees concerned, these factors will need to be looked at both on an organisational and an individual level.

Communicating change

It is important that those involved in the changes – employees and other stakeholders – are informed and that they are involved in decision-making. Communication is the means by which important messages are put across and commitment is returned. Failure here will mean that strategic planning (including resources planning) and the organisation's development and growth will be impeded as the change process becomes stalled. People can often be influenced by education and persuasion. Education is the milder form of social influence because it can help in presenting several different viewpoints, some of which will be unbiased. In this way, the target audience is offered a choice. On the other hand, persuasion can be targeted directly at employees conforming to one viewpoint. It can be used to get employees to accept change such as new working methods and new technology. Other forms that are available include propaganda and indoctrination, although the former is unethical and the latter is extreme and unacceptable in a democratic society. Nonetheless, it may help to be aware of these extreme measures, so ensuring that they are avoided.

Practice Point 5.1   Been there, done that.

Key point: meant with the best of intentions, it is possible for personnel who have been used to a particular way of working to want to continue as before believing that their experience will prove them right.

A college had decided to retain its facilities management in-house after a long process of consultation and some market testing. The main argument given in support of retention was that personnel in the new facilities division had amongst them tens of years of experience of managing the college buildings and grounds. Whilst this was the case, some personnel clearly had entrenched views. Typical of this problem were comments like, 'We tried that in the 90s and it didn't work then, so why is it going to work now?' It was not so much that the personnel concerned were being deliberately obstructive; rather, they had closed their minds to any alternative. If anything, the passage of time had reinforced their own belief in the limited value of doing certain things, because this was the easier alternative. The major challenge for the head of facilities – a newcomer – was to coax them into discussing the reasons why it failed in the past and how they had felt at the time. By persisting with a process of exploring the conditions surrounding a given event, the head of facilities was able to turn the situation around. Now, it was more likely to be a case of, 'We tried that in the 90s, it didn't work then because we were not able to do it this way. Now we can. I am sure that if we gave it a try we would succeed today.'

The process view of change management discussed earlier deserves further elaboration. Clearly, not everyone will be comfortable with graphical or pictorial representations of something they see all around them in the richness of the working environment. In extreme cases, they may see a process model as a crude device that strips away all that is human about work and the workplace. In one sense they are right – models *are* abstractions of reality. To complete the exercise we need to embellish the model, portraying the new order with information that will help people to understand sufficiently what is involved. No process model should, therefore, be posted as the blueprint for the future unless it is accompanied by supporting descriptions of activities, the human and other resources required to perform them, the tools that can be applied to assist in this task and the controls that will be exerted to ensure that the process delivers. Communicating a complete package of information is critical to success.

Responsibilities of those managing change

Implementing planned change brings the change manager directly to the all-important task of protecting the budget. The budget will have presumably been set according to an accepted plan and is an especially challenging situation when the changes involve outsourced services. These will be subject to contracts in which change – sometimes referred to as variations – may be accommodated. There are a number of reasons why change can be necessary, but most significantly we should think about the circumstances where a change can lead to increased cost.

Some changes can be anticipated and resources provided for them, whilst there may be no possibility of predicting others. Circumstances can include:

- Shifting needs in the (client) organisation's programme.
- Unforeseen requirements of external authorities.
- Unforeseen conditions in the workplace.
- Designers or other specialists requiring additions to complete work.
- The change manager simply failing to include certain work.

Arguably, the most important point to bear in mind is that change is generally not welcomed by the client organisation and is distrusted. It is therefore important that changes are allowed for in terms of quality (or performance), cost and time before project initiation so that the client's representative can be forewarned. It is conceivable that the client will understand and accept the need for a change. Change managers must also consider the needs of subcontractors in addition to those of the client organisation. The former should be treated even-handedly to ensure their commitment to the project. In overall terms, certainty and speed are of the essence in change management for ensuring a smooth transition and minimal disruption in workflow. Ensuring the commitment of everyone increases the probability of success.

Resolving cultural conflict

There can be many reasons why change projects fail. Some of the reasons have been touched upon already, but there are others lurking that must be brought out into the open. In these times of international business, travel and worker relocation, it is necessary to consider both the needs of foreign workers and the impact on work of conflict that can arise from different cultures.

The study of cross-culture and its impact on work practices is well documented, certainly at the level of the organisation – see, for example, Hofstede (1991). There is an expanding body of knowledge and literature to support it. Where there is a real weakness is in understanding cultural differences in the setting of a project, particularly major projects involving a multinational team or workforce. When international corporations wish to embark upon change projects in any of their overseas sites they would do well to increase the time and resources allocated to planning – see also Chapter 21.

Case study – EastPoint[1]

EastPoint emerged from a property management department within Colliers Jardine (Hong Kong) Limited with a heritage of more than two decades of business in Hong Kong as a Jardine Matheson company behind it. Over that period it had focused on traditional operations with every day being treated the same as any other. EastPoint undertakes professional management, security and technical duties on a wide range of property infrastructure projects throughout Hong Kong, in Macau, and currently as consultants in China. It manages over 100 million sq ft of property – nearly all of this is the 'common area' of multi-strata, multi-ownership properties typical of urban Hong Kong. These common areas are the frameworks, the approaches and the adjacent areas of buildings that contain a much greater area of residential, commercial and industrial units of accommodation. The organisation estimates that 7% of the population of Hong Kong lives or works in these units and are in its care. It is an important statistic – the organisation has always been concerned about professionalism in managing property, but now it has more to do with caring for the communities of people within these properties. EastPoint is repositioning and innovating within its business to get closer to the heart and soul of these communities.

The innovations that EastPoint have accomplished, through a process of controlled managed change, can be summarised as follows:

- Process re-engineering – delivering tangible products of change that include improved processes for governance, risk assessment, effectiveness and efficiency.

---

[1] now ISS EastPoint Facility Services Limited.

- Business restructuring – redistributing responsibilities and breaking down the walls that had traditionally existed between the established divisions in the organisation.
- Management by projects – adding project management skills and techniques as a prerequisite for business management and for leadership at all levels.
- Documentation to technical publishing standards – striving for clarity, comprehension, visual impression and quality impression.
- Use of proven technology – building information systems and electronic communications that integrate its dispersed business and reduce administrative and transaction costs.
- In-house open learning programmes and mentoring – providing personal workforce training without loss of productivity and with enhanced team effectiveness.
- Young Executive Training Programme – bringing bright minds to bear on research and development issues under seasoned leadership and obtaining tangible results – see also Chapter 20.
- Empowering executive personnel – responsibility for creative leadership in the form of enterprise task groups.

Some of these innovations are now discussed.

Process re-engineering is a broad set of coordinated activities to establish continual process improvements in business governance, risk management, quality standards and performance, and business metrics. As a result, a number of tangible products and techniques have become firmly implanted in the organisation's business. The office policy manual, quality manual and derivative products are best-in-class examples of procedural instruction. Risk assessments of tender submissions are based on Monte Carlo simulation and used to provide upside and downside appreciation of the risks inherent in the tender and pricing sensitivities in real terms.

Business restructuring has taken place in two stages. The property management department was reorganised early to redistribute responsibilities and to break down the walls that had traditionally existed between the established divisions in the organisation. It has given greater emphasis and new direction to the business support functions – for example quality control has been replaced by performance management and work improvement. This has created space for accelerating the development of up-and-coming talent within the organisation. Executive director roles have been defined and are used to empower specific individuals to take up a leadership role in one of three key enterprise areas of the organisation: commercial, operations and business administration. All executive directors report directly to the Managing Director and thereby to the Board.

Management by projects has become the norm for the planning and execution of the actions, small or large, that are required to bring about change in the organisation. Personnel holding strategic roles are given training in project management to an internationally accredited qualification so they are practically equipped to deliver projects on time and within budget.

The Open Learning Programme (OLP) is used to provide property management training to all 3200 employees, using a technical manual and derivative open learning workbooks which were developed as part of a mentoring approach to on-the-job training. The organisation adopted a two-stage approach to producing improved documentation that would provide technical instruction for all personnel. A production team was formed with participation from various grades of operational personnel.

The first task was to refine existing procedures by weeding out non-productive activities and processes, and by ensuring that customer satisfaction was given prominence in operational processes. For these reasons, the paper trails required for ISO quality assurance were discarded if they failed to contribute directly to productivity or customer satisfaction. Performance monitoring was by exception rather than by rule. All pro forma were reviewed for service need, standardised in readiness for porting to electronically enabled processes on the organisation's intranet. The intention was to cut operational procedures to the minimum or otherwise validate them as essential to the business. The second task was to author new documentation that would serve as a technical reference for the organisation. At this stage, a consultant was appointed to design a standard template for the organisation's documentation. These guidelines adopted clear, straightforward English and uncluttered text in readiness for the later production of open learning workbooks and work instruction guidelines.

The task-force effort in the first review of existing documents and editorial rework into new material amounted to 1800 man hours. This produced the draft of 'lean' organisational procedures. A technical writer was employed to author a technical manual from this material, corresponding workbooks for open learning and job specific guidelines for site personnel. Final format according to the layout template and final revisions were done in-house.

Twelve operational areas were identified for the open learning training programme. Each workbook was produced for easy reading. They included simple learning exercises to reinforce the learning process. As such, they are a personal study aid designed by experienced personnel in the organisation. Each workbook relates to sections in the technical manual. It is a reference book on the 'who, what, where, when and how' of the work process. Workbooks are not used in isolation. Users are encouraged to discuss them, to get answers on their questions from more experienced colleagues such as supervisors, or peers, and to make reference to the technical manual.

The OLP is complemented by an in-house training centre, which was introduced in 2001 as a cost saving and work improvement measure. Previously, the organisation's ongoing need for security-related training of building personnel was outsourced. Establishing the training centre has provided:

- An upgrade in the quality of training and on-the-job performance
- A cost saving equivalent to £30 000 annually
- Substantial improvement in the organisation's reputation with the police authority which imposes controls over how property is managed.

EastPoint recognised the improved efficiency and effectiveness that would be achieved by organising its business around workflow management and re-engineered business processes. This action had the added benefit of creating tangible new products and processes that clearly demonstrated business change. It has enabled the organisation to focus on reducing transaction costs within its business operations.

The organisation has also recognised that the nature of the business was changing to community care and, increasingly, the delivery of services at the personal level. Especially important in the context of relationship management is a distribution network that enables delivery of collateral items or messages on a personal basis to 7% of the population of Hong Kong. For EastPoint, the physical distribution network already exists, so the organisation is busy building the electronic network that will enable communications based on B2C intranet technology. Providing personal messaging to individuals to keep them informed and to demonstrate the organisation's commitment to a personal service is seen as offering strategic competitive advantage. It is also one step closer to creating an e-distribution network for the sale of services and commodities that can be distributed by EastPoint's physical distribution network.

Reducing transaction costs through e-enabled integration of a differentiated and decentralised business is likely to add significant value to EastPoint's procurement chain and offers better ways of deploying on-site operational resources. The organisation thus sees strategic competitive advantage from its B2C communications with the people in its communities and from B2B communications with its suppliers and other stakeholders in the business.

As evidence of EastPoint's successful implementation of its planned changes, the organisation has reported a 37% increase in revenue, a 47% increase in profit (EBITDA) and a 92% increase in EVA.

Conclusions

Change is bound to be a major concern and one that can be a force for good and bad. Organisations that are able to apply themselves differently and do so quickly may have an advantage over their competitors. However, this comes at a cost. Time and resources must be invested in planning – there can never be too much. Tools and techniques are available to help in the formalisation of the change process. Change managers do, however, need to ensure that they involve all stakeholders from the outset. Producing a workable plan for change is no fluke; it is the result of hard work that has clear objectives, which can be measured. Change management can be seen therefore as a powerful tool in itself, as it helps the organisation maintain focus on its strategic business objectives whilst identifying and bringing about the operational transformations that will help to deliver them. As the dynamics of the workplace change, so too will facilities management have to change to enable organisations to implement strategies that assume change as a normal feature of business life.

CHECKLIST

This checklist is intended to assist with the review and action planning process.

	Yes	No	Action required
1. Does the organisation have an explicit methodology for managing change?	☐	☐	☐
2. Is this methodology transparent, i.e. does it make the plan for change explicit and will it enable stakeholders to 'buy-in' to it?	☐	☐	☐
3. Is it the organisation's policy to involve stakeholders from the outset?	☐	☐	☐
4. Are major change projects given special status, i.e. do they have separately identified resources and time plans?	☐	☐	☐
5. Is there a communication network for adequately disseminating and gathering information with respect to proposed changes?	☐	☐	☐
6. Is the potential for conflict, arising from cultural differences, recognised by the organisation?	☐	☐	☐
7. Are there policies and/or procedures for dealing with variations to the implementation of a planned change?	☐	☐	☐

6 Human Resources Management

Key issues

The following issues are covered in this chapter.

- HRM issues need to be considered during the development of the organisation's strategic plan and accommodation strategy as an integral part of managing the provision of its support services and facilities.

- Senior management's goal of achieving best value for the organisation needs to be shared by all employees.

- Significant changes in the extent of outsourcing will have an impact on the roles and responsibilities of those concerned, requiring changes to HRM policy and procedures.

- Where applicable, the organisation must make clear its position on the transfer of employees to another employer. Legislation exists in many countries to ensure that employees are not treated unfairly.

- Performance appraisals are needed across the length and breadth of the organisation – there should be no discontinuity between senior management and operatives – and must be linked to the organisation's strategic business objectives.

- Remuneration and rewards for personnel should stem from performance appraisal and the overall success of the organisation – they must not be detached from it.

- Developing the skills and expertise of the workforce can be achieved by providing opportunities for personnel that are identified from performance appraisals.

Introduction

Adopting any significant change to the way in which estates-related and facilities services are provided will have an impact on the culture of the organisation and the nature of relationships with both internal and external parties. This chapter highlights those aspects of human resources management (HRM) that need to be addressed when developing a strategy to improve the value of support services required by the organisation. A key determinant of success for any organisation is the performance of its personnel. For this reason, performance appraisal has become the norm, yet is not always implemented so that remuneration and reward are linked to it and the overall health of the organisation. Here, we deliberately avoid the issue of why some organisations feel it is necessary to steer clear of the connection by showing, through a current example, how performance can be used to forge a closer bond between employer and employees. Developing the skills and expertise of the workforce is touched upon in this chapter, though this is covered more fully in Chapter 20. A case study is used to illustrate the breadth of problems that can be encountered when attempting to bring about change within an organisation that appears to have gone relatively unchanged for many years. Finally, an area of particular concern for HRM professionals and senior management is the transfer of employees from the (client) organisation to external service providers under an outsourcing arrangement. Legislation exists in many countries to safeguard the interests of employees to the extent that they are not treated unfairly as the result of their employment being transferred to another employer. The chapter concludes by illustrating, through a case study, how employees can be successfully transferred from the (client) organisation to a service provider, whilst including some notes of caution.

Dealing with shifting demands for resources

This chapter does not seek to provide a broad treatment of the subject of human resources management (HRM) as this can be found in many other books. Instead, it deals with issues and questions that arise from changes to the current organisational structure and its direction, as would occur if previously retained services were now to be outsourced.

The need for changes in the organisation's current HRM practices will depend upon the extent to which in-house services are to be outsourced to external service providers, as well as the type of policies and practices that are currently in place. Most organisations will probably have already considered many of the issues highlighted in this chapter. The sections that follow act primarily as a check against the main aspects of HRM that need to be reviewed when change is being considered. Particularly important is the need to consult with a competent legal authority on the current position in regard to the transfer of employees from the (client) organisation to external service providers, and this is outlined in a later section.

Appropriate management structure

Any significant change in the number of services that are outsourced will have an impact on the structure of the department or organisation; in the case of outsourcing all estates-related services and facilities management, a core management team is required to control and coordinate the activities of the external parties. In this instance, the role of management changes from direct or hands-on management to the management of the output of others, that is, the performance measurement of deliverables. The main management tasks then become the management of the respective contracts and the definition and development of policy and procedures. In this connection, it is essential to ensure that there is a split between purchaser and provider, regardless of whether or not services are outsourced, with the purchaser acting as the informed client in order to monitor the performance of in-house or outsourced service delivery. These policies and procedures, along with relevant standards, are vital if the respective contracts are to meet the expectations of customers and are not to encourage malpractice or some other kind of irregularity.

The most appropriate management structure will be the one that ensures both control and economy for the organisation over its facilities. This means that organisations will need to determine exactly the number of employees and their functions for managing the provision of services, whether they are outsourced or retained in-house. Clearly, the management of contractors is different from the supervision of directly employed personnel and should not demand the same level of resources. It is acceptable that some personnel will have to be retained even where the organisation has opted for total facilities management (TFM) by a single contractor (see Chapter 13) since the informed client function (ICF) must be maintained (see Chapter 1). Under these circumstances, there is a need for someone to be able to manage the client–service provider interface. The duties involved here can be summarised as:

- Maintaining and enhancing the ICF.
- Defining estates-related and space standard policies and monitoring space utilisation.
- Understanding and monitoring client requirements and likewise keeping clients informed.
- Planning projects involving new or additional works.
- Managing the approvals' process and payments to service providers.
- Measuring the performance of service providers.

Case study – Practical human resources issues

This case study illustrates the potential HRM issues faced by an organisation when outsourcing some or all of its non-core business. It is evident that considerable expertise is required to manage these issues in a way that satisfies both legal and ethical requirements, and avoids alienation and dissatisfaction among the remaining workforce, as part of an enduring focus on optimising the environment for core business interests. The case study is intended to provide a stimulus for the reader to develop a prior understanding of the HRM implications of certain changes in the provision of facilities management services and to exercise the judgement

*required to cope with a situation such as that illustrated here. With such prepara-
tion it should be possible to consider HRM implications in conjunction with the
initial decisions regarding service provision, rather than as a separate issue to be
handled after such decisions have been taken.*

*The resolution to outsource some or all facilities management services must
always be taken in this wider context, for which the fullest possible awareness and
understanding is essential, as the case study reveals. Where the client organisation
is aware that it lacks the expertise to manage such complexity, it can choose to
enlist the help of a facilities management consultant at an early stage. In the case
illustrated, many decisions had been made prior to the involvement of the facilities
management consultant. The consultant was therefore brought in to manage, in
particular, the HRM consequences of the earlier, relatively uninformed, decision-
making process within the client organisation.*

Northen plc has been established for over a hundred years as a mutual
building society, having transferred more recently to full banking status.
In line with competitors, it has undertaken a series of projects to outsource
areas of its non-core business. The bank's facilities management department group premises is now split into two divisions: 'network premises'
and 'head office premises'. Each has adopted a different approach to its
facilities management, creating a 'mixed economy' of service provision
within the organisation.

The network premises section looks after the building maintenance of
all retail branches and a large number of business (administrative) centres.
The management of facilities services has been kept in-house, but all
services have been outsourced at the operative level. A central telephone
helpdesk allows building users to request services and it also monitors
costs and other management information to allow budget management
and forecasting.

The head office premises section carries out a similar task for the bank's
20 or so head office buildings, all located in large cities. Head office premises
runs a mainly in-house operation and provides specific services as follows:

- Engineering – mechanical and electrical (M&E) engineering services,
  maintenance and projects, including heating, air-conditioning, lighting,
  cable laying, generators and installations.
- Building maintenance – building fabric maintenance and projects,
  including condition surveys, decorations, repairs, minor works and
  new build.
- Accommodation services – facilities services including porterage, furniture management and handyman services.

Head office premises has contracted out services such as lift maintenance,
specialist equipment maintenance, pest control, feminine hygiene, grounds
maintenance, cleaning and internal plants. Contracts had been let in bits
and pieces for about ten years; as a result there were over 200 contractors
working in head office buildings. Other facilities services such as catering,

security, conference room booking, chauffeur services, mail and messenger services are provided by the central services department. They do not fall within the scope of any group premises outsourcing project.

Head office premises provides services split into two geographical regions: west and east. Each region is managed by a facilities manager, with responsibility for about ten sites. There are three main buildings in each region, with all having a resident senior engineer, who manages engineering services within the buildings. Of engineering personnel, 50% are bank employees, 40% are employed by a local engineering contractor and 10% are employed by a local plumbing contractor. Contracted personnel have been employed full time by the bank for between five and ten years, and are managed by its senior engineers. The engineering, building maintenance, health and safety and environmental managers report directly to the head office premises manager. They provide policy, expert advice, quality control and a specialist management resource both to head office and network premises.

An accommodation services manager reports directly to each of the facilities managers and manages a mixed workforce of porters and handymen. The latter's role is furniture management, 'churn' and minor works. About half of the handymen are employed by a local joinery contractor and have been employed for a period similar to other contracted personnel. A workshop is also managed by one of the regions and consists of ten self-employed shopfitters, who have worked for the bank for up to 15 years. They carry out office refits and, on occasion, make hand-built furniture.

There are currently two helpdesks, one for each of the regions, but not all buildings are covered by the helpdesk facility. The helpdesks allow building users to call in and report repair requirements or request services. Typical requests include: porters required to move desks, broken lights that need fixing and heating not working. The helpdesk also processes invoices from external contractors and records limited financial data. Management information is not fully recorded and it seems impossible to measure historical costs for service provision.

Generally, the culture in the bank is hierarchical and resistant to change. The notion of a 'job for life' was ingrained in the business. In addition to this, the east region was originally part of a smaller bank that was acquired some years earlier. Its systems are compatible, but there are communication problems between the regions. There is also resistance to the idea that there may be other ways of doing things.

The bank has its own internal union, of which all employees are members. The union is strong, but also has a reputation for working closely with management to resolve personnel issues. Communications can sometimes be difficult, as line managers must liaise with the union via the employee relations department. There is also a tradition of communicating to employees on major issues through the union.

The bank has always paid its personnel above market rates and has been generous with overtime. Additionally, employees enjoy preferential mortgage and loan rates, extended sick leave, a share scheme, performance-related bonuses and a high employer contribution pension plan. Redundancy packages are particularly generous. Group premises employees are proud to work for the bank and consider themselves part of the banking sector as opposed to representatives of other professions and occupations acting within it.

An earlier outsourcing exercise involving security officers was mismanaged. This was not only expensive, but also led to a fragmented security department comprising a combination of in-house and contracted personnel with top-heavy management and inconsistent procedures. As a result, outsourcing is an unpopular concept with management and employees alike.

Group premises went through a series of structural reorganisations in the past and there are a number of rumours circulating about outsourcing and personnel layoffs. Derogatory graffiti started to appear on noticeboards and spurious advice has been generated on the rights of personnel under employment law. Although performance at work is high, morale has steadily fallen.

Deregulation of financial services increased market competition dramatically and the bank embarked on a restructuring programme to increase effectiveness and reduce costs. The decision to outsource the facilities services provided by head office premises has been made at board level and the head office premises manager has been asked to look at the options and make recommendations for providing a more effective and efficient service. Although costs must be reduced it is essential to maintain current high quality standards in the provision of an outsourced service to building users (customers).

Past experience and recognition of the need to manage change effectively have led the head office premises manager to retain a team of facilities management experts to provide advice on outsourcing and the HRM issues involved. The appointed facilities management consultant is therefore faced with two related areas requiring expert help: the continuation of the outsourcing process and its HRM impact. The first area involves helping the client to determine the levels at which outsourcing could be carried out, and advising on the advantages and disadvantages of different options and the appropriate bundling of outsourced contracts. The second area concerns identifying the key HRM issues and advising on how they might be handled. These include deciding who should be consulted concerning the outsourcing exercise, whether TUPE is relevant and, if so, to which employees, and the development of a communication plan.

The particular expertise of the facilities management consultant will be used to supplement the client's existing HRM function, by bringing an awareness of issues in specific relation to the concerns of the facilities management function and, by implication, to the core business which that function aims to support and enhance. From this perspective, the careful and appropriate management of personnel during such changes becomes an essential element in facilities management providing the optimal environment for an organisation's core business.

Employment obligations

Labour markets around the world are subject to varying degrees of control. Increasingly, governments and the legislature are applying more socially minded principles to the matter of employment. The responsibility of employers for their employees has come in for serious attention in efforts to safeguard the latter's rights. In Europe, EC Directives are applicable to all EU member states and prescribe policy and procedures covering the transfer of employees. In the UK, the relevant legislation is the Transfer of Undertakings (Protection of Employment) Regulations 2006 (TUPE). Organisations must establish how TUPE affects their policies, procedures and actions to ensure that they comply with the legislation. Although, for simplicity, the current discussion is set in the context of the UK, the intentions embodied in TUPE do have far wider application.

Employment obligations, both legal and moral, need to be considered carefully before outsourcing. TUPE stipulates that, in the case of directly employed personnel, there should be a consultation period before services are outsourced. In the case of contract personnel, organisations should pass their details to the firms tendering for the contracts. The scope of TUPE extends to cover all subsequent situations where the employment status of personnel is subject to change. It is essential, therefore, for organisations to establish how TUPE affects their policies, procedures and actions to ensure that they comply with the legislation.

The obligation to consult employees is an obligation to consult with elected representatives of those employees, or with any recognised trade union. If there are no recognised trade unions and no elected representatives, the employer has a duty to procure the election of representatives. It is not only representatives of employees subject to transfer who must be consulted, but also representatives of any employees who may otherwise be affected by the transfer. The duty to inform and consult is, therefore, broad and the intention is to involve all stakeholders. The information that must be passed to the employee includes details of the measures the transferee (that is, the new employer) intends to take with regard to the individual's employment.

This is a complex area of legislation and specialist advice should be sought. Consideration should be given both to the management of the process as well as to the inclusion, within tendering documentation, of necessary clauses in order that the mechanism by which TUPE operates can be put in place. In cases where TUPE does not apply, a redundancy situation may arise, and different procedures will have to be observed (and, of course, selection for redundancy must be fair).

Common sense suggests that the best approach to dealing with the transfer of employees is to involve them fully in discussion about their future employment. There are bound to be cynics amongst those facing potential transfer – many will feel threatened – but the only way forward is to keep to a path that strives for fairness. Failure to do so may not only risk a backlash, it might also incur criminal prosecution for those who have disregarded the correct procedures.

Case study – Sun Life

Sun Life of Canada (UK) Limited is a life assurance provider that closed to new business in the UK in 2001. The organisation operates out of a 9500 m² building in the south of England that is occupied by its outsourcing partners and will remain so for the next 20 to 25 years as the existing book of business runs out.

Sun Life outsourced its ICT support and ongoing administrative responsibilities, whilst entering into a sale and leaseback arrangement on the building itself in 2002. The building is effectively, therefore, a multi-let environment with an occupancy profile that includes four separate tenants. Under the individual lease terms, responsibility for running the facility remains with Sun Life, which raises a recovery service charge to the other tenants. The building has been maintained to a very high level, befitting the corporate headquarters of a prominent financial services organisation.

In 2003, Sun Life entered into a partnering agreement with Acuity Management Solutions under an initial three-year agreement for facilities management services. Acuity managed a transition process that included the transfer of 20 Sun Life employees and the novation of an extensive range of supply chain agreements. Following the transition process, Acuity took responsibility for the delivery of facilities services throughout the building, including all demised areas. This includes the management of the tenant relationships and agreement of annual service charges. Described here is the process by which Acuity carried out this transfer and the benefits delivered through the approach that was adopted.

The process of outsourcing the facilities management function for any client has the potential to create tensions that could increase risk of business interruption with a consequential increase in costs. For this reason, Acuity considered it vital to the success of the contract that a carefully managed transition programme was designed and implemented. The programme translated the vision and objectives of outsourcing into a new set of philosophies, processes and systems, and applied them in a systematic way to ensure successful implementation without risk of business interruption.

The overall transition process began during the mobilisation phase, but continued throughout the first six months of the contract. During this important phase, the facilities management team was strengthened by Acuity's own human resources to provide specific skills and experience in the management of change. Taking the outsourcing concept as the starting point the team covered the following:

- Implementation and communication planning.
- Operational audits of existing processes and procedures.

- Process re-engineering of the existing processes and procedures.
- Employee surveys to establish skill levels and identify development requirements.
- Risk and benefit analyses.
- Detailed reviews of the specialist supplier base.
- Asset management and assessment of building improvements, with the associated business cases and their prioritisation.

The whole transition process was the subject of an intensive change management regime to ensure that all the issues raised were dealt with appropriately in a proactive manner.

One of the main objectives of this process was the ability to deliver high-quality services continuously. These services could have been impaired by low employee morale, particularly when the attention of individuals was distracted by their becoming more concerned about the changes and impact on themselves, rather than on the delivery of services. Acuity recognised that managing people through any change process inevitably has its high and low points. Often, expectations are set too high by the new provider wishing to rally its newly acquired personnel. When these high expectations are subsequently not met an already fragile situation is exacerbated.

Recognising the impact and adopting a proactive approach mitigated this threat. Proactive management of the change process ensures that momentum is maintained, particularly as it is a fundamental component in the successful achievement of strategic direction. Whilst a degree of overt or covert resistance is almost inevitable from some affected employees and, to a lesser extent, certain other stakeholders, the introduction of a change manager can provide direction and assist in the overall achievement of progress in a shorter time frame. Whilst senior management commitment is essential, without an identified driver to own and push the change through, progress can, all too often, be slow and painful. Acuity's Account Director adopted this dual role of 'manager and driver'.

The success of the mobilisation process was particularly critical for Sun Life as this represented a first generation outsourcing exercise, with TUPE implications and a relatively short timescale involved. Acuity provided a dedicated mobilisation team that operated in addition to and in parallel with the existing facilities management team. The intention was to establish and document fully the processes, procedures, communications, information and reporting requirements, so that the team could focus on the continuous delivery of high-quality services.

The first step was to establish and confirm with Sun Life the detail of the mobilisation plan. A detailed task list was prepared which allowed both parties to track and report on progress against the plan, in weekly communication meetings, until both parties agreed that the process was complete.

Mobilisation was led by the Acuity Account Director who took responsibility for managing the client relationship from the 'go live' date. The

Account Director was also supported by a fellow director who was involved in one-to-one interviews with each employee. This approach was adopted by Acuity to allow employees access to a director who would not be directly involved in the contract subsequently, but who could act as a mentor should any of the transferring employees have anxieties or concerns which they were uncomfortable raising with their new line manager, the Account Director. In addition, further support personnel were also involved to assist with the technical, health and safety and human resource related issues.

Acuity ensured that a full and open communication process to help employees understand and adjust to the change was followed. A detailed communication plan was adopted and a five-stage process was implemented. Initially, an *Introduction to Acuity* meeting with affected employees was arranged. This meeting described the organisation, its goals, clients and organisational structure; it covered the process, clearly describing the path to be followed and a set of frequently asked questions.

Following this initial meeting, discussions with individual employees were scheduled to explain their position within the organisation, its policies and practices, terms and conditions of employment, and to give each individual the opportunity to raise any queries or concerns. This meeting was conducted in two parts. The first part, with the Account Director, discussed the job, any predicted changes and how work would be managed by Acuity. In the second part, the Acuity Consulting Director discussed terms and conditions, how Acuity manage people and procedural changes, and finally dealt with any queries or concerns.

The time spent with the employees at this stage helped them understand the change and the reasons for it, and was critical in managing their morale during the transition. The objective throughout was to avoid surprises and to ensure that all employees fully understood the process they were going through.

Once the individual meetings were completed, transfer documentation was sent to each transferring employee. This included a statement of principal terms and conditions and the Employee Handbook. In addition, each employee was sent a welcome letter from the Board of Directors. Acuity's induction process was then implemented. Events were organised formally and informally to welcome the transferring employees and to complete the induction process. At every stage of the process, the transferring employees had open access to at least two senior personnel and this approach reduced any lingering suspicion that might have remained from the initial decision to outsource.

Once the transfer had been effected, work continued in reviewing practices and the roles and responsibilities of all personnel, who were given the opportunity to contribute ideas and to identify areas where activities could be carried out more effectively. The Account Director continued to spend a significant amount of time coaching the senior site personnel, providing the support and assistance needed to move from an in-house cost centre to a contributing profit centre.

Twelve months later, the same personnel remain with a site based manager who has developed his skills and successfully made the transition to a broader operations manager with responsibility for a profit and loss account. In addition, the performance management regime implemented by Acuity has demonstrated improving performance month on month together with sustainable savings representing over 10% of the annual budget.

The facilities management team at Sun Life has accepted and met the challenges it faced with commitment and good humour. Whilst initial thoughts of transfer were filled with apprehension, the approach adopted not only reduced anxieties, but allowed individuals to contribute to a process where they could identify the value they were adding. Once the initial trust was established, respect and commitment followed.

Functions, job descriptions and skills

As changes occur in the mode of managing facilities, it is likely that the functions to be performed by personnel will also change. This will mean that job descriptions have to be revised for those with responsibility for managing services. The content of these revised job descriptions will dictate the selection of appropriate individuals for positions. In assigning individuals to positions that require interaction with service providers, including in-house teams, an understanding of operations and performance issues will be required, as well as strong interpersonal skills and knowledge of contracts.

All job descriptions should incorporate a means for evaluating the performance of employees. It is important that job descriptions are accompanied by role-evaluation procedures so that employees and management are aware from the outset what is expected.

The issues highlighted in this book introduce novel ways of operating in a number of areas. These may require managers to develop existing skills further or to learn new skills in order to implement changes effectively. In particular, introducing new information management procedures and systems – many of which are heavily ICT dependent – will require additional training. Difficulties can arise because of the need for employees to adjust to new working practices. Through sensitive handling, the organisation should be able to overcome problems that might arise, using briefings, seminars and training programmes (see Chapter 20).

Managers also need to be aware of the prevailing market for estates-related and facilities services, and what is required to manage service providers effectively. The managers who deal directly with service providers need different skills to those in a line management position. This should be recognised so that training and development needs can be identified (see Chapter 20). In fact, the entire organisation should be subject to continuing professional development (CPD) as an example of its commitment to life-long learning and a drive for continual improvement.

> **Practice Point 6.1   Worth one last try.**
>
> *Key point: the organisation must be prepared to invest in its people, by providing them with opportunities to retrain for new roles and responsibilities.*
>
> When a large city-centre organisation decided to overhaul completely its facilities management, it was faced with some tough choices: make everyone redundant and start over again; transfer everyone on the payroll to a new service provider; or invest in the retraining and reskilling of the workforce. After much discussion behind the scenes, it was agreed that it would be more prudent, at least at the time, to opt for retraining and reskilling. There were many cynics, not only in the organisation's management, but also amongst the workforce. For them, it was a case of having heard it all before. Undeterred, the newly appointed facilities manager decided to take the matter into his own hands. First, there were awareness seminars at which everything was brought out into the open. Next, the workforce was regrouped and refocused on its new challenges and goals. Finally, a permanent communication centre was established and charged with the responsibility for making everything in the facilities directorate, as it was now known, much more visible for everyone. A regular newsletter is now published and distributed to everyone.

Performance appraisal

Management at all levels should be subject to performance appraisal, including those managers who either work for or are part of a service provider organisation. The assessment of the performance of service providers in particular is discussed in Chapter 9. Client representatives (facilities managers and estates managers) who deal with service providers should be set performance objectives that reflect the management relationship with those service providers, along with the actions taken to monitor performance and deal with any shortcomings. This could, for example, take the form of targets for tasks planned and completed over a given period, percentage of response times met and number of tasks needing to be reworked. Where performance depends on the efforts of a group of people, performance at group level should also be addressed either through individual appraisals or at group sessions.

There are many ways in which the performance of individuals can be measured and used to create incentives and to reward excellent performance. A compelling example is provided by EastPoint – an organisation that was the subject of a major case study in Chapter 5. There is a fundamental belief on the part of senior management that all personnel should have a vested interest in the performance of the organisation. With that in mind, personal appraisals are undertaken annually and based upon core competences and key performance indicators (KPIs), which are aligned with the organisation's business objectives. The results of the appraisals have a material bearing on the promotion of individuals and the apportionment of performance bonus payments. These KPIs are in addition to core competences measured as part of a standardised appraisal process. The KPIs for associate directors or heads of divisions and above are customised to suit their specific role and responsibilities. Generic KPIs have been introduced for other grades of professional and managerial personnel, where they are based on business measures linked to the properties being managed and, thus, to customer satisfaction.

Examples of generic KPIs for personnel in support roles are based on five fundamental performance areas and attract equal weight:

1. Core skills – ICT ability, planning and foresight, organisation and team participation.
2. Knowledge management – expertise, consistency, maintenance and time management.
3. Communication – telecommunications, contacts, manner and expertise.
4. Technical documentation – production expertise, adherence to standards and multimedia.
5. Procedures – ISO compliance and office policies.

These can be compared with the KPIs for professional grade personnel, which are also weighted equally:

- Customer satisfaction – ISO compliance rating, customer satisfaction rating and retention/increase in business.
- Professional management – tele-protection compliance, upkeep/satisfaction of manager's diary and director's property inspection report.
- Company performance – debtor control rating, audited accounts and participation in business development.
- Interpersonal skills – communications, turnover of employees, leadership, motivation and self-improvement.

The organisation promotes the development of further skills amongst its personnel through its Training Sponsorship Scheme. This is used to motivate and encourage personnel to upgrade their skills continuously by accredited academic study on a part-time basis in their own time. The scheme is beneficial to the organisation as it increases the knowledge and expertise of its personnel. A subsidy is offered, but paid only when the candidate passes the course examination.

Another approach to accelerating the development of up-and-coming talent is the *Tall Poppies* programme, which has a multifaceted approach covering:

- The development and faster promotion of high performers.
- Increasing the ratio of internal to external promotions.
- Modifying the appraisal process to differentiate individuals by performance.

- The recruitment of a few outstanding graduates as executive trainees to be used as a core resource in process re-engineering, innovation and the production of tangible products for deployment in the business.

The organisation has taken positive action in favour of internal promotion. Approximately 75% of vacancies have been filled through internal promotion, with external recruitment reduced from 75% to about 50% of all vacancies.

The organisation introduces young managerial talent into the business through the vehicle of an Executive Trainee Programme, with the aim of creating a new generation of young executives appropriately trained for promotion to management positions. These personnel enjoy career development through a combination of productive assignments and participation in an Executive Development Scheme within the wider group of which the organisation is a part. These people have proved a highly productive asset to the organisation, having been deployed on a number of business assignments. These are designed to be meaningful to the individual and productive for the organisation. Each assignment is intended to challenge the individual to be creative and to produce new products or re-engineer processes. Their work must be documented and include implementation in the workplace. Two early entrants have since been promoted to assistant manager roles and are pursuing further management qualifications.

Conclusions

HRM is a sensitive area for all organisations. Increasing legislation has added to the burden on organisations to have clear policies and procedures in place, no more so perhaps than in the case of TUPE. These have to be complete and must apply regardless of whether or not a service is outsourced or retained in-house. Organisations need to adopt a management structure that is appropriate to the mode of service provision and understand their obligations as employers. Job descriptions and skills requirements must be made explicit and procedures put in place to appraise and reward performance against measurable outputs or outcomes.

CHECKLIST

This checklist is intended to assist with the review and action planning process.

	Yes	No	Action required
1. Is the organisation's management structure appropriate to the delivery of cost-effective and efficient management services?	☐	☐	☐
2. Have job functions, job descriptions and service requirements been properly described in relation to the provision of management services?	☐	☐	☐
3. Are employees involved in defining job functions, job descriptions and service requirements?	☐	☐	☐
4. Do current arrangements properly recognise employment obligations, as well as the underpinning legislation?	☐	☐	☐
5. Is a well-developed method of performance appraisal in place covering all employees?	☐	☐	☐
6. Is performance appraisal linked to the organisation's strategic business objectives and overall success?	☐	☐	☐
7. Are employees provided with incentives to develop their skills and are they rewarded when they succeed?	☐	☐	☐

7 Policy and Procedures for Outsourcing

Key issues

The following issues are covered in this chapter.

- There is a logical sequence to the outsourcing of services, covering strategy, tender documentation, tendering and contract award. A realistic timescale must be allowed if the overall process is to be successful.

- Outsourcing involves many activities and these have to be managed. A detailed programme should be prepared to help manage the process and to keep all interested parties informed.

- Defining the scope of services is crucial to successful outsourcing, by providing the basis for inviting tenders and administering the contract. A poorly defined scope will lead, almost inevitably, to problems in the management of the service.

- All stakeholders must be involved in the process of outsourcing if their needs, as well as those identified earlier during the preparation of the facilities management strategy, are to be fully addressed and communicated – success depends on commitment to the process from all who could possibly contribute.

Introduction

Once the decision to outsource has been reached, the procedures that follow tend to be somewhat prescriptive, though are certainly not mechanistic. This means that senior management can rely upon legislation, guidelines and practice notes from a wide range of sources. There is benefit from this situation, but there can be disadvantages arising from dogged adherence to procedures that may have been designed for a different purpose. Some interpretation is likely in order to take account of local circumstances, for instance custom and practice, as well as the market. Narrow interpretation of legislation in particular – as we shall see later – risks creating anomalies that can thwart the good intentions that lie behind them. The approach taken here will be one of highlighting current best practice, drawing on guidance from various sources and the authors' research in the field. The chapter begins by examining the general approach to the procurement of works, supplies and services, referred to collectively as services. The procedures apply also to situations where currently outsourced services are being re-tendered and/or rationalised. For clarity, the procedures are followed in chronological order as far as practicable. The objective is to ensure that the following critical success factors are achieved: first, the scope of the services and interfaces with related services are defined; second, the service level required by stakeholders from the outsourced team is clearly specified; third, the outsourced team has the capabilities and skills to deliver the service; fourth, internal departments are recognised as customers and treated as such; fifth, outsourced service provision is provided through a team approach, with each member working towards a common goal; and last, service provision is continually reviewed and improved.

Essential approach

General guidance on procurement can be found in many publications relating to project management; in fact, the subject is covered comprehensively elsewhere. Additionally, reference can be made to Chapter 1 on the risks encountered in outsourcing and to Appendix C, which provides an effective checklist. The organisation should consider risk assessment and risk transfer as an integral part of the process for procuring services. This will mean that risk assessment forms part of the policy and procedures for outsourcing. Risk assessment was covered in Chapter 4, with an example of how to apply it in practice. For a detailed appreciation of risk management see, for example, CIRIA (1996) in which detailed guidance, with practical examples and pro forma, can be followed.

In order to illustrate the outsourcing process, a generic procurement plan is set out in Fig. 7.1 showing the main stages and activities. Each activity is described in more detail below. The plan's aim is to provide an indication of the order and timescales involved in moving from the definition of services to the services actually being provided within the organisation. The plan is divided into three main stages:

1. *Strategy* – covering the definition of services, current arrangements, the position of stakeholders and legislation affecting employment and procurement.
2. *Tender documents* – covering service specifications, service level agreements and conditions of contract.
3. *Tendering process* – covering prequalification, tenderer briefing and assessment, contract award, pre-contract meeting, mobilisation and review.

The timescales will vary according to the scope and scale of services being outsourced. However, many of the critical periods, for instance dealing with legislative aspects, contractual matters, tenderer briefing, tender period and mobilisation, will remain more or less the same for a wide range of

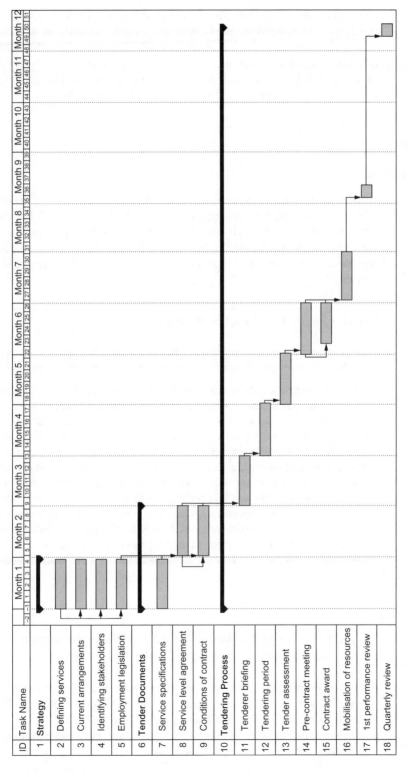

Fig. 7.1   Activities in the procurement of services.

ID	Task Name
1	Strategy
2	Defining services
3	Current arrangements
4	Identifying stakeholders
5	Employment legislation
6	Tender Documents
7	Service specifications
8	Service level agreement
9	Conditions of contract
10	Tendering Process
11	Tenderer briefing
12	Tendering period
13	Tender assessment
14	Pre-contract meeting
15	Contract award
16	Mobilisation of resources
17	1st performance review
18	Quarterly review

contract types and values. The timescale might reduce for activities such as the definition of services, current arrangements, identifying stakeholders, tender assessment and contract award, where the service to be outsourced is of minor economic importance and uncomplicated. As with any exercise of this kind it is easy to underestimate the time required to move from the decision to outsource to the commencement of the service.

Strategy

Defining services

Critical to the success of any outsourcing process is the clear definition of all required services including interfaces – see also Chapter 2. For example, are pest control, waste disposal and sanitary services to be part of the cleaning contract? Such definition is required to ensure that all necessary services are provided and that no gaps exist between the interfaces of each service.

Practice Point 7.1   Falling into the cracks.

Key point: services must have their scope clearly defined, with special attention paid to instances where some services can fall into the gaps between service contracts.

When infestation of the ceiling void above the kitchens was discovered, the immediate reaction was to call in the cleaning contractor. After all, the contractor was responsible for removal of waste and related duties. In the event, the contractor pointed out that any occurrence of this kind was not his responsibility. The contractor appeared to have acted correctly, but there was the understanding, at least in the mind of the facilities manager, that matters like the one encountered were included in the scope of the cleaning contract. The outcome was that the organisation agreed to pay the contractor to remove the infestation and then formally instructed that the revised scope be included within the contract. Fortunately for the organisation, the service contract contained provision for changes of this kind to be made.

Current arrangements

The following base information should be gathered in relation to current services prior to the initiation of the outsourcing process:

- In-house services – number of employees, their grades and employment details (age, starting date, length of service, experience, special skills, salary and benefits), plant and equipment inventory.
- Outsourced services – contract expiry date, contract value, scope of existing services and special features.

Identifying stakeholders

The importance of stakeholders should come as no surprise – previous chapters have underscored the necessity of their early involvement. Stakeholders are those parties with an interest in the services to be provided, such as internal and external customers. In order to secure the success of the process, it is important that they are identified and their requirements understood, with specifications and service levels aligned to their needs (see Chapter 9). While it may not always be possible, given the constraints that may be imposed on the outsourced team to satisfy every requirement or preference, the needs of stakeholders should be ranked according to their benefit to the organisation to ensure that the more significant ones are met.

Essentially, any individual or group with a legitimate interest in the organisation is a stakeholder and these can include:

- The organisation's employees
- External users and customers
- Service providers and suppliers
- Shareholders and non-executive directors
- Neighbours
- General public
- Community groups
- Local councils
- Statutory authorities.

Employment legislation

Prior to proceeding with outsourcing or the re-tendering of services, it is essential to consider the implications of current employment and procurement legislation – see Chapters 6 and 10. In terms of the former, the relevant legislation in the UK is the Transfer of Undertakings (Protection of Employment) Regulations 2006 (TUPE) and the Transfer of Undertakings (Pension Protection) Regulations 2005, which are derived from the EC's Acquired Rights Directive. These regulations protect the contracts of employment of both directly employed personnel and the contractor's employees where the service has already been outsourced. An earlier case study discussed how this legislation applied to the transfer of employees – see Chapter 6.

In relation to directly employed personnel, the organisation's obligations are more onerous and will usually involve a consultation period with employees. Where service provider's employees are concerned, the (client) organisation will normally only be involved in communicating employee details to tenderers – again, see Chapter 6. However, legal precedent is continually being set in this area, for example the definition of a full-time employee. It is, therefore, advisable and prudent to seek professional advice on the specific implications for each service that is to be outsourced.

Public procurement legislation

In addition to employment legislation, public procurement legislation must be addressed, where relevant. In the UK, the implications of the Public Works, Supply and Services Contract Regulations 1995 must be taken into account. The main principle behind this legislation is to ensure that for service contracts above a specified threshold:

- Specifications are non-discriminatory.
- Firms and individuals are selected objectively for inclusion in tender lists.
- The tendering process is transparent.

These principles have, of course, a wider application to best practice procurement. In the EU context, public sector organisations are required by EC public procurement directives to publish tenders for the provision of supplies, services and works over a certain value in the Official Journal of the European Union (OJEU). The contract value thresholds, above which invitations to tender should appear in the OJEU, are as follows (approximate values depending upon categorisation and exchange rates):

- Supplies and services: €499 000 (roughly £400 000)
- Works: €6 242 000 (roughly £5 000 000).

An annual periodic indicative notice is required, covering each priority service category on which it is expected that more than €750 000 (roughly £600 000) will be spent. Public sector organisations, in particular, should check these limits, and establish whether or not they are required to advertise in the OJEU before inviting tenders. Total contract value, regardless of contract period, is the basis of assessment, not annual cost. Some organisations have tried to circumvent this legislation by reducing the size of contracts to below the threshold by breaking them into smaller parcels. Such practices effectively contravene European law.

Whilst it is possible to generalise on the underlying principles, it is not feasible to provide a comprehensive guide to legislation. Appropriate legal advice should be taken and the position on public procurement procedures verified in order to ensure compliance with the relevant legislation in any place and at any time. This should be part of the ICF – see Chapter 1. Responsibilities should also be clearly split between purchasing and provider personnel when in-house tenders are sought in addition to those from external service providers. This will avoid conflicts of interest that might otherwise arise when subsequently assessing tenders.

Tender documents

Service specifications

A service specification quantifies the acceptable standard of service required by the customer and will generally form a part of the contract with the service provider (see Chapter 9). The preparation of a service specification is a prerequisite for the drafting of a service level agreement – see next section. Specifications ordinarily set out standards covering organisation policy, department requirements, statutory requirements, health and safety standards, and manufacturers' recommendations. A specification may also outline the procedures needed to achieve required technical standards.

Service level agreement (SLA)

The SLA builds on the service specification by amplifying, in practical terms, the obligations of each party. Technical and quality standards will usually be defined in relation to industry standards or manufacturers' recommendations, whereas performance will be related to the specific requirements of stakeholders, that is, frequency of activity and response times to call-outs (see Chapter 9). This agreement need only include, at the tendering stage, a framework setting out the overall performance parameters with detailed procedural issues to be evolved and refined during the life of the contract. Whilst the scope must be made clear, detailed day to day operating procedures can only be fine-tuned as knowledge and experience of each service partner is built up over time. SLAs must be kept up to date and avoid locking either party into arrangements and practices that are plainly inefficient or, worse, ineffective.

Conditions of contract

Wherever possible, it is recommended that industry standard forms of contracts are used to formalise legal relationships between the client organisation and contractors. Standard forms of contract may be obtained from a number of sources that include:

- The Chartered Institute of Building (CIOB) Standard Form of Facilities Management Contract (third edition, 2008) – used for a client organisation employing a facilities manager. The contract allows for an adjustable annual fee to be paid, together with reimbursable expenses. It is intended primarily for use in the private sector.
- PACE (GC/Works/10) Standard Form of Facilities Management Contract. The form is designed to help in the procurement of facilities management services and can also be used for the appointment of a contractor as a one-stop shop or as a managing agent. It is suitable for

use in procuring services on the basis of input or output specifications and can be used on one or more sites. It is intended primarily for use in the public sector.

- Chartered Institute of Purchasing and Supply (CIPS) – model form of contract for facilities management of computer operations.
- JCT (Joint Contracts Tribunal) – building contracts for maintenance and small works (the JCT publishes a range of standard forms and variants of them).

The CIOB contract has helped to formalise the nature of facilities management arrangements. Since its original publication in 1999, it has become a popular choice. It outlines and specifies the services to be provided by the facilities manager, and deals with administrative issues – management reporting, personnel changes, etc. – as well as those of a mostly contractual nature, such as obligations, insurances, non-performance and termination. Provision is included for public sector contracts where special conditions apply.

Generally, any amendments required to forms of contract should be clearly stated in the tender documents. Normally, it should not be necessary to amend standard conditions, as to do so might lead to unforeseen events and consequences. If the organisation wishes to amend standard forms, legal advice should be sought.

The purpose of forms of contract is to provide the formal, legally binding framework within which service specifications and SLAs can operate. As such, they should not attempt to restate the contents of specifications and SLAs. Appendix D contains useful guidance on contractual approaches and terms, whilst Appendix E outlines the possible contents and structure of an SLA. In the case of EastPoint – an organisation referred to in previous chapters – the dividing line between SLAs and the contract is clear: the latter includes all annexes necessary to embody the SLAs so that there is no requirement for separate SLAs or service specifications. The organisation's own contract form thus has annexes covering both service specifications and SLAs. In this connection, the latter are intended more as the means for stipulating performance indicators – see Chapter 18.

An important consideration, in terms of contract conditions, is that they should allow for changes to be made as experience of operating a contract grows. SLAs should be reviewed and updated periodically. An inflexible contract, unable to accommodate changes, would represent an unworkable arrangement. Contracts should be seen, therefore, not as straitjackets, but as frameworks within which to operate and develop best practice. As a minimum, contracts should contain clauses that allow for changes to be made to the provision of services, so long as they are not so significant as to alter the overall scope and content of the contract. These clauses should also cover the mechanism for adjusting the contract sum in the event of changes – sometimes referred to as variations – being required and sanctioned by the client.

> **Practice Point 7.2   Form your own conclusions.**
>
> **Risk item:** failure to use standard forms of contract for facilities management or inadequate conditions of contract can lead to serious difficulties.
>
> *Key point: in negotiating contracts with suppliers and service providers, it is essential to ensure that the client's position is properly protected and not compromised. Legal advice should be sought in these matters.*
>
> In one case, an organisation entered into a contract with a service provider only to find later that the terms and conditions were biased in the contractor's favour. The client organisation did not adopt a standard form of contract and, therefore, accepted the contract as drafted by the service provider (the contractor), an established and respected company. A clause in the contract held the client organisation liable for redundancy payments if any of the personnel employed by the contractor had to be dismissed following a decline in the use of certain of the facilities. Subsequently, there was a fall in the use of a particular facility and the organisation had to make substantial payments. An important consideration – in terms of contract conditions – is that they should allow for changes to be made as experience of operating a contract grows. Service level agreements (SLAs) should be reviewed and updated periodically. An inflexible contract – unable to accommodate changes – would represent an unworkable arrangement. Contracts should be seen as frameworks within which to operate and develop best practice. As a minimum, contracts should contain clauses that allow for changes to be made to the provision of services, so long as they are not so significant as to alter the overall scope and content of the contract. These clauses should also cover the mechanism for adjusting the contract sum in the event of changes being required by the client.

Tendering process

Prequalification

Whilst closed (or selective) tendering is naturally preferred by most client organisations, public procurement legislation will demand some form of open tendering. In most cases, however, a certain degree of tenderer prequalification is required to ensure that only competent and capable service providers submit tenders. Open tendering is generally considered suitable for supply-only contracts, notably those involving commodities.

Prospective tenderers are required to comply with basic conditions and provisions. Proof of competence, i.e. track record supported by verifiable details of reference sites, is required, together with evidence of financial and other resources required to perform the service. In the public sector in the EU, the requirements are highly prescribed and open to scrutiny (as well as subject to challenge) – see earlier section on public procurement legislation. In the private sector, clients are usually free to choose their own basis for prequalification, but may be guided by public procurement guidelines as a matter of complying with current best practice.

Tenderer briefing

Depending on the complexity of the services being tendered, it is often useful to organise a tenderers' briefing during the tender period. This can be either formal or informal so long as the latter is conducted on a consistent basis for all tenderers. The object of this briefing is to:

- Show tendering companies the facilities.
- Describe how they support the core business.
- Identify areas of particular concern or sensitivity.
- Explain the principles of the contract.
- Clarify the requirements of the tender submission.
- Answer any questions that may arise.

In the course of these briefings, it is important that tenderers are advised that lowest price will not be the sole factor in choosing between tenders: quality of service will be taken into account. Care must also be exercised in conducting such briefings in order to avoid collusion between parties or allegations that one party is being treated more favourably than others (see Appendix B).

Tendering period

In the public sector, where the value of services to be tendered exceeds the EC public procurement thresholds (see earlier section), the tender period must comply with the duration set out in the regulations. In any event, it is good practice to allow sufficient time for tenderers to consider fully the documentation and allow them to submit a considered proposal. This should never be less than two weeks from receipt of documents. If it should be found necessary to issue an amendment to the tender documents, this should not be less than two weeks before submission of the tender. One of the greatest failings is to maintain a tender receipt date that squeezes the time given to tenderers in which to prepare a properly considered tender. In the worst case scenario, the client organisation could be left with no tenders or just one that is effectively a cover price. This outcome would be wholly unsatisfactory and a waste of time and money.

The procedure for the formal submission of tenders is, for public sector organisations, usually highly prescribed. Adherence to the requirements outlined in the 'invitation to tender' should be followed strictly by tendering companies. Failure to comply with just one aspect – no matter how minor it may seem – could lead to the rejection of the tender without its even being opened. Public accountability and the fears of individual officers leave no margin for negotiation in such an eventuality.

Tender assessment

Sufficient time should be allowed for the assessment of tenders. Assessment criteria should be agreed in advance in relation to technical, quality of service and resource requirements and may also be incorporated in the tender documents. These should be applied to each tender submission in order to shortlist companies for interview, requiring them to make a formal presentation. Additionally, inspection of a company's premises and order books could provide valuable insights into its ability to meet the demands of the new contract. A major consideration is whether or not a company is physically able to perform the service for the tender price. Client organisations should enquire as to the creditworthiness of shortlisted companies and request contact names of existing clients from whom performance references might be obtained.

Clearly, facilities management contracts involve the operation and delivery of services within occupied environments. Consequently, the way in which services are delivered and the manner in which stakeholder communication occurs becomes increasingly relevant. In the authors' experience the choice of the service provider's main representative is a critical component in the identification of an appropriate partner. Effort placed at the interview stage in understanding the strengths, weaknesses and style of the representative and team can provide a valuable insight into the likely relationship to follow. It is recommended that the key representatives are present at interview and that this element is evaluated in its own right.

The concept of least whole-life cost should be used to evaluate tenders alongside risk assessment. Least whole-life cost takes into account the cost of the services over the duration of the contract, including annual price fluctuations, life-cycle cost issues, payback on capital investment and so on. In other words, it is a matter of determining the total cost of each tender, enabling comparison on a like-for-like basis. EastPoint applies a tender assessment mathematical model, based on Monte Carlo simulation, to analyse all standard property, facilities, asset management and engineering contracts. Tender submissions undergo risk assessment of varying depth, covering financial and legal risks as well as the nature of the work itself to determine value. In the future, these two approaches will merge to provide client organisations with whole-life, value-risk assessment.

Practical steps in determining quality and cost

Lowest price is not the sole factor in deciding which tender to accept, although many tenders are accepted on the basis of price alone. Quality should play an equal part in any evaluation if best value is to mean anything. For some contracts it may be difficult to determine the quality of service: rarely can quality or performance be considered in absolute terms. It is possible to take account of quality by judging it against benchmarks established in service specifications or other objective measures.

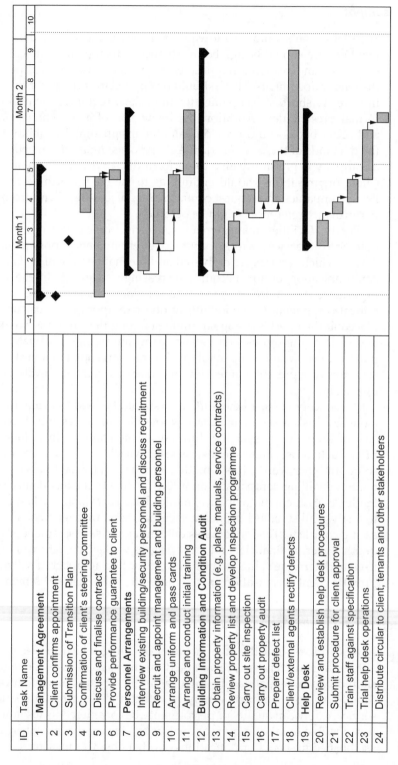

Fig. 7.2 Transition process.

There are other ways in which quality and cost may be judged. For instance, in the case of professional services, one approach would be to operate a two-envelope tender system. Shortlisted consultants are sent model agreements and asked to submit a lump sum tender, along with their time charges for extra work. The first tender describes the quality of service to be provided; the second gives the price. Two separate panels look at the tenders.

A quality panel of, say, four people is convened to rank the tenders, A, B and C according to the quality that they believe each tenderer represents. The panel applies a percentage adjustment (or weighting) to the services offered by each: it is necessary that all panellists agree. Once the quality panel has finished its deliberations, the price panel opens the envelopes containing the price tenders. The decision is then taken to award the contract to the consultant offering the highest quality at the lowest price, based on a simple calculation.

Contract award, pre-contract meetings, mobilisation and review

A pre-contract meeting should be called once the best tender has been selected and the contract has been awarded so as to address the following issues:

- Service provider's plan for commencement and provision of the service.
- Insurance cover with respect to statutory requirements and specific eventualities.
- Contract administration – payments, meetings and other key events.

The service provider should be given a sufficient mobilisation period to marshal all resources, thus ensuring a seamless continuation of service provision. Where the service(s) affected are to be outsourced for the first time, it is recommended that the service provider visit the organisation to explain to users of the service what is expected of them. During this period, it will be necessary to plan for the regular review of the service provider's performance. The frequency of revisions will depend on the duration and complexity of the contract. Typically, three-monthly reviews would be reasonable, though monthly reviews during the early stages might be more appropriate in order to deal with teething problems.

In cases where the organisation's employees have been transferred to a service provider, special arrangements will be required to deal with the transition. This is illustrated in Fig. 7.2.

Ongoing relationships

The relationship between the service provider and the client organisation's representative is crucial to ensuring that the service is provided as expected. Moreover, the client will want to improve the level of performance over time, so sound working relationships are important. Problems that might sour the relationship should be forestalled. For example, the person occupying the role of client representative might also be the person who prepared the unsuccessful in-house tender. Organisations should, therefore, be prepared to make changes to their management, if necessary, to ensure that poor working relationships do not arise as a consequence of earlier decisions – see also Chapters 5 and 6 regarding the acquisition of new skills and the redefinition of roles and responsibilities.

Conclusions

Organisations need to recognise that successful outsourcing of services comes from a process in which policies are clearly defined and procedures are progressive and transparent. Fortunately, there is sufficient advice and published guidance available on how to follow procedures, and detailed aspects of them. Indeed, attention to detail is an essential commodity on the part of client organisations, and this must be matched by those companies tendering for contracts. Thorough preparation and execution takes time and so the organisation embarking on an outsourcing route must plan well ahead and build in adequate time. If followed carefully, procedures that lead to outsourcing can provide a firm basis for the subsequent management and administration of contracts.

CHECKLIST

This checklist is intended to assist with the review and action planning process.

		Yes	No	Action required
1.	Has the base information in relation to current services, prior to the initiation of the outsourcing process, been properly collated?	☐	☐	☐
2.	Have all stakeholders with an interest in the service to be provided been properly identified and consulted?	☐	☐	☐
3.	Have the services to be outsourced been clearly identified and defined?	☐	☐	☐
4.	Has the organisation grasped the full implications of employment and public procurement legislation?	☐	☐	☐
5.	Do the tender documents include full service specifications, the terms of proposed service level agreements and conditions of contract?	☐	☐	☐

	Yes	No	Action required
6. Is the tendering process sufficiently rigorous to allow for proper competition?	☐	☐	☐
7. Are proper tender assessment procedures in place?	☐	☐	☐
8. Are arrangements in place to ensure good ongoing relationships between the service provider and the client organisation?	☐	☐	☐

8 Policy and Procedures for In-House Provision

Key issues

The following issues are covered in this chapter.

- Defining the scope of a service is as important to successful in-house provision as it is to outsourced services – there should be no half measures.

- A poorly defined scope will lead, almost inevitably, to problems in the management of the service with higher supervision costs and a lowering of customer satisfaction: consultation with all stakeholders is essential.

- The organisation must establish the extent of the knowledge and skills that its employees possess.

- Where relevant and appropriate skills are in short supply, retraining and/or recruitment of new personnel will be necessary – again, consultation with stakeholders is essential.

- Customers must be recognised and the relationship between them and the in-house team must be taken seriously and managed professionally.

- Performance monitoring applies equally to in-house and outsourced services.

- A process of continual improvement should be implemented to ensure that productivity and standards of quality and performance are consistently raised.

Introduction

The retention of estates-related and facilities management services might be considered of less interest, even of lower importance, as a topic when compared to outsourcing. In a sector that has grown large on the back of a consistent wave of outsourcing one could be forgiven for seeing in-house provision as having lower economic worth. In fact, nothing could be further from the truth. In most countries, a significant proportion of facilities are competently managed by in-house teams, who consistently deliver customer satisfaction and best value. They have achieved this status by being highly professional and as demanding of their own personnel as others are of external service providers. Some organisations have brought in-house services that were previously outsourced. Our purpose here is not to argue for either in-house or outsourced service provision, since that is entirely a consequence of earlier steps in formulating a strategy, policies and operational plans to deliver best value. The intention is to underline the importance of managing in-house provision to the highest standard. This chapter outlines policy and procedures to be adopted where services are provided in-house. For clarity, the chapter has been set out to follow the process in chronological order. The objective is to ensure that certain critical success factors are met: first, the scope of the services and interfaces with related services must be defined; second, the service level required of the in-house team by all stakeholders must be determined; third, the in-house team must have the capabilities and skills to deliver the service; fourth, the team must treat internal departments as customers; fifth, in-house service provision is provided through a team approach, with each member working towards a common goal; and last, service provision is continually reviewed and improved.

Definition of services

For outsourced services, it is generally recognised that success is dependent upon the clear definition of the services, including their interfaces. In other words, there are 'no cracks to fall down'. This view is also true in the case of in-house service provision, but for different reasons. Where services have been outsourced, definition is required to ensure that all necessary services are provided and that no gaps exist between the interfaces of each service. In-house providers also require clear definition in order to manage their resources effectively. Without obvious delineation of roles and responsibilities, it can be difficult to measure the performance of in-house personnel.

If the customer – taken to be a user department within the client organisation – is unsure as to who is providing which service, it is hard for providers both to achieve and to demonstrate best value. This is also important in the context of avoiding conflicts of interest, because of unclear splits between purchasing and in-house service personnel at the time of preparing tender documents and during the subsequent tendering period.

Identifying stakeholders

As we have now begun to recognise, stakeholders are critical to the success of service provision of any kind. Those affected by the provision of services must be identified, just as they are for outsourced services. It is important for the in-house team to understand the relative influence of the respective stakeholders, as the team will potentially be serving many masters simultaneously. At the same time, it would be wise to avoid embarking upon any path that could conceivably prove divisive and run counter to the organisation's business direction and strategic objectives. The risk of such an outcome is always possible in highly politicised organisations.

In order to ensure the success of the process, each stakeholder's specific requirements must be understood. Whilst it may not always be possible, given the constraints that can be imposed on the in-house team to satisfy everyone, requirements should be ranked according to their business benefit. In this way, an optimal mix can be established, whilst helping to reduce the likelihood of conflict arising from 'political infighting'.

In-house capabilities and skills

The in-house service team must be able to adapt to meet changes in requirements in order to support the core business effectively and provide best value. The ease with which this may be possible will depend upon the skills and capabilities of employees and their willingness to continue in training and development. If necessary, in-house teams may have to recruit new personnel with the necessary skills. Chapter 6 outlined examples of how existing personnel can be motivated and challenged. Retaining and investing in the current workforce should be seen as preferable – and probably less costly and time-consuming – than recruitment.

In technical areas such as maintenance of services installations, many external service providers invest heavily in training to ensure that their personnel are competent and qualified. This is especially so where new legislation and standards come into force and where it is necessary to retain membership of an industry body or association. For a small, in-house team, this may represent a significant time and cost overhead. If the in-house team is to satisfy the organisation's needs this investment must be made.

Departments as customers

The in-house service team probably has the benefit of many years of experience of the organisation, which must not be lost by failing to be responsive to the needs of the customer. Internal departments must be regarded as customers and their needs served accordingly. Furthermore, there should be no difference in the in-house team's attitude towards internal and external customers where the latter could be, for instance, members of the public who are entitled to make some use of the organisation's facilities. A professional approach can and must be adopted and maintained towards all customers. Many organisations have grasped this issue and it has enabled them to provide a focused service that is also responsive.

In-house team approach

It is essential that members of the in-house service team recognise that they should operate in the same way as would an external service provider and that they will be judged on a similar basis. Given that the organisation's management may be looking periodically at the market for external service provision, it makes sense for the in-house team to operate in a business-like way so that it can compete fairly if the need arises. Most organisations manage to do this, but the weakness is in maintaining a consistent level over time. One of the biggest threats to the in-house team's success is from complacency, which is easily noticed by customers.

The in-house team should be examined for its efficiency and effectiveness. The constituent personnel must operate as a team if they are to deliver a value-adding service. The starting point for engendering team spirit is through sharing common goals and objectives. In the UK, the government has promoted the establishment of customer charters that set out the type and level of services that can be expected in a number of service sectors. Many private sector organisations do likewise. This kind of SLA has the added benefit of articulating the objectives to be achieved by the team. By sharing common goals and key objectives, and working as a team, additional benefits can result. This will help the in-house team measure up to the organisation's expectations, as well as its own. Care must be exercised, however, in ensuring that customer charters are not seen as some kind of management fad or, worse, as a concoction of imperatives written in superlatives. Such a mistake will easily attract the cynics.

Service provision reviewed and improved

The in-house service provider must be proactive in looking for areas where value can be added. It should not regard service levels as permanently fixed, but as providing the basis for refinement. The provider's expertise can help to assess whether or not the perceived service levels are, in fact, the most appropriate. This is particularly relevant in the case of response times when ordering work. If informed discussion can take place as to real needs as opposed to perceived needs, the service, with its corresponding resource levels, can be designed to meet those needs. This value-adding activity can enable the in-house team to differentiate itself from outsourced competitors, and intimate knowledge of the organisation can be used to good effect. That said, knowledge of the organisation is no compensation for a service that does not deliver against customer needs and expectations.

Many support service processes are labour intensive and consist of a high volume of low-value activities. ICT could therefore be of help to the in-house service provider by improving communication and producing appropriate management information. Through the use of low-cost ICT tools, in-house service providers can measure how they are performing against the service level agreed with each identified customer type or group. Thereafter, by means of continual improvement, increases in performance can be compared and reported against a benchmark – see Chapter 18. This activity should extend to a comparison with external service providers both to assess the relative competitiveness of in-house provision and to gain new insights into the business and the disciplines that constitute facilities management.

Conclusions

Many of the stages and issues that an in-house team should consider are comparable to those that apply to outsourced services. The difference lies in the clarity of roles and responsibilities that are usually more obvious in the latter by virtue of a procurement process that has been followed preceding the award of the contract. The in-house team should try to achieve the same position both for the benefit of its customers and its own management needs. This, in turn, will permit more ready measurement of performance. Retaining services in-house has to be the primary goal for the in-house team. It is only likely to reach that goal if it delivers customer satisfaction and best value, and can demonstrate both.

CHECKLIST

This checklist is intended to assist with the review and action planning process.

		Yes	No	Action required
1.	Have all stakeholders in the provision of services been identified and consulted?	☐	☐	☐
2.	Are the services to be provided in-house properly defined?	☐	☐	☐
3.	Are the roles and responsibilities of those providing the services properly defined?	☐	☐	☐
4.	Has the organisation clearly assessed and identified current in-house capabilities and skills and augmented those that might be lacking?	☐	☐	☐
5.	Has the role of departments as customers been recognised?	☐	☐	☐
6.	Is there a clear division between the ICF and in-house service providers?	☐	☐	☐
7.	Are proper arrangements in place for the review and improvement of service provision?	☐	☐	☐

9 Service Specifications, Service Level Agreements and Performance

Key issues

The following key issues are covered in this chapter.

- Stakeholders must be involved from the outset in specifying the kinds of services required and the level of performance that will be acceptable to them, both from in-house and external service providers.

- Service specifications and service level agreements (SLAs) are tools for managing the quality, performance and value of services provided.

- A service specification is a document that quantifies the minimum service that is acceptable if the customer's requirements are to be met. It provides a benchmark against which the standard of service delivered to the customer can be assessed.

- An SLA is a commitment by the service provider (in-house or outsourced) to the customer to deliver an agreed level of service. It should specify rewards and penalties, yet retain flexibility so that the customer's changing requirements can be taken into account should circumstances arise.

- Service providers should be involved in the process of updating and improving SLAs and service specifications in order to draw upon their experience of actually providing the service.

- Performance monitoring of service providers involves reconciling the level of the service delivered to the customer against agreed standards and targets set out in the service specifications and SLAs.

- Procedures for correcting any discrepancies between service levels require the joint participation of the client organisation and service provider.

- If internal quality targets are to be met, quality-of-service criteria need to be incorporated into contracts with service providers. Contracts should stipulate that payments will depend on the performance of the provider in reaching these targets.

- The organisation should describe its performance requirements in terms of factors that are critical to successful service provision. Key performance indicators (KPIs) can then be used to measure deviations from specifications and SLAs.

- Performance reporting across the broad and complex areas within the facilities management function demands ICT support and has led to the emergence of the facilities management 'dashboard'.

Introduction

Service specifications and service level agreements (SLAs) are essential tools in facilities management irrespective of whether services are outsourced or retained in-house. They provide the working guidelines for both client organisations and service providers to focus on the services that should be provided, where, when and in what ways. Since they are intended to bridge the gap between customer requirements and expectations on the one hand and the delivery of a response in the form of services on the other hand, they have a pivotal role in the facilities management process. Moreover, they become the centre of attention when one party feels that the other is failing to meet an obligation. In a positive light, they can provide clarity, certainty and motivation to succeed. They should also be seen as something that is capable of improvement and, by implication, something that is bound to change over time. This chapter reviews the use of service specifications and SLAs arising from the requirements of stakeholders. It identifies the purpose of each and the ways in which they are expected to contribute to the effective management of services provision. These documents provide the organisation with the means to monitor performance and a basis for rewarding excellent results, as well as penalising those who fall short. The issue of quality assurance – including the operation of a quality management system – is discussed and advice offered on the broad approach that should be taken.

Stakeholders' interests

A recurrent theme in this book is that of stakeholder involvement. In this and following sections, we see that the client organisation has a responsibility for engaging stakeholders in the framing of individual service specifications and SLAs. Identified stakeholders should be involved in specifying their requirements and the level of performance that will be acceptable. This means:

- Involving stakeholders, as far as practicable, in defining and detailing their requirements through, for example, the use of questionnaire surveys and by contributing to the drafting of service specifications and SLAs.
- Prioritisation by stakeholders of their requirements.
- Controlling stakeholder input and changes once the specification has been agreed.

The organisation may find that it is defining and detailing its requirements for the first time. In such cases, there is a risk that it might unknowingly specify a higher level of service than was received in the past and that, consequently, tenders may turn out to be higher than forecast. Value management, a technique for ensuring that real needs are addressed, can be used to guard against over-specification, whilst allowing standards to be raised over time. This is a broad philosophy as opposed to a prescriptive means for identifying and eliminating excess cost. The organisation should consider adopting value management principles at a strategic planning level – see Chapter 2 – and then apply value engineering principles to eliminate attributes of service that add cost, but no value. There is ample literature on the interrelated subjects of value management and value engineering – see for example Kelly *et al.* (2002, 2004). The use of value engineering workshops is generally advocated in the literature and is widely practised on building and civil engineering construction projects large and small. What is important is the discipline of questioning the need for, and assumptions embodied in, all attributes of service provision and ensuring that only those adding value, or required to support those that add value, are included. In these ways, stakeholders' interests should be correctly incorporated into service specifications and SLAs.

Rationale for service specifications and SLAs

Service specifications and SLAs are formal documents that together set out:

- Customer expectations of the quality, performance and value of the services to be provided in a clear and unequivocal manner.
- Minimum acceptable standards of the service and the customer's requirements that have to be met.
- Output or performance-oriented measures, concentrating on what is to be provided as opposed to how.
- The agreement between the service provider and the customer for providing a range and target level of services.

In practice, SLAs are often made by parties within an internal market, that is, between the departments or other operational units in an organisation, and act as a type of contract. This type of contract is not necessarily accompanied by a charge for the service. SLAs are also highly applicable to situations where services are outsourced. Here, the SLA supplements the contractual arrangements and is the starting point for developing a partnership relationship. In a previous chapter, we observed that the organisation adopted the practice of including service specifications and SLAs as annexes to the contract. Client organisations are bound to approach this matter differently depending on external factors and the legal advice they receive on the whole question of contracts. What is important here is to emphasise the standing of service specifications and SLAs in binding the parties' intentions together.

What is a service specification?

A service specification is a document that quantifies the minimum acceptable (technical) standard of service required by the customer and will generally form a part of the contract with the service provider. The production of the service specification is a prerequisite in the negotiation and drafting of SLAs and should set out:

- Internal standards – relating to corporate or department policy, as well as those that have been adopted on previous contracts.
- External standards – covering conformance to statutory requirements, international standards, health and safety legislation, industry standards and manufacturers' recommendations.
- Procedures with which the service provider must comply in order to achieve the required technical standards.

Performance and quality targets

The extent of detail in the specification will depend on the importance and complexity of the service or asset item. This is bound to be an area of concern for the organisation. Quality, as we are aware, manifests in many ways. If users (as customers) were asked to write down what quality meant to them in the context of a facility, there would be as many different definitions as there were users. In order to overcome this potential problem, facilities managers need to spend time working closely with customers to elicit their views of what quality means to them. In many instances, it will be possible to substitute the word performance for quality. This is not meant to avoid the issue of defining quality; rather it is a pragmatic and realistic way of focusing on what exactly their customers expect and, therefore, mean by quality. In the context of service provision, quality is something that can be defined, detailed and determined as due performance. For example, the quality of cleaning of, say, offices can be stated in terms of either what the customer will accept as clean or how often the act of cleaning must be performed. Ensuring that worktops are always free from dust is an example of a performance requirement and a target to be achieved. It also says something tangible about the quality of service being provided. The example is simple, but not trivial, as it is illustrative of how we are able to express quality and then communicate it in terms that people not only understand, but are also able to follow through into practice.

What does a service specification contain?

Drafting specifications can be a job in its own right. Fortunately, advice and information on how to write specifications are available from a number of sources and will generally follow accepted practice. Table 9.1 shows the typical format of an example service specification. For some services, trade associations provide guidance to their members and offer model forms of specification. Common sense dictates that any model will require some adaptation to suit the organisation or contract in hand; in other words, for model read standard.

The approach to specification writing can vary depending on whether or not a prescriptive view is taken or one that is performance-related – the

Table 9.1   Contents of an example service specification.

Section	Contents
Part 1: Terminology	1.1 Definition of terms used
Part 2: Areas/items/services	2.1 Scope of areas/items/services covered by specification
Part 3: External standards	3.1 Statutory requirements 3.2 Manufacturers' recommendations 3.3 Industry-accepted best practice
Part 4: Internal standards	4.1 Corporate/department requirements 4.2 Previously accepted standards
Part 5: Categorisation of areas/items/services	5.1 Detailed procedures for each category 5.2 Frequency of procedures for each category

former is based on inputs and the latter is based on outputs. In the case of a cleaning contract, for example, the specification could describe the standard of cleanliness to be achieved in terms of the maximum amount of dust or debris that is permitted to remain following cleaning. Below are two extracts from an example service specification for cleaning showing, first, prescriptive specifications and, second, performance requirements.

Practice Point 9.1   Timing can be everything.

Risk item: specifications that are overprescriptive, concentrating on procedures not outputs.

Key point: specifications need to focus on outputs and not the procedures that are carried out in delivering those outputs.

The times of inspections and maintenance of items at a cargo-handling facility were rigidly set out in a programme in the maintenance contract. On a number of occasions, the contractor was unable to carry out the work on the dates specified, as it would have seriously disrupted the operation of the facility. The programme was developed without taking into account the need for certain items to be kept operational under very busy conditions. A programme that was more flexible in its times would have ensured that the required number of inspections per annum was carried out and the equipment at the facility was adequately maintained.

Example of a service specification – cleaning of open-plan offices

Prescriptive specification: daily tasks

1. Empty rubbish containers and bins (clean as required). Collect all rubbish and waste material, place in receptacle provided by the contractor and remove to the nearest designated disposal point.

2. Sweep floors using appropriate antic-static mop sweeper, leaving floors clean and free from visible dirt, dust and smears.
3. Lift primary matting and vacuum beneath.
4. Vacuum all soft floors and carpeted areas (loose or fitted). This is to include all raised areas, stairways, etc.
5. Spot clean hard floors.
6. Spot clean tables, desks and chairs.

Prescriptive specification: weekly tasks

1. Damp wipe furniture, fittings and horizontal surfaces.
2. Using high-speed vacuum floor-polishing machines, spray clean hard floor areas with an approved cleaning agent and maintainer, and then use an appropriate brush or pad until floor is cleaned and polished.

Performance-based requirements

1. Ensure that bins and other containers for waste and rubbish are emptied regularly so that they are not allowed to remain full – deposit at the nearest designated disposal point.
2. Do not permit the contents of bins and other containers to pose a threat to health or allow them to detract from the normal enjoyment of space by users.
3. Ensure that all floors are maintained in a clean, enduring and non-slip state, free from debris and other deleterious materials.
4. Do not permit spillage, contaminants or other deleterious materials to remain on floors.
5. Ensure that all work surfaces, fittings and other furnishings remain free from accumulated dust and other debris, and are maintained in a condition that does not detract from the normal enjoyment of space by users.
6. Do not permit spillage, contaminants or other deleterious materials to remain on work surfaces, fittings and other furnishings.

There are obvious differences between the two approaches. The prescriptive specification – because it dictates what shall be done – will ensure that the cleaning of the specified areas and items will take place on a daily and weekly basis come what may. For example, floors will be cleaned and work surfaces wiped over whether or not this work is necessary – at least in theory. In the performance-based approach, the contractor (service provider) is able to schedule cleaning according to need, which arises from patterns of use, access hours, weather, etc. More likely than not, the performance-based specification will deliver the quality of service required for less money than the prescriptive approach.

Apart from these differences, there is the issue of flexibility. Prescriptive specifications are, by definition, restrictive and probably incapable of change once the contract is running. The performance-based approach, on the other hand, avoids this problem by setting clear targets which the service provider can use to determine the most appropriate operational response. Detractors of the performance-based approach would argue that the minimum effort will be put into the cleaning and that, at least, with the prescriptive approach one can see the work being performed at specified intervals. However, this line of argument is flawed, because the aim should be to ensure that the workplace is cleaned without inconvenience to users. In this particular sense, cleaning should not interfere with enjoyment of the workplace. When performed at the highest level, with all services being delivered as required, facilities management can be regarded as the 'invisible service'.

What is a service level agreement (SLA)?

An SLA is a statement of intentions existing between the service provider and the customer – the recipient of the service – setting out a specified level of service. The agreement is formalised by producing a document that describes the following:

- Name of each party
- Roles and responsibilities of each party
- Scope of services that are to be provided
- Quality and performance-related targets
- Time-related targets
- Prices and rates – broken down as necessary
- Resources required
- Method of communication and interaction between customer and service provider
- Change procedures.

The SLA may be of a general format – applicable to a number of services or facilities – or it may be customer, facility or service specific. In any event, it will incorporate relevant service specifications.

Development of SLAs

The customer will have certain expectations about the level of service that the service provider should deliver. These expectations need to be translated into formal requirements and targets. In the development of these targets, the service provider should be involved and the agreements developed jointly, so that targets are both appropriate and practicable. An example of a target is where the response to a problem, for example the failure of a light fitting or photocopier breakdown, should be within a specified period that is practicable for the service provider and toler-able for the customer. Stakeholders need to specify what their tolerance threshold is for rectifying a range of failures or malfunctions, and they need to be realistic.

Table 9.2   **Contents of an example SLA based on a total facilities management service.**

Section	Contents
Part 1: Agreement details	1.1 Name of parties to the agreement 1.2 Date agreement signed 1.3 Effective date of agreement 1.4 Period of agreement
Part 2: Scope of services – the service specification	2.1 Management of maintenance of buildings, plant and equipment, external landscaping 2.2 Management of minor building works 2.3 Management of accommodation services 2.4 Management of utilities and telecommunications
Part 3: Delivery times, fees	3.1 Service priority categories and times 3.2 Fees and payment
Part 4: Performance	4.1 Submission of performance reports 4.2 Performance measures
Part 5: Customer/service provider interface	5.1 Communication 5.2 Incentives and penalties 5.3 Customer's rating and feedback 5.4 Procedures for revising SLA

What does an SLA contain?

The SLA can contain details and targets relating to all or some of the items listed earlier. In principle, the document should identify those measures that the customer will use to judge the level of service received from the service provider. These measures will generally fall under the following aspects of the service:

- Quality
- Performance
- Delivery/response time
- Charges for services
- Nature of the interaction with the service provider.

The SLA can also set out the procedure for incorporating any changes that occur in these targets. Table 9.2 shows the top-level contents of an example SLA – typical sections of an SLA can be found in Appendix E.

Example contents of an SLA are given below. This illustrates the kind of requirements that might be drafted to deal with the submission of performance reports and the measurement of performance.

Example of a service level agreement (SLA)

(Adapted from original information provided by IBM and Johnson Controls.)

Performance reports

Service performance reports will be completed by the service provider each month on the last working day. Whilst it will be the service provider's duty to complete the reports, the client's appointed representative will furnish the service provider with a master service performance record sheet. These records will register the following items:

1. Maintenance details – incidence of maintenance-induced failures, adherence to agreed planned preventive maintenance (PPM) schedules.
2. Job card – responses and actions within service level.
3. Security – compliance with security procedures, absence of misuses or losses.
4. Cleaning – completion of all specified items.
5. Safety – completion of all recorded action items.
6. Space and facilities planning – space database kept up to date, users informed of progress.
7. Reception – procedure for dealing with visitors is followed.
8. Reprographics – photocopiers serviced within four hours.
9. Stationery and printing – orders fulfilled on a timely basis.
10. Fax service – availability of service maintained.

Operations and service assessment

Operations and service assessment will be undertaken adopting the same procedure as for service performance records. This assessment will record the following items:

1. Effective communication – timely reporting and prompt response to requests.
2. Documentation – complete, sufficient, on time and maintained.
3. Additional work – positive attitude, flexibility and proactiveness.
4. Image – general housekeeping and staff appearance.
5. Management and coordination – efficient use of resources and protection of client interests.
6. Process and methods of work – innovative proposals and effective solutions.
7. Supplier relationships – control of supplier performance and quality of supplier performance.
8. Feedback – space utilisation opportunities, with advice on locations.
9. Financial – fully evaluated proposals, with well-structured business cases.

Performance measures

The following performance measures will apply to monthly service per-formance records:

- Criteria met or exceeded – yes (score 1), no (score 0), for each item.
- Total service performance must be not less than 8 at each monthly assessment.

The following performance measures will apply to operations and services assessment:

- Criteria exceeded, met or failed – exceed (score 2), meet (score 1), fail (score 0), for each item.
- Total service performance must be not less than 9 at each monthly assessment.

The above performance measures will be used to determine overall contract performance for the service provider.

Critical success factors and key performance indicators

In determining the criteria for measuring the performance (or fulfilment) of an SLA, the organisation should consider those factors that are critical to success. Critical success factors (CSFs) are those actions that must be performed well in order for the goals or objectives established by an organ-isation to be met satisfactorily. Within each CSF will be one or more KPIs. The purpose of KPIs is to enable management to understand, measure and control progress in each of the CSFs. For example, an organisation may have set a goal of providing the highest-quality service that ensures each internal customer receives best value. A CSF in achieving that goal would be 'agreed SLAs'. Here, a KPI might be 'published service level agreements' to show clearly what has to be achieved and then, subsequently, to say what has been achieved.

In another example – an internal perspective on productivity – a CSF would lead to KPIs that highlighted abortive work, backlog and ability (or inability) to perform tasks concurrently. Measures of productivity would include:

- Percentage of total work completed at a given time
- Percentage of activities planned against unplanned
- Percentage of total hours by customer type
- Breakdowns against planned preventive maintenance hours.

Where customer perspectives are concerned, a CSF could be quality for which one of the KPIs would be complaints (or the lack of them) that, in turn, would give a measure of the number of complaints over time or, alternatively, a satisfaction rating.

When establishing CSFs and KPIs, it is vital that they correspond to goals and objectives that are aligned to the organisation's business strategy. Without this alignment, successful attainment of service levels may contribute nothing to the success of the core business. It is not just about doing things right, but doing the right things. KPIs are seen as a valuable tool in this regard and have infiltrated all areas of business in the public sector as well as in the private sector. In practice, there will be many CSFs and KPIs that interact and combine to bring about a culture and methods that aim to achieve best practice. Performing at the top end of these measures would bring an organisation to the point of achieving best practice and, with that, best value in the management of its services and facilities.

Practice Point 9.2   ICT helps to spread the workload.

Key point: monitoring the times, costs and other performance data for a large number of low-value activities can be time-consuming and counterproductive, unless ICT is used.

An organisation had decided that, as part of its performance monitoring of the in-house services team, records should be kept of each and every activity performed. The initial reaction from the in-house team was that they would probably spend as much time filling in forms as doing their jobs, perhaps even more. Although initially reluctant, the team was persuaded to use spreadsheets as part of an office automation suite. The manager set up a template on his spreadsheet that was then used to provide the team with paper forms for recording data, which they then keyed in at the end of the day. After some weeks, the team began experimenting with the spreadsheet's wizard function to help generate some useful graphs. These were used subsequently to present to senior management with the information it had been wanting for some time. Even so, the team felt that it was still spending too much time in logging information and then transferring it to the spreadsheets on the office PCs. Usually, they had to allocate around one hour at the end of each day. After making enquiries with a local computer store, the team acquired several PDAs, which came complete with software and an interface to the office PCs. Within the week, the team had automated the data capture routine and reduced the entire daily ritual to a few minutes.

Once the link between KPIs, CSFs and the objectives and goals of the organisation has been established, attention must then be given to performance reporting, in particular the progress of an organisation along the path to achieving its objectives. Historically, the facilities manager spent many days at the end of each month and the beginning of the next compiling the information required to report to the client organisation. Today, the availability of information systems greatly assists in this work. As the breadth and complexities of reporting have increased, so has the demand for obtaining regular updates on progress with the aim of working and reporting in real time. ICT applications have developed significantly and solutions exist for pulling together disparate performance data, but the challenge of turning data into relevant and timely information remains.

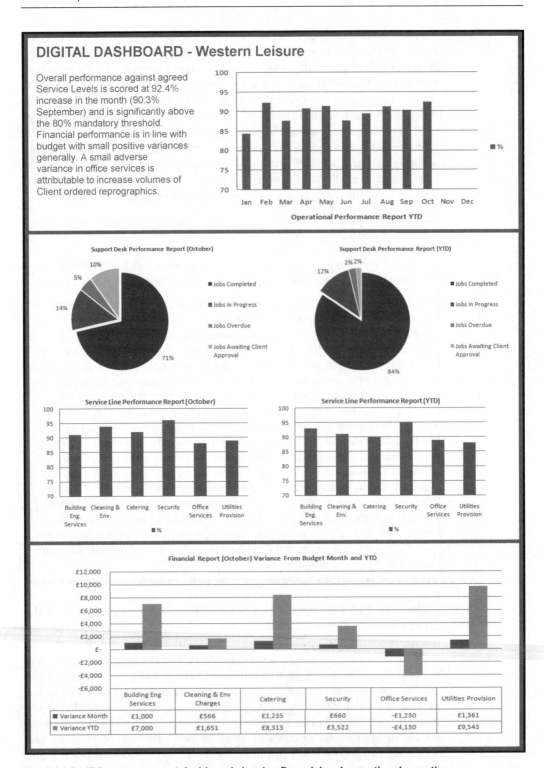

Fig. 9.1   Facilities management dashboard showing financial and operational reporting.

Corporate intranets and the technology supporting them have provided the key to unlocking the potential of this information in real time. In the past, delivering management reports using data from across the organisation has only been possible with the support of large corporate systems. The development of web-based, front-end reporting has allowed timely, comprehensive reporting to become a cost-effective reality and has been marked by the arrival of the facilities management 'dashboard'.

The dashboard uses the principles of *The Balanced Scorecard* (Kaplan and Norton, 1996) to compile a view of operations. Since its conception, the scorecard has been adopted by a variety of organisations as a critical performance management tool. Whilst simple in its underlying principle, the tool can be likened to the instruments in an aircraft cockpit. For the pilot, the instruments provide multiple views of the operation of the aircraft and progress towards its destination. A pilot would not be satisfied with merely knowing about the aircraft's speed or even altitude; equally, direction alone would be insufficient. The pilot needs a wide range of data to fly the aircraft safely to its destination. The scorecard aims to provide the organisation's managers with information provided in a simple manner that affords understanding and insight at a glance.

The dashboard adopts the same approach as the scorecard, based on a cascading or 'drill-down' technique as a means for measuring the performance of operations. The images in Fig. 9.1 show the dashboard, with drill-down views of both financial and operational reports.

Facilities managers who have experience of reporting in this dashboard style appreciate the benefit of responsive real-time information and the advantage this confers in reporting status to the client organisation.

Performance monitoring

The customer's view of the quality of a service or product is based on tangible and intangible factors, both of which are important. Tangible factors are those that can be objectively measured, such as the time taken to deliver an item, the charge made and the level of operational performance. Intangible factors include those that are more subjective in nature and, therefore, more difficult to measure: for example, the utility of the item to the customer, its adaptability and advantages over other types or merely the courtesy of the service provider's personnel. The difficulty of quantifying some factors should not preclude measurement as they can be as important as those that are easily measured. The organisation should, however, be cautioned against imposing too many or overly demanding performance measurements and excessive monitoring on service providers as this risks becoming counterproductive. A sensible approach is to concentrate on the KPIs. Table 9.3 suggests performance measures that could be used and Table 9.4 a possible scoring scheme.

In practice, the overall performance of a service provider can be determined by monitoring adherence to standards and targets under the following headings:

Table 9.3   Example performance measures for planned and unplanned maintenance.

Element	Service	Output/measure	Perspective
1	Planned maintenance performance	Tasks planned in period Tasks completed in period Time taken per task Mean time taken per task Resource attendance in period Number of tasks reworked Percentage of tasks reworked of total tasks in period Service delivery resource utilised	by customer by building/location by building/space type by service provider by asset type by asset
2	Unplanned maintenance performance	Number of breakdowns/faults in period Percentage response times met Number of breakdowns/faults completed in period Number of breakdowns/faults outstanding in period Time taken per breakdown Mean time taken per breakdown Number of tasks reworked Percentage tasks reworked of total tasks in period	by customer by building/location by building/space type by service provider by asset type by asset
		Asset availability in period Downtime in period Unplanned stoppages in period Service delivery resource utilised	by customer by building/location by building/space type by service provider by asset type

- Conformance to regulations and standards
- Quality-related and performance-related targets for service delivery
- Expenditure limits
- Time-related targets
- Interaction between customer and service provider.

Performance data can be collected in a number of ways. For example, the service provider may complete worksheets and job reports, or feedback from customers might be sought actively in the form of comments on worksheets, complaints and customer surveys. Once the organisation has collected these data they should be used to complete a scoresheet, similar to that presented in Table 9.4, at regular intervals. This should be undertaken for a sample of the services delivered by each service provider based on KPIs. These will be given in the SLA and contract and will provide a basis for measuring performance in a way that involves both the service provider and the customer. On the scoresheet in Table 9.4, column 4 (actual level of service delivered) contains the service provider's measurement of the service or product, based on data and information held by the service provider's organisation. These measures will relate to response times to

Table 9.4 Example of unplanned maintenance service scoring scheme (report of faulty lighting on section of floor of main building).

(1) Service criteria[+]	(2) Agreed target level of service (targets in SLA or specification)	(3) Value[+]	(4) Actual level of service delivered	(5) Value	(6) Customer satisfaction	(7) Value
Regulations/standards	Work carried out according to health and safety regulations using certified products	10	Work carried out according to health and safety regulations using certified products	10	Satisfied	10
Performance/quality	Fault to be rectified so that it is prevented from reoccurring. Minimise level of disruption to users	20	Fault diagnosed and problem rectified. Minor disruption to building users	18	Concern over disruption to work	12
Delivery time	*Minor lighting fault* Max. response time = 2 hours Max. service time = 4 hours (Total delivery time = 6 hours)	10	Response time = 3 hours Service time = 2 hours (Total delivery time = 5 hours)	8	Concern over delay in response	5
Delivery expenditure	*Minor lighting fault* Total cost = £120.00 to £250.00 (range)	10	Total cost = £200.00	10	Satisfied	10
Customer–service provider interaction	Keep customer informed of status of work and likely completion time	20	Customer informed that fault had been rectified following completion of work	16	No contact between report of fault and completion	14
Overall service delivery	Work to be carried out according to the targets given above	70	Work carried out satisfactorily, within agreed cost; however, not within agreed response time	62	Work and cost satisfactory, delivery time and contact unsatisfactory	51

[+] = Each activity is assigned a weighted agreed target level of service value. Actual level of service delivered and customer satisfaction values are determined relative to this base value.

fault reports, customer surveys, charges made for services and measures of quality levels. Customer satisfaction relates to the customer's view of the level of service delivered, based on records held by the organisation. Reasons for any discrepancies between the three values in Table 9.4 then need to be established and corrective action taken as necessary. This will entail the active involvement of the client organisation and the service provider.

Practice Point 9.3   A fair return.

Risk item: absence of, or poor arrangements for, incentives improve performance.

Key point: performance-related systems that aim to raise the standard of service delivery should be based on a fair distribution of rewards and penalties.

An organisation intended to introduce a performance measurement system in its contract with a security contractor as a means for improving the level of service it received. During early discussions with the service provider, the organisation proposed that incentives in the form of bonus payments were awarded for improved performance and penalties imposed for substandard performance. However, in later discussions, the organisation revised the system so that good performance was recognised, though not accompanied by financial rewards, whilst financial penalties for poor performance were retained. At that point the security contractor withdrew from the discussions, claiming that there was no real incentive for workers to raise their performance beyond the minimum specified.

The service provider's level of service delivery will be, to a greater or lesser extent, affected by the quality system that the client organisation has in place. The satisfactory performance of the service provider will be more assured if the quality system is geared to the levels of service performance established in the SLAs. In other words, the ways in which quality and service performance are measured, in accordance with the SLAs, should reflect those incorporated in the client organisation's quality system.

Updating service specifications and SLAs

Service specifications should not be regarded as fixed statements of service requirements, but as a basis for continual improvement as circumstances and customer requirements change. Experience will reveal how better results and improved value for money can be achieved by a change in specification. Service providers should be involved in the process of updating and improving service specifications and SLAs in order to draw upon their experience of providing the service. If necessary, visits to other facilities might be necessary to provide insights into how improvements are possible. These actions will ensure that the organisation is able to determine if the specified service was obtained and so draw lessons for the future. At all times, it is essential that the requirements set out in the service specifications and SLAs should be incorporated into the contract with service providers.

Quality system

If the client organisation is to receive a satisfactory level of service, not only should it have a quality system in place, it must also require the same of its service providers. In fact, service providers' quality systems should form an integral part of their service provision. To add value, service providers have to apply the principles of quality assurance in order to enhance service provision through a reduction in errors and reworking, and as an effective means for handling customer complaints (non-conformance), action and feedback. A quality-assured approach can save money. The assessment of a tenderer's quality system should therefore be one of the criteria used by the client organisation in its assessment of tenders.

A common misconception is that a formal quality system is administratively burdensome, costly and, therefore, unnecessary. If a quality system were to be seen as simply generating paper or adding a layer of administration then it has been misunderstood or misapplied. Formal recognition through accreditation under ISO 9000/9001: 2008 is important in underscoring the organisation's commitment to achieving total customer satisfaction and that it is prepared to open its system to external scrutiny. By means of a third-party audit – in addition to periodic internal audits – the organisation is more likely to meet this commitment and, furthermore, be able to demonstrate it visibly.

The approach advocated in this book is sufficient to provide a basis for a quality system, embracing the entire facilities management function within an organisation. A quality system normally consists of a policy statement and a quality manual with procedures. The policy statement is the organisation's explicit commitment to a quality-assured process embodying its services. The quality manual provides a detailed interpretation of the way in which each of the quality standards is to be met within the context of the operations of the business. The procedures, not surprisingly, explain the detailed steps that must be followed in order to comply with the quality system. For a system to be effective, it needs to be applied as work is being done. Thus, for example, logs and reviews should not be completed retrospectively. Contract documents should incorporate quality-of-service criteria and stipulate that payments will depend on the provider meeting these criteria. These contractual provisions should ensure the quality of services or products of service providers. The issue of penalties and incentives relating to performance standards should be considered following performance reviews.

Conclusions

Service specifications are an integral part of the facilities management process and combine with SLAs to define the quality and/or performance required from a service. Both are fundamental to the business of effective facilities management, irrespective of whether or not the service is out-sourced or retained in-house. Time spent in preparing accurate service specifications and SLAs that reflect customer (and other stakeholder) interests will be repaid amply in the future since contracts will be easier to manage and less prone to misinterpretation. A quality system should be adopted by the organisation as a necessary part of its facilities management and used to support the work of managers and service providers alike. This will ensure, as an absolute minimum, that a consistent set of standards is applied as a basis for seeking continual improvement.

CHECKLIST

This checklist is intended to assist with the review and action planning process.

	Yes	No	Action required
1. Have identified stakeholders been involved in specifying their requirements as to the level of performance that will be acceptable?	☐	☐	☐
2. Have service specifications and service level agreements been prepared?	☐	☐	☐
3. Have the critical success factors and key performance indicators for the provision of services been identified?	☐	☐	☐
4. Have the requirements for facilities management reporting been agreed?	☐	☐	☐
5. Are proper arrangements in place for performance monitoring of service provision?	☐	☐	☐
6. Does the facilities management strategy provide for the updating of service specifications and service level agreements?	☐	☐	☐
7. Is a quality system in place in the client organisation?	☐	☐	☐
8. Is the existence of a quality system on the part of tenderers adopted as a criterion for the assessment of tenders?	☐	☐	☐

10 Health, Safety and Environment

Key issues

The following issues are covered in this chapter.

- Compliance with employment and health and safety legislation applies to everybody in the workplace. It includes shared parts of buildings and the grounds in which the organisation's buildings are set.

- Sustainability, environment management and corporate social responsibility (CSR) have risen dramatically up the agenda in boardrooms with a consequential impact on the role of the facilities manager.

- A competent person must be appointed to the organisation or act as a consultant to assist in implementing and complying with health and safety legislation, whether services are retained in-house or outsourced.

- A general policy statement must be produced by the organisation and this must be communicated to all stakeholders.

- An organisation and administration management method for implementing the policy must be produced and its effectiveness measured.

- A growing body of legislation affecting workers and the workplace is appearing – client organisations must not only be aware of their responsibilities, they also need to ensure that their service providers comply too.

- Policies, detailed safety rules and safe working practices to ensure compliance with health and safety legislation must be devised, implemented and reviewed regularly.

- Not all health and safety issues have a legislative dimension – a growing area of concern is that of stress at work. Today, the courts are sympathetic to the plight of workers who succumb to stress-related illnesses.

Introduction

Employment today is framed by a large body of legislation designed primarily to protect the rights, health and safety of employees. The point is that it is morally unacceptable for people to be exposed to unnecessary and avoidable risks and hazards at work. Moreover, the nature of work should not be such that it leads to a reduction in the quality of life. The onus is on organisations – irrespective of type or size – to comply with legislation for the protection of employees. Where services are outsourced, the client organisation cannot escape responsibility, even if it believes that certain legislation does not apply directly to it. Steps must be taken to ensure that the organisation is fully compliant. Far from being a minefield – a word sometimes used alongside 'begrudging acceptance' – employment and health and safety legislation can be used positively to help define working arrangements including those relating to facilities management. Looked at from this end of the telescope – so to speak – it is likely to be easier to comply with the requirements than attempt to work around them. Organisations have become more accountable for their actions. This accountability extends beyond those of an employer for employees and into a wider role in local communities. This shift is reflected in corporate social responsibility (CSR) policies and practices which, in addition to their impact on communities, extend to the environment generally. In a practical sense, the facility manager is likely to become a key figure in translating the intentions of the legislation into policies and procedures for the workplace. This chapter discusses issues that can help the organisation ensure it provides a safe and healthy place for internal and external users. It reviews the legislation and describes the characteristics of a well-managed health and safety regime. The review is set in a UK context, although its principles are paralleled elsewhere, not least in other EU member states and countries whose legal system is similar to that of the UK. Checklists are included to indicate the scope of matters for which attention is required. Whilst every care has been exercised in identifying relevant legislation, it should not be regarded as a complete guide to employment and health and safety law. The organisation should verify the extent to which any legislation applies to it.

Sustainability and environmental issues

Sustainability is a balancing act between nature and the pursuit of an ever-higher quality of life. Competition for scarce resources has created new global pressures, with evidence of climate change increasingly concentrating minds on reducing manmade impacts. Energy efficiency has long been recognised, if not practised, and this is now accompanied by a wider environmental concern. Yet it is only relatively recently that a whole-life perspective on buildings and other facilities has been adopted, and this has largely been achieved through enforcement of legislation. A more recent example in the EU is the Energy Performance of Buildings Directive (EPBD), which establishes a comparative energy performance measurement for buildings over 1000 m^2 floor area. EPBD requires the latest energy performance rating to be prominently displayed in the publicly accessible space – typically the entrance lobby. Ultimately, all buildings will be required to display a rating certificate, enabling closer awareness of energy consumption. Since buildings are believed to account for 30–40% of a nation's energy consumption, of which wasted energy accounts for a similar range, the scope for energy saving is enormous. Given a choice between two otherwise identical buildings, it is realistic to expect the one with the better energy performance rating to be preferred.

Relevant legislation

In the UK, the principal legislation is that contained in the Health and Safety at Work Act 1974. Where organisations have industrial workshops, additional legislation applies, for instance the Noise at Work Regulations 1989; and where building works are carried out on the premises, the Construction (Design and Management) Regulations 2007 (CDM) will also apply. Current legislation will be progressively tightened. CDM therefore marks only the beginning of a major push at reducing accidents and the hazards that lead to them. Organisations must recognise that safety management is a significant item on the agenda for operating a facility of any description.

General policy

The organisation must have a general policy on health and safety. The requirements of this general policy are:

- To provide and maintain as far as is practicable, a healthy and safe place of work.

- To take responsibility for compliance with relevant legislation including, in the UK (in alphabetical order):
    o Construction (Health, Safety and Welfare) Regulations 1996
    o Control of Noise at Work Regulations 2005
    o Control of Substances Hazardous to Health Regulations 2002 (amended 2003 and 2004)
    o Corporate Manslaughter and Corporate Homicide Act 2007
    o Disability Discrimination Act 2005
    o Electricity at Work Regulations 1989
    o Employment Relations Act 2004
    o Fire Precautions Act 1971
    o Fire Precautions (Workplace) Regulations 1997 (amended 1999)
    o Health and Safety at Work Act 1974
    o Health and Safety (Display Screen Equipment) Regulations 1992
    o Health and Safety (First Aid) Regulations 1981
    o Health and Safety (Safety Signs and Signals) Regulations 1996
    o Manual Handling Operations Regulations 1992
    o Personal Protective Equipment (PPE) Regulations 1992
    o Provision and Use of Work Equipment Regulations (PUWER) 1998
    o Regulatory Reform (Fire Safety) Order 2005
    o Reporting of Injuries, Diseases and Dangerous Occurrences Regulations 1995

o   The Construction (Design and Management) Regulations 2007
o   The Management of Health and Safety at Work Regulations 1999
o   The Working Time (Amendment) Regulations 2003
o   Work at Height Regulations 2005 (amended 2007)
o   Workplace (Health, Safety and Welfare) Regulations 1992.

Organisations need to be aware that their responsibilities for health and safety extend beyond their employees to the extent that no activity should pose risks to visitors or persons outside the premises. The organisation has responsibility for anybody and anyone who is affected by the action of an employee, and the organisation's policy statement and risk assessments must reflect this. It is necessary to appoint a person who can be judged to be competent in implementing and ensuring that the organisation complies with health and safety legislation. Employers must have access to a 'competent person' (who could be an employee, service provider or other contractor, even a consultant) and must ensure that he or she has adequate training, time and resources to discharge his or her duties under health and safety legislation.

Corporate social responsibility

Corporate social responsibility (CSR) is a concept whereby organisations consider the interests of society by taking responsibility for the impact of their actions on stakeholders of all kinds – shareholders, customers, employees, suppliers and communities – as well as on the environment. The concept imposes obligations that extend beyond statutory legislation by effectively mandating the organisation to take steps to improve quality of life for its employees and their families, and for the local community and society at large.

CSR is subject to debate and criticism, with proponents arguing that there is a strong business case. Conversely, critics argue that CSR is a distraction from the fundamental role of business and some even regard it as cheap publicity. In another sense, it can be seen as a voluntary code that avoids governments having to step in and impose their law on business organisations.

In practice, CSR means that organisations must understand the consequences of their decisions, not measured merely in short-term profit and loss, but in the impact that they have in the wider community and on the environment. Organisations must take CSR seriously, indeed, they have an obligation to do so. More astute organisations will have decided to be proactive and, therefore, have defined their responsibilities, strategy and policies for achieving CSR objectives. A good example from the property world is The British Land Company – one of the UK's largest real estate investment trusts (REITs) – and a publicly quoted corporation. In addition to fulfilling its ethical and moral obligations as a quoted company, it has sought to integrate CSR objectives into its business philosophy. Whilst remaining as an influential property developer and investor intent on profitable growth and increasing shareholder value, it has targeted reductions in its carbon footprint through its existing portfolio and developments in progress. This transparency and willingness to contribute to local communities set companies such as British Land apart from those looking to ease their corporate conscience with one-off, philanthropic contributions. The key, as with many aspects of the 'green agenda', is sustainability. The corporation's initiatives are summarised in an annual CSR report that demonstrates the breadth of commitment, with initiatives ranging from water harvesting in shopping centres to the desire to become carbon neutral.

A few years ago, organisations that were considered to be environmentally responsible were those that encouraged their employees to reduce energy consumption through good housekeeping. Today, efficient energy management is considered a hygiene factor for any new or refurbished facility. Today's targets are the achievement of excellence in sustainability. What achieves a standard such as the BREEAM 'Excellent' rating for a building is a complete package of measures – sustainable design and materials, with a supply chain that has environmental goals aligned to those of the client organisation.

Facilities managers should be at the heart of an organisation's CSR strategy and policies, because they are expected to act as the custodian of many CSR objectives. Their task is to balance the demands of the facility with the need to deliver sustainable initiatives that they may even have helped shape in the initial design concept. Since information is vital for demonstrating that proposed initiatives are progressing towards their objectives, the facilities manager has a pivotal role to play because services are the source of much of this information. The facilities manager should be an active member of the CSR team in establishing a pathway between the CSR strategy and the physical delivery of CSR objectives.

Organisation and administration

It is necessary to identify responsibilities as imposed by legislation at all levels of management and supervision, and not just for those employees who are directly involved in the day-to-day management of facilities; for example, the purchasing manager and members of senior management will have roles to play. Care should be taken to apportion responsibility in line with authority, with resources to cover the administration procedures for dealing with accidents and contingency plans for handling power cuts, bomb alerts, flood and fire. Safety representatives from all user bodies should always be involved.

Proper consideration should be given to provide information about substances, plant and machinery to employees and to updating this information. Additionally, training in health and safety responsibilities for all employees should be provided.

Workers' rights

There is a plethora of legislation stemming from the European Parliament that is enacted in each of the EU member states. Of these, The Working Time (Amendment) Regulations 2003 affords workers rights and protection regarding, as the name suggests, time spent at work. The basic rights and protection that the regulations provide are:

- A limit of an average of 48 hours a week which a worker can be required to work (though workers can choose to work more if they want to).
- A limit of an average of 8 hours work in 24 which night workers can be required to work.
- A right for night workers to receive free health assessments.
- A right to 11 hours rest a day.
- A right to a day off each week.
- A right to an in-work rest break if the working day is longer than 6 hours.
- A right to 5.6 weeks' paid leave per year.

These Regulations have proven particularly contentious amongst employers and employees alike and it is possible that some modification will occur – though is difficult to predict what exactly this will be. It is important, therefore, to check the current situation before either offering contracts of employment or renewing existing arrangements. Where services are outsourced, the organisation needs to ensure that service providers do not break the law. If they do, the client organisation may find itself culpable.

There is also the matter of minimum wages – another enactment from the European Parliament – which is covered in the UK by the Employment Relations Act 2004. Client organisations need to be aware of the current national minimum wage and impending changes as they might apply to their own departments and to service providers under contract to them. Legislation aside, client organisations cannot turn a blind eye to what they suspect to be worker abuses of any kind. Apart from the illegality of what may be happening there is also the issue of morality and the motivation of others who may be affected by malpractice. A European Commission proposal for a Directive on (temporary) agency work is under discussion, at the date of publication of this book, and is bound to add to the weight of legislation faced by employers in the coming years.

Disability discrimination

Organisations must take account of the special problems faced by disabled persons and others with special needs, and should make certain that appropriate measures are taken to ensure their health and safety in the workplace. This may involve adaptation of existing means of access to, and escape from, buildings. Organisations should seek professional advice on how their buildings and other facilities comply with relevant legislation.

In the UK, the Disability Discrimination Act 2005 (DDA) recognises the many kinds of disability that affect people. In any society, the proportion of the population with some kind of disability is significant. The DDA takes into account the needs of people with disability affecting, in particular, mobility, sight and hearing. Although widely understood in terms of intent and requirements, the DDA has been overlooked by many UK-based employers, notably those employing 15 people or fewer, who were previously largely unaffected by its scope. Now, all organisations are required to make 'reasonable adjustments' to their businesses: for instance, providing access for physically handicapped people and taking other steps to ensure that no one is excluded by reason of a disability. Although many organisations of this size are unlikely to have their own formal facilities management arrangements, most of the principles that apply to larger organisations will also apply to them. Full enactment of the legislation has removed any distinction or excuse for not making adjustments to businesses. The requirements extend beyond building-related alterations to include changes in customer information to ensure that, for example, people who are visually impaired are not disadvantaged. The intention of this and other legislation is to ensure all-inclusiveness. In other words, no one should be excluded from buildings, transportation or any other facility because of a disability.

Safety rules and practice

Organisations will need to assess the risks to the health and safety of employees and anyone else affected by the activities of the organisation (for example, employees, customers, visitors and the general public) and devise means for implementing preventive and protective measures. Assessment must cover planning, organisation, control, monitoring and reviews. There is a close link between risk assessment and arrangements specified in the policy statement.

With a policy and a management system in place, organisations must monitor and review arrangements to achieve progressive improvement in health and safety. Improvement will be enhanced through the development of policies, approaches to implementation and techniques of risk assessment.

The following checklists will help organisations to monitor their adherence to, and progress against, health and safety legislation.

Organisation

- Are policy, management and organisation, safety rules and procedures in place?
- Are these details available to all employees and other building users?
- Have arrangements been made for consultation with employees and other user bodies?

Noticeboards

- Is the safety policy clearly displayed?
- Is the health and safety law poster displayed?
- Is a copy of the employer's liability insurance certificate displayed?
- Are the names of trained first-aiders displayed?
- Are emergency procedures displayed?

Accident reporting

- Is an accident book held on the premises?
- Are employees and other building users aware of the location of the accident book?
- Are internal accident report forms held?
- Is the Health and Safety Executive (HSE) leaflet, *Everyone's Guide to RIDDOR*, available?

Training

- Have all those with health and safety responsibilities received specific health and safety training?
- Have all employees attended a general health and safety awareness course?
- Are records maintained of training undertaken?
- Are there employees who have received specialist training, for example NEBOSH national general certificate in occupational health and safety?

First aid

- Is a current list of first-aid personnel and their locations displayed on each notice board?
- How many first-aid personnel are there and how are they spread throughout the buildings?
- Does each first-aider have an adequate first-aid box?
- Who keeps top-up supplies for first-aid boxes?
- Who is responsible for inspecting all first-aid boxes for their contents, visibility and availability?
- Who organises first-aid training?
- Which organisation supplies first-aid training?
- Are records of first-aid training adequate and up to date?
- Are treatment record sheets available by each first-aid box or located with the accident book?

Fire precautions

- Is there a fire certificate for the buildings?
- Who has delegated responsibility for fire precautions?
- How often are evacuation drills carried out?
- Are full records of these drills kept, including building clearance times?

- How often are fire alarms tested and are full records of these tests maintained?
- How often are smoke and heat detectors tested?
- Is this in accordance with manufacturers' recommendations or fire certificate?
- Are full records of these tests maintained?
- How often are fixed hose-reel and sprinkler systems (if applicable) tested?
- Are full records of these tests maintained?
- Do the drills and tests comply with the conditions of the fire certificate?
- Are records kept of visits from the fire officer?
- Is there a service contract for the maintenance of fire extinguishers and other fire control equipment?
- Are there adequate fire extinguishers of the correct type?
- Is there at least one fire warden for each floor?
- What training, practice or regular meetings are arranged for fire wardens?
- How often are the offices inspected in relation to fire precautions?
- Is there a procedure for notifying the fire authority of alterations to buildings?

Statutory risk assessments

- Have assessments been carried out for all display screen equipment workstations?
- Is there a valid risk assessment for the premises?
- Have all hazardous substances been assessed under the Control of Substances Hazardous to Health Regulations 2002 (COSHH)?
- Have any other assessments been carried out, for example, lifting of loads and personal protective equipment (PPE)? – see also points below.
- Are the control measures specified in the risk assessments being adhered to?

Inspections and audits

- How often does the facilities manager or other person with delegated responsibility inspect the offices for physical hazards?
- When was the last inspection carried out?
- When was the last audit of procedures carried out and by whom?

Work equipment

- Who is responsible for arranging annual lift/elevator inspections, where applicable?
- Are the premises' electrical installation and all portable electrical appliances and equipment tested by a competent person, as required by the Electricity at Work Regulations 1989, with the results of those tests and any necessary remedial action properly recorded?

- Are there procedures for inspecting and maintaining all work equipment?
- Is the use of potentially dangerous work equipment restricted to author-ised persons and are those persons properly trained?

Personal protective equipment (PPE)

- Have assessments been carried out to determine the requirements of employees?
- Have records of these assessments been kept?
- Is all necessary PPE available?
- Are records kept of PPE issued?
- Have employees been trained in the use and maintenance requirements of PPE, if applicable?
- Has adequate storage for PPE been provided?

Off site

- Have risks associated with visiting other sites or working outside been assessed?
- Is a procedure for lone working defined and in use?
- Are employees aware of these procedures and have they been trained in them?

Employing contractors (service providers)

- Are contractors used for window cleaning, maintenance, electrical installation and so on?
- Is there a 'contractors on site' policy document that all contractors must read and then sign as evidence of their awareness of their duties and obligations?
- Do contractors carrying out work on the premises complete a health and safety questionnaire before they are engaged?
- Who vets these questionnaires and on what basis is it decided that a contractor is competent to carry out the work?
- What information is given to contractors on emergency procedures, safety rules and access?
- Who is responsible for ensuring compliance with CDM?

Notices

- Are all necessary compliance and safety signs in place?

Stress, employees and the organisation

Whilst organisations might strive for more from fewer workers, the reality is that people are capable of giving only so much before serious (and sometimes irreversible) damage sets in. At best, this limits organisational effectiveness; at worst, it can lead to conflict, sickness and even litigation. In fact, there is strong evidence to link 'organisational ill health' with employee sickness, absences, high labour turnover and low productivity. Moreover, stress, which can be directly related to job and organisational problems, is thought responsible for 60–80% of all workplace accidents. Work-related stress is now a common reason for absenteeism. The collective cost of stress to organisations in terms of absenteeism, reduced productivity, potential compensation claims and so on is colossal. Stress-related absences are ten times more costly than all other industrial relations disputes put together. Factors within the workplace causing stress include:

- Unsatisfactory working conditions – poor quality internal environment (air quality, light/daylight and temperature), physical location or individual posture.
- Mental and physical overload from excessive work-related demands – long working hours, lack of breaks, working weekends and curtailed or cancelled holidays.
- Role ambiguity and inconsistency in management style – poor senior management (leadership) that causes confusion and discord.
- Responsibility for other personnel – assuming a position for which one is ill-equipped or unsuited.
- Unsatisfactory working and personal relationships – conflict or tensions between individuals or groups.
- Under-promotion or over-promotion – failing to reward or, conversely, moving personnel to new positions where they are unable to cope.
- Poor organisational structure/culture – ineptitude in managing the social infrastructure to the extent that personnel become disillusioned, downbeat and distrustful.

Things are likely to get worse as reorganisations, relocations of personnel, redesign of jobs, and reallocations of roles and responsibilities make changes to the normal way of doing business in the coming years.

The hidden costs of stress caused by not adequately creating an environment that enhances the well-being of employees are manifest in a lack of added value to the organisation's products or services and the costs of rectifying underperformance. Study of work stress has tended to concentrate upon ways in which the individual can cope with or adapt to stress. Instead, effort should concentrate on how the work environment can alleviate stress. The effort of coping with stress absorbs energy that could otherwise be invested in more productive and satisfying work activities. Williams (2002) discusses the effects of stress on performance and productivity and how to recognise it, manage it and prevent it.

A preoccupation of many managers is how to measure performance, especially in an office environment where production line principles do not apply. This may appear to be a legitimate goal and is one area where the use of ICT has led to electronic monitoring. This has the capacity to provide fairer compensation for performance through more accurate and timely feedback. The links between performance and reward are such that this should be beneficial to productivity. However, negative effects of such monitoring, in terms of worker stress and health problems, can actually mean a decline in productivity. The stress that stems from performance measurement and monitoring would seem to be associated with lack of control, loss of trust, and an increased administrative workload involved in operating such procedures. Placing emphasis on monitoring employee performance closely can therefore create more problems than it solves.

One workers' union has been reported as dealing with 7000 stress-related claims at one time. Transferring employees to more challenging jobs may be how some organisations approach the management of their personnel. That view may not, however, be shared by employees. Moreover, it may bring them into a working environment that damages their health, forcing them into premature retirement and a poor quality of life.

Today, courts are more likely than ever to take a sympathetic view of an employee whose quality of life has been ruined by an inconsiderate or unprincipled employer. In fact, as far back as 1999, a former council employee was awarded over £67 000 compensation for stress at work. This was the first time that an employer had accepted liability for personal injury caused by stress and also the first time that the courts awarded damages for work-related stress. This particular award – other cases have been settled out of court – covers loss of future earnings and the cost of prescription medication. The plaintiff worked for Birmingham City Council for 16 years before being forced to retire on grounds of ill health. She began her career as a junior clerk in the housing department and progressed to become a senior technician. In 1993, she was promoted to housing officer, a job that involved dealing face to face with tenants. The plaintiff asked for training for this new job, which brought her into direct contact with the public for the first time. Training was promised, but never materialised. Not long afterwards, she began to show symptoms of stress, which descended into clinical depression and ultimately forced her to retire. The judge found in favour of the plaintiff and awarded costs against the council in addition to the compensation for loss of future earnings.

Conclusions

Providing a safe and healthy place of work and business for employees and customers not only involves compliance with statutory requirements but also safeguards the people using the organisation's buildings and facilities. These commonsense requirements are generally well defined within the law and so ought to be obvious to competent practitioners. Even so, new legislation continues to appear – much of it initiated in the European Parliament and/or by its executive, the European Commission. Rights of workers now extend into areas affecting working time and all-inclusiveness. For client organisations, there is the additional requirement to ensure that where outsourcing has taken place (or is about to), service providers are not in breach of the legislation. As important is the need to avoid arrangements that become divisive and counterproductive. Another area of concern is the now recognised and growing incidence of stress, which is classed as a major industrial disease. Facilities managers should be alert to hidden dangers in the workplace. Guidance in this and other important areas of health and safety cannot be exhaustive and so the organisation must take its own steps to ensure compliance. All organisations are advised to ensure they comply with the relevant requirements by seeking professional advice. Last, corporate social responsibility encourages organisations to become more accountable for their actions and to consider the broader impact of those actions on local communities and the environment.

CHECKLIST

This checklist is intended to assist with the review and action planning process.

		Yes	No	Action required
1.	Are the organisation and its advisers aware of relevant legislation in relation to the management and occupation of premises with particular emphasis on health and safety issues?	☐	☐	☐
2.	Have the organisation's requirements for implementing health and safety legislation been properly identified and arrangements made for their proper organisation and administration?	☐	☐	☐
3.	Has a proper assessment of the risk to health and safety for employees and all others affected by the activities of the organisation been completed?	☐	☐	☐
4.	Have the means of implementing appropriate measures been devised?	☐	☐	☐
5.	Have responsibilities for health and safety matters been identified and placed?	☐	☐	☐
6.	Are the premises able to accommodate people with disabilities of different kinds, i.e. mobility, sight and hearing?	☐	☐	☐
7.	Are the organisation and its advisers aware of the factors that can lead to stress-related illnesses and are they making sufficient efforts to eliminate them?	☐	☐	☐

11 Workplace Productivity

Key issues

The following issues are covered in this chapter.

- Productivity in the workplace is a focus of attention for most organisations. The balance between the demands of work and the well-being of the individual is paramount if productivity is to be maintained or enhanced.

- A key factor in realising productivity gains through ICT is that the organisation must be structured to take advantage of the technology and to optimise the contribution of those who use it.

- There are essentially two ways in which the work environment can impact on productivity – enabling it or hindering it.

- Environmental factors affecting productivity include air quality, noise control, thermal comfort, privacy, lighting and spatial comfort. Not all of these are entirely negative in their impact.

- Factors related to sick building syndrome are exacerbated in the high-tech workplace.

- Environmental characteristics that influence work at the individual level include architectural properties – size of office, number of walls, ergonomic factors, heating and light.

- The issue of control is one that is continually referred to in a variety of contexts. The use of individual environmental control systems can increase productivity.

- Realising that people engage in different activities, and how they do so, then matching the space and facilities to the activity is a critical element of an integrated workplace strategy.

Introduction

The last 10–15 years have seen renewed interest in understanding the factors that impact upon productivity in the workplace – generally taken in the context of the office environment. There is now substantial literature on the subject, and a range of issues so diverse that it is difficult to summarise succinctly; however, many themes and issues recur, not least the difficulty of measuring the actual impact of various factors on worker productivity. Nonetheless, evidence does exist of factors that are acknowledged as contributing positively to worker productivity, though arguably fewer than exist in relation to detrimental or negative impacts. Design issues feature strongly in this chapter and some insights are provided as to the kinds of working environment that could bring about useful contributions towards raising productivity. Findings from studies in a variety of specialist fields concerning workplace efficiency tend to be stronger on assumptions about how work should be structured and what will be the future trends than on practical advice as to how these might be addressed. A commonly propagated view, as to the impact of a combination of measures and improvements in areas affecting productivity, is that a substantial gain may be possible – perhaps to the extent of 50%. The basis of this view is examined. Understanding how productivity is affected by various actions is covered under four headings: work itself, the organisation, communication and working environment.

Measuring productivity

There is a growing body of literature on factors affecting productivity in the workplace, with a particular bias towards those factors which impact on decisions regarding the use of space – for a broad treatment of the subject see, for example, Clements-Croome (2000). Most of the factors affecting productivity are consistently identified in literature covering specific and general workplace issues, even where there is sometimes an admission that the particular claim is unsupported by empirical evidence. In some cases it is not possible to amass such evidence, due to difficulties in measurement. In fact, one overriding consideration is the agreement that productivity in the office – as opposed to the factory – environment is extremely difficult to measure. This should not, however, be allowed to be an obstacle to attempts at identifying factors affecting productivity because of another issue which is subject to widespread agreement: the possible gains from a combination of improvements in all suggested areas affecting productivity could be substantial, perhaps to the extent of 50%.

Particular difficulties in isolating and measuring the relationship between productivity and the physical setting do not imply that the latter is minor. It is generally agreed that 'any programme to increase the productivity and effectiveness of office-based work should employ the design, management, and quality of the work environment to maximum advantage' (Aronoff and Kaplan, 1995). The environment is, however, only one aspect: workers experience the office as a whole, including the physical, psychological and management setting, with each aspect affecting the others. For this reason, the remainder of this chapter is split into sections covering productivity factors relating to:

- Work itself
- The organisation
- Communication
- Working environment.

Most emphasis will be given to working environment, where the issues raised in the previous sections will be seen to impact. This is achieved by reviewing findings in a variety of specialist fields impacting on workplace efficiency and considering professionals in the facilities management sector. Unfortunately, the literature tends to be stronger on assumptions about how work is now structured and, therefore, suggestive of future trends, than on practical advice as to how these might be addressed.

Work itself

In today's business environment employees are not simply under pressure to 'work smarter, not harder' but to do both. A more apt saying is 'lean and mean'. Idle time is pushed out as the means for work intensification are sought, not always with a view to quality rather than quantity, the latter still being easier to measure (Thompson and Warhurst, 1998).

There is general agreement that the nature of work has undergone significant changes in the last few decades. Major changes include a shift of the workforce from a concentration on production to service industries. The vast majority of workers are now employed in offices: as many as 80% are now white-collar workers. This remarkable shift immediately highlights a disquieting point: production industries have been able both to achieve and to measure substantial productivity improvements whereas performance levels in office work, as far as it is possible to measure them, have lagged significantly, in spite of substantial investment in ICT. Given the high percentage of white-collar workers, this is a disturbing state of affairs and indicates the pressing need to achieve greater productivity. This also explains the growing interest in organisational effectiveness, which becomes of national economic interest when it is shown that the country concerned lags in international competitiveness.

The work that is concentrated in the office sector has also changed. It is generally agreed that the workplace of today is likely to be a high-demand environment, subject to fast and continual change, increasing demands and fewer resources. With moves towards downsizing, restructuring and re-engineering, and initiatives such as total quality management, and an atmosphere of perpetual change, prompted by changes in consumer demands and increasing personnel and accommodation costs, jobs have tended to become less individual and isolated and more multi-activity and integrated. It is already becoming clear that an increasing number of people will also be expected to pursue multiple careers. Advances in ICT have facilitated such changes and many routine tasks have been taken over by computer-based systems. These moves have been paralleled by advanced manufacturing technologies in the factory environment, in both cases increasing the psychological or cognitive demands of modern work. There is a move away from non-interactive routine work towards both more collaborative and more highly autonomous styles of working. Much routine work is becoming automated or exported to lower cost economies. The large number of call centres and other technical functions outsourced to low wage countries is clear evidence of this trend.

In some cases, greater job diversity has been achieved; in other cases simply greater workload and responsibility taken on by a diminishing workforce are resulting in longer hours and/or more intensive work. The technology which has enabled such advances has also supported advances in monitoring some aspects of performance, thus increasing the pressure to perform, which in turn adds to stress.

It is often argued and generally assumed by many analysts that the majority of work now done in offices is 'knowledge work' and consequently it is the productivity of the knowledge worker that must be maximised. Creative knowledge work demands a combination of highly concentrated individual work alongside interactive teamwork. Knowledge workers tend to pursue their own interests and see their own value. If their needs can be accommodated within the workplace they can boost productivity within a more collegial form of management, which involves the sharing of information, delegation and the encouragement of upward and horizontal communication. Coordination is now based on collaboration between technical and professional groups, which retain authority over their own work. This is part of the flattening of hierarchical structures and also of the move towards teamworking focused on problem solving and continual improvement in a culture of trust and empowerment.

Worker morale is of obvious importance to productivity. This has previously been linked to issues such as security, routine and stability in job tasks. While this remains true to a large extent, future demands of workers from their work are more likely to focus on independence and creativity. Added to this is the increasing flexibility of working patterns and practices that many organisations are now offering their employees. The following are options open to some workers, often in combination:

- Homeworking or telecommuting
- Flexible working hours
- Out-of-office working – use of satellite centres and the concept of the virtual office (see Chapter 3).

The options have been enabled by technological change, which involves not just a change in the way a job is done, but also a major social transformation in the nature and/or location of the workplace. This flexibility is seen as being mutually beneficial to individuals and their organisations.

There is considerable evidence in various areas of the positive impact of control on the job satisfaction and general well-being of the individual. Conversely, lack of control is detrimental. Given the links seen between satisfaction, well-being and productivity, discussed below, it can be agreed that this type of flexibility will be beneficial all round. Moreover, there is evidence to suggest that working away from the office leads to higher levels of productivity, subject to the nature of the work, the individual and the alternative environment. It is also most beneficial if conceived as part of an integrated workplace strategy.

There is assumed to be a link between personal satisfaction with one's workplace and the effectiveness of the individual and the organisation. The validity of the satisfaction/productivity model is backed up by research, which suggests a relationship between employee satisfaction and the factors of absenteeism and turnover, although the relationship to productivity, while consistent, is not as strong as might by expected. A third variable, rewards, seems to determine the relationship. Good performance may lead to rewards, which in turn can lead to satisfaction; however, this way of looking at it would then say that satisfaction, rather than causing performance, is actually caused by it.

There are two types of reward: extrinsic (pay, promotion, status, security) and intrinsic (personal satisfaction). For this reason, it is more important for the organisation to look at the match between satisfaction and performance rather than addressing satisfaction in itself. The match seems to depend on the perceived equitable distribution of rewards. This may have an impact on issues of space quality and allocation. Reward is not usually linked to professional achievement, but to managerial hierarchies, on the basis of which enclosed, high-quality spaces are allocated as visible status symbols as opposed to being allocated according to quality of performance as a means for rewarding productive workers.

There is a need to focus on the environment in relation to the ease of task performance, rather than in relation to a given job. Ease in accomplishing work affects productivity directly, but also appears to affect motivation and, therefore, performance through its influence on intrinsic rewards. Moreover, 'task performance and work satisfaction are optimised when job demands are high enough for the work to be challenging and interesting, but not so high as to be overwhelming' (Aronoff and Kaplan, 1995). Although factors related to job satisfaction may not be the same as those related to job performance, both impact on productivity and are, therefore, of consequence for the organisation.

In exchange for the removal of restrictions, workers are now required to demonstrate their added value and to do whatever is necessary to achieve the organisation's goals. We can now look at the impact of the organisation on productivity and how this has changed in recent years, as part of changes in the nature and pattern of work.

The organisation

The virtual organisation is now a reality, but not commonplace. Many changes have been taking place that make the forward-looking organisation of the present highly differentiated from the traditional organisation. European organisations in particular have experienced a wave of domestic and cross-border mergers, acquisitions and strategic alliances, as well as restructuring from privatisation or in response to increasing market competition. Reorganisation has an immediate productivity impact in terms of time involved in recruiting or reassigning staff, moving staff and/or furniture, re-establishing and resuming work. The traditional hierarchical pyramid has been squashed to accommodate more horizontal communication and empowerment. The move to flatter and leaner organisational structures has increased the workload and demands on the individual employee. An atmosphere of uncertainty and a need for continual adaptation to new working practices and managerial styles and work cultures, combined with concerns over job security in the move towards short-term contracts, have led to increasing degrees of job-related stress. Chapter 10 discussed factors giving rise to stress amongst workers.

At the beginning of this chapter, we commented on the difficulty of measuring performance in the office environment. The pervasiveness of ICT has led, *inter alia*, to electronic monitoring which has the capacity to provide fairer compensation for performance through more accurate and timely feedback. The links between performance and reward are such that this should be beneficial to productivity. However, negative effects of such monitoring, in terms of worker stress and health decline, can mean a reduction in productivity. Stress from performance measurement and monitoring would seem to be associated with lack of control, loss of trust, and an increased administrative workload involved in operating such procedures. The continuing emphasis placed on closely monitored employee performance, linked to reward and advancement, rests uncomfortably alongside empowerment and participative management, especially if employees are not consulted on targets or the selection of performance criteria.

Focus on the employee as a resource, particularly the soft approach, sees the potential that can be realised in the workforce through training and development, and through cultivating employee commitment to the organisation. This last emphasis will require the physical work environment to be more supportive of the human resources strategies adopted by the organisation. This is particularly evident in the case of flexibility, where the built environment must be able to support the demands for individual and organisational flexibility in order to respond to changes in the marketplace.

Communication

The drive to achieve more efficient realisation of office assets and to promote productivity becomes more feasible with ICT and, in particular, networking. The impact of advances in ICT should be self-evident. However, the effect on productivity is less so, at least in the office environment. Whereas technology has facilitated remarkable increases in productivity in manufacturing, it has had little impact in the office sector and has not provided immediate payback on the high costs of its implementation. Unlike the manufacturing sector, where automation rapidly increases production, technology in the office is likely to increase productivity only to the extent to which users integrate it into their way of working. A key factor in realising productivity gains is that the organisation must be structured to take advantage of the technology and to optimise the contribution of those who use it. The greatest productivity gains are only likely to be achieved when ICT has been used to restructure workflows so that inefficiency and waste are driven out.

ICT has been responsible for some important changes, such as removing the functional and spatial division between headquarters, back office and customer face-to-face offices, leading to greater flexibility in work patterns. Adjacency planning has become less constrained by the demands of physical workflow, with emphasis now given to clustering work activities that require similar background environments, services and equipment. Value can be added to office use by improving productivity through the more effective application of ICT and greater flexibility in its use. For example, the organisation can choose to manage work in a variety of settings, on multiple sites and even across time zones – the location of call centres overseas is but one example.

With up to 80% of office workers reckoned to be knowledge workers, typically spending around 70% of their time on communication activities, they need a mixture of periods of quiet concentration, to allow for creative or complex thought, and collaborative work. The group element enhances individual capabilities and it is therefore critical for their success that they are able to communicate and collaborate as necessary. Moreover, people can learn from each other in informal situations, by working alongside people with whom they do not normally share space. Many organisations now plan adjacencies to take advantage of unanticipated opportunities created by social interaction.

Work environment

There are essentially two ways in which the office environment can impact on productivity: through enabling it or through hindering it. The ways in which the environment adversely affects worker satisfaction and performance are fairly well known and empirically established. Less is known of, or certain about, the ways in which the environment can positively impact on productivity, other than in removing the factors that adversely affect it.

The many issues known or believed to affect production include, but are not restricted to:

- Prevention of diseases and accidents, resulting in reduced costs.
- Reduction of sick leave and lower personnel turnover.
- Improvement of communication – consent on the topic of working conditions.

- Commitment of workers and improvement of industrial relations.
- Enhancement of quality.
- Improvement of productivity and efficiency.
- Better position in the labour market – more attractive jobs.

Seven aspects of the work environment have been identified from the perspective of users:

1. Indoor air quality
2. Noise control
3. Thermal comfort
4. Privacy
5. Lighting comfort
6. Spatial comfort
7. Building noise control.

In the above context, the physical environment for office work is believed to account for a variation of some 5–15% in employee productivity (Rostron, 1997). These aspects or factors are now discussed. In this connection, it is important to bear in mind the complexity of the factors and the difficulty of uncovering the root cause of most problems affecting workers. In a book of this kind, we can only hope to provide a summary.

Environmental factors having an impact on productivity

Indoor air quality is one of the major areas of dissatisfaction amongst workers. It is an umbrella term for a variety of factors that include ventilation, pollutants and moisture. Stale air is a common complaint and arises from inefficient ventilation. Natural means of ventilation can often alleviate problems caused by a low rate of mechanical (i.e. forced) air changes; however, the subject is complex and cannot be discussed comprehensively here. Indoor pollution sources that release gases or particles into the air are a significant cause of indoor air quality problems. Inadequate ventilation can increase indoor pollutant levels by not bringing in enough outdoor air to dilute emissions from indoor sources and by not carrying indoor air pollutants to the outside. High temperature and moisture can also increase concentrations of some pollutants. In fact, moisture is a widespread problem often linked with mould growth, resulting from spores that drift through indoor and outdoor air continually. When mould spores land on a damp spot indoors, they may begin growing and digest whatever they are growing on. The way to control indoor mould growth is to control moisture.

Noise and vibration at high levels can be both physiologically and psychologically harmful; they can obstruct communication and mentally disturb the worker, resulting in job performance impairment and/or accidents. When noise distraction is a problem, people rate it as a serious hindrance to productivity, although they do not claim the absence of noise to be an important benefit. Even so, some level of background noise is, in fact, thought to be beneficial to concentration. Noise at inappropriate levels increases mistakes and slows work rates. People also tend to use more simplistic problem-solving methods. Thus, as noise distraction becomes more troublesome, people not only work less effectively, they think differently, leading to a quality cost as well as a productivity cost. Noise causes breaks in concentration, making it harder to address tasks that require sustained concentration and reducing the ability to make creative leaps. It also interferes with the ability to differentiate relevant issues from those that are unimportant.

Thermal comfort tends to receive the highest number of complaints in most user surveys. Overly cool conditions make people restless, impairing concentration and increasing error rates, particularly for demanding mental tasks. Being too warm can cause weariness, sleepiness, a reduction in performance and a tendency to make mistakes. Fluctuations in temperature can be even more troublesome.

The biological effect of light is significant not only on visual task performance, but also in controlling physiological and psychological functioning of the human body. As with many other factors, the ultimate effect of light and lighting on human well-being is determined in part by individual perception and satisfaction.

Aesthetic choices in office design affect human behaviour and job performance, influencing workers' perceptions of the work environment, how quickly they tire and how tolerant they are of physical stressors. Considerations regarding interior design must therefore take into account the idiosyncrasies of the human visual system. Extremes of contrast are, in particular, visually fatiguing. However, people with certain kinds of visual impairment may benefit from contrasting colour schemes that pick out important objects. White light switches, on a white background, may not be easily found, for example, even if the designer has located the switches where they are expected to be.

Sick building syndrome

Factors related to sick building syndrome (SBS) are exacerbated in the high-tech workplace. Offices with more than two symptoms per person of SBS are likely to show general productivity losses. The reported effects of SBS may combine with other job-related factors to produce an overall sense of dissatisfaction. This means that the concentration of research and business efforts and expense on maintenance and cleaning may be misplaced in the search for improved productivity. Moreover, psychosocial problems may actually lead to susceptibility to symptoms through increased stress in working environments.

Minimising the constraints placed on employees at their workstations will increase social and economic productivity. The more choice people have, the happier and more productive they become. The reason why many people underperform is because their behaviour and degrees of freedom are systematically reduced by decisions over which they themselves have no control – decisions usually taken higher up the organisation.

Environmental characteristics that influence work at the individual level include architectural properties – for example size of office, number of walls, ergonomic factors, heating and light – and architectural attributes, that is, people's perceptions of architectural properties. The very design of workplaces might be creating ill-health. In fact, health and stress problems are greater in high-demand, low-control environments than in high-demand, high-control environments.

The issue of control is one that is continually referred to in a variety of contexts. It surfaces in connection with the work itself and within the organisation and is a major factor concerning productivity in the context of the working environment. Control of one's working environment includes temperature, lighting and ventilation, as well as choice and configuration of furniture. The use of individual environmental control systems can increase productivity by up to 7%. However, the modern office often acts against this, with top-down (or external management) control over functions such as heating and ventilation.

Design implications

An investigation into the influence of the working environment on self-reported productivity found that most respondents considered that the office had a direct influence on their well-being and productivity. They felt that productivity in particular would rise by 10% if environmental conditions were improved. Generally, an improved fit between the physical setting and the work process, both at the individual and the organisational level, should improve performance directly, but also indirectly contribute to future successful job performance by enhancing the intrinsic rewards of the job – performance leads to satisfaction leads to performance.

The design of workspace must address not only employees' lower order needs, such as safety and physical comfort, but also higher order needs such as self-esteem. Once environmental needs are satisfied, the individual becomes dominated by the unsatisfied needs and environmental conditions cease to be important to the individual's current concerns. Instead, issues such as amenity, view, décor, space provision and furniture standard come to the fore in the context of status and self-fulfilment.

Whether a better workplace improves individual performance or more productive workers gravitate to organisations with better work environments is not entirely clear. Yet there are measurable productivity benefits to be gained by improving the physical working environment. Problems may, however, arise as much from the perception of space, such as open plan layouts, as from the reality, including its perceived inferiority to enclosed spaces occupied by managers. Consequently, interventions that alter such perceptions might be a productive approach.

Whilst open plan settings are intended to offer greater flexibility, it is often the case that this flexibility is not utilised, as the upheaval involved is itself considered counterproductive. Minimising the disruption to productivity caused by constant reshuffles can be achieved through such planning measures as the 'universal footprint' or the fixed service spine. The former limits the number of different office sizes to facilitate movement of staff; the latter mixes rigidity and flexibility, enabling quick reconfigurations to facilitate different types of activity with minimum disruption. Within the universal footprint, as in other schemes, furniture may also be standardised but with individuals able to choose a personalised combination from a standard range of components. This results in a degree of equity, essential to employee satisfaction, as well as direct productivity benefits in matching the tools to the task and the individual. Worker preference for private spaces even for routine tasks and the level of worker satisfaction achieved by this may be more important to productivity than the benefits of social contact provided in less private spaces. A moderately arousing setting benefits monotonous or dull tasks, while a non-arousing setting benefits more complex ones.

Realising that people engage in different activities, and how they do so, and matching the space and facilities to the activity is a critical element of the new workplace. There are reports of improvements in productivity following reorganisation which took place with user involvement. Organisations can maximise the productivity of their workforce through such a choice of settings that allows individuals and teams to select the one most suited to their task needs at any given time. Allocated workspace cannot be optimal for all activities, all of the time.

Unconventional working arrangements

One approach to revising space utilisation is to abandon designated spaces or workstations in favour of shared facilities, within schemes such as 'hot-desking' and 'hotelling'. This is not always the best way to increase the productive use of office space, in spite of the obvious cost savings. More can be achieved by zoning space, so that, for example, special 'touch down' places, accessible to everyone, are set aside for concentrated, group or specialist work. This can offset some of the problems associated with open plan offices. In order to maximise the productivity benefits of the non-territorial office, the initiative has to be business-driven rather than cost-driven. The former will involve a fundamental rethinking of organisational structure, performance measurement and business processes.

The productivity increases offered by telecommuting and other new work arrangements can only be maximised if the right sort of space is provided in the office for the times when workers are there. If the office cannot offer appropriate support then productivity gains may be negated. Appropriate support may involve turning the traditional concept of the office inside out. The primary function of the central office space might become support of communication and interaction. Areas for individual, concentrated work would become the support space for the more team-oriented interactive spaces. A system of loosely coupled settings linked physically by the movement of employees and the electronic movement of information could maximise productivity in an organisation with this approach to work. The need for an integrated workplace strategy to accommodate and support new modes of work is paramount.

One large office may appear an efficient option in terms of running costs but there is evidence that decentralisation and the fragmentation of the organisation into several smaller centres is beneficial to job satisfaction and organisational well-being. Hindrances to communication include screening, too little space provided at individual workstations so that impromptu group interactions cannot take place there, and little or no other provision for meetings. Designs that actively support teamwork, collaboration and chance interaction may be highly beneficial to productivity within an organisation which values that approach.

These ideas have come together in the total workplace concept, guided by three principles: breaking down barriers to encourage functional diversity and mixing people who would not normally mix, increasing stimulating and beneficial exposure to differences and diversity; access to the physical resources necessary for effective work, with environmental equity; and varying the optimal setting for accomplishing work according to variations in an individual's work over time. This also encourages spatial mobility between office locations and increases the potential for chance interactions.

Design features that can contribute to this scheme include suitably located activity magnet areas, such as places for breaks designed to create the right kind of behavioural force fields, shared services, and information centres to place the employee's contribution in the wider organisational context and promote contributions to company thinking and development. This concept of the total workplace takes a dual approach to effecting productivity: it accommodates the worker to the greatest extent in some respects, while encouraging mobility and interaction through not making every facility as accessible as possible. Other steps could include dedicated project team rooms, saving time spent on assembling and disassembling material and facilities before and after each meeting. A combination of such spaces with private workstations to accommodate concentrated individual work, plus the clustering of services, may also bring about higher performance from these potentially productive groups.

Conclusions

Proper understanding of worker satisfaction and performance in the office environment requires examination of a complex set of interacting subsystems, including physical environmental factors, job characteristics, organisational factors, sociocultural characteristics and past experience of workers. More detailed operational definitions of the variables being investigated (such as noise, space, health, privacy, satisfaction and pro-ductivity) must be developed. This has not prevented a considerable amount of literature developing on these topics as the root problem that must be addressed and becomes ever more urgent, as also does the need to justify investments in the office environment. Improving one aspect, such as the physical setting, while ignoring others may send conflicting messages. Moreover, the work environment can only operate productively if all aspects are considered as part of an integrated workplace strategy. The high-performance workplace is much talked and written about, but is barely evident. There are so many factors contributing to productivity that prov-ing a cause and effect relationship is bound to be problematic. Decisions on the quality of the office workplace demand informed judgement. Whilst it remains elusive to be able to predict reliably the returns on facility invest-ments of the kind outlined, the evidence that a better work environment promotes better performance is more than superficially compelling. The overriding message is to strike the right balance between maximising com-munication and space for quiet reflective work; between group, team and project work, and confidential or individual work; and between group areas and individual access to daylight, aspect and ventilation.

CHECKLIST

This checklist is intended to assist with the review and action planning process.

	Yes	No	Action required
1. Has the organisation undertaken any formal measurement of productivity in the workplace?	☐	☐	☐
2. Is the organisation aware of the factors that can lead to dissatisfaction with the workplace?	☐	☐	☐
3. Is the organisation continually monitoring the quality of the internal environment?	☐	☐	☐
4. Are workers' concerns about the work environment taken seriously and incidents properly investigated?	☐	☐	☐
5. Have steps been taken to minimise negative impacts upon worker well-being?	☐	☐	☐
6. Has the organisation taken steps to maximise beneficial aspects of the workplace?	☐	☐	☐
7. Has the organisation adopted a flexible policy in relation to the workplace, e.g. working hours, off-site locations and non-traditional office layouts?	☐	☐	☐

12 Building Intelligence and Smart Systems

Key issues

The following issues are covered in this chapter.

- The extent and complexity of building engineering services in a modern building – responsible for the security, safety, comfort and health of users – require a control regime that can respond rapidly to changing conditions and demands.

- Building automation is the broad term used to cover the smart control of building engineering services: it does not in itself constitute an intelligent building.

- Intelligent buildings have been touted for more than two decades but are arguably no closer today to the notion of intelligence than they were then.

- Buildings have to be designed intelligently if they are to satisfy legislation and owners' needs in sustainable development including energy efficiency and zero carbon – technology-enhancement alone is not enough.

- Knowing how a building is behaving in terms of the conditions existing within it and immediately outside it are vital to successful facilities management. Sensors can provide reliable data and detect changes in operating conditions rapidly, no more so than where fire, smoke or intrusion are involved.

- Smart devices – most notably radio frequency identification (RFID) tags – are finding their way into many industrial sectors and their use is spreading to the architecture, engineering and construction (AEC) sector in general and facilities management in particular – significant opportunities await for reducing costs and creating added value.

- RFID can be regarded as a disruptive technology because it has the potential to force structural changes in the procurement of buildings and facilities. Many applications can already be found.

- Intelligent systems, based on RFID active tags and other smart devices, provide the infrastructure for the next generation of building automation. Autonomous agents can interact and build powerful knowledge bases on the performance of facilities and the systems within them.

Introduction

The concept of building intelligence has been debated for at least the past two decades. There are many examples of buildings that are able to respond, even anticipate, the needs of users. Buildings can be equipped with a high level of technology that allows decisions to be taken without manual intervention. Smart sensors and controllers are now routinely incorporated into the design of building engineering services, allowing energy use to be managed more efficiently. A degree of autonomous control can thus be used to create and maintain an internal environment for the safety and comfort of users, and to monitor and secure the immediate surroundings. The idea that buildings can act intelligently *per se* is fanciful, but it does help us to explore concepts and pursue research that can contribute to a better built environment in the long run. Building intelligence should therefore embrace the idea that we design intelligently and that we provide users with a secure, safe, healthy and comfortable environment. These two concepts would seem compatible, but are they? As we strive for more technology in our buildings do we, in fact, move in the opposite direction to the goals of sustainable development? Buildings that are required to be energy efficient also consume materials and products that may deplete natural and scarce resources. Moreover, the technology to control our buildings has to be manufactured at some cost to the environment. We need to take a whole-life view of buildings and be sure that there is a demonstrable net gain to the environment. The purpose of this chapter is not to debate the rights or wrongs of current practice, but to understand how, from a facilities management perspective, we can satisfy a number of competing interests. Significant in this respect are smart devices that are small enough to be attached to components and parts, or embedded in building structures and fabric. They promise to change our perception of how supply chains should be organised and where the real value can be created in design, construction and facilities management.

Building engineering services

For some new facilities, more than half of the capital cost can be ascribed to building engineering services: HVAC, lighting, power, transportation, fire and security systems. For others, it will still be a significant cost. Control over these installations is vital if the facility is to perform optimally and not exceed targets for energy consumption or reduce user comfort, amongst other concerns. Our aim here is not to describe the usual range of engineering services as it would be impossible to do justice to such an expansive subject in a single chapter. Instead, we discuss some of the issues of concern to facilities managers.

For any building or facility to function correctly, there must be information on the conditions within and immediately outside it, and then the means to do something about them. There has to be sensing, control and monitoring across a range of services and this can only be managed using computer-based technology. Whilst technicians and managers will make the final decisions, they need timely and accurate information. It is impractical to understand fully what is going on inside a major facility without having information and data organised in such a way that services can be controlled and their performance regulated as necessary.

Building automation systems

Building automation implies a computerised system that oversees and controls building operations, energy and safety management. Whilst it is possible in theory to integrate all functions into a single system, practical and economic considerations make such a development unlikely despite claims from vendors. Site visits have confirmed the difficulties faced by software developers and control engineers in producing robust systems to meet the satisfaction of facilities managers. Nevertheless, an integrated approach is both desirable and inevitable. For most purposes, a user interface with access to separate systems – HVAC, power, lighting, fire and security – is the more likely scenario. Such arrangements are reliant upon high-speed communications and, of necessity, require significant wiring up of the building or facility based on standards such as ASHRAE's BACnet or the proprietary LonTalk.

A building automation system typically maintains the indoor climate within a specified range (e.g. a set-point of 21°C, ±2°), as well as managing other energy-saving measures such as controlling lighting based on occupancy. In addition, the system would be expected to monitor plant and equipment and overall system behaviour for signs of failure or deterioration in performance.

There is a close connection between building automation systems and the concept of the intelligent building – discussed in the next section – to the extent that some would argue they are one and the same. As we shall see, building automation systems are an important part of the broader picture.

Intelligent buildings – Smart buildings

Smart buildings and technology-enhanced real estate are other terms for the intelligent building and show the association of technology with intelligence. Providing a high-level of connectivity for users within a facility and a means by which they can communicate readily with the outside world can be vital for organisations. Even so, a wired-up building is no more intelligent than one that is without such paraphernalia. A building that is designed to use natural means of ventilation and cooling cannot be dubbed unintelligent. Passive systems are no less worthy of our attention than active or mechanically assisted systems. Many new buildings do, in fact, combine both passive and active systems, utilising nature's forces when conditions allow and intervening with manmade systems when required.

Intelligent buildings use technology to improve the internal environment and support functions for users. Security, safety, health, comfort and accessibility can improve productivity and provide a satisfactory customer experience. The major benefits of intelligent buildings are seen as (CABA, 2002):

- Increased individual environmental control leading to higher value building, leasing and rental potential.
- Managed energy consumption through zone control on a time-of-day schedule.
- Upgrading and modifications to control systems from standardised systems wiring.
- Control of building systems after hours via PC, PDA or telephone.
- Tracking of occupant after-hours system.
- Tracking of service/replacement history of individual zone use.
- Control of changes to telephone, security, LAN, wireless devices, parking and building directory from a single user interface.

This focus on technology can be viewed in terms of the characteristics of the intelligent building. In the context of office or similar buildings, we can differentiate three broad categories of system:

1. Building automation systems
2. Office automation systems
3. Communication systems.

The second and third can be combined under the heading of workplace automation; either way, all three are about technology.

Office automation systems are focused on employee productivity and include:

- Computer workstations (PCs)
- Digital storage and archiving
- Office productivity software
- Technical and specialist software
- Scanning and printing equipment.

Communication systems can be seen in terms of:

- Private telephone exchanges
- Voice over internet protocol (VoIP), teleconferencing and video-conferencing
- Satellite communications
- Virtual private networks
- Instant messaging, email, intranets and extranets.

The dependence on technology is understandable; however, we need to add a further characteristic that stems from our concern about intelligent design. *Responsiveness to change* is a fundamental requirement for any intelligent building and this characteristic could just as easily be applied to other types of building. No building is going to support the organisation within it if change is not possible or cannot be achieved without significant upheaval. Predicting the future is impossible, but anticipating change and having the means to accommodate it is a sign of intelligent design. Too many buildings – even some under construction today – have a fixed purpose and adaptation will prove difficult. Evidence is all around us in the form of modern buildings facing redevelopment for the singular reason that there are no potential tenants willing to take them on.

Some people would argue that buildings have changed comparatively little over two millennia, certainly when we think about how just about everything else has changed. In a world where products seem to be designed for ever-shorter life cycles and often become obsolete before their time, buildings represent a kind of permanence. Yet significant change has taken place in just a few years as legislators and more and more owners demand buildings that are designed intelligently. Here, we are talking of sustainability and the construction of, for example, zero carbon buildings. Green or eco-friendly buildings – there are several terms – have become a reality.

Smart tagging, sensing and control

Progress is often made by very small steps. One technology that has begun to affect industry generally is that of smart tagging – a process in which tiny devices or tags holding unique information are attached to a component or part. The tags are encoded with data that can be read by a scanner in close proximity. Their size and reducing cost means they can be easily fixed to individual components and parts during manufacture and then used to monitor their journey through the life cycle of the object into which they become incorporated. In theory, it is possible to uniquely identify every component or part in a building and to use that information to monitor performance in use.

Inventory management and equipment monitoring are amongst current applications for these smart devices, also known as radio frequency identification (RFID) tags. Future applications include guided control of equipment and tags that can communicate fatigue or excessive stress in structural members, as well as important information for safety management purposes. Maintenance applications probably hold the key to accelerating the use of RFID in facilities management. RFID tags could be used in the management of the completed facility, thereby bringing justification for expenditure on the RFID system and, importantly, adding value to the facility by automating, or at least simplifying, the facilities management process. Unfortunately, the cost of implementing RFID solutions remains relatively high and there has been slow take-up across the breadth of the AEC sector including facilities management. Some manufacturers of components have, however, begun using RFID tags for tracking within their own production processes; the tag-fixed components are not normally removed and remain available for use in the building construction and operational phases. Penetration of the technology into other industries is likely to help in bringing costs down to a level where the attachment of tags to building components and systems becomes normal practice.

Value creation

The drive towards more efficient design, construction and facilities management is well illustrated by considering the value chain, which follows the life cycle of a building from raw materials through to the management of the completed facility. Construction projects less frequently follow the conventional (i.e. linear) model where completed buildings are handed over to the owner through a snagging process, after which the constructor can simply walk away. Today, it is not uncommon for the constructor to retain a measure of control either as part-owner or as the operator of the asset or facility, as would occur under various integrated procurement routes. In this way, the cost-efficiency of the completed facility becomes the constructor's responsibility and so it is as important to manage the facility as if it were the construction phase – perhaps more so.

RFID is well placed to provide solutions for inventory control and location that conform to recognised data exchange standards and that will provide efficient links across multiple suppliers. Even so, open source software is more likely to trigger adoption than proprietary software where licensing costs are likely to maintain artificially high end-user prices.

Two important factors have, therefore, revealed themselves for the successful application of RFID in the AEC sector including facilities management.

- The cost of the technology will be better justified when its use is spread across more than a single process. It is the final stage in the supply chain, use or operations where significant benefits to the client organisation could be produced by the use of information and communication technology (ICT) (including RFID and similar devices).
- RFID technology must conform to standards across industry and the sector, so that multiple suppliers, especially small firms, can participate in the project partnership – this aspect is particularly important in facilities management where many small firms are engaged.

Technical issues

Read-only tags are generally used for simple identification purposes, and derive their power from radio frequency energy received (induced) from the reader; they can store only a limited amount of information that cannot be altered. These passive tags are the simplest form of RFID, but nevertheless have far greater capacity for storing information than barcode labels. Present generation RFID tags can typically accommodate up to 96 bits of data. Since bar code labels are only capable of identifying that the item is, for example, a particular specification of window, door, pump, control or item of furniture, RFID tags could identify exactly which one of the batch it was together with its production history.

The simple read-only tag is not, however, limited to 96 bits. The unique product identifier can be hyperlinked to unlimited additional information, such as manufacturing batch and production history, product handling instructions, storage or delivery instructions, expiration dates and other details. Read/write tags, on the other hand, generally require battery power (i.e. they are active tags), which limits their operational life; but they can support large memory arrays (32MB is possible) that can be changed/updated to accumulate the history of a product as it moves from manufacture into service.

Sensor-coupled tags are a recent development, allowing a sensor-measured value to be transmitted to the reader in place of the tag's stored memory contents. Temperature sensors, for example, can be buried in freshly poured concrete to capture in situ temperatures, thus allowing concrete maturity to be tracked. A hand-held reader allows reliable records of the curing process to be logged without the necessity of cables.

One of the most important differentiators between bar coding and RFID tagging is the ruggedness and environmental performance of the electronic tags. RFID tags can operate effectively in temperatures ranging from −40 to +200°C and can perform under rugged conditions and even when dirty. Although radio frequency devices do not require line-of-sight and can transmit through almost any material, metals may cause signal attenuation. As metal is a familiar material on construction sites, such signal degradation could constitute a limitation. The RFID tag's orientation and fixture methods may have to be altered so that the tag can be clearly identified. New RFID technology claims to align the tag's antenna and a non-insulated metal material in such a way that the metal actually amplifies the signal of the RFID tag. Second generation RFID devices based on ultra-high frequency (UHF) offer up to 4 m proximity scanning, allowing readers to be fixed on ceilings or within ceiling voids for tracking objects in a zone or fixed to desks for tracking objects inside boxes (without the need to open and verify contents).

The manufacturing process for RFID devices has been developed further to produce tags as flexible printed circuits, increasing their ruggedness and reliability for many applications. The flexible circuits can be produced on reels as 'smart labels' complete with adhesive backing.

The *Mu-chip* manufactured by Hitachi in Japan is claimed to be the world's smallest RFID chip. It uses the 2.45 GHz frequency (same as for *Bluetooth* devices) and has a 128 bit ROM capable of identifying trillions of unique objects. At 0.4 mm square it is small enough to be embedded in packaging and paper. Applications include electronic numbering of products for manufacturing, distribution, consumption, tracking and recycling. It is expected to have a major impact on logistical efficiency, construction supply chains and the maintenance of building fabric and building engineering services installations.

Cyber-agents and intelligent systems

As noted above, technology is recognised as an increasingly integral component of value creation. As an example, EDI (electronic data interchange), which uses the internet as a communication medium, has reduced administration costs and increased flow performance enabling:

- Work management tracking of progress and response to reactive repair or complaints.
- Asset management maintenance tracking using plant and equipment identifiers.

As RFID becomes implemented widely in products, the extended use of tags in virtually all aspects of construction and facilities management can be envisaged – from inventory control, security, maintenance of building engineering services equipment through to cleaning. Just as with the EDI example above, RFID will find application in many areas of the value chain. A number of examples are given below of applications under development that could use RFID (and related technical concepts) for effective and automated management of construction processes (on and off site) and operational facilities.

Applications of smart systems technology

Secure access and monitoring

Management of facilities requiring control of access may use RFID tags attached to employees' ID badges; this method is already in use in many facilities to permit/control employee access to specific areas. An EU project, OPTAG, has developed this concept to track the movement of checked-in passengers through airports. It is estimated that passengers and their baggage cause some 10% of delays at European airports and this figure is likely to grow as security tightens and as passenger numbers and aircraft sizes increase. This system will be able to locate to within one metre those passengers carrying an RFID device issued at check-in; those who do not turn up at the gate on time can then be found quickly. Active tags will be used, transmitting two short-burst signals every second and the tags, which will be recycled, could be mass-produced at low cost. Airports are not the only facilities that could benefit from such a system once developed; the concept will find management applications in many facilities, including hospitals, public administration buildings, galleries and museums.

Delivery logistics and materials tracking

Future materials tracking management systems may be able to provide owners with the ability to determine construction progress and materials delivered by simply walking around a site where all materials are identified and tagged using an RFID system. This would guarantee more accurate estimates of the number and quantity of delivered goods and enable reliable monitoring of 'percentage work complete'.

An early example of materials tracking was developed in the EU project, *FutureHome* (Wing and Atkin, 2002), as a logistics delivery agent system for use at site gates. The project demonstrated the use of cyber-agents in combination with e-tags performing as an automated site information management system. The cyber-agent supports information gathering of the material delivery process and is able to make decisions for planning and control of construction processes. The system shows the way to several improvements, such as in the following examples.

- Reduction of costs incurred from wastage of materials, theft and check-in waiting times for material.
- Agent technology will enhance communications by informing the driver immediately where the material is to be placed. The agent will confirm delivery of the material with the supplier via the internet and the supplier's website or email address as soon as the material is sent through the delivery gate. The site engineer will be informed as soon as material has arrived on site and can respond and issue further instructions if necessary. If there are any discrepancies, the driver will be informed, as will the supplier. The key point to note is that this communication will be immediate, so any problems can be resolved as soon as they become apparent.
- Time savings will result due to efficient document management. There should be less paperwork, no invoices for the delivery personnel to complete, as all will be automated by the agent. Information will be provided electronically and will include instructions for the vehicle driver to follow. Multiple handling of documents will be significantly reduced.

Document tracking

RFID technology can be used for rapid document tracking, essential in the construction phase to identify the latest version of files and drawings, and also in the facilities management phase to locate original-build specifications and layouts. Each document is tagged with an adhesive smart label (RFID printed circuit) that contains a unique ID together with human-readable information. The file description is entered into a database along with its tracking number and can be assigned certain parameters like expiration date, permitted movement and personnel authorised to see it. Over time, the database could build up an audit trail of the handling and workflow history of each document file.

Product life-cycle tracking

Manufactured components of all kinds are already using RFID tags for tracking their progress through production and delivery processes. The same tags should be suitable for continued use during the life cycle of the component. A useful illustration of this development comes from the tyre company, Michelin, which is now providing product lifetime identification for tyres. RFID tags embedded into tyres are used to identify the manufacturer's name and plant, store the time and date of manufacture, tyre dimension and pressure specifications – other data can be added later.

The same thinking can be applied to buildings and facilities for use with virtually any equipment that requires regular servicing, functionality checking and logging, safety inspection and recording etc. The safety application is significant, as automated digital record-keeping can provide regular unbiased records that are virtually tamper-proof. RFID tags containing pertinent safety information, including regular test records, could be attached to safety equipment such as slings, safety harnesses and belts, scaffolding and hardhats. Similarly, containers of hazardous materials can carry their own handling instructions and usage records in an attached read/write tag.

Location of buried services

Buried pipes and cables can be located using attached RFID tags, so long as the read-range is not exceeded. For plastic pipes, a more suitable technology (nanotechnology) uses magnetic nanoparticles during production of the pipe. It is possible to introduce conductivity into plastics by simply mixing in conductive nanoparticles in the production process. Thus, magnetic nanoparticles can be used to introduce a unique magnetic signature to plastic items which can then be scanned like a barcode. In the AEC sector, this would allow simple and accurate location and identification of underground services such as gas and water pipes, communication cables, etc. If the magnetic signatures are repeated at regular intervals along the entire length of the pipes and cables, they can be tracked throughout the site.

Sensor and network combinations

RFID active tags can be interfaced to networked sensing systems to add further capability to the basic read or read/write tag data function. Wireless networks in a facility, a hospital for example, will allow real-time location of vital mobile assets. This provides an ability to find equipment immediately and also improves asset utilisation, as well as reducing theft. Tags with integrated sensors provide not just simply electronic barcode data, but also measurements of physical parameters such as temperature, shock (acceleration) and even GPS-enabled tracking. Such sensors can be applied to buildings and other structures to prevent or, at least, warn of fatigue or failure. Sensors will be deeply embedded within these structures, supplying data when scanned for shear, strain, pressure and other forces that can affect them, using wireless networks to return the scanned results to a data centre, thereby saving the expense of sending out safety inspectors and engineers to monitor the structures.

Building energy management and climate control

An efficient building energy management system is one that provides lowest cost energy, by avoiding wasted energy and delivering optimal comfort conditions to users. By monitoring space within the facility and taking measurements of conditions outside, information from different sources can be integrated in a centralised control function.

Networked RFID devices with physical sensors complement other developments in sensor networks. These combine recent advances in sensor miniaturisation, wireless communication, and micro-system technology to form networks of tiny autonomous sensors that can make accurate measurements of environmental parameters such as temperature, humidity, light, acceleration, etc. without the necessity of laying cables. Building energy control systems are generally restricted to prestige projects, as the wiring and signal conditioning costs for the many sensors are prohibitive, but the development of these relatively inexpensive devices using wireless communication across their network brings the possibility of accurate climate control for all buildings down to individual house level.

One centre of development is the University of California at Berkeley, where the next generation of these devices will be as tiny as a few cubic millimetres, and termed 'smart dust'. Existing designs, known as 'motes', are a few cubic centimetres in size, and are already being marketed for building energy control and many other applications. Similar devices, *BTnodes*, are under development in Europe, based on *Bluetooth* communications technology.

A problem common to both these developments is battery life – the devices switch on only for brief periods to update measurements and use very short-range communications by passing data from one device to the next across the network. For many applications in the built environment, it is impractical to change batteries and some form of solar or other energy support is needed.

Sensor networks, RFID included, can involve the handling of very large quantities of data, and the limited processing capabilities of the mote or BTnode devices require a back-end infrastructure for processing and storage of results. This could well be provided by connection to an external network, the internet for example, linking to a remote database system. Agent technology can be used to minimise data movement, and to provide local control functions where required. In a building management system such functions could provide security alarm functions and detailed energy management at room level.

The future of these devices, once the problems of miniaturisation and cost have been solved, is seen as a fundamental solution to one of the most pressing economic problems of today – runaway energy costs. Once distributed around a building, the sensors would form a network relaying data about each room's temperature, light, humidity, occupancy, etc. to a central computer that would regulate energy use in the building, optimising the energy delivery to each room and using passive heating and ventilation control methods wherever possible. The emerging smart-energy technology could save significantly on electricity costs, as buildings currently drain away more than a third of the total energy supply of some countries.

Conclusions

Building engineering services can represent the larger share of the capital cost of new buildings and facilities. They are also responsible for a significant share of the total cost of operations, second only to the cost of employing people. For this reason, we need to take a hard look at how efficiency and economy can be balanced. Building automation systems provide the means for managing performance and take us some way towards the concept of the intelligent building – an energy-efficient, responsive facility. Integrated building systems, communications and controls help to create a facility that can provide the owner and users with an environment that is secure, safe, healthy, comfortable, flexible and effective. As we become more attuned to the environmental imperative and the need to minimise energy consumption, building automation will take on greater significance, but it will not provide all the answers. Designing intelligently has to be given a higher profile, too. At its heart is the ability to sense, control and monitor conditions internally, and this applies equally to existing buildings. The advent of low-cost, smart devices (e.g. RFID tags) provides both opportunity and reward, with few risks. The extent of applications indicates that although it may be slow starting, RFID and its associated sensing and networking technologies are likely to have a major role in facilities management. The comprehensive monitoring it brings may even be seen as invasive and, indeed, there are issues of privacy associated with the technology. People tend to accept, albeit reluctantly, speed cameras along roads and CCTV cameras monitoring our movements, so there is unlikely to be substantial opposition to the onward progress of this ultimately beneficial technology.

CHECKLIST

This checklist is intended to assist with the review and action planning process.

	Yes	No	Action required
1. Is a secure, safe, healthy and comfortable environment being provided for users?	☐	☐	☐
2. Do the facilities have efficient sensing, control and monitoring of the building engineering services?	☐	☐	☐
3. Has the organisation's energy use been properly investigated – is it thinking and acting ahead of legislation?	☐	☐	☐
4. Is there opportunity to integrate monitoring and control of otherwise separate systems?	☐	☐	☐
5. Has the organisation assessed the extent of responsiveness to change in its facilities and how it can cope with change?	☐	☐	☐
6. Has the potential for smart tagging been investigated?	☐	☐	☐

13 Facilities Management Service Providers

Key issues

The following issues are covered in this chapter.

- There are four types of service provider arrangements in the marketplace: managing agent, managing contractor, managed budget and total facilities management – and there are variations on them too.

- The degree of flexibility of service provision enjoyed by the client organisation will vary with each type and is a factor that has to be taken into account.

- All types of service provision attract costs in managing and administering contracts.

- The organisation needs to weigh the risks and costs of the different types of service provision and to have based this on reliable data from the marketplace and information from service providers.

- The employment of a total facilities management company – effectively providing a single point of responsibility – whilst attractive, will not relieve the organisation from managing the contract and the interface between the contractor and customers. There are bound to be costs in connection with the management of even a single appointment.

- Novel solutions and their providers have entered the marketplace and include support of a temporary or long-term nature.

Introduction

Selecting a particular type of service provider is in the same bracket as deciding whether or not to outsource – for some, the answer may appear obvious, but this might not be so. In a similar manner to that adopted for approaching the question of outsourcing, the organisation should look closely at the types of provision available and make an objective decision. For simplicity, the four main types of service provider range from additional support for the client organisation to full support in providing anything the organisation might want. There will be variations in these types according to particular circumstances, but they are, otherwise, the most common. Each of the types attracts its own supporters and detractors, and there is distortion in the marketplace as to what is being offered. However, the real issues are those concerning risk for the client organisation, both financially and in damage that could be done by, for example, a careless service provider or subcontractor, and the management and administration required to support the subsequent service contracts. Whilst these are clearly important considerations, pursuit of these points is peripheral to the main substance of this chapter and, indeed, this book. In any event, the organisation should maintain awareness of the state of the market for facilities management, although any market testing should be done with sensitivity – see earlier discussion in Chapter 4 – as part of its ICF. Whatever type of service provision is ultimately selected, the client organisation must do so on the dual criteria of likely customer satisfaction and best value.

Preliminary approach

The opening assumption is that the organisation will have determined which services to outsource and will have done so by taking account of the market for facilities management – see Chapter 4. Earlier actions will have established whether or not the market is capable of delivering what is required by the organisation. An important consideration should be the bundling of individual services in a way that will provide best value. There are two aspects to consider. First, client organisations will have worked out how best to arrange their outsourcing to ensure that best value is likely to be achieved. Second, service providers will take a commercial view on what is profitable for them. Bundling of services can prove to be an attraction for service providers; likewise, carving up the totality of facilities management into very small contracts may not. It is also useful to recognise that arrangements which may involve a lot of subcontracting and, possibly, sub-subcontracting, can confer a financial disadvantage because cost is added at each point in the supply chain without necessarily adding value. Preliminary enquiries will, however, help to establish the most advantageous approach to the bundling of services, as well as militating the likelihood of redundancy occurring in the supply chain. This can be achieved by considering various combinations of services for which indicative quotations can then be sought – although the points in Chapter 4 regarding market testing should be noted.

The organisation will also need to consider the attributes of service provision that are important to them so that they are able to identify the most suitable service provider – again, see Chapter 4. Qualitative criteria can be used to help in weighing different attributes of service and provide a basis for subsequently judging the suitability of service providers before an invitation to tender and, thereafter, in assessing tenders.

The organisation's representatives should be appraised of the financial standing of any service provider before entering into a contract with them – see Chapter 7. Credit references should be sought in addition to performance references from existing clients. Failure of a service provider, large or small, will have implications for the client organisation. Whilst it is never possible to eliminate the likelihood of this happening, its occurrence can be minimised by taking up references with reliable sources.

Types of service provision

Service provision ranges from an agent, acting largely in a consultancy capacity, to a contracting company providing a complete portfolio of services. The decision as to which is the most appropriate will depend on requirements – identified earlier in the process – as well as the risk tolerance (or aversion) of the client organisation. Important in this regard is to appreciate that the marketplace is continuously evolving the nature of facilities management services as firms compete for their share of business by devising novel ways of delivering customer satisfaction and best value.

Essentially, four types of service can be distinguished. They range from the use of an external organisation or individual who manages the client organisation's own employees, through the appointment of a contractor to manage some or all service providers, to an arrangement where all facilities are managed by an external entity offering a single point of responsibility. Fig. 13.1 shows the four main types in terms of their contractual and management (communication) links.

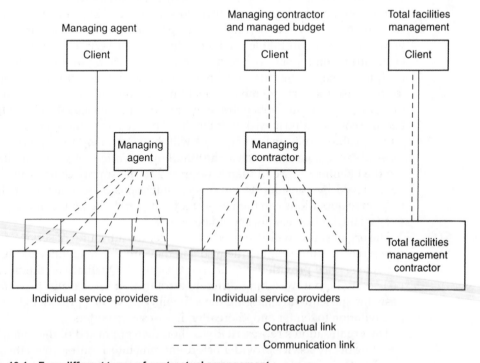

Fig. 13.1   Four different types of contractual arrangement.

Managing agent

This arrangement is adopted when the organisation has determined that it does not wish to hand over control of its facilities to a contractor, yet does not have the skill or expertise with which to manage them efficiently and effectively. By bringing in an external organisation to manage the facilities, the organisation is essentially appointing a client representative. This person – almost invariably the appointment will specify an individual – will act almost as if he or she were part of the permanent establishment of the client organisation. The client representative (managing agent) will perform better and more reliably if performance criteria are laid down, in fact, as would apply to an in-house manager. Under this arrangement, contracts with service providers will be with the client organisation.

There are distinct and, perhaps, obvious advantages in adopting this arrangement. Both the agent and the various service providers (contractors) can be selected on the basis of competitive tendering. Moreover, the appointment (or reappointment) of the agent should not affect contracts with service providers or vice versa. Dissatisfaction with a given contractor would not place other contracts at risk; indeed, it could positively assist in those cases where poor performance has had a knock-on effect.

The managing agent approach offers considerable flexibility for the client organisation to find and then hold on to the combination of contracts that suits it best. There is no reason why services should not be part in-house and part outsourced. The managing agent role attracts particular significance since the client organisation would be using the agent to contribute expertise and exercise judgement when deciding between in-house and outsourced service provision. There are, however, potential disadvantages for organisations that adopt this approach. For example, it is possible that gaps might occur between the scope of the various contracts, including that of the managing agent. Even so, managing agents can be made responsible for ensuring that the scope of service contracts is such that gaps do not occur.

From a risk perspective, the organisation is moderately exposed. It may have to accept the possibility of introducing an uncertain combination of risk factors by its own selection of contractors (including the managing agent) on an individual or piecemeal basis. The reasoning here is that a number of contractors coming together for the first time will place extra demands on the managing agent. Sound relationships between different contractors are needed if services are to be provided properly and facilities are to operate efficiently. These relationships may take some time to develop. A conscious effort will therefore be required on the part of the managing agent to integrate the work of the different contractors in such a way that they become moulded into a single, efficient team.

Some words of caution are necessary. The client organisation may find that administration costs increase as the number of separate contracts rises. Allowance must be made for these when evaluating outsourcing as an option – see Chapter 4. Risks can be mitigated and administration reduced by appointing the managing agent first and requiring that he or she establishes the suitability of service providers. In deciding to embark on this route, the organisation should allocate adequate resources to planning and implementation.

Case study – Facilities management in the public sector

This case study describes a facilities management consultant engaged in a managing agent role in the public sector. In addition to illustrating general and specific issues in facilities management, the case study illustrates the importance of a well-developed informed client function (ICF) and of managing relationships between facilities managers and their various customers. The requirement for compulsory competitive tendering led a UK government department to outsource all non-core business and to bring in a facilities management expert to help define and manage the services, which the department would itself procure and contract. This followed an earlier decision to rationalise the department's property portfolio, reducing it to six occupied buildings in central London, thereby forming part of a complete overhaul of property and facilities management within the department. Initially, the facilities management of two buildings was outsourced, with the remaining four buildings subject to market testing a year later. As a result of this two-stage process, two different facilities management consultants became involved, creating an unusual situation, which will be discussed below. The case study focuses mainly on the management of the group of four buildings forming the basis of the second tendering exercise.

As a result of these two initiatives, many personnel were lost from the facilities management function, such as it was, and a new structure was imposed constituting an ICF. The client had previously given little attention and even less prestige to the facilities management function, which had been resourced mostly by lower-grade civil servants. As neither management nor personnel viewed the existing roles as career positions, there was a high turnover. With the new regime, more high-rank officers were involved, with specific responsibility for specialist areas, including procurement. There were also two liaison officers, each acting as the first point of contact for one of the managing agents. Once these positions had been established, the personnel affected tended to remain, providing a degree of continuity and consistency previously lacking in the facilities management function.

The flagship building, approximately 150 000 sq ft (14 000 m^2) in size, was in central London. It accommodated the ministers, top civil servants and various departmental divisions within the ministry. The building was also occupied by equivalent ministers and civil servants attached to another ministry, for which facilities services were provided by the host. The remaining three buildings were 150 000 sq ft, (14 000 m^2), 100 000 sq ft (9000 m^2) and 60 000 sq ft (5500 m^2) in size respectively, all accommodating further departmental divisions as well as an affiliated government agency.

A straightforward tender document was advertised on the basis of an open competition as required by law. The services to be managed were wide-ranging, as shown below. With the client's ICF now well established, the requirements as stated in the tender document were clear. However, it was necessary for the consultants tendering to be 'intelligent' in interpreting and understanding the full range of services required and the associated personnel and other costs. An organisation unused to providing facilities management services – perhaps operating out of a building surveying or quantity surveying firm – might be unable to appreciate the full implication of all items and would thus provide a tender based on a partial understanding of the work involved. For this reason the development of the ICF prior to tendering this key function is doubly critical; first, so that clarity can be achieved in tender documents and, second, so that clients can be intelligent in their choice of consultant.

The consultant already managing the first two buildings tendered unsuccessfully for the remaining four. A second consultant was awarded the contract to provide facilities management on a managing agent basis. The initial contract was for a period of three and a quarter years, after the three-month mobilisation period. The consultant would then be required to re-tender in open competition.

Under this managing agent arrangement the client remained a contract principal with the service provider and procured all service contracts. The facilities management consultant's role was to manage facilities service contracts on the client's behalf. These contracts were:

- Security
- Cleaning
- Mechanical and electrical engineering services maintenance
- Catering
- Post and messenger services
- Inter-building minibus
- Furniture supply
- Stationery 'just-in-time' supply
- Air, train and taxi travel.

In opting for a managing agent arrangement, the client fulfilled its need to retain overall control. It was also aware that it would have to carry and manage the risk. Part of the careful establishment of the ICF was to ensure that it was in the best position to do so. While the client procured all the services, the managing agent helped with the analysis of requirements, the development of specifications and the assessment of tenders, as a facilities management expert.

The contract allowed the managing agent substantial licence in the approach to managing the facilities. The combination of the well-developed ICF and the facilities management expertise of the managing agent meant that this caused few problems. Service contracts were more specific, but did not have clear input and output specifications and only basic descriptions of the work to be performed under each contract. This approach, and the reluctance on the part of the client to provide adequate prior information and familiarisation with the buildings, led to problems for the managing agent from the tender stage onwards. These restrictions prevented tenderers from providing client-specific specifications. The standard specifications submitted had then to be customised later on an 'exchange' basis. Items that the contractor claimed not to have included, but which were specifically required by the client, were 'traded' for tasks incorporated in the standard specification, for which the client had no need or priority.

In the three-month mobilisation period, the managing agent recruited personnel necessary for its role, while the buildings were still run by civil servants. When established, the facilities management team of 11 people comprised a facilities manager, a deputy with building surveying skills, a building manager in each building and a mechanical and electrical (M&E) engineer to manage the M&E contractor and also project work. Personnel were supported by a central team providing a helpdesk, financial planning and reporting, purchasing, space planning, project management, performance measurement and review, as described below.

Helpdesk

A three-person helpdesk team took responsibility for handling calls from the two departments occupying the buildings, which housed 2000 people. Initially, the helpdesk was a manual system, with instructions and required completion date issued by fax to contractors and job completion information handled similarly. The client required every helpdesk instruction received to be followed up on completion by the issue of a job satisfaction sheet to the person initiating the helpdesk call. Satisfaction levels were recorded and analysed for inclusion in the managing agent's monthly report.

The set-up was perceived by the managing agent to be overly bureaucratic, but was insisted upon by the client. Although placing a high value on feedback, the client was not prepared to resource the helpdesk to the extent of providing appropriate ICT, as requested by the consultant. In the absence of special application software, the consultant used part of a standard software system to support the recording and analysis of helpdesk data.

Financial planning and reporting

The facilities management consultant was responsible for formulating annual budgets for each building and tracking expenditure against a variety of expense heads. All financial processes complied with the client's financial procedures and government-imposed timetables. In order to ensure compatibility with the client's financial systems, the consultant was given access to the client's finance package and was able to extract data for post-processing on spreadsheets.

Purchasing

The helpdesk team was also responsible for purchasing a wide range of services and supplies from the contractors on site and other service providers and suppliers. The team's duties covered obtaining quotations where necessary, order placing, delivery recording and invoice reconciliation. The client provided purchasing software and training in its use. For audit purposes, none of the consultant's personnel were authorised to carry out more than one action in the supply chain process.

Space planning

Building managers were assigned responsibility for the management of space in their buildings, covering minor to major moves, from receipt of a move request to completion. To assist the building managers, a space planner would produce layout drawings using CAD software. Space usage by cost centre was recorded in a CAFM database. The client selected the software and also provided full training in its use for the consultant's personnel. Building managers also specified and purchased furniture and chairs from a call-off contract.

Project management

The consultant was required to manage both minor and major M&E and fabric maintenance projects ranging in cost from a few thousand to a million pounds. Projects included the installation of fan coil units throughout one building, new fire alarm and public address systems, energy management data collection systems, major refurbishment and redecoration. Contracts for substantial projects were generally arranged separately from the main facilities management contract.

The day-to-day management of facilities was left to the managing agent, with the client adopting a 'hands-off' approach other than for exceptional circumstances and other critical actions. Each month, the facilities management consultant would prepare a report covering expenditure against budget, project work, contractors' performance, health and safety record, accidents and new initiatives. There was constant monitoring and measurement of performance, although the consultant's fixed monthly fee did not depend on it. Rates for various types of service provision were agreed upon. The consultant had responsibility for purchasing, but this was via the client's own arrangement and out of a specific budget.

Performance measurement

In order to monitor the performance of the primary service providers (main contractors), the consultant devised a performance measurement system. Each month, building managers and on-site contract managers would meet to review the month and plan future actions. This meeting would include an assessment of the previous month's performance based on helpdesk information and the building manager's own assessment of other issues. Although neither the facilities management contract nor the service contracts allowed for penalties for poor performance, failing contractors would reflect poorly on the managing agent, which might be critical at the point of re-tendering. Although this did not prove to be a serious issue, there was the potential for a conflict of interest. High expectations and the drive to raise and maintain standards, on the part of building managers, inevitably led them to register criticism when contractors underperformed; however, these criticisms could suggest too easily that the managing agent was not performing well. Although there were fixed measures against which service provider performance could be judged, there remained a degree of interpretation and the opportunity for inconsistency in the assessment.

Review

There were several aspects of this particular arrangement which were relatively unusual, but which illustrate issues that both client organisations and consultants need to consider and to manage. First, as explained above, two consultants were involved, each doing much the same tasks in different buildings. Each had his or her own approach and style, as well as overall organisational objectives. These did not necessarily cause conflict between the two managing agents, but were an extra factor for the ICF to manage. The two consultants reported to different heads within the government department; thus, the responsibility for managing any potential conflict rested with the client.

Some services had of necessity to be managed by cooperation between the two facilities management consultants. The contract manager had to report to and deal with representatives of two different companies with two different management styles. Moreover, contractors, who sometimes had difficulty in coping even with the idea of facilities managers, found dealing with two different managers in relation to one service problematic. This was exacerbated by one consultant, who aimed for more of a TFM approach and, therefore, had somewhat different objectives in guiding the management of service providers. Moreover, the different approaches of the two consultants highlighted the need for awareness of a further, more typical, division. There were effectively two customers: the ICF and personnel using the building and requesting services. One consultant focused attention on the former based on a perception that – particularly within the public sector – budgets were of prime importance. This perception extended to the need to 'look after' the ICF, providing sufficient contact, reassurance and moral support. Although this consultant became aware of a weakness in the area of customer care, in the meantime its contract manager was receiving the full support of senior personnel from the consultancy, who retained contact with the ICF. The other consultant focused attention on those actually requesting and using the services, being responsive to their needs at the expense of directly supporting the ICF. The contract manager was largely left to get on with the task without either interference or obvious support from senior personnel within the consultancy. In retrospect it is clear that it is essential to manage both areas, to balance the political with the practical and for both parties to manage relationships in order to get the most out of them.

During the contract period, one consultant, in competition with the other, won extra business with the client, covering the management of some of its minor buildings at other locations. This work constituted a separate contract, but at the point of re-tendering it was included in a consolidated facilities management package for which a single consultant was appointed, as part of the client's developing awareness of its optimal facilities management requirements.

Managing contractor

Under this arrangement there is one contract between the client organisation and the appointed contractor (primary service provider). Subcontractors (secondary service providers) will be under contract to the managing contractor and so will not have a contractual relationship with the client organisation. This means that the organisation has a single point of contact with the contractor on all matters pertaining to service provision. Thus, if a service falls below the required performance for work carried out by a subcontractor, the organisation need only direct its complaint to the managing contractor. However, as the chain of command is longer, delays in receiving prompt action may occur. Although the subcontractors are contracted to the managing contractor, the organisation should protect its position by reserving the right to approve the selection of subcontractors.

Since there is a single point of contact, there should be a sizeable reduction in paperwork and fewer payments. Gaps in service provision should be eliminated because the managing contractor is required to ensure that they simply do not occur. By using a managing contractor to undertake some or all of the work, with the support of subcontractors, the organisation is able to mitigate much financial risk. The managing contractor is generally paid a fee, usually expressed as a percentage of the value of the expenditure managed, and this can, of course, be related to performance. The organisation is, despite the limitation of being in just one contract, able to see where its money is being spent because open-book accounting is usually adopted in which the client organisation has access to the contractor's premises, books and records, including invoices from subcontractors.

The right to access is necessary as the managing contractor may insist on larger trade discounts than are acceptable, or may demand some other preferential terms that are not consistent with best practice. In these cases, the managing contractor's approach may result in poor performance by the subcontractor and, therefore, poor service to the organisation. Open-book accounting also ensures that there are few misunderstandings as to the cost of services. Under this arrangement it will, however, be more difficult to make changes to a contract, once it is formalised, than would be the case under the managing agent arrangement, unless the changes are provided for in advance in some way.

Managed budget

The managing agent model, whilst still valid for many organisations, does not fit with the culture of some, notably those that have invested in enterprise-wide management (ICT) systems and that wish to reduce the number of transactions. The major objection is the requirement to establish purchase ledger accounts for service providers (suppliers), although a managing agent handles all but the payment process.

In order to overcome this objection the managed budget model was developed in which a managing contractor takes responsibility for the payment of all suppliers and provides a consolidated invoice at the end of each month. A management fee is agreed, which is larger than that found in the managing agent model, since turnover from specialist subcontractors goes through the managing contractor's accounts. The management fee is based on a combination of the resources as deployed and the value of budgeted expenditure – all subcontract invoices and contract-specific employee costs are processed without any markup. Usually, the managing contractor places an element of the management fee at risk, subject to the attainment of pre-agreed service levels. For discretionary expenditure, such as stationery and couriers, a simple handling charge can be added to the invoice.

Contractually, the managed budget approach is similar to the managing contractor model. However, important differences lie in the apportionment of risk and in an improved relationship between the client organisation and managing contractor. Through the removal of a supply chain 'markup', and remuneration based upon a management fee, the kind of friction that might otherwise build up between the two parties is alleviated. The benefit of the managing agent model in providing access to professional advice, with management working alongside the client, results in little or no conflict of interest. There is also the further advantage of fewer transactions to be processed, thereby reducing administration for the client organisation.

Total facilities management

Under this arrangement, the client organisation is able to pass the full responsibility for managing its facilities to a single organisation for a fixed price. This does, however, require the organisation to provide the contractor (service provider) with sufficient scope to be able to manage the various services efficiently. While total facilities management might appear to provide an ideal solution, because it provides a single purchasing point for the organisation, the reality can be that the contractor actually subcontracts all or most of the work. Since there is just one contract – that between the organisation and the total facilities management contractor – there is the chance that terms and conditions between the contractor and subcontractor do not mirror those of the main contract. Difficulties can arise because terms and conditions that are embodied in the contract between the client organisation and the contractor may allow for situations that are not subsequently recognised in the contract with the subcontractor or vice versa.

The total facilities management contractor may be better able to offer a more complete and competitive solution to an organisation's needs than in the case of the managing agent or managing contractor. Relationships built up over years between the contractor and (specialist) subcontractors may mean that efficient working relationships are established from the start. Total facilities management can provide a sound solution, but only if the organisation is prepared to spend time in identifying the right basis for such an arrangement and then in selecting the best contractor.

In practice, things can go wrong. Reasons include the contractor's relationship with subcontractors. For example, as with the managing contractor arrangement, the total facilities management contractor may insist on larger trade discounts than are acceptable or some other preferential terms that are not consistent with best practice. Also, during the currency of a contract, the contractor may decide to change subcontractors. These decisions are not always made to improve performance; they may arise because the contractor is seeking to increase margins through the employment of a cheaper subcontractor. As with any change, newly appointed subcontractors – for whatever reason they are employed – will undergo a learning process. In this case, the client organisation should ensure that the procedure for assigning or subcontracting is open to inspection and that they have the right, under the contract, to prior approval before such assignment or subcontracting. Open-book accounting should also be in place.

In terms of risk, the organisation is only moderately exposed and can derive a good deal of comfort from knowing that there is a single point of contact and less administration. Value for money may not be quite as good as in the managing agent approach, although the additional cost of organising and managing many more individual contracts in that approach must be taken into consideration.

Evolution in the nature of service providers

In the early 1990s the UK government – following the demise of its Property Services Agency (PSA) – awarded a number of contracts for property management on the basis of a managing agent contract. The scope of these contracts was narrow, but it allowed various government departments to employ professional consultants to advise them on the most appropriate ways of managing their estates. During what was a time of transition, the approach proved beneficial and expenditure plans for the estates were developed, providing a commercially sound basis for future strategies. In the private sector, the basis of the contractual relationship was what was termed a total facilities contract (TFM) with a single organisation providing the range of services required. The popularity of TFM spread and other public sector contracts were awarded on this basis. More contractors moved into the marketplace from different disciplines, seeing the potential to increase their margins and enter into long-term agreements.

Over the years, the criteria by which client organisations have valued the benefit from their facilities management contracts have changed. It is no longer enough to use the one service provider, one invoice approach as the basis of a strategic decision, neither is it 'base cost' as many clients have subsequently found. The TFM model has proved to be inflexible, lacking in visibility and requiring a high level of policing. In many cases, because the types of organisation involved in this work originate from a particular service delivery background, they will seek to 'self-deliver', with the emphasis placed on the number of operatives on site to achieve their return. Consequently, the focus is on task management and not the strategic management of the client's portfolio or relationships. Typically, contracting organisations have sought to make a return on the supply chain they lead, usually expressed as a percentage of the value of the subcontracted element. An argument supporting this can be developed where the main contractor is bearing risk or adding something unique to the process. However, the desire to improve overall margins results in the addition of a traditionally accepted markup to this element, irrespective of risk or value added. Market pressures, as described earlier, have driven the questioning of such contractual arrangements and the conflicts of interest that arise through the application of a percentage based markup. Client organisations are looking to achieve a partnership-based relationship where returns are agreed in advance and both parties work together to innovate and reduce cost.

The trend depicted in Fig. 13.2 shows evolution towards serviced workplaces. The number of serviced office providers has increased in the marketplace and can provide greater levels of flexibility using a 'menu of prices' geared to levels of service provision. However, for major organisation this does not need to be externally provided. It can be delivered internally where there is a desire to change and as long as financial controls are also put in place. Where a serviced environment is priced appropriately and recharged it can provide business units with real information that can enhance decision-making. Evidence suggests that the old habits of liberal space usage are quickly reformed when the true cost is revealed. Space is a valuable and significant component of the facilities cost equation and this is where the greatest opportunities for cost reduction often lie. Even so, the opportunity to tap this potentially rich seam is dependent upon the appetite of the organisation to change as well as having the resources for this purpose. Implementing a successful flexible working arrangement requires information which under a typical TFM relationship is in the

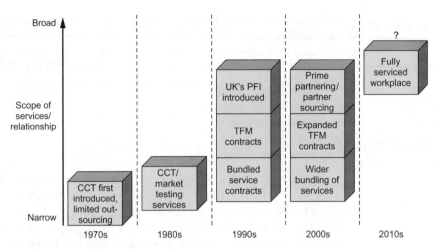

Fig. 13.2   Evolution in service provision.

hands of the service provider, not the client. Facilities management service providers can offer expertise in these areas, but the key to this lies in the level of management expertise deployed on the contract and in the congruence of its objectives with those of the client organisation. Traditional arrangements have inhibited this congruence, with commercial imperatives often driving the service provider in another direction.

Determining the best approach

The choice of which approach works best for the client organisation will depend on many factors. If the procedures outlined in Chapter 4 have been followed, the organisation should be able to see which approach is best and proceed with confidence. Competition in selecting the best value option has to be the criterion applied to all situations. Whether the organisation chooses to manage all service contracts itself – perhaps through an appointed managing agent – or passes the responsibility to a third party, there will be risks and cost involved. The organisation must decide which risks it is prepared to take and at what cost, and which risks to pass to someone else for what may well be a higher sum. Flexibility is a factor that has to be taken into account, along with the attendant cost and risk.

The selected approach should be one that will provide best value for the organisation and its customers. Total facilities management has obvious attractions, but it will not relieve the organisation from managing the contract and the interface between the contractor and its customers. In deciding between the approaches, the organisation must consider carefully how to ensure that customer needs are fully addressed. The best value solution should not be one that compromises on customer satisfaction.

Finally, the client organisation must always take into account the track record of any contractor, subcontractor or agent it may be considering, together with an understanding of the particular expertise the contractor or agent can offer.

Conclusions

There are basically four ways of procuring facilities management services from the marketplace. The first involves the employment of a managing agent under contract to the organisation, acting as the client's representative. The second is the appointment of a managing contractor. This differs from the managing agent in that the contractor takes responsibility for engaging and managing the various services contracts for a fee. The third – managed budget – is a variation on the former two approaches and hands the burden of multiple transactions to a managing contractor. The last is where a single point of responsibility is established, with one contractor providing all services. The best approach for the client organisation will be the one that is most closely aligned to its needs as previously defined, as well as the one that delivers best value. If the ground is thoroughly prepared beforehand, the choice of option will be obvious and uncomplicated. Attention can then turn to the selection of the best service providers. If it is not straightforward then some shortcoming in the steps leading up to selection is probably to blame and the organisation may have to re-examine its earlier decisions and assumptions.

CHECKLIST

This checklist is intended to assist with the review and action planning process.

	Yes	No	Action required
1. Does the organisation understand the types of service provision available and, in particular, the distinctions between the managing agent, managing contractor, managed budget and a total facilities management approach?	☐	☐	☐
2. Is the organisation clear about its own role in managing each type of service provider?	☐	☐	☐
3. Is the organisation aware of the current market for services and how this might impact on its selection or approach?	☐	☐	☐

		Yes	No	Action required
4.	Has the organisation followed an appropriate procedure to identify which approach would best suit its current requirements?	☐	☐	☐
5.	Has the organisation understood where the balance of risks lies for the type of service provision selected?	☐	☐	☐
6.	Has the organisation taken all the necessary steps to verify the capabilities and financial standing of the service providers it intends to select?	☐	☐	☐
7.	Has the organisation checked the position regarding the use of subcontractors by the (proposed) contractor (or service provider)?	☐	☐	☐

14 Managing Service Provider and Supplier Relationships

Key issues

The following issues are covered in this chapter.

- All service providers and suppliers have to be managed – the nature of the relationship between the client organisation and providers/ suppliers is where it varies.

- Buying a service without concern for the ensuing relationship might be to ignore a useful source of skill and expertise – competent service providers and suppliers have much to offer if the conditions are conducive to their offering expertise.

- Cooperative relationships with service providers and suppliers can provide greater certainty of provision without being non-competitive or compromising on quality or performance.

- Partnering is the most common form of cooperative relationship for managing service providers and suppliers – it is not, however, an answer for all needs and situations.

- For public sector organisations, partnering should be seen as an entirely acceptable alternative to competitive tendering provided it too has a competitive element.

- Cooperative relationships imply working toward goals that have to be shared by the client organisation and service provider (or supplier) alike.

- Continual improvement is a necessary part of the culture of cooperative relationships and one that must include measurable targets in all arrangements including partnering.

Introduction

As a reflection on how the world has changed and, in particular, how relationships in commerce and industry have developed, we might be tempted to say that a chapter devoted to managing relationships would have been unnecessary some years back. Service providers (contractors) were awarded contracts on the basis of competitive tenders and instructed to perform. Fortunately, business culture has changed and with it the simple realisation that a successful contract outcome depends on the willing – as opposed to enforced – cooperation of service providers. This chapter considers how the client organisation can get the best from its service providers and suppliers. Rather than seeing them as simply a source that can be tapped as and when required, the organisation can use them to help produce greater economy and higher levels of customer satisfaction through less waste and a generally more efficient process – see also introductory comments in Chapter 1 on establishing and maintaining good relationships. There are many ways of bringing about a culture of cooperation and formalising it in workable procedures and practices. Over the past decade, partnering has emerged as, arguably, the most distinct type of cooperative arrangement. Introduced originally in some quarters as a means for reducing adversarial behaviour, it has developed rapidly to become a sophisticated technique for delivering customer satisfaction and best value; moreover, it lays the foundation for a process of continual improvement – see also Chapter 18.

Service providers and suppliers

There is an obvious distinction between the provider of a service – taken to include the supply of labour and equipment, as well as materials – and the supply of goods or materials alone. However, in this chapter the term 'supplier' is taken to mean service providers too – the term is all-embracing and is in keeping with current practice that sees supplier management as a critical success factor for organisations of all kinds.

Suppliers have traditionally been regarded simply as someone or somebody paid to provide. Where a supplier is responsible for something that can be provided easily by many others, such as cleaning, there may seem little need to bother about a relationship beyond that of a straightforward commercial arrangement. However, this ignores the possibility that the supplier's knowledge about products and processes could be used to reduce waste and raise productivity. Clearly, where the supplier is of economic significance to the organisation, it makes sense to explore ways in which unnecessary cost might be eliminated. Having a close working relationship with the supplier can achieve this goal, yet does not necessarily risk being non-competitive.

The term 'supplier' therefore needs to be broadened to embody any person or organisation external to the client organisation who can contribute to its success or failure. A contract cleaning company is a clear example, but so is an architectural practice working on a refurbishment programme. Each has a relationship with the client organisation and this has to be managed to ensure the success of the contract.

Types of relationship

When considering the nature of the relationship that an organisation should have with its suppliers, it is important not to focus on contractual arrangements until a sensible basis for working with a supplier has been found. Contractual arrangements should not override how a given product or service should be provided. Relationships with suppliers can be improved by incorporating incentives for levels of performance that exceed agreed targets and by making use of the expertise that many suppliers undoubtedly have. Successful relationships will come from treating suppliers as partners even where there is a contract based on traditional price competition in which different terminology prevails.

Partnering is a practice that has become popular across the breadth of the real estate and AEC sectors, including, therefore, facilities management. Some see it, erroneously, as the means by which they can avoid tendering competitively for a service. The aim is to build a business relationship that is founded on trust. It is not a way of working around financial constraints. Partnering aligns the objectives of the customer and supplier in an attempt to maximise the benefits to both. For the client organisation, there can be savings from not having to tender repeatedly; for the supplier it can mean regular work from a customer whose requirements are better understood than they would otherwise be. Business arranged in this way can bring about significant savings over the medium to long term. A comparison of partnering with a traditional contracting arrangement is given in Table 14.1.

The essence of partnering is that the client organisation decides to work with a select number of firms or individuals who will share the work in a prescribed area. This is easy to achieve for a regular and large procurer of new facilities, for example. For other types of organisation, the opportunities to partner are more limited, although they do exist in the sense of sharing with someone or somebody who will provide a real gain for the client organisation. Partnering could exist in transportation services and vehicle maintenance or where related organisations collaborate on the bulk purchasing of utilities supplies to form a procurement consortium. Such arrangements create an economy of scale that can provide smaller organisations with better value for money than under an arrangement where they attempt to negotiate on their own. An additional benefit from this kind of collaboration is that expertise and risks are also shared.

Table 14.1   Partnering compared with a traditional contracting arrangement.

Partnering	Traditional contracting
Innovative, not so well developed	Established, well developed
Ability to negotiate on price	Difficult to negotiate on price
Close interaction between parties	Arm's-length relationship
Quality improvement possible	Quality likely to be minimum specified
Proactive contractor response	Reactive contractor response
Disputes less likely	Disputes common
Long-term benefits	Short-term gains

Practice Point 14.1   A clean sweep.

Key point: A partnering arrangement can allow organisations to benefit from the expertise of service providers to everyone's benefit.

An organisation had long held the view that cleaning was a generally straight-forward activity for which there was an accepted approach. This tended to mean that the contractor's supervisor would requisition supplies of cleaning agents and other consumables as and when required from a local supplier. On the operations front, there was a daily pattern which, though not perfect, was accepted as the way things were done. For some time, the facilities manager had been wondering how she could reduce what appeared to be a wasteful and, therefore, expensive approach. The time was fast approaching when the organisation was due to test the market for a range of services, including clean-ing. The facilities manager took the initiative to talk to a couple of local service providers who were working on various office developments on the nearby science park. After a short time, it became apparent that the organisation was probably paying far too much for its cleaning – it was buying in expensive and perhaps unnecessary agents and consumables and the frequency and timing of a large amount of cleaning was unnecessary. In the event, the facilities manager asked all three service providers to consider bidding for the cleaning contract on the basis that the successful contractor would be asked to enter into a partnering arrangement. Whilst a contract would still be in place, there would be flexibility to explore ways of improving quality and performance and reducing cost. Two of the three accepted the invitation.

What kind of relationship is needed?

Few services or supplies are of exactly the same degree of importance. Failure in certain of them could prove disastrous – for instance, a failure to test electrical appliances – whilst other types of failure might be tolerated or at least a means found to minimise their impact. It is therefore important for organisations to recognise where the kinds of suppliers with whom they are dealing lie within the matrix in Fig. 14.1. Locating suppliers in the correct position within the matrix focuses attention on the kind of relation-ship that has to be managed (Gadde, 1996). Procedures will then need to reflect the different emphases that are required of the relationship. In this way, it should be possible for client organisations to achieve higher levels of service from suppliers.

Understanding the kinds of relationship that are possible is only the beginning. The organisation will need to adopt appropriate controls and incentives that may well differ between sets of relationships. It should be possible for the organisation to devise relationships with individual suppliers that are more closely aligned with the needs of both parties. For example, the relationship demanded of a cleaning contract might embody incentives for ensuring that areas are cleaned in ways and at times that provide maximum flexibility for building users. The extent of the

Economic significance of service
provider/supplier

	Major	Minor
Close **Degree of integration** Loose	Cleaning, security	Helpdesk
	Electricity, gas	Condition survey

Fig. 14.1   Locating service providers and suppliers according to their relationship.

requirements might be so complicated that without a close working relationship – perhaps founded as a partnering arrangement – the quality of service expected might be unattainable. Extensive dialogue and discussion may be needed before a deep understanding can be reached.

In another example – that of the helpdesk – a well-managed service for responding to enquiries and complaints could yield worthwhile savings for the organisation. For instance, helpdesk employees who are well versed in technical procedures and competent in some aspects of problem solving could obviate the need for further action, by providing timely advice on how to deal with problems concerning heating, ventilation or other aspects of engineering services. Savings from the avoidance of calling out service operatives could amply repay the cost of providing the helpdesk. However, helpdesk personnel would need to be specially trained to perform in this way; consequently, the organisation may then have to pay more for their services. Establishing a close working relationship with the service provider – or assessing the capabilities of prospective providers – would seem sensible. In terms of controls, the service provider could be rewarded for reductions in the costs of calling out service engineers and, if the situation arose, penalised for failing to deal promptly and sensibly with enquiries – see Chapter 17 for further comment on providing incentives.

In other areas, for example, the supply of a utility such as electricity, there may be little point in attempting to bring about a closer working relationship other than in arranging consortium purchases. Generally, the greater the involvement or interaction of the client organisation with the supplier, the more indirect costs there will be.

Contractual arrangements and partnering

Contracts generally serve two main purposes: they identify the service to be provided in terms of scope, quality or performance, cost and timing, and they apportion risk. Partnering arrangements are, however, concerned mainly with the way in which the work will be carried out. In this way, partnering should theoretically be achievable with any method of procuring services. However, while no procurement route can compensate for an adversarial approach, some approaches may be more readily adapted to certain aspects of partnering such as gain-sharing – see next section.

Certain kinds of partnering relationship have no contract at all and it has been claimed that a formally binding contract can inhibit the partnering process. In most cases, however, a standard form of contract is used, even when partners declare business objectives that appear contrary to the principles of partnering. This view is to be expected as partnering is still somewhat new to many client organisations and a contract is seen as a form of safety net.

While contracts can embrace some aspects of a partnering approach, such as gain-sharing, others, such as ideas of cooperation and goodwill, may be less easily expressed within them. Other issues concern the accommodation of long-term partnering arrangements in workable contractual terms. For instance, contracts to undertake future work may be rendered void because of uncertainty, since it is not possible to predetermine the value of future work and many factors can come into play even over a short period. However, this does not preclude non-binding framework agreements – those covering a number of contracts over a specified period – that stipulate terms on which the parties intend to contract and the type and extent of the services and/or work envisioned.

Partnering charters can be used to outline the client organisation's philosophy, commitments and the goals of the arrangement. For some organisations, partnering charters are regarded as vital support for its contracts. Partnering charters can also be used to indicate ways of overcoming problems, establish roles and responsibilities, and define clear lines of communication. That said, the relationship between a partnering charter and the contract may appear unclear. Put simply, the contract defines the rights and duties of the parties and to some extent covers the process implicit in delivering the specified service. However, a partnering charter does not sit on top of the contract, but is complementary to it and vice versa.

EastPoint has adopted the use of partnering charters, notably in its approach to cooperative development with strategic partners. Embodied in one such example are the following commitments:

- Establish clear benefits, objectives and milestones.
- Share documentation of process development and manuals to increase efficiency.
- Maintain confidentiality and intellectual property rights on all matters.
- Establish a long-term relationship based on a successful outcome for both parties.
- Reduce administration costs and raise productivity.

These commitments are followed through by mutually accepted goals, including:

- Trust by way of transparent systems.
- Maintain open-mindedness and receptiveness to change.
- Integrate ideas, systems and people and benefits by sharing.
- Maintain clear communication through effective discussion and openness.
- Achieve continual improvement through flexibility, reviews and innovation.

Gain-sharing

Some partnering arrangements include gain-sharing. This is where cost savings arising from performance improvements are shared between the parties. This can provide an effective incentive for performance that exceeds a given level – see also Chapter 17. In practice, gain-sharing arrangements can be straightforward, with the client organisation and service providers dividing any savings above a target price on an equal basis with the providers liable for 100% of any loss. They can also be more sophisticated, with partners exposed to levels of risk and reward according to their degree of influence on service delivery. Whatever means is devised, a commitment to open-book accounting is necessary if efficiency gains are to be encouraged. There must be no incentive or opportunity for the parties to achieve a higher return through adversarial behaviour or by 'hiding behind the contract'.

Continual improvement

The adoption of some means for measuring the performance of a partnering arrangement is critical to ensuring that its objectives are met. This generally involves the client organisation and service provider outlining the improvements over traditional approaches that the arrangement intends to pursue, together with measures of success in achieving these objectives. In the case of longer-term partnering relationships, targets for performance improvement can be incorporated into the partnering arrangements. With appropriate monitoring and feedback, continual improvement – felt to be central to the whole idea of partnering – can be achieved (Bennett and Jayes, 1998). Some features of continual improvement are easy to identify and address, but others may require more of a change in the culture of the organisation.

While longer-term partnering relationships can evolve targets and maintain an acceptable level of competition between different service providers or suppliers, it may be more difficult to establish performance targets for single contracts of a limited duration. In such cases, benchmarking against similar projects may be useful in identifying possible improvements – see Chapter 18. The initial service provider selection process and subsequent negotiations are therefore crucial in helping to identify performance criteria.

Conclusions

The relationship with a supplier does not end once the contract has been placed. That is just the beginning and it will take hard work to manage the relationship successfully into the future. Ways can always be found to add incentives for both sides to ensure the satisfactory performance of a service or supply. Setting targets as part of a programme of continual improvement is possible. These can be based on gain-sharing to provide an added incentive – see also Chapter 17. In any event, engaging the skill of the supplier in the process – as opposed to traditional arrangements that actively exclude it – can lead to better ways of delivering customer satisfaction at lower cost. Partnering or other forms of cooperative relationship can be entirely appropriate for an organisation in its search for best value. However, partnering is not a panacea and its selection must be based on a well-founded case. Nonetheless, it can be a perfectly acceptable arrangement even in the public sector, where there is rightful concern about the probity of contractual arrangements. Partnering can succeed so long as there is a competitive element to it; the latter does not invalidate the approach, rather it improves the prospects for delivering best value.

CHECKLIST

This checklist is intended to assist with the review and action planning process.

		Yes	No	Action required
1.	Has the organisation identified its key suppliers?	☐	☐	☐
2.	Does the organisation understand the economic significance of each of its service providers and suppliers?	☐	☐	☐
3.	Has the organisation differentiated between the type of relationships that are possible and are these sensitive to the nature of the service/supply and customer needs?	☐	☐	☐
4.	Has the organisation considered instances where partnering, or some other cooperative arrangement, might be preferable to traditional, competitive tendering?	☐	☐	☐
5.	If the organisation is in the public sector, has it examined the arguments for and against partnering and has it therefore come to a decision based on fact and objectivity?	☐	☐	☐
6.	Are appropriate strategies in place for managing relationships with suppliers?	☐	☐	☐
7.	Is the organisation benefiting from consortium arrangements for the supply of utilities, or has it at least examined the economic case for them?	☐	☐	☐

15 Managing Specialist Services

Key issues

The following issues are covered in this chapter.

- What exactly constitutes a specialist service may be open to debate amongst organisations and their facility managers. Even so, the idea that some services are beyond the usual range of facilities and estates-related applications means that we can legitimately refer to them as specialist.

- Information and communication technology (ICT) services represent an area of need for most organisations that has evolved rapidly over the past decade. To ensure continuity of its core business operations, the organisation may need to consider specialist ICT service provision. Security and data protection are key concerns and areas where specialists may have expertise to contribute.

- Health care services can be an emotive subject in the context of outsourcing, but this reaction tends to result from confusion between clinical and non-clinical services. Apart from off-site diagnostics, the majority of services are related to medical and ancillary equipment and informational systems of various kinds.

- Security and protection services are closely aligned with building intelligence and may involve a mix of on-site and off-site support. Providing users of facilities with a safe and secure environment has become a concern of many organisations, not least those in high-profile sectors and locations.

- 'Custodial services' is not a euphemism for prisons. A wide range of specialist services is available, with providers working in conjunction with the authorities who are then able to concentrate on their core business instead of diverting scarce resources to support services.

- Professional services can cover myriad disciplines. The more familiar include architectural and engineering services, but others may be encountered depending on the nature of the organisation's core business and its facilities management strategy. Involving an outsourcing partner can bring benefits that would be hard to realise if the service were contained totally in-house. Having access to a pool of expertise can provide the organisation with on-demand specialist skills.

- Any outsourcing involves risk and there are important considerations facing organisations that opt to contract with specialist service providers. Legal and financial implications figure strongly in any deliberations, as do questions relating to indemnities and insurance.

- No service can be expected to deliver customer satisfaction unless its scope is specified correctly. The performance of service providers is a key issue and the need to have robust service level agreements (SLAs) is paramount, not least when dealing with a service that might be complex and unfamiliar in terms of its performance.

Introduction

Not all services required by an organisation in support of its business are the same – some will demand special consideration. As the scope of facilities management increases so must our understanding of how to handle additional or unfamiliar services. Our purpose in this chapter is not to imply that the definition of facilities management should cover all the services discussed or to advance arguments for outsourcing, but to provide an understanding of the particular challenges that arise from the organisation taking responsibility for specialist services. The question of whether or not these services are to be classed as part of facilities management is not one for the authors to answer, but for the organisation to determine, just as it must differentiate between its core and non-core business. What will be core to one organisation will be non-core to another for good reason. Likewise, what one organisation might regard as part of the normal territory of service provision, another may see as novel and highly specialised and thus deserving of particular treatment. What matters is that the service to be received by the customer is precisely what is agreed. Many specialist services will be automatically contracted out, as there is little prospect of their being managed in-house. In some cases, the decision could easily go one way or the other. In practical terms, the response of the organisation will be mostly one of building on the firm base of managing services provision outlined in earlier chapters. This chapter also considers lesser-known issues to which the organisation must be alerted with respect to individual services.

ICT services

Information and communication technology (ICT) spans a wide spectrum of needs and services, for example, the provision of desktop computers, employee training, accounts and payroll functions. At one end, the organisation may rent space on a service provider's web server; at the other end, just about every facet of ICT support may be in the hands of an external provider. Moreover, the provider's service may involve the use of facilities away from the organisation as well as inside it. Server centres and helpdesks are more likely to be located off site. Most will be located with services for other clients of the service provider – an issue that must be considered as there could be a potential conflict of interest or risk of breach in security. The penultimate section in this chapter discusses these and related issues.

ICT services can be considered in terms of:

1. Infrastructure (data centres, networks and customer services)
2. Applications packages
3. Performance and security.

The tendency may be for organisations to focus on the first and second aspects when considering, for instance, the possible outsourcing of in-house services. As financially expedient as that inclination may seem, the last – performance and security – ought to be the primary concern: the other two are means to an end. No good is served if the organisation is paralysed by the failure of mission-critical systems and the services they support. Even a few hours of downtime of a system could spell disaster for the organisation. At this point, it is too late to look at the fine print in a service level agreement (SLA) that promised 99% uptime.[1] Another issue could be malicious attacks for which the service provider is not adequately protected or for which the customer is responsible for appropriate preventive measures.

SLAs for ICT, in particular web-based services, are stacked in favour of service providers. The question of consequential losses, or rather compensation for them, is specifically excluded. From the customer's perspective this may seem unfair to say the least, however, for a service provider the consequential losses faced by just one customer could ruin its entire business. The advice is to choose service providers with great care and seek proof of service delivery through performance data and references from existing customers. Arrangements for backing up data and, as importantly, for restoring data after a failure, are crucial matters. Backups alone do not help the organisation recover from a failure if the time taken to restore data runs into days.

A further issue relating to quality of service provision is that sometimes it is difficult to pinpoint where the fault lies in a system (here we are using system in its widest context). A server can be unresponsive, yet the problem could be caused by the local network or even the customer's own network. As data systems and networks expand, management of them can become more complicated. Nonetheless, capacity and function tend to run ahead of demand for services. As a rule of thumb, the larger the service provider, the more comprehensive the services on offer; the smaller the

---

[1] This translates into roughly 1 hour 45 minutes of downtime in a week. If that were to occur during the working day it could result in a huge loss of business or an even worse outcome.

provider, the fewer the services and, therefore, the more the customer has to work to integrate the different systems involved. The downside is that larger service providers may offer less flexibility, requiring customers to adapt their approach or systems and accept particular brands of hardware or software. Smaller providers can be very flexible, yet may lack knowledge of what is required.

IT infrastructure

With changes in technology sometimes outpacing many organisations' ability to keep up, the idea of another party's taking responsibility for providing and maintaining its infrastructure can be attractive. The benefits to organisations from outsourcing their ICT include:

- Economies of scale from larger equipment purchases.
- Multi-vendor capability for a range of platforms.
- Personnel with knowledge of different platforms and operating environments.
- Up-to-date support tools and technology.
- Ability to implement solutions on demand to suit requirements.
- Integration of helpdesk services.
- Lower total cost of provision (over product life cycles) compared with many in-house options.

Against these benefits, the organisation needs to consider some possible disadvantages:

- Less choice of product and brand
- Vendor/provider lock-in
- Erosion of core competences
- Over-dependence on an outsourced partner
- Remoteness of support personnel
- Steadily increasing costs year-on-year.

Taken together, the perceived benefits and disadvantages can be evaluated to arrive at a decision, indicating the best value option for satisfying customer needs.

ICT applications

Understanding how to get the most out of applications is a perennial issue for organisations of almost any kind. Service providers and vendors can be expected to be more familiar with the workings of specialist applications than an in-house team unless the latter has been involved in joint development or testing – perhaps as an alpha or beta test site. Since packaged applications are intended to support or extend the capabilities of employees, any loss of productivity or performance can prove costly. Savings in support can prove to be a false economy, so it is essential to be clear about what support is really necessary and what is optional.

The benefits of outsourcing packaged applications can be seen in terms of:

- User support, including customer queries
- Solutions to application-related problems
- Enhancements, customisation, upgrades and associated user training.

Factors such as scale, volume and criticality of operations, number and complexity of applications and skill levels will need to be taken into account when evaluating options: these are, in effect, some of the attributes of specialist services.

ICT performance and security

One of the most specialist services within the ICT arena is performance and security testing. Despite its importance, relatively few organisations seem aware of the dangers they may be facing and the cost and time involved in recovery following an incident. Apart from the risk of malicious acts, employees can compromise system integrity without realising they are doing anything untoward. Unfortunately, some organisations only discover the need for performance and security once they have suffered an unforeseen incident. Typical services include:

- ISO 27001:2005[2] compliance audit
- Network and system resilience (load and stress, scalability and volume, endurance and soak tests)
- Server penetration
- Forensic services
- Migration assurance
- Business continuity testing
- Risk analysis
- Disaster recovery testing
- Developing security policies and procedures.

Problems may never surface under normal operating conditions and the organisation can be blissfully unaware of the danger lurking once a basic condition changes. The aim of tests for load, stress, scalability, volume and endurance is to be sure that systems can cope with changes in operational parameters. Predicting how and when a system might fail sets an upper limit on user demands and performance delivery.

---

[2] ISO 27001:2005 is designed to ensure the selection of adequate and proportionate security controls that protect information assets and give confidence to interested parties.

Most organisations rely on client–server architectures for their ICT infrastructure. The vulnerability of servers is something that must be assessed through periodic testing, not least after any upgrading beyond minor patching of the operating environment. Servers that support work groups internally within the organisation may suffer few threats. Those that create a firewall between internal systems and the outside world are in the front line and are likely to be under continual attack from malicious agents. Web servers are similarly vulnerable and will become a target for hackers and organised crime if there is any possibility that the databases running on them hold financial or personal data. What is regarded as low level data by the organisation can be targeted all the same.

Most attacks are caused by automated and persistent agents, not by a lone hacker, with many going undetected. As discussed above, recovery following a failure or other serious incident can take time and prove expensive in resources. This is undoubtedly an area where prevention is better than cure. Once the full extent of risk exposure is known, many organisations will act very quickly to involve specialist service providers. Moving mission-critical systems into secure facilities is the first step; bringing in expert personnel to advise on data management follows a close second.

Health care services

Of all the specialist services that might be suitable for outsourcing, health care is often the one that evokes the most impassioned reactions. Our primary concern here is not with clinical services, but support for them. Even so, we know of cases where clinical services are outsourced, although not in the conventional sense. A shortage of certain skills (e.g. radiologists) in some countries can be alleviated by using practitioners in different time zones and may even succeed in speeding-up a diagnosis. There is a fine line between engaging contract workers and outsourcing a service – a situation that can apply in many fields.

Generally, health care services cover the provision of:

- Clinical systems
- Patient transport services
- Information systems
- Administrative systems
- Practice management systems.

The first of these warrants particular attention. In some countries and health care regimes, the maintenance of clinical systems can be included in the facilities management remit. This means that the service provider is responsible for ensuring the correct functioning of equipment within limits sets by the manufacturer, and will handle sterilisation, recalibration and testing of equipment and appliances. Whilst the idea of engaging such a specialist under a facilities management contract can be worrisome, there is nothing irrational about it. If health care facilities are to be available when needed, each contributory service must be managed correctly. Coordination and control over what happens must fall to someone; so why should this not be the facilities manager? There is a huge difference between performing work oneself and coordinating the efforts of others.

Telemedicine or tele-care[3] is becoming increasingly common and with it comes the need to provide adequate facilities (especially infrastructure) for medical practitioners and patients. There is a role here for the facilities manager to ensure that conditions provided at the centre and those available in the home are compatible. ICT will play a part, perhaps one that is significant. Again, we come to the same question: if the facilities manager is not to manage the integration of services then who is?

Security and protection services

The protection of people and property is a major concern for individuals, organisations and governments alike. Security and personal safety are high on the agenda and are likely to remain so. Many buildings and other facilities were designed and built during times when the real threat of an illegal or terrorist act was remote. Today, people's awareness is heightened and organisations must take very seriously the potential threats in a rapidly changing and increasingly uncertain world.

It is essential to design a secure environment, but all too often organisations create facilities that are not. Specifically, measures have to be put into place to:

- Detect, deny and impede intrusion.
- Initiate an appropriate response.
- Provide accurate information and data for analysis.
- Provide evidence to support criminal prosecutions and civil actions.

These services may require specialist service providers and reliance on remote surveillance, bringing in another specialist alongside those who might already be responsible for security. ICT figures highly in these arrangements. In this sense, there may come a point at which the in-house provision of security and protection can no longer cope realistically with potential threats from innumerable sources and the level of technology that must be provided.

Whilst it is easy to dwell on the negative aspects, a greater concern for security and protection should translate into a feeling of safety and comfort for users. The best employers are generally those who have assured the security and protection of their facilities and employees without being

---

[3] Tele-care in the home is the subject of a research and development project idea discussed in Chapter 21.

intrusive. Most people recognise the necessity, even if they are reluctant to welcome it. In preparing service specifications and SLAs, organisations would do well to engage all stakeholders and so be more confident of mitigating any additional measures that greater security and protection bring. Chapter 12 on building intelligence covers aspects of the design, engineering and technology in this specialist area.

Custodial services

Not many organisations have need of custodial services, although an increasing number are affected by the requirement to contain persons who pose a threat or who may have already committed an unlawful act. Public facilities are typical of locations under threat from those on the fringe of law-abiding society. Transportation hubs – railway stations, airports and ferry terminals – are examples where the movement of people has to be controlled. If national borders are involved, the demands on the organisation multiply. Stadiums and other facilities where the public gather in significant numbers will also fall under this umbrella. The law can be complex and professional advice needs to be sought by the organisation on its duties and obligations to protect the public, employees and property.

Where custodial services are required, the most likely response will be for the organisation to contract with a specialist service provider rather than attempt to develop its competence in-house. Typical of the services offered are:

- Reception duties
- Post-charge administration (e.g. fingerprinting, photographs and DNA swabs)
- Drug testing
- Detainee care and catering
- Forensic medical services
- Interpreter services
- ID parade support.

Care needs to be exercised in drafting SLAs and in the related areas of risk, performance measurement and financial management for anything in the area of custodial services. Again, professional advice should be sought, including dialogue with the authorities.

Professional services

The scope for professional services is wide, and what might be regarded as specialist will have much to do with the organisation's business strategy and internal competences. Typical in the range of outsourced professional services are:

- Accountancy
- Law
- Recruitment
- Architectural and engineering design
- Landscape design (internal and external)
- Vehicle fleet management
- Insurance
- Travel.

The extent to which these might be managed in an overall facilities management remit will vary considerably, often depending on the likely scale of the service or size of contract, as well as the organisation's facilities management strategy and policies. For illustrative purposes, we can consider recruitment since, on the surface, it may not appear to be so specialist. A large facilities management operation may share some responsibility for recruitment of its employees with the human resources department because of the demands from the 'soft' side of facilities management. Outsourcing recruitment services:

- Allows human resource managers to concentrate on managing internal processes.
- Avoids the conflicts of interest that can arise over internal applicants.
- Enables screening and testing of applicants, using diagnostic tools which may not be available in the organisation.
- Brings knowledge of the marketplace, talent availability and current remuneration packages.
- Assists in objectively selecting applicants for appointment based on merit.

Performance and service level agreements

As with any service – in-house or outsourced – performance is paramount. In many cases, the outsourced service takes place on the provider's premises and may not be accessible to the organisation or its facilities manager for reasons of security or simply because it is in a remote location – possibly on another continent. The location where the service is performed can become a stumbling block in decision-making; in others it will be immaterial. Nonetheless, it is important to be objective and not allow irrational arguments to influence decision-making. For instance, the desire to gain access to the facility where the service is performed may be impractical and so it is important to be realistic about the benefits from pursuing such an approach. A situation could occur, for example, where servers are hosted in a secure facility. Being able to point to one's servers may be reassuring, but hardly constitutes a proper assessment of the service to be provided. A more meaningful approach would be, for example, to undertake a penetration test to determine if the server is secure and stable.

A more serious concern is how SLAs are drafted. For some specialist services, it may be that the provider enjoys a favourable position in the market because, for example, it has few competitors and can be more selective about the businesses it is prepared to consider. In these cases, it may be that the contract has to be signed on terms that are slanted in favour of the service provider. Terms that appear onerous will need careful examination as part of an overall assessment of the service and the provider. As discussed earlier in this chapter, failure to perform could put the organisation in a vulnerable position.

Risks, insurance and indemnities

The most obvious risk for the organisation is in the outsourcing of a service that is not fully understood or defined, with the result that the service is not provided as expected. Given the nature of the services described in this chapter, it should be obvious that a full risk assessment must be carried out before embarking on any path that might lead to the engagement of specialist service providers. Moreover, mission-critical services should not be outsourced until all risks have been fully analysed, assessed and mitigated. Other considerations, and thus risks, are in the relationships between the specialist provider's personnel and those of the in-house team and wider organisation. There are many interfaces – organisational, physical, technological and contractual – and these must be identified and managed correctly.

There is a tendency for some people to adopt the mindset of 'out of sight, out of mind' over specialist services, especially where a significant part (or, indeed, all) of the service is executed off site. In such cases, over-reliance on a service provider could prove damaging and, in certain cases, the organisation may be held jointly liable or culpable. Obtaining an indemnity from the service provider is one way of reducing risk and, thus, financial exposure for the organisation. It may also be possible to take out insurance to cover consequential losses arising from the failure of the provider.

There is also the possibility that, despite best efforts, SLAs may prove unworkable and some compromise or understanding may have to be reached between the organisation and service provider. All of this effort will take time and money, and even then it may not produce a satisfactory outcome. Errors and negligent acts (e.g. data loss, financial loss, reputation loss and medical negligence) can have wide repercussions and it may not be possible to indemnify or insure sufficiently in all cases. Close scrutiny of the specialist provider's financial and social standing, current assets and liabilities, ownership structure and business models are amongst the factors that have to be considered when contemplating outsourcing.

16 Information Systems Management

Key issues

The following issues are covered in this chapter.

- In the delivery of a service, from specification to remuneration, much information will be generated. It comes at a cost as well as having a value, and is not something we can or should ignore.

- Information is the lifeblood of facilities management; without it the organisation is not in control of its actions and is unlikely to be able to account for them. Managing information correctly is a contributing factor to the success of facilities management.

- Maintenance systems are a traditional part of information systems in facilities management, with detailed recording of information and data possible through low-cost technology.

- Planned preventive maintenance is a long-standing tool for ensuring that systems and components do not fail in service; more could be done to integrate them with other systems to provide coverage of, and support for, the facilities management function.

- Computer-aided facilities management (CAFM) is used to plan and manage the use of space and has proven popular; even so, it represents an intermediate technology that is likely to give way to building information modelling (BIM).

- BIM enables all physical and operational attributes of a building to be modelled in a way that is universally recognised, opening up opportunities for owners and vendors alike. BIM has moved out of the research world into practice and is being mandated by some governments for new buildings.

- Most progress in the effective deployment of information systems is likely to be made on new-build projects, but opportunities for retrospective action applied to existing buildings is likely to follow.

Introduction

The delivery of a service is also the delivery of information. In managing our facilities, we need to know about the spaces to be serviced, the services to be performed and the performance of those services. Whether or not technology is an enabler or responsible for driving our desire for yet more information is largely irrelevant. Owners, managers and service providers want to know more about how their facilities and services are meeting their needs. No longer is it enough to report on what has been done; organisations and providers are looking for ways to anticipate demands to optimise their approach to facilities management. Information has become a commodity – and a valuable one – with which to inform decisions and shape actions. Information is the lifeblood of facilities management, without which the organisation will fail to deliver its promise to customers; too little information and the facilities management function will be starved, too much and it will be overwhelmed. This chapter looks at how information is being used to transform our understanding of how to manage our facilities. It should be seen as a powerful tool to replace educated guesswork with objective reality. The history of information systems in facilities management reveals a largely reactive role, with the notable exception of planned preventive maintenance. Yet even this development fails to deal with the underlying goal: a single, integrated life-cycle information model of the facility, complete with records, diagnosis and prognosis.

Information management

Information management is more than document management; it is a means to inform, influence and implement actions in the workplace and, unlike document management, is dynamic. Moreover, it is not merely a matter of technology. Information management is what organisations must use to provide themselves with an edge over their competitors. Having information ahead of events is a key to success and survival. In the context of facilities management, information can be used to control the use of resources and determine whether or not they have been spent judiciously. The plain truth is that facilities are needed only if the organisation requiring them cannot do without them. In other words, we need the facts to speak for themselves. Having information that can be relied on is a fundamental precept of management.

Traditionally, information tended to follow events and was often incomplete and inaccurate from the lack of a systematic means for handling it. The conventional view was that information was all much the same and could be treated as such. An accounting mentality prevailed with action more as a reaction to any problem that arose. Facilities management has to be ahead of events if it is to support the core business. Information needed to make a decision about what to do tomorrow has to be at hand today. Given that condition, it is realistic to expect information to be incomplete and less than accurate. What is important is that a decision can be made and the means to achieve that have to be found. Compliance with a statutory requirement, on the other hand, requires time to produce complete and accurate information; it is not possible to finish something one day and account for it fully the next. People also expect to receive what they are promised and within reasonable time and for nothing to be missing.

In the above simple examples, we should accept that to regard all information as if it were the same regardless of need, application or context is plainly wrong. In accepting this principle, it must follow that information systems which do not differentiate between types of information or need are clearly not capable of supporting management. In this regard, four aspects of information management deserve attention:

- Processes
- Resources
- Technology
- Policies and standards.

Processes have to be defined if they are to deliver information to enable the facilities management function. A close coupling between business processes and the facilities management process is therefore essential; otherwise, the golden rule that facilities management is there to support the core business is broken. For this reason, it is advisable to map the organisation's business processes to include facilities management. Instead of being separate, i.e. a stand-alone function, it should be fully integrated into the organisation's business processes. Atkin and Björk (2007) have described such an approach, where the facilities management function is integral with the organisation's business processes and cannot be divorced from them (see Fig. 16.1). A process has to be understood if it is to be capable of improvement and the usual means for portraying a business

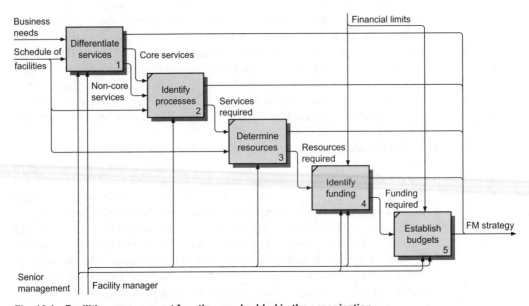

Fig. 16.1   Facilities management functions embedded in the organisation.

process is a model or map drawn in accordance with a recognised international standard such as IDEF0.[1]

Process models are part of the analysis and design of many industrial methods and practices. In facilities management, the use of process modelling is relatively unknown at this point, but is not without proponents. Process models can provide owners and their facilities managers with a means to define decision-making and determine improvements to their current procedures and practices. The implication is that the design of processes should precede the drafting of procedures. Since procedures tend to focus on specific areas, it is essential that they are contextualised and enabled by the correct information and appropriate controls.

A hierarchical process model that portrays the broader context and which is explicitly top-down is more likely to be inclusive than a set of procedures that have been assembled from different sources, no matter how well developed. Concentrating on devising the best procedures, without taking account of the underlying processes, is likely to result ultimately in an inferior plan. This situation highlights the paradox in current thinking about best practices, where the summation of such practices is expected to yield improved efficiency and fewer wasted resources and missed deadlines. Yet it may obscure simpler, more effective means for achieving the organisation's goals in service delivery. A process model can provide transparency and a means for sharing an understanding of what is needed and how it might be accomplished. In this way, decision-making can be shared and questioned in an attempt to define the basis of 'fit for purpose' procedures, which can then be operationalised with the support of information and communication technology (ICT).

Resources are the means by which information is captured, processed and exchanged. In Chapter 15, we discussed ICT infrastructure as part of a specialist service, along with some of the considerations associated with it. Additionally, organisations must recognise that different personnel are needed to provide the service and to support it in use. These may seem to be one and the same; however, providing a service is not enough: employees in the organisation must be able to perform their work efficiently and effectively. The cost of implementing an information system to support facilities management could be equal to the cost of the initial development or greater.

Technology is the classic 'moving target'. It is never going to be possible to keep at the forefront unless substantial funds can be committed and, frankly, that is not a good use of money for most organisations. Individuals can easily justify buying a new computer and may have to answer to no one; however, organisations must adopt a rational and cost-conscious approach to any purchase. Even so, it is unlikely that the technology needed to support the facilities management function would be significant

---

[1] Integrated DEFinition, where IDEF0 is the standard for business processes and IDEF3 is for workflow.

by corporate standards. The demands placed on central ICT services by the facilities management function should therefore present little concern.

Policies and standards are in a sense two sides of the same coin: policies strive for internal order and consistency, whilst standards aim for commonality and interoperability. Standards can be mandatory, but many are not. The organisation's facilities management plan will lay the ground for applying policies followed by procedures that comply with relevant standards and codes. The intention is not to impose a brake on the organisation; on the contrary, policies and procedures are there to help it deliver reliable services through a more certain process.

Factors for success

Organisations need to ensure that information is accurate, reliable, up to date, complete and consistent. Often, this is far easier said than done. As we have observed above, it is not simply a matter of processes or technology; much also depends on resources in the form of people and money, guided by standards and policies. Taken together, these four aspects can help the organisation succeed in its facilities management, because the approach complements that of corporate management.

Other contributory factors include:

1. Access by employees at all levels to information needed to do their jobs.
2. Seeing information as an asset to be exploited through sharing within the organisation and in commercial arrangements with others.
3. Assuring privacy, security, authenticity and integrity of information.

Whilst the above could easily apply to almost any kind of organisation, in the context of facilities management employees need to be kept informed of matters that affect them in the workplace; health and safety is an obvious example. Managers also need to be able to use information about their facilities in their dealings across the organisation and in contractual arrangements with others externally, subject to matters of privacy and security. Organisations that take these matters seriously will benefit from the more effective management of information resources and systems:

- Adds value to the services delivered to customers.
- Reduces risks overall.
- Reduces the costs of business processes and service delivery.
- Stimulates innovation in internal business processes and service delivery.

Information categories

Information is not, as we have implied, one homogeneous mass. To understand its nature and thus appreciate its value, we can consider two distinct categories.

- *Structured data* are pieces of information held digitally in databases and used to support operations. They cover details about the facilities, customers, service providers, suppliers and other resources inside and outside the organisation.
- *Unstructured data* include non-digital forms of images, drawings, contracts and paper documents generally.

The obvious implication is that, in time, all information will be captured digitally, as only in this way can it be fully utilised. Information that is non-digital is difficult to share and risks being lost. Of course, steps have to be taken to assure the integrity and protection of digital data.

Information auditing

An ever-present function for organisations is that of auditing. No organisation can escape some form of audit and most will have to observe statutory checks for compliance. The perception is that audits are used to uncover some irregularity or malpractice, which is true; however, the practice of information auditing has wider benefits. In the context of facilities management, information auditing is used to:

1. Analyse the organisation's business objectives in the context of its facilities management operations to determine if they are aligned.
2. Define its facilities management information needs.
3. Maintain a searchable inventory of information.
4. Identify information deficiencies and surpluses.
5. Measure the cost and value of information.
6. Exploit the potential of information internally and externally.

Information about how well, or not, the organisation's facilities are supporting its business is knowledge that has a value. When harnessed, information can be a ready source of knowledge about the organisation. The cost of its collection and processing can be significant so it is important to know if information is being handled needlessly, such as might occur where too many key performance indicators (KPIs) are being reported. The point here is that KPIs should be, by definition, the significant few and not the trivial many. Reporting on every aspect of operations might seem to be putting management firmly in control, but it has to know what to do with that information.

Document management

A long-standing application in information management has been document management. The latter term is often used incorrectly to mean the same as the former; however, it has a narrower scope that normally covers scanning, distribution, search and archiving of correspondence, memoranda, reports and publications. Nonetheless, distinct advantages include the need for less physical space, although in a hardware context duplicate servers may be required – one active and one passive – each on different sites. The related issues of data protection and copyright must be considered. Control must be exercised over which third-party documents, notably publications, can be legally captured and distributed in an electronic system to avoid copyright infringement and potentially heavy fines or awards for damages.

Planned preventive maintenance

Maintenance of buildings and engineering services is a long-standing interest within the facilities management field. Indeed, the discipline of facilities management emerged from building maintenance management in many countries and still occupies a high position on management's agenda. Planned preventive maintenance (PPM) is a schedule of actions aimed at avoiding breakdowns and failures. The objective is to avert failure of equipment and components in service and to improve reliability by replacing worn parts. Tasks include inspections, equipment checks, diagnostics, adjustments and overhauls at specified intervals. Service personnel can record wear and other forms of deterioration so they know when to replace or repair worn parts in order to avoid failure. It is not, however, confined to mechanical and electrical engineering services and extends to cover the building's fabric, finishes and furnishing. Periodic painting to protect building components and finishes is a common task within PPM; in a few cases, it can be a continuous operation.

Scheduling maintenance activities can be accomplished in a variety of ways. On the simplest level, it can be a diary or calendar entry. For more complex facilities, a dedicated planning and scheduling system might be used, with or without a supporting database. Some systems are purpose-built to deal comprehensively with PPM and may support data exchange with other systems and packaged applications. The decision on which system to adopt should be made as part of a broader evaluation of information systems within the facilities management function. There are bound to be differences in the features offered in proprietary systems and the extent to which data can be exchanged between them – this aspect is also important in a corporate context. The previous chapter discussed issues in relation to 'vendor/provider lock-in' and other constraints from which it should be clear that a decision taken in isolation may well result in a system in isolation.

Case study – ICEconsult

The company specialises in developing ICT solutions in facilities management and has become a major player in the Icelandic market where it is established. In the mid-1990s, there was considerable discussion in Iceland about the poor

*condition and maintenance of buildings and other structures. The state's research
fund awarded a grant that enabled the company to develop software tools
specifically for building maintenance management.*

The first version of the company's software concentrated on the outdoor
maintenance of structures and was launched in the late 1990s. The market's response was that whilst the software was appropriate for consultants it was not suitable for facility managers. Development began on an
improved version that would better meet the needs of facilities managers.
The company began to collaborate with a number of end-user companies
and institutions on the development of solutions for various processes in
facilities management. More than a decade later, this collaboration continues,
and the tools developed have become extensive and widespread in use.

The early versions of the tools were PC-based and ran as stand-alone
solutions on the Microsoft Windows platform, which meant that each
installation had to be set up on individual computers on the customer's
premises. The arrangement was based on the customer's ICT department
supporting operational use. The software was designed around the collection and recording of information and data about buildings, such as drawings, photographs and quantities. Internal work processes dealing with
services (inspections, space management, cleaning and energy monitoring) were not included.

In their enthusiasm, the company's customers, almost without exception, focused on collecting every last detail without first considering what
was really needed and who would have to maintain the information and
data. In parallel, there was considerable 'forgetfulness' on the part of the
customers' ICT departments in servicing this 'support system' for the 'support department'. The nature of facilities management also meant that
users of the software were spread out geographically, near the buildings
for which they were responsible; as employees of large real estate owners,
they tended to be located throughout the country. A PC-based solution
where client software was installed on each PC and then connected to a
network was always low on ICT departments' list of priorities. Moreover,
the support service it represented was naturally not seen as part of the customer's core business operations. Under these circumstances, it proved
very difficult to keep users satisfied.

As use of the internet grew and became commonplace, the company
started to offer a networked solution. The number of users grew quickly,
and in just over three years 2000 were registered. In response to this dramatic change in the business landscape, the company changed its business
model and began offering a fully hosted service, effectively operating as
an applications service provider (ASP). This kind of software service is
known variously as on-demand software or software as a service.

Since customers' support departments can assess the service directly,
there was no longer any need for ICT departments to act as an intermedi-
ary. This change accelerated the development of facilities management ICT
solutions; soon, the software included features for inspections, deviation

recording, planning, quality control, leasing and rentals, space management, energy monitoring and helpdesks. As one customer put it: 'It was as though the software had made its support department leap 50 years into the future.'

The company received a further boost following a legislative change which obliged municipalities to establish sinking fund accounts to cover the maintenance of buildings and other structures. Auditors had deemed the greatest risk in municipalities' annual accounts to be poor maintenance of buildings and other structures. Today, the company hosts details of 10 000 buildings and structures in Iceland and Denmark. The company has further developed ICT-supported facilities management processes to help its customers obtain safety and quality assurance certification under ISO standards.

Computer-aided facilities management (CAFM)

Managing the use of space can be a major feature of some facilities management groups and planning for different uses can increase demands on resources at all levels. For some the extent of change can be a priority and, as discussed in Chapter 5 on change management, change can be regarded as entirely normal. Having tools available to plan and explore the impact of changes can represent a significant productivity boost for organisations that must routinely redeploy resources to meet shifting demands and needs in the workplace.

The use of computers in spatial planning can be traced back to the 1970s, so there is nothing new in terms of applications. What has happened is that facilities management can benefit from technology developed for other industries and the market for computer games. It is easy to dismiss 3-D computer games as irrelevant, but the market for them has provided the impetus for hardware and software developers, and put pressure on vendors to offer these applications at better prices. There is no reason why we cannot model the spaces in our buildings to create virtual reality (VR), which is precisely what is happening. Not all buildings are 'designed by computer' and a model of the facilities – buildings plus processes and people – may not be available digitally. Creating a digital model retrospectively can be expensive and it may take a long time, but will provide benefits for even longer.

Computer-aided facilities management (CAFM) is a fusion between space planning and 3-D computer-aided design (CAD) to support the planning and monitoring of physical space and the activities in it. These graphics-based systems model both the geometry and attributes of three-dimensional spaces. Most CAFM software packages are based on a CAD front-end (e.g. Autodesk's AutoCAD and Bentley's MicroStation), linked to a relational database back-end such as Microsoft SQL or the open-source package, MySQL. Typically, the database contains non-graphical attribute data of the spaces and objects associated with them. The database can be searched and reports generated to suit user needs. Histories of changes can be mined to provide insights into patterns of use that can help us understand employee social interaction and networks. These are important for creating workplaces that enhance end-user experience, and provide the organisation with highly effective spaces.

Linking scheduling software to the database of a CAFM system to handle the time dimension creates what is known as a '4-D' simulation that can be used to plan, schedule and optimise changes. The advantage is that proposals for change can be tried and tested in the computer before they are made. Other dimensions, such as cost and energy performance, can be added to provide further modelling of facilities and conditions within them. The collective term for this technology is n-D. As time passes, CAFM and building management systems (BMS) (as discussed in Chapter 15) will converge. Ultimately, facilities will be modelled digitally in a single system from inception with the impact of design on operations closely scrutinised. Information will not need to be handed over in the conventional sense, as the model will evolve through the different phases over the project life cycle. Owners and developers already have to demonstrate to planning authorities the environmental and other impacts that their new building or facility will create, bringing us closer in practice to the goal of sustainable development.

Building information modelling

CAFM can be thought of as an intermediate technology. Everybody is free to use it as they wish and for whatever purpose they choose. To make a real breakthrough in terms of creating digital models requires consensus on the conventions used to define such models. A building information model (BIM) is an information or data representation containing geometry, spatial relationships, geographic information, quantities and component properties. Systems, assemblies and sequences are shown in a relative scale. Overall, BIM can be used to simulate the building life cycle including construction and facility operation. By classifying the structure of such models universally, owners and their project teams, including suppliers and service providers, can define the attributes unambiguously, enabling product data to be exchanged between designers, suppliers, constructors and operators. BIM has been pursued for three decades or more in various forms, yet has only recently begun to be taken seriously by owners.

Vendors of CAD systems are incorporating BIM into their software based on their own definitions or industry foundation classes (IFC) developed under the auspices of the IAI (International Alliance for Interoperability). IFC models for the architecture, engineering and construction (AEC) sector provide a common format for the exchange of data throughout the life cycle of a building. This step raises expectation of an accelerated take-up of BIM for all new buildings. In Finland, new buildings must be created from a BIM and more countries are likely to mandate the use of BIM. In other words, a building or other facility has to be built digitally before it can be built physically. One day, all buildings will be subject to this requirement: the question is, when? Those who cast doubt on this prediction should recall the persistence of those who, a decade or so ago, insisted that not everybody in business would need their own PC. Today, many people have more than one, if laptops, PDAs and smart phones are included. The real challenge is how to deal with the existing stock of buildings and other facilities in a way that will not be prohibitively expensive. Technology will no doubt help to make the breakthrough.

BIM applied to existing buildings

The use of BIM retrospectively has much to offer to create facilities data, asset registers, maintenance and service data, as well as service procurement data, although it can be expensive to set up.

Project example – Sydney Opera House

The iconic Sydney Opera House (SOH) has been used to test the feasibility of BIM technology for the exchange of data between applications in facilities and asset management. The Cooperative Research Centre (CRC) for Construction Innovation and the Australian Government's *FM Action Agenda* chose SOH as the focus of its Facilities Management (FM) Exemplar Project and collaborated with industry, government and the research community to develop strategies in three areas:

1. Digital modelling
2. Services procurement
3. Performance benchmarking.

An underlying motivation was that if SOH could demonstrate the benefits of BIM then it would be possible to use it on less complex and new building projects. As the SOH's construction predated the CAD era, there were no digital models of SOH's structure. An objective of the Sydney Opera House FM Exemplar Project was to create one from an existing computer-aided architectural design (CAAD) model and then to add various properties about the spaces, rooms, furniture and other features in the building. The resultant IFC model would then be used to test various strategies and scenarios.

The structural model created by Arup, the international engineering firm responsible for the original design, was exported from Bentley's MicroStation in IFC format. That file was then imported without loss of data into Graphisoft's ArchiCAD, a 3-D architectural modelling package then extended by the addition of rooms and other features and attributes. Users can interact with the model, which is displayed graphically alongside its non-graphical attribute data. The project involved the definition of a number of schemas (or building information specifications) covering various facilities and asset management applications, and focused on a range of issues including:

- Reusability of a standardised BIM for facilities management.
- Potential to integrate different sources of data.
- Ability to cope with business-related data.
- Interfacing with proprietary software.

A demonstrator was developed to show on-screen how data could be exchanged through the IFC model to support facilities and asset management applications. Overall, the R&D (research and development) team found that the exchange of geometric data was reasonably accurate and concluded that IFC-based exchange was possible with a selection of common BIM-based applications. Whilst the demonstrator was based on a partial BIM, it was felt there was sufficient proof that IFC-based exchange could be scaled up and extended to support a wider range of applications. SOH is a credible, working example of retrospective BIM, where benefits to the owner and customers/end-users have accrued from optimised use of space and energy consumption.

Conclusions

Information management might not be regarded as a particularly important function, but it is essential to the efficient and effective practice of facilities management. Information is needed to control and measure the performance of services, amongst other things. It amounts to far more than reporting on past events; it should be used to ensure that facilities management works ahead of events to anticipate owner and end-user requirements. Information management is, in effect, the glue that holds facilities management together. Without it, we cannot be sure how services are performed or even if they are the right ones. In looking ahead, we need to acknowledge the key role of anticipatory strategies, such as planned preventive maintenance. This activity is hardly new and must remain at the fore of considerations by decision makers. Normally, things fail while in use and not at any other time. Having comprehensive information on our facilities enables us to plan, schedule and optimise tasks. Increasingly, 3-D CAD technology is used to model the use of space, as well as enable new building and facility designs to be scrutinised for compliance with building codes and energy performance requirements. The emergence of international standards (i.e. IFC) for defining buildings as assemblies of spaces and components with properties and purpose will quicken the pace of development of BIM and their respective systems. As progress is made on the new buildings front, attention will turn increasingly to existing buildings and facilities.

CHECKLIST

This checklist is intended to assist with the review and action planning process.

	Yes	No	Action required
1. Does the organisation have an information management plan as part of its facilities management?	☐	☐	☐
2. Has the facilities management function been defined explicitly in the form of a process model or map?	☐	☐	☐
3. Has the organisation undertaken an information audit to determine the value of its information and any deficiency in its provision?	☐	☐	☐
4. Is planned preventive maintenance (PPM) an integral part of the organisation's facilities management and is an appropriate system provided for this purpose?	☐	☐	☐
5. Does the organisation have a policy of capturing comprehensive digital information on all its facilities and assets?	☐	☐	☐
6. Is the organisation making use of available computer-aided facilities management (CAFM) technology for managing its spaces?	☐	☐	☐
7. Is the organisation aware of the benefits of building information modelling (BIM) and the likely changes in legislation mandating its use?	☐	☐	☐

17 Contract Management and Financial Control

Key issues

The following issues are covered in this chapter.

- The organisation needs to develop its ICF if it is to manage contracts and control finances – this applies irrespective of whether or not services are outsourced.

- Procedures should be transparent and follow accepted accounting standards.

- Actions must be performed according to the contract and at intervals stipulated therein – this is not only to ensure compliance with the contract but to ensure prompt payment to service providers and suppliers to avoid cashflow problems.

- Service providers should receive reimbursement or attract penalties appropriate to their performance against the service specification and SLA.

- In-house service providers should be assessed against the same criteria as external providers. Any changes that are required should be controlled in accordance with the principles of the original contract.

- Contract costs should be monitored against both the budget and tender price on a basis that is appropriate to their duration and size.

- The level or extent of contract review should be appropriate to the value and complexity of the contract. For most services, this period should be 12 months unless otherwise agreed as part of a specific public–private partnership arrangement – see Chapter 19.

Introduction

In keeping with previous chapters, the subjects of contract management and financial control follow largely in chronological order within the overall facilities management process. If earlier procedures have been followed carefully, the management of contracts should be – in the sense of their administration – relatively straightforward. Sufficient precedents exist for contract administration, largely in the context of monitoring, control and, where necessary, corrective action. Contract management and financial monitoring are, however, aspects of facilities management that can represent a significant resource issue for client organisations, not least because they are ongoing commitments. As such, they will always involve a minimum level of resource whether services are outsourced or retained in-house. In these respects, the role of the ICF – see Chapter 1 – is one that should develop over time as working knowledge accrues of how contractors perform – mostly service providers in this context. For the purpose of this work, contract management and financial monitoring include contract conditions and terms, payments, cost monitoring, performance monitoring, change control, contract administration and review. Together they offer a sufficiently broad treatment of this stage in the process to enable the client organisation to put effective controls in place. Even so, there may well be additional procedures – most likely linked to the organisation's own accounting provisions – that will necessitate further development of some functions.

Contract conditions and terms

The guiding principle is that in all cases, payment must be dependent upon performance. Contracts should define, therefore, how payments are to be adjusted when performance deviates from what is acceptable. Given that facilities management is about the provision of services, rather than tangible products, it is important to see reimbursement as something that should vary according to the performance of the service provider. This will mean that the client organisation has to define the level of poor service delivery at which reduced payments are no longer a sufficient redress and the client can terminate the contract. In this connection, contracts may need to contain a clause stating that, if the client organisation does terminate the contract, the service provider can go to arbitration or some other cheaper and quicker alternative dispute resolution method. Appendix D outlines how contracts should be approached and what terms should apply.

Payments

The client organisation will need to be aware of the implications of cash-flow both for itself and service providers. Whilst the organisation might be expected to have up to date financial information and so be appraised of its cashflow position, service providers may not be so well supported. It is likely to prove beneficial, therefore, for service providers to submit a cashflow forecast for their service provision before the contract comes into effect and to keep this up-to-date. This tends to be less of an issue in general facilities management contracts; however, forecasts or allowances for reactive works and discretionary expenditure items can be useful. Taking these issues into account will mean that both the client organisation and service providers will know what their likely pattern of payments will

WESTEN LEISURE COMPLEX		**Month:** 6
Contract: Mechanical & Electrical Maintenance	**Service provider:** Emeny (Contractors) Ltd.	**Ref:** ..PPM01 . . . .
Covering period:		**Payment no:** 6
Annual contract sum: £449,000.00		
Gross values to date: • Planned contract services • Changes to planned services • Unplanned/reactive services	£176,000.00 £ 22,000.00 £112,000.00	
Sub-total		£310,000.00
Less previous		£236,000.00
Payment due:		£ 74,000.00
VAT @ 15%		£ 11,100.00
Total amount due:		£ 85,100.00
Authorised by:	**Date:**	
. . . . Supervising Officer		

Fig. 17.1 Monthly payment form.

be. This will also help in measuring actual performance against forecast performance. Regular payments to service providers are essential to ensure that they do not fail financially. It is dangerous to assume that a large service provider will always have funds flowing in from other contracts. Sometimes too many clients think the same, resulting in the failure of the service provider.

The structure and format of payment documentation should be clear and simple; an example is shown in Fig. 17.1. The advantage of the format is that as the gross value of services is recalculated each month any overpayment in a previous month will be automatically taken into account without the need for credit notes. In addition, the value of planned contract services and any changes in them are clearly identified.

Cost monitoring

A report should be completed by the client organisation in order to ensure that contract costs are monitored and controlled systematically. An example format is shown in Fig. 17.2. This should incorporate all monthly payments to service providers, as referred to above, as well as the anticipated final account. The use of an accounting system – failing that spreadsheets or a database management system – can easily improve the efficiency of this process and is a highly recommended practice.

WESTEN LEISURE COMPLEX

Month: 6

(A) Service or service element	(B) Annual contract sum	(C) Changes	(D) Anticipated out-turn account (B + C)	(E) Gross value of service to date	(F) Comments
Planned preventive maintenance	449 000	22 000	471 000	176 000	PPM programme behind schedule
Unplanned/reactive services	–	112 000	112 000	112 000	High level of reactive repairs
Total	449 000	134 000	583 000	288 000	

Fig. 17.2   Cost control report form.

The complexity and value of the particular service contract should determine the frequency and detail of the report. Some contracts may need a one-line item; whereas, for example, expenditure under a mechanical and electrical engineering maintenance contract may be broken down into the following elements:

- Planned preventive maintenance
- Unplanned/reactive services
- Special equipment maintenance
- Performance-related payments.

Performance monitoring

In order to ensure the continued performance of the service provider against the service specification and SLA, a performance scoresheet should be completed regularly by the organisation so as to arrive at an agreed rating for each provider. An example format for a performance scoresheet is provided in Fig. 17.3.

The above performance rating can be applied to a performance-related payment table that would reward the service provider for exceeding the specification – if the organisation has previously agreed that enhanced performance is to be sought – and penalise the service provider for not meeting the specification's minimum requirements. The level of detail in the table must be commensurate with the size and complexity of the service provided. However, the golden rule is to concentrate on KPIs – those that can be determined and analysed cost-effectively.

WESTEN LEISURE COMPLEX			Month: 6
Item Service criteria	Priority weighting	Monthly rating	Score (weighting × monthly rating)
01 Planned Preventive Maintenance Regime	5	2	10
02 Response Times to Breakdowns	5	0	0
Total score			10
Performance rating % (**Actual total/maximum** × **100**)			50%

In this simple example, the scoring is based upon the following:
0 = service does not meet specification
1 = service meets specification
2 = service exceeds specification
A more detailed scoring system can, however, be employed where a specific measurement system has been agreed.

Fig. 17.3   Performance scoresheet.

The importance of maintaining continuity of service is one aspect of performance that may require special attention, particularly in the case of mechanical and electrical services. Persistent non-functioning of such services could have dire consequences for the client organisation. Financial penalties to cover the losses that might be faced by a serious failure have to be carefully considered. However, it is important to set these in the context of the value of contracts. For instance, it would be unreasonable to expect a service provider to accept a level of penalty so onerous that any failure would discount all payment.

Change control

The client organisation must be able to control changes if it is to be fully in charge of managing its facilities. It is suggested that the organisation:

- Approves all changes before they are implemented.
- Before approval, identifies all possible risks together with the impact of the proposed change – see Chapters 1 and 5.
- Only allows a designated member of management, or nominated representative, to grant authorisation to proceed with a change.

In any event, changes should be avoided unless the consequences are agreed beforehand. Where they are necessary, their cost should be based on tendered prices and rates. Where this is not possible, it should be clear that the contract administrator will value the additional works at market rates. The evaluation of changes should always be consistent with the conditions of contract.

Contract administration

Diligent contract administration is essential if the organisation is to achieve continual improvement in the management of its facilities. Successful contract administration includes the following key practices:

- Roles and responsibilities should be clearly defined and allocated, with responsibility for the supervision of service delivery vested in the ICF.
- Every contract (and therefore contractor) should have its own contract manager.
- A helpdesk (or central coordination point) should be set up to manage the interface between customers and service providers, regardless of whether the service providers are in-house or outsourced.
- An open-book agreement can be put in place under which the client organisation will have the right to inspect the service provider's accounts for the contract.
- Frequent meetings should be held with service providers to discuss performance in the early days of the contract, in order to deal with teething problems – as the contract progresses, the need for such meetings should diminish.

Contract review

In the case of outsourced service provision, contract review is necessary in order to establish if the decision to outsource is still valid in terms of the organisation's facilities management strategy, current market conditions and the performance of the service provider. The necessity for reviews will have been built into the SLA and formalised in the contract, although here we are concerned primarily with an internal review. The frequency of contract reviews will depend on the size and complexity of the contract – as reflected by the nature and scope of service provision – with more frequent reviews likely during the initial period. The following matters must, however, be addressed in each case:

- Comparison of tendered costs against actual costs.
- Current performance rating.
- Ideas for improving and/or providing better value for money and increased customer satisfaction.
- Prompt highlighting and discussion of contentious issues, thereby avoiding escalation and further dispute.

Practice Point 17.1   Passing the buck.

Key point: the need for roles and responsibilities to be clearly defined – within the client organisation and the service provider – is highlighted by the following arrangement.

A contracted facilities management company was impeded in its ability to deliver a timely, best value service due to overlapping roles within the client organisation. Although a contract manager had been appointed to act as the client representative and was the single point of contact, the contractor's facilities manager regularly had to consult a number of in-house managers in the client organisation before a decision could be made. On one occasion, the repair of an item of mechanical plant was delayed because the contracts manager had to approach three in-house managers before finally receiving authorisation for the works to go ahead.

Conclusions

All contracts must be managed. This requirement applies both to formal contracts with external contractors and to informal contracts (SLAs) with in-house service providers. The principles and procedures must be appropriate to the contracts being managed and provide a realistic level of flexibility. Whatever approach is taken, valuable resources will be consumed in managing the contracts and in ensuring that the correct financial controls are exercised. Important in this latter connection is that due account should be taken of the organisation's wider accounting practices, especially in the public sector where controls to guard against irregularity are in place.

For these reasons, it is inappropriate to prescribe a single approach here; rather, best practice dictates that customer-related and financial measures should be considered. It is possible to derive hundreds of performance measures for services, but only KPIs should be captured. To do otherwise would divert valuable resources away from where they are needed most and prove a distraction to an otherwise competent service provider.

CHECKLIST

This checklist is intended to assist with the review and action planning process.

	Yes	No	Action required
1. Is the organisation satisfied that its facilities management service contracts properly define the level of payments that should be made and how they should be adjusted when the contractor's performance deviates from that defined as acceptable?	☐	☐	☐
2. Has the organisation considered the cashflow implications both for itself and service providers in relation to its management of contracts?	☐	☐	☐
3. Is the organisation providing resources at an appropriate level to support its contract management and financial control?	☐	☐	☐
4. Are appropriate cost monitoring and control arrangements in place?	☐	☐	☐
5. Are arrangements in place to enable the continued assessment of the performance of service providers against service specifications and SLAs?	☐	☐	☐
6. Are adequate controls in place in relation to the agreement of any changes to the service specification and SLAs?	☐	☐	☐
7. Is the organisation satisfied with its contract administration and audit arrangements?	☐	☐	☐

18 Benchmarking Best Practice

Key issues

The following issues are covered in this chapter.

- Benchmarking is one tool of many that can assist managers in their pursuit of improvement, but it is also one that is widely understood and applied.

- Benchmarking is an external focus on internal activities and is aimed at supporting the drive towards best practice through objective comparisons and insights gained as a result of studying best-in-class organisations.

- For benchmarking to work successfully, it has to be stakeholder-driven, forward looking, participative and focused on quality or performance.

- Benchmarking can work well between organisations that might otherwise regard themselves as competitors.

- The organisation needs to recognise that the gains from benchmarking with other comparable organisations far outweigh the perceived disadvantages.

- Goods or products can be compared objectively, along with the processes that create them. Facilities management offers no such simplicity and relies on policies and procedures that may not be well defined and/or are poorly documented in comparison.

- Benchmarking methods are relatively easy to understand and apply – in the specific case of facilities management there are simple and accessible ways of undertaking benchmarking.

Introduction

More than a decade has passed since benchmarking came to the fore in a wave of new management thinking, conventions and tools designed to improve the fortunes of business organisations. Views differ on the success achieved by the new wave, with some dismissing it simply as a fad. This is both true and false. Business process re-engineering is a case in point, having been promoted by many as an all-or-nothing solution to an organisation's ills. Aping the mantra of management gurus is bound to have its dangers. For each organisation that failed to respond to its treatment, there have been hundreds that have benefited from a critical review of what they had been doing – often with little or no change – for years. No convention or tool can be good for all organisations in all situations. More importantly, new tools do not necessarily lose their effectiveness because of the passage of time; some are simply the victim of new fads. For many people and organisations – clients, consultants and service providers alike – benchmarking has a value. That is not the same as saying it is the only tool or the one that can give all the answers. However, in the right hands, it can be as powerful as it is simple: benchmarking is not rocket science. The primary purpose of this chapter is to show why benchmarking should be an appropriate tool for facilities management, how it can be applied and how it relates to best practice. Knowing how an organisation is performing is vital. Without such knowledge, it is difficult to measure the effects of any improvement. Benchmarking is about establishing the norms for performance in terms of financial, organisational, innovation and change management and customer focus. People tend to have notions of what things might cost, how long they might take and what they should expect. Benchmarking is chiefly concerned with formalising these notions. In making organisations look out from themselves, the exercise also directs energy towards serving the organisation's best business interests and away from internal conflict.

Pursuing continual improvement

Benchmarking is a tool for supporting a process of continual improvement. Its objective is to identify current performance in relation to best practice in areas of concern to the organisation. In this context, it is about measuring performance in the underlying processes of facilities management. This means, for example, establishing how much the organisation is paying for its services and supplies. Typical in these respects are the costs of energy – electricity and gas – and other utilities (for example, water, sewerage and telecommunications), as well as domestic services like cleaning and security.

The organisation needs to appreciate that benchmarking should not be used simply to compare costs of services but, where appropriate, to measure the effectiveness of the process that leads to those costs and a given performance. As was shown in Chapter 2, the facilities management strategy and its resultant plan will outline the means for measuring whether or not business needs have been met and cost optimised. If the optimal cost level is to be measured, the organisation must be able to compare the costs of different methods of delivering the required performance. Benchmarking can also be used to measure the effectiveness of in-house practices against external practices in related organisations or industrial sectors and against an organisation identified as achieving best practice in the area under scrutiny.

Benchmarking provides management with a tool for making decisions about policies and procedures in regard to how services should be procured, i.e. whether they should be outsourced or retained in-house. It is neither complicated nor expensive to apply, and may be a relatively easy route to establishing and then recording key performance indicators (KPIs). Since many organisations lack basic information on their own estates-related and facilities services, benchmarking can provide the necessary focus to enable such information to be gathered objectively and relatively painlessly. In these cases, cost or price and quality or performance of service should become the primary targets for study if the organisation is to be sure of achieving best value and have a basis for pursuing continual improvement.

Organisations that have raised the profile of facilities management, perhaps as the outcome of re-engineering their business processes, and given it the clear mandate of adding value, need to know whether or not their objective is being achieved. Benchmarking can supply the answers not once, but at intervals as the organisation pursues improvement. Continual comparisons with organisations recognised as achieving best practice allow the organisation to recognise and close the gap between its own performance and that of the best practitioner.

Benchmarking practices

The origins of formalised benchmarking are well documented (Leibfried and McNair, 1994): it is 'an external focus on internal activities, functions or operations in order to achieve continuous improvement'. The main purpose is to measure quality of service, and the processes that support it, against the organisation's goals and aspirations and best-in-class organisations in other sectors. In these cases, it is likely that the best practitioner is better, because what it does is different.

A benchmarking study begins with an analysis of existing activities and practices within the organisation. These processes have to be properly understood and measurable before comparison can take place with another organisation – if you cannot measure it, you cannot improve it.[1] Usually, benchmarking is a one-on-one activity; that is, it is used by one organisation to help identify improvements in its own processes by exchanging information – often in a workshop – with another. The activity is normally a collaboration of mutual benefit, however strange it might seem to look so closely at one's competitors and vice versa. Competitors can provide not only the challenge, but also the insights into how performance can be improved and costs reduced.

In partnering arrangements – especially those where an organisation is going to share business amongst a few select suppliers – the necessity of benchmarking becomes all the more apparent. Continual improvement is an integral part of any partnering relationship, without which there can be no purpose served – see Chapter 14. By comparing a partner's performance against other service providers, it is possible to provide the

---

[1] Attributed to Lord Kelvin (1824–1907).

stimulus for improvement. This can effectively replace the stimulus provided by the competitive tendering of each new contract. Concerns that a partner might have about feeling exposed are unlikely to arise, since all partners are aware from the outset about the arrangements to be adopted and have signified their acceptance of them by entering into a partnering agreement.

Measuring performance

Performance measurement is at the centre of good facilities management. Benchmarking begins by identifying perceived critical success factors (CSFs), typically the strategies, roles and processes existing within the organisation. Preliminary questions are:

- Who is involved in delivering the service?
- Why are they involved?
- What are they doing?
- Why are they doing it?
- Is what they are doing adding value?

The last question recognises the need to add value to the services provided to the customer.

In offering an approach to benchmarking there is bound to be the danger of appearing too prescriptive. The organisation should apply the approach outlined below having regard to any practical issue that might be an obstacle. Authors will differ on their prescription for benchmarking. Here, we identify eight steps in a benchmarking exercise:

1. Identify the subject of the exercise.
2. Decide what to measure.
3. Identify who to benchmark within sector and outside.
4. Collect information and data.
5. Analyse findings and determine gap.
6. Set goals for improvement.
7. Implement new order.
8. Monitor the process for improvement.

Step 1 – Identify the subject of the exercise

- Agree on the objective(s) of the exercise.
- Decide on who to involve internally.
- Define the process (core business or otherwise).
- Identify the scope.
- Set the limits for the exercise.
- Agree on the process.
- Produce a map or model of the process.

Step 2 – Decide what to measure

- Examine the elements of the process.
- Establish measures of performance.
- Verify that measures match objective(s).

Step 3 – Identify who to benchmark within sector and outside

- Identify main competitors and 'rising stars'.
- Agree on those to benchmark.
- Identify out-of-sector comparisons.
- Identify best-in-class outside own sector.

Step 4 – Collect information and data

- Draft a checklist or questionnaire.
- Pilot the questionnaire.
- Conduct structured interview(s).

Step 5 – Analyse findings and determine gap

- Score answers/responses and weight them, as necessary.
- Analyse qualitative responses.
- Summarise findings.
- Measure gap between one's own performance and others.

Step 6 – Set goals for improvement

- Identify goals for performance improvement.
- Establish criteria for judging performance.
- Draft action plan with milestones for improvement.

Step 7 – Implement new order

- Draft new procedures.
- Communicate procedures to all stakeholders.
- Train those affected by the new order.
- Implement new process(es).

Step 8 – Monitor the process for improvement

- Conduct regular review meetings.
- Observe progress of best-in-class comparison.
- Determine if any corrective actions are required.
- Document changes and communicate them to all stakeholders.

Benchmarking facilities management

Many organisations now routinely collect data and engage in their own benchmarking of the costs of energy, water, maintenance, cleaning, security, etc. Some organisations also participate in benchmarking clubs involving similar organisations and in arrangements with very different kinds of organisation. Commercial enterprises have been set up to bring together organisations seeking to benchmark; some universities have even become involved in benchmarking within key sectors. The success of some initiatives is, however, unclear. The organisation should look very closely, therefore, at the costs of getting involved against the likely benefits.

Facilities management as a recognised discipline is not only relatively new, but also has great potential for reducing cost and increasing service levels over the long term. Mechanisms for benchmarking can and should be built into newly defined facilities management operations, whether services are retained in-house or outsourced. One example of benchmarking the overall approach to facilities management that an organisation takes is described below. It is based on a validated model of best practice facilities management and has been tested with a large number of organisations across different sectors.

The Micro-Scan*fm* diagnostic tool enables senior managers to review, discuss and modify its facilities management in the light of responses to a detailed questionnaire, which is held and analysed by computer. Micro-Scan*fm* provides an opportunity to understand and assess the scope for business improvement and to highlight the potential gain. It does this against four separate perspectives.

1. *Customer* – how do customers see us?
2. *Financial* – how is the function managed to achieve best value?
3. *Operational* – how efficient and effective is the delivery of estates-related and facilities services?
4. *Innovation* – how does the facilities management function continue to improve and assist the core business in creating value?

The overall approach is consistent with that of the perspectives adopted in *The Balanced Scorecard* (Kaplan and Norton, 1996). Areas of potential improvement are identified easily and can be monitored over time to gauge the extent of improvement achieved. *The Balanced Scorecard* relies upon the minimum amount of information that is necessary in order to obtain a balanced view of the organisation's performance. Micro-Scan*fm* adopts the same approach through 80 questions, the answers to which can then be compared across respondents and organisations. Thus, it is possible to compare understanding, attitude and actions within a single organisation as well as across many.

The baseline (or benchmark) against which scores are calibrated is that of best practice. This is established from industry sources and is reviewed periodically so that recalibration of the tool can be undertaken as required.

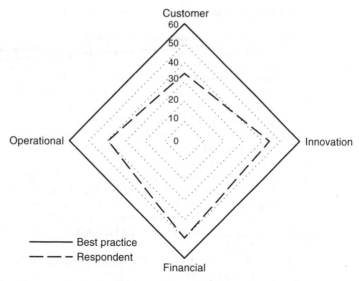

Fig. 18.1 Comparing one organisation with best practice.

In this connection, it is important to appreciate that understanding develops over time and so today's best practice will not necessarily be tomorrow's best practice. The diagrammatic presentation of the scores resulting from an individual analysis is shown in Fig. 18.1. This reveals at a glance where an organisation (or respondent) needs to direct attention. Likewise, it can confirm that current initiatives are measuring up to the pursuit of best practice.

The four perspectives have shown themselves to be purposeful and aligned to both the facilities management strategy of organisations and their strategic business objectives. The idea that one can have strong financial controls and yet be less concerned about, say, customers, is easily highlighted. Balance across all four perspectives, as shown by best practice organisations, can be the only sensible path to follow. In this respect, it is not a matter of having the right answers, but more a case of knowing where improvement lies and how this might enable the organisation to close the gap on best practice. Examples of the many issues that stand behind the four perspectives are information technology, human resources management, education and training, and customer satisfaction. Typical questions used in dialogue with users are given in Table 18.1.

Micro-Scan*fm* has been constructed so that each element in its dialogue with a user – typically a facilities manager – relates to a CSF. Quantitative analysis of a more detailed series of questions could be added to enable actual performance to be measured against best practice. However, the aim is not to provide measures of performance, but to guide facilities managers and their organisations to understand better how they are thinking and behaving now. Developing that understanding is the cornerstone of the Micro-Scan*fm* tool.

Table 18.1   Example dialogue taken from Micro-Scan*fm*.

1. We allocate our budgets based on a priority of needs.
2. We measure improvement by achieving lower costs this year than last.
3. We conduct tendering competitions for all services and supplies over a specified minimum contract value.
4. We require our in-house services costs to be compared against the costs of buying in the same services.
5. Our service contracts are procured on an annual basis.
6. We form cooperative relationships with our major suppliers and service providers.
7. We seek the advice of external consultants in areas where we do not have the expertise ourselves.
8. We manage our services effectively by leaving them with the same provider.
9. We retain in-house as many of our services as possible.
10. We assess the cost-effectiveness of all services whether in-house or bought in.
11. We are more concerned about value for money than cost or quality alone.
12. We have indicators for measuring the cost-effectiveness of all services and supplies.
13. We compare the costs of our services and supplies with those of organisations similar to ourselves.
14. We compare the costs of our services and supplies with those of the best organisation irrespective of their business sector.
15. We undertake skills audits to determine our management needs in regard to facilities and services.
16. We have explicit procedures for buying in services and supplies.
17. We produce service level agreements for services and supplies.
18. We measure the performance of our service providers whether in-house or outsourced.
19. We have up-to-date specifications for our services whether provided in-house or outsourced.
20. Our data on the costs and performance of services are held centrally and are readily accessible.
21. Our data on the costs and performance of services are held electronically.
22. We apply service level agreements to assist in measuring the performance of services provided in-house.
23. We are able to show what our space utilisation is.   . . . *and so on*

Against each of these questions, respondents are required to indicate the extent of their actions according to the following:

Always	Frequently	Occasionally	Seldom	Never

Other kinds of benchmarking

Openness in relationships between the client organisation and service providers, whether as part of a formal partnering arrangement or not, is essential to the successful operation of facilities management. The role of ICT in facilitating the efficient transfer of information cannot be underestimated in this respect. Information management is essential to achieve margins and therefore to create client satisfaction. As such, it is a major tool in the

strategic management of facilities. For this reason, research has been undertaken to identify the level of ICT use in support of facilities management.
The ICT use and performance of ten organisations, in relation to facilities
management, was charted against the industry norm and an international
organisation whose achievements were accepted as representing current
best practice. The selection of an acceptable example of best practice for
comparison is one of the most difficult aspects of benchmarking, and those
conducting the benchmarking exercise should look as widely as possible
to find an organisation suitable for valid comparison.

The research in this instance looked at the application of ICT in relation
to the following six areas of facilities management:

- Strategy, policy and procedures
- Strategic management
- Building and engineering services management
- Environmental management
- Domestic services
- Administration and service support.

Anonymity of the organisations was maintained in the published
results, although each participating organisation was shown how its own
performance related to those of others in the exercise. Descriptive information regarding current use of ICT and future plans was also volunteered
by participants and made available in the final report for general benefit.
Fig. 18.2 shows a typical chart generated from the study as used to provide
feedback to the participating organisations.

The findings show how the benchmarking exercise, despite having measured organisations against their competitors, can be of mutual benefit to all
participants without threatening commercial sensitivity or competitiveness.

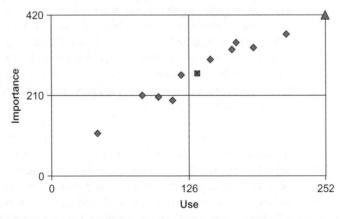

**Fig. 18.2   Comparing the performance of organisations within sector against
best-in-class out of sector. The graph shows the positions of benchmarked
organisations (use against importance) relative to best-in-class (top right) and the
sector average denoted by ⊠.**

Moreover, as the process is directed at technical and general managerial processes, commercially sensitive information is unlikely to be exposed.

Other methods of providing objective comparison of performance have been devised and are widely implemented. Their supporters claim considerable success and this is not in question. What is important is that the organisation understands its processes implicitly – in this context those of facilities management – and is able to apply tools that lead to answers consistent with its declared business strategy. For some organisations, benchmarking is able to provide a simple and direct solution, but for others more developed tools and techniques, such as *Six Sigma*, are deployed (Pande *et al.*, 2000). *Six Sigma* is used to help companies improve customer satisfaction, profitability and competitiveness through a focus on the customer by the disciplined use of facts, data and statistical analysis – the term itself refers to a statistically derived performance target. The whole approach is more demanding and more rigorous than that of the benchmarking methodology outlined above. In the right hands, *Six Sigma* can deliver benefits for the client organisation.

Case study – Diageo

Diageo plc is the world's leading premium drinks business with headquarters in the UK. Over the past five years the organisation has achieved strong growth in both turnover and profitability. It is highly regarded among financial institutions and has become the benchmark company for its sector.

This dramatic growth has been achieved through a combination of increased market share from its own range of brands – for example Guinness, Pimm's, Johnnie Walker, Smirnoff and Gordon's – and also the addition of new products through company acquisition. However, the consequence of this has been an unprecedented amount of change throughout the business with many challenging demands being placed on support functions.

The objective for each of Diageo's acquisitions has been to grow the revenue base of the products involved, through increased sales and clever marketing to expand the number of market segments for which a particular product has appeal. Significant growth has been achieved in turnover, which has dwarfed the corresponding increase in the cost of support functions. Consequently, these functions have escaped any significant attention.

The organisation is faced with major challenges in continuing to grow at the same rate, with market share proving harder to increase and the lack of attractive targets to acquire at a reasonable price. The focus more recently has been on targeting waste reduction and increasing efficiency and through these two elements to reduce its cost base.

Facilities management is gaining greater visibility and although not represented by a single function, the different regions within Europe are collaborating and sharing knowledge with greater frequency. Initiatives in the south-east of England in particular have created an outsourced management model which in turn has generated significant savings in the order of 20%. Even so, such savings must be sustainable and continued effort is required to drive out any inefficiency.

Diageo has recognised that significant differences still remain between the various geographical regions within Europe. This was highlighted through a benchmarking study, which compared both cost and quality of service provision. Large disparities exist between sites in terms of service levels and, ultimately, cost. The key to achieving cost-effectiveness is to ensure that the services offered are appropriate and fit for purpose. However, within the real estate portfolio, differences exist between the use of sites, ranging from breweries to distilleries to commercial offices. The challenge for Diageo is to obtain a degree of homogeneity, whilst recognising that the sites themselves will always have their differences.

After careful consideration, a unique approach was developed that would allow a degree of diversity whilst still applying a consistent approach to service levels. If the facilities management function could come up with a framework and achieve consistency, yet retain a degree of flexibility, Diageo was confident of further efficiency. The approach was to develop a set of guiding principles for services that could be agreed with the principal stakeholders. These principles would in effect be a set of rules by which the level of each service could be set. Local differences to these rules would be permissible, but had to be justified by the business case.

A steering group chaired by the Facilities Director for the south-east of England was set up with representation from Scotland and Ireland. The group received its mandate from the Board with further direction from a group of sponsors from within the human resources function to whom facilities management reported.

The steering group decided that whatever approach was taken it had to be inclusive. Diageo commissioned the services of a facilities management consultant to assist and considered how best to go about this challenge. The group, aided by the consultant, developed a process to review each service and then to pilot one of the simpler services. The process had four key elements:

- Rationale
- Cost drivers
- Comparators
- New service definition.

The rationale sought to challenge historical custom and practice by considering the service in the light of Diageo's core values. It sought to ask 'Why is the service provided or needed?', 'Who does it benefit?' and 'How does this service drive value for the business?' The link to Diageo's core values was important as custom and practice had allowed incremental rises in service levels with corresponding cost increases. Any change downwards would be difficult to implement and to get senior management 'buy-in' unless a disconnection with core values could be demonstrated.

Once the rationale was proven, it then became important to understand what the primary drivers of the service were. By gaining an understanding of these drivers, Diageo could analyse the service and thereby enable the later brokering of service levels. Examples of such drivers included, in the case of security, the extent and level of technology used, the number of guarding hours required, pay rates and adoption of *The Working Time Regulations*. Each service has unique drivers, as well as generic drivers applicable to the majority of services.

Understanding the cost base provided valuable information; however, a geographically dispersed portfolio meant that it was also necessary to understand the current situation site-by-site. The primary purpose here was to identify notable differences for further measurement. This provided an internal means of benchmarking which was then supplemented by an understanding of other organisations, ideally within Diageo's sector, but also out of sector where world-class organisations could be identified.

The last activity within the process was to consider the service in the context of a new facility. If this service were to be specified for the first time how would it be defined and what typically would be included? The steering group piloted this new approach for the provision of a health and fitness service. It proved workable and immediately identified the disparities from site-to-site and the level of service provided by others. The next step was to set up this initiative as a specific project. This was managed by the consultant with support from the steering group and ownership of the service by nominated facilities managers in each geographic region. The first workshop proved to be difficult to complete. Whilst the facilities managers were motivated to work through it and make significant effort, they found initially that the process was hard to grasp.

Further examples were developed and two subsequent workshops proved successful, with the output of a service standard framework endorsed by the project sponsors. Diageo has benefited from this project and is now in a position to continue this work reconciling the cost of service provision against 'fit for purpose' service levels.

Conclusions

There are many tools at the disposal of managers and organisations that are pursuing improvement. Each will have its proponents and detractors. Benchmarking is not a new invention and so has the benefit of being tried, tested and refined. Other methods that have been touted as the route to improved organisational performance are associated with it. Benchmarking should be taken on its own merits and for what it is – a relatively simple tool to apply so long as the user understands the process that is to be measured. There is no one form that benchmarking can take and it is neither exclusively quantitative nor qualitative; it can be both. Benchmarking has a place in providing management with a tool for continual improvement, especially when formal market testing is inappropriate. It provides a simple, but effective, means for measuring performance and cost, leading to a better understanding of best value. It can be applied easily and can produce immediate benefits as soon as the results are available. Several examples of successful benchmarking are now in the public domain and it is likely that more will appear in the future. With this in mind, it will pay most organisations to consider active participation in benchmarking clubs or associations, or even to mount their own benchmarking initiatives and exercises.

CHECKLIST

This checklist is intended to assist with the review and action planning process.

	Yes	No	Action required
1. Is the organisation aware of benchmarking as a tool for helping to effect improvement in a (business) process?	☐	☐	☐
2. Has the organisation evaluated or adopted other objective methods for assessing and comparing performance as an alternative to straightforward benchmarking?	☐	☐	☐
3. Does the organisation appreciate the importance of benchmarking as a means for measuring its effectiveness in achieving best value in its facilities management?	☐	☐	☐
4. Has the organisation made arrangements for the benchmarking of its facilities management performance in terms of the quality of services delivered?	☐	☐	☐
5. Are appropriate arrangements for measuring performance in place?	☐	☐	☐
6. Has the organisation considered cooperating with other organisations or joining or forming benchmarking clubs to help assess relative performance in key areas?	☐	☐	☐

19 Public–Private Partnerships

Key issues

The following issues are covered in this chapter.

- A public–private partnership (PPP) is an arrangement that brings together a public sector need with the skill and expertise of private sector actors to deliver a solution.

- The Private Finance Initiative (PFI) is the UK government's mechanism for PPPs.

- The PFI represents an opportunity for public sector organisations to procure services, or the buildings and infrastructure to provide those services, whilst leaving the risks of asset and infrastructure ownership and maintenance to the private sector.

- Facilities management is an essential part of any major PPP/PFI project proposal and a key to its successful outcome – this may also apply to smaller schemes.

- Consideration can be given to incorporating facilities management for separate or additional sites within proposed capital schemes. This should, however, be subject to an initial feasibility study to determine potential efficiency gains.

- Although private investment arrangements continue the policy of out-sourcing facilities management services, the former can have wider implications.

- Best value considerations must apply at each stage – it is essential to demonstrate that best value is likely to be achieved and to define the means for measuring it.

- Properly defined output specifications are required so that it is clear what is to be provided.

- A common form of PPP/PFI project is that of a design, build, finance and operate (DBFO) scheme that is likely to extend for up to 30 years.

- Although there are many potential benefits, the relative newness of such projects means that their long-term implications may not yet be fully apparent.

Introduction

Public–private partnerships (PPPs) are not a recent phenomenon. They first appeared hundreds of years ago and many governments around the world have long established the practice of sharing the risks of major projects for public benefit with the private sector. This chapter considers how organisations can ensure that opportunities for private investment and partnership can be fully and effectively considered in plans to develop or improve the quality of their facilities. The Private Finance Initiative (PFI) launched back in 1992 is the main mechanism for this within the public sector in the UK. However, PFI principles also have application in projects within the private sector, as well as outside the UK, as a type of PPP. Important here is to stress that the PFI is a particular type of PPP – not the other way around. The aim of the chapter is to show the relationship between facilities management and private investment and partnership, specifically within the context of new capital schemes. Private finance arrangements offer a chance to challenge traditional practice, yet also have the potential for problems that must be recognised and properly addressed. When first introduced, the greatest interest in this kind of project was found amongst consultant architects, consultant engineers and construction companies, each seeing an opportunity to create work. A more developed understanding today recognises the pivotal role that facilities management and, therefore, service providers play. Ensuring that the design of the proposed facility – the creation of the asset upon which the proposed function will be performed – will not cause financial problems requires expertise of the kind that, possibly, service providers are best able to provide. Even so, caution is advised, as all PPP projects stretch out into the distance. 30 years can be a long time over which to sustain a loss instead of a profit.

Public–private partnerships (PPPs)

Interest in PPPs – the PFI in the UK – has been rising steadily over the past decade to the point where it has become a sector in its own right, supported by a market in secondary financing. This new market provides the means to refinance a project once the asset is in use, enabling the equity partners to trade their shareholding and exit cleanly. This is especially important for construction companies whose business planning horizons would not normally extend beyond a few years. PPP are concerned with the delivery of services, which in most cases happens over a long period, perhaps 20–30 years. The characteristics and extent of services are dependent upon the authority of the public sector body involved and how a given service fits into its business plan, i.e. core or non-core activities. Regardless of the object of the PPP, the public sector body is withdrawing from activities that formerly have been carried out within its own organisation. It has, therefore, a strong interest in ensuring satisfactory quality and performance in the outcome. The risks and responsibility for delivering and managing the product or system during operation are, to a large extent, transferred from the client organisation to a private sector actor. Thus, attention is turned from the perceived needs of the client to the provision of customer-related services. This creates a different situation for actors in the AEC sector to those traditionally experienced where, in the main, they have been largely content with short-term commitments, investments and returns.

The definition of a PPP – as broad as it is – together with the wide perception of partnerships has given rise to a large number of arrangements that could be legitimately termed PPPs. To make matters more confusing, the term PPP is also used in a narrower sense in attempts to describe the characteristics of specific projects. Thus, in order to provide a description of how PPP applies to the AEC sector, it is necessary to break down the term into more manageable categories.

A PPP is essentially a method for procuring capital projects, to enable enhanced service delivery, but where capital expenditure in the present is converted to an expenditure commitment in the future. An external company will usually design, build and operate the facility, by sponsoring a project and holding an equity stake in it. The financial interest that the sponsor holds in the project helps to ensure efficiency. In this sense, in particular, it is easy to see how the principles of a PPP are transferable to other types of organisation.

Several broad types of partnership can be differentiated. They are, however, general and there will be projects/arrangements that can overlap two or more categories. These categories of partnership are briefly presented below.

1. Public sector assets are sold to the private sector in the belief that private sector finance and management can increase the value of the asset and thereby give the taxpayer better value for money.
2. Shares in state-owned businesses are sold to the private sector, with the state retaining either a minority or majority stake of the business. This could be done with or without the use of legislation or regulations in order for the public sector to retain control of the business. The main objective of this kind of PPP is to improve the overall achievement of the business by bringing in private sector finance, managerial and marketing skills.
3. The public sector uses private finance and managerial and marketing skills so as to exploit the potential of public assets, both physical and intellectual, that cannot easily be sold or in which the state wishes to retain ownership.
4. Arrangements where the public sector contributes to the funding of private sector projects/establishments that are considered to be of public benefit, but which are not capable of fully funding themselves on the capital markets.
5. Arrangements where the public and private sectors under joint management combine their assets, finance and expertise in order to pursue common long-term goals and shared profit.

6.   The public sector contracts services, with defined outputs, from the private sector including the construction and maintenance of the required facilities and/or infrastructure.

The UK government's PFI includes projects that lie within all six categories presented above and accordingly some projects will not feature estate or construction work.

Procurement and contractual approach

In order to describe the particular project's contractual arrangement, terms other than PPP are used. Generally, the various kinds of contract are given three or four letter abbreviations, most of which are not so easily differentiated. Indeed, some of them are confusingly alike. It is more important, therefore, to understand the main characteristics of projects than it is to be able to match a specific project directly to a contract abbreviation. Nonetheless, most of them are presented below.

- BOOT – Build, Own, Operate and Transfer
- BOR – Build, Operate and Renewal of Concession
- BOT – Build, Operate and Transfer
- BRT – Build, Rent and Transfer
- BTO – Build, Transfer and Operate
- DBFO – Design, Build, Finance and Operate
- DCMF – Design, Construct, Manage and Finance
- MOT – Modernise, Operate and Transfer
- MOOT – Modernise, Own, Operate and Transfer
- ROT – Rehabilitate, Own and Transfer

A short description is given below for the two most common: BOT and DBFO.

- BOT – Build, Operate and Transfer is by far the most widespread and it is not uncommon for literature to use the term to represent all types of PPP project. BOT and BOOT are often used interchangeably, although there is a marked difference between them. These types of project are characterised by the major part of the payment for the private sector coming directly from customers in the form of user fees of one kind or another.
- DBFO – Design, Build, Finance and Operate, and to a certain extent DCMF, are the most common for projects where private sector revenues come exclusively, or to a large extent, from a public sector body.

Generic PPP project set-up

A PPP brings together a large number of stakeholders, each with its own agenda, priorities and goals. This plethora of overlapping – and potentially

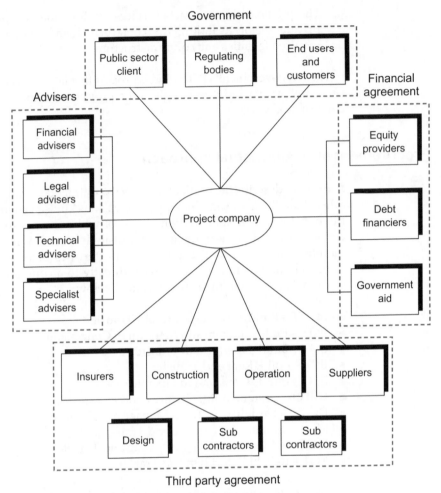

Fig. 19.1   Generic PPP project set-up (Leiringer, 2003).

conflicting – interests ensures that any PPP will abound with contracts and agreements. The exact nature of these and their interrelationships are, of course, specific to the project in hand, but there are some common features. A generic project set-up is presented in Fig. 19.1. The rest of this section deals with the main actors and their roles in a generic PPP project as presented by Leiringer (2003).

The public sector client

It is a government's responsibility to provide essential services for society. To help in this task, the government typically sets up a wide range of institutions. The exact division and legislative empowerment of these public sector bodies vary from country to country. The following could, however, be considered generic:

- Governmental departments
- Governmental agencies
- Local authorities
- Municipalities
- County councils
- Single purpose agencies.

One of these actors will become the public sector client in the project. It is this body that contracts with the private sector for the delivery of a service over a specified period and it is not uncommon that the public sector client creates a client's representative organisation whose primary task is to monitor the project.

Regulating bodies

Depending on the nature of the service that is contracted, the project will – apart from the particular sponsoring public sector client – also come under the jurisdiction of one or several other public sector bodies. These could be anything from governmental departments or agencies to local authorities or single purpose agencies. The size and statutory powers of the public sector bodies involved that claim regulatory jurisdiction vary widely. Each has its own standards and regulations and, in certain cases, the relationships between the bodies are quite complex.

Customers/end-users

There would be no need for – and, in fact, no interest in – a project if there were no demand for the service that it could provide. Of importance here is the relationship between use of, and payment for, the service. A distinction is made between paying customers and indirectly paying users. If users pay for the service they are called customers. If the service is paid for by other means, such as through taxes, the users are deemed end-users of the service.

The project company

The company – known as the concessionaire – is the legal entity that tenders for, develops and supplies the required service(s). The precise form of this entity will depend on the circumstances at hand, taking into account fiscal, accounting and legal issues as well as the physical nature of the required facility and service. In some cases, the project company could be an existing company that takes on the project by itself – on the balance sheet – or a subsidiary of a larger company established to undertake PPP projects. However, it is far more usual that it takes the form of a special purpose vehicle (SPV), established either in the form of a consortium or as a joint venture for undertaking the project. Arrangements exist to make it possible for companies of different sizes, financial strength and objectives to participate in the SPV. Participation is grounded in the added value of the skills that a company brings to the consortium/joint venture and the members are dependent on the nature, size, scope and complexity of the project. Projects that involve more than a modest amount of construction will most commonly have a construction company as a shareholder, with the same being true for the operational phase and for the operators.

Equity providers

The equity providers in a project own that project. Equity is the lowest ranking form of capital in the project and the claims of the equity investors are therefore subordinate to those of the project's debt financiers. Hence, the equity providers bear the greatest risk of loss if the project is unsuccessful. This risk is balanced by a greater return than that of the debt lenders – they stand to gain the most if the project performs better than expected. The principal equity investors are the members of the project company, although several other parties might contribute. Equity providers can be divided into three groups:

1. Long-term providers – the organisations responsible for construction and operation, major suppliers of technology and some specialist investment funds and banks.
2. Retail or institutional providers – these tend to be institutions such as superannuation funds, life insurance companies and fund managers without controlling interests in the business.
3. Quasi-equity providers – these are mainly risk capital funds and institutional investors that do not have a controlling stake in the project company.

Debt financiers

Debt finance is, as mentioned above, senior to equity. It also distinguishes itself from equity in the sense that it is secured against the assets of the project. Accordingly, the return expected by the debt financiers is lower than that of the equity providers. The debt financiers have no controlling stake in the project company, but they have considerable leverage in issues concerning project execution. A project usually has a mixture of short and long-term loans. Once the project is operating, a syndicate of commercial banks generally provides the long-term debt. The short-term loans – they are sometimes referred to as bridging loans – are used to finance the construction phase. Several different kinds of financial institutions are capable of providing short-term finance.

Bonds

There is also the possibility of obtaining finance by raising bonds. Bond-holders generally do not have any interaction with the project company after the bond has been issued and do not exercise any control over the execution of the project.

Government aid

Government aid is by no means normal in PPP projects and it can take a wide variety of forms. Usually though, it consists of the provision of equity or additional debt financing and various forms of guarantees. In addition to host governments, institutions like the World Bank, European Investment Bank (EIB), European Bank for Reconstruction and Development (EBRD) and various development finance institutions provide aid.

Design and construction contractors

The construction contractor will normally be signed to design and build the asset. Depending on the size and scope of the project it could either be a single construction company that takes on the work by itself – with or without the additional hiring of designers – or a consortium of design and construction companies. Either way it is usual that responsibilities are passed on to a variety of subcontractors. It is common that the main contractor has a stake in the project company.

Operators

If the contracted service includes the operation of the asset then this would normally be contracted out to a specialist operator. In these cases, it is usual that the operator would be part of the project company. Operation is normally divided into soft and hard services and it is not unusual that the operator has one or more subcontractors. In the case that the service provided is of a maintenance character, it would be likely that the construction contractor, or else a major, dedicated service provider, takes on the role of the operator.

Suppliers

The role of supplier is very much dependent on the required service and the characteristics of the built asset. Strategic suppliers and suppliers of major components and/or large technology owners usually take a part in the project company.

Insurers

Insurance is sought to cover as many commercial risks as possible. It is often the case that all or a significant part of the insurance cover is reinsured with other insurers. These can be either local/domestic or international and a mix of them is usually preferred.

Legal advisers

Due to the complex nature of the projects and the large number of agreements that have to be agreed and later interpreted, the need for legal advice is crucial. Both public and private sector parties use specialist legal advisers.

Financial advisers

Financial advisers are retained by the public sector client as well as by the project company and will also have expertise in risk management.

Technical advisers

Technical advisers are used by the public sector client as well as by the project company, irrespective of whether or not the construction contractor has a stake in the company. The financiers in the project may also retain technical advisers in order to oversee the design and any changes during the project life.

Specialist advisers

The competences of specialist advisers vary from project to project and could include, for example, transportation engineers, behavioural scientists and clinicians.

Main types of service provided

In PPP projects one of the most significant problems will be caused by the different interfaces between the public and private sector actors. These interfaces will vary according to the authority vested in the public sector actor and this will, in turn, influence the nature of the contracted service. Four broad groups of PPP projects, each with rather distinct operating characteristics can be identified, where the operator provides:

1. A facility for a single client, most probably a public sector body
2. Services directly to the customers (public or private)
3. Several different, but interrelated, services to a single client
4. Several different, interrelated services to a variety of customers.

Payment mechanisms

The choice of payment mechanism is a key factor that will inevitably affect the project set-up. There are three typical approaches in which the private sector collects revenues depending on the service that is provided and who is considered to be the customer. Whichever form is used, its influence on the management of the project is highly significant.

- Revenue streams are collected from customers, e.g. users of a sports centre or toll road.
- Revenues are collected from the client organisation, e.g. a road with shadow tolls.
- Revenue is provided by a combination of the above.

There is a marked difference between a toll road where all revenue is collected from the end-users and a prison, where the revenue could be collected according to the availability of cells and the quality of service provided.

Facilities management and private sector participation

In terms of new capital schemes, a PPP (or PFI) project offers public sector bodies the opportunity to procure the design, construction, finance and operation of their new facilities from one provider and to transfer the attendant risks. This enables the client organisation to concentrate on its core activities. Facilities are, therefore, designed with proper consideration for their management by a party with a vested interest in the long-term success of the project.

In any new capital proposal, especially those involving private sector investment or partnership, due consideration must be given at the feasibility stage to the extent of potential facilities management provision. Facilities management will need to be provided on a best value basis and the means for demonstrating this has to be included in any study.

In all cases, it will be necessary to assess whether or not facilities management is appropriate for inclusion and, if so, in what ways. This can cover those situations in which the bundling of services for other buildings or sites might make the proposal more attractive because of economies of scale. Equally, it may be that facilities management is not suitable for inclusion and so should be left out, perhaps because of implications for the organisation's overall facilities management provision. Additionally, the organisation may consider other variations to service provision, such as partial facilities management involving selected services only. Whatever is decided, the organisation will need to demonstrate that it has considered the relevance of facilities management to a proposed new capital scheme and the options available for its delivery. A sound articulation of the case for and against, as appropriate, should be provided.

The organisation will need to consider the mode by which facilities management should be supplied. This refers to the choice between in-house service provision and outsourcing. The same assessment criteria as apply routinely to determining which of these paths to follow also apply to assessing capital scheme proposals for private sector investment and partnership. It is vital to assess risk transfer, including the risks of in-house service provision.

This kind of private investment arrangement continues the policy of outsourcing support services for facilities management, although it differs from outsourcing in that the private sector is involved as a provider of a capital asset as well as a provider of services. It also has accounting implications that can be beneficial to the client organisation.

Output specifications

Earlier chapters – notably Chapters 9 and 14 – have proposed procedures for specifying service requirements. In any capital scheme proposal likely to include private sector investors or developers, it is essential to advance consideration of facilities management to the point where all of the issues and likely actions have been examined. The thoroughness that should apply to specifying service requirements without direct private sector participation should apply to the same extent to those schemes with it. The organisation may find this easiest to achieve when contemplating an entirely new scheme unencumbered by past arrangements.

Relevance and benefits of private investment and partnership

The benefits of private investment and partnership to facilities management within the public sector can be summarised as follows:

- All types of organisation have the potential to simplify their procurement of capital schemes and subsequent operations.
- The client organisation can transfer responsibility and risk to a single provider and concentrate on its core business.
- Consideration of the operation of new facilities can be built in at the design stage – the input of reliable life-cycle cost data into the design is at the heart of successful arrangements.
- A long-term focus can be built into the project, thus avoiding the dangers and costs of short-term, reactive facilities management.
- Since the operational period will far exceed the design and construction periods, facilities management receives higher priority as its importance to the successful and efficient operation of the organisation's core business is recognised.
- The focus on the overall package can ensure integration between design, construction, finance and operation, avoiding the pitfalls of other, more fragmented approaches to the procurement and maintenance of new capital schemes.

Partners need to work towards common goals within a long-term relationship of openness, trust and compatibility. Private investment and partnership can add real value to the organisation's core business if the provider:

- Is focused on the long-term needs of the customer.
- Can translate those needs into an efficient design for the facility with maximum flexibility for future change.
- Specifies a solution that optimises the life-cycle costs of both the facility and the support services, thereby minimising cost.
- Works in partnership with the customer to deliver services aligned to (changing) needs.
- Enables the client organisation to maximise its efficiency and effectiveness, thereby adding real value rather than simply cutting costs.
- Offers a solution as part of a transaction that covers risks at minimum cost and is financed at the least rate of interest to provide both best value and a more affordable outcome.

Risk and private investment

The crucial criteria for assessing direct private sector involvement in capital scheme proposals are best value and risk transfer. The opportunity to transfer all risks inherent in the design, construction and operation of a new facility may be very tempting. However, a balance has to be struck between the two so that the client organisation should not be seeking the maximum risk transfer, but the most appropriate in securing best value. Risk transfer will always attract a cost. The principle of optimal risk transfer has an impact on value assessment, as any change in risk apportionment will have an impact on the total cost of the project and therefore on value achieved. In this instance, of course, best value is to be looked for in the full duration of private sector involvement, which, as we have seen, could be up to 30 years. Value in the context of facilities management services is therefore linked with the wider concern for best value in the total project. However, as the period of operation will far exceed that of design or construction, facilities management becomes a focus for best value and risk issues.

The contractual documentation required for private finance projects will deter or rule out those contractors who do not have a balance sheet able to cope with the contractual liabilities involved in creating the asset and operating a service on the back of it. While this is useful in the selection of suitable partners, the chosen contractor will look for profit margins that are commensurate with the risk. In turn, the risk issues that must be addressed in advance increase the complexity of the tendering process.

Problems with private investment and partnership

The potential benefits of private investment arrangements inevitably bring associated problems, including the following:

- The arrangements for private investment remain complex and therefore difficult to comprehend fully, as well as expensive to implement.
- The relative novelty of these schemes means that they suffer from the legal and financial complexities associated with any new type of transaction.
- The accounting complexities need to be resolved into a simpler set of principles – it is vital to make well-advised judgements concerning which party carries the asset in each case, as wrong decisions can prove costly and embarrassing.
- Few contractors are substantial enough or financially prepared to accept the risks; consequently, there may not be sufficient choice of contractors to ensure true competition and interested companies may enjoy premium pricing.
- Some contractors have limited their long-term risk exposure to notional liability for future defects – focus must therefore be centred on the long-term service issues rather than on the short-term construction project.
- The attractions of risk transfer may discourage its careful consideration on the twin bases of affordability and best value.
- Users may be especially intolerant of any deterioration in service and performance where it is known that the facilities have been organised with their long-term maintenance and operation in mind.

Conclusions

Public–private partnerships (PPPs) have become commonplace in many countries, including the UK where its particular enactment is the PFI. A new sector engaging in PPPs has emerged and is providing rewarding opportunities for construction companies and facilities management service providers. Private sector participation in one form or another is likely to be increasingly important for the financing, provision and management of capital scheme proposals within public sector bodies. It also has potential benefits for the private sector. Facilities management is a key element in all DBFO proposals, of which those schemes under the UK PFI are typical. Client organisations are free to consider many options, but they must always demonstrate rigour, especially in the areas of risk transfer and best value. It will also be important to ensure that appropriate priority is assigned between capital procurement, financing and facilities management aspects of project proposals. Ensuring that services can be maintained over the long term requires much 'up front' thinking and planning. This has had one unexpected benefit – it has forced project design and construction teams to confront life-cycle costs at the design stage. In this way, it has ensured that facilities management becomes a key input during early design as a strategy for delivering customer satisfaction and best value.

CHECKLIST

This checklist is intended to assist with the review and action planning process.

	Yes	No	Action required
1. Is the organisation aware of the relevance and benefits of public–private partnerships to its own business, irrespective of whether it is a public or private sector body?	☐	☐	☐
2. Where relevant, is the organisation aware of the nature of PPP/PFI projects in terms of project set-up, actors involved and mechanisms in regard to the handling of risk and finance?	☐	☐	☐
3. Where relevant, is the organisation aware of the options for pricing the service created by the asset and how this will generate a return on the investment for the term of the concession?	☐	☐	☐
4. Where relevant to UK organisations, have the requirements of the PFI been met in terms of considering facilities management provision?	☐	☐	☐
5. Have the risks affecting partnership projects been identified and assessed?	☐	☐	☐
6. Are the organisation's facilities management requirements properly reflected in the output specifications for partnership schemes?	☐	☐	☐
7. Is the organisation aware of the balance between best value and risk transfer in assessing partnership proposals and the facilities management elements contained therein?	☐	☐	☐

20 Education, Training and Professional Development

Key issues

The following issues are covered in this chapter.

- Facilities management has emerged as the fastest growing profession within the breadth of the AEC sector.

- Core competence in facilities management covers, amongst other things, real estate management, financial management, organisational management, innovation and change management, and human resources management.

- The necessity of the ICF should be a major factor in the drive to have personnel who are trained to act as competent client representatives, irrespective of whether or not services are outsourced.

- The organisation must be committed to the training and development of its workforce, especially, in this context, its facilities managers.

- The organisation should adopt recruitment policies that recognise the specialisation of facilities management, and seek individuals who have undergone appropriate education and training and who are prepared to undergo continuing professional development (CPD).

- Education and training in facilities management is available in the university sector, up to the level of Master of Science, with a larger number of institutions supporting research.

Introduction

The last decade has seen enormous advances in the facilities management profession in the UK and many other countries – except the USA, perhaps, where it has had a longer presence. Even so, it cannot yet be described as a fully established discipline in the way that architecture, civil engineering and surveying can. However, the rate at which the discipline and the sector have developed – and continue to develop – suggests that its status will continue to rise, bringing it to the point where it is on a virtual par with these other professions. The aim of this chapter is not to map the history of facilities management or the professional discipline that has emerged, but to discuss the educational, training and development framework and the needs of aspiring professionals and technicians seeking a career in the field. Since the subject of facilities management has come late to the broader real estate, architecture, engineering and construction curricula it may lack general agreement on its educational base and the professional training that should accompany or follow it. Nonetheless, facilities management has become recognised as a subject and discipline in its own right and one that can now be studied to postgraduate level in many universities around the world. From our perspective as authors – one an academic researcher, the other a practitioner – we have tried to present an interpretation that is informative and purposeful, without attempting to steer the reader in a particular direction. As the various professional institutions evolve their approach to facilities management for the benefit of their membership, institutions dedicated to the discipline strive for their own recognition at the highest level. As authors, our approach is, we trust, one of objectivity and impartiality. In this connection, we freely discuss the needs and opportunities for education, training and professional development in facilities management, without trying to fit them into any institutional framework.

Backgrounds of facilities managers

Many of today's facilities managers are not graduates from schools or departments of facilities management. Instead, they are likely to have a real estate or construction-related discipline and career behind them. Architects, civil engineers, building services engineers, surveyors, builders and accountants have become today's facilities managers. For many, facilities management might have been seen as a new opportunity or, simply, a necessary role to perform in a rapidly changing world. Consequently, they may not have the background or experience for the job. That is not to say they are not performing well. Moreover, it does not follow that those from real estate architecture, engineering or construction backgrounds are better equipped to undertake the work of a facilities manager. In fact, research has suggested that the three main attributes sought by employers of facilities managers are integrity, organisational skills and communication skills. Successful facilities managers are those who are able to combine knowledge and skill in estates-related matters with an understanding of organisations, people and processes. A good architect does not necessarily make a good facilities manager; understanding how a building works is not the same as ensuring that it is safe, secure and enjoyable for customers and/or end-users.

Facilities management is not just about looking after buildings. As the definition in Chapter 1 implies, it is the creation of an environment to support the primary function of the organisation. Knowing how people within an organisation make use of a building – moreover, how those people can perform at their best – is the key to understanding facilities management.

For these reasons alone, it is possible to justify the need for specialised education and training in facilities management.

The organisation needs to be an informed client – again, see Chapter 1. As such, the ICF should be a major factor in the drive to have personnel who are trained to act as competent client representatives, irrespective of whether or not services are outsourced. Where organisations find expertise lacking they should adopt recruitment policies that recognise the specialisation of facilities management and then seek individuals who have undergone the appropriate education and training.

Growth of a professional discipline

For those who are engaged in facilities management, it will probably come as no surprise that it is the fastest growing professional discipline within the breadth of the AEC sector. The last decade has, in particular, witnessed a breakthrough both in numbers of qualified persons and in an acceptance by clients, customers and other interests of facilities management as a profession demanding a separate identity and a clear recognition of the competence offered by both professionals and technicians.

Inevitably for a discipline that has grown out of the ranks of, *inter alia,* building services engineering, there is a strong belief in the need for a solid grounding in building services engineering, real estate (or property) management and/or contract management. These basic building blocks of the discipline cannot be denied, but today they are accompanied by several other subject areas that give both breadth and depth to facilities management. Taken together, they constitute the original core competences of facilities management.

Core competence in facilities management

Setting aside the historical background to the development of the discipline for one moment and, therefore, the particular competences that have been drawn in over the years, we can see that facilities management draws on a body of knowledge that spans science, engineering, the humanities and social science. Architecture, engineering, construction, technology, management, law and economics are the fields in which its core competence was founded. Yet facilities managers need to be able to take a physiological view of buildings – rather than a purely anatomical view – and this means a greater familiarity with softer issues than those of a technical, engineering nature. In practice, this means that facilities managers have to understand how buildings and other constructed facilities behave and function as environments to support people in their work (and in their homes). A fundamental characteristic of the environment is change, and so one of the main competences that facilities managers should have is an ability to manage change.

Other competences include organisational management, financial management and customer service. It is the interaction of these that establishes facilities management as a unique discipline. Traditionally, it may have been considered that a good education and training in one of the estates-related disciplines was enough, but those educated in one of those specialisations may well lack appreciation of organisational behaviour and human resources management, and how innovation and change can be managed effectively. Core competence in facilities management therefore covers:

- Real estate management – building performance, environmental services and workplace design.
- Financial management – accounting, finance, purchasing and supply, and legal aspects.
- Organisational management – organisational structure, behaviour, processes and systems.
- Innovation and change management – technology, ICT and information management.
- Human resources management – motivation, leadership, employment law, health and safety.

Studying facilities management

Many organisations and universities see facilities management as a serious subject for undergraduate and postgraduate study. Even so, there are comparatively few degree courses worldwide, although that position is changing. Providing a basis for the study of facilities management in a way that is both rigorous and relevant to the needs of business and society at large really does require the support of universities, with practitioners making it clear that they value a university education. Of course, not all study is aimed at an initial qualification, no matter how high in academic terms it is placed. In the case of facilities management, there is a need to offer and encourage more open access for those who are intent on studying, but for whom formal entry qualifications do not exist.

Many universities and colleges recognise the need to provide in-service education for those already working full time in a facilities management capacity. The opportunity to undertake a degree programme on a part-time basis avoids the piecemeal approach of short courses that, collectively, can lack a coherent conceptual framework. Whether studying part time or full time, undertaking a structured programme of specialist study also allows facilities managers to share and compare experiences with fellow students to the benefit of all participants. Universities are also active in research and consultancy in various aspects of facilities management, and these activities feed back into the degree programmes and courses offered. This ensures that universities are abreast of the latest developments in what is a new and continually developing discipline. It is also possible to pursue doctoral research in a large number of universities, even though there may not be any taught postgraduate courses in the same university.

Some university courses offer facilities management as an optional module or specialisation within broader undergraduate and postgraduate programmes. Whilst the number of single degree programmes might be limited at present, the continuing growth in this sector will ensure that facilities management's voice is not lost.

Facilities management training and personal development

Many organisations invest significantly in the training and development of their personnel. We can think of training as being concerned primarily with the acquisition of new skills and extending individual capability, or updating existing skills and reinforcing individual capability – emphasis here is on the short to medium term. Development on the other hand is focused more on instilling interpersonal and other human-centred abilities and tends to follow a longer-term path. Additionally, we might see training as imparting detailed know-how, whilst development is concerned with broader, cross-cutting concepts. From this description, it should be clear that the two go together – training on its own is not enough.

Training in the private sector typically covers such areas as:

- Facilities operations management – budgeting, purchasing, costing centres, internal charging, critical success factors and key performance indicators.
- Leading and motivating the facilities management team – human motivation theory and practice, and impact of organisational culture.
- Optimising space usage and disposing of surplus space.
- Managing change – coping with new legislation and the changing workplace.
- Workplace productivity.
- Technological innovation, ICT and systems.
- Benchmarking costs and performance.
- Service level agreements and their management.
- Managing heating, cooling, comfort and energy costs.
- Healthy buildings.
- Performance-based partnering services contracting.

Professional institutions have, to varying extents, recognised facilities management as an area into which some of their members have moved and in which opportunities for work and institutional membership exist. Architects, engineers, surveyors and builders have laid claim to facilities management, although none of these has a natural or automatic entitlement. A weakness would be if one were to believe that technical skills were all-important. The authors would contest that view, arguing that a broader base of skills is needed to cope with the many facets of facilities management today and into the future – see earlier comment.

In support of this view, we would point out that, over the years, IFMA has adapted its definition of facility management to reflect a broader range of interests and disciplines. Moreover, as a discipline that helps client organisations cope with change, it must involve people who understand softer issues. None of this is meant to imply that people with a good technical background cannot make good facilities managers, but it will require a mind that is able to adapt to new concepts and be capable of handling problems for which there may be no express formula or 'route map' to follow.

In Chapter 6, we examined a broad range of initiatives introduced by EastPoint, including its Training Sponsorship Scheme, which is aimed at developing the skills of its personnel. The scheme is used to motivate and encourage personnel to upgrade their skills continuously by attending accredited academic study on a part-time basis in their own time. Another of EastPoint's initiatives is an Open Learning Programme (OLP), which has been introduced company-wide to bring about a consistent approach to on-the-job training. Developing this in-house capability has led to significant, continuous cost savings and an upgrading in personnel training and on-the-job performance. Site-based property management training is now provided to all personnel using a technical manual and derivative open-learning workbooks – developed as part of EastPoint's mentoring approach to on-the-job training. The OLP covers a variety of subjects from customer service to personnel recruitment and selection.

Initially, 12 operational areas were identified and have been developed into workbook format for the OLP. Each workbook relates to sections in EastPoint's technical manual, from customer service and quality, through building security, to financial analysis. The workbooks are produced for easy reading, cover a variety of topics and contain simple exercises to reinforce the learning process. Each exercise is designed to make the participant stop and think about a particular point or concept that is explained in the text.

New recruits enter the ongoing programme as soon as they join and are provided with their first workbook. Written assessments – arranged by the human resources department – are undertaken before the next workbook is distributed. At each facility, a site-based professional is selected and appointed to be a coach or mentor and to assist frontline personnel in their self-study. There are also training sessions to reinforce learning for professional grades, enabling them to benefit through sharing practical work experience with peers. The satisfactory completion of the OLP is now included in the company's annual appraisal of employee performance.

Continuing professional development (CPD)

CPD (continuing professional development or continuous professional development) has become accepted as a necessary feature of holding a professional qualification, i.e. retaining membership of a professional institution. Our purpose in using this language to describe what should be welcomed by all as a perfectly reasonable way of keeping abreast of new developments is to draw attention to a common difficulty, even frustration, for professional institutions. Once qualified, many institutional members feel it unnecessary – for whatever reason – to give proper account of their ongoing learning and personal development. From a client perspective, it matters that the people it employs, directly or through agency, are competent in their work. Those who bother to be appraised of new developments should fear nothing, but this is, of course, a purist view. Most practitioners are busy people. Even so, this can be no excuse for failing to invest in an up-to-date understanding of their work and how it can be improved.

In their attempt to promote their members' moves into facilities management, professional institutions encourage and mount courses to support CPD in the discipline. In this respect, the institutions are fulfilling a valuable role in ensuring that those members who are working in the field, or who may wish to do so, are receiving up-to-date training. Although useful, these efforts cannot substitute for a comprehensive and rigorous education, training and development programme. There is a need for facilities managers to be kept up to date in many areas, especially in health and safety matters where legislation is moving quickly. It is important, therefore, for facilities managers and key colleagues to have access to continuing education and information regarding current best practice.

The future for facilities managers

The enhanced status of facilities management within organisations has raised the profile of the facilities manager, and it is set to rise yet further as the discipline develops and its full potential is realised in practical and financial terms. The particular combination of skills required in a facilities manager means that suitably qualified managers can command increasingly high salaries. Under arrangements such as PPP, including the UK's PFI – which seem likely to continue for a long time to come – the expertise of the facilities manager in the operational phase becomes invaluable. For this reason, well-qualified and experienced facilities managers may also become involved in private investment schemes in a consultancy capacity because of the detailed knowledge they possess about the services derived from facilities over their whole life cycle.

Conclusions

Facilities management has emerged from an indistinct past to become the fastest growing profession in the broader AEC sector. It owes its good fortune – if one can call it that – to the increasing awareness amongst real estate owners and customers of the value that well-managed facilities can bring to the core business. At the same time, the discipline of facilities management has evolved to embrace softer issues, but without ignoring the engineering and science base that remains a cornerstone of the profession. In a continuously changing world, facilities management is likely to evolve in line with changes in corporate real estate management, legislation affecting employment and the workplace, especially health and safety, and the management of change. Whatever happens, distinct core competences must be present within those managing an organisation's facilities at any given time. Where they are not, retraining or recruitment of appropriate resources will be necessary. Facilities managers can earn recognised qualifications through many universities, institutions and centres. Facilities managers and those closest to them will need to keep abreast of developments in all areas of their work and be able to prove that they have done so.

CHECKLIST

This checklist is intended to assist with the review and action planning process.

	Yes	No	Action required
1. Is the organisation aware of the competences that must be instilled in their facilities management personnel for them to operate successfully?	☐	☐	☐
2. Has the organisation implemented a programme of training and development for its personnel that matches its strategic (business) objectives?	☐	☐	☐
3. Have the core competences required for the successful implementation of a facilities management strategy been identified and are they available within the organisation?	☐	☐	☐
4. Are identified core competences brought into the organisation's criteria for the recruitment of facilities management personnel?	☐	☐	☐
5. Is the organisation aware of the extent of information that is freely available for supporting continuing professional development and has it satisfied itself as to the quality?	☐	☐	☐
6. Are there sufficient arrangements in place for continuing professional development, both for the organisation and its service providers?	☐	☐	☐

	Yes	No	Action required
7. Is the organisation examining trends in the marketplace, so that it can introduce the most appropriate training and development to meet the challenges likely to be created by those trends?	☐	☐	☐

21 Innovation, Research and Development

Key issues

The following issues are covered in this chapter.

- Innovation is not the same as change management, but has a close relationship to it, with each supporting the other to a certain extent.

- Innovation is not invention – innovation is when an act, such as the implementation of a new method, product or service begins to have a positive impact on the environment.

- Innovation is not research and development – the latter provides the vehicle or capacity for enabling innovation to take place by providing answers to questions and solutions to problems.

- Facilities management represents a combination of disciplines focused on improving the quality of life and work – these disciplines should include research and development.

- Areas in which innovation is needed are many, but in focus here are those relating to flexible corporate real estate, healthy living, sustainable communities and tele-care in the home.

- The research and development challenges are many, but not beyond means – most of the challenges have to do with conventional attitudes and business models, none of which are immune from questioning or change.

- Delivering just some of the outcomes promised under the research themes would make a dramatic difference to the quality of life and work.

Introduction

Facilities management is testament to the notion that change – particularly the introduction of new services and disciplines – can occur in business and that, consequently, there can be a positive impact upon the environment. Innovation is a process that has a close relationship with managing change – itself the subject of Chapter 5. Many novel ways of dealing with estates-related services have been covered in this book, some of which are outcomes from organisations that are strongly focused on innovation. This is not some academic pursuit, but should be the mission of organisations to ensure that they keep abreast of important changes external to themselves – on the one hand – and to create and then satisfy new markets on the other hand. Increasingly, innovation is occurring as the result of formal research and development (R&D), not a process of trial and error. Recognition of facilities management as combining a number of disciplines does not preclude those of research or business development. On the contrary, these are key competences that must exist within the organisation or to which it must have direct access externally. This chapter explores some current concepts, which – in their desire to improve the quality of life and work – will require changes to be made to how things are done now as well as introducing entirely new ways. This will take the form of four themes, each equating to a distinct aspect of quality and performance improvement.

Change and innovation

Innovation is not some nebulous activity performed in laboratories – it is a process for helping an organisation, its customers and the wider society to benefit from something that is new. All organisations must have, otherwise they must create, a culture of innovation. This is necessary if they are to cope with future changes and, perhaps more importantly, pre-empt those shifts that exert unwarranted pressure on their organisation. Change management is about helping organisations move from where they are today to where they want to be tomorrow – so too is innovation. The distinction is that change management can provide the context for enabling the results of research and development (R&D) to find their way into daily use. Whilst R&D is a key part of the innovation process, it is only one of three broad phases – see Fig. 21.1. The first of these identifies with business needs and the last with the commercial exploitation of the results of R&D. All too often, the efforts of R&D produce results that are not 'picked up' and so they fail to be implemented. Innovation, as a process, recognises that there must be a phase of implementation during which the results of R&D – in providing a solution to a problem identified earlier – can be successfully exploited. This usually means – if it is an in-house situation – that personnel will have to do things differently. Worse for them is that they may find their roles and responsibilities have to alter significantly. Making adjustments to the current organisation in order to exploit an innovation – be it a new product, working method or ICT system – will involve managing change – see Chapter 5.

Innovation and research and development

Research and development provides the vehicle for meeting challenges and for enabling innovation to take place; but it does not guarantee that

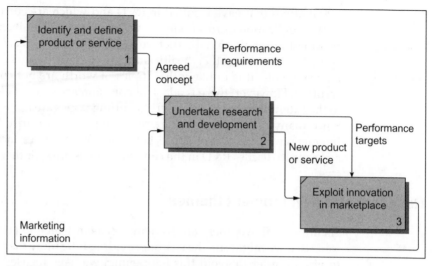

Fig. 21.1   Where R&D fits into the innovation process.

innovations will appear. The relationship between innovation, research and development and commercial exploitation is briefly discussed.

Innovation is not invention, although some things might be discovered or created by individuals in the normal course of their work; but neither is it serendipity. Innovation is when an act, such as the application of a new material or product, or the introduction of a new method, impacts positively on the environment. In other words, it is a process that enables something new or novel to be created. For innovation to succeed, it has to be formally recognised within the organisation. It is not a covert activity or moonlighting on company time. In most large corporations, innovation is the process by which they are able to retain and build market share, by bringing new products and services to the marketplace before their competitors. For this to happen there has to be an organisational structure and culture that encourages innovation across the board – everyone in the organisation is capable of something.

Innovation is not a department or unit with the organisation, although R&D personnel may need to be co-located. There is a distinction between making everyone in the organisation conscious of innovation and charging particular personnel with having to solve problems before any solution can be developed. No matter what money is spent on R&D it cannot be used as a reliable indicator of an organisation's propensity for innovation. Clearly, there is a relationship between the resources available to perform R&D and the chances of producing innovative products or services. In facilities management – taken in the broadest sense – there are considerable sums of money being spent on R&D. This is not intended as any kind of judgement on the efficacy of the R&D being performed or the innovation processes of which it forms a part; merely it is to observe that researchers are active in trying to find answers to questions and solutions to problems identified by their own or another organisation.

Initiatives that have resulted in R&D and which are current at the date of the publication of this book are wide-ranging. They include questions relating to organisational structure and culture, workplace productivity, security measures, other health and safety, and design of all-inclusive environments. It is unlikely that topics of worth are not currently under scrutiny. However, there is a lack of cohesion across the fields of research to the extent that, for example, cross-cutting issues are not well addressed. Since many of the problems are at the interfaces or arise because of an interaction or interdependence between two or more factors, it seems apposite to discuss R&D in the context of focus areas or themes.

Research and development themes

As implied above, there are so many areas in which to conduct relevant R&D that we might run the risk of providing little more than a catalogue of topics. In order to avoid this happening, we have focused on four areas where innovation is desperately needed and which must be supported by R&D if technological challenges and other barriers are to be overcome. The areas are concerned with living, working, health and community, and arise in the form they are presented because they are cross-cutting, multi-disciplinary and directed towards the needs of people.

These four areas translate into the themes of flexible corporate real estate, healthy living, sustainable communities and tele-care in the home, and are outlined below:

1. Flexible corporate real estate – providing highly serviced, re-configurable space that responds to the needs of different customers over short lifetimes.
2. Healthy buildings promoting future living – innovative solutions for delivering affordable, safe, adaptable homes.
3. Sustainable communities – workable sustainability concepts, real estate and infrastructure.
4. Tele-care in the home – utilising innovative housing and advanced ICT to deliver medical care.

Each of these themes is now discussed, including an indication of the problems to be solved by a coordinated R&D response.

Flexible corporate real estate

Businesses demand highly serviced workspaces and total flexibility. In response, industrialised building systems have been developed to provide the levels of engineering services and ICT that are needed in modern commercial buildings. Flexibility is generally claimed, but is often limited to changes in office layouts and workplace settings. Sometimes flexibility can amount to little more than demountable internal partitioning and system furniture. Building systems that can offer reconfigurable, serviced space, without adverse effects on the structure or services installations, would represent a breakthrough in space provision, reduce waste, raise profitability and avoid premature obsolescence. This implies designing building systems to provide a choice of multi-configurable components or products to shape not only the spaces of today, but also the spaces required tomorrow.

The manufacture of customised products from standardised components – the concept of mass customisation – is a common approach in many industries in order to create variants of products that satisfy different customers' needs. To be competitive and remain so, especially in inter-national markets, the real estate sector faces the challenge, amongst other things, of creating design concepts that take advantage of advanced manu-facturing methods and that are adaptable to local conditions. The discipline of modularisation helps to identify how product variance, component life cycles, maintenance and replacement costs and intervals can be used to create concepts for modular building systems that are adaptable to a variety of real estate needs. A more realistic account could thus be taken of the design life for various concepts and questions in regard to reuse and recovery. The research would also lead to significant transfer of techno-logy from manufacturing into the AEC sector.

Building obsolescence is a characteristic that can occur for many reasons, including technical limitations, premature failure and shifts in fashion. In their day, many buildings represented the (then) state-of-the-art, but as time passed and the demands placed on them changed so did their useful-ness and attraction. There is no guarantee that buildings and other facilities constructed today will not suffer a similar fate, unless they are deliberately designed with change in mind. But even that may not be enough. The increasing focus on whole-life costs – primarily the concern for energy use and, now, 'zero carbon' – brings into question some long-standing and basic assumptions. A design life of 50 or 60 years is rarely questioned, yet buildings designed 20 years ago may have reached technical (or another form of) obsolescence.

Present needs are not capable of extrapolation over decades. A plausible approach would be, therefore, to develop design concepts and real estate products that have deliberately defined lives more in step with the growth patterns of the businesses they are intended to support. This is likely to mean products that are easy to refurbish, reconfigure and relocate. This kind of flexibility most likely requires a redefinition of what it means to be a real estate owner, at least in the context outlined here. Ownership or rental will be too simplistic a decision when it is possible for organisations to offer total service packages that include all manner of support for the knowledge workers that are housed in their space.

The aim of the research required in this area is primarily to create manufactured modular products that provide a rapid response to the need for highly serviced, flexible space. The specific objectives would be to:

1. Define innovative service concepts that support business growth, whilst minimising risk exposure for businesses, especially SMEs.
2. Develop novel concepts for scaleable real estate solutions, based on high levels of service provision and reconfigurable space.
3. Develop know-how to support the rapid deployment (and redeployment) of robust, state-of-the-art ICT infrastructures anywhere.
4. Devise workplace strategies that support building occupants in their work, making them more efficient and content with their conditions.

Fig. 21.2 illustrates the relationship between these objectives.

Research should explore and define service concepts that adapt to, or better still anticipate, shifts in the marketplace and that provide low risk exposure for businesses, especially SMEs. The concept of networks of knowledge-based enterprises could be used to create access to human resources for selected industrial sectors – in terms of specialist skills and knowledge – so that both physical and virtual proximity are taken into consideration. The research should adopt an 'inside-out' strategy for defining end-products, relying heavily on the preferences of users to guide design decision-making. The nature of workplaces, as spaces that are conducive to productive knowledge-intensive activities, requires an indoor environment to match. Moreover, this must be capable of satisfying the various needs of all facility occupants. The kind of real estate that is likely to satisfy these needs is highly ICT-serviced, reconfigurable and relocatable, matching the pattern of growth for knowledge businesses.

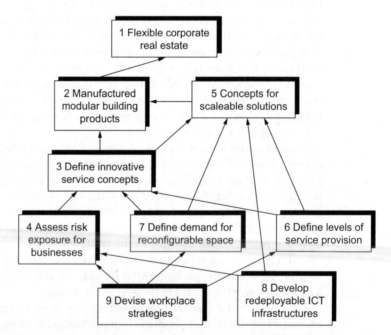

Fig. 21.2   Relationship between R&D objectives in achieving flexible corporate real estate.

The technical feasibility of these concepts will need to be fully explored including modularisation, methods of assembly, fixing and disassembly. The focus should be on how to produce real estate solutions in terms of designs that can be adapted according to product variance requirements. Additionally, they must allow for maintenance, replacement and upgrading to be done economically over the building life cycle. ICT infrastructures will need to be designed and tested for their efficacy in supporting worker and organisational mobility.

A substantial proportion of new buildings will never experience the full service life for which they were designed. This is not a UK or even European phenomenon, but a global problem. Delivering business support is predicated on the use of many resources of which real estate is both obvious and primary. As such, real estate must provide an effective platform for businesses to develop and grow, so that flexibility – in the sense of adaptability – becomes paramount. The scale of the problem of creating flexible real estate products is enormous and is only likely to be tackled by a major push on the part of leading real estate developers, owners, users and providers. Overturning opinions in the AEC sector that are fixated on permanent structures – albeit with scope for adaptation – which are built to last several lifetimes will not be easy. The task will, however, be made easier by demonstrable action on the part of major players in the sector, especially real estate developers and owners, and forward-looking manufacturers.

The areas of competence required for this research include, but are not restricted to:

- Workplace design
- Virtual design environments
- Modular building system concepts
- Modular building components
- Large-scale production of buildings
- Field-factory automation systems
- Control systems
- Mobile technology.

Healthy buildings promoting future living

Housing is the fundamental right of all people, yet gross distortions in housing conditions and in the balance between supply and demand exist across the world. This situation is not peculiar to poor regions. Affluent countries fail to provide decent and affordable housing for all and this is an impediment to the advancement of modern and just societies. There are many excuses for this failure, but fewer for effecting workable solutions. A central theme is that housing must not impair the health of its occupants, yet there is evidence of ill-health from recurrent problems such as moisture penetration, emission of harmful chemicals and, inexcusably, lack of basic amenities. In the future, houses must do more than provide shelter and protection – they must contribute to a minimum standard of living for everyone and eliminate conditions that give rise to building-related illness. Furthermore, housing must not be used to define strata in society. All households must have access to modern services, and ICT in particular, otherwise the digital divide will become a reality for many people.

Maintaining control over the condition and functioning of homes and alerting occupants – and others with a legitimate interest – to the hidden dangers is fundamental to this thinking. Providing the means for monitoring and controlling the condition of buildings, especially housing, over the life cycle would represent a major breakthrough in preventive maintenance and servicing of the built environment. Technology is already capable of providing many solutions, for example the introduction of embedded technology into factory produced components. However, the application outlined above needs careful examination, development and testing of prototypes and feedback from full-scale demonstrators. In this regard, the workability of any new approach and products is unlikely to be assured by scale models – people's health is too important an issue for this kind of treatment. The scope of this research thus includes mechanisms for monitoring and control throughout the life cycle, by the use of embedded technology. Access to information on the condition of one's home should be readily available and should be provided to authorised third parties. The use of embedded technology is not, however, confined to the occupancy phase. Tracking of components from manufacture through transportation and incorporation into the building can provide valuable histories for use in diagnostics and preventive measures, and has been discussed in Chapter 12. A term that could have been adopted here is that of 'smart homes'; however, this would not necessarily convey the importance of healthy homes and living.

Households change over time: they grow and contract and their tastes and requirements alter. Generally, homes stay much the same, apart from minor alteration and periodic redecoration. The life cycles of households and homes could not be more out of step. Housing may be regarded as having to serve future generations, but when it fails to serve the present something has to be fundamentally wrong. Adaptation to new services and upgrading of the building fabric, services installations and interior fittings are needed for many homes. Retrofitting is an option for existing buildings. However, replacement with new buildings may be the only option where decay and obsolescence are too far advanced. Clearly, the mistakes that have led to this situation must be avoided in new buildings. For this reason, an implicit assumption is that the manufacture of customised products from standardised components – the concept of mass customisation – will provide the platform for modularised house building on a major scale. This is needed if people are to have affordable, decent quality homes that are equipped for twenty-first century living. Moreover, homes must be capable of adaptation in a controlled and relatively easy way to provide different configurations of space to suit households at different stages in their development.

Often, people have to move to another home if the present does not satisfy needs. For many people, however, this may not be an option, either because they are unable to afford such a step or simply because they wish to remain within their community. In other words, housing provision must be driven by people's needs. The implications of this closer alignment of the needs of households with the provision of housing amount to a radical departure from traditional house building concepts in which largely conventional methods of construction can, quite literally, build in obsolescence. Furthermore, the speed with which new or replacement housing can be built is unlikely to be satisfied by a traditional construction response.

The primary aim is to produce sustainable, healthy homes that protect, support and stimulate occupants in their formal and informal activities. An implicit aim is to ensure that past mistakes in mass housing are not repeated. The specific objectives are to:

1. Define users' needs – housing developers, owner-occupiers and tenants – as a basis for developing housing concepts and support systems.
2. Develop housing solutions based on high levels of service provision, low energy consumption and reconfigurable, extendable space.
3. Develop natural or passive methods for heating, cooling and ventilating that can be used alongside active systems and all necessary control regimes.
4. Develop methodologies for the correct selection of building materials, products and systems and the detection of harmful materials and potential emissions.
5. Develop systems using state-of-the-art sensing and navigational technology to support the tracking and interrogation of products and components, including support from internet-based cyber-agents.

Fig. 21.3 illustrates the relationship between these objectives.

In spite of improved understanding of how to eliminate problems in buildings, especially multi-storey housing, building failures are all too prevalent. Much of the blame can be laid at the door of design teams in omitting to consider the broader implications of their work and in the lack of systematic feedback from projects past and present. The research should, therefore, re-engineer the process of design and production to include tools for the systematic gathering of performance data and for detecting potential failures. For example, the quality of the indoor environment can be assured through a variety of measures including, for example, methods for selecting the most appropriate components and for warning of the potential of harmful emissions.

Research should also examine the use of natural or passive methods for heating, cooling and ventilating the spaces within buildings so that the relationship between air quality and the energy used by more active methods can be better balanced. The efficient co-existence of these two approaches has to be determined so that effective monitoring and control strategies

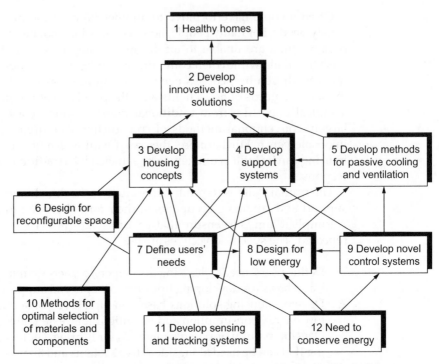

Fig. 21.3   Relationship between R&D objectives in achieving healthy buildings.

can be developed, ensuring that optimal comfort conditions are provided. The incorporation of embedded technology should be examined in the context of providing knowledge of how the building and its systems are functioning. The interconnectivity between different ICT infrastructures and standards for communication, for example Ethernet, BACnet, LonTalk and Bluetooth, are central to this approach and questions in regard to their deployment will need to be carefully examined. This has to operate in parallel with the ongoing development of industry standards for product information to provide data for embedded technology. The use of internet-based cyber-agents – 'search and do' agents – to assist in the coordination and control of the entire design, construction and facilities management process needs to be investigated further. The aim should be to provide real-time support to occupants and other stakeholders such as maintenance crews.

The quality of housing in most countries is highly variable, with a significant proportion of dwellings lacking one or more basic amenities. A radical overhaul of the housing supply market is required if a serious impact is to be made. Traditional methods of house building have to be complemented by large-scale manufactured housing programmes through which affordable, decent quality homes that reflect owners' and occupants' preferences are produced on a wide area basis. Mobilising the supply chain to support such an ambitious, but vitally important, initiative will necessitate the inclusion of major industrial companies and the collaboration of large municipal authorities. Inevitably, this means that major players are needed, at least for the production, delivery, installation and commissioning of these products.

The areas of competence required for this research include, but are not restricted to:

- Occupant needs in healthy buildings
- Home automation
- Building automation
- Embedded technology – sensors and communications
- Building technology and quality assurance
- Modular building system concepts
- Modular building components
- Control systems
- Logistics
- Supply chain management.

Sustainable communities

The concept of sustainable communities is not new. However, achievements are few and far between, with some questionable practices included in them. Advances in greener sources of energy, higher standards of building leading to substantial energy saving, and a perceivable shift in the attitude of people towards the environment bode well for a major push aimed at establishing workable sustainability concepts. Significant changes in demand and in the use of energy cannot, however, continue without further action or incentive. Demonstration of how entire communities can work successfully must be actively considered. It is not enough to show how novel concepts can work in a selection of specially commissioned 'show houses'. Zero carbon schemes designed for large settlements must be implemented and must be clearly seen to work economically and socially, as well as technically. Demonstration seems to be one of the few ways in which it is possible to change people's attitudes to energy use and other activities that impact negatively on the environment.

Buildings are responsible for such a major proportion of energy consumption in any nation that it is an obvious and legitimate target for action. How they are designed and constructed is an important subject and one that cannot escape a root and branch review based on workable sustainability concepts. Realisation of *Kyoto* and European Community targets for CO_2 reduction and decreased energy consumption are only likely to be achieved by a concerted effort to implement new standards in design, construction, heating, power and waste disposal. Furthermore, such effort has to bring together a package of measures that can be tested, proven and released to the wider community. A coordinated action is necessary to avoid sub-optimal solutions emerging, where gains in one area are negated by losses in another. Balancing community interests will require that many trade-offs have to be considered and adjustments made to ensure an overall optimal solution. In this way, it will be possible to demonstrate a holistic approach to sustain-ability that could be then replicated across a wide geographical area.

This thinking is aimed at the challenge of designing and building entire communities where the environment is subject to proactive management. In most cases, this is likely to be targeted at the regeneration of existing communities; typically, those areas where communities are living in poorly maintained conditions. Although action is needed across a broad front, the main focus is operational energy efficiency and, in particular, the use of materials having a low energy input requirement. The need is to reduce energy use to such a low level that by the addition of green sources of energy it is possible to provide a net gain to the wider community – the concept of zero carbon building. This requires new design philosophies driven by the need to consider combinations of design concepts that minimise initial environmental impact and the longer-term consumption of resources.

The approach emphasises the ecological and economic dimensions of sustainability and also takes into consideration social and cultural questions. The emphasis is upon communities and, as such, a holistic account has to be taken of the planning and realisation of mixed use settlements, where housing is just one part – albeit an important one. In the case of urban regeneration, the intention must be to revitalise decaying areas, by offering decent, affordable housing incorporating space for work, health care, community services and shopping. Benefits from such regeneration are likely to include lower crime, improved health and a better economic base for the area. At the other end of the scale, recreational interests can be shaped to provide novel solutions to the need for new and greener sources of energy. The entire ecosystem for settlements of up to 1000 people has to be considered. On this scale, it may be possible to balance resource demands with renewable supplies of energy and to prove the viability of the concept of sustainable communities in which life can be seen to be as normal and unrestricting as possible.

The primary aims are to bring about achievable actions in reducing the impact of real estate and construction on the environment and to create a net contribution of energy to the wider community. The specific objectives are to:

1. Identify concepts for environmentally friendly design and construc-tion that are achievable in practice, without detriment to owners' and occupiers' needs.
2. Define and develop knowledge management systems to support intelligent search for and analysis of appropriate know-how and tech-nology in regard to sustainability.
3. Develop tools and techniques for generating, evaluating and syn-thesising design solutions based on whole-life costs and minimal environmental impact.
4. Demonstrate the workability of the above concepts through full-scale buildings and infrastructure that minimise environmental consumption and that make a net contribution to the wider community's energy needs.

Fig. 21.4 illustrates the relationship between these objectives.

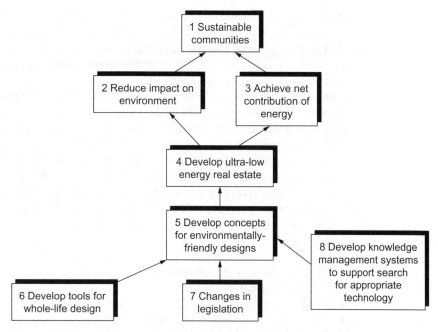

Fig. 21.4   Relationship between R&D objectives in achieving sustainable communities.

Legislative changes are pending and these should be examined to determine the timetable for conversion to practices that are consistent with the goal of zero carbon. Concepts for environmental design that minimise impact on the environment and the consumption of scarce resources in the construction of new buildings – as well as in the refurbishment of existing buildings – need to be investigated. This will require support from tools and techniques for selecting the most appropriate materials and components in terms of whole-life cost and 'carbon neutrality'. These will require further support from knowledge bases used to select components that carry official labelling, certifying their compliance with environmental codes, and offering advice on relevant financial or other incentives, for example tax breaks or rebates, for exceeding minimum code requirements.

Research is also needed to examine successful examples of combined heat and power, and district heating, concepts that have, for instance, stood the test of time in many towns and cities in Scandinavia. A further dimension that affects existing communities will be to devise strategies that strive to keep people in their homes until such time as they can be moved directly into new accommodation adjacent to their existing location. This approach will avoid breaking up the very communities that one is trying to retain.

Measures to advance sustainability concepts and to introduce them into the community cannot be expected to succeed on the back of piecemeal initiatives that address parts of a wider problem. The idea that one might bring about sustainable communities through a succession of minor measures that provide incentives to individual homeowners and occupiers is unrealistic. Wholesale change is required and, therefore, this can only be done on a scale that has the opportunity directly to influence entire communities. Another aspect is that of involving all the necessary expertise and other ingredients that are needed to turn a working concept into a real community. This can only be done on the scale of a major project in which demonstration on an equally large scale can be performed. Whilst there is little doubt that specific examples of novel technologies and approaches are scaleable, there is both a credibility and integration gap to fill. The project should aim for a full-scale community in order to demonstrate working concepts so that replication can take place. True breakthroughs in establishing lasting actions are only likely to occur if the scale is real and convincing for ordinary people, as much as it is for other stakeholders.

The areas of competence required for this research include, but are not restricted to:

- Building design for zero carbon
- Engineering infrastructure
- Timber technology
- Modular building system concepts
- Fuel cell technology
- Photovoltaic technology
- Energy sources and management
- Energy systems infrastructure.

Tele-care in the home

People are affected by their surroundings and, especially, by the condition of their homes. When people are healthy, a less than ideal setting may amount to little more than irritation; but when people are elderly and/or in poor health, conditions in the home can have a significant impact. Poor building conditions lead to poor health; conversely, good conditions can promote good health. The starting point for tele-care is a healthy building into which can be introduced medical and ancillary equipment to allow people to be treated and cared for in their own homes. There are sound economic as well as medical arguments for treating people in their own homes. However, this cannot take place without serious investment in both housing to suit and technology to enable medical care to be correctly received. Inevitably, this will mean that new buildings will have to be produced with such features and then maintained properly.

Retrofitting of the existing housing stock is also possible, but success is more likely when homes have been designed to take these features into account. Since an individual's needs are likely to be different to any other, a strategy for delivering technologically enhanced real estate is needed. The adaptation of homes to accept a range of support functions and care regimes will call for a rethink of how dwellings can be equipped or re-equipped to deal effectively with these challenges. One concern, amongst others, will be to minimise the impact upon the occupant/patient arising from changes to the original layout, functionality and appearance of the home. Furthermore, changes will need to be reversible if it is subsequently shown that an alternative arrangement is better suited.

The design of all-inclusive buildings and other facilities is a developing field, as opposed to an exact science in which all parameters are known. In addition to the provision of medical support, there is likely to be the need for homes that are responsive and which, as underscored above, do not adversely affect health. Many of the arguments and recommended solutions advanced for affordable, healthy homes would apply here, particularly in the context of enabling technology against the background of mass customised products that are economical, defect free and of a decent quality.

Homes equipped with ICT and medical apparatus could provide care, monitoring and education to patients who would otherwise have to be admitted to hospitals or other care facilities. Medical practitioners would be able to maintain continual contact with patients, enabling them to be treated in their own home and avoiding the trauma and expense of hospitalisation. The problem is one of designing and delivering both a home and a care environment – through the provision of modern, highly serviced, ICT-enabled housing – that can accommodate the equipment required for home telemedicine. Given the right kind of setting and conditions, there is no reason why medical equipment that was previously found in health care centres and hospitals could not be adequately installed, protected and maintained in a person's home.

The development of mobile technology provides an important element in the provision of tele-care services, especially since mobility in the home is likely to be a key issue and one where the occupant/patient might face restrictions on movement. Another aspect of concern is coping with an ageing population and one where the proportion of older people will become increasingly significant in the coming years. The approach advocated offers a realistic alternative to moving people from their homes to health care centres and hospitals and then back again, and repeating the cycle many times over. The economic and social arguments are powerful, and there is sufficient technology to ensure this can be achieved. However, the latter has to be placed within a process that is purposely designed for tele-care purposes. It is not enough to graft it on to existing practices for procuring buildings that will house the elderly and/or people in poor health.

The primary aim of this project is to develop a range of innovative housing products that can provide a secure and safe environment into which tele-care services can be introduced. The specific objectives are to:

1. Define users' needs (i.e. housing developers, owner-occupiers, tenants and medical practitioners) as a basis for developing inclusive environments and support systems.

2.   Develop housing solutions, based on high levels of service provision, low energy consumption and reconfigurable, adaptable space.
3.   Specify the characteristics of the indoor environment in terms of function, amenities, climate and support for medical and ancillary equipment.
4.   Create branded products that are acceptable to national health departments and the medical professions and demonstrate this to all stakeholders, not least the elderly and infirm.

Fig. 21.5 illustrates the relationship between these objectives.

The research necessitates extensive investigation of the means for delivering medical care in the home. It is not enough to scale down the facilities of a professional health care facility or simply to modify existing housing products. A detailed investigation of how elderly or infirm persons can be properly supported in their homes has to be undertaken. Questions of mobility and dependency will need to be addressed if housing solutions are to be real solutions to the needs of a growing proportion of the population. The interaction between such occupants and their surroundings needs careful examination so that workable solutions arise. It goes without saying that people should not be prisoners in their own home. The technical feasibility of the overall concept will need to be fully explored and this will extend to modularisation, methods of assembly, fixing and disassembly. Special attention will need to be paid to the added complexity arising from the incorporation of medical and ancillary equipment.

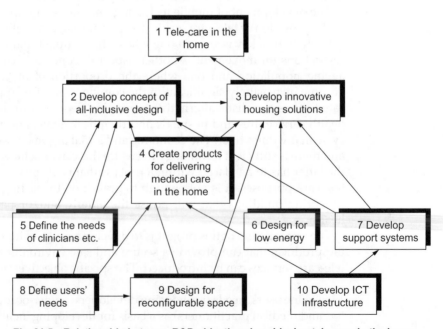

Fig. 21.5   Relationship between R&D objectives in achieving tele-care in the home.

The growing proportion of the population and, hence, the housing market that serves (or should serve) the elderly or infirm is in need of radical overhaul. Attempts to provide health care regimes for people in their own homes are, in many countries, generally limited to the well off with little commercial interest in extending this to the social and mass housing sector. A concerted effort that would bring together the many interests, bodies and disciplines in this area is needed. The success of tele-care in the long run will depend largely upon how effective housing solutions are at catering for the needs of their occupants. This will require that the research results are adequately demonstrated so that practical solutions, as well as the concepts, can be replicated. Important too is that proprietary rights are not allowed to prevent the maximum penetration of tele-care housing products into the marketplace.

The areas of competence required for this research include, but are not restricted to:

- Design of inclusive environments
- Tele-care concepts
- Sensors and controls
- Telemedicine – equipment and communications
- Mobile technology.

Conclusions

The need for innovative thinking and practices within organisations in any sector is generally recognised. This has, of course, to include facilities management, which combines many disciplines which bring their different skills and expertise to bear on solving problems to enable the quality of living and work to advance. Further research and development (R&D) is required, but not before precise needs have been identified and agreed. This chapter has attempted to show through examples – four of them in detail – the very kind of R&D that is required now to enable the quality of living and work to rise to more acceptable levels. Some long-standing conventions and assumptions must be challenged. These include questioning the rationale for building life cycles that are out of step with the needs of industrial and commercial real estate owners and users. Also of concern is the fragmented approach to dealing with sustainability – something that is talked about, yet for which there seem to be too few examples of real progress 'on the ground'. There are many other problems that must be solved. The most important of these is, arguably, the design, construction and management of buildings and other facilities to provide good quality conditions for living and work. Facilities management, in combining many disciplines, has the potential to deal competently with the crosscutting issues that are involved. Experts with deep knowledge are needed, but they must be coordinated by others who are capable of seeing the bigger picture.

CHECKLIST

This checklist is intended to assist with the review and action planning process.

		Yes	No	Action required
1.	Has the organisation a recognised strategy or policy regarding innovation?	☐	☐	☐
2.	Is the organisation promoting a culture of innovation amongst its personnel?	☐	☐	☐
3.	Has the organisation a structured means for dealing with the process of innovation?	☐	☐	☐
4.	Has the organisation examined the case for accepting different life cycles for its buildings and other facilities?	☐	☐	☐
5.	Has the organisation produced a strategy for dealing with the imperatives of energy reduction and sustainability?	☐	☐	☐
6.	Are the buildings and other facilities owned or operated by the organisation truly 'fit for purpose' and, if not, are steps being taken to make them totally acceptable?	☐	☐	☐
7.	Is the organisation satisfied with the level of ICT support that it presently has and the arrangements for supporting personnel in their homes, as well as in their normal place of work?	☐	☐	☐

Appendix A

Glossary

accommodation strategy
An objective assessment of the space needs of an organisation and how these will be satisfied – see also space management.

action research
A branch of scientific discovery in which the research life cycle is compressed to deal with subjects undergoing dynamic change; often involves iterations of key stages.

added value
Tangible gain from a decision, action or procedure that exceeds its monetary equivalent, e.g. a specified service might be performed at its most economical cost yet still provide further benefit from, say, the manner in which customers' other needs are satisfied – see also best value.

alpha test
Simulated or actual operational testing of software by potential users or independent test team on the developer's premises.

as-built
Term used to define the actual state of a building at completion and often used in conjunction with another term, e.g. as-built drawings.

asset management
Systematic process for maintaining, upgrading and operating assets, combining engineering principles with sound business practice and economic rationale – a close relation of facilities management.

assets
Sufficient human, physical (e.g. property) and financial resources to enable an organisation to discharge its obligations under its charter or mission statement.

attitude surveys
A means for measuring the perceptions, expectations and experiences of people for the purpose of objective analysis.

audit (internal)
Measurement and verification of the practices, procedures, policies and decision-making within an organisation with the aim of improving its operational efficiency and effectiveness.

B2B
Business to business; a term used to describe the nature of electronic (web-based) commerce (transactions) – see also B2C below.

B2C
Business to consumer; a term used to describe the nature of electronic (web-based) commerce (transactions) – see also B2B above.

BACnet
Data communications protocol for building automation and control systems – an ASHRAE, ANSI and ISO standard protocol.

benchmarking
An external focus on an internal process to provide an objective comparison of performance or achievement.

best value
Relationship between cost/price and quality which is optimal for a given organisation or customer – not to be confused with lowest price.

beta test
Testing of software undertaken by people outside the developer's team to ensure the product has few faults or bugs – follows alpha testing.

BIM
Building information modelling or building information model – an information or data model containing geometry, spatial relationships, geographic information, quantities and component properties accumulated throughout the building's life cycle.

Bluetooth
Short-range, international wireless communication protocol based on the 2.4 GHz frequency band, enabling electronic devices to be paired for the purpose of data exchange.

BREEAM
UK's Building Research Establishment Environmental Assessment Method – the first widely accepted scheme for the appraisal of the environmental impact of a building's design. The original scheme has been expanded to cover many kinds of building design.

briefing
Eliciting, giving or receiving instructions and information required to initiate or inform a desired action or process.

BTnodes
Tiny devices for sensing and control based on the *Bluetooth* communication protocol.

building automation systems
Integration of separate building engineering services installations into an effective and efficient system which can be controlled from a (single) user interface – a distributed control system.

building energy management
Optimising the use of energy in a building or facility, which relies on sensing of, and control over, spaces and the environmental conditions within them.

building engineering services
Mechanical and electrical installations, including HVAC (heating, ventilating and air-conditioning), transportation, electrical power, lighting, fire protection, security and communications.

building intelligence
Characteristic of a building that has been subject to technological enhancement and which is capable of some degree of sensing and control in anticipation of, and response to, user needs – see also intelligent building.

business continuity
Arrangements for ensuring that the organisation is able to continue its operations in the event of an incident that would otherwise threaten its business survival.

business infrastructure management
Support system of an organisation enabling it to undertake its business.

business process re-engineering (BPR)
Fundamental rethinking and radical redesign of business processes to bring about dramatic improvements in performance.

CAFM
Computer-aided facilities management, where computer-aided design is integrated with database management to provide an environment in which the dynamic behaviour of an organisation can be planned, observed, modified and maintained.

change management
The process, tools and techniques to manage the people side of business change to achieve a required outcome and to realise that change effectively within the social infrastructure of the workplace.

client
Organisation that specifies needs and procures estate-related and facility services by means of a facilities management agreement. The client has a general and/or key function in all stages of the relationship with the service provider.

communication systems
Technology used to enable digital data transfer.

compliance audit
Selection of adequate and proportionate security controls to protect information assets and give confidence to interested parties.

continual improvement
Recognising that today's performance is not enough to meet tomorrow's challenges – striving to raise standards.

contract management
Ensuring that service providers perform according to their commitments.

contracting out
A particular type of outsourcing, where work is undertaken by a contractor as opposed to being carried out in-house.

corporate real estate management
The discipline and practice of making a financial return from real estate without changing the organisation's core business.

CSF
Critical success factors are those attributes of a service that determine whether or not its objectives and priorities have been met – see also key performance indicators.

custodial services
Range of services in the management of persons subject to official control under the terms of relevant criminal justice legislation.

customer
Organisational unit that specifies and receives estate-related and facility services within the conditions of a facilities management agreement.

customer focus
Recognising that without customers there is no business and that they can be anyone with a legitimate interest in the organisation, e.g. own personnel, general public, funding agency, service providers and suppliers.

cyber-agents
Autonomous or semi-autonomous, internet-based applications used to initiate, monitor and control a process.

data integration
The principle that data are entered once only into a computer-based system enabling more than one application to share those same data.

de-layering
Removing supervisory or management grades within an organisation where there is no real or perceived benefit from their continuance. The effect is to flatten the hierarchy to bring the most senior managers closer to the customer.

demobilisation
Phase during which estate-related and facility services as specified in the facilities management agreement transfer back to the client or to a new service provider.

design briefing
Process of translating the client organisation's business and functional requirements (as instructions and information) into the design of a building or facility.

disaster recovery
Planning of operations to take account of circumstances that would pose a significant threat to the organisation's continuation in the event of an incident – see also risk management.

document management
Control over the generation, distribution, storage and archiving of information, usually taken to mean a computer-based system.

downsizing
Reducing the scale of an operation or process to a level in keeping with the demands placed upon it.

due diligence
Compilation, appraisal and validation of information about an organisation required for assessing accuracy and integrity.

EBITDA
Earnings before interest, taxes, depreciation and amortisation.

empowerment
Providing personnel (and others under one's control) with the ability to make decisions that will affect their own work and personal development; *synon.* effective delegation.

end-user
Person receiving facility services on a permanent or temporary basis.

energy audit
Measurement of the amount, rate and cost of energy consumed in operating a facility in order to achieve acceptable conditions – usually contains a comparative element.

environmental audits
Assessment of the extent to which a system or organisation conforms with legislation and practices designed to protect the environment.

environmental protection
Taking steps to ensure that the consequences of actions, operations and processes do not harm or in any way pose a threat to the ecosystem.

escalation path
Procedure to ensure that problems unresolved within an agreed time are quickly brought to the appropriate level of responsibility for resolution.

EVA
Earned value added.

facilities audit
Determining the extent to which the provision of existing properties and other facilities match needs within an organisation – see also accommodation strategy and space management.

facilities management
Integrated process to support and improve the effectiveness of the primary activities of an organisation by the management and delivery of agreed support services for the appropriate environment needed to achieve its changing objectives.

facilities management agreement
Document and/or contract stating the conditions for provision of estate-related and facility services between clients and external service providers, as well as internal service providers (in-house team).

facilities management brief
Document for embodying the estate-related and facility services required by the client organisation and used to inform the design, construction, commissioning and operations process.

facilities planning
Phase within facilities management for examining the case for changed or new facilities and the subsequent programming of design and construction.

facility
Physical asset supporting the activities of an organisation.

facility management
Term used interchangeably with facilities management.

facility service
Support provision to the primary activities of an organisation, delivered by external or internal service providers. Service related to space and infrastructure, people and the organisation.

framework agreement
Formal arrangement between a client organisation and two or more contractors establishing the terms of contracts to be awarded in a given period.

hazard assessment
Identification of a potentially dangerous or threatening occurrence and its subsequent assessment against legal requirements under health and safety legislation – see also risk assessment.

helpdesk
A point of contact for requesting information and action in response to a facilities-related need – does not have to be a physical location, but can be, for example, a reception centre.

human resources management (HRM)
More than a personnel function, HRM, as it is often known, takes account of the needs, motivations and welfare of people in order to help them realise their potential.

ICF
The informed client function, ICF, enables the organisation to strive for best value and total satisfaction in its facilities management by focusing on agreed core competences.

IDEF
Integrated DEFinition, where IDEF0 is the standard for modelling business processes and IDEF3 is the standard for workflow.

if ... then
Used in predicting the future; a type of conditional statement in which one event or occurrence triggers another, e.g. if global warming continues then governments will be forced to impose a carbon tax.

IFC
Industry foundation class or classes – data elements representing the parts of buildings, or elements of a process, containing relevant information about those parts. IFCs are used by computer applications to assemble a computer-readable model of a building or facility.

information management
An organised and structured approach to handling information and data so as to ensure that the right information is provided to the right people, at the right time and in the right format.

intelligent building
More than a building that has been 'wired-up', rather one that affords a high level of support for its users through the use of technology and a design that takes account of the inevitability of change – also referred to as technology-enhanced real estate.

intelligent client or customer
See informed client function, ICF.

interoperability
Electronic exchange of data between different applications and use of those data.

Investors in People (IIP)
A UK scheme for encouraging and rewarding innovations in the workplace that lead to personnel realising their potential.

Just-in-time (JIT)
Just-in-time delivery is regarded as one of the factors in the successful transformation of many industries. This lean production method ensures that inventory levels are kept to a minimum thus lowering levels of waste and releasing cash flow.

KPI
Key performance indicators, KPIs, enable an organisation's effectiveness, in meeting its objectives, to be measured objectively. Usually, two or more KPIs will be linked to a critical success factor – see also CSF.

learning organisation
An entity that has as its underlying principle the will to learn from those outside and to use the knowledge it generates in doing business to help it improve its processes.

letter of intent
Note or memorandum setting out a clear intention to take a certain course of action or to enter into a formal agreement.

logistics
Timely and efficient distribution of goods and other resources to where they are needed.

LonTalk
Protocol for control of networked devices used in building automation systems over media such as twisted cable, power lines, fibre optics and radio frequency – an ANSI standard protocol and part of the technology platform called LonWorks.

managing agent
Individual or organisation appointed to act on behalf of another to manage a service whose performance may be the subject of separate contracts.

mega trends
Tendency towards specified events in the future that are predicted to have a significant impact on the way we do things, e.g. governmental action on global warming that affects the way we live.

metric
Measure, benchmark or statistic used for comparative purposes often given as an output per unit of measurement, e.g. x tonnes per hour.

mobilisation
Phase to establish and implement all resources, systems, data and procedures prior to taking responsibility for the services to be delivered, as specified in the facilities management agreement.

mote
Tiny RFID-derived device for sensing its environment and communicating data to other such devices and controllers for effecting prescribed action. Part of a technology loosely referred to as 'smart dust'.

Mu-chip
Tiny RFID device developed by Hitachi, using the 2.4 GHz frequency band (same as for *Bluetooth* devices), containing a 128 bit ROM capable of identifying trillions of unique objects.

nanoparticle
Object of a size between 1 and 100 nanometres that behaves as a whole unit in terms of its transport and properties.

nanotechnology
Engineering at the atomic and molecular level, i.e. materials or devices 100 nanometres or smaller.

norm
Standard, model or pattern regarded as typical.

office automation
Collective term for the information systems, both hardware and software, used to support employee productivity in the office.

open book
Transparent exchange of relevant information between the client organisation and a facilities management service provider.

outsourcing
Placing one or more non-core services in the hands of an external organisation or contractor – see also contracting out.

partnering
A method of working with suppliers (and service providers) to enable both parties to share in the benefits arising from a close working relationship that strives for cooperation and improvement. This method can and should still contain a competitive element, but can be an effective counter to traditional adversarial working practices.

penetration test
Check of a computer server's integrity and stability during a simulated attack from a malicious user.

performance-based payment
Payment based on agreed output criteria.

performance indicator
See KPI, key performance indicators.

PEST
Political, economic, social and technological; used to establish a framework around which discussion can focus on those external factors affecting an organisation.

PFI
The private finance initiative (PFI) is a type of public–private partnership used by successive UK governments to secure private investment in projects for public benefit – see also public–private partnership, PPP.

planned preventive maintenance
An organised approach to scheduling work and other actions needed to avert failure of components and parts in service and of the fabric and finishes in a building or facility. Tasks include inspections, equipment checks, diagnostics, adjustments and overhauls.

post-occupancy evaluation (POE)
Post-occupancy evaluation is a method for establishing the extent to which users are satisfied with their facilities and, by implication, how closely reality matches the brief. The term is perhaps inaccurate, since 'post' could imply that the occupants have moved out!

primary activities
The distinctive and essential competences of an organisation set within the context of its value chain. The distinction between the primary activities and support services is decided by each organisation individually and has to be reviewed continually.

procurement
Used generally to refer to the process of inviting, selecting, awarding and paying for goods or services supplied to an organisation. This is nowadays taken to be part of an organisation's supply chain.

public–private partnership (PPP)
An arrangement where the public sector enters into an arrangement with the private sector to create an asset and/or service for public benefit, such as a school, hospital, road, bridge, etc.

quality circle
An opportunity for personnel of different grades to meet informally, sometimes outside working hours, to discuss ways of improving the performance of their tasks and the effectiveness of their decision-making.

real estate
Property in the form of buildings and other structures in which individuals or organisations can take an interest or holding; more generally, land, including the air above it and the ground below it, and any buildings or structures erected on it.

RFID
Radio Frequency IDentification – often used in conjunction with the word 'tag' to refer to a (generally) tiny device containing readable data concerning the properties of the object to which it is attached. More sophisticated devices can also write data.

rightsizing
Establishing the most appropriate structure and resources for an organisation – see also downsizing.

risk assessment
Part of risk management wherein hazards, events or the likelihood of events occurring are identified and their impact evaluated.

risk management
Taken to include risk assessment, but extended to include dealing with the associated risks by the adoption of a given strategy. This can include, for example, holding the risk, transferring it or eliminating it altogether.

scenario analysis

A technique used by corporate strategists and planners to help them think in a structured way about the future by building different descriptions of how the future might be. In the process this may pinpoint key actions for the organisation if it is to secure its goals.

service level agreement (SLA)

An SLA deals with how the service specification shall be translated into actions that achieve the required result and will include the means for dealing with evaluation of performance, incentives and penalties.

service provider

Organisation that provides the client with estate-related and facility services within the terms of the facilities management agreement.

service specification

Lays down what a specified service shall be and can be either prescriptive, where the process necessary to achieving a given result is outlined, or performance-based, where the service provider is given outputs or measures that must be achieved.

sick building syndrome

A condition affecting the users of buildings that disappears after they stop using the building and which cannot be attributed to a specific factor; once identified, it is no longer sick building syndrome.

Six Sigma

A technique for improving customer satisfaction, profitability and competitiveness through a focus on the customer by the disciplined use of facts, data and statistical analysis – the term itself refers to a statistically derived performance target.

smart device

Piece of equipment that performs specific tasks and is controlled by a user interface; increasingly, a sensor and controller that can sample, measure and communicate data, enabling an appropriate response in an electro-mechanical system.

smart homes

A term used to label housing in which technology is used to support occupants and other users – see also intelligent building.

sourcing

Determining the source of the delivery of an estate-related or facility service from inside or outside the organisation.

space management

The process by which better use is made of available space, matched to needs. It ensures there is more intensive and extensive use of existing accommodation and that there is a reduction in the need to procure or acquire additional space, whilst maintaining flexibility in response to users' needs.

stakeholder
Any individual or group having a legitimate interest in the activities of the organisation, including its facilities management.

structured data
Information and data in digital form that can be searched and archived.

SWOT analysis
Strengths, weaknesses, opportunities and threats; a framework used to focus attention on the essential characteristics of an organisation; usually drawn as a cross, with each issue in a separate quadrant, where the aim is to list all possibilities and to examine any correlation between the lists.

tag
Small device attached to an object containing data about that object – see RFID.

tele-protection
The use of information and communication technology to support security and other measures aimed at safeguarding people and property.

total facilities management (TFM)
Total facilities management is where a single entity takes responsibility for all facets of facilities management. In reality, this entity may, however, subcontract some of the more specialist elements.

total quality management (TQM)
An approach to work where the aim is to do things right first time, every time. This has little to do with the administration of quality assurance schemes and has more to do with the motivation of individuals to give of their best and accept no compromises.

totally serviced workplace
Serviced and fully operational facilities, enabling users to begin or resume work immediately.

uncertainty
Events that cannot be foreseen or quantified, unlike a risk for which some assessment might be made – see also risk management.

unstructured data
Information and data in non-digital form, such as photographs and drawings, being held on paper.

value
Worth or utility; also a way of expressing the relationship between quality and cost – see best value.

workplace productivity
Concerned with the extent to which the working environment (surrounding an individual) contributes towards or detracts from the amount and/or quality of work undertaken.

zero carbon building
Minimisation of carbon emissions from a building through energy efficiency, using micro-generation and low or zero carbon energy technology to move towards energy self-sufficiency. A zero carbon building will pay back the carbon expended in its construction by exporting zero carbon energy to the grid.

Appendix B

Prevention of fraud and irregularity in the award and management of contracts

Definitions

Fraud may be defined as the use of deception with the intention of obtaining an advantage. Corruption is the giving or receiving of money, goods or services for favours provided. The risks of fraud and corruption can be reduced by awareness of their nature and good procurement practice.

Fraud should be deterred. Prevention is always preferable to detection, and strong preventive controls should therefore be applied.

Risks

Facilities management services have long been considered to carry a high risk of fraud, corruption and other irregularity. The frauds can take a number of forms, some involving collusion with the client organisation's personnel or agents.

One fraud risk is the 'ringing' of contracts, whereby a group of contractors conspires to form a ring for submitting tenders ostensibly in competition but, in fact, having arranged among themselves which firm will bid the lowest. Even the lowest tender will be overpriced. The aim of the ring will be to win the majority of the contracts available and share them.

Frauds can be perpetrated in the execution or pricing of work for new contracts. This can take a variety of forms from failure to perform to specification, to deliberate falsification of suppliers' invoices or labour records leading to overpayment for services. Maintenance contracts also provide opportunities for a contractor to claim for more work than has been done, with or without collusion.

The pricing of contracts not let by competitive tender carries the risk that costs may be deliberately overstated. This can be a particular problem in 'cost plus' contracts and in small value non-competitive contracts which can add up to large amounts of expenditure over the year.

Particular care needs to be taken about the acceptance of gifts, hospitality and other benefits, and to ensure there is no conflict of interest in the award of contracts.

Key principles of control

There are a number of basic principles of control to minimise the risk of fraud in estates-related services and facilities management procurement.

Separation of duties

Duties should be separated to ensure that no single member of staff has control over the award and procurement process for contracts. For example, there should be a separation of duties between ordering the work, certification and authorisation of payments. Failure to separate duties is one of the most common elements of fraud in this context.

Organisations should also ensure that all staff are aware of the risks of fraud and of their responsibilities for reporting any fraud or suspicions of fraud to the appropriate level of management. One option is to set up an internal fraud helpline.

Authorisation

All transactions or specified activities should be approved or sanctioned by a manager or other responsible person before they are undertaken. Limits for these authorisations should be specified. Authorisation seeks to ensure that proper responsibility is taken for all transactions and activities. Authorisation should ensure that delegated limits are complied with, and provide an independent scrutiny and consistency in the procurement process.

Competitive tendering

Contracts should normally be let by competition. A decision not to use competitive tendering should require a higher level of authority.

Regular supervision

There should be positive supervision of the procurement process including regular and unannounced checks of transactions. In addition, managers should carry out pre-commitment checks to confirm the need for the service, that the type of contract is appropriate, and that estimated costs are realistic.

Record-keeping

Appropriate records must be kept to enable every decision and transaction to be traced through the system. The requirement to keep proper records is an important deterrent to fraud.

Documentation

Standard documentation, in the sense of being uniform and consistent, can help to enforce conformity with procedures and legal requirements.

Budgetary control

Budgetary control matches resources and costs to responsibilities for objectives and outputs. Managers should be fully accountable for the achievement of their objectives and targets. Budgets should be closely linked to planning and review procedures to ensure that proposed expenditure is essential. This will help to minimise the risk of fraud.

Indicators of fraud

The following may indicate the occurrence of fraud in the tendering and award of contracts for estates-related services and facilities management:

- Contracts that do not make commercial sense.
- Contracts that include special, but unnecessary, specifications that only a favoured supplier could meet.
- Consistent use of single-source contracts.
- Split ordering to circumvent contract conditions.
- Contractors who are qualified and capable of tendering, but who do not do so for no apparent reason.
- Unusual patterns of consistently high accuracy in estimating tender costs – this is used to deflect the attention of auditors and senior managers who tend to look for adverse rather than favourable variances.
- Withdrawal, without obvious reason, of the lowest tenderer, who may then go on to become a subcontractor of a high tenderer.
- Patterns in tenders from a group of firms, for example, fixed rotation of the lowest tender.
- A contractor tendering substantially higher on some tenders with no logical cost justification.
- Tender prices appearing to drop whenever a new tenderer submits a bid.
- Obvious links between contractors tendering for these works, for example, companies sharing the same address, having the same directors, managers and professional advisers.
- Acceptance of late tenders.
- Disqualification of a suitable tenderer.
- Change in tender after other tenders are opened, often by the drafting of deliberate mistakes into the initial tender.
- Poor documentation of the contract awarding process.
- Suppliers awarded contracts disproportionate to their size.
- Contracts awarded to contractors with a poor performance record.
- Unexplained changes in contract shortly after award.
- Successful tenderer repeatedly subcontracting work to companies that submitted higher tenders.
- A consistent pattern of the same winners and losers (from the tender lists).
- Undue patronage, by consistently favouring one firm or a small number of firms over others.
- Close personal relationships between staff and suppliers.

Table B.1 Risks and controls in the award of contracts.

Activity	Risk	Control
Scoping of contract	The contract specification is written in a manner which favours a particular supplier.	Use of contract panel consisting of technical, end-user and purchasing representatives, to ensure that more than one person is involved in drawing up the specification.
Contract documentation	Conditions of contract are changed to accommodate a favoured supplier and/or exclude competitors who cannot meet the varied conditions.	Standard contract conditions and specification to be used. Any variations to be approved by senior management.
Setting evaluation criteria	Original evaluating criteria are changed after the receipt of submissions to ensure that favoured suppliers are shortlisted.	Use evaluation criteria as agreed by the contract panel prior to tendering. Where EU procurement directives apply, evaluation criteria are required to be stated in advance.
Selection of tenderers	The selection of a group of tenderers with a view to ensuring that the favoured tenderer will win.	Selection by panel against clearly defined and objective criteria; where applicable, in accordance with the requirements of EU procurement directives.
Tendering	Contract rings – repeat orders using narrow source list. Links between contractors – uncompetitive tendering.	Firms should be selected by someone other than the member of staff commissioning the work. Widen the sourcing list by the introduction of new firms and examine tender records for a pattern of pricing and tenderers who have been awarded contracts. Check for links in names, addresses and telephone numbers plus tendering partners.
Tender evaluation	Collusion to ensure that the favoured supplier is chosen.	Technical and commercial evaluation to be carried out independently by the contract panel.
Post-tender negotiations	Modification of favoured supplier's tender to ensure that it is successful.	Where necessary, identify reasons for negotiation and negotiate with a minimum of two suppliers.
Single-source procurement	Overstating of prices.	Competitive tendering and advance purchase planning. Tight budgetary control and a comprehensive system of price checking.

Table B.2   Risks and controls in the management of contracts.

Activity	Risk	Control
Contractual correspondence	Altering terms and conditions to suit favoured supplier.	Contract terms and conditions will be the procurement team's responsibility and may not be altered without senior management approval.
Contract management	False claims for work not carried out or exaggerated claims for actual work done.	Clear audit trail with written records. Authorisation of changes, by senior management, to original document. Site checks, random and systematic.
Claims negotiation	Assisting the contractor to justify claims.	Claims negotiation should be carried out using professional advisers.
Certification of completion	Inadequate certification may lead to overpayments or payment for work not carried out.	Clear separation of duties between ordering the work, certification and authorisation for payment. Ensure that certified documents are not returned to the originator.
Authorisation	Contract splitting to keep contract values under particular staff member's authorised financial limit.	The splitting of contracts should not be allowed unless authorised by senior management. Managers' and supervisors' checks and sampling should be constructed to detect this.
Acceptance of documentation to support claims	Documentation has been modified or fabricated.	Act on original documents. Do not accept copies/faxes. Do not accept use of correction fluids etc. without obtaining satisfactory explanation for any amendments.
Supervision	Payment for work not done and duplication. Failure to monitor daywork on site. Duplication of names on more than one return or 'ghost' workers. Work paid for under one contract and provided in a different format on another contract. Lack of separation of duties, failure to report gifts and hospitality or conflicts of interest.	Good site supervision and audit of site diary. Look for similar work in same building and enforce contract management controls. Separate duties; ensure hospitality rules are formulated and understood; have clear conduct and discipline code, including conflicts of interest and penalties; take disciplinary action against those staff who fail to declare a conflict of interest.
Security of documents	Duplication and manipulation of accountable documents.	Restricted access to accountable documents, such as works and stores orders, tender documents and claim forms. Serial numbering should be used.

Declarations of interests

Staff and management should be required to declare any personal interests in proposed contracts, and appropriate administrative arrangements to facilitate this should be put in place. 'Relevant interests' for this purpose could include not only financial interests but also interests such as membership of public bodies or closed organisations. The duty to decline would also extend to the interests of persons closely connected with the manager or staff member, such as his or her spouse/partner and the close family of the individual or of the spouse/partner.

Risks and controls

A formal request to the tenderer to sign to the effect that no fraud or corrupt practice has occurred when developing the tender could be introduced at invitation to tender acknowledgement stage or at submission. This has two effects:

- *Deterrent* – the contractor is alerted to the fact that the client is aware of the risk of fraud and will be on the lookout for any evidence that it has occurred.
- *Protective* – it ensures that should something fraudulent come to light there can be no excuse that the contractor was not aware of the policy of the client organisation.

Organisations will need to handle such a declaration with sensitivity so as not to impair good working relationships with suppliers or service providers. Tables B.1 and B.2 show the risks of which organisations should be aware, and suggested control factors that can be used to minimise the risk.

Adapted from *Estates and Building Services Procurement: Prevention of Fraud and Irregularity in the Award and Management of Contracts* (HM Treasury, 1996).

Appendix C

Risks involved in outsourcing

Planning to outsource

- Are the objectives for outsourcing correctly identified?
- Is the service to be outsourced adequately scoped and defined?
- Are the in-house costs of delivering the business to be outsourced adequately calculated?
- Will adequate competition be generated from credible contractors?
- Does the outsourced management team have the right number and mix of skills?

Shortlisting of potential contractors

- Are there appropriate evaluation criteria?
- Are there adequate safeguards against corruption or bias in the evaluation?
- Is there sufficient expertise on the evaluation team?

Negotiating contracts

- Are customers' needs translated into business requirements?
- Are measures of contractor performance defined?
- Are appropriate penalties for unsatisfactory contractor performance included in the contracts?
- Is the organisation's contract protected against the contractor's making excessive profits?
- Are the contingency arrangements that would apply in the event of disasters defined?
- Are there adequate safeguards against the commercial failure of the contractor?
- Are termination arrangements specified?
- Are there adequate safeguards to protect the confidentiality of data?
- Are there appropriate arrangements for the control of assets?
- Are there plans for transferring staff in an orderly fashion?
- Is adequate audit access provided for in the contracts?

Tender assessment

- Have the evaluation criteria been tested thoroughly?
- Have the contractors' price proposals and their experience in delivering equivalent business been tested thoroughly?
- Are there safeguards against corruption or bias in the selection of contractors?
- Is there sufficient expertise in the evaluation teams?
- Are there safeguards against the possibility of legal challenge by contractors?

Contract award

- Are there adequate skills in the negotiating team?
- Is the significance of contract terms properly assessed?
- Are there safeguards against disruption to existing business prior to the handover of business to the successful contractors?

Contract management

- Are there adequate arrangements to manage the contracts after award, including performance monitoring and price-control mechanisms?

Adapted from *Outsourcing the Service Delivery Operations* (HMSO, 1996).

Appendix D

Contractual approach and terms

- The contract should normally be for a period of three to five years. Organisations may wish to include a provision for the option of extending this by a further one to two years.

- Organisations should ensure that contract documentation is consistent with the specification.

- Organisations, especially those in the public sector, should ensure that their contract provisions are in line with the Central Unit on Procurement's (CUP) *Guidance Note 42* (CUP, 1993). The updated form of contract by the Chartered Institute of Building (CIOB) should also be considered.

- The contract should include provisions for:
  o Organisations to retain ownership of, and access to, all relevant records and knowledge.
  o The arrangements for another contractor to take over the service at short notice in the event of the financial failure of the contractor.
  o The handling of changes in the organisation's requirements.
  o Full disclosure of all data via an open-book arrangement which gives the client organisation access to all the contractor's premises, systems, books and records.
  o The organisation's right to check the qualifications and competences of the personnel the contractor proposes to use and to approve any appointment beforehand.
  o Requiring the contractor and any subcontractors to have in place quality assurance or quality management systems.
  o Contingency arrangements.
  o The arrangements for the transfer of assets at the start and end of the contract.
  o The mechanisms for dispute resolution.
  o The arrangements for handover to a succeeding contractor at the end of the contract.

- If the contract involves a one-off transfer of assets to the successful tenderer, it should include a clawback provision to allow the organisation to share the benefit if the contractor then sells them on. The contract should contain clear and precise terms which:

o   Detail the service levels and performance standards the contractor is required to meet.

o   Define performance monitoring arrangements and the associated information requirements.

o   Link payment to performance.

o   Detail any remedies in the event of default of whatever nature.

- Organisations may wish to guarantee the expected workload for the first few years of a contract, in order to generate enough interest from potential tenderers. If TUPE applies, the contract should stipulate that, at the end of the contract, the existing contractor will have to provide other tenderers with information about the staff who would transfer to them under this.

- The contract should set out the pricing regime:
  o   Fixed price for items or tasks which can be defined fully
  o   Variable price for those which cannot
  o   Arrangements for sharing savings.

- The payment structure should provide the contractor with an incentive to perform well, for example by:
  o   Paying nothing until the required performance standards are met.
  o   Making subsequent payments dependent on the continued meeting of these standards.
  o   Structuring payments to provide incentives to improve performance.
  o   Making good identified failures at the contractor's cost.
  o   Recovery of costs incurred by organisations in rectifying poor performance.
  o   The removal of particular services from the contractor.
  o   In exceptional circumstances, the right to terminate the contract.

- Client organisations should require appropriate third-party protection in the form of parent or associated company guarantees, performance bonds, and evidence of the appropriate insurance cover.

- The contract should normally reserve the client organisation's right to terminate the contract in the event of a change in the controlling interest in the contractor.

- The contract should ensure that the contractor cannot assign any part of the contract to a third party without the client organisation's agreement.

- Contracts should be consistent internally and with each other.

- The contract should be flexible enough to cope with any client-approved changes in user requirements over the course of the contract.

General conditions of contract for the provision of services

1. Definitions
2. Services
3. Recovery of sums due
4. Value added tax (VAT)
5. Bankruptcy
6. Racial discrimination
7. Transfer, sub-letting and subcontracting
8. Corrupt gifts and payments of commission
9. Drawings, specifications and other data
10. Use of documents, information, etc.
11. Disclosure of information
12. Law
13. Arbitration
14. Official Secrets Act (condition that would not apply outside the public sector)
15. Security measures
16. Approval for admission to government premises and information about workpeople (condition that would not apply outside the public sector)
17. Observance of regulations
18. Safety
19. Accidents to contractors' servants or agents
20. Special health and safety hazards
21. Liability in respect of damage to government property (condition that would not apply outside the public sector)
22. Contractor's property
23. Intellectual property rights
24. Patents
25. Default
26. Insurance
27. Duty of care
28. Design liability
29. Issues of government property (condition that would not apply outside the public sector)
30. Personal injury and loss of property
31. Hours of work
32. Occupation of government premises (condition that would not apply outside the public sector)
33. Contractor's organisation
34. Break
35. Facilities provided
36. Duration of contracts
37. Variation of requirement
38. Contract documents
39. Amendments to contracts

40. Monitoring and liaison meetings
41. Price
42. Price fixing
43. Lead-in costs
44. Payment
45. Payment of subcontractors
46. Availability of information
47. National Audit Office access (condition that would not apply outside the public sector)
48. Transfer of responsibility
49. Quality assurance

Appendix E

Sections for a service level agreement (SLA)

1. Definitions
2. Services
3. Value added tax (VAT)
4. Subcontracting
5. Resolution of dispute
6. Default
7. Duty of care
8. Hours of work
9. Occupation of premises
10. Agreement holder's organisation
11. Break
12. Facilities provided
13. Terms of agreement
14. Variation of requirement
15. Agreement documentation
16. Amendments to agreement
17. Monitoring and liaison meetings
18. Price
19. Extensions
20. Allocation of costs
21. Transfer of responsibility

References and Bibliography

Aronoff, S. and Kaplan, A. (1995) *Total Workplace Performance: Rethinking the Office Environment*. Ottawa: WDL Publications.

Atkin, B. and Björk, B.-C. (2007) Understanding the context for best practice facilities management from the client's perspective. *Facilities*, **25** (13/14), 479–92.

Barrett, P.S. and Baldry, D. (2003) *Facilities Management: Towards Best Practice*, 2nd edition. Oxford: Blackwell Publishing.

Bennett, J. and Jayes, S. (1998) *The Seven Pillars of Partnering*. London: Thomas Telford.

CABA (2002) *Technology Roadmap for Intelligent Buildings*. Ottawa Continental Automated Buildings Association and National Research Council.

CIRIA (1996) *Control of Risk: A Guide to the Systematic Management of Risk from Construction (SP125)*. London: Construction Industry Research and Information Association.

Clements-Croome, D. (ed) (2000) *Creating the Productive Workplace*. London: Spon.

Gadde, L.-E. (1996) *Supplier Management in the Construction Industry: Working Papers*. Gothenburg: Chalmers University of Technology.

Hofstede, G. (1991) *Cultures and Organisations: Software of the Mind: Intercultural Cooperation and its Importance for Survival*. New York: McGraw-Hill.

Kaplan, R.S. and Norton, D.P. (1996) *The Balanced Scorecard: Translating Strategy into Action*. Boston, MA: Harvard Business School Press.

Kelly, J., Morledge, R. and Wilkinson, S. (2002) *Best Value in Construction*. Oxford: Blackwell Science.

Kelly, J., Male, S. and Drummond, G. (2004) *Value Management of Construction Projects*. Oxford: Blackwell Publishing.

Leibfried, K.H.J. and McNair, C.J. (1994) *Benchmarking: A Tool for Continuous Improvement*. London: HarperCollins.

Leiringer, R. (2003) *Technological innovations in the context of public–private partnership projects*. Doctoral Thesis, Department of Industrial Economics and Management, Royal Institute of Technology, Stockholm.

Pande, P.S., Neuman, R.P. and Cavanagh, R.R. (2000) *The Six Sigma Way*. New York: McGraw-Hill.

Rostron, J. (ed) (1997) *Sick Building Syndrome: Concepts, Issues and Practice*. London: Spon.

SMG (2006) *Space Management Project: Summary*. 2006/42, UK Higher Education Space Management Project, Space Management Group. London: University of Westminster.

Stationery Office (2000) *Public Private Partnerships: The Government's Approach*. London: Stationery Office.

Thompson, P. and Warhurst, C. (eds) (1998) *Workplaces of the Future*. Basingstoke: Macmillan.

Williams, S. (2002) *Managing Workplace Stress*. London: John Wiley.

Wing, R.D. and Atkin, B.L. (2002) *FutureHome – A Prototype for Factory Housing*. Proceedings of 19th International Symposium on Automation and Robotics in Construction, SP989, Washington DC: National Institute of Standards and Technology, 173–8.

Index

3rd edition

EVENTS
MANAGEMENT

principles & practice

Razaq Raj, Paul Walters & Tahir Rashid

SAGE

Los Angeles | London | New Delhi
Singapore | Washington DC | Melbourne

Los Angeles | London | New Delhi
Singapore | Washington DC | Melbourne

SAGE Publications Ltd
1 Oliver's Yard
55 City Road
London EC1Y 1SP

SAGE Publications Inc.
2455 Teller Road
Thousand Oaks, California 91320

SAGE Publications India Pvt Ltd
B 1/I 1 Mohan Cooperative Industrial Area
Mathura Road
New Delhi 110 044

SAGE Publications Asia-Pacific Pte Ltd
3 Church Street
#10-04 Samsung Hub
Singapore 049483

Editor: Matthew Waters
Assistant editor: Lyndsay Aitken
Production editor: Victoria Nicholas
Proofreader: Andy Baxter
Indexer: Elizabeth Ball
Marketing manager: Alison Borg
Cover design: Francis Kenney
Typeset by: C&M Digitals (P) Ltd, Chennai, India
Printed in the UK

First edition published 2009. Reprinted 2010 and 2011

Second edition published 2013. Reprinted 2013, 2014 (twice) and 2015 (twice)

Library of Congress Control Number: 2016954965

British Library Cataloguing in Publication data

A catalogue record for this book is available from the British Library

ISBN 978-1-4739-4827-3
ISBN 978-1-4739-4828-0 (pbk)

At SAGE we take sustainability seriously. Most of our products are printed in the UK using FSC papers and boards. When we print overseas we ensure sustainable papers are used as measured by the PREPS grading system. We undertake an annual audit to monitor our sustainability.

CONTENTS

PART 3: EVENTS MARKETING AND MEDIA

PART 1

EVENTS CONCEPTS
AND MANAGEMENT

1

INTRODUCTION TO EVENTS MANAGEMENT

In this chapter you will cover

This chapter provides an historical overview of the events and festivals industry, and how it has developed over time. The core theme for this chapter is to establish a dialogue between event managers and event specialists who need to have a consistent working relationship. Each strand of the chapter will be linked to industry best practice where appropriate. In addition, this chapter discusses the different types of events that exist within the events management industry. Specifically, the chapter will analyse and discuss a range of events and their implications for the events industry, including the creation of opportunities for community orientated events and festivals.

THE HISTORICAL DEVELOPMENT OF EVENTS

Events, in the form of organised acts and performances, have their origins in ancient history. Events and festivals are well documented in the historical period before the fall of the Western Roman Empire (AD 476). They have an important function within society, providing participants with the opportunity to assert their identities and to share rituals and celebrations with other people. Traditionally, special religious holy days have been celebrated, for example, Christmas and Easter. Sovereign rulers and other leaders have often organised events as a way of controlling the public, as was especially the case in the seventeenth and eighteenth centuries.

In modern society, it may be argued that traditional religious and national festivals are no longer viewed as the key focus for community celebrations. Modern western society instead tends to create events which celebrate *individual* milestones, anniversaries and achievements. Birthday parties, wedding celebrations and house warming parties are all ways in which we get together.

These days, events are considered to make a key contribution to the cultural and economic development of the countries that hold them. Events can have a major impact on the development of cultural tourism in the host communities.

A festival can be defined as a gathering of a community or an event which is centred on some theme and held annually or less frequently for a limited period of time. Historical and cultural themes are now often used to develop annual events to attract visitors and create cultural images in the host cities by holding festivals in community settings. Increasingly, larger events and festivals are not specifically designed to address the social and cultural needs of any one particular group but instead are often developed because of the economic benefits they will hopefully bring, primarily through tourism. Such festivals attract increasing numbers of local, regional and international visitors and thus may help to develop links with the global community.

Festivals and celebrations in local communities have generally been accepted and recognised as making an important contribution to society. These local festivals create entertainment for residents and visitors, but also contribute to a sense of community, building bridges between diverse community groups and giving them an opportunity to come together and celebrate their history and the place they live in.

TECHNICAL DEFINITIONS OF EVENTS MANAGEMENT

In order to understand more fully the large array of events that take place today it is important to begin by examining their objectives. Any dictionary definition of an 'event' will include a broad statement, such as 'something happens'.

The word 'event' also has specific meanings in medicine, philosophy or physics. In such disciplines we are concerned with happenings or incidents beyond the will of man or woman. When we couple this term with the concept of 'management', the definition of which includes words such as 'organisation', 'administration' and 'control', we begin to see an 'event' as a purposeful human creation. For events to be managed, they must therefore involve other people, and have a predetermined purpose and a location.

Event management can therefore be defined like this:

Event management is the capability and control of the process of purpose, people and place.

It follows, then, that events themselves can be defined as 'happenings with objectives'.

The prime objective for an event can be strictly defined. An objective may be quantitative and financial, for instance to sell tickets and produce a profit. There may also be less tangible, qualitative objectives relating to the thoughts, feelings and emotions, during and after the event, of those attending it. These would be key objectives for a wedding or a private party.

In the next chapter we will look more closely at event objectives and in particular their role within the event planning process. In this section, however, we will explore the way in which 'event objective components' can help us to analyse the full range of international events currently being staged.

Event objective components are the building blocks of event objectives. They are divided into the three categories derived from our earlier definition of event management: purpose, people and place (see Figure 1.1).

So, in order to understand the range of events, we can attempt to classify them by their objective components. But, the process produces so many permutations and overlaps that in the end we must conclude that events cannot be precisely classified. One positive conclusion, though, is that all events involve a community. This community can be local or international; it may be a certain business community or a cultural community.

If we look at events on a scale ranging from the individual to the global, a private and personal event, such as a wedding anniversary or birthday, involves the community of family and friends at a particular calendar date in the individual's life for the purposes of celebration. Culture and community are both expressed and enhanced through the social interaction of the event. At the global end of the scale, an event such as the Olympic Games in London in 2012, or the FIFA World Cup in Brazil in 2014, will probably involve every possible component somewhere in its tiered objectives and stakeholders. This is due to the complexity of such major events, which actually consist of a whole series of events in one. Looking at our diagram of event objective components (see Figure 1.1), we can identify the culture, carnival and celebration of the opening and closing ceremonies; the many competitors; the corporate elements; and the positive changes these events bring to citizens, communities, city and country.

Community, or communities, is thus the most important of the event objective components. Communities include the international track athletics or football communities; the expatriate and descendant communities, such as a city's Irish or Caribbean communities who come together

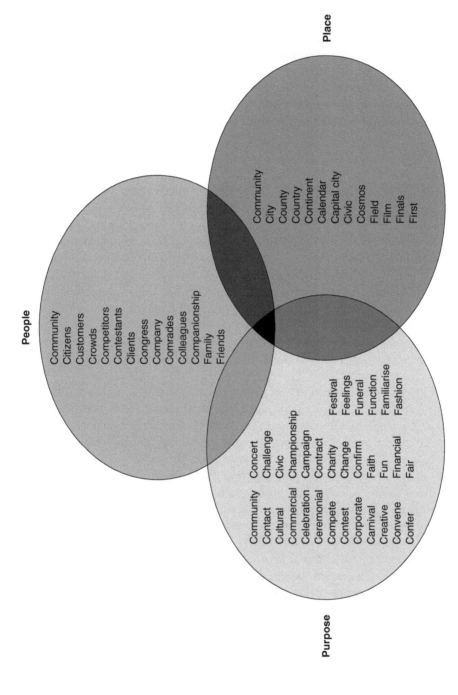

People

Community
Citizens
Customers
Crowds
Competitors
Contestants
Clients
Congress
Company
Comrades
Colleagues
Companionship
Family
Friends

Place

Community
City
County
Country
Continent
Calendar
Capital city
Civic
Cosmos
Field
Film
Finals
First

Purpose

Community   Concert   Festival
Contact   Challenge   Feelings
Cultural   Civic   Funeral
Commercial   Championship   Function
Celebration Campaign   Familiarise
Ceremonial   Contract   Fashion
Compete   Charity
Contest   Change
Corporate   Confirm
Carnival   Faith
Creative   Fun
Convene   Financial
Confer   Fair

Figure 1.1 Event objective components – the 'C's and F's' of events

to celebrate St Patrick's Day or Carnival; or any field of commerce, such as the UK utilities industry business community. Events are all about the vast and varied communities of people of the world. Events are where people commune!

SIZE OF EVENTS WITHIN THE SECTOR

Modern events vary enormously in terms of their scale and complexity and the number of stakeholders involved, ranging from community festivals to major sporting events.

The larger the event, the more objective components it will have, due to the numerous sub-events and stakeholder events which make the whole. This is particularly true, for example, of events such as the Olympic Games. Figure 1.2 shows the different types of events that have been developed around the world by organisers ranging from individuals to multinational organisations.

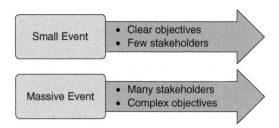

Figure 1.2 How the size of an event links to its complexity

There have been considerable changes in the nature of festivals over the last decade. Where they previously tended to be associated with key calendar dates, particular seasons and heritage sites, there is now a much broader and more diverse range of festivals and events taking place all over the world. The revolution in festivals has been stimulated by commerce. The changing demands of local community groups have increased business opportunities for event organisers and local businesses.

Festivals play a major part in the economy of a city and local community. Such events are attractive to host communities, since they can promote a sense of pride and identity among local people. In addition, festivals can play an important part in promoting the host community as both a tourist and commercial destination. Events can help to develop the image and profile of a destination and may attract visitors outside of the holiday season. They can also generate significant economic impacts, contributing to the development of local communities and businesses, providing support to those who pursue economic opportunity, and supporting key industrial sectors.

Festivals provide an opportunity for local people to develop and share their culture. If we understand 'culture' to mean the personal expression of community heritage, we can see how festivals may create a sense of shared values, beliefs and perspectives within a local community. The peoples and communities that host festivals also offer their visitors a vibrant and valuable cultural experience. Events enable tourists to see how local communities celebrate their culture, and also give them an opportunity to interact with their hosts. This not only meets their leisure needs but can increase their understanding and appreciation of the local culture and heritage.

AN EVENTS INDUSTRY

There is some debate as to whether an events industry actually exists. Those who work exclusively in exhibitions view themselves as part of the exhibition industry; those who work in live music might define themselves as part of the music business. Others, such as wedding organisers, may see themselves as part of a standalone industry.

The common link that binds all of these diverse event organisers together is the multitude of suppliers who rely on events for all or part of their business. A ticket printer's trade exclusively depends upon orders from events, be they sporting, cultural, musical or corporate. In order to prosper, a professional sound company needs contracts with event venues and event organisers, ranging from contracts for sound systems installed permanently in churches or nightclubs, to those set up temporarily for a concert or conference. A printer may have a wide range of other customers, but event businesses that need posters, flyers and brochures may account for a significant part of their work. Events can also be a component of an hotelier's business, if the hotel is available for use as a venue for meetings or conferences. Yet business tourism is a vital part of the UK tourism industry and it is one of the largest industries in the UK economy, generating around £19 billion per annum from 180,000 businesses and employing over 1.4 million people across the whole tourism and events sector. Over the last ten years it has provided growth and employment for the UK and European economies. In addition, tourism is a vital source for the event and hospitality industry, especially where delegates are attending large MICE (meetings, incentives, conferences and exhibitions) events. For example, it is forecast that Britain will have a tourism industry worth over £275 billion by 2025. It is predicted that the tourism sector will grow by 3.8 per cent annually through to 2025, which is significantly greater than the overall growth rate for the UK economy and much faster than sectors such as manufacturing, construction and retail. A record 34.4 million visitors from overseas visited the UK in 2014 and spent a record £21.8 billion. This is an increase of 5 per cent compared to 2013 (www.visitbritain.org/2016-forecast [online]).

VALUE OF AREAS OF THE EVENTS INDUSTRY

Estimating the financial value of such a diverse UK events industry is a very difficult task. The typology of events shown in Figures 1.3 and 1.4 breaks the events industry down into different sectors and sub-sectors, some of which have information more readily available than others. These facts and figures, however, do take full account of the importance of events in economic and employment terms.

The UK Conference and Meeting Survey (UKCAMS, 2015 [online]) estimates that conferences and meetings generated £21.4 billion in 2014 and there were an estimated 1.28 million business events in 2014, which is similar to 2013 but the average size of the events was larger compared to 2013. Furthermore, in 2014 there was an average of 366 business events in the UK compared to 356 events in 2013 and 373 events in 2012 and most of these events (61 per cent) were held in hotels and 20 per cent in multi-purpose venues (UKCAMS, 2015).

The music festival and concert sector is worth more than £1.3 billion annually with 6.5 million music tourists. However, this figure increases to £2.2 billion when indirect spending is included. It is estimated that 41 per cent of live music audiences are music tourists. Furthermore, music tourists from overseas spend an average of £657 each during their visit to the UK. It is also estimated that 24,251 full-time jobs are sustained by music tourism. According to former Prime Minister David Cameron, 'Music is an industry that is an international success story and we should go on backing it' (www.ukmusic.org). It is not just the exports but also the people the music industry employs in the UK, the growing music tourism, with people coming to Britain to listen to great acts. *Wish You Were Here* (UK Music, 2016 [online]) describes the UK's ambition to attract 40 million visitors by 2020. The report says that music tourism already contributes to the economy, but the music industry can play a much greater role in helping Britain achieve this target. By 2020 VisitBritain targets earnings of £31.5 billion from inbound tourism. An increase in music tourism has the potential to benefit every part of the UK.

Sports events would merit an in-depth study in their own right, such is the range of both events and stakeholders. Given that many sporting events are part of international competitions, it can be difficult to define the boundaries of the market within the UK alone. The clearest example is perhaps Premier League Football – the UK's most popular sport in

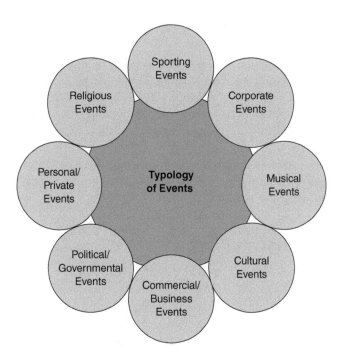

Figure 1.3   Typology of events

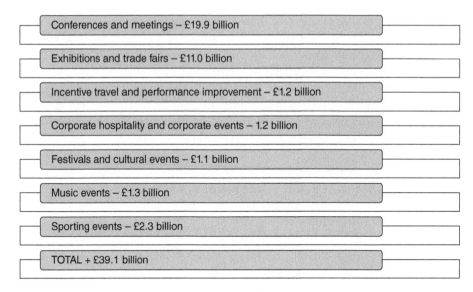

Conferences and meetings – £19.9 billion

Exhibitions and trade fairs – £11.0 billion

Incentive travel and performance improvement – £1.2 billion

Corporate hospitality and corporate events – 1.2 billion

Festivals and cultural events – £1.1 billion

Music events – £1.3 billion

Sporting events – £2.3 billion

TOTAL + £39.1 billion

Figure 1.4   The value of Britain's events sector direct spend by segment

Source: www.businessvisitsandeventspartnership.com/news/bvep-press-releases/242-bvep-launches-events-are-great-britain-report [accessed 24/10/2016]. Reproduced by permission of the BVEP.

terms of spectator admissions and television viewing. The Football Association Premier League, comprising of 20 clubs, contributed around £725 million to the Exchequer in 2010, but now contributes £1.3 billion per year in terms of income tax and national insurance contributions (This Is Money, 2011 [online]).

The most revealing figure is the increase in the value of the broadcasting rights contract between the Premier League and Sky broadcasting. The domestic broadcast revenue has grown from £633,000 per game in 1992 to a staggering £6.53 million in 2014. In addition, overseas broadcasting contributes huge amounts of revenue. For example, NBC in the USA paid US$250 million for the right to broadcast the Premier League for three years (Royal Statistical Society, 2014 [online]).

There is also a core group of companies and organisations that work across these various specialist sectors of the events industry. These organisations, known as 'event support services', constitute the foundation of the industry.

DIFFERENT TYPES OF EVENTS

Religious events

The largest event in the world in terms of actual attendance is the Hajj in Makka, Saudi Arabia. This annual event is a pilgrimage, which is sacred to the Muslim faith; it is the fifth and final pillar of Islam and is undertaken by approximately 3.4 million people each year (Saudi Arabia

Information Resource [online]). This figure not only includes the world's largest number of 'religious tourists' who fly in from all over the world, but also the large numbers who converge upon Makka from within Saudi Arabia and neighbouring countries. Papal visits are another example of large religious events. When Pope John Paul II visited Ireland and the USA, he said mass to a million people in Dublin, New York and Boston.

These enormous gatherings of people share the objective components, drawn from Figure 1.1, of faith and feelings, culture, community, ceremony and contact.

The dates of such religious event experiences become etched into the memory of the people attending, alongside their feelings and emotions. The same is also true of individual religious events such as Bar Mitzvahs. A Jewish male automatically becomes a Bar Mitzvah after his thirteenth birthday. The popular Bar Mitzvah cerebration is a relatively modern innovation and the elaborate ceremonies and receptions that are commonplace today were unheard of as recently as a century ago. The Bar Mitzvah is a celebration of the Jewish faith by friends and families, and the local Jewish community.

A Bar Mitzvah takes place on a Saturday shortly after the boy's thirteenth birthday. Saturday is the Jewish Sabbath, a day of rest and spiritual enrichment. The boy is called upon to lead sections of the weekly service at the Synagogue. This may be as simple as saying the blessing but often involves much more and varies from congregation to congregation. The boy then often makes a speech which, tradition dictates, begins with the phrase, 'Today I am a man'. His father responds by reciting a blessing, thanking God for taking the responsibility for the son's sins from him (www.barmitzvahs.org).

The religious service is nowadays invariably followed by a reception and celebration. It is this event which is also a cultural and indeed a personal event; however, this celebration would not take place without the religious ceremony. Bar Mitzvahs have the function of convening a community to celebrate their faith. They can rival weddings in terms of size and scale and are consequently significant to the events industry.

Cultural events

Some cultural events have a religious aspect and some may be held for commercial reasons. However, the primary purpose of such events is the celebration or confirmation of culture. Cultural events, such as concerts or carnivals, incur costs. They also create important economic opportunities and impacts, though a district, town or city may not directly benefit from a festival's balance sheet. For example, Liverpool's Matthew Street Festival is held every year at the end of August at a cost to Liverpool City Council; yet the event generates £30 million for the local economy (Liverpool Culture Company [online]).

At one level, cultural events facilitate the integration and inclusion of smaller communities of families and friends within the wider community. On another level, they allow outsiders and tourists from different cultures to join and share in the process. For example, St Patrick's Day parties are held not only in Dublin and Belfast but also in New York, Boston and around the world. While these events are a celebration of Irishness, they also give anyone that wishes to the opportunity to enjoy Irish food, drink and music.

Musical events

Musical events range from the Glastonbury or Roskilde Music Festivals to the Last Night of the Proms in the Royal Albert Hall and all manner of concerts and performances in between. Musical events are often commercial in purpose but they are also about culture and fashion. They can even be concerned with change or charity and they are a celebration of creativity. A concert is about a shared feeling, fun with friends and new companions. Music festivals in particular promote a sense of belonging to the crowd.

An example is T in the Park, which has become Scotland's leading music festival. The first festival was at Strathclyde Country Park on the outskirts of Glasgow in 1994; however, in 1997 T in the Park moved to a more central location at Balado near Perth. This larger and more easily accessible site certainly enabled T in the Park to grow. The event now features hundreds of musicians from many countries around the world. They perform a wide range of popular music on four different stages to a combined audience of over 85,000. This takes place every year on a weekend in early July. In 2011, 45 per cent of people buying tickets for T in the Park came from outside Scotland, making the event one of Scotland's larger annual tourist attractions.

The event is strongly supported by the local council and surrounding communities, thus it does not experience the licensing problems of some comparable events in England. In 2004, T in the Park became the only festival in the UK to have been awarded a three-year licence for the second time. T in the Park has a large number of stakeholders with different objectives. For the organisers, DF Concerts, and the title sponsor, the Scottish lager brand Tennents, the event's purpose is commercial. Yet to its audience, it is a celebration of music and specifically of the Scots' love of music and partying which they wish to share. This is what gives the event its atmosphere. The event is about country but it is also about fun; it is the date on the calendar for the popular music community of Scotland. The event's objectives now go beyond the commercial ones it began with. Scotland's First Minister, Jack McConnell, when attending T in the Park in 2003, said: 'It is great to see so many young people enjoying themselves. The festival is very valuable to the Scottish economy and it symbolises the modern Scotland we want to portray' (www.tinthepark.com).

Sporting events

These range from the largest of international events to local leagues and competitions for communities and children. Their purpose is contest, challenge and competition but they also involve companionship, camaraderie and colleagues. They can often take the form of a championship, where there are displays of differing skills or prowess depending on the sport. Examples range from the US Open Golf Tournament or the Formula One Grand Prix Drivers' Championship to a city's schools' swimming gala, and countless others, both large and small.

As professional sports men and women are often very well paid and as some sports attract large numbers of spectators, including huge global television audiences, there is invariably a strong commercial purpose in any large sports event. The success of teams or individual sports men and women from a community, city, county or nation is often a cause for great celebration, particularly if not expected. A perfect example is Greece's victory in the 2004 European Football Championships in Portugal. This had a very positive impact upon Greek national pride, which continued throughout and after the Athens Olympics. Sports events may therefore have political significance. With so many stakeholders and such high stakes, sports events require a high degree of professional events management.

Manchester City Council successfully bid for the staging of the 2008 UEFA Cup Final. It took place on 14 May, and was part of the Manchester World Sport 08 programme, a long-term strategy to bid for and host many international sporting events in 2008. The Northwest Regional Development Agency calculated that Manchester's 08 programme of sport attracted over 317,000 visitors to the city, and was worth an estimated £23 million in terms of financial impact. Manchester City Council and its partners commissioned Ipsos MORI North, in conjunction with Experian, to research the economic benefits. In that same year Manchester won the accolade of the world's top Sport City at the SportBusiness Sports Event Management Awards, ahead of Melbourne, Berlin, Doha, Moscow and New York.

Personal and private events

Personal events are celebrations of special occasions with friends and family. These could be viewed as a subsection of cultural events because when they are cross-cultural the format of weddings or funerals may vary. But the celebration of the union of two people, or the mourning and respect at the passing of a life, are the oldest and most widely practised events. Many other life stage celebrations occur, linked either to age or achievement, including birthdays, anniversaries, graduations and homecomings. These events concern family and/or friends and their purposes are celebration and feelings.

Political and governmental events

From annual party political conferences and trade union conferences to events held by specific government departments, these events may be commercial in that they can be costly to organise; but the profit they seek is not financial currency but political change. As the media play a major part in such events, some, especially the party conferences, have become contests. This can range from subtle internal contests, played virtually behind the scenes, to blatant competition for public opinion and future votes between opposing parties on the stage provided by the attendant media.

In order to drive ticket sales and engage with their audience successfully, most events may require some form of media alliance, and none more so than political conferences. Without a media broadcaster(s) attached to the event, essential political messages may be lost at the point of delivery. As the national broadcaster the BBC has a moral undertaking to present fair and objective coverage on all media platforms.

Commercial and business events

These often involve a whole section of industry or business. Exhibitions tend to be the most complex type of event within this category since each stand can be regarded as a sub-event, particularly where new products or services are being presented. Every stand has its stakeholders and all are competing for customers or clients. These events are key points on the calendar at which an industry convenes or confers in order to coordinate campaigns, make contacts and agree contracts. The overriding purpose is thus commercial.

Major exhibitions such as motor shows or, the largest of all, air shows are such spectacular events that, alongside bringing together the crucial business buyers and manufacturers, they also attract many thousands of members of the general public who pay for tickets. A good example of this is the British International Motor Show. By 1978, the motor show had out-grown the London exhibition facilities and was moved to the then new Birmingham National Exhibition Centre (NEC). Attracting around 700,000 visitors annually, the British International Motor Show now ranks alongside similar international motor shows in Detroit, Brussels and Turin. Since 2006, it has been back in London, at Battersea Park (www.britishmotorshow.co.uk).

Business events also include 'association events' – the annual conferences of a very wide range of professional and business associations. From dentists to banking, ocean technology to e-marketing, all spheres of human industry and endeavour have at least one association conference.

Corporate events

Events of this type involve just one single business, company, corporation or organisation. They may include annual conferences, product launches, staff motivation events or awards ceremonies. They draw their audience from within the organisation and often include an 'incentive' element in their choice of venue or location. Their purpose may be to give colleagues the space and place to confer in order to create change within the organisation. Key tasks may include considering competitors, clients or customers, reviewing the challenges faced by the organisation, and generating creative solutions to those challenges.

Special events

The term 'special events' is used to describe events that are first class or extraordinary in terms of the widespread public recognition they receive. Special events enrich the quality of life for local people and attract tourists from outside the area on account of their uniqueness.

Special events sometimes become synonymous with and dependent on the place where they are held. For example, the annual Edinburgh International Festival, which is a prime example of a special event, would not hold the same prestige should individual festival organisers ever decide to move any of its components to another city.

The primary goal of special events is to develop recognition for the local community and festival organisers. Examples of such events include Notting Hill Carnival, Bradford Festival, Berlin Love Parade, Toronto Street Festival and the Queen's Golden Jubilee celebrations in the UK. Such events create images for the tourism market and attract visitors to the location. A city wanting to upgrade its infrastructure or its political image may also use a large-scale event as a tool to generate funds from corporations and higher levels of government.

The host community benefits from special events both socially and economically. Yet special events are also typically dependent on a large outlay of public monies, which may arise not only from hosting them but also from bidding to host them in the first place. Despite the enormous costs and benefits for host communities, the full impact of special events, socially and environmentally as well as economically, is rarely calculated.

Special events range in size from small community fairs to large-scale sporting events. Community and local festivals can be classed as special events, since they can create a cultural and social environment for tourists who are attending the event. Major cities use special events to celebrate the city and highlight what it has to offer in terms of sport, music, culture and art.

Leisure events

Large-scale leisure events are capable of attracting substantial numbers of visitors, gaining global media coverage and reaping vast economic benefits for the hosts. There is generally a competitive bidding process to determine who will host such large-scale events as the Olympic Games, the FIFA World Cup and the Commonwealth Games.

Events on this scale are extremely important for the host community, not only because of the number of visitors, but because they create legacies, which may continue to have an impact on the host community long after the event has taken place. The bids for large-scale sporting events often incorporate urban regeneration goals into their strategies in order to justify the high costs of such events to all stakeholders, especially the local community. Large-scale leisure events are linked to government funding programmes, which enable the construction of facilities and infrastructure, and the redevelopment and revitalisation of urban areas. This process creates a physical, economic and social legacy which may have long-term benefits for the local communities. Law (1993) suggests that such events:

> act as a catalyst for change by persuading people to work together around a common objective and as a fast track for obtaining extra finance and getting building projects off the drawing board. (1993: 107)

Leisure events can act as a tool for urban regeneration, since through them host cities are given the opportunity to present new or promote existing images of themselves and thus enhance their profile on a global scale. Improving the image of the location as a destination will attract tourists to the area and hence generate future local employment in the tourist industry.

Crucially, leisure events provide an opportunity to acquire funding to regenerate cities and develop new facilities. The planning for these events should include a legacy plan to ensure that local communities continue to benefit from the event and associated investments in the future. This should consider the urban regeneration and social impacts of the event on host communities, identifying any adverse effects and ensuring that benefits to the surrounding communities are not squandered. How new facilities are utilised once the event has moved out of the host city is of great importance, as improper planning can mean they may not be used to their maximum potential. The facilities for the Commonwealth Games in Manchester in 2002 were fully utilised, since it was agreed at the planning stage that the main stadium would be handed over to Manchester City Football Club and that the athletic village would be passed on to the local authority to provide accommodation. In this century, with competitive bidding for large-scale sporting events by local authorities, countries and cities, it is no longer acceptable to stakeholders for central and local governments to host a large leisure event without developing a comprehensive post-event strategic plan.

There has been much discussion over who benefits most from large-scale leisure events and whether the costs and benefits are shared equally by the different stakeholders. It is clear, for example, that such events can produce tangible benefits for governments and businesses, especially within the tourism industry. The non-tangible benefits for the community are less self-evident, aside from the privilege of participating in the mega event in one way or another.

Community festivals now play a significant role in generating income for local businesses and attracting tourists to the local area. These economic impacts have increased considerably over the past decade as the festivals have grown in size. The expansion of information technology and media networks has contributed to the development of these events and the industry which promotes and runs them. Festival organisers now utilise these new communication tools to advertise their events to wider audiences. Festivals now attract visitors from all over the country and from other countries, not only for the duration of the festival but also possibly, as a result of the media attention attracted by the event, in the longer term. A festival can, however, bring both positive and negative associations to an area; but if the positive impacts are stronger, it can help to develop a sense of local pride and identity. Examples of this include Glastonbury, Reading Festival and the Edinburgh Festival. These events have all taken the host community's name and have therefore reinforced the relationship between event and host community.

LOCAL AUTHORITIES' EVENTS STRATEGIES

Many local authorities are using events to position their destinations in the market, and thus support their cultural, tourism and arts strategies. Over the last decade, local authorities' strategies have begun to state the importance of festivals in promoting tourism and developing the social and economic cohesion, confidence and pride that connect local authorities with the communities they serve. Through events, councils can secure political power and influence among the local residents and businesses. Local authorities undertake the development and direct delivery of festivals to pursue specific economic and community development objectives. Given their responsibility for public spaces, they have some advantages in presenting outdoor public events.

Manchester City Council (and the North West Development Agency) put forward a Major Event Strategy after hosting the 2002 Commonwealth Games. The prime objective was to encourage international events to come to the city, and also to build on the existing events to attract a greater number of visitors. With five bespoke venues built, one upgraded site and a total spend of £160 million it would be inconceivable not to extract the potential long-term economic benefits from those venues. The strategy consisted of a number of objectives to become a destination city, and can be summarised as follows:

- to ensure that the region can take maximum advantage of, and be adequately prepared for, staging and bidding for major events
- as far as is reasonably practicable, to manage intra-regional competition to avoid wasted effort and resources
- to develop a regional mechanism for sharing and developing expertise in the staging and bidding for major events
- to develop evaluation tools to consistently measure the impact of major events and guide investment decisions
- to provide a strategic framework to support bids to national and international organisations for the funding of major events in the Northwest
- to maximise the opportunities to secure engagement and funding from the public and private sectors. (North West Development Agency, 2004)

To acquire the international status of a destination city it was imperative for Manchester to have an International Festival. This event came to market in 2007 as a biennial festival. In 2007 it had £6 million support from Manchester City Council and a number of business-related, Manchester-based stakeholders to offset the financial shortfall.

Local authorities in the UK are developing event-led strategies in cities and using events to serve as marketing tools to boost the national and international profile and image of their cities, so as to attract hundreds of thousands of visitors every year. There are many public and private companies and agencies in the UK events sector at present, working to deliver successful events and festivals. Local authorities are increasingly promoting awareness of the events industry and the role it can play to provide inspiration and ambition to local communities to deliver large festivals and events on an international stage.

Although not all local authorities have an explicit event-led strategy, many can be seen to use events and festivals as marketing tools to achieve some of their goals and objectives. Events and festivals can promote urban regeneration and enhance the profile of the city. The international hosts of major sporting events have all experienced positive benefits in terms of their economic and social development. For example, the London Olympics in 2012 had a major impact on the local economy and the city as a whole.

CORPORATE EVENTS STRATEGIES

The corporate events sector has been the fastest growing industry in the UK over the last decade. Corporate events are used by companies to attract and maintain customer loyalty, to raise their business profile, and to increase the motivation level of their workforce to maintain high standards. Over the last decade, companies have become increasingly strategic in their planning of corporate events so as to maximise their impact on business profile. They may, for example, hold a team-building activity at a unique time of year or link their event to a specific ritual, ceremony or large-scale sporting event.

Corporate events can be broken down into two main types, as shown in Figure 1.5.

Large-scale events may include sports events such as the Olympic Games, the Commonwealth Games, Royal Ascot, the Grand Prix and the FA Cup Final. They also could include cultural and lifestyle events such as the Notting Hill Carnival, the Berlin Love Parade, the Chelsea Flower Show and major music festivals.

Corporate hospitality can be defined as events and activities organised for the benefit of companies who want to entertain clients, prospective clients or employees at the company's expense. A variety of options for entertaining are available, including evening receptions and dinners with a private view of current exhibitions.

Corporate hospitality events are a form of non-financial reward to employees and are increasingly being used by companies in order to motivate employees, to foster team spirit and secure employee loyalty in the long term. Corporate hospitality events may include cultural, team-building and sporting events. The increasing demand for high-quality and high-profile corporate hospitality events has enabled the expansion of events management companies around the world who specialise in organising them. Corporate events are big business within the UK market and have an estimated value of £1.2 billion in direct spend (BVEP, 2014 [online]).

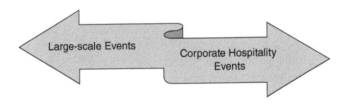

Figure 1.5   Two main types of corporate event

COMMUNITY FESTIVALS

The concept of 'community' has complex social, psychological and geographical dimensions and there are divergent views as to what constitutes a 'community'. Traditional views of 'community', as defined by the parameters of geographical location, a sense of belonging to that locality, and the mix of social and economic activities within the area, have been supplemented with greater degrees of complexity by analysts. 'Interest communities' rely not on the focus of place, but are anchored in other characteristics, such as ethnicity, occupation, religion, etc. This type of community thrives on social networks and social/psychological attachments. Britain has always been a multicultural society and people with diverse histories, beliefs and cultures have settled here. People from South Asia, Africa and the Caribbean initially arrived in the UK after the Second World War to help meet labour shortages. These multicultural communities now play an important role in enhancing the cultural diversity of Britain. Multi-cultural communities are spread all over the country, with approximately 30 per cent settled in the sub-region of Yorkshire and Humberside.

Clearly, while some communities might have a shared locality and common interests, there are underlying complexities which have ramifications for public policy-making, particularly in terms of community development goals. A misconception of what 'community' is, or a lack of precision or understanding regarding some of these elements, can lead to imprecise and ulti-mately unsuccessful and wasteful policy initiatives.

Community festivals now play a significant role in income generation for local businesses and create tourism for the local area. The expenditure in the local economy is more likely to *support* supplier jobs in tourism-related sectors of the economy rather than *create* new jobs; however, many other factors will also have an impact.

Community festivals or cultural events are those produced primarily for the community and only secondarily as a tourist attraction. There are various reasons for organising community events, including celebration of religious festivals such as Diwali. Community events can be part of regeneration schemes aimed at giving communities a sense of involvement and com-munity spirit. Community events are organised by members of the community, community leaders and professional event managers or festival producers. These events are often seen by government and community leaders as a way of improving communication between various sections of the community.

In addition to creating community cohesion, such festivals and events have the potential to improve the economic life of the host destination, by developing employment, trade and busi-ness, by investing in the infrastructure, and by providing long-term promotional benefits and tax revenues. Events and festivals not only generate significant economic benefits, they also provide host destinations with the opportunity to market themselves nationally and interna-tionally, bringing people from diverse backgrounds to the destination for the duration of the event or festival. As a result, they have the potential to provide host destinations with a high-status tourism profile and may enhance the links between tourism and commerce. Events may do this by improving the image of a place, by generating economic impacts, such as the devel-opment of local communities and businesses, by providing a tourist attraction, which may overcome seasonality, and by supporting key industrial sectors.

The economic impacts of events are the most tangible and therefore the most frequently measured impacts. Economic impacts can be positive and negative. The positive effects may include visitor expenditure, investment in infrastructure and increased employment. Examples of negative economic impacts include price inflation for goods and services to cash in on the influx of visitors, or local authority-funded events which run at a loss leading to an increase in local Council Tax. The latter actually occurred following the 1991 World Student Games in Sheffield. The economic impact of the World Student Games was not fully realised due to a lack of foresight from the major stakeholders. Bramwell (1997) made reference to the fact that mega events can be significant assets to a host city if and only if there is a strategic plan. However, he notes that for Sheffield, a strategic plan – the Friel plan as it was known – was not rolled out until 1995 and looked at events as a means to drive tourism to the city.

CHARITY EVENTS

Charity events have developed as a major provider of employment for event professionals. The alignment of a celebrity and a media channel orchestrated around a worthwhile activity can bring forward consumer support, revenue and media attention. The organisation of 8, 10 and 12 kilometre runs in cities throughout the UK has become commonplace in raising awareness and finance for a particular cause. The most prominent of these, which is recognised by the International Association of Athletics Federations (IAAF) and was endorsed by them in 2010, is the Bupa 10 km city run televised by the BBC. This event does not carry charity status; however, a large percentage of the runners are doing it to raise funds for a particular charity.

The charity sector has expanded substantially over the last two decades. There were nearly 200,000 registered charities in the UK in 2014 that raised and spent close to £80 billion a year. Together they employed more than a million people (*Daily Mail*, 2014 [online]). Data supplied by the Charity Market Monitor (Pharoah, 2008) also gives an overview of government support, which shows that there is a disparity in the amount of support depending on the type of charity and its turnover.

> Total government funding represents 35.7% of the sector's earnings. Charities with an income of between £100,000 and £1 million rely most on government funding, while charities with an income of less than £10,000 rely the least (9.2%). There has been a shift from grants to contracts since 2002. (Philanthropy UK, 2011 [online])

SUMMARY

In this chapter we have explored the ways in which events and festivals have changed over the years. In the past, festivals were associated with key calendar moments, linked specifically to particular seasons and heritage sites. Events and festivals have been revolutionised to meet the commercial needs of the market in response to the changing demands of local community groups and increased business opportunities for event organisers and local businesses. Local authorities are now using events as a major tool to promote their city and are justifying their bids for large-scale sporting events on the grounds that these form part of their regeneration strategies. Events and festival managers are now using historical and cultural themes to develop annual events to attract visitors and create cultural images in the host cities by holding festivals within community settings. Such events provide an opportunity for local people to develop and share their culture, enhance their own values and beliefs and promote local culture to visitors and tourists.

In addition, the typology of events has been thoroughly examined and many examples of diverse events have been discussed. The focus in this review has been on the objectives of these different events, or to be more precise, the components that make up their objectives, in terms of people, place and purpose. This chapter has identified the most fundamental of these objective components as being that of 'community' in all its many applications. There is no doubt that events and festivals do achieve economic goals and develop community cohesion through their functional role in attracting visitors to the area. We have also noted that the spending by visitors on local goods and services has a direct economic impact on local businesses and that these benefits pass more widely across the economy and the community. On the other hand, cultural tourism does not take into account the loss of local beauty, environmental degradation and the effects it has on the local people of the host communities through their direct and indirect involvement with tourists. In addition, events and festivals can play an important part in promoting the host community as both a tourist and commercial destination. Events and festivals can help to develop the image and profile of a destination and may attract visitors outside of the holiday season.

The various sectors of the events industry have been introduced. These include both specialists who organise a huge range of different events and the core event support services who are subcontracted to work across these different events.

Discussion questions

Question 1

Discuss the value of religious events to the communities in which they are held.

Question 2

Critically discuss the role festival events play in generating tourism.

Question 3

In your opinion, why has there been an increase in charity events and how do they benefit the events industry? Give reasons for your answer.

Question 4

Identify and discuss the benefits of political events to the cities and towns in which they are being held.

Question 5

Investigate the influence corporate and hospitality events have on the local community and regional tourism.

Question 6

Identify and discuss any problems that are associated with sporting events and their impact on the local economy.

Case study 1: Manchester Parklife Music Festival

The city of Manchester holds one of the fastest growing festivals in England that attracts musical fanatics and electronic enthusiasts. In the last five years Parklife festival has grown significantly and now takes place at Heaton Park on June 11 and 12th. Over the weekend, 50,000 people will come out each date to dance, play, sing, and groove to good music.

However, in recent years Parklife has come under criticism from local people against the festival. The festival organisers are leading a charm offensive to reassure neighbours about potential safety problems. Organisers have delivered 11,000 letters with details of security arrangements. For the first time, they will have a security team dedicated to the arena and a community team – responsible for behaviour outside. Throughout the weekend, people will be able to visit the centre or phone, email or tweet with their concerns.

Enquiries will be dealt with by 120 workers who are a mixture of police, security officers, parking monitors, cleansing staff, noise monitors and transport managers. They will be joined by officials from Rochdale, Bury and Manchester councils responsible for street selling, taxi licensing and the sale of alcohol.

The number of security staff patrolling the streets around the park has been increased and some of the workers will be on bicycles so they can get to flashpoints quickly. A no-parking zone will be twice the size of last year and residents of the streets affected will be given parking passes.

Critics have also accused organisers of not helping local businesses and organisations, so event leaders have pledged to buy as many goods as possible from near the park from local suppliers. Event management students from St Monica's RC High School's sixth form college will be invited to watch a sound check and Bury-based charity Jigsaw will receive a donation.

Jon Drape, chief organiser of Parklife, said: 'Working with a wide range of organisers, we have put a tremendous amount of work into making sure that all the concerns that were brought to us about last year's festival will be addressed. This is a radical plan and we are 100-per-cent confident of getting this right and we want people to know that, over the weekend, we will be approachable and eager to help with any issue, however large or small'.

Cllr Alan Quinn said: 'I had many concerns about the event and I am content that the organisers have done enough to prevent most problems that may occur and react well to anything that does trouble residents over the weekend'.

Cllr Andrea Simpson added: 'I'm really encouraged that the organisers have listened and taken on board everything that has been put in front of them'.

Source: adapted from *Bury Times* (2015) www.burytimes.co.uk/news/12959201.Parklife_Festival_organi sers_go_on_charm_offensive_to_ward_off_problems/ [accessed 24/10/2016]

Case study 2: Fundraisers – 'Stop firefighting and see the fire'

Central to the debate on how fundraising will look in ten years' time is our ability to look back. We need to reflect on the past ten years, where mass participation events and online giving replaced door-to-door collections as the mainstays of local community fundraising. Innovating and trend watching are the tools in the kitbag of those local charities who have fared best over the past decade and similar tools will be needed to survive the tough years ahead.

Much will be said about harnessing technology in fundraising for the future and no doubt it will be crucial. The right news feed on Facebook can transform a charity from local to viral in one click, which can be useful but not necessarily if you want to appeal to your local audience. Charities need to know their donor profile and understand how to tap into their local demographic.

Crowdfunding on a local scale could be the next big thing in local community fundraising and new technologies that are creating opportunities to advertise locally via TV and smartphones could be lucrative. This month, Sky TV launched its Adsmart business – an initiative which plans to serve tailored adverts to viewers featuring local stores and services. This kind of targeted, affordable advertising could prove a real bonus for local charities.

Collaboration is another way to keep local charities fit for the future. With almost 200,000 charities in the UK and thousands deregistering each year, survival of the fittest might mean finding a like-minded running partner. We are currently part of a consortium of 23 North West hospices who have collaborated on a new Granada TV advert. It is the first of what we hope will be many collaborative partnerships across the hospice movement.

Charity events are evolving, too. Once it was enough to copy events, or re-invent successful ones with a new twist. Nowadays, local charities pride themselves on taking a national event and bringing it 'local'. My big tip for the future is to watch how charity events evolve locally. We recently ran a Strictly Come Dancing event with a twist – asking the 'celebrities' of our local community to become amateur dancers – pairing them with a pro until they could compete in a gala competition. Funds were raised through sponsorship and audience voting on the night.

Preparing for the future is the biggest challenge. Staff and volunteer morale in local charities is more important than ever so charities must invest in staff and take time out to innovate and keep abreast of the best ideas. Local charity fundraising is often too focused on the fire-fighting to see the fire. We need to find space – mental, emotional, sometimes even a separate physical space – to be able to innovate; it can't just be tacked onto an already full to-do list.

Source: adapted from Houghton, Claire (2014) www.theguardian.com/voluntary-sector-network/2014/feb/04/10-years-time-local-charity-fundraising [accessed 13/10/2016]. Copyright Guardian News & Media Ltd 2017.

FURTHER READING

British Tourist Authority (BTA) Available at: www.visitbritain.com.

BVEP (2014) 'BVEP Launches Events Are GREAT Britain Report', press release. Available at: http://goo.gl/CyLzJr [accessed 30/04/2016].

Daily Mail (2014) Available at: www.dailymail.co.uk/news/article-2835947/The-Great-British-rake-really-happens-billions-donate-charity-Fat-cat-pay-appalling-waste-hidden-agendas.htm [accessed 30/04/2016].

Getz, D. (2005) *Event Management and Event Tourism*, 2nd edn. New York: Cognizant Communications Corporation.

Glasson, J., Godfrey, K., Goodey, B., Van Der Berg, J. and Absalam, H. (1995) *Towards Visitor Impact Management: Visitor Impacts, Carrying Capacity and Management Responses in Europe's Historic Towns and Cities*. Aldershot: Avebury.

Goldblatt, J. (2002) *Special Events: Best Practices in Modern Event Management*, 3rd edn. New York: International Thomson Publishing Company.

Hall, C. (1994) *Tourism and Politics: Policy, Power and Place*. Chichester: John Wiley & Sons.

Raj, R. and Morpeth, N.D. (2007) *Religious Tourism and Pilgrimage Management: An International Perspective*. Oxford: CABI Publishing.

Royal Statistical Society (2014) Available at: www.statslife.org.uk/sports/1713-how-much-is-the-premier-league-worth [accessed 29/04/2016].

The Guardian (2011a) Available at: www.guardian.co.uk/commentisfree/2011/aug/07/are-pop-festivals-over-debate? [accessed 09/09/2011].

This Is Money (2011) Available at: www.thisismoney.co.uk/money/news/article-2032122/Are-footballers-good-economy-Premier-League-tax-1bn-UK-season.htm [accessed 29/04/2016].

Tomlinson, J. (1991) *Cultural Imperialism: A Critical Introduction*. Baltimore, MD: The Johns Hopkins University Press.

VisitBritain. Available at: www.visitbritain.org/visitor-economy-facts [accessed 28/04/2016].

Yeoman, I., Robertson, M., Ali-Knight, J., Drummond, S. and McMahon-Beattie, U. (2004) *Festival and Events Management: An International Arts and Culture Perspective*. Oxford: Butterworth-Heinemann.

2
EVENTS DESTINATIONS MANAGEMENT

In this chapter you will cover

This chapter introduces the concept of events tourism. Events tourism and tourism destinations are intrinsically linked. Cities and regions throughout the UK and the European Union have developed strategic policies for encouraging tourism when associated with festivals and events. Festivals attract cultural tourists to local community events and promote enriching exchanges between tourists and residents. Where there are established migratory travel routes, and communities which have emerged through patterns of diaspora and immigration, these are sites which are often able to host particularly distinctive festivals and events. The case studies within this chapter explore the development of cultural tourism and multicultural festivals and events within the UK, and the positive contribution that these events play in solidifying community relations.

EVENTS TOURISM

Events and festivals play a significant role for towns and regions. Historically, events were staged for the benefit of the local community and were concerned with key calendar moments and seasonal activities (Buch et al., 2011). The purpose of hosting events therefore, concerned social and cultural benefits not economic ones. In more recent years, local events and festivals are being used as a destination marketing tool and a mechanism to enhance tourism development (Derrett, 2004). There are many economic benefits to be realised from events tourism and events can be big business for destinations. Getz (2005) identified several travel motivators for tourists which fell into four categories: physical, cultural, interpersonal and prestigious/status, and argued that events were able to satisfy all of these motivations.

Festival organisers are now using historical and cultural themes to develop annual events to attract visitors and create cultural images in the host cities by holding festivals in community settings. The desire for festivals and events is not always specifically linked to the needs of any one particular group. Events are often developed because of the tourism and economic opportunities they present, and also the social and cultural benefits they offer. Many researchers have argued that local communities play a vital role in developing tourism through festivals.

Governments now support and promote events as part of their strategies for economic development, nation building and cultural tourism. In turn, events are seen as an important tool for attracting visitors and image building within different communities. According to Stiernstrand (1996), the economic impact of tourism arises principally from the consumption of tourism products in a geographical area. According to McDonnell et al. (1999), tourism-related services, which include travel, accommodation, restaurants and shopping, are the major beneficiaries of events.

As far as events and tourism are concerned, the role and responsibilities of the government, private sector and society in general have significantly changed over the last decade. Where previously the state had the key responsibility for tourism development and promotion, we are now in a world where the public sector is obliged to reinvent itself by relinquishing its traditional responsibilities and activities in favour of provincial, state and local authorities. This suggests that festivals impact on the host population and stakeholders in a number of ways, including social, cultural, physical, environmental, political and economic. All of which can be both positive and negative.

The current trend in almost all regions of the world is towards semi-public but autonomous tourism organisations engaged in partnerships with both private sector and regional and/or local authorities. Together they have a role to play in the development, organisation and promotion of destinations. Host organisations, in marketing terms, reach niche as well as mass audiences, not simply through increasing visitor numbers at events but by creating powerful associations with the destination in the mind of visitors. In this respect, multi-cultural communities have a key role to play in creating narratives and themes which are the basis for diverse festivals and events. To paraphrase the eminent cultural studies academic, Colin Hall (1994), multicultural events and festivals have the capacity to create linkages between culture, place and identity.

Events and festivals are found in all societies, and are seen as a unique tourist attraction for the organisers and destination image-makers, constituting one of the most exciting and fastest growing areas within the tourism industry. The phenomenon known as 'event tourism' origi-nated in the 1980s. Event and festival organisers recognised the opportunity to enhance the development of event tourism as a brand to attract consumers and also to reassure the tourists that they will get the promised benefit from the chosen destination. The approach, as Getz (2005) explains, advocates a mixture of science and art:

> Actual mechanisms of image-making are part science and part art. The science is in researching the needs, motives and perceptual processes of potential customers. The art is producing an event or products to meet the needs and in effectively communicating the strengths of the attraction. (Getz, 2005: 369)

Getz (2005) believes that many countries and destinations fail to recognise the advantages of events and are often unable to manage negative images and publicity. Getz (2005) also states that due to rising competition, tourist regions and communities should strategically plan in order to achieve their environmental, social and economic objectives.

Events have the potential to generate a vast amount of tourism when they cater to out-of-region visitors. Although definitive data on the impact of event tourism is not available due to the com-plexity and diversity of the industry, Key Leisure Markets (2001) claim that day trips in England are worth more than domestic and inbound tourism combined. A report commissioned by Deloitte states:

> [the] report offers a snapshot of the UK leisure sector, which is worth £117 billion in revenue, accounts for 7.4% of GDP and has grown 5% annually since 2010. (Deloitte, 2016b [online])

Key Note's report for 2010 states that the market for leisure activities outside the home was valued at £60.4 billion in 2009, representing 7 per cent of total consumer spending.

A London Borough of Lambeth council report (2015) further supports the argument that the UK events industry since the 2012 Olympics has increased, generating over 530,000 full-time jobs, and was worth over £36.1 billion in 2012, increasing to £42.2 billion by 2015 and to £48.4 billion by 2020.

In addition, festivals have an important role in the national and host community in the context of destination planning, enhancing and linking tourism and commerce. Festivals have become more of a tourist attraction over the last ten years, which has had a great economic impact on the host communities. The events industry has developed due to the expansion of information technology and media networks. Festival organisers now utilise these new communication tools to advertise their event to a wider audience.

Community events are developed to create cross-cultural diversity within the wider community and to enhance economic value for local ethnic minority communities. Events such as African and Caribbean carnivals and Asian melas have given the local communities a sense that they are of long-term cultural benefit to the host city. Such events can promote cross-cultural understanding and social integration among local communities and visitors.

CULTURAL TOURISM

Cultural tourism is defined by the International Cultural Tourism Charter in the following way:

> Domestic and international tourism continues to be among the foremost vehicles for cultural exchange, providing a personal experience, not only of that which has survived from the past, but of the contemporary life and society of others. (ICOMOS, 1999 [online])

Culture can be seen as a sense of identity; it also refers to the importance that individual people place on local and national social organisations, such as local governments, education institutions, religious communities, work and leisure. Cultural tourism describes tourists who take part in cultural activities while away from their home cities. The purpose of cultural tourism is for travellers to discover heritage sites and cultural monuments on their visits. Keillor (1995), in an address to the White House Conference on Travel and Tourism, best described cultural tourism by saying:

> We need to think about cultural tourism because really there is no other kind of tourism. It's what tourism is ... People don't come to America for our airports, people don't come to America for our hotels, or the recreation facilities ... They come for our culture: high culture, low culture, middle culture, right, left, real or imagined – they come here to see America. (Keillor, 1995 [online])

The theme of culture has grown over the last few decades but no clear definition of culture has been accepted. Culture in modern-day terms is generally seen by governments, large organisations and individual people as a product to develop their own standing in a given market. Tomlinson (1991) explains that there are a plethora of definitions, and that culture can encompass aspects from these different definitions. Culture is wide ranging; as Yeoman et al. (2004) state, it ranges from high culture, such as the arts, to popular culture, which embraces diverse subjects such as football, music and television.

Reisinger and Turner (2003) argue that:

> Culture is a multivariate concept. There are many definitions of culture. These definitions of culture are complex, unclear and there is no consensus definition that can be widely accepted. The majority refer to culture in psychological terms. There is a dominant culture that influences the majority of people, and there are subcultures with regional differences. (2003: 16)

For Colin Hall, the term 'culture' includes:

> the social practices which produce meaning as well as the practices which are regulated by those shared meanings. Sharing the same 'maps of meaning' gives us a sense of belonging to a culture, creates a common bond, a sense of community or identity with others. (1995: 176)

Moreover, cultural tourism relates to those individuals or groups of people who travel around the world, to individual countries, local communities and individual events and who seek to experience heritage, religious and art sites to develop knowledge of different communities' ways of life. This can include a very wide range of cultural tourist experiences, for example, performing arts, visits to historic sites and monuments, educational tours, museums, natural heritage sites and religious festivals. The model in Figure 2.1 shows the process through which cultural tourism attracts visitors to different destinations and famous heritage sites.

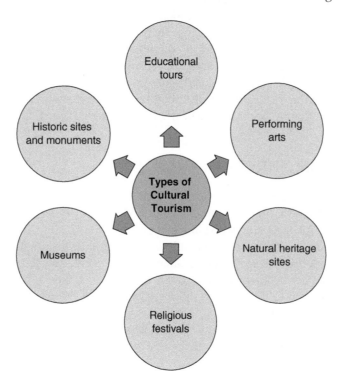

Figure 2.1 Types of cultural tourism

The future of event tourism in developing cities or countries relies significantly on event tourism strategies. Therefore, it is important for governments to develop clear and effective event tourism planning strategies. It is also important for destinations and countries to understand the potential needs and expectations of customers/tourists, and to introduce the consumer decision-making process for events. As levels of tourism in the future are difficult to predict, it is essential that governments and other related authorities do not rely on certain events to attract tourists, but have a variety of future event tourism strategies in place to increase cultural tourism. Moreover, it is difficult for some countries or cities to control negative images of their destinations and events through the media. So it is important for governments to avoid negative media publicity for their destinations and to encourage event tourism through highlighting the cultural elements of the country or city. Festivals and events can play a major role in generating a positive image of a destination, and amending negative images of a country can be important both economically and socially for the host community.

Strategic decisions made by a variety of governments in the past have resulted in poor support from the local community. Therefore, it is important for governments to work with local communities to attract visitors to cultural and heritage sites. Also they need to improve transport, accommodation and food facilities in the tourism areas. Governments should provide tax breaks for those companies which are catering for local and international tourists to the destination.

Event tourism allows locals to become independent. Government laws allow the locals to make and sell handicrafts, to rent rooms from their own housing, as well as to cook for tourists. This is an advantage both to the local community as well as to the country's economy. Government strategies, with support from locals, involve regular improvements of heritage buildings, such as museums, churches and large sports facilities. They provide facilities for visitors, ensuring that the locals are not disturbed by tourist activity in the area. Events can be used to develop community pride and self-sufficiency as well as intercultural communication.

NICHE TOURISM THROUGH EVENTS

Many researchers, including Raj and Musgrave (2009), Yeoman et al. (2004) and Kim (2002 [online]), have contested that local communities play vital roles in developing tourism through cultural festivals, sporting events and hallmark events.

On the other hand, in spite of the tremendous increase in tourism and events, cultural festivals are now assessed by visitor numbers attending the event, and the tourist experience is disregarded and treated as an economic tool to generate income for event managers and organisers. This can disguise the wider significance of festivals in establishing the link between culture, identity and place (Hall, 1994).

Richards (2001) argues that event-led strategies which market the 'cultural capital' of towns and cities have to consider balancing benefits between tourists and residents, warning of the pitfalls of 'social spaces' being utilised for commercial gain and competitive advantage over other urban centres. Event-led strategies, according to Richards (2001: 62), create 'the danger, however, that the city will become trapped on a treadmill of investment, requiring a constant supply of events to ensure visitor flow'. He suggests the possibility that more appropriate and sustainable strategies should focus on improving the 'cultural capital' of a city, which might benefit both residents and tourists. The inference is that the 'hijacking' of contested social spaces creates environments for events and tourism to the exclusion of community needs (Richards, 2001: 14).

Festivals can be big business for a destination. Festivals become part of destination tourism strategies because they can bring in new money to the local economy. It now seems the importance of cultural events is higher than ever. Festivals can act as a spectacle in attracting tourists' attention and concentrating their focus on a particular city during a short, intense period. This can enable the hosts to showcase their destination on a world stage and highlight key attractions and activities they offer. Therefore, local authorities are using events to position their destinations in the market, and thus fulfil their cultural, tourism, festival and arts strategies – see Raj and Morpeth (2007), Yeoman et al. (2004), Hall (1992).

DEVELOPING COMMUNITIES' CULTURE THROUGH EVENTS/FESTIVALS

The revolution in festivals has primarily been driven by the need both to meet the changing demands of local community groups and to address the increasing business opportunities for event organisers and local businesses. Festivals are attractive to host communities because they help to develop local pride and identity for the local people. In addition, festivals have an important role in the national and host community in the context of destination planning, enhancing and linking tourism and commerce. Some aspects of this role include: events as image-makers, economic impact generators and tourist attractions; overcoming seasonality; contributing to the development of local communities and businesses; and supporting key industrial sectors.

Organisers and communities hosting a festival provide the visitors with a vibrant and valuable culture. In addition, culture is the personal expression of community heritage and community perspective. Festivals also provide support to those who pursue economic opportunity related to sharing community culture with the broader world. UNEP (2002 [online]) suggest that cultural tourism is boosted through the development of festivals and events. Tourism can add to the vitality of communities in many ways. One example is that events and festivals in which local residents have been the primary participants and spectators are often rejuvenated and developed in response to tourist interest. Local authorities in the UK and other countries have provided grants and support for local festivals to add additional activities to cater for visitors. Priority is given to those events and festivals which include some of the themes in Figure 2.2 in their events.

The prime objective of local authorities' support for festivals and events in their area is to create economic wealth for the local economy. Tourism plays a critical role in providing jobs and income for many local communities. In addition, visitors to an area are likely to visit more than one place, and this creates more revenue for the local community and local businesses.

Event tourism over the years has developed into a massive income generator for local communities. Visitors are staying longer in urban areas and spending per head has increased, having a positive effect on the local communities. However, getting visitors to stay for an extended period in an urban area is much harder than it first appears. Unless the area is renowned for its history or culture, many cities do not own the credentials to bring in tourists on a regular basis. Large sporting events are one of the key areas for countries and cities to create events tourism. A sporting event generates global exposure and raises interest from local and international visitors. Large sporting events can act as a spectacle in attracting the world's media attention and concentrating their focus on a particular city during a short, intense period – enabling the hosts to showcase their destination on a world stage and highlight key attractions and activities they offer. Large sporting events are extremely beneficial for cities to promote themselves as a tourist destination and to enhance the visitors' experience. According to UNWTO (www.unwto.org), international tourist arrivals grew by nearly 7 per cent in 2010 to 940 million compared to 2008. In particular, as destinations attempt to differentiate their brands and engage visitors at a deeper level, unelected officials, namely destination marketers, may find themselves not only deciding how the events they host will present the destination and how they want the world to relate to their own destination, but also what the destination wishes to say about the world.

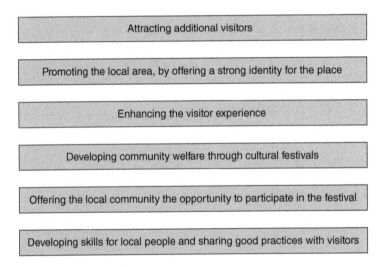

Figure 2.2   Essential activities for events visitors

Case study 1: The Bradford Festival

The annual Bradford Festival Mela was first held at Peel Park in 1988. In 2013 the event moved to City Park as part of a relaunched Bradford Festival programme. An intoxicating festival in its own right, the Bradford Festival is the largest mela outside Asia and a rare blend of party and pleasure trip. The Bradford Festival has created a unique image in the city since its inception. The festival perfectly illustrates its unique role in the communities where it brings people from different cultures together demonstrating various forms of expression. This also brings with it pride and traditional Asian arts to the city of Bradford.

The Bradford Festival attracts 80,000–100,000 people over two days. This has a great economic impact on the city of Bradford when local small businesses in particular gain vital revenue from the festival. Visitors spend large amounts of money during the festival and this outweighs the social and physical problems that are encountered by the locals.

Moreover, Bradford Festival brings the local community together to celebrate the diverse cultures within it. Over the last decade the Bradford Festival has become a major multicultural event for the city of Bradford and has demonstrated the advantages of cultural diversity to the rest of British society. In addition, the festival has created significant economic impacts for the local community and enhanced local businesses that benefit from the actual event.

The Bradford Festival over the years has developed into an international event that attracts audiences from the UK and throughout the world. It attracts family and friends

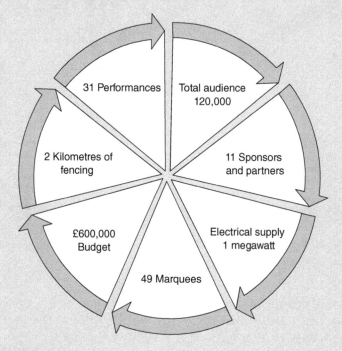

Figure 2.3 Bradford Festival key facts

Source: Bradford Mela (2011)

(Continued)

(Continued)

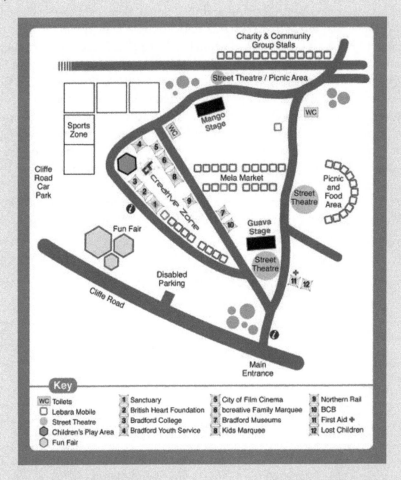

Figure 2.4   Bradford Festival Mela site plan

Source: Bradford Telegraph and Argus (2009)

from abroad due to the large South Asian Community in Bradford. They often pick festival time to visit close family and friends in the city, which increases the tourism in the area. Councillor Adrian Naylor, Bradford Council's executive member for regeneration, stated:

> Bradford Mela, the first in Europe, helped give the city a worldwide recognition. In terms of businesses this is a great showcase, as you walk around you see everything, from the voluntary sector to the private sector. (*Bradford Telegraph and Argus*, 2009 [online])

The visitors to the festival provide great financial support for the local economy by overnight stays in the city, which generates direct income from the festival for local businesses. The festival also has a major impact on the host city by creating extra employment for the period leading up to the event and even after the event has taken place. The data in Figure 2.3 highlights the actual benefits the event brings to the city.

The Bradford Festival has developed into one of the centrepieces of the Bradford International Festival programme. The Festival has offered a cultural display over the last 28 years to attract tourists and build the image of the city of Bradford. Figure 2.4 gives the site plan for Bradford Festival Mela 2009. In recent years many local businesses have been inspired by the Bradford Festival to hold stalls at the Mela market.

The Bradford Festival now attracts tourists from different community groups and creates cultural experiences for the visitors in a general context. Traditionally, the Bradford Festival depended on local visitors. In its early years the Mela attracted over 95 per cent of local people to the festival. This image has changed over the last decade and now 42 per cent of visitors attending the event come from outside the city of Bradford. Some of the visitors come from as far away as countries like Pakistan, India and Bangladesh. Other cities in England have adopted a similar approach to the city of Bradford to develop cultural festivals similar to the Bradford Festival, to create an enhanced image, reputation and status among South Asian communities to help attract visitors to their area.

Without any deliberate planning, the festival has become a PR event for the Asian community and added an educational focus for other cultures to understand the different aspects of South Asian communities. Finally, Bradford Festival has created an image to enhance tourism for the City of Bradford.

MANAGING VISITORS FOR EVENTS

Hosting and staging events as part of tourism strategies to promote destinations has become an increasing focus for tourism agencies and national governments around the globe over the last decade. From staging international events to promoting community festivals within localities, events can shape tourist perceptions of a region and can shape the geography of the imagination.

By analysing event provision within tourism, insights can be gained into not only what the destination wants to present to visitors but also what the destination aspires to be. Events thus serve to provide potential visitors and other nations with an insight into a country's vision of their past, present and their future.

Community festivals provide displays of local cultures deemed appropriate for the eyes of passing audiences. Mega event hosting can raise the status of a country and offer an opportunity for it to showcase its cultures and aspirations on a global stage. Events have become part of an image-making process, playing a critical role in positioning destinations against their competitors.

Events can be marketed to reach niche as well as mass audiences, not simply through increasing visitor numbers at events but by creating powerful associations with the destination in the minds of visitors. These associations may be connected to the nature of events, such as religious festivals, but event associations can also result in an overall perception of a country or locality as 'dynamic', 'youthful', 'historic', 'sporting', 'showbiz', etc. The case study below looks at the destination management of Manchester by the local authority.

Case study 2: Manchester as a tourism destination

The North West region of England, and in particular Manchester with the City Council as the main driver, set out a strategic model to drive the economy forward and for Manchester to become an international destination by 2010, benchmarking the city alongside New York, Barcelona and Paris, etc. Manchester has a population of approximately 2.5 million inhabitants and is considered to be the second city in the UK after London.

Of the five objectives written in 2003, festivals and events were given prominence as an objective to enhance the city and region. In 2007 Manchester City Council launched the Manchester International Festival to the world market, a biennial festival of original and new work. It is an international cultural and arts festival which has become the signature event for Manchester. In January 2004, Manchester City Council approved a £2 million underwriting of the Manchester International Festival. This funding was also complemented by money from the Arts Council of England and the North West Development Agency. Early economic impact studies estimated that the festival contributed £34 million to the Manchester economy, also supported by the private sector with a potential audience of 270,000.

Financial backing for this event was detailed in the Manchester City Council report and resolution in 2007.

Committed or contracted sponsorship deals have been obtained of £2.5m towards the target of £2.8m, together with public funding of £1.5m, consisting of £1.25 from the Arts Council and £0.25 from Salford City Council. There is a broad level of engagement with local business and the Festival has been awarded the prestigious Lever Prize by the North West Business Leaders Team which offers not only a prize of £10,000 but a programme of collaboration with top business leaders across the north west. (Manchester City Council, 2007 [online])

An independent evaluation of the first International Festival in June–July 2007, by Morris Hargreaves McIntyre, was titled *The Ascent of Manchester* (2007). The report showed through quantitative research that the festival had attracted 200,930 attendees, created 34 jobs, and it was estimated that the festival achieved an economic impact value of £28.8 million.

CULTURAL AND ECONOMIC IMPACTS

Events have several types of impacts on the host city, ranging from cultural and economic, to social and environmental. Events have both positive and negative impacts on their host cities, but emphasis is often focused on economic analysis. It is the role of event organisers to focus on impacts other than the purely economic ones that may be created by the event.

The impact of events on host cities is changing in accordance with significant developments in the events market during the past ten years. Consequently, post-event evaluation is extremely important not only to review the situation but also to identify and manage the impacts in order to assist in maximising future benefits. However, it is quite common for event managers to pay so much attention to the financial impacts of the events that they can become myopic concerning other possible impacts occurring during the event. It is important for the event manager to realise this potential situation and identify and manage both positive and negative impacts resulting from the event.

Economic values are often placed on the benefit of publicity obtained for the event, which may occur before, during and after its occurrence. Column inches and advertising costs are used to quantify such impacts.

Undoubtedly, in addition to creating community cohesion, festivals and events potentially give greater economic life to host destinations, by developing employment, additional trade and business development, investment in infrastructure, long-term promotional benefits and tax revenues. Events and festivals not only generate significant economic benefits, they also provide host destinations with the opportunity to market themselves nationally and internationally bringing people from diverse backgrounds to the destination for the duration of the event or festival. As a result, they have the potential to provide host destinations with a high-status tourism profile. Economic impacts of events are the most tangible and therefore the most often measured impacts. Economic impacts can be positive and negative, but the positive economic impacts of events are visitor expenditure, investment in infrastructure and increased employment.

EVENT DESTINATION SECURITY AND ECONOMIC GROWTH

Since the terror attacks on the twin towers in New York on 11 September 2001 the pressure on destinations to attract tourists against their competition has increased, compounded by the fact that the US and North American region was competing for a smaller tourist market. Increasing terrorism around the world is making it incredibly difficult for tourists to avoid destinations associated with risk. Terrorists are now targeting tourist destinations, making it increasingly problematic for destinations to hold major sporting, music and cultural events. Therefore, terrorism is creating a serious tourism crisis for event managers who organise and manage large-scale events. It became clear that while leisure travellers were altering travel plans, adventure tourists and Europeans in particular appeared to be less sensitive to security concerns. The swift change in trend and direction required a rapid and effective response and would prove a catalyst for a move away from advertising and towards events as a more powerful mechanism to 're-image' destinations for the target markets. The focus for tourism boards was to continue presenting the destination as pristine and untouched but also to actively encourage more adventure/eco-tourists and Europeans to visit the USA. In order to represent such images on such a scale, the tourism boards had to go beyonds advertising. Over the last two decades the events industry has grown faster than any other creative industry, regardless of the many setbacks identified in the Figure 2.5.

The events industry in the UK is contributing about £58.4 billion in gross domestic product (GDP) and employing over 530,000 full-time equivalent (FTE) people (Eventbrite, 2015). Figure 2.6 provides details of the economic value of the events sector. The events sector is affected by world terrorism, economic downturns and international conflicts. Events are becoming a powerful destination development tool for event organisers in order to 're-image' or 'image' destinations.

The 'nostalgia motivation' is where tourists visit sports-related attractions such as stadiums and sport museums. Such a trend manifests itself in many ways from tours of Olympic stadiums to see the Eiffel Tower in Paris for instance to the 'Beckham trail' in the London Borough of Waltham Forest which enables visitors to follow in the foot(ball) steps of David Beckham. Sports event tourism involves spectating at sports events. However, the nature and size of the event may not necessarily need to be 'mega' in order to provide imaging opportunities. And while travel to the destination is identified in this segment, the value of watching sporting events from home cannot be underestimated.

Many leading researchers argue that globalisation has led to a competitive marketplace for tourist destinations, and the culture and heritage of a destination is what offers the authenticity and unique selling point that attracts visitors (Raj and Vignali, 2010; Richards, 2001; Hall, 1992). Festivals and events represent the host communities' sense of place and identity, and there has been growing interest in this concept (Derrett, 2004). Emphasis has been laid on hosting local events and festivals due to their appeal to visitors who want to experience the authentic local culture. Events started by the local community therefore can evolve into events of significance, in terms of economic and social benefits for the host region.

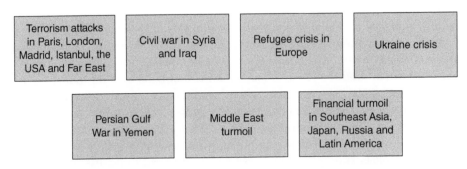

Figure 2.5   Destinations and conflicts

SUMMARY

Over the last two decades the events industry has been growing very fast and local authorities have identified the importance of using festivals to stimulate tourist demand. Many countries have realised the positive effects that event tourism can have. Countries such as the USA, Australia and China have all attracted a wide variety of events, such as the Olympic Games, which have contributed to the development of the country as well as increasing the number of annual tourist arrivals. Examples such as these have shown that events are definitely an effective tool to attract tourists, not only at the time of the event but in the future as well.

This chapter has suggested that events tourism has increased through the development of local festivals which provide economic and cultural benefits to the local area. It was found that social and economic factors contributed to events tourism growth in these festivals. The Bradford Festival and Manchester International Festival have become major tourist attractions for local, regional and international visitors.

Festivals have contributed to the development of events and cultural tourism. Festivals attract events tourists to local community events to promote cultural exchanges between tourists and residents. Events tourism brings benefits to cities, but these benefits are not being analysed in any great depth. Tourism festivals have major effects on the local economy directly and indirectly. The spending by visitors on local goods and services has a direct economic impact on local businesses and these benefits also pass more widely across the economy and the community.

Discussion questions

Question 1

Evaluate and examine evidence of community cohesion and community disharmony in relation to cultural festivals.

Question 2

Examine public safety, police presence and density of people and their effect on the host community during festivals and events.

Question 3

Critically develop a strategic approach for how to deliver an iconic festival that residents will be proud of and visitors will engage with as part of their cultural festival.

(Continued)

(Continued)

Question 4

Critically evaluate the long-term economic impact of outdoor events on host cities.

Question 5

Explore and discuss the potential benefits that events bring to the hosting community in terms of cultural, social and economic impacts.

Question 6

Critically evaluate the success of the autonomous tourism organisations engaged in partnerships with both the private sector and regional and/or local authorities.

Case study 3: Seattle International Film Festival (SIFF)

Seattle International Film Festival (SIFF) is the largest and one of the best attended film festivals in North America. Taking place over three weeks in late May and early June, SIFF shows more than 400 feature films and documentaries at a wide variety of venues throughout the city. SIFF also operates a year-round venue, and coordinates and hosts numerous events throughout the year.

The challenge

It takes well over 700 active volunteers and at least 100 paid/regular, contract and hourly staff to run festival operations each year. Like most festivals and seasonal events, many SIFF volunteers are new and need to be brought on-board quickly but in a productive manner. With such a steep volunteer ramp-up prior to each event, online scheduling and recruiting tools that require minimal training are critical.

For example, in order to host over 400 films across multiple screening venues, and also to stage numerous industry parties, special events, and other activities, SIFF requires at least 4,500 positions to be scheduled and reliably filled by qualified volunteers and staff members. Such roles include: usher, box office, theater operations, special events and hospitality, office/clerical, promotions, and dozens of others.

Shiftboard event scheduling software

The Shiftboard hosted software system provides SIFF round-the-clock scheduling and communications for the festival. SIFF is one of Shiftboard's earliest not-for-profit customers, having used the system for event scheduling since 2005.

Designed and updated for the unique, ever changing SIFF look and feel, the system includes:

- Web registrations, group communications, and complete access to online scheduling 24 hours a day, seven days a week – from any web browser
- Color-coded schedule views, sign in sheets, email reminders and confirmation for upcoming shifts
- Ability to view, print and report entire schedules from a single source

Monica Hinckley, SIFF's volunteer coordinator for two consecutive years, says that scheduling continues to get easier. 'Getting people on the system went exceptionally well this year. Everyone within the SIFF organization uses Shiftboard, our paid workers and volunteers. Being user friendly and flexible, everyone, including our most loyal retirees and senior citizens say to me, "Shiftboard is great!"'

Hinckley also says that Shiftboard has made a huge difference compared to what the volunteer coordinator's job has traditionally been. 'Typically, managers had to ask the volunteer coordinator to schedule shifts for them,' she explained, 'but now we have at least 10 team managers on our Shiftboard site, each of whom can schedule and communicate directly with their volunteers any time of day.'

Hinckley uses Shiftboard reporting and signing sheets every day. 'I use the visual charts to see where and when I need people and also to compare my current coverage expectations to any previous years' results.'

Source: www.shiftboard.com/casestudies/event-management/event-scheduling-seattle-international-film-festival.html [accessed 13/10/2016]

Case study 4: Notting Hill Carnival

Notting Hill Carnival (NHC) is about people coming together, celebrating and having fun. NHC presents a wonderful atmosphere – it combines Caribbean music and art forms with Caribbean food. NHC merges the vibrant colours of parading costumes and sounds of the Caribbean with the terraced streets of London, creating cultural diversity in the local community.

Over the August bank holiday weekend, there is a large influx of people into the Notting Hill area; in 2013, approximately one million people attended (Royal Borough of

(Continued)

(Continued)

Kensington and Chelsea, 2013 [online]). This presents many problems for local residents as it prevents them from carrying out their day-to-day activities. Batty et al. (2003) suggested that the number of people in the streets during NHC presents many challenges. The strategic review identified that the impact of this on the Notting Hill area was problematic and sought to minimise this through recommending parts of the event be contained (Greater London Authority, 2004).

Both community cohesion and community disharmony have surrounded the NHC celebrations from their very beginnings. NHC has had a chequered past with violence, crime and anti-social behaviour often being associated with the event. The police presence at the carnival is often high and it has been portrayed within the media that NHC is an unsafe event. *The Guardian* (2011b) reported:

> Up to 70 floats are expected to take part in the children's day parade amid a heavy police presence. Officers are manning knife arches on London underground links around the capital ... about 16,000 officers will be deployed across the capital for the duration of the carnival.

The police attendance figures for NHC for 2009–2013 are presented in Table 2.1.

Table 2.1   Police attendance figures for NHC

Year	2013	2012	2011	2010	2009
Sunday	5827	5941	5500	4626	4961
Monday	6810	6582	6500	5729	5618

Source: adapted from Royal Borough of Kensington and Chelsea (2013)

The table shows that the police presence at NHC has been significantly large over the five years. Each year the police report on what criminal activity has taken place during NHC. In 2013, it was reported that 279 arrests were made during the event (The Voice, 2013). This highlights that there are some negative impacts for the host community and NHC can bring anti-social behaviour and crime into the area. The Royal Borough of Kensington and Chelsea (2013) conducted an environmental impact and community safety report which showed the number of complaints received by residents regarding noise.

Source: adapted from Raj, R. and Simpson, H. (2015) 'Exploitation of Notting Hill Carnival to increase community pride and spirit and act as a catalyst for regeneration', *Journal of Hospitality and Tourism*, 13(1): 27–47.

FURTHER READING

Deloitte (2016) 'Leisure sector grows to £117 billion as UK consumers prefer pleasure to shopping'. Available at: www2.deloitte.com/uk/en/pages/press-releases/articles/leisure-sector-grows-to-117-billion.html [accessed 21/11/2016].

Dwyer, L., Mellor, R., Mistillis, N. and Mules, T. (2000) 'A framework for assessing "tangible" and "intangible" impacts of events and conventions', *Event Management*, 6: 175–89.

English Heritage (2000) *Tourism Facts 2001*. Swindon: English Heritage.

Eventbrite (2015) Available at: www.eventbrite.co.uk/blog/uk-event-industry-in-numbers/ [accessed 13/10/2016].

Getz, D. (2005) *Event Management and Event Tourism*, 2nd edn. New York: Cognizant Communications Corporation.

Greater London Authority (2004) *Notting Hill Carnival: A Strategic Review*. Available at: www.london.gov.uk/moderngov/Data/Culture%20Sport%20and%20Tourism%20Committee/20040310/Agenda/5%20Notting%20Hill%20Carnival%20PDF.pdf [accessed 21/11/2016].

Key Note (2010) *Leisure Outside the Home Market Review 2010*. London: Key Note.

Leslie, D. (2001) 'Urban regeneration and Glasgow's galleries with particular reference to the Burrell Collection', in G. Richards (ed.), *Cultural Attractions and European Tourism*. Oxford: CABI Publishing, pp. 111–34.

Richards, G. (ed.) (2001) *Cultural Attractions and European Tourism*. Oxford: CABI Publishing.

Seattle International Film Festival (2015) Available at: www.shiftboard.com/casestudies/event-management/event-scheduling-seattle-international-film-festival.html [accessed 13/10/2016].

3

EVENT ENTREPRENEURSHIP

In this chapter you will cover

The aim of the chapter is to provide an overview of entrepreneurship in the events industry. Theories of entrepreneurship will be discussed in order to identify the prime methods and techniques which would help event managers to develop the necessary skills and attitudes to deal with the challenges and at the same time take advantage of the new opportunities presented by the evolving events industry.

The events industry is a key player within the key economic sector of creative industries. The events industry mainly includes the designing, promoting, advertising and delivery of an event, but also includes a range of supporting professions and boundary industries.

Most entrepreneurs start their first venture in their own field of interest and expertise. This implies that emerging entrepreneurs with event skills (particularly event management graduates) are more likely to identify an opportunity within the events industry. Therefore, it is important that, as a prospective event entrepreneur, you should understand the full extent of the events industry and where you might find potential business opportunities.

Despite the global economic downturn and the challenges and opportunities presented by the emerging economic superpowers like India and China, the events industry in the West is still thriving, with plenty of opportunities for innovative and intuitive event entrepreneurs.

WHAT IS ENTREPRENEURSHIP?

The word *entrepreneur* is widely used both in everyday conversation and as a technical term in management and economics. It is a French word dating back to the 1700s, and originally referred to an individual commissioned to carry out a particular commercial project by someone with money to invest. This was often an overseas trading project and carried with it risk for both the investor (who could lose money) and the entrepreneur (who could lose a great deal more). Therefore the chance of risk with entrepreneurial activity is evident from the start.

Since then the term has evolved to mean someone who undertakes a venture, particularly starting a new business. This meaning is central to the understanding of the word entrepreneur in the English language, although the French would prefer to use *créateur d'entreprise* (creator of an enterprise). From the word entrepreneur, a number of concepts have been derived such as *entrepreneurship, entrepreneurial* and *entrepreneurial process*. Entrepreneurship is what an entrepreneur does. It is more of a process, a way of doing things that transforms innovation into market opportunities or competitive advantage. The entrepreneurial process is the means through which new value is created as a result of the project – the *entrepreneurial venture*. Entrepreneurial is an adjective describing how entrepreneurs undertake what they do.

Nevertheless, there are many definitions of entrepreneur found in the management and economics literature and it is certainly a task to provide a concise and unambiguous definition. Endeavours to define it have concentrated on utilising the abilities that portray the entrepreneur, using those procedures and events which are a part of entrepreneurship, and using those outcomes that entrepreneurship leads to. Most of the existing definitions are a mix of these three. For instance:

> An entrepreneur is a person who identifies an opportunity or new idea and develops it into a new venture project. (Burke, 2006)

In this respect, enterprise is an outcome of entrepreneurship, i.e. the organisation created is an enterprise. However, to some people it is basically about using enterprise to create a new business, and in this respect enterprise is a means of entrepreneurship. It is important to note here that it is generally accepted that entrepreneurs are agents of change and that they provide innovative and creative ideas for enterprises to grow and make profit. They act to create and build a vision from virtually nothing, thus being enterprising.

Taking into consideration the above ideas, therefore, the event entrepreneur is the key innovative person who is managing the entrepreneurial process. This will usually involve planning, organising, promoting, directing, controlling, managing and delivering an event with the help of team members, together with handling the associated business risks.

Entrepreneurship is acknowledged as the driving force behind innovative change in society and the events industry is no exception. Taking the definition above, an event entrepreneur can therefore be defined as someone who sets up a new event venture. To achieve this, the event entrepreneur needs to spot new commercial opportunities and determine the needs of the customers by co-ordinating the resources to deliver an event.

ENTREPRENEURSHIP TODAY

Today, with the internet boom, entrepreneurs represent one of the most dynamic forces in the economy. It is they who are driving the technology boom, which in turn is driving much of the world's economic growth. This makes entrepreneurs very important from a macro-economic perspective. Entrepreneurs, therefore, are an economic phenomenon that has a major impact on the global economy and thus as the globalism of business becomes even more widespread, this impact will be felt even more deeply. Entrepreneurs are already becoming a major force in developing nations and in the economy worldwide.

The scope of what entrepreneurship involves will continue to change and evolve, and yet there are some common issues of how to start a business, how to finance the business, how to share our business with the community and how to learn from each other. Something that is common for all entrepreneurs is the challenge of starting their own business, be it through inventing something, looking for a new idea within a business, finding the right opportunity to break into a business or buying into a franchise. This involves planning and organising all the aspects so that the goals can be achieved. All entrepreneurs are also faced with financing their entrepreneurial enterprise. Even intrapreneurs (those who are entrepreneurial within an existing organisation – internal entrepreneurs) usually are faced with financial hurdles within corporate rules. So unless the funding for the venture comes from your own pocket, getting money is a challenge that requires preparing funding proposals or applications to be written and/or presented for loans and venture capital. There is so much information written about these stages of an entrepreneurial venture that sorting the good from the bad is an overwhelming challenge in itself.

CHARACTERISTICS OF ENTREPRENEURS

Integral to the concept of entrepreneurship is the ability to take action. It is this ability which sets entrepreneurs apart from others. In addition, a wide range of competences are seen as entrepreneurial and useful to entrepreneurs. These include knowledge, skills and personal traits such as those shown in Figure 3.1.

Furthermore, many pieces of research over the years have shown that entrepreneurs are risk-takers, or more willing to engage in risky activity. That is, people with a higher risk-taking propensity are more likely to exploit entrepreneurial opportunity because risk-taking is a

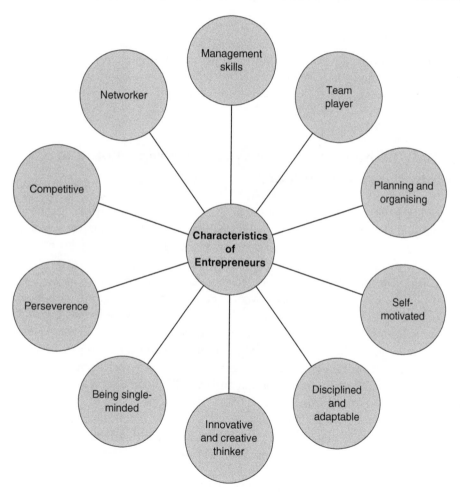

Figure 3.1 Characteristics of entrepreneurs

fundamental part of entrepreneurship. Aspects of risk-taking among entrepreneurs include investing their own money, leaving secure jobs and the stress and time associated with starting and managing a business. Kobia and Sikalieh (2010) argue that enterprising individuals seek to realise productive opportunities and consequently function in uncertain environments.

TYPES OF ENTREPRENEURS

Although potentially anyone can become an entrepreneur, it may be of interest to examine some demographics such as age, gender and race in their relative roles in entrepreneurship.

Young entrepreneurs

It is evident from several studies that entrepreneurs are most likely to be between the ages of 25 and 40 when creating a new venture. In fact, studies have also shown that entrepreneurship can emerge even among young people between the ages of 8 and 24. This is illustrated by the case study below.

Case study 1: The best ways for young entrepreneurs to break into the sports industry

While graduate programmes continue to churn out students with degrees in sports management, the competition for a select number of jobs remains rampant. Separating yourself is key to get a widely coveted position in the sports event industry.

You have to put yourself in the best opportunities to meet people already in the industry. Attend as many live sporting events as you can and learn how the arena and stadiums operate.

Study the different promotions, giveaways and in-game entertainment each team offers.

Any sports enthusiast can easily start their own blog to provide fan insight and opinions. This is an inexpensive way to get started covering your favourite teams and players. Throughout the year, there are hundreds of tradeshows and conventions that bring together industry leaders. The Sports Licensing Show, the Surf Expo, the Golf Industry Show, the Cynopsis Sports Business Summit and the MIT Sloan Sports Analytics Conference are just a few of the bigger ones.

Most of these shows bring out keynote speaker panels and moderated Q&A's that allow attendees to pick the brains of top thought leaders and learn valuable lessons. Bring plenty of business cards to these events as you never know who you may run into.

Source: adapted from www.inc.com/darren-heitner/best-ways-for-young-entrepreneurs-to-break-into-the-sports-industry.html [accessed 17/10/2016]. Republished with permission of Mansueto Ventures LLC, from 'The Best Ways for Young Entrepreneurs to Break into the Sports Industry', Inc.com, Darren Heitner, 30 November 2015; permission conveyed through Copyright Clearance Center, Inc.

Women entrepreneurs

Women's entrepreneurship has been on the rise to the point where women are opening their own businesses faster than any other segment of small businesses start-ups. In the United States they account for 29 per cent of all enterprises. Although a very high percentage of women-owned businesses are in the retail sector, women are now branching out into male-dominated industries such as mining, manufacturing, construction and transportation. This rise is further illustrated in the case study below.

Case study 2: Women-owned businesses are proliferating in United States

Women-owned businesses are proliferating faster than men-owned businesses in the United States, according to The American Express OPEN State of Women-Owned businesses Report.

Between 1997 and 2011, when the number of businesses in the United States increased by 34%, the number of women-owned firms increased by 50% – a rate 1.5 times the national average. As of 2011, there are over 8.1 million women-owned businesses in the United States, generating nearly $1.3 trillion in revenues and employing nearly 7.7 million people, the report found.

Despite the fact that the number of women-owned firms continue to grow at a rate exceeding the national average, and account for 29% of all enterprises, women-owned firms only employ 6% of the country's workforce and contribute just under 4% of business revenues. Further, the employment and sales growth of women-owned enterprises between 1997 and 2011 (8% and 53%, respectively) lags the national average (17% and 71%).

'Within the population of women-owned firms, we see steady growth but a lack of progress up the size continuum,' American Express said in the report. 'And, when comparing like to like, small- and midsize women-owned firms are keeping pace with the national average – and are topping the very sluggish growth seen among men-owned firms in the 1997–2011 period. However, something is putting women-owned firms off their stride as they grow larger; they fall behind toward the end of the entrepreneurial marathon, when entering the 100-employee and million-dollar "anchor leg" of the race.'

Source: adapted from http://entrepreneurs.about.com (2011) [accessed 21/2/2017].

Minority entrepreneurs

Certain ethnic minorities have shown a greater propensity than others, including the indigenous populations, to engage in self-employment. Minority entrepreneurs such as Asians,

Chinese and Eastern Europeans find starting their own businesses to be a way out of poverty and a chance to move up the class system. For instance, historically, in the UK it was the Jewish community who led the way in starting their own businesses after the Second World War, followed by Asians from the Indian sub-continent and China in the 1950s and 1960s. Then it was the turn of Asian-Africans who arrived in the 1970s followed by Eastern Europeans who came to the UK after the opening of the European Union borders. Interestingly, what is common among most of these groups is that they possessed some kind of entrepreneurial characteristics from their home countries and took advantage of the opportunities presented by the open UK business systems. Research has shown that there could be many factors in their success including culture, religion, family, network support, determination, commitment and hard work.

Asian people were twice as likely to be involved in autonomous start-ups as compared to their white counterparts. However, these Asian entrepreneurial activities have historically been in low-profit, low-growth industries such as minority ethnic retail and clothing (Rashid, 2006).

Family-owned businesses

A family-owned business can be described as one that is run by two or more members of the same family, and where the family has overall financial control of the business. These are an integral part of many economies.

Copreneurs

Copreneurs are couples who start and own their own business. Each one brings a special expertise to the enterprise and both are regarded as equal in terms of ownership and decision-making. To some this may be a recipe for divorce. Nevertheless, couples should set rules and clearly define their roles very early on at the start of the business in order to reduce friction and conflict. One key area to address is to keep family matters separate from business matters and have family time set aside from the business.

Corporate entrepreneurs

Three types of corporate entrepreneurs can exist within organisations: the intrapreneur, the venturer and the transformer (Bolton and Thompson, 2003).

The intrapreneur is the enterprising person in the organisation. They are the innovators who develop new products, new services, new processes, new market opportunities and new distribution channels. They are already open to change and are often the instigators and champions of change in large organisations.

The venturer is the next level up in the entrepreneur hierarchy. They have the talent to spin off a new business from an existing one. They either leave an established business to start up a new one; or they seize an opportunity when companies develop new ideas which do not fit into their existing set-up but still have growth potential; or they come to a decision that some businesses within their portfolio would be better off by divesting.

The transformer is the growth entrepreneur in the corporate world. They are the leaders at the top of the entrepreneur ladder and have the expertise and skills to lead transformation in large corporations.

THE ENTREPRENEURIAL PROCESS

The entrepreneurship process gives us a framework to understand how entrepreneurs create wealth and helps us to make sense of the detail in specific ventures. According to Wickham (2006) the process is based on four interacting contingencies: the entrepreneur, the market opportunity, a business organisation and resources (see Figure 3.2).

The entrepreneur is the person, or team of entrepreneurs, who is at the centre of the process and drives it. Entrepreneurs may be individuals or they may act as a team and have different roles and responsibilities. They may be from the same family, copreneurs or an existing management who have started their own venture after a management buyout.

Opportunity in the marketplace is the gap which has been left by existing players and is recognised by the entrepreneur either to serve customers better than they are being served at

Figure 3.2   The entrepreneurship process

Source: Strategic Entrepreneurship. Harlow: Financial Times/Prentice Hall © Phillip Wickham 1998, © Pearson Education Limited 2001, 2004, 2006.

present or to do something differently. The role of the event entrepreneur involves researching the market for those opportunities and possibilities which have not been exploited. However, in all situations, it is important that the customer recognises that the new offering by the entrepreneur is something of enough value to them that they are willing to pay for it.

The organisation is the new business created by the entrepreneur, in which the activities of different people need to be coordinated to supply the innovation to the marketplace. The entrepreneurs within these organisations often show strong and charismatic leadership.

Resources can be thought of as tangible assets and intangible assets. Tangible assets include: money, people who contribute their efforts, machinery and production equipment, buildings and vehicles. Intangible assets include: brand names, knowledge and skills of people, company reputation, and customer and supplier goodwill. All these resources can be subject to investment. The entrepreneur plays a key role in attracting the investment to the venture and using it to build up these assets effectively to supply the innovation to the marketplace competitively and profitably. Figure 3.2 illustrates the entrepreneurial process.

STARTING A NEW EVENT BUSINESS

As part of the entrepreneurial process the question is often asked by an entrepreneur: should I start a new event business or buy an existing one? In this section we examine the pros and cons of both.

Starting a new venture is not easy and accepting that at the outset will avoid any disappointments and regrets. It is to be expected that working patterns will change substantially, the hours may be irregular and the business may take precedence over everything else including family and friends. This is when support from family and friends will be really crucial, especially at the beginning, when the going is tough and the road is hard.

One of the challenging questions a budding event entrepreneur may have is: 'What kind of event business can I start easily and will it be successful?' This is a very difficult question to answer, as it depends on the entrepreneur, trends at the time, the global national and regional economic situation and the needs of the market. However, most successful ideas for starting a business come from identifying gaps in the market or problems that people face. Potential event entrepreneurs could begin asking and answering the following questions:

- What skills and capabilities do I possess?
- What business experience and expertise do I have?
- What is my rationale and motivation for starting a new business?

It is so important to seek answers to these questions and evaluate thoroughly your talents, skills, experiences and contacts to see if these could be translated into a successful business.

Further points to consider when starting a new event business include:

- Research whether there is a market for your new event idea before embarking on the venture.
- Who are your customers and where are they?

- Carry out a feasibility study to find out whether to pursue your event business idea or not.
- Identify who are your potential competitors. Improve upon their weaknesses and avoid trying to compete against their strengths.
- Seek out trends in events that are just beginning and take advantage of them quickly.
- Develop a business plan and design a long-, medium- and short-term business strategy.
- Consider starting the venture from your home but be professional at all times.
- Always try to negotiate the terms and conditions of any contract.

Another possibility is to consider starting a venture in an event management area that you are familiar with, and that you have given clear thought to in terms of its uniqueness. You could use existing contacts and networks for advice and help while searching around for a variety of sources for financial backing. It is important to cover the financial bases really well as it's no longer the employer's money which is on the line but your and/or your investors' money.

BUYING AN EXISTING EVENT BUSINESS

The trend of buying an existing business and making it more profitable is growing among entrepreneurs. This is particularly popular among displaced workers who are ambitious to become entrepreneurs, and among large corporations which are seeking out specialist small businesses to provide them with innovative products in new markets.

Many entrepreneurs are not the creative types in starting a new venture but are more successful in buying existing businesses and turning them around by growing them and making them more profitable. They have the flair to recognise good business opportunities when they see them and revitalise and revolutionise them rather than creating new businesses from scratch. Buying an existing business is a good idea when the business opportunity is thoroughly analysed, thought through and matches the existing expertise and experience of the purchaser.

Although the advantages of buying a new event business outweigh starting one from scratch, the disadvantages should not be ignored (Table 3.1).

Table 3.1 The advantages and disadvantages of buying an existing event business

Advantages of buying an existing business	Disadvantages of buying an existing business
<ul><li>Risks associated are lower</li><li>Lower asset costs</li><li>Seller may finance whole or part of the business</li><li>Buyer has clearer idea of the operations</li><li>The business may have established markets</li><li>There is a history of the business</li><li>Established suppliers</li><li>Established customer base</li><li>Seller may provide management training to run the business</li></ul>	<ul><li>Market is saturated and there is intense competition</li><li>Hidden costs associated with the business</li><li>Seller is dishonest and may back out</li><li>Inadequate market potential</li><li>The business is not worth much</li></ul>

SUMMARY

This chapter has presented an overview of entrepreneurship in the events industry. An event entrepreneur is the key innovative person managing the entrepreneurial process, particularly starting a new business such as a wedding planning or conference organising enterprise.

Entrepreneurship is an activity which leads to the creation and management of a new organisation designed to pursue a unique and innovative opportunity in the marketplace. Although there are many characteristic traits of an entrepreneur, the most important is the ability to take action and risks. Moreover, entrepreneurs are people who have a strong need for self-realisation and independence.

Research has indicated that most entrepreneurs are between the ages of 25 and 40; women represent the fastest growth segment in the start-up of new businesses; and ethnic minorities such as Chinese, Asians and Eastern Europeans have shown a greater propensity than others to engage in self-employment.

Although there are advantages and disadvantages in deciding whether to start a new event business or to buy an existing one, as an entrepreneur you should consider your existing skills, capabilities, experience and your motivation. Careful consideration and planning given to these points should reduce the failure risk of the new event enterprise.

Discussion questions

Question 1

Explain how entrepreneurship has changed in recent years.

Question 2

Discuss the characteristics of an event entrepreneur.

Question 3

Evaluate what has contributed to the rise of women entrepreneurs in the events industry.

Question 4

Imagine you are an events consultant and have been approached by a client to provide advice on whether to open a new event business or buy an existing one. What would you advise and why?

Question 5

Discuss the type of entrepreneurs that can be found in corporate events organisations.

Question 6

A new graduate has decided to convert his hobby of arranging parties into a career in the wedding planning business. What advice would you give to the new graduate on how to go about starting the business?

Case study 3: Ivvy

Lauren Hall's only been in Australia a few years, but already has plans to become the first female entrepreneur to build a $1 billion business.

She's preparing to officially launch the next version of her all-in-one events management platform Ivvy in the coming months, incorporating a real-time trading platform for the events industry.

Described as, 'The Wotif of the function space and event supply chain', the platform is also seriously scalable and already working with some of the largest hotel chains in the world. It's the kind of locally developed technology you can't help but get a little excited about, especially given its potential to disrupt industries.

But it's certainly not an overnight sensation. Hall's been working on the platform, in some shape or form, for seven years. A serial entrepreneur in her home country South Africa, she's also got the kind of back story that underscores an unshakable resilience and drive for success.

Hall arrived in Brisbane in 2008 with two young children and a husband, but no money and no local connections.

She'd walked away from millions of dollars in funding in South Africa in order to call Australia home, as well as everything she'd personally invested in a previous version of Ivvy and a number of other businesses. She describes the move as, 'committing economic suicide', but as the only choice for protecting her family.

She's now an Australian citizen, and believes she has a lot to give. Based on the Gold Coast (she liked the 'Surfers Paradise' in the name upon looking at options on where to live) and now running Ivvy out of the old Billabong headquarters in Varsity Lakes in the Gold Coast, she works closely with co-founder and Ivvy Chief Technology Officer, James Greig.

She draws on a background in programming, accounting and marketing in order to develop ideas and attract funding, but ultimately it's her hard work ethic and formidable attitude that gets what she needs done.

(Continued)

(Continued)

'There are no one hit wonders in technology, it takes years to build these things', Hall says, having brought part of the IP over from South Africa, before rebuilding it in a more robust and highly scalable way locally here.

It also takes a great idea. For Hall, the idea to build something for the events industry came from the frustration of creating and managing events herself. 'The processes that I had to go through with my team in sourcing venues, sourcing suppliers, collating the data, going back to clients, and then securing it all was so frustrating', Hall says, discussing event-based work she did in a previous business.

That frustration hit new levels when Hall was asked to manage a major event for 1,000 people. Having worked frantically to meet a tight deadline, she found that when she went to confirm the relevant suppliers for products and services, more than 50% had pulled out, including the venue.

'That was in October 2006, and right then and there I said I need to source a solution to this fundamental problem: access to real time data to allow organisers to be able to compare for and pay people for these products and services in real time'. She built the first prototype in South Africa, started working initially with one organisation before having some of the country's biggest banking institutions and employers mandating it as their procurement system for events.

I went on this huge journey, originally funding it myself and then required external capital to complete the technology and scale the business. Without my team and my shareholders none of it would have been possible. It was really an, 'imagine if we could do this,' to have this live data and simplify the process.

That was my desire, it's taken me seven years. And it's now going to change the entire way people manage, procure and secure their services and suppliers for events.

Hall says she's wanted to build businesses since asking her father for $10 as a nine-year-old and being told that 'money doesn't grow on trees'. She decided she never wanted to have to ask for money again, and never did – working a number of jobs in order to help fund the life she wanted.

Source: © Women's Agenda. Used with kind permission.

FURTHER READING

Barringer, R.B. and Ireland, D. (2015) *Entrepreneurship*. London: Pearson.

Kobia, M. and Sikalieh, D. (2010) 'Towards a search for the meaning of entrepreneurship', *Journal of European Industrial Training*, 34(2): 110–27.

Rashid, T. (2006) 'Relationship marketing and entrepreneurship: South Asian business in the UK', *International Journal of Entrepreneurship and Small Business*, 3(3/4): 417–26.

Wickham, P. (2006) *Strategic Entrepreneurship*. Harlow: Financial Times/Prentice Hall.

4

HUMAN RESOURCE MANAGEMENT

In this chapter you will cover

This chapter aims to provide an overview of human resource management (HRM) for festivals and events. Theories of HRM will be discussed in order to identify the prime methods and techniques which can help event managers to develop the necessary skills and attitudes to deal with employees in the workplace. In Japan, the recognition that people should be seen as a key resource within strategic plans changed attitudes to employment and resulted in increased quality for Japanese products and business practices. This allowed Japan to challenge for industrial dominance. This example suggests that people are indeed the key asset of any organisation and that the management of people has to be at the heart of any strategic issue, rather than a necessary inconvenience.

HUMAN RESOURCE MANAGEMENT

Over the last hundred years or so human resource management (HRM) has become a distinct feature in organisations. HRM has its origins in studies of Japanese firms undertaken by American academics interested in the development of the Japanese manufacturing industry. They discovered that Japanese personnel policies revolved around performance, motivation, flexibility and mobility (Blyton and Turnbull, 1992).

HRM is the process of organising and effectively employing people in pursuit of organisational goals. Dessler has stated that HRM refers to:

> the policies and practices one needs to carry out the people or human resources aspects of a management position, including recruiting, screening, training, rewarding and appraising. (2000: 2)

According to Krulis-Randa, HRM involves the following characteristics:

- A focus on horizontal authority and reduced hierarchy; a blurring of the rigid distinction between management and non-management.
- Whenever possible, responsibility for people management is devolved to line managers – the role of the personnel professional is to support and facilitate in this task and not to control it.
- Human resource planning is proactive and compound with corporate planning; human resource issues are treated strategically in an integrated manner.
- Employees are viewed as subjects with a potential for growth and development; the purpose of HRM is to identify this potential and develop it in line with the adaptive needs of the organisation.
- HRM suggests that management and non-management have a common interest in the success of the organisation. Its purpose is to ensure that all employees are aware of this and committed to common goals. (1990: 136)

Whatever the characteristics of HRM in event organisations, the planning process for human resources needs to be carried out carefully in order to fulfil the needs of the different types of event organisations.

FLEXIBLE ORGANISATIONS

A pulsating organisation is one whose workforce increases and decreases with demand. This means that the organisation must be flexible, with a core of permanent workers and a periphery of other staff. Due to the peripheral nature of temporary workers they will raise their own management issues.

In a corporate hospitality organisation, for example, the number of temporary staff used means that the organisation will be pulsating and therefore flexible. Flexibility can be placed into two distinct areas: functionally flexible labour and numerically flexible labour (Goss, 1994).

Functional flexibility

Functional flexibility allows employees who are multi-skilled to perform various jobs and roles.

A corporate hospitality organisation will operate with both functional and numerical flexibility due to the fluctuations in its labour demands. Functional flexibility could refer to an employee who, in the time leading up to the event, was responsible for the logistical operations, but during the event is required to perform as a section manager due to their prior role being completed.

Numerical flexibility

Numerical flexibility in terms of corporate hospitality will refer to the many agency staff employed solely for an event's duration. This is numerical flexibility because they are not required before and after the event.

The fact that numerically flexible staff are employed for short periods raises issues of how to achieve maximum output from them, how to build effective relationships, and how to have high service levels.

THE HUMAN RESOURCE PLANNING PROCESS

Human resource strategy

Many activities are involved at this stage of events management including job analysis and job descriptions.

Job analysis

Job analysis is a very important part of this stage of the HR planning process. It includes defining a job in terms of specific tasks and responsibilities and identifying the abilities, skills and qualifications needed to perform it successfully.

The level of the job analysis process will be different from event to event; however, some small-scale events that depend on volunteers may simply attempt to match people to the tasks in which they have expressed an interest. Under these conditions, it is nevertheless still important to consider factors such as skills, experience and the physical abilities of the volunteers.

Job description

This is another result of the job analysis process that you need to be familiar with if you are to effectively match people (both employees and volunteers) to jobs. A job description is a statement identifying why a job has come into existence, what the holder of the job will do, and under what conditions the job is to be conducted.

Policies and procedures

Policies and procedures are required to provide the framework in which the remaining tasks in the HR planning process take place, including: recruitment and selection; training and professional development; supervision and evaluation; termination; outplacement; re-employment; and evaluation. Stone states that policies and practices serve to:

- reassure all staff that they will be treated fairly (e.g. seniority will be the determining factor in requests by volunteers to fill job vacancies)
- help managers make quick and consistent decisions (e.g. rather than a manager having to think about the process of terminating the employment of a staff member or volunteer they can simply follow the process already prescribed)
- give managers the confidence to resolve problems and defend their positions (e.g. an event manager who declines to consider an application from a brother of an existing employee may point to a policy regarding employing relatives of existing personnel if there is a dispute). (2011: 163)

The event manager needs to make sure that policies and procedures are communicated to staff and that they are applied. Furthermore, resources will need to be allocated so that the policy and procedure documents can be stored, accessed and updated/modified when needed.

Recruitment

Recruitment is about making sure that the right staff are taken on to do the right job. For large events, it is more than likely that there will be a budget for this purpose in order to cover costs such as recruitment agency fees, advertising, travel expenses of non-local applicants and search fees for executive placement firms. For smaller events, in reality, however, event managers will have few resources to allocate to the recruitment process.

Once the right staff are recruited, event organisations need to provide the appropriate training and development.

Legal rights of employers and employees

The Health and Safety at Work Act 1974 has direct links with UK and European regulations. It states that if you have five or more employees, a health and safety policy must be in operation, with a clear health and safety certificate displayed at a location visible to all employees. The employer, apart from developing a health and safety policy, is also required to undertake a full risk assessment of the working environment for all employees. Consideration should also be given to employees where working conditions may endanger their health. Therefore, an occupational risk assessment could be part of the health and safety policy. The organisation can seek insurance once a full health and safety policy has been developed and introduced to all employees and a risk assessment has been carried out.

Employers' liability insurance is compulsory for all businesses with employees under the Employers' Liability Compulsory Insurance Act 1969. If your organisation has employees based abroad they must also be covered by your company insurance. In general, the minimum level of insurance cover for any UK business is £5–10 million. However, insurance liability may fluctuate depending on the type of business, and the type of event planned, managed and delivered. Organisations have a legal responsibility to inform employees and to display a copy of the employers' liability insurance certificate. This certificate must be displayed where all employees have access to it. There are some exemptions to employers' liability and one area is where family members are employed.

The Information Commission must be notified if an event company stores personal data on employees, and in particular where a Criminal Records Bureau (CRB) clearance is required. The vast majority of event companies actively partake in direct marketing, but personal information, such as contact details, held by a company can only be used once authorisation has been obtained from each individual. Websites that have an option to collect personal data must protect the individual's rights. You can find more information about health and safety, and public liability, in Chapter 8.

Another piece of legislation, concerning employing security at events, is the Security Industry Act (SIA) which arrived on the statute book in 2001, and was implemented in 2006–7. The main purpose of this legislation was to remove/clean up rogue security companies that permeate the leisure and entertainment industry. It also has a further remit linked to seven other licensed activities.

It is vital to ascertain the legal status of security personnel employed at the venue when your organisation approaches a venue for the purpose of securing it for an event. Once you have undertaken these operational and legal requirements, it is then the responsibility of the company to issue employment contracts that meet UK and European legislation on employment rights. Any employer must be fully aware of the minimum wage, human rights, disability discrimination, equality and race discrimination legislation when selecting employees and during staff development/training and awareness.

Training and professional development

The prime motive for event managers should be to treat individuals as a vital asset and enable them to make maximum contribution to the organisation. This can only be done if the individual is educated and fully trained on the job. Training is the most vital tool which can motivate and enhance the knowledge of the workforce.

Therefore, it is important to help new and current staff to develop new skills that will help them to contribute to the overall goals of the event organisation. Training courses and workshops for staff can be set up which address different skills and areas of development and enhance the knowledge of staff for the future. Figure 4.1 shows what the training programmes should include.

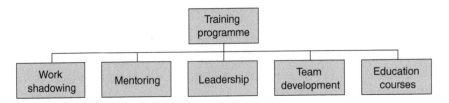

Figure 4.1   Training programme for event managers

If your organisation addresses training and staff development issues you are much more likely to have satisfied employees, and also to avoid high rates of staff turnover, which is a notorious problem within the events industry.

Boella and Goss-Turner (2005) have stated that an employee needs to develop and effectively achieve their role by developing the following:

- knowledge required for the job
- skills developed over the years
- attitude towards the job.

The authors describe how these can only be improved upon by effective training and clear mentoring to achieve the required task. Providing clear and effective training to the workforce helps the organisation to achieve the set tasks quicker and more effectively.

Mullins (2013) describes how training is a key element in the ability, morale, job satisfaction and commitment of staff, which will lead to improved levels of service and customer satisfaction.

The events and festival industry is very complex and changes in line with the nature of the event. For this reason, it is important for events organisations to offer on-the-job training and appoint individuals according to their skills and knowledge. To support this, the US Department of Labor has outlined the role of human resource professionals as follows:

> In an effort to enhance morale and productivity, limit job turnover, and help organizations to increase performance and improve business results, they also help their firms effectively use employee skills, provide training and development opportunities to improve those skills, and

increase employees' satisfaction with their jobs and working conditions. Although some jobs in the human resources field require only limited contact with people outside the office, dealing with people is an important part of the job. (US Department of Labor, Bureau of Statistics, 2011 [online])

The importance of training is unquestionable but it is not always sustainable within events due to the short period of time staff are required and the flexible nature of the organisation. Due to the strong customer focus of both the events and the hospitality industry, much of an employee's time will be spent at the customer interface. This means that much training may be considered 'on the job' (Boella and Goss-Turner, 2005). In the context of corporate hospitality at large-scale events, this may place extra pressures on managers who themselves may be unfamiliar with the event.

The need for orientation at events is evident, due to the large amount of staff on site and their temporary nature. Within a permanent sustained corporate culture, orientation takes the form of socialisation and can be described as acquiring a firm's cultural perspective and an understanding of others' expectations and their personal role boundaries (Foote, 2004). If this understanding is not reached then it may lead to misconceptions and a dysfunctional organisation.

This poses the question: 'How can you best help orientate a temporary employee who is arriving at an event on the morning it goes live?'

Supervision and appraisals

Training employees in the supervision function may be carried out through a variety of means, including having potential supervisors shadowing an existing supervisor, developing a mentoring system, or encouraging staff to take professional courses.

One of the main tasks of supervisors and managers is that of performance appraisal. This normally involves evaluating performance, communicating that evaluation and establishing a plan for improvement. The main outcomes of this process are a better event and more competent staff and volunteers.

Once an appraisal has been conducted there should be a follow-up review. This will allow the supervisor or manager to review job responsibilities and how these responsibilities have been carried out, and also to find out whether performance has improved. Training should be provided for managers/supervisors involved in this process.

Part of the appraisal system also involves rewards which, in the case of paid staff, come in the form of salaries, bonuses, profit sharing, promotion to other jobs or other events, and benefits such as cars and equipment usage (e.g. laptop computers). A range of options also exists to reward volunteers for their efforts. These include:

- training in new skills
- free merchandise (e.g. clothing, badges, event posters)
- hospitality in the form of opening and closing parties, free meals/drinks
- certificates of appreciation
- opportunities to meet celebrities, sporting stars and other VIPs

- promotion to more interesting volunteer positions
- public acknowledgement through the media and at the event
- free tickets to the event.

Discipline also needs to be considered by managers. Thus it is useful to have in place specific policies and practices that reflect the seriousness of different behaviour/actions, and these should be communicated to all staff (paid and voluntary). A disciplinary policy is likely to begin with some form of caution and end with dismissal. It also needs to be noted that many of the approaches to disciplining paid employees (e.g. removing access to overtime) are not applicable to volunteers. Approaches that may be applied to this group include reassignment, withholding rewards/benefits, and simple admonition by a supervisor.

Retaining personnel in event organisations

Retention of staff is a fundamental issue in most organisations. But this is a specific problem for event organisations because they are different from other organisations in the way they pulsate. Event organisations often transform their structure overnight, expand personnel by significant numbers for an event, and then reduce to their original size in a matter of weeks. This pulsating feature places unique and specific demands on event managers in relation to retaining personnel. For example, for major sports event organisations, there are three quite distinct stages in the operating cycle and there are different elements that need to be taken into consideration by managers in each stage. The three stages are: lead-up to the event, during the event and post-event (Hanlon and Jago, 2004).

In the lead-up to the event stage, an event can be put at risk if key personnel depart. Since in many events most personnel are seasonal, minimal notice is required before such staff can leave, which has the potential to pose problems. During the event itself, loss of staff can be unfortunate. Many part-time personnel involved in events generally begin to look elsewhere for employment in the concluding stages of the event. Some personnel may even leave during the final days of the event. The nature of the three stages means that major sports event organisations require more complex and tailored retention strategies than might be necessary in other organisations. Hanlon and Jago (2004) recommend that in order to overcome these problems organisations should have a guide illustrating their retention practices, which recognises that different strategies are required for various personnel categories at different stages of the event cycle. This would assist event managers to optimise performance. In addition, they suggest that the proposed strategies are made available to all personnel.

Termination of employment

Occasionally, event managers will be faced with the need to terminate the services of an individual. This may be necessary in circumstances where an employee violates the employment contract (e.g. repeatedly arriving late at the workplace) or under-performs.

This may also arise when economic or commercial circumstances of the organisation conducting the event are such that it needs to let staff go (e.g. insufficient revenue due to poor ticket sales).

Evaluation of the process

A regular review is necessary to see how well the HR planning process is working. To carry out such a review it is necessary to obtain feedback from relevant supervisory/management staff and from organising committee members in the case of a voluntary event. A specific time should be set aside to analyse the extent to which the process and its individual parts achieved the objectives. Once the review has been done, revisions can then be made to the process for subsequent events.

HRM THEORIES

What motivates staff and how can they be encouraged to pursue excellence? Some staff may be motivated by empowerment, others may be motivated by promotion, while others may be motivated by a pay rise. These questions can be answered by understanding the various theories of human resource management.

Empowerment

Knowing your job role leads to another management issue, this being empowerment. This can be described as permitting staff to undertake duties and accept responsibilities which were previously practised by management (Mullins, 2013).

This description is consistent with the HRM idea that empowerment will increase efficiency by removing unnecessary layers of management. In the live event context, empowerment is associated with the art of delegation.

Delegation involves the passing on of authority and responsibility throughout the structure of an organisation (Mullins, 2013). It can be conducted at an organisational level or at an individual level.

Empowerment may concern management as it could lead to various control failures due to a more remote management style (Boella and Goss-Turner, 2005), but it is also possible that it will lead to a more positive and committed workforce due to them having more control over the way in which their roles are performed.

Commitment

The next HRM issue to consider when managing temporary workers is the theory of organisational commitment. This is a contentious issue as its main purpose is to develop an employee to be committed to the organisation and their work.

The basic assumption underlying this theory is that if you are committed to the organisation and believe in its objectives and goals, it is likely you will perform well for them. However, in order for you to be committed to the organisation, what must the organisation first deliver to you? In relation to events an employee may not be committed to the organisation, but might be committed to the event or the work they are responsible for. It is therefore the organisation's responsibility to enhance and maintain this commitment.

To develop commitment an organisation must fulfil the needs of its employees. This will be a hard task to achieve as each employee will be different and have different needs, and they will also have different expectations referring to the psychological contract.

Diversity

This leads to the issue of workplace diversity. Diversity can be defined as follows:

> Valuing everyone as individuals – as employees, customers and clients. (CIPD, 2011 [online])

The Chartered Institute for Personal Development places diversity into three separate types as shown in Figure 4.2.

1. The first type is social diversity, which relates to demographic differences such as age and race.
2. The second type is informational diversity. This acknowledges the differences in people's backgrounds, such as knowledge, education and experience.
3. The third type is value diversity. This refers to the difference in people's personality and attitudes and is also known as psychological diversity.

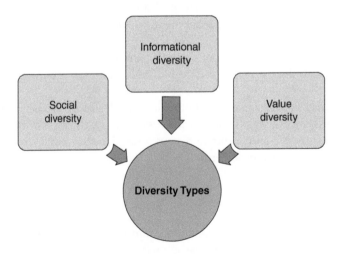

Figure 4.2   Three diversity types

Diversity is an issue that runs parallel with the other HRM theories and practices. It is an element that needs managing simply because it is the make-up of an events workforce. An employee's background, age, experience and race may impact on their motivation, commitment and how to achieve the maximum output from them.

As a manager, you can help with the issue of diversity by taking the following actions:

1. Examine your own styles of behaviour, beliefs and attitudes.
2. Consider your own feelings and reactions to people.
3. Be a role model.
4. See things from other people's perspective.
5. Be honest with staff.
6. Make sure that everybody feels part of a team.
7. Look at how flexibly you treat your staff.

Motivation

Motivation is one of the key factors in every individual's daily life. It is important to understand that motivation underpins an individual's ability to perform their duties. For this reason an employee's level of work performance is determined by their ability and their motivation, which has been developed through job satisfaction and individual needs. Theories to help understand motivation have been developed through carrying out studies in the workplace.

Motivation is a very complex concept and there is no universal answer for ascertaining which motivation theory applies to any given individual. Carrell et al. define motivation as:

> the force that energizes behaviour, gives direction to behaviour, and underlies tendency to persist, even in the face of one or more obstacles. (2000: 127)

Maslow (1943) provides a theory of individual development and motivation. The idea behind this is that people want better living standards and job satisfaction, and they will always desire more. This desire is dependent upon what they already have. Maslow suggests that this desire can be arranged into a hierarchy, which he named *the hierarchy of needs*. This is shown in Table 4.1.

Table 4.1   Maslow's hierarchy of needs

Type of need	Examples
1 Physiological needs	Develop self-satisfaction of hunger, food, shelter and sex
2 Safety and protection	Look for security and stability, feel secure and safe for the future
3 Social (support)	To care for others, love and be loved by others, developing social activities and friendship
4 Self-esteem (respect)	Admiration, self-respect, good opinion
5 Self-actualisation	Developing self-confidence and fulfilling individual potential capabilities

In this model, each need or level has to be satisfied for the person to be motivated in order to progress to the next level. The first three levels are seen as deficiencies. They must be satisfied in order to compensate for a lack of something. In contrast, satisfaction of the two higher needs is necessary for an individual to grow emotionally and psychologically.

However, the problem with this model is that, when it is applied to a work situation, many of the needs could be considered personal and are not necessary for motivation at work. It should be noted that Maslow's theory relates to individual life and not just to work behaviour (Mullins, 2013). Furthermore, it has been argued that the Maslow model is now outdated, and does not sit well alongside modern thinking on managing organisations.

Nevertheless, it is important to understand that an employee in any organisation will attend work in return for a salary or wage that has been agreed in advance. The level of effort from each employee will be different, because it will depend on the individual's motivation. In addition, Maslow's model has implications for human resource managers in that if the organisation can give individuals reasonable pay and competitive wages or salaries according to national requirements, and also provide the workers with a safe and clean working environment, this will satisfy the basic needs of individuals.

Expectancy theory

Expectancy theory focuses on the need to link performance outcomes to rewards that are valued by employees. Expectancy theory is really a framework for performance management.

Its main premise is that the motivation of an employee is determined by the perceived strength of the link between (see Figure 4.3):

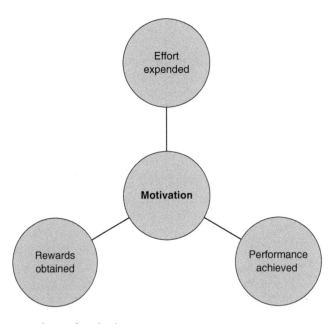

Figure 4.3   The expectancy theory of motivation

- effort expended
- performance achieved
- rewards obtained.

Expectancy theory linked with Maslow's hierarchy of needs provides a strong theoretical base for motivating factors in relation to temporary staff.

The social aspect to work

Supportive working relationships and social interactions with work colleagues can be strong motivating factors. These tie in with both Maslow's hierarchy of needs and the expectancy theory of motivation.

The social elements at corporate hospitality events will have a bearing on motivation, whether it is workforce-to-workforce interaction or workforce-to-customer interaction.

SUMMARY

Human resource management is a process of staffing and organising the right kind of people that will benefit the organisation and the event. As a manager, you need to understand that this is a process of integrated activities including: human resources strategy, policies and procedures; recruitment; training and professional development; supervision and appraisal; termination; and evaluation. Why are these activities and techniques so important? Perhaps it is easier to list the personnel mistakes that managers need to avoid. For example, hiring the wrong people for the job – both paid and volunteer; experiencing high turnover; finding that staff are not performing to their best; wasting time with useless recruitment and allowing a lack of training to undermine the organisation's effectiveness.

The final part of the chapter discussed the issues of empowerment, commitment, diversity and motivation, examining Maslow's hierarchy of needs for understanding what may motivate an individual, and expectancy theory for understanding motivation at work.

Discussion questions

Question 1

Why is it important to consider the legal rights of employees in the events industry?

Question 2

Write a job description for volunteers for a music festival you are organising.

Question 3

In your opinion why is there a high turnover of staff in the events industry?

(Continued)

(Continued)

Question 4

Identify the benefits of empowering staff in an event organisation and how this may give your company a competitive advantage.

Question 5

Discuss the type of training that you may need to provide for volunteers that you have hired for a community event.

Question 6

What steps would you consider in making sure that your staff is from a more diverse background.

Case study 1: What is it like working in event management?

Martin Jack is managing director of event management company Think Different Events.

Get stuck into events by volunteering – it is valuable experience and can lead to a job: Many event organisers, probably most, are always on the look out for volunteers to support their events. Obviously the larger ones such as the Olympic games, music and film festivals and so on are well known but within the business-to-business world there are a wide range of events such as conferences, product launches, award ceremonies and so on where on-site and other support is required. I realise the term volunteer means you are offering your services for free, but by showing a willingness to support events, gaining valuable knowledge in the sector and so on you are putting yourself in the shop window when real and paid event jobs do become available – gaining valuable experience at the same time.

It's important to manage your work load to avoid burning out: In our experience event organisation is very much like an exponential curve. It starts slowly and gradually and as the event nears the workload builds and builds until the event itself, when you are trying to appear calm on the outside but running about daft on the inside making sure everything is going well, if not you're firefighting, and then before you know it the event is over. You don't actually become relaxed, if anything you're totally deflated with little energy left. If you don't manage this properly with yourself and your team then you can burn out. If you don't manage the pressure, you make bad decisions. If you make bad calls, you exert more pressure on yourself. Entering the events industry is not an easy option. It's hard work no matter what role you have. The client expects a great event, the audience a quality experience and you are responsible for various aspects of this.

Make a name for yourself first before aiming for high-profile events: There are events where the great and the good are wined and dined and there is a great razzmatazz around the event. However this is the sexy aspect of the sector, one which a lot of people may aspire to. The reality is that you can only get so many people organising these events. I think people can improve their chances if they widen their scope initially, get that valuable experience, work up the career ladder and one day have a key role in the high-profile events. It's far too much of a risk to the project manager on these events to have staff who don't have the experience.

Rob Davidson is a senior lecturer at the University of Westminster, where he runs a master's degree in Conference and Events Management.

Master's degrees can help show you have a commitment to an events career: More and more graduates, in a wide range of subjects, are doing a master's course in events management to get in-depth knowledge of the events industry, as well as a way of showing their commitment to a career in this business and making their job applications stand out above the others. A growing number of UK universities are offering such postgraduate courses and you can see a list of these on the Association for Events Management Education (AEME) website, since most UK universities offering events courses are members. If you decide to go ahead and study this subject, I would recommend that you get as much practical experience as possible during your studies – volunteering to help at events and so on. That will look good on your CV.

Networking is essential so get yourself out there: Networking is key to getting that first job (and subsequent jobs) in events, and that's why we strongly recommend our students to join one of the industry associations so that they can meet and interact with events professionals at seminars, conferences and so on. Most of our students join the UK chapter of Meetings Professionals International and regularly attend functions and evening seminars run by that association. It's not expensive for students – it costs €40 – and it gives them something else to put on their CVs that demonstrates their commitment to this industry.

Alan Newton is group supplier relations manager at meetings, events and communications company Grass Roots.

Enjoy the event – but remember you're at work: Don't feel pressured into drinking. It is one thing associated with the events industry but it's not an expectation. It's important to retain your professional image and remember that you are still at work. If you're concerned about having too much alcohol, then you need to consider your own willpower. We expect our staff to enjoy themselves but, at the same time, to remember they are representing the company and to behave in a professional, business-like manner.

(Continued)

(Continued)

What to do when things go wrong: What all these situations require is a calm and level head and an ability to methodically and logically look at the solutions. You need to provide your clients with the feeling of safety and assurance in your experience and expertise to deliver a suitable solution. Things go wrong all the time because we're human and we work in a very human and people-orientated industry. It is always the manner in which issues and disasters are dealt with that leave their mark and your legacy.

Sarah Gordon is event manager for Thames Valley University.

There are some skills a course can't teach: I'm a huge advocate of education. I work in the education sector and think it is crucial, however, experience and key skills are just as – if not more – important. Particularly when working in events. Not many courses can teach patience, common sense, the ability to stay calm and collected when chaos swarms around you.

Glamour isn't guaranteed – but this is a hugely rewarding job: The hours are long, your social life will disappear a little when you're busy and it isn't anywhere near as glamorous as people think – however, it is hugely rewarding and the benefits are immense. I've been lucky enough to be involved in some fantastic events which are great fun and make it all worthwhile.

Justine Kane is an event management professional with more than 12 years experience. She joined us on behalf of Event Management Training.

Having an unrelated background doesn't have to be a hurdle: Lots of different backgrounds are considered for the industry. I have placed postgraduate students of mine with a physics background in roles. I think if you do have a degree, or have experience, in a different background it does help a lot to do a course in events so that you show you are serious about the transition and also that you have the knowledge. It would probably bode well for your own confidence in the area when in interviews and actually in a role so you feel like you know what you are talking about. There are certain skills that a good event manager possesses (being organised, people person, flexible and so on) which can be transferable no matter the trained experience. Do not let this be a hurdle for you because it does not need to be.

Source: www.theguardian.com/careers/what-is-it-like-working-in-event-management [accessed 17/10/16]. Copyright Guardian News & Media Ltd 2017.

Case study 2: Volunteering at a music festival

Oxfam stewards

If you want to get yourself to any of the big-hitting British festivals (think Glastonbury, Bestival, Reading and Leeds), as well as a bunch of great smaller ones, such as Shambala and Boomtown, then you need to apply through Oxfam. The money Oxfam generates by running the service goes back into its charity work and it raises £1m each summer through festival work. Applications to steward open in spring but you should register your interest now in order to get a reminder. You will need to provide details of a referee and pay a deposit in order to apply.

Work Exchange Team

In the States, the Work Exchange Team does a similar job to Oxfam, organising festival volunteering opportunities for music fans across a large number of American festivals, including the Californian music and arts festival Coachella and magical dance rave-up Electric Forest in Michigan. Again, you earn your ticket through shifts and the roles you take on will vary from festival to festival.

Festivals abroad

SXSW festival

The week long 'music, film and interactive' festival and conference in Austin, Texas, has become the darling of the hip, tech-savvy, entrepreneurial start-up world. It's a huge event that runs each year thanks to 3,000 volunteers. The festival welcomes out-of-town volunteers, making it a great way for a newcomer to dive into one of America's great modern cultural events. Out-of-town volunteers need to work a minimum of 30 hours throughout the festival as part of the conference crew or complete a minimum number of shifts with the production teams, with roles involving everything from technical support to registering visitors. Depending on the hours you work, you will earn wristbands giving you access to various parts of the festival. Limited hotel discounts are also available for volunteers.

Outlook festival

If you want to combine amazing music with a beach holiday, electronic bass-fest Outlook – this year featuring Lauryn Hill and Busta Rhymes – is one of several in Croatia that takes volunteers. Roles include everything from box office to decor, and applications open in the spring.

Electric Picnic

A leftfield festival in Ireland, which combines top musical acts (last year the line up boasted Fatboy Slim and Björk) with art, performance and comedy. Volunteers need to pay a deposit equal to the value of a weekend ticket, shifts last six-to-eight hours and volunteers need to clock up 24 hours over the course of the festival.

(Continued)

(Continued)

Sundance

It is one of the world's most-respected independent film festivals and every year more than 1,800 volunteers help make it happen. Sundance, which takes place in Utah each January, requires volunteers to help run everything from shuttle stops to theatre entrances. Volunteers from around the world are welcome to apply and will get the chance to see world premieres of new indie flicks in return for their hard work, as well as getting food vouchers and a golden ticket to the staff and volunteer opening night party.

Melt!

This rapidly expanding rock and electronic music festival in Germany relies on volunteers to help its 20,000-capacity event run smoothly. Volunteers must be able to speak German but the work provides an insight into the backstage workings of a large event and the organisers give out certificates for anyone using the experience as a step into the music industry.

Source: adapted from www.theguardian.com/travel/2014/feb/25/how-to-volunteer-music-film-arts-festival [accessed 17/10/2016]. Copyright Guardian News & Media Ltd 2017.

FURTHER READING

Blyton, P. and Turnbull, P. (1992) *Reassessing Human Resource Management*. London: Sage.

Boella, M. and Goss-Turner, S. (2005) *Human Resource Management in the Hospitality Industry*, 8th edn. Oxford: Elsevier Butterworth-Heinemann.

Carrell, M.R., Elbert, N.F. and Hatfield, R.D. (2000) *Human Resource Management: Global Strategies for Managing a Diverse and Global Workforce*, 6th edn. Dallas, TX: The Dryden Press.

Dessler, G. (2000) *Human Resources Management*, 8th edn. London: Prentice Hall International.

Foote, D.A. (2004) 'Temporary workers and managing the problem of unscheduled turnover', *Management Decisions*, 42: 863–74.

Goss, D. (1994) *Principles of Human Resource Management*. London: Routledge.

Hanlon, C. and Jago, L. (2004) 'The challenge of retaining personnel in major sport event organizations', *Event Management*, 9(1–2): 39–49.

Kandola, R. and Fullerton, J. (1998) *Diversity in Action: Managing the Mosaic*. London: Chartered Institute of Personnel and Development.

Krulis-Randa, J. (1990) 'Strategic human resource management in Europe after 1992', *International Journal of Human Resource Management*, 1(2): 131–9.

Mullins, L.J. (2013) *Management and Organisational Behaviour*, 10th edn. London: Pearson.

Stone, R.J. (2011) *Human Resource Management*, 7th edn. Brisbane: John Wiley & Sons.

PART 2

EVENTS FINANCE
AND LAW

5

FINANCIAL MANAGEMENT IN
THE EVENTS INDUSTRY

In this chapter you will cover

The aim of this chapter is to provide clear-cut explanations of accounting terms for event managers/businesses, enabling you to familiarise yourself with the financial management process. Financial management effectively controls growth and should be carried out by event organisations for the protection of creditors and shareholders and to keep the company in business. Finance is at the centre of every business and at the heart of management; it is concerned with everything to do with obtaining money for an organisation and recording and controlling how that money is being spent. The most important point to remember for event managers, even if you have no direct responsibility for managing financial resources, is to be aware of the financial procedures that are used in your organisation, particularly for those items which cost money or which generate cash for the business. The chapter also discusses the budgeting process for event managers to understand in order to manage the financial activities of organisations.

THE PRINCIPLES OF FINANCIAL MANAGEMENT

Financial accounts are concerned with classifying, measuring and recording the transactions of a business. At the end of a period (typically a year), financial statements are prepared to show the performance and position of the business, through the systematic recording, reporting and analysis of its financial transactions.

Traditionally, finance is split into four major accounting disciplines, as highlighted in Figure 5.1.

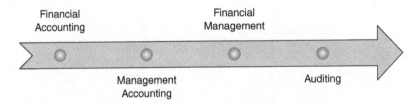

Figure 5.1   Traditional accounting disciplines

Financial accounting is a technique which involves recording the results and financial position of a business. Financial accounting reports on how the organisation has performed in the previous accounting period or year. The information is based on what has already happened. It is only concerned with summarising the historical data that has been collected over the year. Financial accounting is mainly concerned with financial reports which are produced at the end of each period for external users and shareholders.

Management accounting provides information to managers for day-to-day decision-making, as well as for short- and long-term planning. Management accounting produces detailed information for each department; it is also responsible for preparing budgets and helping the managers and board to set prices for their products.

Financial management is a method used to analyse the future for management and to help managers to make better long-term decisions for the organisation. In addition, it helps the management decide where to obtain money and to choose the best options for the use of the monies available to an organisation.

Auditing is an evaluation process for organisations to maintain quality control and also provide an assessment of an organisation's internal control. The generic definition of an audit is an assessment of a system, process, product and business. The role of the auditor is to carry out the financial audit as a part of the investigation. The purpose of the audit, which is designed by the law-making bodies, is to determine whether financial statements which are produced by companies are fairly presented in accordance with International Financial Reporting Standards (IFRS), Generally Accepted Accounting Principles (GAAP) or by the individual countries' own legal requirements.

In the UK the audit is carried out under the Companies Acts 1985, 1989 and 2006. The annual accounts of a limited company must be audited by a person independent of the company. In theory, the company should appoint chartered or certified accountants to carry out an annual investigation of accounts prepared by the company.

Each year the auditor will investigate the accounts prepared by the company. He or she will then complete a report explaining the work that has been done and noting whether or not the accounts show a 'true and fair view' of the company's performance. If the auditor agrees with the annual accounts, he or she will state that the work has been carried out according to the auditing standards as laid out in the Companies Acts. If in the auditor's opinion the accounts show a true and fair view, this is called an **unqualified audit report** (in other words it is a clean report). If the auditor disagrees with the company's board of directors in the preparation of the company's accounts, it is the responsibility of the auditor to ask the company's board of directors to make changes and report to shareholders at the annual general meeting, setting out the concerns on which he or she has disagreed with the board of the directors. In accounting terms this is called a qualified report.

Under the Companies Acts, the auditor must investigate and compile his or her report on four key financial statements, as shown in Figure 5.2.

In addition, the auditor's report needs to be included as a part of the final annual accounts for the company. Therefore, it is also important that the auditor addresses the reports to the shareholders, not to the directors of the company or anybody else within the company.

Figure 5.2   Fundamental statements for an auditor's report

THE REGULATORY FRAMEWORK OF ACCOUNTING

In the UK the preparation of financial accounts is governed by the Companies Acts 1985, 1989 and 2006, particularly for limited companies. The UK is (EU) a member of the European Union currently and companies need to comply with legal requirements which are set by the EU. The regulatory framework is based on three main accounting laws.

Company law

Company law provides the legal framework within which businesses operate in the UK. The Companies Act 1985 brought together all the previous Acts. This Act was amended on the enactment of the Companies Act 1989. The Companies Act 2006 repeated certain parts of the 1985 and 1989 Acts and inserted new sections.

Limited companies are required by law to prepare financial accounts for each financial year for shareholders and other groups who are interested in accounts. Under the Companies Acts, financial accounts need to be registered with the registrar of companies and available for inspection by any member of the general public. The published accounts need to be lodged with the registrar of companies within four weeks of the end of the financial year.

Limited companies are required to keep all accounting records and accounting files for each accounting period with Companies House. Under the Companies Act 2006, company directors are responsible for preparation of the accounts and ensuring that accounts are delivered to Companies House within the given time period. If accounts are not delivered on time, directors can be penalised for late submission.

The annual return which is submitted by the company is a snapshot of company information giving details of its annual financial activities and providing details of its chairman, directors, company secretary, registered office address, shareholders and share capital. Each year Companies House sends an annual return form to the company's registered address asking for any changes during the year to be noted, and that all details should be checked. The form needs to be signed off by the company secretary and returned within 28 days with a fee.

The legislation also requires directors to produce accounts which show a true and fair view of the company's accounts for the accounting period and which highlight the financial position at the end of the period. The board of directors needs to sign off the annual accounts, and the independent auditors then attach their report. The accounts are presented to the shareholders of the company at the annual general meeting. Once the accounts have been adopted by the members they are sent to Companies House for the registrar to file.

Accounting standards

In the UK, apart from company law, the key principles or regulations which affect accounting procedures are derived from guidelines issued by the professional accounting bodies. The accounting standards were devised in the UK and around the world due to the need to standardise the ways in which companies' accounts are measured. The accounting standards had the effect of narrowing the areas of difference between each company, and standardising the preparation and presentation of accounts. This helped to eliminate deliberate manipulation of accounts and also served to enhance comparability between companies. The Accounting Standards Board (ASB) was set up in 1970 to crack down on the manipulation of published accounts that were being presented to shareholders. This was the first step taken by the UK government and professional accounting bodies to protect investors in the wake of accounting scandals. The ASB introduced Statements of Standard Accounting Practice (SSAPs) for companies to follow in 1973.

Following the recommendations of the Dearing Report in 1990, accounting standards are now governed by four accounting bodies (see Figure 5.3). The Financial Reporting Council (FRC) took over the responsibility for financial accounting standards on 2 July 2012. Financial accounting standards were formerly developed by the ABS and are contained in Financial Reporting Standards (FRSs).

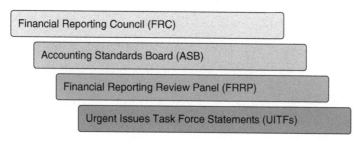

Figure 5.3   Accounting bodies

Over the last 25 years, the ASB has revised the SSAPs, replacing them with FRSs. While some of the SSAPs have been superseded by FRSs, some remain in force. Before 1990, SSAPs were the major accounting standards being used by companies. As these contained a number of loopholes, they have now been replaced by FRSs.

Soon after it started its activities, the ASB adopted the standards issued by the ASC, so that they also fall within the legal definition of accounting standards. These are designated SSAPs.

The Financial Reporting Council has issued revised Financial Reporting Standards in the UK and Republic of Ireland from 1 January 2015. The revised standards are applicable for accounting periods beginning on or after 1 January 2016. Below are the main FRSs and SSAPs used by sole traders, partnerships and limited companies in the UK.

Financial Reporting Standards (FRSs)

FRS 1 (Revised 1996) – Cash Flow Statements

FRS 2 – Accounting for Subsidiary Undertakings

(Continued)

(Continued)

FRS 3 – Reporting Financial Performance

FRS 4 – Capital Instruments

FRS 5 – Reporting the Substance of Transactions

FRS 6 – Acquisitions and Mergers

FRS 7 – Fair Values in Acquisition Accounting

FRS 8 – Related Party Disclosures

FRS 9 – Associates and Joint Ventures

FRS 10 – Goodwill and Intangible Assets

FRS 11 – Impairment of Fixed Assets and Goodwill

FRS 12 – Provisions, Contingent Liabilities and Contingent Assets

FRS 13 – Derivatives and Other Financial Instruments: Disclosures

FRS 14 – Earnings per Share

FRS 15 – Tangible Fixed Assets

FRS 16 – Current Tax

FRS 17 – Retirement Benefits

FRS 18 – Accounting Policies

FRS 19 – Deferred Tax

FRS 20 (IFRS2) – Share-based Payment

FRS 21 (IAS 10) – Events after the Balance Sheet Date

FRS 22 (IAS 33) – Earnings per Share

FRS 23 (IAS 21) – The Effects of Changes in Foreign Exchange Rates

FRS 25 (IAS 32) – Financial Instruments: Presentation

FRS 26 (IAS 39) – Financial Instruments: Recognition and Measurement

FRS 27 – Life Assurance

FRS 28 – Corresponding Amounts

FRS 29 (IFRS 7) – Financial Instruments: Disclosures

FRS 30 – Heritage Assets

Statements of Standard Accounting Practice (SSAPs)

SSAP 4 – Accounting for Government Grants

SSAP 5 – Accounting for Value Added Tax

SSAP 9 – Stocks and Long-term Contracts

SSAP 13 – Accounting for Research and Development

SSAP 17 – Accounting for Post-balance Sheet Events

SSAP 19 – Accounting for Investment Properties

SSAP 20 – Foreign Currency Translation

SSAP 21 – Accounting for Leases and Hire Purchase Contracts

SSAP 24 – Accounting for Pension Costs

SSAP 25 – Segmental Reporting

International accounting standards

In 2003 the UK government announced that from January 2005, all UK companies will be able to use the IFRSs as an alternative to UK accounting standards. In addition, EU law currently requires all listed UK companies to use International Accounting Standards (IASS) following the 2006 Act, when preparing their consolidated financial accounts.

UNDERSTANDING FINANCIAL STATEMENTS

Trial balance

The trial balance is a schedule which lists all the ledger accounts in the form of debit and credit balances to confirm that total debits equal total credits.

The balance sheet and trading and profit and loss account are prepared from a list of the various balances, which then produces a trial balance. Traditionally, the trial balance is derived from the ledger accounts at the end of the financial year or accounting period. These accounts are drawn up by the owner or the accountant for the business. The business accountant records every single transaction that takes place in the business during the year.

In reality, the accountant or book-keeper for the business will use a technique called double entry book-keeping with which to write up individual transactions in the ledger of accounts.

The accountant needs to enter every transaction over the year twice in the books of annual accounts. This double entry process results in the forming of a trial balance for the business. In return, this equation balances both sides of the trial balance.

Total debit £ amount + total credit £ amount

Traditionally, businesses use the following principles in preparing a trial balance:

- Find the balance of each account on the ledger account.
- Businesses should record the ledger account balances in the right column of the trial balance.
- Once the ledger account balances have been recorded on the trial balance, then each column can be totalled.
- Then both totals of the two columns of the trial balance are compared, to see if they match with each other or not.
- If the totals do not match, then the book-keeper or financial record keeper may have made a mistake in the ledger accounts.

This proof that debits and credits match the ledger accounts offers the business the opportunity to verify that the individual accounts are correct and accurate. It helps the accountant to prepare the final account with clear and effective proof that the accounting information is correct and efficient for the year. It is vital for businesses that the correct debit balances have been entered into the debit column and the credit balances are entered in the credit column of the trial balance.

The trial balance is used by the accountant to put together the final accounts and at the same time uses the legal framework to ensure that the accounts meet requirements of the Companies Acts 1985, 1989 and 2006. Businesses need to produce a working trial balance at the end of the year, usually using a layout such as the one shown in Table 5.1.

The balance sheet

The balance sheet is one of the main financial documents used by any company, and provides information about its financial state. A balance sheet is a financial snapshot of the company's financial situation at any given moment in time. It is one of the financial statements that limited companies and PLCs produce every year for their shareholders.

Essentially, a balance sheet is a list of the assets, liabilities and capital of a business. In addition, the purpose is to show the financial position of the organisation on a certain date during the year. Under the Companies Acts 1985, 1989 and 2006 the balance sheet needs to be produced at the end of the company's financial year. An example layout of a balance sheet for a sole trader is shown in Table 5.2.

Table 5.1   Example layout for a working trial balance

Trial balance for a logistic event as at 31 December 2015

	DR	CR
Event income		
Sales		303,500
Capital		145,780
Event expenditure		
Purchases	93,800	
Motor expenses	7,800	
Office expenses	17,510	
Premises	100,500	
Motor vehicles	25,435	
Fixtures and fittings	18,645	
Light and heat	3,200	
Debtors	39,765	
General expenses	6,570	
Creditors		51,340
Bank	37,985	
Cash	7,890	
Drawings	13,400	
Stock at 1st Jan 2014	34,500	
Salaries and wages	67,950	
Rent and rates	25,670	
	500,620	**500,620**
Stock at 1st Jan 2015	31,200	

Traditionally, a balance sheet is divided into two halves, the top half of the balance sheet shows where the money is currently being used in the business, and the bottom half of the balance sheet shows how the money has been raised by the business.

Fixed assets

Long-term assets are known as fixed assets. A fixed asset is an asset purchased for use within the organisation and which helps the business to earn income from its use on a regular basis. Examples would be machinery, equipment, computers and so on, none of which actually get used up in the production process.

Fixed assets = Property + Machinery + Equipment

Table 5.2   Example layout of a balance sheet for a sole trader

Balance sheet as at 31 December 2015			
Fixed assets			
Land and building			XXX
Fixtures and fittings			XXX
			XXXX
Current assets			
Stocks	XXX		
Debtors		XXX	
Cash in hand	XXX		
		XXXX	
Current liabilities			
Creditors		XXX	
Bank overdraft		XXX	
Net current assets			**XXXX**
			XXXX
Long-term liabilities			
Long-term loan			XXX
			XXXX
Capital			
Capital as at 1 January			XXX
Profit for the year to 31 December 2015			XXX
			XXXX

Current assets

Short-term assets are known as current assets – assets which are used on a day-to-day basis by the firm. In the balance sheet layout shown in Table 5.2, the fixed assets are followed by current assets. The current assets are items which are owned by the business. The purpose of current assets is to turn them into cash within one year. In addition, current assets are continually flowing through the business at regular intervals, so these are assets which can be quickly changed to liquid cash. The current assets may include cash in hand and in the bank, anything owed to the business by debtors, any advance payment of bills, stock and so on.

Current assets = Stock + Debtors + Cash/Bank + Prepayments

The current assets are shown on the top half of the balance sheet, and the current liabilities are subtracted from them to show net current assets.

Long-term liabilities

In a balance sheet, just like the fixed and current assets, long-term liabilities and current liabilities are shown separately. The long-term liabilities are debts which are not payable within the one-year period. Under the terms of the Companies Acts 1985, 1989 and 2006, limited companies must show any long-term liabilities by using the term **creditors** (amounts falling due after more than one year). The amounts can be owed to suppliers, creditors, employees or the government. In addition, if the business receives money in advance of an event taking place, they have a liability to carry out the event or service.

Long-term liabilities = Bank loan + Long-term creditors

Current liabilities

Current liabilities are the short-term debts of the business, which are due to be paid within one year, and usually refer to amounts owed to creditors or suppliers. Under the terms of the Companies Acts 1985, 1989 and 2006 limited companies must show their current liabilities by using the term **creditors** (amounts falling due within one year).

Current liabilities = Creditors + Accruals

Capital employed

The other half of the balance sheet includes capital employed. Capital employed is debt owed to the business owners. The three main areas which are shown on the balance sheet under this heading are: the amount invested by the owner(s) in the business; the profit earned by the business during the year; and the amount of money which has been drawn from the business by owner(s) for personal use (also known as drawings).

Moreover, capital employed is considered as a liability by company accountants, because this is money owed by the business to the owner(s). Finally, on the balance sheet, the owner(s) equity is shown as a liability, as illustrated in Figure 5.4.

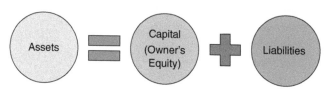

Figure 5.4   The owner's equity is shown as a liability on the balance sheet

Profit and loss account

The profit and loss account differs significantly from the balance sheet. The profit and loss account is a record of the firm's trading activities over a period of time, whereas the balance sheet is the financial position at a given moment in time.

The purpose of the trading account is to measure the actual gross profit on trading of the business over the last 12 months. This is done by taking the total sales for the year minus the cost of sales (cost of goods sold). An example of a trading account is shown in Table 5.3.

Table 5.3 The trading account

Sales		97,800
less **Cost of sales**		
Opening stock		12,300
add Purchases	43,900	
less Discounts received	3,450	40,450
		52,750
less Closing stock		11,340	41,410
Gross profit		56,390

The purpose of a profit and loss account is to define the gross profit of the business by deducting from it all the genuine expenses incurred in running the business over the last 12 months and arriving at a net profit for the given period. There are a number of different types of expenses that are incurred during the year in a business cycle, which are deductible from gross profit.

Table 5.4 Example of a profit and loss account for a sole trader

Gross profit			**56,390**
less **Expenses**			
Lighting and heating	1,230		
add Accrued electricity	189	1,419	
Wages		11,600	
Rent and rates	10,200		
add Rent owing	1,200		
less Rates prepaid	560	10,840	
Telephone	355		
add Accrued	35	390	
Insurance	980		
less Prepaid	105	875	25,124
Net profit			31,266

The profit and loss account looks at how well the firm has traded over the time period concerned (usually the last six months, or the last year). It shows how much the firm has earned from selling its products or services, and how much it has paid out in costs (production costs, salaries and so on). The net of these two is the amount of profit the business has earned. An example of a profit and loss account for a sole trader is shown in Table 5.4.

The basic principle of a profit and loss account is to show the net profit of the business for the financial year, that is, any money which is left after all relevant business expenses have been deducted from the gross profit (Table 5.5).

Table 5.5   Example layout of a trading, profit and loss account for a sole trader for the end of a financial year

Trading, profit and loss account for the year ended 31 January 2016

Sales			XXX
less **Cost of sales**			
Opening stock	XXX		
add Purchases	XXX		
less Closing stock		XXX	XXX
Gross profit			**XXX**
less **Expenses**			
Lighting and heating	XXX		
Wages	XXX		
Rent and rates	XXX		
Telephone		XXX	
Telephone		XXX	
Insurance		XXX	
Total expenditure			XXX
Net profit			**XXX**

Put simply, in order to understand the concept of a profit and loss account, you can use the formula in Figure 5.5 to calculate the net profit.

Gross profit – Expenses = Net profit

Figure 5.5   Formula for net profit

As indicated in the profit and loss account, the expenses are those which have been incurred in the business over the last 12 months. These are expenses which are not included in the trading account. The expenses for a sole trader are not classified into any category; however, for a limited company expenses are classified into three main categories:

- Selling
- Administrative
- Distribution.

Table 5.6 shows an actual example of a trading, profit and loss account and a balance sheet, for the Logistics Events company, for the year 2015.

Table 5.6   Example trading, profit and loss account and balance sheet for Logistics Events, 2015

Logistics Events

Trading, profit and loss account, for the year ending 31 December 2015

	£	£	£
Sales			303,500
less **Cost of sales**			
Opening stock		34,500	
add Purchases		93,800	
		128,300	
less Closing stock		31,200	97,100
Gross profit			206,400
less **Expenses**			
Lighting and heating	3,200		
Salaries and wages	67,950		
Rent and rates	25,670		
i. Office expenses	17,510		
ii. Motor expenses	7,800		
General expenses	6,570		
iii. Drawings	13,400		
			142,100
Net profit			64,300

Logistics Events

Balance sheet as at 31 December 2011

Fixed assets

Premises	100,500
Fixtures and fittings	18,645
Motor vehicles	25,435
	144,580

Logistics Events			
Balance sheet as at 31 December 2011			
	£	£	£
Current assets			
Stock	31,200		
Debtors	39,765		
Cash at bank	37,985		
Cash in hand	7,890	116,840	
Current liabilities			
Creditors		51,340	
Working capital (or net current assets)			65,500
			210,080
Financed by:			
Capital			145,780
add Net profit			64,300
			210,080

Accounting ratio analysis

The financial ratio analysis is the most essential information contained within financial statements, besides the trading, profit and loss account, and the balance sheet. The financial ratios are a mathematical analysis of a company's final accounts and help the shareholders, investors, creditors and board of directors to understand how well the company has performed over the last financial year. The financial position of the business needs to be measured in order that the key stakeholders within the company are able to appreciate how the business has performed during the financial year. The only way you can enhance the key stakeholders' understanding of how the company is performing is through ratio analysis.

Ratio analysis is a technique which compares crucial relationships between numbers in a readily understood form (usually a percentage). It is essential for an event organisation to carry out evaluation of the performance of the business or event, to examine the profitability, growth, return on fixed and current assets, return on equity capital and general expenses of the business. This will provide an indication for the company to compare the financial performance of the business with other companies in the industry. It is important to understand that ratios on their own are not particularly useful. You need to be able to compare ratios over time or against other ratios to be able to build up a useful picture of the performance of the company.

Ratio analysis compares company financial accounts to generate vital figures by using the following techniques.

- **Performance ratios**: these include profit, capital employed and turnover.
- **Liquidity ratios**: these are concerned with the short-term financial position of the company.

- **Gearing ratios**: these are focused on the long-term financial position of the company.
- **Investments ratios**: these are concerned with the return for the shareholder.

(See Table 5.7.)

Table 5.7   Business analysis ratios

Type of ratio	Ratio
Performance	Profit margin
	Return on capital employed ratio
	Days sales in stock
	Asset turnover
Liquidity and gearing	Current ratio
	Acid test ratio
	Shareholders' equity ratio
	Gearing ratio
	Interest coverage ratio
Investments	Earnings per share
	Dividend yield
	Dividend per share
	Price/earnings ratio

Profitability ratios

These ratios help the business and key stakeholders to judge how well the firm has performed in terms of profit over the last 12 months. Profitability ratios are expressed either in terms of the profit earned on sales, or the profit earned on the capital employed in the business. In addition, profitability ratios relate to a company's ability to earn a satisfactory income. A company's profitability is closely linked to its liquidity because earnings ultimately produce cash flow. The key profitability ratios are explained below.

Profit margin ratio

The profit margin ratio measures the level of profit compared to the sales of the firm for the financial year. It therefore shows the percentage profit on the sales. It can be measured as either a gross or net profit margin.

$$\text{Gross profit as a percentage of sales} = \frac{\text{Gross profit} \times 100}{\text{Sales}}$$

$$\text{Net profit as a percentage of sales} = \frac{\text{Net profit} \times 100}{\text{Sales}}$$

Return on capital employed ratio

The return on capital employed ratio measures the level of profit of the firm compared to the amount of capital that has been invested.

$$\text{Return on capital employed} = \frac{\text{Net profit (before tax)} \times 100}{\text{Capital employed}}$$

Liquidity ratio

The liquidity ratio measures the liquidity of the firm. The business needs to ensure that it has enough liquidity in place to meet all it commitments. The liquidity ratio shows whether the firm has sufficient assets to convert into liquid cash to meet the business commitments for 12 months, and it is important for the business to not have all their assets tied up as capital.

Current ratio

The current ratio is calculated by dividing the current assets by the current liabilities.

$$\text{Current ratio} = \frac{\text{Current assets}}{\text{Current liabilities}}$$

Acid test ratio

The acid test ratio excludes stock from the current assets, but is otherwise the same as the current ratio.

$$\text{Acid test ratio} = \frac{\text{Current assets} - \text{stock}}{\text{Current liabilities}}$$

Gearing ratios

Traditionally, all businesses have to borrow money regardless of the size of the business. If the company wants to expand, it needs to borrow money from banks or other financial institutions. In addition, most businesses fund their investment from profits they have made from the business over the years. The other means of investment is by the issue of shares. In reality, most of the investment need is met by borrowing money from banks. The only disadvantage of borrowing money for business is that the business has to pay interest on the sum which has been borrowed, regardless of whether the investment is a success or not.

The key stakeholders and potential investors look at a set of accounts to assess how big that risk is and they use gearing ratios to analyse business stability in the industry.

Shareholders' equity ratio

This ratio measures and determines how much shareholders would receive in the case of a company going out of business (liquidation).

$$\text{Shareholders' equity ratio} = \frac{\text{Shareholders' equity} \times 100}{\text{Total assets}}$$

Interest coverage ratio

This measures how easily the company can pay its interest out of its profits.

$$\text{Interest coverage ratio} = \frac{\text{Profit before interest and tax}}{\text{Periodic interest charges payable}}$$

Investment ratio

The investment ratio is key for current and potential investors, and measures a standard return on investors' equity.

Price/earnings ratio

This ratio measures the market price per share compared to earnings per share and is useful for comparing the value placed on a company's shares in relation to the overall market.

$$\text{Price/earnings ratio} = \frac{\text{Market price per share}}{\text{Earnings per share}}$$

Dividend yield ratio

The dividend yield ratio measures the rate of return an investor gets by comparing the cost of his or her shares with the dividend receivable.

$$\text{Dividend yield ratio} = \frac{\text{Dividend per share} \times 100}{\text{Market price per share}}$$

BUDGETING PROCESS FOR EVENT MANAGERS

The budgeting process is a vital tool for event managers to understand in order to carry out the financial activities of their organisations. Event managers need to develop a budget, this is one of the first and most important tasks in managing an event. The budgeting process is a vital part of the event management activities and enhances the ability of management and employees to see budgeting as a tool to control revenue and expenditure. It is important for event managers to develop skills and strategies that cultivate and maintain effective control over the income and expenditure of the event, regardless of the size or type of the event.

The budgeting process helps event managers to establish whether the event will make a profit or loss, and provides an indication for management of whether total costs will be covered by the event. Therefore, organisations should not make any commitments to run an event until sufficient budgeting has been undertaken to establish the viability of the revenue and expenditure. The budgeting process provides event managers with the opportunity to carefully match the goals of the organisation with the resources necessary to accomplish those goals. The budgeting process is used to communicate information to individuals who are accountable and responsible for an event, enabling them to make effective decisions.

One of the most essential elements of the budgeting process is the event budget, and event managers need to develop the skills to prepare an event budget.

Event budget

The budget is designed to show the expected cash income and expenses during the specific event or period. It is the most important tool of any event manager. A budget provides a guide to managers to project income and expenses for the event and gives an early indication of whether the event is going to make a profit or loss. A budget is illustrated in Table 5.8.

Table 5.8 Event budget

Income	
Event ticket sales	41,300
Sponsorship	7,680
Funding from local government	1,200
Bar/canteen	8,500
Total event income	**58,680**
Expenditure	
Advertising	3,900
Catering	4,500
Equipment	4,590
Office costs	2,500
Printing	2,005
Event cleaners	1,340
Venue costs	5,000
Staffing cost	18,500
Event security	6,500
VIP hospitality	1,790
Total event expenditure	**50,625**
Surplus/profit	**8,055**

Event managers can use the example in Table 5.8 to control the activities of the organisation as closely as possible. It illustrates the importance of carrying out a budgeting process to plan and control various sections of the organisation in order to achieve the desired outcomes.

SUMMARY

In this chapter it has been suggested that understanding finance is vital for event managers. It is important to understand the principle of financial statements of a business, and also the legal, financial and accounting concepts which are governed by the Companies Acts 1985, 1989 and 2006. In order to understand financial accounting, it is important to look at finance as a whole, and to see where it fits in the organisation. Under UK law, limited companies need to produce annual accounts, which must be audited by a person independent of the company. This will provide a clear and effective process for companies to report their annual return within the given framework. In theory, the company should appoint independent chartered or certified accountants to carry out an annual investigation of accounts prepared by the company.

The FRSs issued by the ASB have been changed over the last 15 years to close the loopholes that were left open by the SSAPs. Over the years, financial reporting requirements have been getting more detailed and so updating is necessary to enhance the structure for large companies to report accurate information.

Ratio analysis provides a means of comparison for event managers and organisers. The financial position of the business needs to be measured in order that the key stakeholders within the company are able to appreciate how the business has performed during the financial year, in line with other competitors in the industry. Ratio analysis provides investors with a clear and effective comparison of financial data for the company's financial activities for the year. In addition, ratio analysis is a prime technique to help managers and event organisers to assess and evaluate how well the event has performed in terms of profitability. Ratio analysis compares crucial relationships between numbers in a readily understood form (usually a percentage). Finally, the chapter has discussed the budgeting process for event managers as a vital tool for event organisers; it helps the organisation to plan and control the expenditure for the event regardless of it size. The budgeting process helps event managers to make key decisions based on financial data generated through a cash budget.

Discussion questions

Question 1

The information in Table 5.9 was extracted from the books of V2000, as at 31 December 2015.

Prepare a trading and profit and loss account for the company, for the year ending 31 December 2015.

Table 5.9 Accounts information for V2000, 31 December 2015

Sales	3,500,000
Purchases	950,000
Vehicles hiring cost	70,000
Trade debtors	43,500
Trade creditors	55,000
Capital	800,000
Security charges	75,000
Salaries	315,000
Lighting and heating	19,500
Stationery	3,500
Sundry expenses	89,000
Vehicle expenses	29,955
Postage	575
Telephone	6,750
Insurance	8,500
Rent	109,000
Equipment hire	204,500

Question 2

The information in Table 5.10 was extracted from the books of Global Events Management Limited, as at 31 October 2015.

Prepare a trading and profit and loss account and a balance sheet for the company, as at 31 October 2015.

(Continued)

(Continued)

Table 5.10 Trial balance for Global Events Management Ltd, as at 31 October 2015

	DR	CR
Event income		
Cash sales (usually tickets)		£86,550
Credit card sales (usually tickets)		£30,800
Sponsorship		£10,600
Fees from clients		£4,500
Donations		£940
Capital		£60,500
Expenses		
Director's salary	£32,000	
Event assistant's salary	£18,500	
Employer's National Insurance and tax	£7,400	
Office rent	£15,350	
Office rates	£1,650	
Office telephone	£1,400	
Water rates	£1,760	
Mobile phones	£955	
Electricity	£2,150	
Gas	£2,355	
Company advertisement and promotion	£1,560	
Motor expenses	£5,390	
Public liability insurance	£2,500	
Bank charges at 1% pa	£750	
Creditors		£14,360
Stock at 1 November 2014	£16,600	
Depreciation on car	£7,000	
Depreciation on computer	£600	
Premises	£45,000	
Motor vehicles	£7,500	
Fixtures and fittings	£9,530	
Debtors	£5,200	
Bank	£23,100	
	£208,250	**£208,250**
Stock at 1 November 2015	£16,575	

Question 3

a   Investigate and explore the difference between 'fixed' and 'current' assets.
b   Critically evaluate ratio analysis and discuss different types of ratios.

Question 4

a   Explain and discuss the difference between financial accounting and management accounting.
b   Critically explore the differences between private and public limited companies.

Question 5

The information in Table 5.11 was extracted from the books of World Events Ltd, as at 31 March 2015.
   Prepare a profit and loss account for the company for the year to 31 March 2015.

Table 5.11   The trial balance of World Events Ltd, as at 31 March 2015

350,000 Ordinary shares of £1		350,000
6% Preference shares £1		70,000
Dividends: ordinary	15,000	
Preference	5,900	
Taxation	29,000	
Interest paid	7,500	
Bank loan	60,000	
Admin cost	43,000	
Turnover	250,500	
Cost of sales	170,500	

Question 6

Calculate the current ratio and acid test ratio for Logistics Management Ltd, using the trading and profit and loss account and balance sheet, as at 31 December 2015, as shown in Table 5.12.

Question 7

Calculate the gearing ratio and dividend yield ratio for Logistics Management Ltd, using the information in Table 5.12

(Continued)

(Continued)

Table 5.12   Trading and profit and loss account and balance sheet for Logistics Management Ltd, as at 31 December 2015

Logistics Management Ltd

Trading and profit and loss account, for the year ending 31 December 2015

	£	£	£
Sales			45,600
less **Cost of sales**			
Opening stock		5,468	
add Purchases	19,565		
less Discounts received	1,568	21,133	
		26,601	
less Closing stock		3,456	23,145
Gross profit			22,455
less **Expenses**			
Lighting and heating	4,567		
add Accrued electricity	120	4,687	
Wages		7,890	
Rent and rates	3,190		
add Rent owing	560		
less Rates prepaid	145	2,775	
Telephone	206		
add Accrued	67	273	
Insurance	1,405		
less Prepaid	105	1,300	16,925
Net profit			5,530

Logistics Management Ltd

Balance sheet as at 31 December 2010

Fixed assets			
Van			4,000
Fixtures and fittings			8,500
			12,500
Current assets			
Stock		3,456	

Logistics Management Ltd

Balance sheet as at 31 December 2010

	£	£	£
Debtors	5,780		
Cash at bank	7,675		
Cash in hand	64		
Prepaid	250	17,225	
Current liabilities			
Creditors	3,469		
Accrued	747	4,216	
Working capital (or net current assets)			13,009
			25,509
Financed by:			
Capital		29,194	
add Net profit		3,719	32,913
less Drawings			7,404
			25,509

Case study 1: Broadstairs Big Top

Broadstairs Folk Week has recently considered an option to replace the annually hired marquee with a more innovative temporary structure. This has a 500 flat floor seating capacity and they have rented it for the last six years from Dover Marquees for around £4,000 per week, including transport and labour for putting it up and taking it down.

They have an ambition to purchase a new structure for their own festival and then rent it out to other festivals and events when not in use. Their business model relied on an application for funding from the Foundation for Sports and the Arts which unfortunately has just been turned down. They are unsurprisingly keen to find another public sector supporter although the model could, in theory, work without public investment.

Broadstairs have approached Roustabout Ltd to purchase a Big Top structure suitable for their site in Pierremont Park. Broadstairs recognise that they don't have the skills or

(Continued)

(Continued)

experience to operate the structure and have asked Roustabout to consider storing, maintaining, hiring and installing it for Folk Week, and for other events at a hire charge.

The cost of the structure would be £43,500 and Roustabout estimate that it could be rented out at £2,000 for a typical 7–10 day period, giving a payback time on the capital cost of 22 weeks. They further estimate that there might be a market for 4–5 weeks' hire a year in addition to the Folk Week, resulting in a 5–6 year payback period. In addition, installation costs a further £2,000, depending on location, which is borne by the hirer. However, Roustabout would be required to store and maintain the structure and make a profit for operating it. This might leave Broadstairs with £1,000 profit per hire.

The problem with this approach is that the Broadstairs site is unusual and the structure they want will need to be purpose built. Although it can be used for other hirers, the potential to achieve 22 weeks' hire over its lifetime might be limited. Broadstairs are not able or willing to raise the investment commercially, and providing public funds would save them £2,000 a year, and potentially give them a further income stream of £4–5,000 a year if the project achieved its targets.

The risk:return ratio for this type of project is not sufficient for it to be of interest outside a publicly funded model.

Source: SEEDA (South East England Development Agency), 2009 [online].

Case study 2: Rio 2016 Olympic and Paralympic Games

Financial position

The media has consistently quoted a large multiplier effect for the 2016 Olympics. A report by Haddad and Haddad calculated a 4.26 multiplier. Projecting that for every $1 USD invested, $3.26 will be generated until 2027, or $51.1 USD billon. Often times the use of multipliers to indicate economic benefit is exaggerated; this seems to be the case for 2016. Tommy Andersson states that multipliers are often inflated 10–90 per cent. Total economic impact of mega-events is difficult to measure and there are a number of studies with varying numbers. On average, the economic impacts of Olympic Games are under $10 billion. The inflated numbers projected to the general public about total expected outcome may only disappoint Brazilians. Much profit received in terms of profits does not go back to the public, it goes to shareholders and investors. Public funding is sacrificed to host mega-events; increased taxes and spending cuts in other areas are not taken into account.

Barcelona is consistently quoted as the gold medal winner in terms of Olympic hosting successes, but many host countries have not been impacted like Barcelona. Montreal in 1976 and Athens in 2004 are examples of games that have left the host countries with large financial debts. The financial status of Greece is the center stage of the Eurozone. One-fourth of their current budget deficit was spent on the Olympics. While blame cannot be solely placed on hosting the Olympics, the events may have contributed to the country's financial woes.

Many of the facilities built for the Greek Games, are currently sitting unutilized, yet use public funds for maintenance and operation. The 2000 Games in Sydney have a similar story, underutilized stadiums and facilities are still costing $40 million USD a year, as of 2009. The use, or lack thereof, of facilities for post-mega-events is troubling. Brazil hosted the 2007 Pan American Games, which actually helped Brazil secure the Olympic Bid. However, facilities built for the Pan Am Games took large amounts of funds from Federal Workers Fund among other public programs, and are sitting empty. Some of the buildings were even built on wetlands, sank, and required additional investment to save the building. A few of the Olympic Stadiums and venues are to be built on the same wetlands, due to lack of available space in the city. This shows a lack of consideration of where facilities are located and further the ignorance of post-Olympic usability. Other high-cost stadiums sit empty, but are not up to Olympics standards, thus requiring further investment for 2016. In all these cases the governments uses public funding from taxpayers to build arenas that do not benefit the public after the games. Obviously the expected outcomes of continuous inflow of money for Athens and Greece were not enough to provide funds for post-game upkeep. Questioning where public funds for the Olympics would have gone, is valid. Funding for the Olympics can be validated to a certain extent with tourism, international attention and prestige. It can even be argued that a mega-event is the only motivation that some governments have to invest in infrastructure. The difficulty is deciding when the amount of public funding negatively impacts taxpayers.

Analyzing what Barcelona did differently from Montreal is difficult. Both cities made significant investments in infrastructure. In fact, all non-United States games after Montreal made large investments in infrastructure. As with all other host-countries, Brazil hopes to be a 'Barcelona', but the key to success is finding the right formula. Infrastructure is important, but proper planning and exact execution seem to be where countries come up short. Mega-events are exciting and are something Brazilians are pleased to be a part of, but the expected long-term benefits of the infrastructure, social, and economic projects are problematic.

Source: adapted from Seven Pillars Institute (2016) [online]. This article was first published by Seven Pillars Institute for Global Finance and Ethics, www.sevenpillarsinstitute.org and is republished with the permission of the Institute.

FURTHER READING

Dyson, J.R. (2010) *Accounting for Non-Accounting Students*, 8th edn. London, Pitman.

Elliott, B. and Elliott, J. (2011) *Financial Accounting and Reporting*, 14th edn. Harlow: Pearson.

Glautier, M. and Underdown, B. (2001) *Accounting Theory and Practice*, 7th edn. Harlow: Financial Times Press/Prentice Hall.

McLaney, E. and Atrill, P. (2014) *Accounting and Finance: An Introduction*, 7th edn. Harlow: Pearson.

Weetman, P. (2010) *Financial and Management Accounting: An Introduction*, 5th edn. Harlow: Financial Times Press/Prentice Hall.

Wood, F. and Sangster, A. (2008) *Business Accounting 1*, 11th edn. London: FT/Pitman Publishing.

6

COSTING, PRICING AND CAPITAL IN THE EVENTS INDUSTRY

In this chapter you will cover

This chapter will examine the accounting methods a company uses for its internal reporting and decision-making, in order to give event managers sufficient financial knowledge to manage the company. One of the most important aspects of management accounting is to provide the managers and board of directors of companies with information related to its costing. The reason why costing information is important is that it helps managers to understand and know what selling price would lead to a profit. The chapter will also explore the relationship between profit and investment expressed through a measure referred to as capital investment appraisal. Capital investment appraisal methods consider the rate of return, and they therefore overcome the main weakness of cost-oriented methods by focusing on profit and taking account of the investment necessary to generate that profit.

CLASSIFICATION OF COSTS

Management accounting is a management information system for analysing past, present and future data for decision-making. Cost accounting is defined by the Chartered Institute of Management Accountants (CIMA) as:

> that part of management accounting which establishes budgets and standard costs and actual costs of operations, processes, departments or products and the analysis of variances profitability or dual use of funds. (Association of Accounting Technicians, 1990: 3)

Traditionally, the elements of costing for events organisations are classified as shown in Figure 6.1.

The organisation incurs a number of different costs when it produces products or in carrying out a service. Under the cost accounting system these costs need to be split in various ways. One way is to split them into fixed costs and variable costs as highlighted in Figure 6.2.

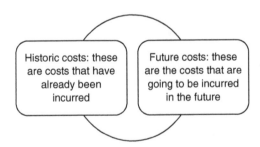

Figure 6.1 Traditional costing concept for events

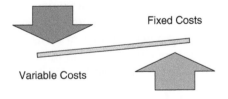

Figure 6.2 Fixed and variable costs

Fixed costs

Fixed costs are not related to products or services. These costs are totally independent of the company's output. Fixed costs have to be paid out by the company regardless of whether the company has produced any activity or not. Fixed costs remain fixed for a period and are unaffected by the increases or decreases in the level of activity produced by the company. Fixed costs only change with the time span; as the span increases, the fixed costs increase too. By keeping fixed costs under control, the business can enjoy a very healthy profit and achieve successful development in the future. Figure 6.3 demonstrates fixed cost classification.

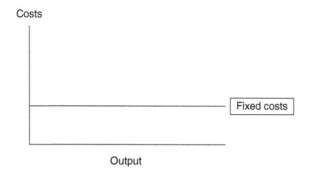

Figure 6.3   Fixed cost classification

The most common fixed costs include the following:

- business rates paid to the local authority
- interest paid on bank loans
- rent paid for the use of buildings or venues
- staff costs for a permanent member of staff
- company liability insurance.

Variable costs

Variable costs depend on the level of production or service being provided. Variable costs change with the level of activity being carried out by the organisation, and so they will change with the size and type of event. Variable costs are hard to control and are determined by the level of activity being produced or sold. By controlling the variable costs the organisation can create more effective and efficient products or services. It is important for event organisations to bear in mind that the larger the event or festival, the larger will be the variable costs to control. Figure 6.4 demonstrates variable cost classification.

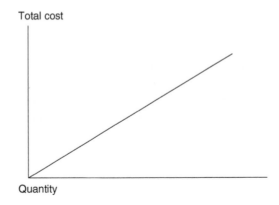

Figure 6.4 Variable cost classification

The most common variable costs include the following:

- hiring the venue
- printing of marketing material
- advertising
- guest speakers
- weekly wages paid to the staff working on the event
- gas and electricity bills.

Managers need to bear one important element in mind regarding fixed and variable costs. The clear difference between fixed and variable costs lies in whether the amount of costs incurred will rise as the level of activity increases during the period of the event, or whether the costs remain the same during the event, regardless of the level of activity.

TRADITIONAL COST ACCOUNTING CONCEPTS

It is important for managers to analyse and classify costs according to the purpose for which each cost is being used. The following are the most common cost concepts the management accountant and costing managers are concerned with:

- **Total cost**: the sum of all items of expense which have been incurred in the process of the event or festival or in providing services to customers.
- **Standard cost**: the target or budgeted cost predetermined by the management or business prior to starting the event. The standard cost is estimated by the management in advance and then it is compared to the actual costs incurred during the event or activity.
- **Marginal cost**: determined by the level of activity, the fixed cost under this concept is considered separately.

- **Direct cost**: the cost which is directly related to the specific event or service. The direct cost is easily traceable within the event cost. For example, direct costs would include staff working on the event, security, equipment hiring and advertising for the event.
- **Indirect cost**: the opposite of direct costs, indirect expenses cannot be traced to the finished product or event. These are costs which are incurred in the business or for the event from its start to its finish. This may include office expenses which are not related to the event. For example, salaries of company directors, rent, rates and insurance for the whole year cannot be directly related to one particular event.
- **Functional cost**: the cost which relates to a specific event or festival. It is the cost that is attached to an area of operations in a business. This could be security, administrative, marketing, personnel and development costs.
- **Controllable and uncontrollable costs**: this accounting method provides management with clear guidelines in advance as to which costs are controllable and which costs are uncontrollable by management action.
- **Incremental cost**: this is incurred only when the individual event or project is undertaken. The incremental costs include both additional fixed costs and variable costs arising from the individual event or festival, besides standard costs that are already being incurred by the business.

MARGINAL COSTING

In the marginal costing concept, only variable costs are charged as the cost of sales and contribution is calculated by accountants. They ignore fixed costs and overheads. Under marginal costing, fixed costs are treated as period costs and fully charged to the period in which they are incurred. CIMA defines marginal costing as:

> [a] principle whereby variable costs are charged to cost units and fixed cost attributable to the relevant periods is written off in full against the contribution for that period. (Association of Accounting Technicians, 1990: 221)

It is impossible to calculate marginal costing without working out contribution. The contribution is the difference between the revenue achieved during the event and the marginal cost of the event.

Contribution per event ticket can be defined as: selling price less variable costs. Total contribution can be calculated by businesses as shown in Figure 6.5.

Tables 6.1 and 6.2 look at operating statements set out in a marginal costing format. Notting Hill Carnival and Leeds Film Festival host annual events in London and Leeds, which each have variable costs and fixed costs.

Marginal costing is a management accounting system for business managers to analyse the company's individual costs. It distinguishes between fixed costs and variable costs and can be compared to the absorption costing method.

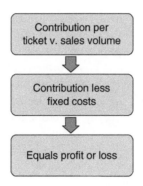

Figure 6.5 Contribution formula

Table 6.1 Notting Hill Carnival operating statement, marginal costing format

	Volume	Per ticket	Total
Sales	12,000	£60	£720,000
Variable costs	12,000	£38	£456,000
Contribution per ticket	**12,000**	**£22**	£264,000
Fixed costs			£87,000
Profit and loss			**£177,000**
Notting Hill Carnival's break-even point		£87,000	
		£22	£3,955

The advantages of using marginal costing by accountants and business managers for pricing the product or service are as follows:

- Marginal costing is simple to understand compared to absorption costing.
- It provides information for managers and boards of directors for short-term decision-making.
- It helps businesses to focus on achieving the break-even point.
- It calculates the difference between sales volume and variable costs.
- It helps managers to avoid having to make different allocations for fixed and variable costs.

Table 6.2   Leeds Film Festival operating statement, marginal costing format

	Volume	Per ticket	Total
Sales	170	£35	£5,950
Variable costs	170	£23	£3,910
Contribution per ticket	170	**£12**	£2,040
Fixed costs			£840
Profit and loss			**£1,190**
Leeds Film Festival's break-even point		£840	
		£12	£70

- Fixed costs are charged fully to the accounting period in which they have been incurred.
- Under marginal costing, by not charging fixed overheads to the cost of the production or event, varying of charges per ticket is avoided.
- Marginal costing also eliminates large balances overdue in the overhead control account and provides greater flexibility for management to control the overheads.

However, there are disadvantages of using marginal costing methods:

- Under the marginal costing method it is difficult for management to raise prices for event ticketing, if the contribution per ticket is set too low at the start of the event.
- Marginal costing can create a high risk for management when setting the ticket prices, because it may not recover the company's fixed costs set at the beginning.
- If contribution is set very low at the start, it can cause businesses to make major losses at the end of the event.
- The division of costs into fixed and variable is difficult to understand and sometimes provides misleading impressions of results to management.
- The marginal costing concept does take into account that stock and works in progress are understated. By not including the fixed costs in the actual event or service it can affect the organisation's profit.

ABSORPTION COSTING

Absorption costing is the opposite of marginal costing. Under absorption costing the full cost is passed on to the event or service. It does not disregard the fixed cost from an individual event or service. In absorption costing, the fixed cost is included in the pricing of the event or service; under marginal costing the event or service is valued at the variable cost only.

The prime difference between marginal costing and absorption costing is that under absorption costing all costs incurred during the event are allocated to particular costing areas, for example, direct costs, indirect costs, semi-variable costs and semi-fixed costs, etc. In addition, absorption costing allocates all indirect costs more accurately to the specific cost area where the cost was incurred during the event or service.

For example, let's look at the operating statements again, this time set out in an absorption costing format (see Tables 6.3 and 6.4).

The advantages of using absorption costing for pricing the event or service are as follows:

- Under absorption costing the fixed production costs for events are incurred in order to make an output, therefore it is fair to charge all output with a share of costs that have been incurred during the event production process.
- Absorption costing is the technique which helps management to take into consideration all the costs that have been incurred during the production of an event or service, regardless of its nature. Particularly, it takes into account fixed costs, where marginal costing techniques ignore the fixed costs involved for each event or product.

Table 6.3   Notting Hill Carnival operating statement, absorption costing format

Notting Hill Carnival produced 15,000 tickets for the event

Direct production cost £20 per ticket

Direct labour £11 per ticket

Fixed costs are £95,000 a month £ per ticket

Sales are 14,000 tickets at £60 per ticket

	Per ticket	Total
Sales	£55	£550,000
Cost of sales:		
Direct production cost	£20	£200,000
Direct labour	£11	£110,000
Overheads	£6	£90,000
Total cost of sales	**£37**	**£400,000**
Profit and loss	**£18**	**£150,000**

Table 6.4   Leeds Film Festival operating statement, absorption costing format

Leeds Film Festival produced 120 tickets for the event

Direct production cost £12 per ticket

Direct labour £11 per ticket

Fixed costs are £600 a month £5 per ticket

Sales are 110 tickets at £40 per ticket

	Per ticket	Total
Sales	£40	£4,400
Cost of sales:		
Direct production cost	£12	£1,440
Direct labour	£11	£1,320
Overheads	£5	£600
Total cost of sales	**£28**	**£3,360**
Profit and loss	**£12**	**£1,440**

Disadvantages of using the absorption costing method:

- The fixed cost is carried over to the subsequent accounting period under the absorption costing technique.
- Absorption costing is dependent on the levels of output of the business, which vary from one accounting period to another.
- This practice does not provide clear and effective cost per unit prices, because it depends on the existence of fixed-cost overheads, which may not be related to the same period.

CONTRACT COSTING

Contract costing is the name given to job costing where contracts are to be carried out at a sophisticated level between the supplier and the customer. The company draws up a formal contract for each large piece of work that is undertaken.

Contract costing provides the company with an up-to-date picture of expenditure and revenue associated with specific and large-scale contracts or projects. The majority of contracts are carried out away from the company's head office, therefore it is important for organisations to keep separate records for each individual contract which has been agreed. From the accounting point of view, each contract or project is regarded as a separate unit or product. Large contracts may take a long time to complete, and the time period for large-scale contracts is hard to predict at the initial stage. The contracts may even be spread over two or more accounting periods. However, problems may arise within contract costing in the following areas:

- adding overheads
- identifying direct costs
- dividing the profit between different accounting periods
- difficulties of cost control
- identifying indirect costs.

Therefore, it is important to have some clear guidelines in place, and to make sure that standard documents are used by the management to record the costs of each contract. In addition, very specific rules are laid out by the Companies Act 2006 for disclosing long-term contracts in a company's financial accounts. These rules need to be followed for internal management accounting purposes by the management.

THE STRUCTURE OF A CONTRACT

A standard contract should cover the following areas:

- the period of the contract
- the specification of the contract
- the location of the work of the contract
- the agreed price for the contract
- the end product of the contract
- the agreed date for the contract to finish.

Once the structure of the contract has been agreed by both the parties, it is important to work out the total cost for the contract. This can be done in three different ways:

1. Total cost for the project.
2. Pricing based on stages of the contract.
3. Time scales for the contract.

The central focus for the costing is to bridge the gap between customer and supplier by providing an up-to-date financial picture of the contract at each stage to both parties. In addition, the contract costing brings together both the financial accounting functions and the operational activities of the business, by anticipating any potential problems and taking action to rectify the situation.

Contract costing is the main accounting method used by events and festivals organisers to bid for large-scale events or to subcontract the work out to individual clients. This method was used, for example, for bids for the Commonwealth Games, the FIFA World Cup, the Olympic Games, and also for large music festivals.

BREAK-EVEN ANALYSIS

Break-even analysis is one of the most common techniques used by management accountants. Under this technique the costs are categorised into fixed and variable costs. The break-even analysis technique does not compare the total fixed and variable costs with sales values or revenue. Instead, it looks at points at which neither profit nor loss occurs, that is, it analyses the point at which sales revenue covers all expenses. At this stage no profit is being made by the festival organisers, but loss will begin to show as soon as the sales revenue begins to fall below the break-even point. Break-even analysis provides clear and very effective information to management about expected future costs and sales revenue for decision-making processes. This technique is used by management accountants to help managers to plan the budgets for future activities.

The break-even point can be calculated arithmetically by managers or budget planners by using the formula which takes the number of tickets that need to be sold in order to break-even compared to total costs, then divides it by the contribution per unit (see Figure 6.6).

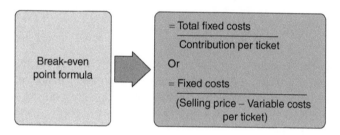

Figure 6.6   Break-even analysis point

However, break-even points can also be calculated by representing figures as a graph. Let's look at a worked example (see Table 6.5 and Figure 6.7).

Table 6.5   A graphical approach to break-even

Real Festivals Limited sell events tickets at £100 each. They pay the festival organisers' company £60 for each ticket.

Office and admin costs are £4,000 however many are sold.

With only a little thought we can produce a table like this:

	Quantity sold	
	0	200
Sales (£)	0	20,000
Variable costs	0	12,000
Fixed costs	4,000	4,000
Total costs	4,000	16,000

The next step is to produce a chart from the figures in this table (see Figure 6.7)

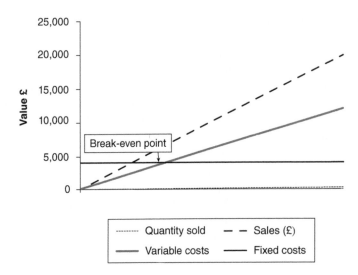

Figure 6.7   Break-even festival ticket sales

The various cost levels of activity are shown on the same chart as the sales revenue, variable costs and fixed costs. The festival fixed costs and variable costs make up the total costs (the straight line parallel with the X axis). The sales revenue appears on the dashed line through the origin of the graph. Figure 6.7 indicates the break-even point at the intersection of the revenue and total costs lines.

THE ROLE OF CAPITAL INVESTMENT DECISIONS

Capital investment appraisals relate to the future and look at the ways in which organisations can make a strategic financial decision on whether to invest in or decline to take part in a project. They also provide an organisation with the opportunity to choose between a number of different projects which are available to invest in. Capital investment appraisal techniques are used by accountants to analyse and collect the information for senior managers to make better decisions.

Event organisations operate in a dynamic environment and must gain competitive advantage over their competitors through continual improvement. The development of large-scale events will require investments of capital expenditure to meet the demand. The amount of money can vary between businesses, for example it may be thousands of pounds for a small event organisation or millions of pounds for a large-scale event organisation, but the amount is usually substantial relative to the size of the organisation. This factor dictates that decisions on capital investment should be thoroughly explored and all options and consequences clarified.

Drury (2015) states that once the organisation has committed to the investment, the decision is often irreversible, increasing the risk for the organisation and putting a greater emphasis on the need for extensive analysis prior to the decision being made.

Investments usually involve the allocation or reallocation of resources to a project or product which will benefit the organisation. This could involve replacing or updating equipment to improve efficiency, expanding the existing organisation through office space or resources, or establishing a new area of business to gain market share. If capital resources are restricted, this results in strategic business units (SBUs) within the company bidding against one another to have their proposal accepted. A successful proposal will gain not only investment and development of that SBU, but will lengthen its product life within the organisation. In addition, capital investment decisions cover a wide range of projects to produce cash flow for years. For example, the main type of projects may include:

- research and development projects
- replacement of existing assets
- expansion of existing services and products
- new services and products
- property
- large advertising campaigns
- social and welfare programmes.

Figure 6.8 shows the four methods which are used by senior management in the events industry. Each method will be discussed and simple examples provided of how to work out the calculations and apply them to your own organisation.

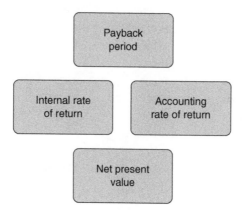

Figure 6.8 Capital investment techniques

Payback period

This is a simple method of calculating how long it will take before the cash inflows from an investment are equal to the sum of any costs incurred, including the initial capital investment. This is the most tried and trusted method among managers and financial accountants. The payback method refers to initial investment in the project and provides analysis to the management team as to what date the investment will start to make a profit. Projects which achieve payback within the target period are accepted.

The payback period is calculated by dividing the total initial investment by the expected annual inflow. For example, if a company invested £100,000 and expected to have an annual income of £25,000, then £100,000 divided by £25,000 would give a payback period of four years.

However, if the cash inflow varies per year, as is likely due to demand, then the payback period is calculated using a cumulative total of cash inflows (as shown in Table 6.6). The initial investment is shown as a negative and when the cumulative total turns positive the payback period is reached. This often occurs part way through a year but the rounded estimations shown in Table 6.6 are acceptable, due to the uncertainty attached to the prediction of future income.

Table 6.6 indicates the calculated payback period, describing how many years it will take to recover the original investment outlay from the cash flows which result from an investment project.

The application of the payback period method in Table 6.6 favours the acceptance of project B, as the initial cost would be paid back in less time. However, this method also reflects that the total profit gained by project A is lower than project B.

Table 6.6   Payback period calculation

Year		Project A		Project B	
Cumulative year		Annual	Cumulative	Annual	Cumulative
0	Cost	(100,000)	−100,000	(100,000)	−100,000
1	Cash inflow	24,000	−76,000	18,000	−82,000
2	Cash inflow	18,000	−58,000	26,000	−56,000
3	Cash inflow	21,000	−37,000	40,000	−16,000
4	Cash inflow	16,000	−21,000	14,000	−2,000
5	Cash inflow	16,000	−5,000	16,000	14,000
6	Cash inflow	25,000	20,000	11,000	25,000
		20,000		25,000	

$$\text{Project A}: 5 + \frac{5,000}{25,000} \text{ years} = 5.2 \text{ years}$$

$$\text{Project B}: 3 + \frac{22,000}{24,000} \text{ years} = 4.1 \text{ years}$$

Advantages and disadvantages of payback period

Advantages

- It is a popular method compared to others, due to its simplicity.
- Managers favour this method, it is easy to understand and calculate.

- This method is more objectively based; it uses projected cash flows rather than projected accounting profit.
- It favours fast-return projects and reduces time-related risks for the organisation.
- It saves management time otherwise spent in calculating forecast cash flows for the whole of a project or event.

Disadvantages

- The payback period does not take into account the time value of money.
- Under the payback period rule, if the two projects or events are similar, the project or event which has the shorter time period will be considered.
- It ignores the end values of the project and wealth maximisation.
- It presents the problem of ambiguity: at what point do you start counting the cash flows?

Accounting rate of return

The accounting rate of return (ARR) can be defined as the ratio of average profits to the initial capital invested. The average rate of return also expresses the profit which has been generated from a project as a percentage, after taking away depreciation. There is no clear definition for ARR and different authors provide different definitions of profits and capital cost.

ARR is also known as 'return on capital employed' (ROCE), or 'return on investment'. These terms can be defined differently, causing confusion.

Pike and Neale (2006) define ROCE as indicating an organisation's efficiency in generating profits from an 'asset base'. ROCE is concerned with the comparison of profitability and capital employed within a single year. This is likely to fluctuate, increasing in profitability as the project becomes established. On the other hand, ARR finds the 'average rate of return', or annual percentage of profit, over the entire life of the project.

In Table 6.7, project B has a better ARR value than project A, so would be the preferred investment. However, project B has a higher cash flow in the first three years so would benefit the investor if they have high liabilities as they could be paid back more rapidly.

The ARR technique has no concept of the lifespan of the project or its size. If project B was extended into year seven, yielding a profit of £1,000, this would make the profit seem more attractive. However, the ARR would then decline from 8.33 per cent to 7.42 per cent as it is the average over seven years as opposed to six years. ARR also ignores the timing of cash flows as it works out the average profit per year even though the large returns may only occur in the latter stages of the project's life.

The previous examples use the average investment for the proposal but an alternative ARR technique is:

$$\text{ARR (total investment)} = \frac{\text{Average annual profit}}{\text{Initial capital invested}} \times 100$$

Table 6.7   Accounting rate of return

	Project A	Project B
Accounting profit = ($\sum$ inflows) – initial investment	= £120,000 – £100,000 = £20,000	= £125,000 – £100,000 = £25,000
Average annual profit = accounting profit ÷ n years	= £20,000 ÷ 6 = £3,333	= £25,000 ÷ 6 = £4,167
Average investment = (initial asset value + closing asset value) ÷ 2	= (£100,000 + £0) ÷ 2 = £50,000	= (£100,000 + £0) ÷ 2 = £50,000
ARR (average investment) = Average annual profit × 100 Average investment	= £3,333 × 100 £50,000 = 6.67%	= £4,167 × 100 £50,000 = 8.33%

Both are acceptable methods and give appropriate results when applied correctly. Confusion can be caused, however, if the same equation is not applied routinely and to all proposals, as the result from each produces wide variations and could lead to a wrong investment decision.

Drury (2015) states that the ARR method is inappropriate as it is based on profits instead of cash flows; profits are not equal to cash flows because financial accounting profit measurement is based on the 'accrual concept'.

Advantages and disadvantages of accounting rate of return

Advantages

- It is easy to understand and calculate.
- It is a popular method due to its simplicity.
- It is simple for managers and business planners to understand, because it is expressed in percentage terms.

Disadvantages

- It ignores the time value of the money.
- It ignores the timings of inflows and outflows of cash generated from the project.
- There is no standard concept of calculating accounting rate of return.
- It uses the concept of accounting profit; profit can be very subjective and is not appropriate for capital investment decision-making, because cash is generated by the project.
- It does not help managers to make investment decisions, because it does not give very clear and definitive answers.

Discounted cash flow methods

Discounted cash flow (DCF) can be worked out by the following equation:

$$PV = \frac{FV}{(1+r)^n}$$

PV: Present value of cash flow

FV: Future value of cash flow

r: The required rate of return/interest rate

n: The number of years until the cash flow takes place

For example, Project A receives £21,000 in year four of the investment, if this had a required rate of return of 5 per cent then the actual value would be:

$$\frac{25,000}{(1+0.14)^4} = £20,575$$

These manual calculations can become lengthy if the investment lasts for a number of years, so discount tables containing annuity factors are produced by HM Treasury in *The Green Book* to simplify the method (HM Treasury, 2011).

For the previous example, using this table and cross-referencing three years with a discount rate of 10 per cent gives the following equation:

£25,000 × 0.823* = £20,575

(*The Green Book* shows the discount rate for four years at 5 per cent is 0.823.)

This published discount rate contains a small margin of error due to rounding but makes the DCF method of appraisal a lot more accessible to non-accountants. However, it is advised that a declining long-term discount rate should be used for investments of over 30 years due to uncertainty about the future. These long-term discount rates are shown in *The Green Book*. A higher percentage can also be used when calculating high-risk investments to give a more cautious present value.

The two main techniques within the discounted cash flow group are: net present value and internal rate of return.

Net present value

The net present value (NPV) appraisal method utilises discounted cash flow to estimate the current total value of future inflows compared with the initial investment. If, when the total cash inflow at present value is subtracted from the total cash outflow at present value, the grand total is negative, then the investment should not be made; but if it is positive, the organisation should accept the proposal.

NPV explains whether the capital would be worth more if invested for several years, or whether it would be worth more lent into the capital market. Theoretically, this means if the NPV was zero then the investor should be indifferent.

This concept of present value clearly helps the company to assess the return of a project at the initial stage, by using the NPV technique to look at cash flows expected in future years. The value of money varies over time and between different nations. This happens due to changes in interest rates and inflation. It is important to understand the concept that the current value of £1 will not be the same in future years. It is important to work out how much present capital will be worth in the future. NPV ignores any depreciation as the full cost of the asset is treated as the initial investment, so it would mean 'double-counting' the cost.

The formula for calculating NPV is:

$$NPV = \frac{FV1}{1+r} + \frac{FV2}{(1+r)^2} + \frac{FV3}{(1+r)^3} + \ldots\ldots + \frac{FVn}{(1+r)^n} - I$$

NPV: Net present value

FV: Future value of cash flow

r: The required rate of return/interest rate

n: The number of years until the cash flow takes place

I: Initial investment

By applying the discount factor of 4 per cent to projects A and B, both have positive NPVs so should be accepted. When compared with a higher discount rate of 10 per cent, as shown in Table 6.8, project A remains acceptable yet project B makes a loss. The NPV for project A,

Table 6.8   Net present value with a 4 per cent discount rate factor

Year		Amount	Discount factor 4%	Present value	Amount	Discount factor 3.5%	Present value
0	Cost	−80,000	1	−80,000	−80,000	1	−80,000
1	Cash inflow	20,000	0.962	19,240	19,000	0.962	18,278
2	Cash inflow	19,000	0.925	17,575	15,000	0.925	13,875
3	Cash inflow	20,500	0.889	18,225	36,000	0.889	32,004
4	Cash inflow	14,000	0.855	11,970	16,000	0.855	13,680
5	Cash inflow	12,000	0.822	9,864	12,000	0.822	9,864
6	Cash inflow	27,000	0.79	21,330	8,000	0.79	6,320
			NPV =18,204			NPV =14,021	

Table 6.9   Net present value with a 10 per cent discount rate factor

Year		Project A			Project B		
		Amount	Discount factor 10%	Present value	Amount	Discount factor 10%	Present value
0	Cost	(100,000)	1	(100,000)	(100,000)	1	(100,000)
1	Cash inflow	28,000	0.9091	25,455	21,000	0.9091	19,091
2	Cash inflow	23,000	0.8264	19,007	28,000	0.8264	23,139
3	Cash inflow	20,000	0.7513	15,026	38,000	0.7513	28,549
4	Cash inflow	18,000	0.683	12,294	15,000	0.683	10,245
5	Cash inflow	18,000	0.6209	11,176	9,000	0.6209	5,588
6	Cash inflow	35,000	0.5645	19,758	9,000	0.5645	5,081
				NPV =2,716			NPV =−8,307

using a discount rate of 10 per cent from *The Green Book* is shown in Table 6.9. The ARR method suggested that project A would have a profit of £12,000 but the NPV approach shows that in reality the investment would only make a profit of £2,716.

Advantages and disadvantages of net present value

Advantages

- NPV allows management to compare and analyse a number of different projects with the same discounting factor.
- NPV considers all the cash flows which have been generated from the projects.
- NPV takes into account the time value of money.
- NPV takes into account the risk of future cash flows.
- NPV ensures that the organisation gains maximum return from the investment.

Disadvantages

- NPV is very complicated to calculate and understand.
- It is difficult to apply the appropriate discounting rates.
- NPV is time consuming.

NPV allows a decision-maker to compare a number of projects with the same risk factor. A negative aspect is the assumption that the cash flows occur at the end of the year, which is often false. In addition, it is difficult to say that any investment appraisal method can give definitive guidance to a decision-maker as to whether to invest in the project or not. NPV merely acts as a guide for managers to analyse the future cash flow.

Internal rate of return

The internal rate of return (IRR) is one of the most important methods among investment appraisal techniques for analysing the future cash flow of a project. In other words, it is a capital budgeting method used by companies to make financial decisions as to whether to invest in the project in the long term. IRR is used by managers to access a positive return from the investment.

IRR calculates the capital investment return on each individual project. If the project produces a positive IRR that is higher than the rate of the interest, it helps the organisation to make better decisions and to compare alternative options.

Moreover, IRR can be defined as the discount rate which gives the net present value of zero to different sets of cash flows. IRR is a method of working out the discount rate of a project. This can be used when there is a predefined discount rate and the decision-maker wishes to know if the project meets or exceeds this target.

> If the project's IRR exceeds the comparison rate (cost of capital) accept the investment; if IRR is less than the comparison rate, reject the investment. (Brayshaw et al., 1999: 63)

IRR is calculated by calculating the value of r when the NPV is zero.

$$\frac{FV1}{1+r} + \frac{FV2}{(1+r)^2} + \frac{FV3}{(1+r)^3} + \ldots\ldots + \frac{FVn}{(1+r)^n} - I = 0$$

This equation can be rearranged if the project only lasts for a year, and is simple to work out:

$$\frac{FV_1}{1+r} - I = 0$$

$$\frac{FV_1}{1+r} = I$$

$$FV_1 = I(1+r) = I + Ir$$

$$FV_1 - I = Ir$$

$$\frac{FV_1}{I} - I = r$$

FV: Future value of cash flow

r: The required rate of return/interest rate

n: The number of years until the cash flow takes place

I: Initial investment

If the investment is for a period of two years, the equation can be solved using a quadratic equation. However, when an investment is for several years the equation is a lot more complicated.

$$\frac{FV1}{1+r}+\frac{FV2}{\left(1+r\right)^{2}}+\frac{FV3}{\left(1+r\right)^{3}}+.......+\frac{FVn}{\left(1+r\right)^{n}}-I=0$$

This complex polynomial equation can be solved using computer programs. For example Table 6.8 shows project B with a positive NPV with a discount factor of 4 per cent and Table 6.9 shows project B with a negative NPV with a discount factor of 10 per cent.

Therefore the IRR discount factor must lie between 4 per cent and 10 per cent.

IRR = 4% + (difference between the two discount rates × $\dfrac{\text{positive NPV}}{\text{NPV range}}$)

= 4% + (6% × $\dfrac{14{,}021}{22{,}328}$)

= 4% + 7.8

= 7.7%

This shows that for project B to be accepted the discount rate, or rate of interest, must be below 7.7 per cent. In a stable economy this is possible, but risk factors such as reliance on demand can be used in conjunction with discount factors. IRR enables decision-makers to calculate the level of interest a project can withstand, and competing projects with the highest resilience will have greater appeal. In addition, IRR is a very difficult technique to use in the industry, due to the nature of the method and practical difficulties which are attached to this technique of investment appraisal. NPV and IRR will usually show the same result when carried out on an investment proposal, and will indicate whether it should be accepted or rejected. Unlike NPV, however, IRR calculates the average discount per year, and does not allow for different discount rates to be used in different years.

Advantages and disadvantages of internal rate of return

Advantages

- IRR uses the time value of the money.
- IRR is a break-even discount rate used by management accountants to analyse future cash flow.
- The IRR method is more popular than the NPV method among managers.
- Compared to NPV the IRR method is easier to use and more understandable to managers in the industry.
- IRR is a method used by firms to minimise errors in the calculations obtained by using NPV.

Disadvantages

- IRR often provides unrealistic rates of return compared to NPV.
- IRR expresses the return in percentages rather than in forms of currency.
- IRR is time consuming compared to the payback method and ARR.
- IRR ignores the scale of investment, it only takes into consideration the percentage derived from the project.

INVESTMENT APPRAISAL METHODS USED IN BUSINESSES

Over the past two decades research has shown an increase in the use of the more sophisticated methods of investment appraisal involving discounted cash flow, NPV and IRR. However, these techniques are still less popular in smaller companies. This may be due to the companies' lack of understanding, or because smaller companies concentrate on short-term investments and so do not take account of the difference in value of money.

Although the payback method ignores profits, it is still widely used in UK industry as it can be a comprehensive, simple argument used by a manager to convince others, who do not have a financial background, that a certain proposal should be accepted. This is emphasised by companies' focus on profits; projects with larger profits seem more attractive despite the decreasing value of money.

The proposed projects for investment can be independent (unrelated to the acceptance or rejection of other projects) or mutually exclusive (which precludes the acceptance of one or more alternative projects). As resources are limited, however, projects may have to be adapted as capital is shared, and this can endanger the effectiveness of that investment.

Decision-making process in investment appraisals

When any decision is made, be it large or small, it will go through a type of decision-making process. The formality and time taken to carry out this process will vary according to the implications of the decision and the investment required. For a non-biased capital investment decision a formal procedure should be adhered to and applied to each proposal to ensure the correct proposal is accepted.

Time can be a major factor in how the decision process is carried out. If a company is reactive, then they will want to reach a decision quickly to maintain competitive advantage in the dynamic environment. However, if the organisation is proactive the time period will be extended as they are predicting changes and planning for them rather than making decisions after the change has taken place. This is beneficial as they can apply a more extensive decision-making process and ensure that all proposals are considered equally and any elements of risk are considered.

Capital investment appraisal methods provide a quantitative analysis giving a firm logical basis from which a decision can be made. However, it is important to note that capital investment appraisal methods are only part of the final decision and other factors must be taken into account.

Strategic decisions are subject to external and internal influences. This makes it difficult to come to a non-biased decision but by following a routine process it is more likely that the project that offers the greatest benefits for the organisation is accepted.

The application of capital investment appraisal methods enables a company to set benchmarks and have a standard of comparison; it also helps the management to make better strategic decisions. This is due to an extensive proportion of businesses using the same investment appraisal techniques to enhance business growth and develop benchmarking tools; all of this helps businesses to compare their performance with other competitors and internal managers.

Accounting managers and experts in financial investment extensively consider this decision process; however, strategy texts put heavy emphasis on past financial analysis instead of ways to direct capital expenditure. Prior to carrying out an investment appraisal there must be a strategic need for the project, therefore strategy is interlinked with the investment at all stages of the decision-making process.

Therefore, strategic management involves making investment decisions by identifying, evaluating and selecting the projects that are likely to help the business to have greater impact and have a competitive edge. Capital investment appraisal helps the senior management to make the right decisions and these techniques have been proven successful over the years. As Idowu states:

> The question to address is whether or not the future returns will be sufficient to justify the sacrifices the investing entity would have to make. (2000: 1)

For this reason, strategic investment decision-making helps managers in all elements of cost – benefit analysis and ensures that future capital can be raised through future returns, to invest in the business for future growth.

The time factor can be a major element for any decision-making process. In modern events management, decision-making needs to be quick in order to prevent competitors from securing market share, which results in little benefit for a business. However, if the organisation is being proactive the time period is extended and techniques like capital investment appraisal can be applied. A successful event company should have processes for both types of decision to ensure resources are allocated correctly, competitive advantage is maintained and future development projects are feasible. Capital investment appraisal can be initiated due to an environmental change or it can be used for an idea at development stage; it can therefore be either reactive or proactive. However, due to the nature of capital investments, in which a large amount of resources may be utilised and in which the cost may be recouped over several years, the organisation must go through a methodical process to ensure the correct decision is made.

The identification of an investment need by the organisation is the primary step. This is achieved through a thorough internal and external strategic analysis of the company. A company analysis is an imperative preliminary to the evaluation of investment projects as this will determine the financial and other resources available.

It is important to note that capital investment appraisal is only part of the decision-making process and other factors must be considered. These are often intangible and so are more difficult to measure.

SUMMARY

This chapter has critically evaluated the process of cost accounting. Costing is a vital tool for any company, regardless of its size or business activities. The main aspects of cost accounting are to provide information which will be useful for the board of directors, managers and employees of the organisation. In reality, the majority of them are not economists or accountants. The other reason that cost accounting information is important is that it helps managers to understand and know what selling price would lead to a profit. When looking at the individual costs, it is important for the costing manager or director to analyse and classify the costs according to the purpose for which the cost will be or has been used.

Traditionally, costs are broken into direct or indirect, but there are several other ways of presenting the costs. The types of costing classification used by managers will depend on the purpose of the exercise. In addition, organisations will also use the marginal and absorption costing methods to calculate final costs. The marginal costing method only takes into account variable costs, whereas absorption costing takes into account total costs.

Another technique which has been explored in this is chapter break-even analysis. This is the most common technique used by management accountants. In this technique the costs are categorised into fixed and variable costs. The break-even analysis technique compares the total fixed and variable costs with sales values or revenue achieved, and focuses on the point at which neither profit nor loss occurs.

The development of large-scale events will require investments of capital expenditure to meet the demand. The amount of money can vary between businesses, but because the amount can be substantial relative to the size of the organisation, all decisions on capital investment should be thoroughly explored and all options and consequences clarified.

In this chapter four traditional methods of capital investment methods have been explored. There are similarities between all four models. NPV and IRR are more sophisticated methods of investment appraisal involving detailed calculations and taking into account the time value of the money. However, these techniques are less popular in smaller companies, which may be due to the companies' lack of understanding, or because smaller companies concentrate on short-term investments and so do not take into account the difference in value of money.

Discussion questions

Question 1

Mercure Festival Ltd

The following information relates to three possible capital expenditure projects for Mercure Festival Ltd.

Because of capital rationing only one project can be accepted.

		A	B	C
Initial cost		£320,000	£260,500	£180,000
Expected life		5 years	5 years	5 years
Scrap value expected		£20,600	£13,900	£6,000
Expected cash inflows		£	£	£
End year	1	75,000	140,000	20,000
	2	80,000	90,000	40,000
	3	95,000	75,000	60,000
	4	65,000	65,000	80,000
	5	55,000	40,000	55,000

The company estimates its cost of capital is 10 per cent and discount factors are as follows.

Year	0	1.00
Year	1	0.91
Year	2	0.83
Year	3	0.75
Year	4	0.68
Year	5	0.62

Calculate the following:

a) The payback period for each project.
b) The accounting rate of return for each project.
c) The net present value of each project.

(Continued)

(Continued)

Question 2

Explain and critically discuss the drawbacks of the average rate of return method of investment appraisal.

Question 3

Discuss and explain the importance of capital investment appraisal decisions. Critically evaluate the following three investment appraisal methods.

a   Payback period.
b   Internal rate of return.
c   Net present value.

Question 4

Explain and critically analyse the importance of pricing strategies for Mercure Festival Ltd.

Question 5

Explain and discuss the distinction between fixed and variable costs for event managers.

Question 6

Outline the major principles underlying break-even analysis for Mercure Festival Ltd.

Case study 1: Corporate Events Ltd

Senior management of Corporate Events Ltd have identified that there is a strategic need for replacement of their sound and lighting equipment to be acquired in one of their production departments. They have to make a choice between two models of the sound and lighting: model 1 is called Super and model 2 is called Deluxe. They are unsure as to which of the two models they should buy. They want you to use the three following investment appraisal techniques.

1   Payback period.
2   Internal rate of return.
3   Net present value.

You are required to recommend which of the two models is better under each appraisal technique and to explain briefly why you have recommended one in place of the other under each technique.

		Super	Deluxe
Cost		£500,000	£800,000
Net cash inflow		£	£
Year	1	250,000	150,000
	2	100,000	200,000
	3	100,000	250,000
	4	50,000	100,000
	5	150,000	100,000
	6	100,000	250,000
Scrap value		20,000	80,000

The cost of capital is 12 per cent and Corporate Events Ltd depreciates all its fixed assets on the straight-line basis. By cost of capital is meant what it costs to raise the required finance for the project. Corporate Events Ltd is an events production company with many large departments that each make separate musical lighting for events. One department makes marquees. Corporate Events Ltd is planning to invest in new machinery which will develop marquees for clients.

Case study 2: Leeds West Indian Carnival

The West Indian Carnival is an annual event celebrated in Leeds since the 1960s. The carnival is one of the oldest Caribbean carnivals in Europe. The carnival has created a multicultural spirit for people of all races and nationalities to attend the event during the August bank holiday each year since 1967. The event is held on the August Bank Holiday weekend from Sunday to Monday.

Originally the Leeds West Indian Carnival used to go into the city centre: that tradition changed during the 1980s. The carnival has outgrown the original concept and now it takes place around Chapeltown and Harehills.

Behind the colour and music of the carnival there is a deeper meaning rooted in the experiences of Caribbean people arriving in England around a time of great change in the late 1950s and early 1960s. So it was a search for identity, for community and belonging that led to the carnival being developed in the early 1960s in the area of Chapeltown and Harehills in Leeds

(Continued)

(Continued)

In 2004 over 80,000 people enjoyed the mixture of local and international talent. This magical event was mixed with the wonderful smells of Caribbean cooking. In the afternoon over 100,000 people watched the carnival procession.

One of the most essential developments within the Leeds West Indian Carnival is the economic impact of the carnival on the host community of Leeds. The carnival has a great economic impact on the local community: the revellers come from all parts of the country and as far as the Caribbean. Local businesses can gain substantial financial rewards during the carnival weekends. It is a great income generator for local businesses, and the local community benefits from the carnival festival well before the carnival weekend itself.

The festival has to try to work out the cost of each of their products. This is vital for them in setting their prices.

You are employed as an Event Organiser in the Events Department of Leeds West Indian Carnival. There is a small team of full-time staff in the Events Department which has been given the responsibility of organising the festival. You are heading up this team and will report to the Head of the Events Department.

As is usual in organising, planning and managing any major event, many organisations and individuals will be involved at some or all stages of the event – local officers of the council, local politicians, commercial organisations, outsourced services, emergency services, volunteers, local communities, commercial sponsors, etc.

When contemplating long-term costing and pricing strategies, event managers face two key questions:

1   How can managers develop standard approaches to all costing and pricing activities across the festival, while maintaining flexibility to satisfy local requirements?
2   What level of investment should be approved for human resources development?

FURTHER READING

Alkaraan, F. and Northcott, D. (2006) 'Strategic capital investment decision making: a role for emergent analysis tool?', *The British Accounting Review*, 38(2): 149–73.

Atrill, P. and McLaney, E. (2015) *Accounting and Finance for Non-specialists*, 9th edn. Harlow: Pearson.

Brayshaw, R., Samuels, J. and Wilkes, M. (1999) *Financial Management and Decision Making*. London: International Thomson Business Press.

Burns, P. (2005) *Corporate Entrepreneurship*. New York: Palgrave Macmillan.

Butler, R., Davies, L., Pike, R. and Shaap, J. (1993) *Strategic Investment Decisions*. London: Routledge.

Drury, C. (2015) *Management and Cost Accounting*, 9th edn. London: Thomson Learning.

Lumby, S. and Jones, C. (2000) *Investment Appraisal and Financing Decisions*, 6th edn. London: Chapman & Hall.

Watson, D. and Head, A. (2013) *Corporate Finance: Principles and Practice*, 6th edn. Harlow: Pearson.

Weetman, P. (2010) *Management Accounting*, 2nd edn. Harlow: Financial Times/Prentice Hall.

7

PROJECT MANAGEMENT AND FINANCING

In this chapter you will cover

This chapter will investigate and explore the theories and practices that are associated with project management, as appropriate to the events management industry, and will also evaluate a range of techniques that are available for event managers in the context of organisational transformation and density. In addition, the chapter will look at the different sources of finance and the wide range of fundraising strategies available to event managers. This should enable event managers to understand, negotiate and make decisions regarding the financial opportunities that may be presented to them.

PROJECT MANAGEMENT WITHIN THE EVENTS INDUSTRY

Project management has been a cornerstone of all projects that have been implemented since the early days of major projects such as the construction of the Hoover Reservoir Dam and the Manhattan Project (Luecke, 2004). Today, project management is applied to all kinds of activities and even the events industry is discovering the benefits and realising the significance of project management. Over the last two decades expectations about the quality and efficiency of events have increased (GCB, 2009 [online]), and some discussion is needed as to which project management tools are most suitable to ensure the successful planning and control of events. It is questionable whether the importance of project management grows with the complexity of an event, or whether project management offers planning and control tools which contribute to the success of any kind of event, no matter what size or scale. Undoubtedly, the more complicated and long-lasting the planning of an event is, the more essential it is to introduce methods guaranteeing its progress and success.

As several leading authors such as Getz (2005) emphasise, every event has to be completed by a specific date, and its budget is limited and closely linked to its quality and performance. Organising an event can thus definitely be characterised as a project. So, we now need to investigate to what extent the application of project management can contribute to more successful events. For event managers to be successful in managing an event they must approach it as a project to be managed. Therefore, it is important for event managers to ask for the event proposal from the client to see if the project is suitable for the company to undertake. The event proposal contains the main information in relation to project requirements and resources needed for project. The event proposal template in Table 7.1 contains information to be provided by the client such as the background of the event.

Table 7.1   Event proposal template

Name of project

Name of contact person

Background to the project

Goals and objectives

Scope of the project

Target audience

Partners/supporters

Risks and key assumptions

Budget

Time scale

Event date

The event can be seen as an asset, the ultimate deliverable that has to be presented to the customer. The way of producing an event can therefore be defined as the management through which the progress and success of the ultimate deliverable (the event) has to be guaranteed.

THE PROJECT LIFE CYCLE

Project management approaches generally divide the project life cycle (PLC) into a number of phases, in order to support a project's progress and success. Figure 7.1 summarises the six fundamental framework phases of the product life cycle for an event.

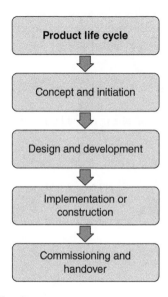

Figure 7.1 Fundamental framework of project management

To correctly apply these phases to the events industry it is necessary to define them briefly.

Concept and initiation: The two most important things to be covered in the first phase are to establish 'a need or opportunity for the product, facility or service' and to conduct a feasibility study, to assess whether or not the project is realisable.

Design and development: If it is decided that the project is to go ahead, the second phase is concerned with very important tasks. Undoubtedly, failures in this phase will have very damaging impacts on a project as discrepancies within the planning process will affect a project's quality and time management.

Implementation or construction: The third phase uses the outcome of the second phase to implement the project. Effective management is very important here as monitoring and controlling will be undertaken throughout this phase. The reason for this is the interdependence between the parameters of time, budget and quality – any shortfall in one of these parameters will very likely endanger the whole project.

Commissioning and handover: The fourth and final phase 'confirms that the project has been implemented or built to the design' and in the end terminates the project (Burke, 2006: 28). Luecke (2004) stresses that learning from experience is also a very important activity of this phase. For the events industry, this phase offers a great opportunity to assess the ways things have been done in order to improve for future projects, as a lot of events take place annually or might at least repeat within a few years.

This short definition of the PLC reveals how dependent all these phases are on each other. Every end result of one phase determines the success and progress of the following. As events, just like any other project, are in most cases organised over a long period of time, it is best to divide the planning of an event into several phases.

THE EVENT LIFE CYCLE

The PLC of events is called the event life cycle (ELC), and is considered to have five phases (as shown in Figure 7.2).

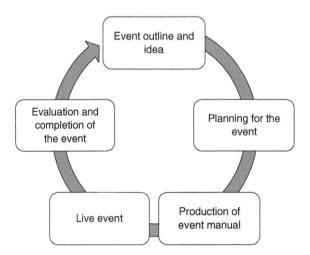

Figure 7.2   The event life cycle

The aim of the different phases is to provide clarity to the confusing tasks involved in events management. The most important action of the last phase is learning for the future. Understanding how the different phases overlap and determine each other, in the opinion of authors like Goldblatt (2002), can only be improved by experience, since the basic framework of, for example, planning, leading, designing, marketing, controlling, budgeting, staging and evaluating an event does not necessarily depend on the type of event. Remember, every event is unique and therefore sets new standards.

Event outline and idea: The outset phase of the ELC is concerned with the presentation of the project's idea, for which objectives have to be set. This phase can also include a feasibility study to determine whether the event is realisable or if the idea has to be rejected. According to this, the outset phase clearly offers decision-makers the opportunity to evaluate if any investment in a potential event should be undertaken or not.

Planning for the event: The planning phase supports event organisers with clearly structured plans and schedules if developed and implemented in the right way. Better coordination means that any risks and dangers can be identified before they seriously affect the successful completion of an event. Well-conceived and detailed plans and schedules facilitate an event's planning and as there is only one opportunity to get it right, the planning phase should provide events industry professionals with security and clarity to successfully plan, control and implement an event. Thus, it is at this stage where project management tools can be deployed to contribute to an event's success.

Production of event manual: The implementation phase deals with the monitoring and controlling of all actions undertaken and furthermore offers the opportunity to compare the initially set objectives with reality. It is this phase that offers events industry professionals the opportunity to intervene and adapt plans to the objectives, to ensure they do not steer off course and endanger an event's success.

Live event: In this phase the event takes place. Any last-minute difficulties have to be solved on site. If serious problems and risks have not been worked out in the planning or implementation phase there is hardly anything that can be done to bring the event to a successful termination. This stage of the ELC clearly reveals how important it is to have a well-structured plan for an event. Dividing the organisation of an event into different phases reduces pressure, provides an overview and the opportunity to react early enough if potential threats and risks might arise.

Evaluation and completion of the event: It is important for event managers to take the completion of an event very seriously, because to do so always helps in the preparation for future events. Therefore, event evaluation becomes an important part of this phase, helping to improve future performance. The evaluation and completion of an event means more than just paying the bills and closing the venue. It is an opportunity to evaluate an event's success and to improve the way an event is planned, monitored, controlled and brought forward.

As shown above, using the ELC to divide the organisation of an event into different phases provides clear structures and support to successfully organise the event.

PROJECT MANAGEMENT TOOLS AND EVENTS

What tools does project management have to offer to guarantee an event's success? Which phases can be supported and what limitations might exist which could weaken or endanger an event? Project management is built upon a diverse number of project management tools. However, some project management tools might be more efficient and beneficial than others. The choice of appropriate tools depends on the kind of project. The most common project management tools used in the events industry include:

- breakdown structures
- the critical path method
- the Gantt chart.

These are usually initiated and applied in the planning phase of an event or project, which again emphasises the fact that the planning phase is the most important one within the ELC. The following sections will look at each of these tools in more detail.

Breakdown structures

There are five tools within this category: work breakdown structure (WBS), resource breakdown structure (RBS), contract breakdown structure (CoBS), location breakdown structure (LBS), and breakdown by sub-projects. Let's look at each of these in turn.

Work breakdown structure: The WBS is a suitable tool for successfully handling and structuring events. The graphical subdivision of an event into manageable work packages is an important feature of the WBS, which leads to benefits such as the improvement of communication or the early identification of risks and uncertainty factors. The WBS also provides clear structures which support all team members with explicit ideas about their responsibilities.

Resource breakdown structure: The RBS subdivides the event in terms of the total resources available. Resources like money or human resources are issues which have to be considered and treated with greatest attention, as, for example, failing to budget properly will surely endanger the successful completion of any event.

Contract breakdown structure: The CoBS simply helps to understand the relationships between large numbers of contractors that might exist in an event. It also facilitates the setting of priorities in favour of an event's success as some stakeholders are more or less important, and able to express their expectations of an event.

Location breakdown structure: Large-scale events often include a wide spread of work over different locations. To stay on the top of things the LBS supports a listing of the physical locations of the work.

Breakdown by sub-projects: The subdivision of a big event into several smaller sub-projects is a measure to keep lines clear and to identify risks as early as possible. The process and structure of the event is demonstrated graphically, so that every team member is able to reconstruct the project's progress.

Application to events

The various breakdown structures show that there are many ways of subdividing an event. Therefore, the choice of the right breakdown structures depends on the kind of event. Events feature characteristics which demand continuous monitoring and control, so breakdown structures can help to improve the way an event is handled and planned. The WBS can help managers to address the fact that events are characteristically non-routine, as potential risks can be identified, eliminated or minimised before they harm an event substantially. However, breakdown structures do not provide a time flow, which in the case of events is very important as deadlines have to be met.

Critical path method

The critical path method (CPM) helps to determine the total time needed to accomplish a project and to identify critical tasks which might endanger a project's completion on time. To make use of the CPM, the WBS has to be first transformed into a networking diagram.

In this context the networking diagram (Figure 7.3) can be seen as an extension to the WBS. Although both are a graphical presentation of an event, the networking diagram is more suitable to demonstrate dependencies and to provide certain activities with the time needed to accomplish them (Lock, 2001).

Activities are marked with the latest starting time (LST) and the earliest finish time (EFT) to determine whether a specific task can be delayed without delaying the project as a whole. Any delay on the critical path will delay the whole event. These are valuable features as most events are characterised by fixed end-dates, and events industry professionals are expected to meet the deadlines. Any delays might evoke costly miscalculations which in return will weaken stakeholders' satisfaction and future business.

Therefore, effective communication among all parties concerned when staging an event is important. Applying the CPM supports the early identification of critical tasks and any misunderstandings can be eliminated before any damaging consequences occur. All in all, the CPM is an indispensable tool for event planning, and in fact it becomes even more important as the complexity of an event increases. Nevertheless, the WBS and CPM might also provoke some issues. Shone and Parry (2010) stress that the application of these tools might hinder team members in free thinking, collaboration and the use of their own creativity as both the WBS and CPM provide 'ultimate' plans which permit no variances. Therefore, the right balance between fixed plans and room for manoeuvre has to be found to prevent the planning of an event from becoming self-driven.

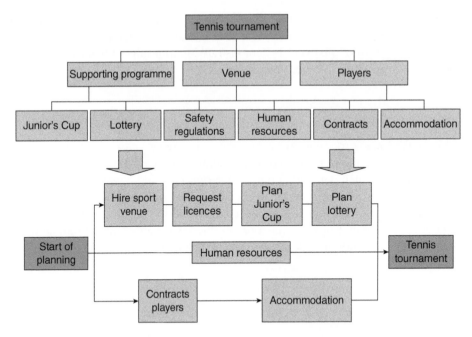

Figure 7.3 WBS into a networking diagram

The Gantt chart

Another widely used project management tool is the Gantt chart (GC), which is named after its inventor, Henry Gantt, an American engineer and social scientist.

A definite advantage of the GC is that it puts all activities in a time-sequenced order. This helps to identify the different tasks and in deciding on how long they should take, that is, when they should be completed. It assists events industry professionals in developing scenarios that might occur if critical tasks are delayed. Another very valuable characteristic of the GC is the simple act of thinking through an event which increases the awareness of all work that has to be done.

IDENTIFYING SOURCES OF FINANCE FOR EVENTS AND FESTIVALS PROJECTS

Event managers rarely have the pleasure and luxury of sufficient funds to sustain their current and planned business expenditure. However, they need to obtain sufficient funds in order to compete within the industry, and must therefore look to external sources of finance to meet their business obligations. Generally speaking, there are two methods of raising money for business development. Firstly, there is business equity, which covers funds invested by the owner of the business, shareholders and any other interested parties. Secondly, there is debt, which is generated by borrowing the money through banks, trade credit or leasing. The business needs to pay this money back to the lender at some point in the future.

The most common sources of business funding are outlined below.

Internal sources of finance

Personal savings

Personal savings are most commonly used to raise funds for businesses. The savings invested are normally those of the business owner, partner or shareholder and this type of financing is frequently found in small businesses or businesses which are at the early stages of their development. Investing substantial personal savings in a business can help to demonstrate commitment to external finance providers.

Sales of assets

Businesses may decide to sell some of their surplus fixed assets in order to raise funds for current or future projects, to expand the business or to pay off debts. By selling fixed assets, the organisation can avoid borrowing, which would mean incurring interest charges and increasing the overall liability of the business.

Retained profit

Using retained profit is the simplest method by which a business can finance its own activities. The retained profit is the money which has been generated by the business in the past through net profit and which has not been spent on any other project or activity. Retained profit is typically used by businesses to help them to buy new assets or to expand in other ways. Sometimes business owners save profits to provide security during any difficult periods in the future.

External sources of finance

Bank loans

Borrowing money from the bank is the traditional method used by businesses to raise funds for their current and future projects. Interest must normally be paid on any money borrowed from the bank. There are different forms of bank loan which are available to businesses. It is generally more difficult for new businesses to secure cheaper rates of interest; these are usually only offered to reputable businesses with good track records. The business will need to repay the bank loan in regular instalments, with interest rates being set according to the Bank of England rate. Typically, banks charge businesses interest rates of at least 4 per cent above the Bank of England rate.

There is an endless range of loans on offer, to suit all types of businesses. These vary according to:

- the amount required by the business
- the length of time over which the business will repay the loan
- the type of interest rate being charged by the bank (e.g. fixed or variable).

Choosing the right type of interest rate is very important for the business in the long run. This can be difficult, since both fixed and variable rates have advantages and disadvantages. For example, taking out a fixed rate loan means that the company can accurately predict the size of the monthly repayments. On the other hand, repayments on a variable rate loan can fluctuate if the base rate changes in line with the Bank of England rate. In addition, the banks charge individual customers different rates, usually ranging between 3 per cent and 4.5 per cent on top of the Bank of England rate.

Overdrafts

An overdraft is the most common form of debt available to businesses in the short term. An overdraft is easy to arrange and does not have a minimum borrowing term. It is a flexible method to use in order to finance a business shortfall over a short period. The money can be drawn down by the business fairly quickly and repaid over the period agreed with the bank manager; interest rates and ease of borrowing will depend on the state of the business and on the history of the company. If a company has no previous track record, banks will require some form of security, perhaps involving the assets of the business or the personal property of the owner. Where a business uses its assets to secure an overdraft, this clearly limits its ability to sell these assets or to use them to secure any other sources of finance. However, if the business has a good track record, an unsecured overdraft facility is easy to arrange.

One of the main advantages of this type of borrowing is that the debt can be paid off at any time without incurring a penalty. On the other hand, an overdraft is repayable on demand from the bank. Since overdrafts are given and the interest rate set according to the status of the individual account, new customers are normally charged more than long-standing customers. Overdrafts are one of the most expensive forms of finance since the interest rate is usually higher than that set for medium- and long-term borrowing and a business arrangement fee of between 1 per cent and 2.5 per cent of the agreed overdraft facility is commonly charged. It is therefore important only to use the overdraft facility for a short period of time.

Leasing

Leasing is the most common method of obtaining assets, such as backstage equipment, vehicles or computer equipment, without immediate large-scale capital expenditure by the company. Traditionally, the leasing company buys and owns the assets and claims any capital allowances due against them. A number of different types of leasing agreement exist within the market. The two most commonly used by businesses are:

- finance leases
- operating leases.

The finance lease is a form of loan repaid by the company in monthly instalments through-out and up to the end of the economic life of the product. An operating lease is an arrangement whereby the product is used by the company for less than its full economic life and the leasing company therefore takes the risk of the equipment becoming obsolete during this period. Normally, the leasing company will pay for the maintenance and insurance of the product.

The main benefit of leasing an asset is that the business does not have to pay a deposit or a large amount of money up front. This allows the finance to be spread over time in monthly or quarterly instalments that are generally fixed and means that costs can be shared with other parts of the business. This can make it much easier for small and medium-sized companies to manage their cash flow and plan their use of capital over the year.

Business angels

Business angels are individual investors who provide finance to support either the start-up or further growth of businesses which can demonstrate the opportunity for good future returns. Private investors are usually individuals who are prepared to make a long-term investment of £50,000 or more in promising businesses which are at a very early stage in their development. Business angels usually select local companies or those which are of personal interest to them in which to invest. Some business angels also have specific knowledge of the business and can bring a great deal of added value.

Generally, investments by business angels take the form of share capital (as defined on page 145) in exchange for a share of the business and its future profits. It is their intention to help the business develop and they may join the board of directors in order to safeguard their investment and provide support, knowledge and guidance.

Corporate sponsorship

Corporate sponsorship is another method of finance used by events and festivals. It may take the form of cash donations, goods or services from a large corporation in return for specific opportunities to promote their business. These may include using a corporate logo on promotional materials, displaying a special corporate banner at the event or calling the event by the corporate name.

Formal stock markets

The formal stock markets method is the most efficient and proven technique used by large corporations to raise finance. Large organisations have a clear advantage over smaller ones since, once their listing has been established on the stock market, shares in the company can be bought and sold readily and thus become more stable and liquid assets. At the same time, being listed on the stock exchange provides the individual shareholders and company with a better rating on the stock market.

Moreover, once the company's shares are registered and held publicly on the stock market, the stock exchange imposes conditions and rules upon the business, which the company's board of directors have a duty to follow by law.

In the UK, various types of stock market listings are available. The type of listing normally depends on the market valuation of the company being floated on the stock exchange. Figure 7.4 describes four traditional world stock markets.

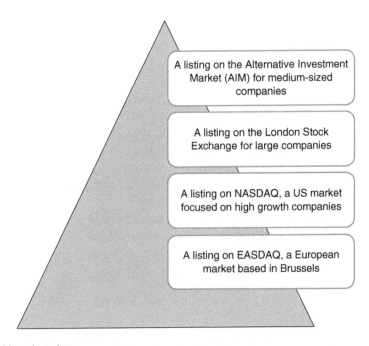

Figure 7.4   World stock markets

Debentures

A debenture is a loan which is given to an organisation for a long period of time, by a wealthy investor. Money is lent on a secured basis and with interest rates that may be either fixed or floating. Debentures usually have a number of different conditions attached with regard to interest rates, security and, most importantly, the preferential treatment that debenture holders are given over external shareholders. The debentures are normally rolled over to future periods if the company fails to make a profit; however, even if a company makes a loss, they will still need to pay interest charges to the debenture holder.

Moreover, debenture holders have the right to receive their interest payments before any dividends or interest are paid out to external shareholders. Secured debentures are usually tied to one specific asset like a building or a particular activity, such as a special event.

Share capital

This is the simplest method by which a company can raise finance. However, this option is only open to those companies which are listed on the stock market. This method normally involves a permanent interest-free loan, given in exchange for a part share in the ownership and profits of the business. The share capital scheme is used by investors to buy shares in individual companies through the stock market without stipulating fixed interest rates for their investment. The only payment they will get is their share of the profit, in the form of dividends, at the end of the financial year.

There are a number of types of share capital in each company. The voting rights of shareholders at the end of the financial year are determined by the grade of shares that they own. The ordinary shareholders are the least powerful; whereas the preference shareholders have stronger voting rights and also receive their fixed dividend before any other dividends are paid out.

Government grants

Governments are normally very keen to provide support to businesses, both in the form of grants and through the provision of expert advice and information. It is in the public interest that new businesses are started and existing ones developed, since successful businesses provide employment and create wealth for the country by helping the economy to grow. To this end, the UK government has provided finance to companies over the last 30 years, through cash grants and other forms of direct assistance.

Government grants have been made available through a number of different initiatives. Government grants are always attached to a specific purpose or project and it can sometimes be difficult for small and medium-sized enterprises to meet the government's criteria. The government applies very strict terms and conditions to all its grants and if a company does not follow these they may be required to repay the grant immediately. However, the government normally provides clear guidelines and assistance, so companies rarely break the terms and conditions.

Most government grants require businesses to match the public funds they are being awarded. It is important for a business to show that it can provide its share of the total amount before applying to the government for a grant. Businesses normally generate matching funds through retained profits, owner's own funds, bank loans or through partnership.

FUNDRAISING STRATEGIES FOR EVENTS ORGANISATIONS

Financing can take many different forms and a mix of several approaches will increase the event's chances of success. There are various sources from which an organisation can seek funds to put on an event, including individual donations, grants, corporate and business donations, partnerships or sponsorship.

The majority of contributions come from individuals who believe in a project or cause. Sometimes a company may ask the relevant private, community and government foundations for a grant. Grants are donations or interest-free loans that are given to groups or projects in accordance with strict standards and procedures. In order to apply for such funds, the organisation must usually submit a formal proposal.

Corporate and business giving is the other form of fundraising. Creating a partnership with a business to receive cash, in-kind support, product donations or even employee involvement can be a smart move. Businesses of all sizes have resources to offer, if asked in a proper and timely manner. There are two main methods by which a business may donate funds: corporate underwriting is where a business provides cash to cover a specific item in the budget; and corporate sponsorship involves the donation of cash, goods or services by a corporation in exchange for specific marketing opportunities.

Direct-request campaigns are excellent strategies that can be used both to increase contributions and get the word out about the project. Recently, the trend in fundraising has changed from individual involvement to mass communication and public participation.

Successful financing requires a regular programme of communication to keep the company visible to the target audience and the potential funders. A range of media can be developed, including: news releases, television or radio advertising, email newsletters and websites. Such a marketing strategy can have long-term benefits by building a relationship with the public ('friendraising') and saving time later by educating people now about the firm and forthcoming events. A good communication strategy will help the company to focus its energy on raising money (Freedman and Feldman, 1998).

Nowadays, fundraising for events can be a worldwide process, since international mass media enables people of all ages and a wide range of groups and organisations to access both the fundraising programme and the marketing of the event. As a result of this trend, many organisations in both the profit and not-for-profit sectors are turning their attention to the fundraising event business.

Financing through sponsorship and ticketing

Sponsorship is a central source of fundraising for many large-scale events. In the last decade, sponsorship has become essential to the events industry providing the means to finance many events. In today's market sponsorship has also become an integral and recognised part of event operations, with many savvy sponsors fully exploiting the marketing opportunity, often through promotional activity, to enhance the consumer's event experience. Sponsorship managers have recognised that they need to adopt a much more hands-on approach.

Lee et al., define sponsorship as:

> The provision of resources (e.g., money, people, equipment) by an organization directly to an event, cause or activity in exchange for a direct association (link) to the event, cause or activity. The providing organization can then engage in sponsorship-linked marketing to achieve either their corporate, marketing or media objectives. (1997: 161)

It is very clear that large-scale events, such as music festivals and sporting tournaments like the Olympic Games, cannot take place without the commercial support that comes from sponsorship.

Generating revenue through ticket sales

Ticket sales are one of the major revenue-generating strategies for the events organiser to adopt in the modern events market, and are the main source of income generation at events. Ticketing helps the business to overcome cash flow problems which are encountered by events. Selling tickets in advance can provide an organisation with the opportunity to raise revenue early on and potentially ease the cash flow problem in the short term. Selling tickets or charging conference fees in advance increases the opportunities for event organisations to take advantage of this method of raising funds.

Over the years, many large- and small-scale events have generated revenue by ticketing. Figure 7.5 shows the revenue generated by the corporate meetings and events market in the UK.

There are a number of difficulties with the ticketing concept, particularly in setting ticket prices. The event attendees are attracted to the event for several reasons, but one of the main reasons will be the price being charged at the event. Therefore, this can cause major problems especially for the pricing strategies which are set by the events organisers to cover all costs or to break even from the event. The dilemma for organisers is to attract the customer to the event and at the same time cover the cost. For this reason it is important for businesses to raise funds from other sources as well. Some of the common sources which can be used to raise funds are explored in the following sections.

Sales of merchandise

Brassington and Pettitt (2000) describe merchandise as

[a] physical good, service, idea, person or place that is capable of offering tangible and intangible attributes that individuals or organisations regard as so necessary, worthwhile or satisfying that they are willing to exchange money, patronage or some other unit of value in order to acquire it. (2000: 699)

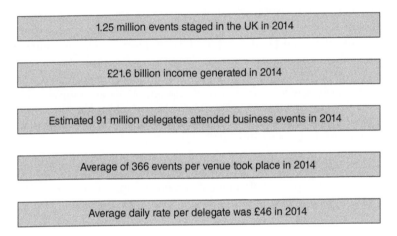

1.25 million events staged in the UK in 2014

£21.6 billion income generated in 2014

Estimated 91 million delegates attended business events in 2014

Average of 366 events per venue took place in 2014

Average daily rate per delegate was £46 in 2014

Figure 7.5 Revenue generated by the corporate meetings and events market

Source: UK Events Market Trends Survey (UKEMTS), 2014. Reproduced with permission of EVCOM (evcom.org.uk). (EVCOM is the official voice of the live event and visual communication industry in the UK. Through training, networking, lobbying and awards, we champion the power and value of communication.)

Events can provide many opportunities for merchandise sales and this is yet another source of income. The most obvious use of merchandise is to generate direct income for the event through sales of programmes, such as at the Edinburgh Festival. Merchandise sales are particularly popular at events as it is a way of combatting their intangible nature. Another benefit of selling merchandise such as programmes is that advertising space in the programme can be sold or offered to sponsors, generating additional funds for the event organisation.

Donations

Donations are sums of money that are given to an organisation, and which do not require any privilege or service in return. In this way they must not be confused with sponsorship. Obtaining donations can also take a substantial amount of time, effort and resources. Donations often need to be requested, either from existing donors (a database of previous donors would ease the process slightly), identified targets or the general public. Charities are the normal recipients of donations (Getz, 2005), which means this method of fundraising may not be particularly useful to other types of event organisations. Edinburgh Festival, however, does list donations in the same category as sponsorship in their accounts suggesting that they do benefit from this area.

SUMMARY

This chapter has explored the key fundamentals of project management. It has analysed the issues that event managers need to consider in order to achieve success during events. The key tools of project management can support event organisers with clearly structured plans and schedules, if developed and implemented in the right way, no matter what size or scale the event happens to be.

Finance is vital to the existence of any business in the industry. In addition to bringing in money, fundraising also helps an organisation to develop relationships with the people who can support it. The basic sources of finance for any business include: personal savings, debt, grants and earnings from business activities. Few business managers have the luxury of sufficient funds to sustain current and future planned expenditure. The approach to raising funds is not the same for each organisation, and this will vary according to the size and ownership of the business. Generally, the longer the business has been running, the easier it will be to acquire finance for it.

Businesses are funded from two main sources of finance: internal funding streams, including retained profit and the owner's own funds; and banks and other financial institutions, which are the principal source of borrowed money for businesses. These institutions apply very strict conditions before they agree to lend money to any organisation. Other approaches to borrowing include leasing, business angels, debentures and government grants.

Discussion questions

Question 1

Critically discuss the importance of project management in events management.

Question 2

Evaluate how project management can support the event manager in delivering large-scale events.

(Continued)

(Continued)

Question 3

Discuss and evaluate how event managers develop techniques of project management into practice.

Question 4

Critically evaluate how event managers can enrich their current and future growth fundraising strategies.

Question 5

Discuss and critically evaluate the role of sources of finance strategies for the Notting Hill Caribbean Festival held in London.

Question 6

Explain and critically discuss why fundraising is important for events and festival organisations.

Case study 1: Co-operative village experience 2012

Increasingly, many sponsors are aware of the benefits of supporting an event via financial assistance as a means to drive their brand to the target audience. However, many corporate organisations have taken it upon themselves to create their own experiential brand experience.

The Co-operative Society, with its history and head office in Manchester, for the second year created the 'village experience' event, as part of its sponsorship of the Manchester Day Parade on 8–10 June 2012, hosted in Albert Square in front of Manchester City Town Hall. The event had a schedule to tour throughout the country attaching itself to major events. It toured between June and September, going to the Royal Highland Show after Manchester, the Royal Welsh Show which had over 200,000 visitors in 2011, Bristol Balloon Fiesta which has a history dating back to 1979 and the Thames Festival London. It is obvious why the Co-operative made a strategic decision to align itself to the type of events on offer. Three strategic reasons explain this method of brand alignment and positioning. Firstly, each of the events listed has a significant history in terms of event delivery over many years and therefore already has a committed target audience.

Secondly, all shows have a strong family appeal directed towards the target audience of families, which is a cornerstone of the Co-operative brand. Lastly, the Co-operative Society can drop into an existing event without needing a significant budget to market their concept. Following this method of dual alignment can raise some issues that relate to the professional delivery of the existing event and thus have a negative impact on all brands attached to the various shows. For example, in 2009 a hot air balloon crashed into a wall in Bristol.

The Royal Highland Show is the only event with a headline sponsor in place. Where there is more than one sponsor at an event and if those sponsors have a similar business profile it could be difficult for the audience to distinguish who has exclusivity and dominance. Therefore it is essential for brands to create an experience beyond the standard branding one can see at most events.

This type of experience is not uncommon for major brands, for example Smirnoff Vodka, adidas and many more have taken to creating the event experience and therefore have a significant amount of control over the means by which customers experience the brand. The Co-operative has many facets to its business and thus requires an experience that it can display and communicate to the target audience. Currently the Co-operative has six facets to their business profile which featured at all event locations in 2012: the bank, travel, pharmacy, electrical, food and legal service. In the village, branding was significant throughout with enough staff to direct participants to various activities; the purpose of the activities was to create a long-lasting experiential experience for customers and research shows this gave a significant return on investment for the brand. Many of the activities were targeted towards children allowing the family atmosphere to take precedence. The activity that had significant coverage at the event was the kitchen demonstration which allowed members from the audience to participate and walk away with a memorable experience.

Case study 2: Event management media sector case study

Overview

A large media client had a requirement to manage and deliver a major event which reached all 3,000 engineers. This was a completely new initiative, which had never been attempted in the company's history. The requirement came from internal feedback which highlighted the need to engage with engineers to help encourage company buy-in, improve motivation, increase staff retention and to inform about future developments and long-term goals.

(Continued)

(Continued)

Activity schedule

Conference Care met with the client, to gain a clear understanding of their requirements and discuss how these objectives could be carried out in the most cost effective and time critical way. Time frames were discussed, roles and responsibilities of both parties outlined in order to clearly define the schedule of delivery for the entire process.

Production schedule and project plan

After the initial briefing, Conference Care and our audio-visual partner, MCL, started work on project documents and concept visuals in line with the meeting objectives. Event materials and tools were created, which showcased a bespoke 'Animated Helix' logo and brand for the event, which became the foundation of all event documentation and created a visual event identity.

The set design was carefully considered, as there were many challenges to overcome: it had to be forward thinking and impactful, durable as it would be travelling all around the UK over the course of three weeks, flexible and adaptable to ensure it would work in five different venues while giving each engineer the same quality experience. The final set comprised of a 12 metre widescreen, colour-matched 1 metre high illuminated light boxes and bespoke branded stage furniture and lecterns.

Pre-approval quotation and project plan

Conference Care worked with the client to deliver an event programme that would work on many different levels. By using our knowledge and expertise we made recommendations about venues, location, event logistics, presentation formats and AV requirements. Recommendations were not exclusive to the initial meetings. We understood that no event was the same and the key to success lies in flexibility. We continuously assessed and measured the effectiveness of the events. From the outset we gave advice on suitability of venues, we made suggestions for logistics such as the transportation of delegate literature to each venue, and during the live show days we reviewed all areas to ensure the best experience each and every time depending on venue constraints.

Production schedules

Conference Care acted as the central point of contact through which all parties could liaise. Our audio-visual partner MCL played a major role in the planning and production delivery, with all communication channelled through Conference Care. This was crucial for the client, as it meant that they had a dedicated team of people ensuring peace of mind throughout the duration of the project. Two different production schedules were created, one for the planning stages and the other for the live event. This critical path highlighted all key milestones and deadlines to ensure that everything was in place for the live event. For the live event, an event schedule was created and detailed all of the intricacies that needed to happen from start to finish.

Project budget breakdown

A project budget breakdown was created, showing the individual cost of each element, including all of the stage and set equipment for each event. Each of the five events was shown line by line, in addition to a full cost for the entire project allowing complete transparency between Conference Care and client.

Content budget

We provided cost effective solutions to maximise budgets. For example, local event staff were employed to assist with the live shows, such as stage and set builders and registration staff. When events form a series, cost savings can be achieved on the delegate registration tools where the template is set up for the first event and then developed for the rest of the series. Where possible delegate literature is recycled; badge holders are collected and re-used for both budgetary and environmental reasons.

Live

Two members of MCL's production team attended the final planning meeting with Conference Care. During this meeting, the Show-Caller and PowerPoint technician met with the client's planning team. The primary purpose of this meeting was to combine the individual files into a draft formal show. Video clips, sound bites and presentations were downloaded and prepared by the production team.

The day was then pieced together slide by slide. Holding slides were created, walk up music was agreed and edited, breakout sessions agreed, visual countdown timers set, video stingers were tested, timed and looped, as well as final amends made to slides to shape the programme to ensure consistency and accuracy throughout.

Creative input and maximising engagement

Conference Care's team worked with the client to format the event. Our creative input with MCL in designing the show visuals and brand identity was pivotal to the impact of the event and was rolled out across all engineer events. Recommendations were given in many areas including timings, format, including seating arrangements and room layouts. In light

(Continued)

(Continued)

of the client's forward thinking technology ethos, we incorporated state of the art presentation 'Spyer Widescreen' technology and 'VersaTile' Video Panels, mirroring the core company values through to the live event delivery.

Post agreement

The client employs 3,000 engineers, with a UK-wide geographical spread. For the purposes of reaching as many people as possible in the fewest number of locations, the UK was broken down into concentrated regions. The final event locations were Bradford, London, Edinburgh and Birmingham.

Logistical challenges

We aided the client with the logistics of getting event materials to each of the road shows in a cost effective manner. MCL's large production trucks were booked for each venue, so we managed the process of having event materials transported and delivered with the rest of the equipment. This ensured things arrived together and were easily traceable without having to locate everything through external courier tracking systems.

Events cascade and measurement

After each event, Conference Care held a de-brief meeting. During this meeting we reviewed all elements of the event, including venue, administration, level of service and support. At this stage, delegate feedback was assessed for both future improvements of the event with the client as well as any potential improvements to our overall event management service.

Post-event, attendee analysis was undertaken to measure the effectiveness of the day. As well as measuring the effectiveness of the corporate messages the other crucial part was to re-assess engineer morale in terms of improving company buy in, morale, motivation and staff retention. All criteria had improved beyond expectation, giving the client an exceptional return on investment. Due to these results, the client is planning to roll out these events to other parts of the business and run them on an annual basis to build on the momentum.

Expectations

Conference Care was the key manager and driver in delivery of the engineer road shows, despite working with several different supporting incumbents. The successes of the events were due to us gaining a detailed understanding of the company, the purpose of the event and desired outcomes. Having this knowledge gave us the insight to be able to proactively offer solutions to ensure expectations were met and delivered.

Source: www.conferencecare.com/clients/case-studies/media-sector-case-study [accessed 20/10/2016]

FURTHER READING

Berridge, G. (2006) *Event Design and Experience*. Oxford: Butterworth-Heinemann.

Burke, R. (2006) *Project Management: Planning and Control Techniques*. Chichester: John Wiley & Sons.

GCB (2009) 'The German Convention Bureau (GCB) celebrates winning the IMEX/GMIC Green Exhibitor Award at IMEX in Frankfurt 2013'. Available at: www.imex-frankfurt.com/press/news-releases/imex-news-releases/2013/05/the-german-convention-bureau-(gcb)-celebrates-winning-the-imexgmic-green-exhibitor-award-at-imex-in-frankfurt-2013 [accessed 16/11/2016].

Getz, D. (2013) *Event Tourism: Concepts, International Case Studies*. New York: Cognizant Communication Corporation.

Glautier, M. and Underdown, B. (2001) *Accounting Theory and Practice*, 7th edn. Harlow: Financial Times Press/Prentice Hall.

Johnston, R. and Clark, G. (2008) *Service Operations Management*. London: Prentice Hall.

Lock, D. (2001) *The Essentials of Project Management*, 2nd edn. Farnham: Gower Publishing Limited.

Locker, K. and Kaczmarek, S. (2013) *Business Communication: Building Critical Skills*, 6th edn. Maidenhead: McGraw-Hill Education.

Luecke, R. (2004) *Managing Projects: Large and Small*. Boston, MA: Harvard Business Press.

Meredith, J.R. and Mantel, S.J. (2009) *Project Management: A Managerial Approach*, 7th edn. Chichester: John Wiley & Sons.

Shone, A. and Parry, B. (2010) *Successful Event Management: A Practical Handbook*, 3rd edn. Andover: Cengage Learning.

UK Events Market Trends Survey (UKEMTS) (2014) Available at: www.evcom.org.uk/uk-events-market-trends-survey/ [accessed 16/11/2016].

8

LEGAL, SECURITY, SAFETY AND RISK MANAGEMENT

In this chapter you will cover

The purpose of this chapter is to give an overview of the standard legal requirements for event organisers. The chapter will present in the first instance a number of pieces of statutory legislation under UK jurisdiction. While the context of the chapter is the UK legal framework, the European market and the wider international business environment will be introduced in order to alleviate any confusion on operating procedures and legal jurisdiction. The chapter will also show that the legal structure for limited companies and the Licensing Act have significant financial impact on international revenue.

LEGAL STRUCTURE FOR LIMITED COMPANIES

To operate as an event organiser within the UK, no formal registration or licence is required at present. Each individual business should look at registering the business through Companies House, under the Companies Act 2006. This particular legislation has direct lineage from the Companies Act 1989. The 2006 Act covers limited and unlimited companies, private and public companies, companies limited by guarantee and having share capital, and community interest companies. The most popular type of company registered by event organisers in the UK is a company limited by guarantee.

Formal registration of a limited company can be done by an individual but a chartered accountant is required in submitting year-end business accounts to Companies House under company law. A company with share capital may require the assistance of a solicitor who specialises in company law in drafting articles for shareholders.

Registering a company not only gives direct access to particular operating company procedures but also allows your organisation to have credible prominence in its particular market. From a consumer perspective, it demonstrates legitimacy and accountability for consumers. Investors will be given protection under company law along with shareholders. Outside contractual relationships with suppliers, agencies, partners and other companies also operate according to a legal framework to establish sustainable working relationships; and, when operating outside of the UK, organisations have legal protection for employees and in contractual disputes. Company annual accounts can be accessed via the gate keeper (Companies House) for a nominal fee by any interested individual or organisation. This information could help in determining the type of business relationship that could be entered into by any outside organisation.

Once your company is registered with Companies House there are a number of legal requirements to meet before the business can become operational. It is not a legal requirement to register your business with the Health and Safety Executive (HSE) or the local authority. However, various types of organisations may require permits or certificates from the local authority, including the Health and Safety Executive, before commencing business operation. From an event perspective, it is advisable to register with the local authority through the HSE website. Where your event has a construction build as part of the event planning process it is necessary to complete an HSE 'Notification of Construction Project Form' which is available from the HSE website. As many outdoor event organisers work with suppliers that have health and safety regulations attached to their particular type of activities, it is advisable to access the HSE website and make sure that you have the necessary information that will enable you to interpret, manage and sign off, where required to do so, work carried out by outsourced companies.

PUBLIC LIABILITY AND HEALTH AND SAFETY REQUIREMENTS FOR EVENTS ORGANISERS

The Health and Safety at Work Act 1974

The Health and Safety at Work Act 1974 states that if you have five or more employees, a health and safety policy must be in operation, with a clear health and safety certificate displayed at a location visible to all employees. The employer, apart from developing a health and safety policy, is also required to undertake a full risk assessment of the working environment for all employees. Consideration should also be given to employees where working conditions may endanger their health. Therefore, an occupational risk assessment could be part of the health and safety policy. The Health and Safety at Work Act 1974 has direct links with UK and European regulations (and this area will be highlighted later in the chapter). Once a full health and safety policy has been developed and introduced to all employees and a risk assessment has been carried out the organisation can seek insurance.

Employers' liability insurance

Under the Employers' Liability Compulsory Insurance Act 1969 employers' liability insurance is compulsory for all businesses with employees. If your organisation has employees based abroad they must also be covered by your company insurance. Company insurance should be obtained from authorised insurers. The Financial Services Authority (FSA) maintains a register of authorised insurers in the UK. Your insurance company may undertake their own risk assessment or ask for a copy of yours. This will determine the level of insurance liability required for any particular type of business. In general, the minimum level of insurance cover for any UK business is £5–10 million. However, insurance liability may fluctuate depending on the type of business, the type of event planned, and how it is managed and delivered. If your organisation has witnessed previous insurance claims, this may affect the overall premium. Therefore, it is the requirement of each organisation to seek further advice and guidance from their insurer for each event if not identified in the organisation's insurance policy.

As a company, you have a legal responsibility to inform employees about and to display a copy of the employee's liability insurance certificate. This certificate must be displayed where all employees have access to it. There are some exemptions to employer's liability and one area is where family members are employed.

For further advice on employee insurance, contact a registered insurance company regulated by the FSA. Further advice can be obtained from the HSE and the Department for Work and Pensions. Self-employed people, regardless of the contractual status between the organisation and the person(s), can also be covered by your employees' liability insurance. This would depend upon the nature and relationship of control that you have with that individual while they are working for your organisation. Within the events industry there are a number of activities by outside individuals or an employee of your organisation that may require individual insurance cover to support their type of work. 'Riggers' by definition undertake very high risk intensive operational procedures, therefore it is essential to ensure that any rigger has full insurance cover that allows them to carry out their type of work. In some local authorities within the UK it is a requirement to obtain a permit before a rigger can undertake their activities.

Freelancers and freelancing within the sector

The UK government has attempted to reorganise and disseminate new procedures and accountability for freelancers and companies who contract freelancers. These new changes are applicable because many individuals within this sector decide to operate freelance and companies increasingly contract individuals under this particular arrangement. The official government website (www.gov.uk/guidance/ir35-find-out-if-it-applies) gives a clear overview of what they consider as the status for a freelancer/contractor:

- they are self-employed or are part of other companies
- they often look after their own tax and National Insurance contributions (NICs)
- they might not be entitled to the same rights as workers, e.g. minimum wage
- the employer is still responsible for their health and safety.

As an employer, the tax and employment responsibilities you have for your staff will depend on the type of contract you give them. An event company can set out a number of contractual arrangements for employees. The most popular and traditional contract of employment falls within two camps, full-time or part-time contract of employment. If employed under these two arrangements an employee can have a written statement of contract of employment but an implied contractual agreement is acceptable within law. With these types of contracts employees are given a number of legal employment rights.

Public liability insurance

Public liability insurance is different and voluntary; it covers against claims made by the general public. As an event company that may manage, produce and deliver events of many types to the general public, it will be essential for you to obtain public liability insurance. This particular cover is made mandatory by many local authorities when applying for a temporary entertainment licence for outdoor events open to paying or non-paying members of the general public.

Data protection

Many organisations today have a legal remit to register their company with the Information Commissioner under the Data Protection Act 1998. The Data Protection Act was brought into existence to address a number of issues; one of the principles was to protect individual personal data held by organisations. It also has a remit to allow individuals to have access to their personal data. The Information Commissioner can provide training courses to staff and assist organisations in developing data protection handbooks and policy.

Where an event company stores personal data on employees and in particular where a Criminal Records Bureau (CRB) clearance is required the Information Commissioner must be notified. A vast majority of event companies actively partake in direct marketing, but personal information held by a company can only be used once authorisation has been obtained from each individual. Websites that have an option to collect personal data must protect the individuals' rights.

Employment contracts

Once an organisation has undertaken these operational and legal requirements, it is then the responsibility of the company to issue employment contracts that reflect and meet UK and European legislation on employment rights. Minimum wage, human rights, disability discrimination, equality and race discrimination should be given full representation when selecting employees and in staff development/training and awareness. The Disability Discrimination Act, as written and made law in 1995, has had a far-reaching impact on event organisers and venue operators. Local authorities, educational establishments and their facilities had specific inclusion, and amendments were made to the 1995 Act for the 2006 edition. Therefore, we now operate within a climate whereby all individuals within society should be given equal chances without prejudice or discrimination.

The 2006 Act states that an organisation must show 'reasonable' effort to meet the needs of everyone in society. Entertainment venues, exhibition halls, conference venues and outdoor spaces have a legal remit to demonstrate that they are working to meet the requirements within the amended Act.

Legal requirements for UK venues

Apart from the initial start-up and legal requirements for that process, the business may need to demonstrate ongoing legislative adherence. This, however, will be reflected in the type of events developed and delivered by the organisation and while the organisation expands. To illustrate this, let's have a look in detail at the legal requirements event organisers need to be aware of when negotiating with a venue.

When an event company negotiates with a venue for the purpose of delivering an event, there are a number of regulations and statutory requirements to meet before final contractual negotiation. It is the responsibility of a representative from the event company to ascertain if the venue meets all the legal requirements and has all documentation necessary. A fire certificate will be granted by the local fire service which allows the venue to be used as directed under the fire certificate. This document may have representations as to the use of materials within the venue such as curtains or drapes, and the requirement of those materials to meet

British Standards on fire retardant capability. A separate fire certificate will also be required for any material that is brought into the venue that does not meet British Standards on fire retardant materials. Under new legislation it is also a requirement for a venue to undertake an independent fire risk assessment. The venue must present a recent and full risk assessment, including a health and safety policy indicating a full emergency and evacuation procedure. An entertainment licence denoting the type of entertainment granted by the local authority with any restrictions associated to that licence should also be presented along with a full alcohol licence and associated certificate which should be displayed at the venue. The event company has a legal responsibility to relay the health and safety and evacuation procedures presented by the venue to all employees of the event company, suppliers or outside contractual staff working within the venue. This information must be presented and understood prior to any outside employee commencing work within the venue.

To accompany any health and safety policy an event organiser must have an understanding of the different types of regulations that will have an impact on the event, staff and venue. The most common group of regulations are known as the 'six pack' and were developed by the EU and represented into UK law. The 'six pack' includes: management of health and safety at work regulations; manual handling operations regulations; display screen equipment (DSE) regulations; workplace (health, safety and welfare) regulations; provision and use of work equipment regulations; and personal protective equipment (PPE) regulations (for more information on these, go to the Unite union website, at www.unitetheunion.org/member_services/health_and_safety/health_and_safety_resources/the_six_pack.aspx).

Food hygiene

Food hygiene falls under local authority control; the Environmental Health Department within the local authority will take full responsibility for the issuing of a Food Hygiene Certificate along with the procedures for checking that each establishment or temporary catering unit(s) continually meets the legal requirements. The Environmental Health Department is also responsible for issuing closure notices and legal proceedings for contravention of food hygiene. Further advice and guidance can also be obtained from the HSE or your local authority.

THE LICENSING ACT AND PERMITS FOR EVENTS/FESTIVALS

The 2003 Licensing Act was introduced to modernise licensing arrangements, to meet European standards and to improve control over places of entertainment. It also extends to temporary entertainment licences along with the sale of alcohol. The 2003 Act only has jurisdiction for England and Wales. In Scotland, entertainment is governed by the Civic Government (Scotland) Act 1982. All applications for entertainment, renewals and alcohol licences in Scotland must be sent to the local authority. For entertainment in Scotland where no fee is charged for admittance an entertainment licence is not required.

In England and Wales the entertainment requirements were previously regulated by the 1982 Miscellaneous Provision Act. The changes brought in by the 2003 Act were broad and far reaching. Administratively, the 2003 Licensing Act gave control of licensing and its administration to the Licensing Department within each local authority. The Licensing Act requires the issuing of two licences, one for the event or building, and a separate and national licence for the individual. A personal licence is valid for ten years and can be obtained from the local authority where the person resides and may only be renewed at the end of the ten-year period by the same local authority. This enables a person to sell or authorise the sale of alcohol. A premises licence under the new Act is valid indefinitely unless it is revoked, or the business decides not to continue in its current form issued under licence. If the building requires a change then a change of use can be applied for via the local authority.

Figure 8.1 shows the four clear objectives within the Act that must be translated into practical operational duties for licensed purveyors of alcohol.

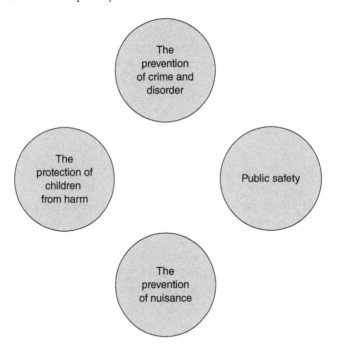

Figure 8.1   Licensing Act objectives

If the local authority or appointed agencies charged with upholding these four objectives obtain evidence that a breach of these objectives has occurred, they have the power to enforce a closure of an establishment or use the full legal due process available.

Alongside that, each holder of an entertainment licence must produce what is known as an 'operational document'. This document should set out the full operational duties related to the event or venue, including substantial information about all regulatory documents that support any particular activity. The document should act as a footprint for any agency, authority or contracted service and above-line management charged with the responsibility for a particular aspect of the event or building. The document should also clearly specify the roles and responsibilities for all parties involved.

Apart from the legislative requirements, each local authority has the opportunity to produce supporting conditions for obtaining and operating a temporary licence within that local authority's jurisdiction. The condition to the licence, as it is usually known within the industry, carries enormous influence on a successful application and continued use of the licence for the agreed length of time. The cost incurred by an organisation for obtaining an entertainment licence will be an internal matter for each organisation. However, each local authority will charge an administration fee for processing an application and each licence will relate to a sliding scale in relation to costs and customer capacity. Another aspect to the application process is the requirement for the organisation applying for the licence to place an advertisement in the classified section in the local newspaper for a period of one month.

The full legislation as passed by Parliament can be accessed at the Department of Culture Media and Sport's website (see www.culture.gov.uk). Not only is it possible to read the full document but a copy of the guidance document associated to the Act is also available.

As part of the event planning experience an organisation may wish to obtain road closure around a building or site which may be in a residential, commercial or non-residential location. For this to take place an organisation or representative must make an enquiry to the local police in the area where the event is taking place. The permit for a temporary road closure order is regulated under the Town Police Clauses Act 1847, section 21. This type of arrangement is generally enforced at outdoor music festivals and the application should be completed early within the event planning process. Where disruption to daily traffic flow is considered to be outside of the norm for that location, consideration of public safety and emergency vehicle access must take precedence.

Entertainment licences

When there is a need to obtain an entertainment licence or temporary entertainment licence with singing and dancing attached to that licence, further legal consideration must be given if live or pre-recorded music is part of the event or played within the facility.

Since the release of the 2003 Licensing Act which superseded the existing legislation, the events industry has argued and discussed the merits of the legislation and its ability to meet the current changes within the sector. In March 2015 the Home Office published 'Revised Guidance issued under section 182 of the Licensing Act 2003'. The four licensing objectives which built the foundation of the 2003 Act will remain:

- prevention of crime and disorder
- public safety
- prevention of public nuisance
- protection of children from harm.

The new guidance gives local authorities the power to depart from the original guidance if they have good reason to do so and can provide full reasons. There is a caveat to this and local authorities must be aware, if they depart from the guidance, it may invoke an appeal or judicial review. Section 5 of the Licensing Act 2003 requires a licensing authority to publish a statement of the licensing policy at least once every five years. Even after publishing a licensing policy the Act allows a licensing authority the right to depart from their own policy so long as they can provide good reason. So how would this work in reality? Some local authority licensing departments have a strict policy on the type of music that can be played within their jurisdiction within licensed venues. If a one-off event applied for a licence and published the play list as part of their licensing application and it was clear it went against the policy, the local authority has the legal power to over-ride their policy and allow the application to be granted without any conditions. The authorisation and permission within the Act also remain the same, and they are as follows:

- premises licence – to use premises for licensable activities
- club premises certificate – to allow a qualifying club to engage in qualifying club activities as set out in Section 1 of the Act
- temporary event notice – to carry out licensable activities at a temporary event
- personal licence – to sell or authorise the sale of alcohol from premises in respect of which there is a premises licence.

It is clearly explained that where a licence application is submitted lawfully to a local authority and that application does not receive any objections from responsible authorities or other persons, the local authority must grant the application.

The new guidance also makes reference to the inclusion of radio communication between clubs and pubs within city centres with a high density of clubs and pubs in order to manage crime and disorder.

Under public safety, there is further guidance for licensed venues to ensure the safety of people when leaving the premises. This may include:

Providing information on the premises of local taxi companies who can provide safe transportation home; and

Ensure adequate lighting outside the premises, particularly on paths leading to and from the premises and in car parks. (Home Office, 2015: 17)

There is greater guidance given to venues where live music emanates beyond the structure of the venue and can have a negative impact on neighbours. It becomes the responsibility of the venue/event to manage the type of noise and the possibility of light pollution. Some licensing authorities have requested that music venues place signs outside as people exit the venue for patrons to be quiet when leaving the venue. Under the new guidance, this can also be a condition within the licence.

Representation within the guidance on the sale of alcohol to children is clear and without ambiguity as to what is permitted or allowed along with the authorities that can prosecute if an offence is brought to their attention. Sections 145–153 within the 2003 Licensing Act highlight this particular area.

The guidance also looks at the sale of hot food, be that from a vending machine or preheated and served on the premises or heated on the premises. The Licensing Act 2003 only covers food that is either preheated elsewhere and sold or heated on the premises and does not include vending machines. To ensure that food is stored and displayed correctly one must work with the Food Standard Agency and follow their specific legislation and guidance.

Where an individual applies for and obtains a personal licence that allows the sale of alcohol, the holder of the licence does not need to be present on the premises or oversee each sale.

The requirement to renew a personal licence was removed from the Licensing Act 2003 by the Deregulation Act 2015. (Home Office, 2015: 19)

With that said every premises licence that authorises the sale of alcohol must specify who will be the duty manager/have responsibility while alcohol is on sale. This needs to be in place so any emergency services or designated authority can make contact with that individual if required. The power of the police to revoke a personal licence remains within the Act and should not be taken lightly by anyone who receives and attempts to carry out their duty under the personal licence.

There are many types of venues which either fall within or have exemption from the licensing authority. Sports stadiums or sports grounds with a retractable or closed roof fall outside of the licensing authority and this also applies to ships and boats, so long as they are not moored or berthed permanently. International airports, ports or hoverports with substantial amounts of traffic are also outside of the licensing authority jurisdiction. Trains and aircraft are also exempt from authorisation by the licensing authority but a magistrate's court can in the interest of public order prevent the sale of alcohol on trains.

To circumvent applying for a personal licence, some organisations under the title of a 'Members Club', with at least 25 members, can apply for a premises certificate which allows them to sell alcohol to their members and guests. Instant members are not permitted under this certificate and individuals must wait at least two days between their application and admission to the club. Individuals on behalf of the club can apply for temporary event notices. Section 62 of the 2003 Licensing Act outlines the general conditions to qualify as a club.

Under the Copyright, Designs and Patents Act 1988, events or venues that provide live music performances to the public will be subject to the requirements of the Act to safeguard writers and music publishers, therefore an application to the Performing Rights Society (PRS) must be made for a music licence. PRS has over forty different tariffs for premises and types of performance. When your venue or event would like to play original sound recorded music it is essential that a Phonographic Performance Ltd (PPL) licence is obtained. PPL represents the record companies who own the copyright in the recording.

Alongside PRS and PPL there is also the Mechanical Copyright Protection Society (MCPS). The main remit of MCPS is to collect and distribute royalties. These charges will be levied against anyone who wishes to record music for TV, radio, websites, feature films and so on.

The guiding principle for the use of live or pre-recorded music at events and venues, where the music will be played to the public, is that there is a cost/tariff and a licence will be required.

As previously mentioned in relation to other legislation presented thus far there are also exemptions regarding the obtaining of the music licence. For further clarification and guidance it is essential to access the MCPS–PRS alliance website for a more definitive discussion (see www.prsformusic.com).

A Video Performance Ltd (VPL) licence is needed for the public playing of music videos. VPL represent the companies who own the 'film' copyright in the music videos themselves. Contact VPL through PRS and MCPS.

UK trademark registration

This next section is not considered to be a legal requirement under UK law. However, to protect the individual identity and integrity of your company, product or event and to secure the merchandising rights, this particular process would be a necessary requirement. The UK Patent Office is where all UK trademark registrations can be applied for and held. This process protects the intellectual design/logo given to a company or event. Registering that design, name, logo or sound gives your organisation immediate protection once the application has been successful. Upon receiving notification from the Trademark Office it is a simple process of filling in a form supplied by the Patent Office at no cost for the merchandising rights.

Obtaining the merchandising rights and permission to produce items under the licence could potentially be a huge income generator for many events as they increase in size, frequency and become successful. This also allows the company to sell the merchandising licence to an agency for the production of official merchandise. With that licence an organisation can also franchise the event/product to any interested party. Further trademark registration must be taken out in each separate country if you consider that your event has an international reach, audience profile and locations.

Registering with the Patent Office is not a straightforward process and it can take up to a year to receive a final application notification. Therefore, a considerable amount of pre-planning in the formulation of a business idea for the intended market is essential.

Not all applications sent to the Patent Office will be approved. There are some names and designs that will never be approved, such as the five rings for the Olympic Games. It is necessary to contact the office with any queries concerning trademark registration. Trademark registration is held within the UK office and has a renewal date every ten years. (Glastonbury Festival was first registered in 1999 at the UK Patent Office, although the festival has been in existence since 1970. It was first licensed as an entertainment event in 1983.) Upon receiving full trademark registration there is no legal requirement to place the official trademark logo on company letter-headed paper or on any communication materials, products or associated items that fall under trademark law.

THE CONSUMER PROTECTION ACT 1987

Consumer protection is essentially a piece of government legislation that protects the rights of consumers. Trading Standards are the authority that will act on behalf of consumers when rights have been infringed. Alongside Trading Standards the Financial Conduct Authority also has powers where unfair terms are represented in consumer contracts.

Within the event management selection process for contractors and subcontractors who supply goods and services at events, it is imperative that all contractors have met the legal requirements associated with their particular task or activity before commencing work or supplying a service. If products that are supplied, sold or used at events are found to be defective when in contact with the consumer, product liability under the Consumer Protection Act will enable a person to request a refund or exchange of goods and in some cases sue for damages. The latter will only come into play when that consumer's rights cannot be resolved via the normal channels of negotiation.

Where an event organiser imports goods into the UK, including from the EU, the liability will rest with the first importer. By placing a company name on a product that gives the impression to the consumer that they are the producer, liability will rest with the company.

Within this type of business arrangement it is vital that the event organiser takes great care in selecting products and services providers who meet all the regulatory requirements under health and safety law including all regulations which support their particular activity. This will ensure that consumer rights are protected at events, thus avoiding refunds, defective products/services or possible litigation.

THE PRIVATE SECURITY INDUSTRY ACT

The Private Security Industry Act arrived on the statute book in 2001. The implementation of this legislation came in 2006–7. The main purpose of this legislation was to remove/clean up rogue security companies that permeate the leisure and entertainment industry. It also has a further remit linked to seven other licensed activities.

When an organisation approaches a venue for the purpose of securing it for an event, it is vital to ascertain the legal status of security personnel employed at the venue. A full list of all licensed security operatives should be logged with the local authority. The local police may also have a copy of the same information. If security checks on operatives are required by event organisers, the local police can assist with that process. It is an offence to employ security staff who have not been trained, security checked by the police or who do not have the appropriate licence to carry out a task. Stewards at events, as titled, have a different operational remit and do not require a licence to undertake their designated operational task. When working within a football stadium, stewards will fall under different licensing requirements and certificates and must be regulated accordingly. The sports industry made a representation for exclusion from the Private Security Industry Act. This was presented on the basis that sporting facilities are governed by the Safety of Sports Grounds Act 1975 and the Fire Safety of Places of Sport Act 1987. The representation was not successful and sporting events remain bound by the requirements of the Act. Adequate training must be given to stewards before permitting them to work.

CONTRACTS AND THEIR LEGAL COMPLEXITY

Another area within the event management remit is to construct contracts which are fair in their content and expected outcomes. Contracts by definition are legally binding agreements. Event managers will ultimately encounter many types of contracts while producing events. Apart from the terms and conditions attached to a contract, a service agreement could also be included. It is necessary to have an understanding of the different levels of contracts available.

Contracts are formulated to ensure that all parties' rights and obligations are not infringed, and if breached they can be enforced in the civil courts usually with an outcome of an award of compensation to the aggrieved party. Contracts can be divided into two main areas: contract by deed, or simple contracts. The majority of event managers will work under simple contracts. These can be written, delivered orally or they may be implied by general conduct.

Another way of classifying contracts is according to whether they are 'bilateral' or 'unilateral'. Bilateral contracts generally relate to the sale of goods. Unilateral contracts are those where an offer is made not to a specific party but to anybody. A unilateral contract can be best explained using the example of a competition online, which is promoted to anyone via a website. When producing an event and working with suppliers a simple contract under a bilateral agreement will be the standard approach. An event provider promises to make available access and an area on the site for the safe erection of a temporary structure. The company supplying the temporary structure promises to deliver and erect the structure within an agreed time frame that meets all the regulatory requirements, and that it will be handed over upon completion of all safety checks.

It has become standard practice for many event providers and suppliers to include a service agreement alongside the contract. The two may have similarities but are different in the general style and approach. As stated earlier, the contract is written from the point of view of upholding rights and obligations. A service agreement is written from the point of view of the delivery of the service or product and all its associated complexities. The service agreement gives a greater understanding as to the level of service or product that could be supplied and its intended use throughout its lifetime at the event. Therefore, any disagreements as to service delivery or product defects have a direct point of reference.

In the early negotiation stage there are a number of elements to consider before signing a contract. A legally binding contract must possess an offer, an acceptance of that offer and due consideration to promise to give or do something for another. The parties must be legally capable of entering into the contract, and knowingly have the capability to carry out the given task or provide the product/service. Consent to deliver on the contractual promise must be without duress or undue influence. On the whole, contracts should be drafted by a legal representative with sufficient knowledge of this particular area of the law. Mistakes in contracts, even down to the name of the individual, can render a contract void.

A breach of contract can occur if one party does not uphold their side of the bargain as set out in the original contract. A claim for unfair contract terms may come about at a later stage if one party believes that the original draft had expectations far beyond the scope that was required.

RISK MANAGEMENT

Risk management, when aligned to health and safety, can be viewed as a mechanism to apply further control and disseminate responsibility beyond the scope of the event. The wider ramifications regarding risk can be seen when assessing an organisation and the risk associated with the stability of the enterprise. Enterprise risk management addresses risks borne out of everyday operational activities. Risk management shouldn't be confused with risk assessment as the two have specific theoretical principles and protocols; risk management has a broader remit. Event agencies have consistently requested the services of companies to undertake a risk assessment; however, risk management is something which many companies overlook. PricewaterhouseCoopers have written extensively on this subject and published a number of guidance documents that cover financial and operational risk, in response to the recent meltdown of the global financial banking sector in 2008, and its subsequent impact on many commercial organisations. This guidance allows an organisation to apply a ten-point plan as taken from the paper titled, *Principles for Enhancing Corporate Governance* (Basel Committee on Banking Supervision, 2010 [online]).

The nature of a commercial business ultimately places an entity in a risk averse environment. The potential survival of that entity is to strike a balance between risk and return for the entire organisation. The Enterprise Risk Management Framework appoints a person to manage risk within the organisation; this is done by applying some basic rules.

It is necessary to establish what a health and safety policy is, why it is required and in what ways it may achieve organisational security. A health and safety policy is a document that sets out a clear working standard for all employees while working on behalf of the company. This document should be written with direct reference to the Health and Safety at Work Act 1974. The policy will set out the company's duty to ensure that individuals can carry out their tasks in a safe environment. It will also specify what is acceptable for employees while undertaking their particular tasks. Acceptable measures may also state that training is to be provided before undertaking a particular activity or using equipment. The document may also be supported with guidance notes that will give an employee further information before commencing a task. The policy can also make reference to regulations to which an employee must adhere 'when completing a task' or 'before commencing a task'. If protective clothing is essential to a particular activity, it should be indicated in the document as a necessity. An event manager should request a copy of the Health and Safety Policy from any organisation that has a contractual agreement with the event company, and where employees are working under the direction of a contractor or subcontractor. By neglecting the health and safety policy an organisation can jeopardise the employee's safety and human rights plus the organisation's ability to remain operational and within the law.

The term 'risk assessment' in today's business climate has more than one function when applied to an organisation. It can protect the employees from harm; it can also ensure customers can use a product/service with a minimum level of risk to themselves and others. Risk assessment concerns the long-term stability of the organisation to carry out its daily business and remain competitive. For all events it is essential that the principles of risk assessment are applied. Figure 8.2 highlights the key HSE guiding principles.

The five steps to risk assessment as presented by the HSE should become the cornerstone of any organisation/event internally and externally. Due to an increase in the litigation culture within the UK over recent years, due diligence on behalf of the organisation to protect employees is considered paramount for many organisations. Where risk assessment is not given sufficient attention, it could have a negative effect on the organisation's insurance liability for employees and customers.

Risk assessment is a legal requirement in the UK in order to execute the 'duty of care' under the Health and Safety at Work Act 1974. It is essential that a risk assessment is fully presented as part of the production process. The risk assessment should be formulated in line with the five key steps set out in Figure 8.2. Upon identifying the activity or task, it is necessary to look at ways of limiting exposure, and removing, controlling or transferring risk. In some documents you may also find a risk rating, which gives further information about the likelihood of the risk accruing and the impact of the risks to person(s) in the immediate vicinity.

By using a matrix, as shown in Figure 8.3, a priority can be established. If likelihood is high, and impact is low, it is a medium risk. On the other hand if impact is high, and likelihood is low, it is medium priority. A remote chance of a catastrophe warrants more attention than a high chance of a hiccup.

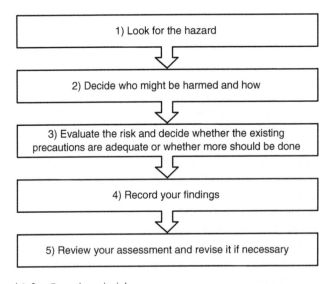

Figure 8.2   Health and Safety Executive principles

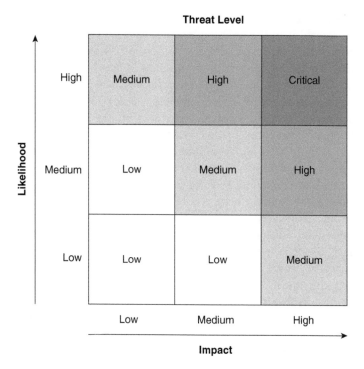

Figure 8.3   Risk matrix

The risk matrix is a more scientific method of developing risk control measures. The document should also highlight who has responsibility for monitoring and controlling the identified risks. For more complicated or hazardous production processes, further guidance will be required by the production company and associated agencies.

Risk assessment is not to be confused with risk management, which should be regarded like any other management function. Risk management should involve the identification, analysis and control of risk which has the potential to threaten assets or the enterprise. The risk assessment document, when presented to the venue, local authority and event manager allows all parties to engage in reasonable discourse to manage production safely. Within the production process it is also essential to document injuries that have occurred as a direct result of any of the risks identified in the risk assessment or the management thereof. The documentation should be in a separate incident log book. With regard to regulation, registration and inspection, event companies with ten or more employees must register their business in compliance with the Social Security Claims Payment Regulations 1987. When a business falls under leisure and entertainment, inspection for health and safety/risk assessment will rest with the local authority. However, the HSE has the authority to inspect fairgrounds. On the other hand, local authority events can be inspected by the HSE if they are on local authority land. If the event business has fewer than five employees there is no requirement under health and safety to produce a health and safety policy for employees.

To improve operational and production procedures, many production companies also include a method statement in the information they give to event managers. This document aims to ensure the duty of care for employees, as do the risk documents. A method statement is given to production personnel before they undertake a specific task to ensure they are fully aware of what to do and how to do it. It sets out a step-by-step approach to completing a task, especially where equipment is required to complete a task or is the finished article. If technical illustrations are required, they must also accompany the method statement. A method statement should either be prepared by the production manager or should accompany equipment. It should also identify all of the tools and supplementary equipment to be used in order to create a safe working environment in which to carry out work. There should be a method statement for each task or operation and copies should be held at the production office on site. This document can also help create a safe working environment and safeguard against insurance claims from employees.

Where an organiser has arranged for an event to be held, whether inside a venue or outdoors, it is essential to obtain electrical test certificates for electrical equipment powered by fuel or mains supply. This process of testing electrical equipment is called a PAT test (portable appliance testing) and it must be signed off by a qualified electrical engineer. It will give a degree of assurance to organisers, venue managers, licensing authorities and production personnel that electrical equipment has been tested and is ready for use. It is not possible to provide complete assurance of the electrical stability of the tested equipment but this process will go some way to ensuring that equipment is safe for its intended use.

From the information presented so far, we can see the fundamental relationship between the production company and the event organiser. Each has a direct responsibility to ensure that individual employees are given sufficient training, information, certification, method statements, insurance, permits, protective clothing and well-maintained equipment to carry out each specific task. All this information should be written down and given to the event organiser and associated agencies (which may include the fire service, local authority and police) in the pre-planning stage of the event.

When the production company is satisfied with the information they have in turn obtained from the site/venue, an official undertaking to commence work will be ordered. Any sub-contracted companies must also adhere to all the agreed documentation and regulations, in accordance with the requirements set out for the main contractor for whom they are working. If sub-contracted production companies have any special requirements, all new details must be forwarded to the relevant organisation.

LEVEL OF RISK MANAGEMENT

With the best planning, risks get identified as early as possible. The level of risk and opportunity to minimise a risk is very high at the start of an event (outset and planning phase), whereas the amount at stake is very low. This relation changes dramatically while the event proceeds, as decisions are made and plans get implemented. Therefore, the opportunity to minimise a risk declines, whereas the amount at stake continuously increases as resources are invested to accomplish the event.

The case study below, of the Bupa Great Manchester Run, provides an example of how risk management can be assessed at large-scale events.

Case study 1: The Bupa Great Manchester Run

The case study provides an overview of the application and results of the risk and vulnerability analysis for a 10km mass participation run in Manchester.

Event format

The Bupa Great Manchester Run is a 10km mass participation road race, and takes place within Manchester City Centre in the month of May on Sunday each year. The event is a joint promotion by Nova Limited and Manchester City Council, and includes:

- an elite wheelchair race
- an elite women's race
- a mass race for an anticipated field of up to 29,600 male and female runners aged over 15.

Each of the events listed above fall directly under the Nova organisation but it has in place its own management team, planning meetings and own event safety plans, plus risk assessment.

On site, the event liaison team (ELT) will coordinate all necessary contractors during the crucial stage of the event set-up. The official start of the race will see operational control fall under the Event Director and Course Director; their task is multifaceted but they have overarching operational decision-making powers for the event. Further delegated responsibility is given to competent individuals who manage the start and finish of the race. To assist with the management and control, the ELT is located in a building to record and respond to all communication traffic and decisions made throughout the event with the assistance of the police, senior medical and senior security operatives. This dual approach to operational management and control, as seen from the on-site Event Director and ELT, has immediacy due to the fast nature of the event and response time that is required to assist and deal with any given situation. This approach to managing the event helps to reduce and respond to known and unknown risks. This particular race has five waves of runners, designed to help reduce congestion on the course, and to allow more space for the competitors during assembly. Each wave leaves at different times, with the elite runners given first position. Runners are placed into waves by a colour-coded system from

(Continued)

(Continued)

information submitted in their online application, based on the time that each individual considered appropriate to finish the race. Before each wave arrives at the start line they have the opportunity to participate in an orchestrated warm-up session. This ultimately helps to reduce the risk for runners who may require medical attention due to muscle spasms during the race and after. To assist in the recording of times for runners, they each have an individual electronic chip which records when they start and complete the race.

For a run of this magnitude, there are many risks for the organisation to contend with. The one which has the highest priority while the run is under way, is the risk that a runner may collapse due to over exertion, a pre-existing medical condition, or due to warm or cold weather conditions. Therefore, it is paramount that the course is set up to mitigate those potential risks.

The 10km race is designed with clear markers for all runners. Showers and water stations are strategically located along the race route, as are medical professionals with full resuscitation equipment (water is positioned and available at the start, finish and at 5km). When runners approach the last two kilometres a fast response medical team are on alert, as past experience has shown that runners tend to require medical assistance during the latter stage of the race.

The risk assessment with the event manual identifies 126 individual risks associated with the event, of which only 20 are marked as medium risk, with the other 106 ranked as low risk. The fact that the event has a significant amount of risk ranked as low is testament to the planning, organisational management and competence of the individuals in the above-line management associated with the event. An event of this nature is susceptible to extreme weather conditions which ultimately increase the risk in a number of specific categories. In particular, there is a risk of dehydration through prolonged and intense heat or humid weather. Extreme rain and cold can decrease the core body temperature dramatically. Where cold weather is a problem, aluminium space blankets are given out before and after the race to keep the core body temperature at a stable level. There is also an area for 7,000 people to have shelter if required.

In situations where the weather can have a dramatic influence on the event, the spectators and more importantly the participants, the event will bring forward a wet weather or hot weather plan. If this has been activated, medium-level risk may be ranked as high if not dealt with immediately, thus having a dramatic effect on a person's chance of survival. It is not a common situation within events of this nature; however, participants have died when participating in road races due to a number of issues such as a pre-existing complication or insufficient medical service/equipment available to assist at any given time. As noted above, through the process of delivering events of this nature, event organisers know that participants have a higher propensity to require medical attention in the last few miles before the finish line. In their online application, participants are asked to inform the event company of any pre-existing medical condition; this is an optional request but may be essential if medical assistance is required. If that medical information is forthcoming the event company can identify that person by a colour code given to them with their official number. If that person requires any medical attention their information is available via a database shared with the medical operatives and above-line management team (ELT). Individual official race numbers given to each participant are directly linked to all data supplied by that person. Therefore, to pass on an official number to another participant increases the potential confusion and risk if a person requires medical attention.

Figure 8.4   The start position for each colour wave

In order to reduce the risk in those areas, there are a number of protocols and secondary checks made to ensure that a person is correctly linked to a given number. Correct information connected to next of kin becomes absolutely essential in the event of a serious incident or a fatality. Figure 8.4 illustrates the start position for each colour wave; they are

(Continued)

(Continued)

released in a controlled manner to reduce the risk of injury to runners and to ensure spectators and TV broadcasters can locate runners by their colour code.

Figure 8.5 gives an overview of the route with a key that indicates crucial aspects of the race design for runners and spectators in the first instance. The distance markers act as sector timers for runners and give the ELT a degree of control for monitoring the times of the last runner in each wave.

Figure 8.5   The Bupa Great Manchester Run route map

SUMMARY

This chapter has outlined many of the regulatory requirements to which event organisers must adhere. In order to keep up-to-date with changes in legislation and regulations, you should register your organisation with the HSE, via their website, which will provide you with regular updates on new legislation and regulations associated to particular activities and organisations. There is a requirement for operational deployed staff at events to have undertaken training courses in key areas such as health and safety, demountable structures, crowd management and licensing law.

Legal and risk management will help to ensure that events are planned, organised and delivered within the confines of the law and operational procedures. Apart from UK legislation, there are regulations, policies, procedures and benchmark standards which you must also take into account in the international market place. Many companies within the events sector have a long history of delivering events across international boundaries. Operating outside of the UK brings with it many new challenges and obstacles. Exporting goods to another destination could render the entire operation redundant if the paperwork is inaccurate. If you have opted for a handler to collect goods on arrival and store them at a secure location, if appropriate use a reputable company that has been fully investigated.

For employees who travel, work and reside within a different international jurisdiction for a month or a year and beyond, it is essential to ensure that insurance covers their entire stay and also the activities they do while they carry out their job. If further insurance is required due to the nature of the location, political situation or potential instability, environmental or otherwise, then seek further advice from your insurance company. Most insurance companies allow for cover outside of the UK but this must be negotiated and continually risk assessed.

Operating an event business requires not only business acumen in setting up the business in the first place. It also involves knowledge of the vast number of operating policies and procedures that are necessary while delivering an event. This is even more the case when the business is supported by contractors and business partners/stakeholders. Setting the appropriate business 'tone' is essential for future growth and long-term partnership development.

Discussion questions

Question 1

Under the 2006 Companies Act name three different types of companies available for registration through Companies House, and indicate which companies require the assistance of a solicitor for the administration and formal registration process.

Question 2

Under the 2003 Licensing Act the police have significant powers in revoking a personal or premises licence. Discuss the specific powers of the police that could allow them to revoke a personal or premises licence.

Question 3

The 2003 Licensing Act has a number of exemptions for applying to obtain a premises licence. Put forward two types of situation where an exemption can be made and state the reasons why.

(Continued)

(Continued)

Question 4

Within the new guidance on licensing issued by the Home Office (March 2015), entertainment venues have a requirement to ensure they take special care when patrons enter and leave a club. Outline the reasons why this is important and the potential negative consequences to the venue/licence if not managed appropriately.

Question 5

In an attempt to reduce the risk to runners at a 10 kilometre run, why is it necessary to increase medical facilities and operatives in the last few miles?

Question 6

What agencies are required to reduce the risk when closing down the roads over a Saturday night/morning for a 10 kilometre run?

Case study 2: Korean Food Fair

Anticipated crowd size: up to 20,000.

Event activities

Food stalls and eating areas, information stalls, speeches and entertainment at main stage, Korean dance troupes, music groups and martial arts demonstrations, amusement rides, children's stage, Hyundai car auction.

Venue description

Beamish St is the main street of Campsie. The fair was held in the area north of the station and the Anzac Mall. Anzac Mall is a paved pedestrian mall, closed to traffic. There is a variety of Korean shops which line the mall and were open during the festival. The event attracts families, with a majority of Korean visitors (over 80 per cent) and the remainder a combination of Chinese and other ethnic mixes. There is public parking in nearby streets. The venue is also readily accessible from Campsie railway station.

Existing facilities

The street litter bins (approx. 55 litre bin inside a metal frame) along Beamish Street and Anzac Mall were supplemented with sixty 240 litre wheelie bins for the event.

Other relevant information

Canterbury City Council has in the past offered free cleaning and waste disposal at the Korean Food Fair as the event is a council-run event. The value of labour and tipping fees is approx. $5,000. For the past two years, the Southern Sydney Waste Board has sponsored the festival by supplying the envirotrays and biodegradable cutlery for use by all of the food vendors via the packaging supplier D&JC Trading. A standard size envirotray was used as a unit of measurement, as all stalls were charging $5 for a selection of foods in the same tray. The food vendors are discouraged from bringing their own packaging and were not charged to use the envirotrays and corn starch sporks (combination of spoon and fork).

Source: www.environment.nsw.gov.au/resources/warr/cs_koreanfoodfair2001.pdf [accessed 01/03/2016]

Case study 3: Outdoor music festival

Staff at a major music festival were exposed to very high noise levels without adequate care for their safety. This was a large music festival with more than 50,000 people present and with two major outdoor stages.
  The following problems were found:

- Security staff were less than one metre from the front of the bass speakers for the main stage.
- Food vans for the main stage were facing the stage and positioned close to the PA delays.
- There was no refuge from the noise. Sound levels in staff rest areas reached or exceeded 79 dB, and there were no quiet areas or refuges where staff were working.
- There was little or no evidence of control of the noise levels that the staff were exposed to, or limiting of the time spent in the noisy locations, or warning of the risks due to the noise.

(Continued)

(Continued)

- Hearing protection had been provided without training on its use. In some cases security staff receiving the highest exposures were choosing not to use any hearing protection.
- Hearing protection had not been considered for staff at the food outlets.

Table 8.1 Daily noise exposure for workers at the festival

Job	Location	Hearing protection	LEP, d dB
Paramedic	Side of main stage	Muffs	100
First aider	Tent at side of main stage	Muffs when outside tent	97
Food service	By PA delays of main stage	None	100
Gate security	Side of main stage	None	101
Gate security	Wheelchair area for main stage	None	95
Door security	Secondary venue tent – 1	None	99
Stage security	Secondary venue tent – 1	Earplugs	108
Door security	Secondary venue tent – 2	None	103
Drummer	On stage	None	104
Bass guitarist	On stage	None	101
FoH sound engineer	Tower approx. 30 m from stage	Earplugs	99
Monitor engineer	Side of stage, behind PA	None	96

Commentary

The use of noise control and hearing protection was inadequate. Both the event organiser and the individual employers were in clear breach of the law.

Under the law employers have a duty to protect their own employees from the risks associated with high noise exposures. In addition, there is a duty to other workers who are also put at risk by their noisy activities. These duties had clearly been neglected.

Exposure needs to be reduced by means other than hearing protection. Where a risk still remains the correct fitting and use of hearing protection needs to be enforced.

Employees have a duty to use hearing protection provided for them if their exposure is likely to exceed 85 dB.

Source: www.soundadvice.info/amplifiedlivemusic/casestudies.htm [accessed 20/10/2016]

FURTHER READING

McKendrick, E. (2007) *Contract Law*, 7th edn. Basingstoke: Palgrave Macmillan.

Murphy, J. (2007) *Street on Torts*, 12th edn. Oxford: Oxford University Press.

Richards, P. (2007) *Law of Contract*, 8th edn. Harlow: Longman.

Silvers, J. (2008) *Risk Management for Meetings and Events*. Oxford: Butterworth-Heinemann.

Tarlow, P. (2002) *Event Risk Management and Safety*. New York: Wiley.

Turner, S. (2007) *Unlocking Contract Law* (Unlocking the Law), 2nd edn. London: Hodder Arnold.

Webster, I., Leib, J. and Button, J. (2007) *The Concise Guide to Licensing*. Leicester: Matador.

PART 3

EVENTS MARKETING AND MEDIA

9

EVENT SPONSORSHIP

In this chapter you will cover

This chapter will look in detail at the process of events sponsorship, investigating the relationship between sponsors and the events industry on local, national and international levels. What are event sponsors seeking to achieve? The chapter will examine tendering and pitching ideas, and also look at the concepts of support, involvement and funding. It will outline the guiding principles for developing and presenting a sponsorship package in line with particular types of events, making clear distinctions between the various types of sponsorship levels within a sponsorship deal. The chapter will also look at the new and emerging trends in sponsorship allocation across the events sector.

THE ROLE OF SPONSORSHIP IN THE EVENTS INDUSTRY

The concept of sponsorship has been developed over the years and is now considered as a specialist area within the marketing framework. Many organisations today employ what is known as a 'sponsorship manager'. This position can either be taken up by an individual (who may also have a team of people working in support) who looks at supporting events as part of the company's strategic vision. Or, alternatively, organisations may employ an individual to acquire sponsorship as part of the event's financial and operational requirements.

Sponsorship comes in many forms and guises. Not all sponsorship deals look to increase market share or competitive edge for the company product or service directly. Indirectly, some companies use sponsorship to maintain a public image. An organisation may find it necessary to maintain their public image by associating their product/service with a particular event.

However, sponsorship is also applicable when an organisation is faced with unacceptable/ negative publicity and therefore adopts a strategy to maintain an acceptable level of public image.

Cadbury, the chocolate confectionery company, saw its milk chocolate sales slip 2.5 per cent in 2006, on the back of a salmonella scare. The recall of 1 million chocolate bars brought an estimated £30 million loss to the company. Cadbury's ten-year relationship with *Coronation Street*, a British TV series, came to an end in 2007. That relationship had achieved marked success for both organisations, as the biggest in terms of financial contribution and the longest TV sponsorship deal in British history. We are not attempting to imply a direct cause and effect scenario here, of a negative impact on a business from its decision to relinquish its sponsorship relationship with a TV series – we do not have the necessary data to make that claim. However, there is room to see a cause and effect situation between Cadbury relinquishing their deal with *Coronation Street* and a drop in sales due to bad publicity via a food scare in chocolate production. With Cadbury no longer part of the sponsorship market, the big food chains in the UK went into a bidding war for the sponsorship rights to that TV series.

SECURING SUPPORT, PARTNERSHIP AND STRATEGIC ALLIANCES

Sponsorship acquisition in its true form within the events industry looks at seeking out an appropriate sponsor, or sponsors, to meet the combined strategic vision of the event and sponsoring company, and in particular where financial assistance is a necessary business requirement for the short- to long-term sustainability of the event. There are also ethical and political issues that should be taken into consideration when researching potential companies.

The combined strategic vision is the level of knowledge and work required in developing a business partnership. This will be looked at in more detail throughout the chapter. Within this model the chapter will demonstrate how to match appropriate sponsorship companies to particular types of event.

When undertaking any type of sponsorship research it is a good idea to obtain historical data on the type of events sponsored by the company you are looking at. You may not be able to see the exact level of financial assistance that the company has given to events overall. However, there are some routes you can use to find detailed financial information. Company accounts, if published via Companies House, could give you some statistical data to begin with. Internal/external newsletters may also carry this information. Articles on the company website, along with local or regional newspapers, where the event has a public image, generates civic pride or has newsworthy appeal, could contain useful information. Industry-related trade magazines may also give a specific viewpoint. These are just some of the areas where information can be obtained and may help to build a picture of the type of events and financial assistance given as part of the sponsorship deal. This invaluable information when analysed could demonstrate a profile of events sponsored, frequency of sponsorship deals, and long-term sponsorship deals including financial assistance. Where the event is attached to local authority resources or a local authority event, information on that type of event should be in the public domain. The Freedom of Information Act 2000 places requirements on public authorities relating to the disclosure of information in order to promote greater openness and transparency. Therefore, information should be accessible through the local authority or stored at the local public funded library. The Manchester Commonwealth Games in 2002 were supported by the local authority and commercial sponsorship. Information on this event is held at the Manchester public library and available via the internet.

Case study 1: Sport Industry Interviews

This sponsorship case study will investigate a different type of sponsorship arrangement, and the trend towards sponsoring an award ceremony within a business context.

On the back of London winning the 2012 Olympics in 2005, the Mayor of London's office set up an event titled 'Sport Industry Interviews'. This event ran for the first time in 2006. The purpose of the event was to address the UK sport industry business leaders and stakeholders on the key milestones, challenges and opportunities ahead in the preparations for the London 2012 Olympic Games.

In the pre-publicity information posted on the website of the Mayor of London's office, a sponsorship package was made available, outlining the sponsorship opportunities for supporting the 2006 Sport Industry Interviews.

The package clearly stated the different types of sponsorship levels and benefits attributed to each option.

The event was by invitation only, for approximately 260 attendees; it was aimed at CEO/Director level key decision-makers in sport. As part of the event there were also the sports industry awards, which have been described by the media as the 'Oscars of the sports world'. The award ceremony received coverage from BBC, ITV, Sky and national newspapers – extensive media coverage which helped to enhance the sponsorship package on offer.

(Continued)

(Continued)

There are a number of reasons as to why any organisation would deem this event worthy of sponsorship. From the point of view of the potential sponsor, the main constituent parts that made up this event were that it was:

- linked directly to the 2012 London Olympics
- organised and represented by Ken Livingstone, then Mayor of London
- covered by three national broadcasters and national newspapers
- offering networking opportunities with major decision-makers in the sports industry
- attended by 260 hand-picked delegates by invitation only
- an established event with a recognised award ceremony
- the largest sport business event in Europe.

The seven points above are considered to be the sponsorship pitch. This information would be translated via printed media or verbal communication to potential sponsors. Alongside this information an event will have a sponsorship package that outlines the different levels of sponsorship deals. These deals are closely linked to financial commitments from a potential sponsor. The different deals within the package will give an indication of the level of exposure prior to the event, at the event and post-event. The level of sponsorship is calculated on the cost of hosting the event and the economic value of media coverage in all areas. Levels of sponsorship deals generally fall within three categories. For this particular event there was one headline sponsorship deal and other multi-layer deals for the award ceremony. As a headline sponsor an organisation has complete confidence that no other company can compete within the same arena. Exclusivity is given to the headline sponsor. This would be demonstrated by areas within the venue where branding opportunities are given. Press and media coverage would also carry the headline sponsor on all communication associated with the event for a given period of time.

It is essential to remember that each sponsorship document must be constructed around the specific and general opportunities that can entice a potential sponsor. Marketing and advertising, along with credible presentation, are what makes the sponsorship package a saleable item. In constructing the package you might want to consider a particular business sector, with a strategic vision that can drive their product/service to a wider audience through association with the event.

MAJOR SPONSORSHIP DEALS

Major sporting events today such as the Commonwealth Games and the Olympic Games can only function effectively with a substantial level of financial funding. Financial support for the

Olympic Games dates back to Ancient Greece, when prominent citizens gave financial support. Historically, the Olympic Games also received funding from the state, as do the Games today in most cases.

In 1924 in Paris, advertising hoarding made its first and last appearance. Four years later the Olympic rights were extended to other sectors. It is now possible for companies involved in brewing to open bars/restaurants within areas where the customers are. Advertising did return to the Olympic Games but not inside the competition areas. In 1936 at the Berlin Olympics television made its first appearance. In 1947 at the London Olympics, television rights were assigned for the first time. In 1994 the Los Angeles Olympics were marketed as the beginning of organised sponsoring of the games by groups of companies. The International Olympic Committee (IOC) set out a marketing plan and divided it into three categories. The three categories were: Major Sponsor, Official Sponsor and Official Supplier; with 34 companies acquiring contracts with the IOC as official sponsors, 64 companies acquiring the right to supply and another 65 being granted authority to use the Olympic symbols. The Los Angeles Olympics television rights were bought by 156 countries. At the Seoul Olympics it was decided to reduce the number of sponsors in order to increase the value of the rights. In 1992 the Barcelona Games continued the reduction of companies acquiring rights. In 1996 the Atlanta Games turned the whole organisational structure upside down. All expenses were covered by private funding, through TV rights, sponsors and ticket sales. TV viewers from 214 nations watched the Games, and 11 million tickets were sold, more than for the Barcelona and Los Angeles Games combined. The Sydney Olympic Games in 2000 only covered 63 per cent of expenses; the rest was covered by the Australian government. It is evidently clear that major sporting events around the globe rely heavily on corporate sponsorship. It also demonstrates that over time sponsorship has developed and become an enormously complicated mechanism in driving a product/service to potential consumers on a global scale, or maintaining the continual presence of a major sporting event. The concepts highlighted earlier for major sporting events have also been grafted onto many of our national and regional events in many business sectors, e.g. the demarcation of categories within sponsorship profiles, the selling of TV rights to acquire substantial revenue, and funding from regional and central government along with associated agencies. Exclusivity deals and service deals are now entrenched within many of the sponsorship proposals/packages in the marketplace today.

EXTERNAL INFLUENCES AFFECTING SPONSORSHIP DEALS

The marketplace for acquiring sponsorship does not operate in isolation and sometimes can be very fragile. It is prone to fluctuation under the influence of geopolitical events. The downturn in the global economy through political or economic market forces has a direct effect on the stock market.

With economic fluctuations emanating from various parts of the globe, there can be both short- and long-term impacts on available financial revenue from corporate organisations listed on the stock market. Within any business, the departments most likely to be affected by these situations are marketing and advertising, where revenue spend is curtailed. A geopolitical event, such as the 9/11 attack on the twin towers in the USA in 2001, can have a major negative economic and ripple effect across the globe. The robustness of the global market and in particular the US stock exchange at that time meant that the world did not experience a recession. There was, however, a downturn in stocks for some businesses and in particular the airline industry. Companies laid off staff at home and abroad, and also reduced their spending in many territories.

Event companies seeking sponsorship must be fully aware of the economic and political landscape before attempting to approach a business for sponsorship. Research is essential and will save time and resources, a valuable commodity for most small-to-medium-sized event companies.

Within this sophisticated sponsorship market, we have what are called 'brand agencies'. Many companies today relinquish the responsibility to place their product/service in a suitable marketing environment. This function is instead passed on to brand agencies, where the strategy is delivered by 'brand managers'. They work on behalf of the client, in essence becoming the gate keepers for managing the product/service. Therefore, these clearly defined processes show that, in order to be successful, sponsorship proposals need to have natural synergy with their intended audience. This must not merely be implied but well documented throughout. Brand agencies, as with the client, on the whole are looking for maximum exposure and return on investment. Therefore, sponsorship proposals must demonstrate a strategy that communicates across all communication channels, enabling the sponsor to maximise investment.

Within the event management tool kit for delivering a sponsor's message via a partnership, we now have what is called 'new media'. This is not just a simple matter of branding on a web page, rather it should be seen as moving towards a fully integrated and interactive procedure, whereby data can be collected and analysed with a view to establishing a method for customer relationship marketing. This will assist the event company and the sponsor in building future marketing campaigns, and where long-term sponsorship deals are in place this method can help to solidify a working relationship.

With this audited data, event companies can back up their proposal with facts and figures to attract future sponsors. Sponsorship has its original heritage in marketing, advertising and public relations; this area of business management works well when marketing campaigns fully recognise the target audience. The proliferation of new media has fragmented the consumer market. Therefore, targeting a consumer or potential audience now needs a sophisticated scientific approach. Audience profiles have become expansive with the digital media network through the internet, digital satellite and cable TV, and digital radio. These communication platforms have become further delivery portals with the introduction of integrated mobile phones. It is essential for event providers to recognise the changing and developing technological landscape and use new media where appropriate to enhance the event experience and acquire synergy with their customers.

NAMING RIGHTS – PART OF THE MARKETING MIX

Within the sponsorship portfolio there are a number of income-generating strategies. Naming rights is a concept that has its historical and commercial development firmly rooted in the USA and dates back over 50 years.

In defining naming rights we need to look at the process in the first instance from the sponsor's perspective. It is a tool to acquire intangible and tangible benefits by purchasing the space and length of time to apply a name to a facility.

> According to a report on SportsBusiness.com, as manager of the venue [Multifunctional Amphitheatre of Quebec] for the next 25 years, Quebecor will pay the City of Quebec CAN$33m (€24.4m/$25.8m) in full when the arena opens. This figure is set to increase to CAN$64.5m if an NHL franchise is secured. (PanStadia & Arena Management [online].)

Within the UK naming rights is a relatively new business concept, with naming rights on sports stadiums within the UK football Premier League introduced for clubs such as Bolton Wanderers with the Reebok stadium, completed in 1997. In 1994, BT Cellnet signed a ten-year deal for £3.5 million with Middlesbrough football club for sponsorship at the Riverside Stadium. In 2006, Arsenal football club opened their new stadium with a £100 million naming rights deal with Emirates Airways; this is the largest naming rights deal in the UK at present. With exclusive worldwide rights the new stadium is officially called 'Emirates Stadium'. This deal will conclude in 2020–21. This deal also included an eight-year shirt sponsorship deal which began in 2006.

Naming rights sponsorship deals have seen a steady increase over the past ten years in the UK. However, the major financial spend is predominantly located within the sports industry.

The live music industry within the UK has also seen an injection of commercial sponsorship for live music facilities. Academy Music Group (AMG) is the UK's largest owner and operator of nationwide live music venues. This organisation was formally known as McKenzie Group Ltd. The management buyout of the McKenzie Music Group in 2004 included the promoters SJM Concerts, Metropolis Music and MCD Productions. This strategy also included bringing online new academy venues in Birmingham, Bristol, Glasgow, Liverpool and Islington.

Within the AMG business portfolio there are now a number of live music venues which carry the naming rights of the Carling beer company: Carling Academy Brixton, Carling Academy Birmingham, Carling Academy Bristol, Carling Academy Glasgow, Carling Academy Liverpool and Carling Academy Islington. Carling Academy Islington opened in 2003, and it is clear that AMG has a strategic direction to acquire and develop venues as part of their business strategy, with the inclusion of sponsors purchasing the naming rights for a period of time. It signifies a new direction for facilities owners and managers to support their financial business model with sponsorship revenue.

> The UK's Creative Industries, which includes the film, television and music industries, are now worth £76.9 billion per year to the UK economy. This massive contribution is an all-time high and equates to £8.8m per hour, or £146,000 every single minute, playing a key role in the Government's long-term economic plan. (DCMS, 2015 [online])

There are many factors that have contributed to the fall in profits for some areas within the music sector. The biggest factor can be seen in the digital revolution and in particular across the internet, with downloadable music from legal and illegal websites. As is indicated from the report, the live music sector, and in particular management and promoting, is still a profitable business (DCMS, 2015 [online]). This can be seen in the case of AMG from the strength given to the business model from the three main partners and the offsetting of financial liability through sponsorship naming rights with Carling Lager.

Naming rights have also filtered into outdoor live music events over the years. From 1997 to the present, the Virgin brand has been working alongside the dual-sited V Festival. V Festival, Carling Festival, O2 Wireless Festival and T in the Park are some of the very few events that have effective naming rights sponsorship deals in the UK.

Of the 100-plus outdoor festivals that pop up in the UK landscape on a yearly basis, less than 5 per cent carry any corporate naming rights sponsorship deals. Evidently there is room for commercial growth in this area along with entertainment facilities.

It is argued that within the UK, as opposed to the rest of Europe, there is a resistance to change. Naming rights are not considered a tangible part of the sponsorship/marketing mix. (See Chapter 10 for more detail on the concept of the marketing mix.)

According to Brand Finance (2015 [online]):

> The most critical success factor in the Manchester United brand's renewed financial potency has been this year's record-breaking £5.1 billion deal for the UK broadcast rights of the Premier League. The deal will cover the three seasons from 2016 and the high price, which represents a 71% increase on the last round, is the result of an accelerating battle for content between telecoms companies BT and Sky.

It is generally agreed that the USA is coming to maturity with regard to naming rights. Therefore, brand managers are looking to Europe for future sponsorship development. Within the European market it is recognised that Germany has the biggest sponsorship market. With that in mind, event providers should be aware of the sea change of corporate sponsorship shifting its focus to the European and the global market. With the assistance of major sporting events which rotate around the globe such as the Cricket World Cup, the UEFA European Football Championship, the Rugby World Cup and many more, awareness of international brands and the tangible benefits that sponsorship can bring is building internationally.

Case study 2: London Marathon

According to Hurwitz and Jowett, part of sponsorship's continued momentum is down to the fact that 76% of people believe brands should 'provide funding and/or be actively involved in the sponsorship of sport and entertainment'. When you break this figure down further it becomes clear that the majority of people want to see active

engagement on the part of sponsors/partners – not just funding. In the case of professional sport, for example, over half of those surveyed by Havas S&E expect brands to
provide funding and get actively involved. (UK Sponsorship Awards, 2014 [online])

It is universally known within academia and the events sector that sport sponsorship consistently receives the highest spend in sponsorship year on year globally.

The London Marathon is a major sporting event, dating back to 1981. An estimated
20,000 people signed up for the race that year; 7,747 were accepted and there were 6,255
finishers. In its first year it was televised by the BBC, consequently 90,000 applications
arrived in 1982, and the race was limited to 18,059 runners. The race has continually grown
each year in terms of numbers and popularity, to become one of London's signature
events. With that growth the BBC has continued with a live broadcast each year. Currently
the event is televised in 150 countries.

A total of 746,635 runners have completed the London Marathon since it started while
a record 35,694 people finished in 2007. (Virgin London Marathon, 2010: 10 [online])

The title sponsor for the first three years was Gillette. The initial sponsorship deal
amounted to £75,000, which continued for another two years. Impressed with the results
and media acclaim, Gillette increased their sponsorship to £100,000 in 1982. In the same
year a major strategic decision by the International Amateur Athletics Federation decided
that athletes should be paid. Therefore, all elite athletes who take part in similar events all
over the world expect to be paid, and this has continued to the present day. This decision
marked a major change in the professional approach surrounding the London Marathon.
From a corporate point of view it raised the event to a higher commercial sponsorship
value. In 1984–88, Mars, the confectionery company, paid £150,000, then £217,000 and
then £350,000 in 1986. This growth in sponsorship allocation went on unabated, so that by
1989–92, six corporate companies were bidding to become title sponsor for the event; ADT
eventually won the contract. This recognition and media attention did not go unnoticed by
the International Association of Athletics Federations (IAAF). They co-opted the event
within the World Marathon Cup in 1991, the third year of the IAAF competition. (Previously,
the event had been held every four years, but after Japan the event was scheduled
biannually.) At the end of the sponsorship deal with ADT in 1992, the London Marathon was
firmly recognised as one of the world's leading marathons. In 1993–95, NutraSweet was
able to capitalise on the success of the event thus far but also pushing it to new levels of
excellence. The race saw an increase in entry figures and a change to the route, with the
new finish line at the Mall, with Buckingham Palace as the backdrop.

(Continued)

(Continued)

The longest sponsorship period in the history of the London Marathon was 1996–2009, with Flora, with 2010–14 seeing a new chapter in the commercial history of the London Marathon. Virgin Money financial services put down £17 million in sponsorship and has taken up the mantle as the new title sponsor (Figure 9.1). Virgin Money put together a strategic plan for runners to raise £250 million by 2014 for charitable organisations – linked via the Virgin Money official website. Money raised goes directly to the designated charities as more and more runners sign up to the Virgin system. As with so many of the previous sponsors, Virgin has also taken the naming rights. As title sponsor Virgin is also in competition with other commercial sponsors/suppliers of the London Marathon. They include adidas, London Pride, Holiday Inn, Lucozade, Realbuzz.com, Renault, Times, TNT, Nestlé Pure Life, and a number of media broadcasters such as BBC Radio 5live and BBC Sport. The obvious commercial relationship for some of the current sponsors is very clear. Nestlé Pure Life and Lucozade provide refreshments at designated water stations throughout the route. As the event is also seen as a destination event within a tourism context, runners, spectators and sport aficionados seek out appropriate affordable accommodation in London, which ultimately draws upon the Holiday Inn association.

Figure 9.1   London Marathon winner 2011

The London Marathon has also seen a significant growth in participants raising money for charities. The organisation was incorporated with charity status in the early years; runners raised £46.5 million in 2007, and this made it the largest single fundraising event in the world. In 2010, it was estimated that over £500 million would have been raised for charitable causes from 1981–2010. In 2010 the London Marathon listed 27 official charities linked directly to the event.

> The Trust has pledged £6 million to help several Olympic facilities after the 2012 Games. (Virgin London Marathon, 2010: 12)

It is quite easy to see why Gillette became the title sponsor in the early years of the marathon, as the target audience at that stage, including the athletes, reflected a high percentage of male participants. Over the years marathons and half marathons have proliferated in the UK, with an increasing amount of female participants. The change in demographics and change in gender split could also be one of the reasons for the increase in charitable donations. To increase the commercial attractiveness of this event, political and social pressure for the UK population to get healthy has seen a significant rise in the number of road races up and down the country. As with the London Marathon, there are a number of similar events that receive significant amounts of commercial sponsorship and media representation from the BBC and other TV broadcasters. This ultimately increases the commercial value for any sponsorship deal.

Case study 3: Dpercussion sponsorship proposal

In 1996 Manchester was targeted by the Provisional IRA. The terrorist bomb attack was not the first on the British mainland, but inflicted substantial structural damage to retail units in the city centre. The result of the terrorist attack was to infuse Manchester with the will to rebuild the areas worst affected. On the back of that redevelopment, the people of Manchester came together a year later through a live music event in Castlefield outdoor arena. In 2007, the event celebrated its tenth anniversary, and is now known as Dpercussion. The event is managed and produced by a local event company, Ear to the Ground. Currently the event is going through an internal process of restructuring and seeking financial assistance through sponsorship and government-assisted grants. In previous years the event in the main was supported financially by Ear

(Continued)

(Continued)

to the Ground. As the event has developed and established itself within the city as a free live music event celebrating diverse music cultures from all areas of Manchester and beyond, it has therefore marked itself within the Manchester calendar of events as the free one-day summer live music festival. A number of companies over the years attempted to associate their product or brand with the event, but not enough to secure its long-term strategic security.

Ear to The Ground developed a sponsorship package, inviting potential sponsors to consider associating themselves to the long-term sustainability of this event. Within this proposal they adopted many of the aspects drawn from the marketing mix.

The document set out to inform potential sponsors of the history of the event and the potential audience figure for 2007.

Specific information about the music content was also included, giving a flavour of the range of musical production. A catalogue of bands listed who previously had made their debut at Dpercussion. Apart from the music the document also gave a description of the diverse forms of entertainment associated with the event.

As with every sponsorship proposal, it included the audience demographics, a vital part of the decision-making process for any potential sponsor. This looked at age range, along with areas of interest, spending potential and lifestyle, etc.

The attendance figure for each year was also given, with reference to a sustained incremental rise. The method behind this approach was to demonstrate the continual success of the event in reaching the target audience in Manchester and beyond.

As part of the visual layout of a document, and where the event has a historical heritage, it is a good idea to include some visual imagery to enhance the proposal. New media processes can also communicate the message beyond the usual marketing/advertising channels. Within the Dpercussion document, the organisation adopted some of the established methods of marketing, juxtaposed with new media techniques.

Areas where new media was integrated include giving the event a Myspace.com home page with a facility to join and become friends of Dpercussion.

With the information from this particular site the event company was able to build a profile of their audience. The event also has a dedicated website with a facility to upload personal information. This audited information is owned by the event provider under the Data Protection Act and is crucial to building a profile of the audience and an advertising campaign if required. It also allows the event organiser to communicate through emails directly to the target audience. Customer relationship marketing (CRM) has become an integral element within the tool kit for event organisers who produce and manage their own events.

Case study 4: Liverpool European Capital of Culture

Exclusivity deals through sponsorship and ambush marketing

The European Capital of Culture was launched on 13 June 1985. Over the years, many cities within the European Union have been given the privilege of holding the title. Liverpool was awarded the title in 2008, following a successful bid to the European Parliament. The previous time a British city had hosted this event was Glasgow in 1990.

This particular event does require a certain amount of finance, which is generally raised through commercial sponsorship, local government funding, central government and associated agencies established to donate financial assistance. Therefore, the organising committee in Liverpool put together a number of categories within their sponsorship package, signifying the level of sponsorship and the benefits attributed to each.

The first category was Official Partner; this category was limited to twelve companies, and with this a sponsor received exclusivity rights across all communication channels including digital and print media. The Liverpool Culture Company responsible for the sponsorship agreements had to ensure that no form of ambush marketing interrupted the sponsor's agreement at any of the events planned. Ambush marketing is a way of usurping the advertising or marketing of another product or service without the authorisation or permission of the negotiated client. In essence, ambush marketing obtains free marketing/advertising rights. The value of a sponsorship deal is sometimes balanced on how well an organisation can ensure that exclusivity is consistent throughout. All major events are susceptible to ambush marketing, given their duration and scope, and the audience attendance at various locations. It may become difficult to manage consistently; adidas achieved ambush marketing at the opening ceremony of the Commonwealth Games at the City of Manchester Stadium. David Beckham, ex-Manchester United footballer, presented the Commonwealth torch to the Queen in the main arena wearing a specially made adidas tracksuit. Adidas was not listed in any format or arrangement within any of the sponsorship categories for the 2002 Manchester Commonwealth Games.

The second category of sponsorship was Official Supporter; at this level an organisation was given the opportunity to enjoy full involvement in the Capital of Culture programme of events. In the first and second categories, hospitality involvement came with the sponsorship deal. It must be noted that hospitality has become a major element of the event experience. For some events it is one of the highlights of the occasion. Hospitality could involve simply supplying beer at an event, or providing a full three-course banquet as part of the celebration. Where hospitality has a role to play within the event experience, consideration should be given and opportunities explored for commercial sponsorship.

Sponsorship at the level which has been discussed in this chapter carries with it an immense knowledge of contractual negotiation to ensure that both parties are fully represented and achieve their desired outcomes. To present and manage a sponsorship deal, lawyers are continually used to draft, negotiate and conclude the process.

SUMMARY

The main focus of this chapter was to illustrate different types of events and assess the sponsorship arrangements, drawing on similarities in the sponsorship proposals and how sponsorship can be obtained.

The chapter highlighted major iconic events such as the Olympic Games, and charted the development of advertising, marketing and sponsorship deals. The chapter also made it explicitly clear that sponsorship acquisition and management has become a sophisticated and complex animal. This was indicated by presenting case studies around some high-profile events such as the London Marathon, Liverpool European Capital of Culture, and a North West regional event titled Dpercussion. The cultural, sporting and music events were selected on the basis of their distinct differences, but they also illustrated similarities in many areas.

One particular similarity was evident in how sponsorship deals are given various categories and associated benefits that meet each category. The chapter also touched upon the emerging trends in sponsorship and in particular naming rights.

An economic viewpoint was highlighted demonstrating the potential for growth within the UK and European market. This was not just connected to sporting and entertainment facilities but included some of the major outdoor live music events within the UK. The chapter also stressed the importance of research by an individual or organisation before approaching a potential sponsor.

Discussion questions

Question 1

Outline and discuss the various categories of sponsorship available within a sponsorship document and explain the need for differentiation in each category.

Question 2

Naming rights is an area within sponsorship that is a recent development within the UK market. Explain some of the cost benefits to an organisation when considering naming a live music facility.

Question 3

Explain some of the global impacts that can have a negative effect on corporate sponsorship for major sporting events.

Question 4

What can be argued as the single contributing factor for sport sponsorship financial allocation over and above any other form of event sponsorship?

Question 5

Put forward a commercial response as to why road races within the UK have become an attractive commercial vehicle.

Case study 5: Managing sports event sponsorship for a national company

The situation

One of New Zealand's largest and oldest life insurance companies had undertaken research which showed it lacked visibility in their largest potential market – Auckland. Having recently undergone a name change, there was a clear need to supplement the usual means of communication through advertising, direct mail and media activity, with sponsorship of a major sporting or cultural event. The new chief executive asked Crabtree Associates Ltd, a public relations consultancy, to assist in obtaining sponsorship rights to New Zealand's biggest fun run, Round the Bays, and if successful, to manage the promotion and public relations programme for the company.

The programme

Crabtree Associates wrote the proposal to the organising committee which secured this sought-after sponsorship ahead of two multinational companies. By this time, the event itself was only five months away – half the normal time frame usually available to organise a programme for an event of such magnitude. The race organisers had also decided to add a new element to the event – a competitive section, which had also to be explained to the public.

(Continued)

(Continued)

The consultants recommended a launch function at which the new logo would be unveiled and, to attract media attention, preceded by a novelty race down the main city shopping thoroughfare. The race consisted of teams of four athletes from various groups and organisations, pulling harness racing sulkies which were 'driven' by the five mayors of the major cities in the region, plus two media personalities and the chief executive of the sponsoring company. This occurred two months before race day proper.

In the lead-up to the event regular weekly news releases were organised, covering aspects of the organisation, personalities involved, new elements which needed explanation and general information. Six radio stations were involved in promoting the event. In the seven days before the race, regular 'phone-outs' were organised with three stations to increase the flow of information.

Crabtree Associates recommended and organised: the building of a 'lighthouse', the company's symbol, which was towed to promotional sites by trailer for display purposes; a huge banner for draping across the frontage of the company's Auckland office block to promote runner registration; banners to be hung on lighting poles and on other high density traffic routes around the city – promoting registration and the date of the event; special T-shirts to be printed; a video of the launch event to be shown to staff at other cities and towns to enthuse them about the event; crisis management when a story broke in the media that barbed wire might be used to 'control' athletes at the start; coordinated placing of signs at the finish and presentation sites.

On the day of the event, two consultants assisted with media liaison, cooperated with organisers, minor sponsors and VIPs, and directed still and video photographers. After the event, the coordinated release of results and photographs to media outside Auckland was organised.

The results

A survey conducted by the client company showed that awareness of the company in its target market had risen by 50 per cent, while awareness of the company as the sponsor of the race stood at 15 per cent. Given the long history of association of previous sponsors – this was regarded as most satisfactory. Staff in the Auckland region expressed their pleasure at being involved in a community event.

Most importantly, registrations increased by over 12,000 on the previous year and the nominated charity received a cheque for $180,000, being the proceeds from registrations – the highest amount ever in the Round the Bays' 20 year history.

Source: Crabtree Associates Ltd [online]

FURTHER READING

Hard, R. (2016) 'Sponsorship categories for fundraising events'. Available at: www.thebalance.com/sponsorship-categories-for-fundraising-events-1223690 [accessed 15/11/2016].

Lee, M.-S., Sandler, D.M. and Shani, D. (1997) 'Attitudinal constructs towards sponsorship: scale development using three global sporting events', *International Marketing Review*, 14(3): 159–69.

Virgin London Marathon (2010) Media Guide. Available at: http://static.london-marathon.co.uk/downloads/pdf/Media_Guide.pdf [accessed 07/01/2012].

10

MARKETING PROCESS, COMMUNICATIONS AND PUBLIC RELATIONS

In this chapter you will cover

The aim of this chapter is to apply marketing process models to the events industry from conception to evaluation, to examine marketing research, segmentation, targeting and positioning of specific events as examples, and to highlight the application of marketing research. The focus will be upon positioning an event favourably in the mind of its target market in order to ensure long-term success.

The chapter will begin with a brief look at the history and theory of marketing followed by a discussion of marketing concepts and marketing research in relation to events. The chapter will then examine the behaviour of consumers and how they can be segmented. A detailed discussion will then follow on the marketing mix and its constituents: product, price, place and promotion, as applied to events. Finally, how events could be positioned within the marketplace to compete successfully and how relationship marketing could be applied to achieve repeat visitors and loyalty will be discussed.

HISTORY AND THEORY OF MARKETING

The *marketing era* could be said to have begun in the early 1950s (see Figure 10.1), when the public appetite for new goods and services appeared insatiable. In western markets consumption rose substantially as prices fell. This was also the period when independent commercial television was launched and this became the marketer's most powerful mass market communication medium. The influence of marketing was such that consumer spending doubled during this time (Egan, 2011).

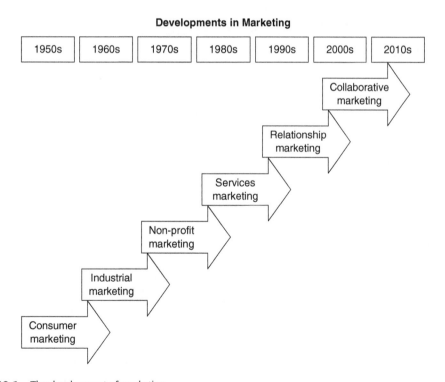

Figure 10.1   The development of marketing

a

Product planning	Personal selling	Display
Pricing	Advertising	Servicing
Branding	Promotions	Physical handling
Channels of distribution	Packaging	Fact finding and analysis

b

Product	Price
Place	Promotion

Figure 10.2 Borden's (a) and McCarthy's (b) models compared

Research in marketing grew in the 1960s and it was during this decade that Borden (1964) introduced the 12 elements of the marketing programme (see Figure 10.2a), which were later simplified further by McCarthy (1978) to what became known as the *4 Ps* of marketing or the *marketing mix* (see Figure 10.2b).

APPLICATION OF THE MARKETING CONCEPT TO EVENTS

Marketing is one of the concepts in management which is difficult to define. If you ask people within a business what they understand about marketing and the role of the marketing department, you could expect to get a variety of answers including:

- Marketing is about advertising.
- The people who work in marketing put brochures together.
- It is the company's sales activities.

There have been numerous definitions of marketing and no single definition is correct. They are simply opinions of how people view marketing. Below are just a few of the definitions which have been used.

> The process by which companies create value for customers and build strong customer relationships in order to capture value from customers in return. (Kotler and Armstrong, 2014: 27)

> Marketing is the achievement of corporate goals through meeting and exceeding customer needs better than competition. (Jobber, 2010: 918)

The above definitions do seem to be different. However, what is needed is an explanation which will apply to every company in every situation. In the UK, the definition given by the Chartered Institute of Marketing is widely accepted:

Marketing is the management process responsible for identifying, anticipating and satisfying customer requirements profitably. (Chartered Institute of Marketing, 2016 [online])

This definition is an elegant description of what marketing means. Of the many definitions that are available it is the most to the point. It emphasises the wide scope of marketing, ranging from the initial identification of customers' needs by means of research, right through to eventual, profitable satisfaction of those needs.

Academic research on marketing in events management has been slow to get off the mark, as Shannon noted in his article when discussing, in particular, sports marketing:

The primary focus of most of the sport marketing publications, to date, appears to be in the marketing communications (advertising/promotion) and consumer behaviour areas of marketing. There appears to be less research in the pricing, product, and distribution/place areas of the marketing mix. These areas provide rich research potential for future studies in sport marketing. (1999: 517)

Taking into consideration the broad definitions of marketing, events marketing can be defined as follows:

Event marketing is a management process to achieve the objectives of an organisation through identifying, anticipating and satisfying the needs of the customers who attend an event and building strong customer relationships.

In order to satisfy the customer an event organisation must identify what business it is in and the purpose it is serving to satisfy the customer requirements.

The following list shows the number of marketing activities that an event manager should undertake to produce a successful event or festival:

- Analyse the target market to establish appropriate event components, or products.
- Establish what other competitive events could satisfy similar needs, in order to ensure their event has a unique selling proposition.
- Predict how many people will attend the event.
- Predict at what time people will come to the event.
- Estimate what price they will be willing to pay to attend the event.
- Decide on the type and quantity of promotional activities needed to inform and attract the target market to the event.
- Decide how the tickets to the event can reach the target market.
- Establish the degree of success for marketing events.

All the above activities are important in the organisation of a successful event. In order to achieve these marketing principles, the business will carry out a series of marketing functions such as:

- managing change
- co-ordinating marketing planning control

- managing the effects of competition
- ensuring the survival of the business.

The success of any business depends on its ability to satisfy the customer. This statement suggests that the main purpose of the marketing function should also be the purpose of other functions within the organisation. The enterprise stands to win or lose by its ability to attain such a goal. To enable organisations to satisfy their customers effectively there are a number of questions which need to be asked:

- Who is our customer and what exactly are his or her needs?
- Who is responsible for satisfying the customer?
- What do we need to 'know' before we can commence the task of planning the process of satisfying customers, now and in the future?
- To what extent do our customers expect us to be creative and innovative in whatever we do?

EVENTS MARKETING RESEARCH AND PLANNING

Marketing research has a specific function which is to aid effective planning and decision-making in markets. It plays an important part in designing and implementation of an effective strategy. There are three areas of activity involved in successful marketing management of events (see Figure 10.3).

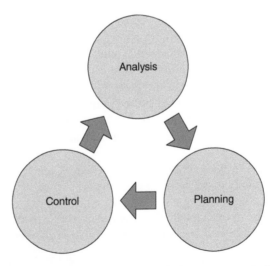

Figure 10.3   The process of designing and implementing a marketing management of events strategy

Analysis

This is a crucial area of marketing. Its aim is to find out about the market in which the company operates or which the company is planning to enter. Through systematic market research, present and future needs can be identified, analysed and evaluated. To gain a comprehensive view of the market behaviour and opportunities both qualitative and quantitative assessments should be made.

Planning

Planning is critical in professional marketing. It follows logically from the analytical approach. From the data derived from the marketing research process, management should be in a position to select markets suitable for exploitation. Products and services designed to satisfy the identified needs of specific markets should then be developed.

Control

Control is the third area of successful marketing. It is important for the productivity of the business or any type of organisation. Standards of performance need to be set and closely monitored. Marketing management should recognise that success in markets depends substantially on total commitment to management control throughout the business and an awareness of the need for specialists in marketing, design, finance, purchasing, personnel, etc., to work together creatively to achieve the objectives of the organisation to which they belong.

THE FIVE STAGES OF MARKETING RESEARCH

There are five sequential stages of the marketing research programme as discussed below.

Stage 1: Brief research

This initial stage is where clients and researchers can identify the marketing problems. Some areas the company or event manager may discuss are: the industry background and the nature of products made by the company; the proposed topic of market investigation; and the extent of market research activities.

This stage is critical because it will determine the type of research and the research activities to be undertaken. At this stage the marketing problem must be clearly defined to enable the survey to be carried out effectively.

Stage 2: Research proposal

Information collected from stage one will be studied by researchers who will then submit a detailed proposal to clients for approval. The proposal should be carefully checked before moving on to the next stage.

The proposal is likely to contain the following information:

- a clear statement of the marketing problems to be investigated
- a definition of the product or service to be investigated
- a definition of the survey population to be sampled
- the major areas of measurement
- the methodology
- the degree of accuracy of the survey findings
- any costs involved in the survey
- any conditions applying to the research survey
- the experience of the researchers.

Stage 3: Data collection

Data can be collected using a number of different methods. The two main areas of data collection are primary and secondary. Primary data refers to data collected at first hand, such as observations, surveys or questionnaires. Secondary data refers to information which already exists. Secondary research is also known as desk research. This information can be obtained internally or externally. The acquisition of secondary data depends on four factors:

- availability
- relevance
- accuracy
- cost.

Each factor must be carefully assessed to ensure that relevant, valid and cost effective information is obtained in specific enquiries.

Stage 4: Data analysis and evaluation

This is one of the final stages of the survey. It involves editing of survey forms, coding of answers and tabulation.

Stage 5: Preparation and presentation of the report

After the first four stages have been completed, the information has to be communicated in an attractive manner. This will usually take the form of a survey report.

ESTIMATING ATTENDANCE AND EVALUATION

Generating accurate estimates of attendance is an important aspect of event evaluation (see Figure 10.4). It is quite simple for ticketed events or restricted number events, but complications can arise when the events are open or semi-open.

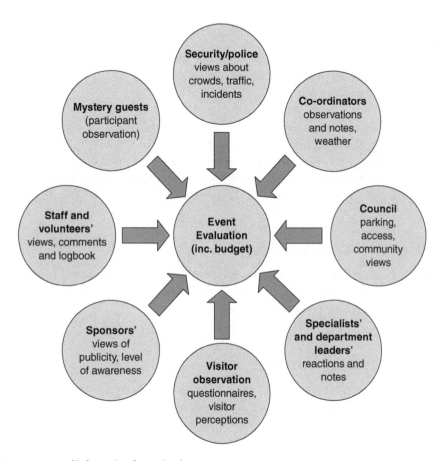

Figure 10.4 Sources of information for evaluation

Source: Successful Event Management: A Practical Handbook, 3rd edn, Shone and Parry, copyright 2001, Andover. Reproduced by permission of Cengage Learning EMEA Ltd.

CONSUMER BEHAVIOUR AT EVENTS

The marketing concept is just as important to the events industry as it is to any other service industry. This is because the service in events is often intangible, separable, variable and perishable.

Why is the service intangible?

Unlike buying a product, the customer cannot pick, touch or try an event before the ticket is purchased, so the customer therefore has to make a decision based on expectations that a need or desire will be met.

Customer expectations may often come from the following sources:

- recommendations from family and friends
- word of mouth
- promotional or advertising campaigns from the marketing organiser, for example through posters, television advertisements, leaflets, etc.
- the brand image of the event.

Before the event, expectations have a great impact on the levels of satisfaction and future purchase behaviour. If customers have high expectations of the event, then once they have attended the event, if it has not met their expectations then future business may be lost. On the other hand, if an event exceeds customer expectations then event managers would expect to see an increase in the sale of tickets in the future.

Why is the service inseparable?

The service the customer receives is inseparable from the consumption of the service. This is due to the fact that production and consumption of the service are inseparable, unlike purchasing a product from the shops and consuming it elsewhere.

Why is the service perishable?

If on the day of the event or festival the weather is not as expected – for example, if the event has been organised outdoors and it is wet and windy – the attendance level would be affected, and unsold tickets may not be sold at a later date when the weather improves.

Why is the service variable?

The event service is variable because people have different perceptions of the same event. This is because when markets are tightly segmented into a group of people with a common interest, members of the group may have differing perceptions of the benefits they have received from the event experience. Also, the event service is based on many variables which hamper continuity – artists, staff, environmental conditions, etc.

THE CONSUMER DECISION-MAKING PROCESS

The acronym PIECE helps to explain the customer decision-making process as shown in Figure 10.5.

To influence customers to arrive at a decision about attending an event, marketers need to understand the needs, motives and expectations of their potential customers. Many event organisers do not carry out thorough customer-orientated research as either they believe in their own ability to know what their customers want, or they lack the resources to do it.

The start of the marketing process is to identify which of the customer needs will be satisfied if they attend the event. Many choices are available to customers to satisfy their needs or wants. Events must compete with other forms of leisure and events. There may be barriers which may not allow the customer to take part in the events, for example:

- personal reasons – time, social influences, money
- event-related reasons – location, accessibility, cost.

Events are designed to satisfy all levels of needs, although not necessarily at the same time. People come to events with a variety of motives and expectations but there is no guarantee they will all be met.

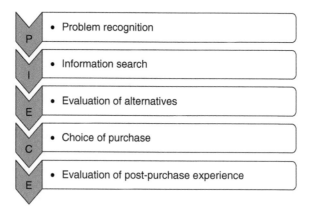

Figure 10.5 PIECE customer decision-making process

THE EVENTS CONSUMER AND SEGMENTATION

The majority of events do not appeal to all consumers, therefore when the event organiser is carrying out marketing planning for an event or festival, an understanding of the behaviour of the visitors must be included. This can be done by identifying market segments.

Geographic segmentation

This is to do with where people who are visiting the event reside. For example, the organisers of a community festival will most likely decide that the local residents should be the starting point of their segmentation activity. However, the event or festival may be of interest to other people outside the residential area, and so the marketing network could be increased to include day visitors from outside the area, domestic tourists both local and national, school excursions and international inbound tourists. The chosen geographic segmentation depends on the experience provided by a festival or event.

Demographic segmentation

Demographic segmentation is about the measurable characteristics of people including:

- age
- gender
- occupation
- education
- income
- cultural economic group
- socio-economic group.

Men and women have different needs, which some event organisers may arrange to cater for in order to satisfy them. The age of the consumers can also affect the way they look at life, their attitudes, values and interests. When events are organised they may often be targeted at more than one generation, thereby creating a desire for people to attend events as families and spend quality time together.

The particular stage that consumers are at in their life cycle will often determine the type of event or festival they will attend. For example, 'empty nesters' in socio-economic groups AB will tend to visit cultural events featuring quality food and drink, whereas consumers with families would be more interested in attending events which cater for both adults and children.

Psychographic segmentation

This is another method which event organisers find useful when planning event segmentation. This is based on the consumers' lifestyles and their values.

Psychographic segmentation has many limitations for the marketer. One of the main limitations being that it is very difficult to measure lifestyle segments quantitatively. This method can, however, be useful for marketers when trying to identify the characteristics of the target market.

THE EVENTS MARKETING MIX

The marketing mix is the term used for the four marketing variables the company can control when organising events. The marketing mix consists of the 4 Ps: product, price, place and promotion.

When marketers are deciding on a marketing plan for an event, they can control any of the 4 Ps to enable them to make the event a success. This can only be done when they have carried out some market research and analysed the results to find out who their potential customers are.

Product

Products are usually considered to be tangible. That is to say, consumers can see the product, look at its appearance, touch the product and even try it. However, with events or festivals the product is not tangible. Consumers are not able to do any of these things and have to make a decision whether to attend an event or festival simply from the way the product is marketed.

Often when choosing an event, consumers tend to look at brand names. This helps them because they feel more confident visiting events they know will provide them with the product which will satisfy their needs. As with any other product, events also have different stages. This is known as the product life cycle. The stages are as follows:

- introduction
- growth
- maturity
- decline
- stagnation
- rejuvenation.

For example, an event or festival which is popular today may not continue to have the same benefits in the future, unless the event is changed or organised in a different way in order to keep pace with the expectations of the consumers. By making a change to satisfy consumer needs, the event may be rejuvenated.

Another method marketers could use to attract people to events is to launch a new product into the market which would be of interest to them. In order to bring the new event to the public's attention there would need to be a variety of advertising campaigns to attract the public to attend the event. Once this is done the organisers must try their best to satisfy the needs of their customers, in order to achieve an image which will attract consumers to attend the event in the future and even promote it by making recommendations to family and friends who may have similar interests.

Price

Events organisers need to set prices for their products including admission to the event, merchandise, vendor rentals and sponsorship fees. Even events that are normally free enforce a price on customers in terms of travel costs, lost opportunities and time.

In business terms, price is a simple expression of the monetary value of the product, service or asset. Price is a very important tool for management and key to the marketing mix of the company to gain competitive advantage. A pricing policy needs to be in harmony with the organisation's strategic goals and compatible with the market. Economists argue that price is an exchange strategy between goods or services that pay for the company's expenditure. It is important for events and festival companies to apply a pricing strategy which is achievable and accepted both by the market and by competitors. Another theory of price, stated by economists and marketers, is that the market price reflects the interaction between two different concepts. On the one hand the price is determined by demand considerations based on marginal utility; on the other hand, price is determined by supply considerations based on marginal cost.

In general, pricing can be seen as the use of simple methods to calculate and allocate prices to certain goods or services; in reality it is not simple for companies to manage price. Therefore, it is vital for event managers to understand and effectively use pricing strategies in order to set the price for events, by managing the price in line with the industry.

Place

Place normally refers to the physical location where the event is held, which could be a building, set of venues or space. Within the marketing mix, place also considers the atmosphere and how this may be created through lighting, set and design.

Place could also mean the distribution of event products or how they may be sold to the customers.

Promotional mix

The marketing communication mix is sometimes referred to as the 'promotional mix' within the events industry and consists of advertising, promotion, personal selling and public relations. Marketing communication is an important part of the marketing mix and affects all the other parts of the mix – product, price and place. Therefore, the task of marketing communications is to present the event in the most appropriate manner.

As can be seen above, the role of marketing communications in events management is very important. The following sections will explore marketing communications in more detail.

MARKETING COMMUNICATIONS

The purpose of marketing communications is to provide information to a target audience in a way that encourages a positive response. Integrated marketing communications emphasises the benefits of harnessing synergy across different media types to establish brand equity of products and services in achieving that response. Marketing communications is defined by Fill as:

a management process through which an organisation engages with one another [sic]. Through an understanding of an audience's preferred communication environments, participants seek to develop and present messages, before evaluating and acting upon any responses. By conveying messages that are of significant value, participants are encouraged to offer attitudinal, emotional and behavioural responses. (2013: 18)

This definition has three main themes: engagement, audiences for marketing communications, and response. Taking into consideration these three themes, marketing communications relating to events can be defined as:

the management process of engagement between an event and its audience and how the audience responds to the marketing communications.

But the key question is: how does marketing communications work? There are several conceptual models that are presented in the marketing communication literature but the model put forward in Figure 10.6 perhaps best describes this process. It has eight elements:

1. Sender: the party sending the message to another party.
2. Encoding: putting thought into symbolic forms.
3. Message: the communication channels the message is sent through.
4. Noise: unplanned static or distortion during the process of communication.
5. Decoding: the process through which receivers place meaning on the sender's transmitted symbols.
6. Receiver: the party receiving the message (audience).
7. Response: set of reactions following exposure to/reception of message.
8. Feedback: part of the response transmitted back to the sender.

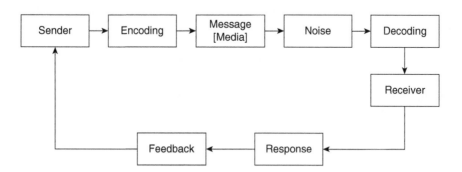

Figure 10.6   Elements in the communications process

In this model the communication is a two-way process, as response and feedback mechanisms are built in and the sender or source may alter the message and media as necessary.

Marketing communications consists of various functions: advertising, sales promotion, direct marketing, personal selling, public relations, online marketing (e-marketing and viral marketing).

Marketing communications works best when these different functions are integrated to achieve the overall marketing goals and thus the corporate goals. In the following sections each function of marketing communications is introduced and commented on in relation to events.

Advertising

Advertising is defined by the American Marketing Association as:

> Any paid form of non-personal presentation and promotion of ideas, goods or services by an identifiable sponsor. (www.marketingpower.com)

The purpose of advertising events is to move the audience along a continuum stretching from complete unawareness of the event to taking action to come to the event.

Advertising communicates information to a large number of recipients, paid for by a sponsor. It has three main aims:

1. to impart information
2. to develop attitudes
3. to induce action beneficial to the advertiser.

For example, an advertisement for a motor exhibition is paid for by the exhibition organisers to achieve a greater number of visitors to the exhibition; a rock group will pay to advertise the concert to sell more box office tickets. It must be remembered that advertising is only one element of the communications mix, but it does perform certain parts of the communication task faster and with greater economy and volume than other means.

How large a part advertising plays depends on the nature of the event and the number of times it is repeated. It contributes the greatest part when:

- the event has features which are not obvious to the customer, i.e. the buyer's awareness of the event is low
- opportunities for differentiating a particular event are stronger than for other similar events
- events industry sales are rising rather than remaining stable or declining
- a new product or new service idea is being introduced at an event.

Planning an advertising campaign

There are six distinct stages in planning an advertising campaign.

Identifying the target audience

The target audience will be determined by the segmentation process, which will define the group that the event is trying to target. Creativity in the ads could be used to highlight mood, atmosphere and environment for brand usage, usually relying on non-verbal communication such as the background setting for an advertisement (indoor/outdoor, relaxed or tense environment, type of music, use of colour schemes, appearance of models, etc.).

Specifying the promotional message

The intended function of the campaign will determine the promotional message that needs to be specified. This function could be:

* to change perceptions
* to stimulate desire
* to produce conviction
* to direct action
* to provide reassurance
* to pass on information.

Each function can suggest an appropriate form for, and content of, the message.

Selecting the media

The medium selected provides access to a certain type of audience. The type of media includes: national newspapers, regional newspapers, magazines and periodicals, posters and transport advertising, cinema, internet and radio.

The medium selected will be the one that is able to contact an optimum number of potential customers for an event at the lowest price. The choice of medium will depend on who the advertiser wishes to reach with the advertising message.

There are advantages and disadvantages with each of the various media types. Television is watched by viewers from all social groupings and is an ideal medium for advertising an event targeting mass consumers. Certain media may reach audiences with special characteristics, e.g. the cinema is visited mainly by young people; many magazines and local newspapers are read mainly by women; and there are trade magazines for certain industries. Events often use flyers and posters which can be mass produced at low cost and widely circulated locally. The size of the circulation for a particular audience is also an important factor in deciding which medium to use.

Another important consideration is the cost of advertising. This consists of:

* the cost of producing the advertisements
* the cost of exposure in the media.

The cost of exposure is often far higher than the cost of producing the advert.

Scheduling the media

An advertisement needs to be repeated several times because many of the target audience will miss it the first time it appears. It has also been found that a larger target audience is reached by advertising in several newspapers instead of just one, and again, in several media instead of just one.

Setting the promotional budget

A budget needs to be set which will meet the objectives for the chosen media to convey the required message. The promotional budget is often linked to sales using:

- a percentage of the last period of sales
- a percentage of the target sales
- a percentage of the target profit.

Evaluating promotional effectiveness

The problem with evaluating the effectiveness of an advertising campaign is that it hardly takes place in a vacuum. Other factors in the marketplace, such as competing events, changing attitudes and price changes, can all affect the advertising effect.

Sales promotion

Sales promotions are largely aimed at consumers, but also can be aimed at the 'trade', e.g. exhibition organisers, wedding planners, festival organisers, the travel industry, etc. Sales promotion is a more cost effective way to communicate with the target markets than conventional media advertising.

One important characteristic of sales promotion is its short-term nature. Rarely does a sales promotion last for more than six months, and the majority last for much shorter periods.

In general, sales promotion seeks to add value to the decision to purchase or attend, and to communicate a sense of enthusiasm. A common type of sales promotion is exhibitions.

Exhibitions

Exhibitions are another form of below-the-line promotional activity. As with many other below-the-line methods they are growing in use and popularity. Exhibit marketing is a rich and flexible promotional practice that spawns new applications and has the power to adapt to changing situations. A recent example of new exhibit marketing is called the 'pop-up store'. This is a temporary retail set-up that may last a few months and is often used for seasonal products and services. The pop-up store is an unusual and novel idea which generates considerable publicity and promotional value. They can be found in major cities, malls and airports and include both mainstream retailers and firms with new products to introduce (Pitta et al., 2006).

Exhibitions come in three basic forms:

1. those aimed at the consumer
2. those aimed solely at the trade
3. those aimed at both.

Most exhibitions start off as trade exhibitions and then after the first week or so when all of the 'trade' business has been conducted they are usually opened up to the public. The public usually pays an entry fee that brings in revenue for the exhibition organiser and helps to pay for the costs of actually staging the exhibition. The general public may have an actual interest in the products and services being exhibited, for example clothes shows, motor shows and home exhibitions. Sometimes the products and services are of little direct interest to the general public. That is, they are highly unlikely to buy any of the products on show, but nevertheless attendance at the exhibition can be a 'good day out' (e.g. an agricultural show or an air show) and the public is prepared to pay for this privilege.

Direct marketing

Direct marketing creates and develops a direct relationship with the event organisers and their consumers on an individual basis. It is a form of direct supply, embracing both the variety of alternative media channels (like advertising) and a choice of distribution channels (like mail order). Direct marketing methods include:

- **Direct mail**: This is the use of the postal service to distribute promotional material directly to a particular person, household or firm. The usage and acceptance of direct mail is increasing rapidly, and with the increasing sophistication of computerisation, advertisers can now segment and target their markets with greater flexibility, selectivity and personal contact. Direct mail can be used to sell a wide range of products or services, and its uses are also varied.
- **Direct advertising**: This is perhaps one of the oldest methods of reaching the consumer, with printed matter being sent directly to the prospect by the advertiser, often by mail, but sometimes through the letter box as a personal delivery, handed out to passers-by or left under the windscreen wiper of a car.
- **Mail order**: Mail order advertising aims to persuade recipients to purchase tickets for an event by post, with delivery of the tickets being made through the mail or other carrier or through a local agent. Thus, it is a special form of direct mail, seeking to complete the sale entirely by mail and being a complete plan in itself. Mail order is a type of direct mail, but not all direct mail is mail order.
- **Direct response advertising**: This is a strategy of using specially designed advertisements, usually in magazines or newspapers, to invoke a direct response, such as the coupon-response press ad, which the reader uses to order.

Personal selling

The sales force is an important part of the communication mix. It engages in 'personal' selling, as compared with the 'non-personal' selling of advertising and sales promotion activities.

The task of selling involves the following:

- communicating the advantages of the event to customers
- securing a sale of the event
- prospecting for additional customers – this involves perhaps visiting prospective customers several times and then making a sales proposition
- gathering information about what customers want from an event.

An important aspect is to decide on the possible size of the sales force but this can be increased or decreased depending on the size of the event. However, management need to have effective, supportive, informative and persuasive communication with the sales force in order to achieve a successful operation.

Public relations

Traditionally, advertising may have been the main communication function in organisations because of budget size. It is increasingly common to find large budgets for public relations (PR).

The Chartered Institute of Public Relations defines public relations as:

> the planned and sustained effort to establish and maintain goodwill and mutual understanding between an organisation and its publics. (CIPR [online])

Public relations and publicity are used interchangeably sometimes. There is, however, a distinction between public relations and publicity. Publicity may be any form of information from an outside source used by the new media. It is largely out of the hands of the organisation as the source of the news item will have little control over how and when the story will be interpreted. While public relations may be concerned with publicity, not all publicity derives from public relations. The responsibility of public relations is to create and influence publicity in such a way that it has a positive impact on the event.

Public relations requires that organisations relate to the public in some manner. In events, for instance, the public could be the media, event organisers, customers, financial investors, employees and potential employees, opinion formers and the local community. The type of audience will depend on the nature of the event but it is critical that the key audience for a particular event is identified.

Functions of public relations

PR carries out a range of different functions and Figure 10.7 identifies a number of these.

In some instances events will need to be created to provide an opportunity for 'hospitality' which can be extended to clients and customers of the organisations. At other times PR will take the form of participation in conferences and exhibitions, the themes of which are relevant to the functions of the company.

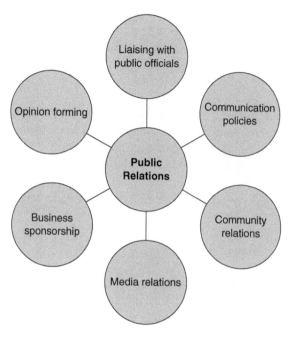

Figure 10.7   Functions of public relations

Online marketing

There appear to be at least three different sources of marketing changes. Firstly, the internet is altering our culture and the ways in which customers react to marketing stimuli. Secondly, the internet is changing the way businesses operate and as a result the speed and style of marketing is changing. Thirdly, this new way of communicating has given rise to e-marketing or internet marketing and viral marketing.

E-marketing

E-marketing can be defined as the use of the internet and related digital technologies to achieve the marketing objectives and support the modern marketing concept (Chaffey et al., 2008). These technologies include internet media and other digital media such as cable and satellite, together with the hardware and software which enables its operation and use.

As a result of e-marketing the nature of the ways in which partners interact has also altered (O'Toole, 2003). McWilliams (2000) stresses that information technology is challenging the power balance in many relationships. For example, the creation of online communities has challenged firms to respond to strong, more vocal, united consumer groups.

Additionally, interactive television (t-commerce) and m-commerce (mobile commerce) facilitated through the new WAP mobile phone technology are yet more examples of remote interfaces through which customers will be able to interact with their suppliers.

Viral marketing

Viral marketing refers to marketing techniques that use previous social networks to produce increases in brand awareness, through self-replicating viral processes. This can be through word of mouth or online. The internet is very effective in reaching a large number of people rapidly.

Viral marketing on the internet can make use of blogs, chat rooms and websites designed to promote a new event. The purpose of viral marketing is to create media coverage using viral stories that is greater than the advertising budget for an event.

Viral marketing is increasingly becoming popular for the following reasons:

- it is relatively easy to carry out a marketing campaign using viral marketing
- effective targeting
- low cost
- the high and rapid response rate.

The main strength of viral marketing is its ability to target a large number of interested people at a low cost.

Viral advertising assumes that people will share interesting and entertaining content. This can be achieved through interactive games, images, funny video clips and text.

Through the use of the internet and email advertising, organisations can have a greater impact in acquiring and retaining a large customer base compared to other marketing tools. Unlike spam mail, viral marketing encourages potential consumers of an event to tell a friend through positive word-of-mouth recommendation.

RELATIONSHIP MARKETING FOR EVENTS

According to Grönroos:

> Relationship marketing is to identify and establish, maintain and enhance and, when necessary, terminate relationships with customers (and other parties) so that the objectives regarding economic and other variables of all parties are met. This is achieved through a mutual exchange and fulfilment of promises. (2007: 29)

Basically, the idea of relationship marketing is that event organisers attempt to develop relationships with visitors so that they will repeat their visit and promote the event to their friends and families. This will result in reduced marketing costs in targeting new customers.

In a general sense, relationships require at least two parties, who are in contact with each other. For example, the basic relationship of marketing is that between an event organiser and visitor. Nevertheless, within an event there will be several other players involved and a relationship may need to be developed between the participants in a network.

EXPERIENTIAL MARKETING

Events are in reality experiential, interactive, targeted and relational, and as such these characteristics are highly appropriate and desirable given the modern marketing environment. These features are consistent with other communication forms, notably within the wider and expanding field of experiential marketing (Smilansky, 2009).

The term experiential marketing refers to actual customer experiences with the brand/product/service that drive sales and increase brand image and awareness. It is the difference between telling people about features of a product or service and letting them experience the benefits for themselves. When done right, it is the most powerful tool to win brand loyalty. Experiential marketing is defined by Lanier and Hampton as:

> [t]he strategy of creating and staging offerings for the purpose of facilitating memorable customer experiences. (2009: 10)

With the right kind of experiential marketing strategy, event organisations should be able to demand a higher premium for their offerings. However, without a real understanding of what experiential marketing entails, the rush to achieve a presence among experience providers has led many organisations to design and implement experiential marketing without proper preparation. Regrettably, with poor planning as to what needs to be achieved through experiential marketing as part of their overall marketing strategy, these event organisations often have ended up dissatisfying rather than delighting event goers.

Therefore, through experiential marketing, the idea is that experiences will positively influence the perception of a brand both during and after the consumption phase of the event. Lanier and Hampton further add that brand experiences must offer 'added value' and fit the 'sign system' and audience profile/expectations of the event concerned (2009: 13). 'Adding value' means that the brand must do more than simply offer a spectacle.

SUMMARY

At the heart of marketing is a focus on meeting the needs and wants of the customer. This chapter has demonstrated that marketing is more than selling and advertising, a misconception held by many within the event and festival industry. The main marketing principles include: anticipating marketing needs and opportunities to stage events; satisfying event visitors' expectations; generating income and/or profit from the event, maximising the benefits to the event organisation; and managing change and competition. Furthermore, marketing involves co-ordinating activities such as marketing research, planning new product development, pricing, advertising, personal selling and developing relationships in order to satisfy event visitor needs and at the same time meet the objectives of the event organisation.

In order to achieve these marketing principles, the event organisation will carry out a series of marketing functions including: co-ordinating planning and control; implementing the marketing mix (the right event in the right place with the right promotion at the right price); and ensuring the survival of the business.

In this chapter the various functions of the marketing communications mix such as advertising, sales promotion, direct marketing, personal selling, public relations, e-marketing and viral marketing have been discussed. When deciding how to properly use the marketing communications mix to meet the marketing objectives, it is important to consider the relative strengths and weaknesses of each component of the mix. It should also be noted that marketing communications is most effective when each of the functions are integrated to achieve the overall aims and objectives of marketing and thus the long-term goals of the organisation. In addition, as an event manager, you should be knowledgeable about the different marketing communications functions so that you can communicate effectively the objectives of the event to the people responsible for the different functions.

Furthermore, the total budget (generally defined in the marketing and/or business plan) needs to be defined first, and a decision needs to be made as to the best way to leverage the different elements of the mix to maximise the return on event organisation investment. The various parts of the mix should be balanced to not only create an integrated approach to event marketing communications but also to ensure that enough resources are in place for each component to be successful.

Discussion questions

Question 1

Explain how relevant price is as a marketing tool as part of the marketing mix strategy. Discuss with examples from an event from your choice.

Question 2

Create a promotional message for an event of your choice to 'stimulate the desire'.

Question 3

Is the marketing communication model discussed in this chapter still relevant in the digital age? Discuss.

Question 4

Discuss how experiential marketing can be applied effectively as part of the overall event marketing strategy.

Question 5

In your opinion, which are the key relational factors for developing a relationship with music concert goers?

Question 6

Evaluate, by giving relevant examples from events, the importance of place as part of the marketing mix.

Case study 1: Aero Hot Chocolate experiential campaign

Nestlé wanted to move into the hot chocolate category with Aero Hot Chocolate. iD, an experiential marketing agency in the UK, was selected to run a nationwide sampling campaign in 2007 to launch the product into the marketplace.

In 2008, once the product was established on the shelves, Nestlé approached iD again to run a bigger, more 'experiential' campaign.

The challenge was to 'develop an integrated through the line marketing campaign that builds on the success of 2007. The activity must champion our key differentiator and key brand attribute; bubbles,' instructed Aero Brand Manager, Vicky Hall. According to Vicky Hall, they really do make a difference to the taste of the product and help reinforce consumer perceptions of Aero Hot Chocolate.

The iD answer

To up the ante after the 2007 campaign, iD built a huge Aero Bubble dome to house an unforgettable bubble-inspired experience. The dome was taken on the road to the UK's key Asda and Tesco supermarkets during a six-week campaign. Using iD trained brand ambassadors, consumers were lured into the bubble dome with dry sample giveaways, an interactive prize-giving floor and lashings and lashings of Aero Hot Chocolate!

The dome acted as a consumer chill-out zone, giving families a place to relax, away from the stresses of the weekly shop.

(Continued)

(Continued)

The result

This was one of the most successful campaigns in iD's history. During and post campaign the sales figures were increased by 3,000 per cent. Importantly, this figure didn't immediately drop once the campaign moved on either – consumers continued to buy the product at all of their locations.

This shows that the campaign opened consumers' eyes but the product won their taste buds – an example of how a great product makes a great campaign.

Aero Hot Chocolate is now the category leading Hot Chocolate product in the UK, kicking Cadbury off the top spot in just its second year in the game. Thanks in no small part to Nestlé's commitment to good, integrated experiential event marketing.

Source: www.utalkmarketing.com

Case study 2: Samsung's Hope for Children

Every year, Samsung hosts a benefit gala to thank its customers and partners for supporting their greatest philanthropic endeavor, the Samsung Hope for Children program. This dedicated program has raised more than $30 million for more than 500 schools, health initiatives and community-based foundations.

The gala hosts Board-level Samsung guests, valued customers, A-list celebrities and global media. The event generates immense media buzz for the program and serves as a unique opportunity to deepen important relationships. After a brief change in venues, Samsung decided to return the Gala to the legendary Cipriani Wall Street® in New York City. GPJ was charged with refreshing, updating and producing Samsung's prestigious event.

Every touchpoint needed to reflect the highest standards, from creative theming, guest experience development and run-of-show to environmental design, scriptwriting, attendee communications and end-to-end event management.

Working closely with Samsung partners, GPJ raised the bar on the Gala, surpassing donation goals and delivering an amazing guest experience that left attendees wanting more. A 70-foot 'blue carpet,' with nearly fifty media outlets and interview-ready press bullpens, set the tone of the evening. From there, Master of Ceremonies Sherri Shepherd of *The View* fame framed an evening that included a fundraising football toss with Drew Brees, Boomer Esiason, Jimmie Johnson and Samsung president Tim Baxter; presenters Chelsea and Bill Clinton; performances by Robin Thicke, Estelle and Matchbox Twenty, the presentation of Ambassador of Hope awards to recipients Tony Bennett and John Legend; and much more. Stunning design treatments coupled with beautiful lighting schemes were key in bringing guests a stylish new experience within a familiar space.

The newly reformatted Gala engaged, entertained and inspired close to 900 attendees while generating 276.6 million impressions in influential fashion, style, entertainment and culture media; streamed live interviews via What's Trending to key influencers, resulting in over 152,000 Samsung-branded content views; and raised a total of $1.5 million.

Source: www.gpj.com/experience-marketing/samsung-s-hope-for-children [accessed 24/10/2016]

FURTHER READING

American Marketing Association. Available at: www.ama.org.

Brown, S. (2009) '"Please hold, your call is important to us": some thoughts on unspeakable customer experiences', in A. Lindgreen, J. Vanhamme and M.B. Beverland (eds), *Memorable Customer Experiences: A Research Anthology*. Farnham: Gower Publishing, pp. 253–66.

Carter, P. (2009) *The Complete Special Events Handbook*. London: Directory of Social Change.

Chaffey, D., Mayer, R., Johnston, K. and Ellis-Chadwick, F. (2008) *Internet Marketing: Strategy, Implementation and Practice*. Harlow: Prentice Hall.

Chartered Institute of Marketing. Available at: www.cim.co.uk/more/getin2marketing/what-is-marketing/ [accessed 21/10/2016].

Chartered Institute of Public Relations. Available at: www.cipr.co.uk [accessed 21/10/2016].

Egan, J. (2011) *Relationship Marketing: Exploring Relational Strategies in Marketing*, 4th edn. Harlow: Financial Times Press/Prentice Hall.

Fill, C. (2013) *Marketing Communications: Brands Experiences and Participation*, 6th edn. Harlow: Pearson Education.

Grönroos, C. (2007) *Service Management and Marketing*, 3rd edn. Chichester: John Wiley & Sons.

Jobber, D. (2010) *Principles of Marketing*, 6th edn. Maidenhead: McGraw Hill.

Kitchen, P.J. and Schultz, D.E. (2000) 'A response to "Theoretical concept or management fashion"', *Journal of Advertising Research*, 40(5): 17–21.

Kotler, P. and Armstrong, G. (2014) *Principles of Marketing*, 15th edn. Harlow: Pearson.

Lanier, C.D. and Hampton, R.D. (2009) 'Experiential marketing: understanding the logic of memorable customer experiences', in A. Lindgreen, J. Vanhamme and M.B. Beverland (eds), *Memorable Customer Experiences: A Research Anthology*. Farnham: Gower Publishing, pp. 9–23.

Morgan, M. (1996) *Marketing for Leisure and Tourism*. London: Prentice Hall.

O'Toole, T. (2003) 'E-relationships: emergence and the small firm', *Market Intelligence and Planning*, 21(2): 115–22.

Pitta, D.A., Franzak, F.J. and Flower, D. (2006) 'A strategic approach to building online customer loyalty: integrating customer profitability tiers', *Journal of Consumer Marketing*, 23(7): 421–9.

Shone, A. and Parry, B. (2010) *Successful Event Management: A Practical Handbook*, 3rd edn. Andover: Cengage Learning.

Smilansky, S. (2009) *Experiential Marketing: A Practical Guide to Interactive Brand Experience*. London: Kogan Page.

Uysal, M., Gahan, L. and Martin, B. (1993) 'An examination of event motivations', *Festival Management and Event Tourism*, 1: 5–10.

www.utalkmarketing.com.

11

BRAND CO-CREATION AND SOCIAL MEDIA

In this chapter you will cover

Brand co-creation and social media have become a major influence within business overall and particularly within the events industry. The world of social media transforms the way event managers communicate with target audiences. Social media have developed into a highly interactive platform via which individuals and consumers share, co-create, discuss and modify user-generated content.

MOTIVATION AND VALUE CO-CREATION

Events and festivals are consumed in a social environment. Participants associate not just with staff and administration components that are arranged and controlled by the event coordinator but also with different customers who share the service setting. The interaction between event participants – both offline and in the online environment – develops into encounters of co-creation. Therefore, co-creation assumes a critical part in evoking positive results for event goers, and in addition guaranteeing the delivery of the event.

There is little agreement between writers on the definition of co-creation and many have defined the term from different perspectives. Prahalad and Ramaswamy (2004) attempt to compare what co-creation is against what it is not (see Table 11.1).

Co-creation is about getting the community outside the event organisation involved in the creation of the event, especially at the idea stage. The participants who may include customers, suppliers and the general population, are made aware that they would be contributing towards the event idea and concept. Through a number of stages, people are invited to contribute, evaluate and refine ideas and concepts concerning the event. Value is jointly created by both the event organisation and the participants.

Table 11.1   The concept of co-creation

Co-creation is not:	Co-creation is:
• Customer focused • The firm trying to please the customer • Customer is king or customer is always right • Delivering good customer service or pampering the customer with lavish customer service • Mass customisation of offerings that suit the industry's supply chain • Transfer of activities from the firm to the customer as in self-service • Customer as product manager or co-designing products and services • Product variety • Segment of one • Meticulous market research • Staging experiences • Demand-side innovation for new products and services	• Joint creation of value by the company and the customer • Allowing the customer to co-construct the service experience to suit their context • Joint problem definition and problem solving • Creating an experience environment in which consumers can have active dialogue and co-construct personalised experiences; the product may be the same but customers can construct different experiences • Experience variety • Experience of one • Experiencing the business as consumers do in real time • Continuous dialogue • Co-constructing personalised experiences • Innovating experience environments for new co-creation experiences

Source: adapted from Prahalad and Ramaswamy (2004: 8)

THE BENEFITS OF CO-CREATION

Benson (2013) explains that collaborating with customers offers many benefits for event organisations including:

- **Increased innovation capacity**: Because you're tapping into the creative and intellectual skill sets of people outside your organisation, you can get more ideas without hiring a whole new team.
- **Increased innovation velocity**: When done right, and if you're using the right technology, you could go from need identification to reviewing innovative ideas and concepts within days – something that used to take months to do.
- **Reduced innovation risk**: People in a co-creation community are typically pre-screened to make sure that they are familiar with the category. These people then vote for submitted ideas. As these people are already familiar with the product and category, you can be more confident about the ideas that the community votes for.
- **Increased flow of quality ideas and concepts into your development pipeline**: Involving a wide assortment of consumers and stakeholders can help give you a consistent flow of ideas and concepts that you can use for new product development.
- **Accelerated time to market with new products and services**: Co-creation's feedback process weeds out misfit ideas quickly so that only the most promising ideas make it to the next steps. This iterative filtering works more quickly than it normally takes during new product development.

Co-creation can help event companies to generate:

- product ideas
- service concepts
- promotional ideas
- brand development.

In a study carried out for the consultancy firm McKinsey, Bughin (2014) researched 300 companies in three European countries to understand the motivation for co-creation. He found that co-creation excelled in three areas:

1. targeting your co-creators
2. finding the motivation
3. focusing on sustainable pay off.

However, event companies using the web and social media to generate ideas from customers in enhancing services and developing new events should take into consideration how to measure the impact of co-creation on their business. While attempts to create events jointly with customers or partners may produce desirable reduced market research costs or increase customer loyalty, the ultimate goal of bringing outstanding events to market remains a challenge. Nevertheless, one of the ways as highlighted above is the importance of brands and how co-creation can assist in developing the brand of an event organisation.

BRANDS

Kotler and Armstrong (2014) suggest that brand managers should plan long-term brand strategies. Working closely with advertising agencies, brand managers create national and international advertising campaigns to build market share and long-term consumer brand loyalty. However, brand loyalty cannot be taken for granted and it is well known that many brands, especially those new to the market, fail. It is often difficult to ascertain why so many fail while others succeed. One reason may be that strong brands succeed because they are developed through co-creation involving different players including brand managers and consumers.

Brands are a means by which a firm can differentiate their goods or services from those of their competitors. Brands act as a promise of consistency and quality for consumers and are renowned for offering a unique set of perceived benefits not found in other products. These benefits potentially simplify consumers' purchase decisions and provide a basis for customer loyalty. Products that most closely match their consumers' need become brands. It is the perceived unique benefits to consumers that give brands their value-adding potential enabling them to demand a price premium. The added value that firms seek from building and owning a brand is known as brand equity. There are four key brand assets from which brand equity is derived. These are:

1. perceived quality of the brand
2. brand awareness
3. brand loyalty
4. brand association.

Boyle (2007) on the other hand suggests that there are five rather than four key brand assets:

1. development of a new product with unique perceived product attributes
2. creation of brand awareness through marketing and other communications
3. consumer interpretation of marketing and other communication to form pre-consumption brand association
4. consumption of the product and the formation of post-consumption associations
5. repurchase and the intensifying perception of unique benefits leading to brand loyalty.

The essence of this process is **branding**. The event is given a character, an image almost like a personality. This could in most cases include a name, the brand, but then other factors may also be included that affect the image, such as the packaging and specifically advertising. The aim is to create a separate market for the brand.

Sign of ownership
Differentiating device
Functional device
Symbolic device
Risk reducer
Shorthand device
Legal device
Strategic device

Figure 11.1   Eight different types of brands

There are no less than eight different types of brands (see Figure 11.1).

In economic terms the brand is in reality a device or a tool to create a monopoly so that the brand owner can obtain some of the benefits which a monopoly would enjoy. Brands are able to sustain a premium price since consumers perceive relevant added value. In this context, most branding is established by promotional means.

Branding policies

In creating a brand an event organisation can take up a number of possible branding policies that would identify a brand. For instance:

- company name
- family branding
- individual branding
- brand extensions
- multi-brands.

In today's world these branding policies can be further developed through promoting the event organisation and individual events through social media.

THE INTERNET AND EVENTS

The rapid diffusion of the internet as a user friendly multimedia information space has contributed to a paradigm shift in the way people interact, learn, obtain knowledge and generally communicate. The interaction and engagement of users are mainly referenced to the second generation of web-based services known as Web 2.0. This enabled the creation of user-generated content and revolutionised users' interaction with organisations, with other users and with information. This change from a 'one to many' channel, to a 'many to many', and concurrently to a 'one to one' channel, has caused a paradigm shift in the way we communicate.

The internet has drastically readjusted the marketing approach for events as it has changed the focus from a mass market approach to a consumer centric approach. Similarly, the consumer rather than the product now initiates marketing activities. Therefore, the internet has allowed products to become more personalised. The internet allows co-creation of event products and services; breaking the geographical distance barrier and allowing availability and accessibility not only regionally but also internationally; reducing excess of information by acting as a platform for development for info-mediaries (i.e. product review sites); providing open pricing because consumers can access and compare prices of competitors.

The growing influence of the internet has led to the creation of the e-consumer, whose behaviour has had an impact similar to the Industrial Revolution, railways or the print press. Today consumer preferences and decision-making processes are not only determined by the traditionally recognised uncontrollable and controllable stimuli, they are also influenced by factors such as the online environment, including controllable factors: interactivity of the website, design and usability, trust and online marketing mix, experience, satisfaction and website interface. The development and popularity of virtual communities is seen as a significant attribute in the development of the internet.

Nonetheless, the internet also has negative implications, such as consumers becoming increasingly self-absorbed, more demanding and time driven, wanting more information, guiding the mode and timing of communication, resulting in increased expectations. Moreover, the intensity of information available on the internet has led to information overload that could have a negative impact on the users' ability to locate the necessary information for their needs.

Web 2.0 has permitted the creation of online communities, establishing a complicated web of interactions, connecting users on a global scale, changing human interactions to virtual dimensions. Such transformation has a significant impact on marketing and consumer behaviour, through consumer empowerment, transparency of information, content generation and the ability to share and publish through various tools and platforms that are easy to use by ordinary people and non-specialists, the opportunity for product co-creation and personalisation, exposing product failures or rewarding companies for product performance and their social responsibility and ethical consideration. In particular, UGC (user generated content) sites represent a form of consumer to consumer e-marketing and can be paralleled to e-WOM (electronic Word of Mouth) marketing, where users share their experiences, opinions and beliefs with others about a certain product or service.

The rise of social media has been considered responsible for the transformation in consumer behaviour, with related implications such as consumer apprehension in traditional mass media and marketing practices, broadening of WOM and consumer empowerment.

SOCIAL MEDIA FOR EVENTS MANAGEMENT

Nowadays social media offer the events industry huge potential in terms of marketing. It is no longer just a passing fashion to be on social media, more and more of us are using social media platforms such as Facebook, Twitter, Instagram, etc., in our everyday lives. The events industry benefits considerably from social network technology.

However, despite the growing popularity of social media, as yet there is no accepted definition to describe the term, possibly due to the immaturity of the concept involved. However, when we talk about social media sites we are referring to sites that allow people to form online communities and share user generated content. Three key requirements are necessary for content to be considered as user generated content or consumer generated content:

1. it is not established through professionals or practitioners
2. it reveals creative effort
3. it is freely accessible.

In a study carried out by Alphen-Schrade (2014) for the social media platform XING, the researcher interviewed 2,000 event organisers in an online survey to understand the use of social media in the events industry. The study found that Facebook was the most popular social media channel among event organisers followed by Twitter and then YouTube.

The point is that not every social media channel is going to be appropriate for all events so you have to identify your target audience and find out the most relevant social media channel to market your event. The relevant social media channel may also depend on the time of communication. For example, Twitter would be the most relevant channel during an ongoing event. The survey also showed that the most important goal for event organisers was to increase the awareness of an event followed by maintaining relationships with current customers rather than winning new ones.

The events industry is continuing to make use of social media activities and trust in social media continues to be strong. Nevertheless, without a coherent social media strategy the effective use of social media is limited.

SOCIAL MEDIA STRATEGY FOR EVENTS MANAGEMENT

A social media marketing strategy is absolutely crucial to the success of social media marketing. From the beginning you should consider which objective you would like to achieve with your social media activities. One goal could be to increase awareness of the event and obtain new customers and another could be to enhance loyalty of your regular customers. In order to measure the success of a campaign it is important to deploy and measure the appropriate indicators. For example, if you are interested in increasing awareness of the event, then you could determine the number of followers you hope to gain through the campaign within a certain period.

Relevant social media channels

In order to identify the relevant social media channels for the campaign you must understand the 'buyer persona' and then choose the appropriate social media channel. Buyer persona is when we try to understand all of our customers or consumers and we describe and speak to them collectively. The buyer persona identifies that we are not just interacting on a one-to-one basis with each customer but instead targeting definite groups of customers who may share similar qualities, attributes and attitudes. The buyer persona represents all your customers and consumers that you describe (in detail) as part of your strategic planning. The buyer persona also recognises that your customers are never all the same and that their combined interests and motivations may vary between themselves and over time, in relation to you and your products and services.

Therefore, when we consider which type of social media platform we should use to promote the event, we need to consider the buyer personas we are targeting. For instance, for conferences, seminars and trade shows the social media campaign will predominantly target professional networks using LinkedIn.

Resources

It is often found that the biggest obstacle to achieving a goal is lack of resources in terms of time, money and staff. You must budget enough resources for the implementation of social media activities in your marketing mix. One of the key aspects of a social media strategy is how to respond and handle feedback and also critical reviews on your social channels. Normally a person is appointed to respond to positive or negative reviews so that the event social platforms are seen to be active.

TYPE OF CONTENT AND SOCIAL MEDIA PLATFORMS

Think about the relevant content that you would like to target to your buyer persona (Alphen-Schrade, 2014). This content should be interesting to the audience but at the same time it should not diverge from your event topic. Draw up a plan and think about which topics you would like to address at which point. This will ensure that you publish new content on your social media channel regularly. The plan should consider the posting of material before, during and after the event. For instance, to increase awareness before the event you could post content regarding speakers and general event updates. During an event, you could communicate short-term schedule changes, highlights and special offers. After the event, you could post information about future events and stay in touch. However, different approaches need to be deployed for before, during and after the event depending on the platform. Adapted from Alphen-Schrade (2014), the following section discusses the activities that could be deployed before, during and after the event for the two popular social media platforms: Facebook and Twitter.

Facebook

Facebook is the biggest networking platform with 1.65 billion users worldwide and over 220 million in Europe in 2016. It is an informal platform focusing on personal contacts and friends, acquaintances and family as opposed to professional contacts. The most common demographic using the platform is the 25–34 age group (29.7%) (Statista.com, 2016a). Facebook represents the biggest reach for event organisers. Even though the potential of Facebook to reach customers can be applied to all types of events, its real potential lies in its usage for festivals, concerts parties and sporting events.

Before the event

If an event organisation does not already have a company profile on Facebook then it should create one as soon as possible. Create a fan page for your events. Make use of the customisation features Facebook offers to create an appealing page. Upload a colour image and a profile picture and make sure these are of good quality. All relevant information in the 'about me' section of the fan page should be completed. This description will be made public underneath the public profile picture. It is important to make the Facebook page attractive and effective to encourage users to share the event with other people on their Facebook accounts and to get maximum coverage. Facebook also enables you to link to a ticket sales page in your event so that users can buy tickets then and there. It is also possible to include website links for the sale of tickets on a website.

Creating a company page as well as an event page gives you the opportunity to communicate via two channels. On the fan page you should market your event and on the event page you should have updates of interesting information for attendees.

While the event is taking place

Facebook is a useful tool for sharing key information about the event while it is happening both with attendees and with wider audiences who are unable to attend the event. This is a vital marketing strategy to attract people to future events. Set up a Facebook page before the event for people to follow your event. Sharing posts is an indirect strategy to communicate information to people who are following the event online.

After the event

To get maximum coverage of your event you should share photos to increase publicity of the event to a wider audience. It will help to capture future audiences for your events. It is vital to review the Facebook account after the event to evaluate how successful it has been and to help inform future marketing initiatives.

Twitter

This micro-blogging platform had 320 million users worldwide in 2016 (Statista.com, 2016b) and is popularly used to tweet during live events. The football World Cup in 2014 is proof of how Twitter is utilised at occasions: 32.1 million messages were tweeted during the final between Germany and Argentina and 618,725 tweets per minute were posted after the final was over. Within seconds the entire world realised that Germany had won the World Cup and Twitter had achieved its most astounding level of activity ever.

This demonstrates the capability of Twitter for live occasions. With live tweets data can be shown in seconds. The 140-character service is a perfect way for communicating on these types of occasions and can be utilised as a part of each of the three phases of marketing of events.

Before the event

It is important to communicate the vital information about your event on social media by sharing details of your Twitter page and hashtag on all your marketing platforms. This could be the company website, other social networking sites, pamphlets and even in your email signature. A hashtag like #eventname gives the chance to package your data. Share all important data about your event by means of Twitter. This could be insights about speakers or the event area.

If speakers at the event are dynamic Twitter users you could tag them in your tweets and possibly get some information about your event. The lifespan of a tweet on the micro-blogging site is much shorter than on other platforms. This is the reason your Twitter activity should be more regular than on other channels. Likewise you should distinguish exceptionally active Twitter users with numerous followers, so called power users, in advance and assemble connections. These power users can be important multipliers for your event.

You should keep your tweets short, as they just comprise 140 characters. Utilise a URL shortening service, for example, bitly.com or https://goo.gl, when posting about sites. You can reach most clients from Monday to Thursday during normal working hours, but try to maintain a strategic distance during weekends or from 3 p.m. on Fridays.

During the event

Twitter is the perfect tool to invigorate users to post live from your event. It is important to share vibrant information through tweets using the event hashtag and set up a Twitter wall (this displays all tweets which include a specific hashtag) for people to follow your event. To attract a bigger audience for your event on social media you should share the information and schedule for your event on twitter.

After the event

After the event is finished you have to begin planning your next event. Make active use of Twitter after the event to promote the following one. Tweet pictures, recordings, press reports, perhaps opinions or voices from the event and react to inquiries and proposals. Each follower of your event is a potential participant at your next event. The new Twitter design gives you a chance to highlight the most essential tweets after an event in a bigger textual style.

SUMMARY

This chapter has highlighted the value of co-creation by involving customers, partners, employees, brand managers and other stakeholders in the development of ideas for events, and development of services and brands. Development of brands through co-creation helps the organisation that owns the brand to create consumer loyalty. The creation of brand loyalty nowadays can be further enhanced through the use of social media. However, event managers need to be aware of the buyer persona of their target audience and deploy relevant social media strategies through the application of the most appropriate social media platforms before, during and after the event.

Discussion questions

Question 1

Critically discuss the creation of brand loyalty by events managers.

Question 2

How can co-creation assist in the development of a brand?

Question 3

How can social media help to promote an event?

Question 4

Create a buyer persona for an event of your choice.

Question 5

How can Facebook be best used before, during and after an event?

Question 6

How can Twitter be best used before, during and after an event?

Case study 1: How do you successfully integrate social media and multi-media with live events aimed at a hard-to-reach B2B audience?

Social media have compounded the speed, intensity and deluge of information confronting people every day. For brands, standing out against this content torrent, let alone making a meaningful connection with a specific audience, is at best challenging and at worst futile.

For a highly regulated sector like financial services, the challenge is compounded; social and content marketing must convey complex information in an entertaining, informative and compliant manner. So, how did we manage to reach almost 2.5 million people on Twitter, attract 600 contributors on social media and attract 300 niche financial professionals to an afternoon-long event held at the British Museum in London?

The answer? A digitally integrated, offline social event. And a serious amount of planning and orchestration.

Who's afraid to be a 'thought leader'?

Too often large brands, particularly the heavily regulated, hide behind compliance as a reason for not engaging in a two-way conversation with their peers and target audience. Their fear is that if they can't control the conversation – whether online or offline – they can't promote a biased, sales-orientated agenda.

This is the old way; it is the antithesis of social media marketing.

At Saxo Capital Markets, we took a different approach with the launch of #TradingDebates, a digitally integrated event designed to provide a platform for informative, intellectually rigorous discussion among a qualified forum of true 'thought leaders'. We supported the event with a mixture of multi-media and real-time social media engagement.

Pre-planning

This kind of social media reach doesn't happen by accident and the integrated campaign took six months to prepare. Social media integration was fundamental (and a key performance indicator) from the outset:

- The event's name was hashtag-inclusive and promoted as such across all online and offline channels: #TradingDebates.
- A Twitter-based competition was launched simultaneously with the event landing page (using TweetBinder contributor rankings) to encourage social media engagement.
- Social media engagement was incentivised by awarding an iPad to participants with the highest impact, most popular, most active and for (number of) original tweets.

- Meaningful white papers, illustrations and infographics on each topic were launched to stimulate online debate ahead of the physical event.
- A Twitter wall prominently displayed streams of social conversations based on keywords relating to whichever panel discussion was taking place at that time.

Influencers – a crucial ingredient

Prior to the event we identified key influencers in the UK trading community (our target audience) by using sophisticated social media segmentation tools. We used social media to reach these influencers and invited them to participate in the #TradingDebates event.

Some contributed blogs on the debated topics were published on the website and promoted through the influencers' own social media, increasing awareness of the event. Others contributed through real-time engagement in the debate on social media, across the afternoon.

A prominent tweet wall positioned above the live panel debates at the event venue allowed participants in the room to interact with highly relevant influencers and peers via social media. The tweet wall displayed the event hashtag but also streams of conversations by keywords relevant to each panel debate, as they happened.

Co-ordination is key

To maximise social media exposure, we pooled the resources of marketing teams across the company and also leveraged the experience of agencies specialised in search, PR and content marketing. To produce a successful, digitally integrated event requires intense collaboration across all of these specialisms.

We determined remits for each team member, dividing up responsibility across all of our social media channels. Some had responsibility for live tweeting the salient points expressed during our panel discussions. Others were responsible for engaging with contributors who took part in the #TradingDebates topics via social media.

In the early days of the internet, Bill Gates famously proclaimed that 'content is king' and key to the future success of any business. Taking a lead from this, our campaign team used a range of illustrations, infographics and thought-provoking articles to facilitate lively discussions on social media with our audience of investors.

It was also imperative that we worked closely with our legal and compliance department, as it is with their guidance we are able to be active across the various media channels.

As our target demographic is a niche of highly sophisticated private and institutional investors, we believe that the inclusion of prominent and relevant disclaimers and risk warnings sends a message of trust and it shows our prospects and clients that we comply with all necessary regulations.

(Continued)

(Continued)

What to do with social data

After the event, we pored over the social data, which provides strong signals about how we can better personalise our communications for this audience and provide the most meaningful content and events marketing specifically for them.

We achieved twice the traditional media coverage during the event month and discovered that our event had produced seven times the number of total tweets, 3.5 times tweets per contributor and triple the social media impact of the *Financial Times*'s Camp Alphaville event, according to Twitter data compiled using Tweet Binder (comparing #TradingDebates and #CampAlphaville).

Although our target audience differed from that of the *Financial Times*, this highlights the level of success attained from our socially integrated event. It demonstrates that for the firms that embrace modern marketing tools and techniques – such as integrated social and content marketing – and do so in a compliant fashion, opportunities abound.

Source: adapted from Uriel Alvarado, *The Guardian* (2014), www.theguardian.com/media/2014/aug/26/case-study-how-to-truly-integrate-social-with-events, 26 August 2014 [accessed 16/04/2016]. Copyright Guardian News & Media Ltd 2017.

Case study 2: XING Events

The company

XING Events is an event management software platform for online ticketing and event registration to purchase event tickets securely and quickly. It is part of Xing AG which is a professional social media business network that connects 12 million members in the XING network in the German speaking countries including Germany, Austria and Switzerland. XING AG was founded in November 2003 by L. Hinrich in Hamburg, Germany. In December 2010, XING AG acquired Amiando AG, Munich-based and Europe's leading provider of online event management and ticketing company. The new acquisition was called XING Events.

XING Events provide support for event organisers before, during and after the event. Before the event organisers are able to target groups with tickets sales, during the event organisers can be supported with customised solutions for all conceivable entry situations and after the event the company provides customer relationship and community management through the XING Group.

XING Events products and services

XING Events focusses on the business sector and professional conference organisers and this is shown in the professional look and feel of the software, particularly compared with their rivals which are not specifically aimed at the business market.

Xing Events provides services from event planning to implementation by creating customised event management solutions that meet their clients' requirements. These services include event marketing to the 12 million potential customers, creating individualised event pages, and targeting potential audiences with marketing opportunities.

XING Events App

The XING Events App was developed in co-operation with Heidelberg Mobil and XING AG. The entry management app is available for iOS and Android operating systems and also as a desktop version. It allows fast entry control by scanning tickets with mobile device cameras for the mobile version or with barcode scanners for the desktop version. Furthermore, the app enables on-site printing of tickets, badges and invoices as well as on-site ticket sales for a smooth entry process. It is designed to enable easy access to all key user data, which can be directly edited as needed and provides real-time statistics about visitor numbers and the use of different entry points.

In November 2016 XING Events launched the ability of its app to give the organisers the opportunity to communicate with their attendees in four important languages – German, English, French and Spanish. However, organisers can present their communication in any other language whether it be for ticket, invoicing, or any email. The makes XING Events the only provider in the world to offer this service at such a scale. The multilingual ticket shop is designed especially to assist international clients to sell their tickets in their own language. It avoids misunderstandings prior to an event that are often the result of language barriers.

According to the Prof. Dr Cai-Nicolas Ziegler: 'Using our products, organisers have sold and accounted more than 8 million tickets for more than 210,000 professional events globally. Most of the organisers are targeting an international audience making it all the more important for them to be able to communicate with their attendees in multiple languages. We are therefore very pleased that our multilingual ticket shop has enabled us to address our organisers' needs as well as those of their attendees, allowing them to present themselves in a professional manner in front of an international clientele'.

XING Events customers

Over the Years XING Events has helped a number of leading organisations including expopharm, Online Marketing Rockstars, BMW Group, DLD Conference/DLD GmBH and ISPO Munich.

(Continued)

(Continued)

ISPO Munich organised by Messe Munchen GmbH, a leading sports fair for over 45 years enlisted the services of XING in 2015 to create a campaign to attract HR managers from occupational health management for the trade fair. Messe Munchen GmbH also required XING to filter prospective trade fair attendees via a pre-registration function to selectively and individually send attendance confirmation. XING provided ISPO Munich with an intelligent solution combining different marketing options which enabled them to increase the reach of the target audience. In addition a XING Ticketing Manager was tailored to the individual requirements of the customer to collect attendee data with the aim of generating high-quality leads.

As an outcome of the campaign Messe Munchen increased their reach to the relevant target segment and at the same time attracted new attendees for ISPO Munich. As a result of the pre-registration, in the ticket shop, the organisers, benefited from 500 new contacts whose data was transferred into its database. Furthermore, Messe Munchen were able to view the 2,500 prospective attendees for ISPO Munich 2016 with a personalised invitation. Following the event, prospective attendees were available to be contacted for accurate targeting opportunities.

Markus Hefter, Exhibition Group Director, ISPO MUNICH stated that the XING Events tailored campaign generated considerable reach with the right target group in a short period of time and attracted a new specific target group for ISPO Munich.

Another of XING Events' customers are BMW Group. BMW Welcomes is a series of events run by BMW Welt which are organised several times a year covering various current topics. The events are exclusive and not open to the public and only limited tickets are available. BMW wanted to reach more potential attendees in a specific segment while at the same time wanting to select prospective attendees via a pre-registration feature and confirm their attendance. The preregistration also needed to include targeted retrieval of specific applicant data.

Through the XING network of potential attendees within German speaking countries, BMW Welt targeted the attendees through a range of marketing tools. The marketing options adopted resulted in increased reach within the relevant target group. The flexible XING Ticketing Manager was adapted to meet the customer's individual needs and combined with an individual data query option, generated high quality leads.

Strategic partnerships

XING Events extended its services through strategic partnerships. In September 2016, XING Events partnered with Submit (www.submit.to), the specialist for submission management, to offer their combined expertise with the aim of offering organisers a smooth event management as well as simplifying the award management to minimise the administrative work.

'Our common goal is to give organisers the best possible support for their event organ-isation and to offer the largest possible service portfolio via a single source. In cooperation with our partner Submit, we are now not only offering event marketing and attendee management but have also added the complex submission and validation process of award shows and ceremonies to our portfolio', says Prof. Dr Cai-Nicolas Ziegler, managing direc-tor at the XING Events GmbH.

Through innovation, acquisitions and strategic partnerships XING Events are continu-ing to provide their customers through an extensive network, services in terms of ticketing, marketing and administration which are keeping the events industry up to date in the digital age.

Sources: www.eventmanagerblog.com/xing-events-review; www.traveldailynews.com/post/xing-events-expands-its-multilingual-ticket-shop; https://en.xing-events.com/erfolgsgeschichten/bmw-welt/; www.exasol.com/fileadmin/content-de/pdf/Success_Stories_Kunden/CSXINGEN0611B.pdf; https://en.xing-events.com/success-stories/; www.incentivetravel.co.uk/agency/36513-xing-events-expands-its-multilingual-ticket-shop; https://en.xing-events.com/?awID=90069; https://en.xing-events.com/fileadmin/user_upload/Pressemitteilung/XING_Events_and_SUBMIT_Join_Forces_to_Form_a_Strategic_Partnership_002_.pdf

FURTHER READING

Alphen-Schrade, M. (2014) *Social Media and Events Report.* Available at https://en.xing-events.com/filead min/user_upload/Infomaterial/XINGEVENTS_SMR_EN_low.pdf. accessed 16/04/2016 [accessed 20/3/2016].

Benson, S. (2013) 'Co-creation 101: how to use the crowd as an innovation partner to add value to your brand'. Available at: www.visioncritical.com/cocreation-101/ [accessed 29/04/2016].

Boyle, E. (2007) 'A process model of brand co-creation: brand management and research implications', *Journal of Product & Brand Management*, 16(2): 122–31.

Bughin, J. (2014) 'Three ways companies can make co-creation pay off'. Available at: www.mckinsey.com/industries/consumer-packaged-goods/our-insights/three-ways-companies-can-make-co-creation-pay-off [accessed 30/3/2016].

Heinze, A., Rashid, T., Fletcher, T. and Cruz, A. (2016) *Digital and Social Media Marketing*. London: Routledge.

Kotler, P. and Armstrong, G. (2014) *Principles of Marketing*, 15th edn. Harlow: Pearson.

Prahalad, C.K. and Ramaswamy, V. (2004) 'Co-creation experiences: the next practice in value creation', *Journal of Interactive Marketing*, 18(3): 5–14.

Statista.com (2016) 'Leading social networks worldwide as of April 2016, ranked by number of active users (in millions)'. Available at: www.statista.com/statistics/272014/global-social-networks-ranked-by-number-of-users/ [accessed 02/05/2016].

12

NEW MULTIMEDIA TECHNOLOGY FOR EVENTS ORGANISERS

In this chapter you will cover

The aim of this chapter is to investigate the technological development of m-commerce (mobile commerce); charting its growth over the past 15 years, thus establishing a relationship with the consumer as a viable marketing avenue for consumer interaction leading to brand penetration. The general term m-commerce will be consistently used throughout this chapter as defined by Balasubramanian et al. (2002). This term denotes commerce using the type of hand-held communication device known as a mobile phone or smart phone.

This chapter will set out and chart the short history of new media and its relationship with the events industry. The chapter will take into consideration events that are considered to be early adopters of this technology, and it will also look at the current audience experience.

The aim of this chapter is to explore the ways in which smart-phone-embedded technology, associated with other media devices, can drive content to a consumer market via a live event. Two case studies will also assist in highlighting the types of events that have embraced new media as a tool to enhance audience experience and help to drive brand performance in a competitive environment.

PROLIFERATION OF NEW MEDIA WITHIN THE EVENT EXPERIENCE

New media as a stand-alone term has many different connotations; its use and potential proliferation is only tempered by the technological capacity of the infrastructure that enables it, coupled with the hardware and software available and the potential knowledge and understanding of the end user. There are a number of factors that will ultimately impact on user experience, such as legislation, permission, privacy and financial outlay. While the term new media has not been disputed and is now part of the global marketing framework, there are many speculative and empirical hypotheses surrounding the technologies and their current applications. This push and pull application will only have full functionality with third and fourth generation mobile devices. It is this 4G technology that has transformed the method of interaction for marketers to communicate and actively engage with consumers. With extensive literature available on m-commerce, this chapter will also illuminate current research theory and demystify the relationship between consumer and mobile technological advancements.

The first mobile phone call in the UK was made on 1 January 1985 on the Vodafone network. In the early 1990s, applications embedded into mobile phones were two-dimensional and appealed to a distinct consumer group who saw ring tones, games, SMS interaction and payment models as attractive features. Mobile operators invested a considerable amount of time and money in software development and handset advancement throughout the mid to late 1990s, which saw a sharp increase in consumer purchasing of mobile phones. Jaap Haartsen and Sven Mattisson developed the Bluetooth application while working for Ericsson in 1994. This software function is a feature in all third and fourth generation mobile smart phones. This technology is also included in headsets and earpieces, digital cameras and computers.

In 1997, the UK had four mobile operators: Orange, Vodafone, Cellnet and One 2 One. They all had licences for second generation mobile networks. Wireless application protocol (WAP) was brought to the market in 1999–2000 by Unwired Planet, a combination of the leading telecommunication companies. This is a technological advancement that allows a mobile user to operate in the same virtual environment as a wireless laptop user, uploading and transferring data, and it became a very attractive option to the consumer and especially the business user. The beginning of the new millennium saw a rapid expansion in the sale of mobile devices and a new generation of phones – also known as smart phones – with applications to enhance the consumer's way of life. On 27 April 2000 the British government concluded the sale of the third generation mobile phone licences for £22 billion. This watershed moment was the start of a technological mobile revolution within the UK market; the mobile handset now had the technological potential to compete with computers. Apart from becoming a viable communication interface, smart phones are also marketed and exploited by the user as a must-have consumer item. Along with the UK, Europe and the international market were also transforming communication protocols with third generation communication licences.

The smart phone revolution in the UK is moving rapidly into a new era, which will position the UK in line with most of Europe and the USA. The 4G mobile licences were auctioned in 2013.

This much-needed capacity ensured the further increase of advertising spend for smart phones, which had overtaken printed media. The increased data service is comparable to the broadband services on today's laptops. The new spectrum on offer was auctioned to the mobile operators in the UK.

The recent advances in software development, commonly known as 'apps' or applications, were pioneered by BlackBerry with the 'phone as a computer'. This was then revolutionised and fully exploited by the Apple iPhone, which now has 90 per cent of the apps market share. Although it had a relatively late introduction into the consumer market, the iPhone has become for many the consumer product of choice. In 2009, Apple launched the App Store, only available to iPhone customers, with a choice of over 250,000 downloadable apps available.

This technology allows a user, or multiple users, to connect through wireless application or mobile internet and draw down updates of a specific nature. It must also be stated that each mobile operator (or mobile platform) has apps designed specifically for their devices. With the software known as app it is now possible to send multimedia files via Bluetooth to mobile phones.

SMART PHONE MARKETING AND COMMUNICATION

Bluetooth and SMS technologies make it possible to send messages to individual mobile phones through which consumers can be called on for action. This might be to respond to a survey, to use a forward link to online information, to receive coupons or other multimedia files, or to be directed to an m-shop through which a mobile transaction (payment) can be made. Through Bluetooth marketing it is possible to create a strong, personalised conversation (targeted according to time, place and need for information or communication). Other advantages are the visual transfer of messages and opportunities for strong interactivity. Other direct marketing characteristics that can be related to Bluetooth marketing include: a forced confrontation level, a limited information exchange, a limited online processing of messages after reactions, and low costs per customer.

To counteract that low cost and high impact there is also the risk of higher irritation levels – similar to cold calling. Current research and case studies have demonstrated that different demographics have significantly different responses to smart-phone-embedded applications.

When Bluetooth marketing is applied, you need to consider a multi-channel approach, and the mobile campaign needs to be supported by an online website or offline follow-ups (preferably in the direct physical environment).

With mobile applications you can facilitate a platform related to an event offering information, and also let visitors communicate and interact with each other in order to create value and relevance to the context of that event. This not only leads to a more valued consumer experience but also to a stronger brand, consumer loyalty and retention.

Consumers are attracted to mobile apps because it is clear who the provider is (an event organiser), what's in it for them (relevance, context, social interaction), that other visitors use it too (consumers tend to show and share it with friends and thus be part of a community), and whether it contains invitations to contribute to get something. Event driven marketing can bring strong results, especially when consumers' own actions invite more interaction. Research from the German-based Brand Science Institute (BSI) showed that mobile users show and share their new apps with friends and families. Each app reaches 14 new people in this way, on average. Also these applications lead to stronger brand recognition than applications and widgets in social networks.

DEFINITION OF TERMS

Mobile applications require an active action to opt in (that is, to download it from an app store), and the user can grant access to be localised and receive updates. Thus marketing and communication becomes a consumer-directed process.

Danish researchers Sundbo and Hagedorn-Rasmussen (2008) define three stages in the development of new experience productions and innovative systems: the *backstage* (where the focus is on all e-business and e-commerce processes); the *stage* (where the created experience is being offered and communicated from the perspective of the producer); and the *frontstage* (where the consumer is going through an experience with others but also actively influencing the participation in and creation of that experience). In terms of the use of digital media for events, we focus on events websites and social media services that are used by the festival organiser. The frontstage in this context relates to the consumer interaction with the created festival, but also to expressing feelings and experiences to and with others. Frontstage is all about socialising, sharing and communication that can be enabled with the use of mobile and social media.

In today's communication market, information is integrated for many users via a mobile device. The level of impact of this integration for users will be discussed as we go through this chapter. One of the most popular functions associated with mobile phones in the second millennium is sending SMS. A modern fourth generation phone has the capability and functionality not only to communicate through the device itself but also to allow the user to acquire knowledge, experience entertainment and earn a living.

To acquire knowledge, entertain and earn is made possible by mobile applications. The advantages of mobile devices are immediacy, simplicity and context. When those are combined with usefulness, we begin to see a different type of software application which has transformed the way consumers use mobile phones.

The theoretical framework around this subject highlights a number of promising areas for discussion, including: user interaction across age, gender and social class boundaries; technology compatibility across mobile operators for push and pull applications; privacy and permission marketing; and behavioural boundaries. All of these will become key areas within a partially unregulated marketing environment.

CONSUMER INTERACTION

One of the intrinsic problems encountered with m-commerce is the inability of the provider to maintain an unbroken connection to any application. This breakdown in service has the potential to seriously hinder sponsorship and brand penetration to the collective consumer group, thus creating an intangible void, loss of trust in technology and also loss of the marketing message. To circumvent this potential inhibitor a number of platforms are incorporating a location sensitive GPS system (Balasubramanian et al., 2002). Next to that fourth generation smart phones are equipped with a camera, compass and access to broadband mobile internet (4G networks). These attributes make it possible to offer personalised information and multimedia applications based on the location of the consumer.

The sixth annual edition of the UK Mobile Consumer survey analyses the current trends in the mobile industry (Deloitte, 2016a [online]).

Some key findings include:

- Almost half of 18–24 year olds check their phone in the middle of the night.
- 27 per cent of smart phones include a fingerprint reader, of which 76 per cent are used.
- Connected home devices still haven't taken off, with just 2 per cent of adults owning smart lights and smart appliances.
- As of mid-2016, almost half of UK adults had access to at least one type of connected entertainment product.
- 4G adoption more than doubled in 2016, from 25 per cent to 54 per cent.
- 31 per cent of smart phone users make no traditional voice calls in a given week. This contrasts with a quarter in 2015, and just 4 per cent in 2012.
- The majority of survey participants have downloaded 20 or fewer apps.
- By mid-2016, almost two-thirds of UK adults had access to a tablet, but penetration growth had slowed down.

In the same Deloitte study on the use of smart phones in the UK, it was found that smart phones can enhance social lives, but overuse can be perceived as anti-social and the cause of arguments. During the day, 18–24 year olds are among the most enthusiastic smart phone users. A third use their devices 'always' or 'very often' when meeting friends, shopping or watching television. Over a tenth use their phones 'always' or 'very often' when eating at home or eating out.

EARLY ADOPTERS WITHIN THE SECTOR

In 2010, V Festival launched their first app, only for Nokia users; 2011–12 saw the app roll out to iPhone, Android, Blackberry. As with the Lowland Festival in the Netherlands, V Festival also introduced a friend finding functionality using the Facebook powered friend finder tool.

Glastonbury Festival launched their first free app in 2010, which also had an augmented reality (AR) feature: by scanning the stage with the phone, the customer can receive specific data on performers linked to the stage in question. This app was designed and promoted in association with the Orange network and available for iPhone and Android users. Early consumer online comments showed that the Glastonbury Festival app received many favourable reports from its users in 2011.

CURRENT TRENDS

Music tourism numbers in the UK increased by 34 per cent between 2011 and 2014, with 9.5 million people travelling to music events in 2014. These music tourists, attending live concerts and festivals in the UK, helped generate £3.1 billion in direct and indirect spending (UK Music, 2015 [online]).

The *Wish You Were Here 2015* report published by the umbrella organisation UK Music highlights the direct impact that music events and this new influx of fans have within every region of the UK, as well as giving practical examples of some of the many festivals, venues and companies that are helping to support this booming music tourism industry, including: Glastonbury, the Isle of Wight Festival, T in the Park in Scotland, Green Man in Wales' beautiful Brecon Beacons, Koko in London, Sheffield's iconic Leadmill venue and the Sage in Gateshead (UK Music, 2015).

It could be argued that event organisers within the UK are late adopters in comparison with our European partners. However, within the UK, V Festival and Glastonbury Festival are early adopters and currently setting the benchmark standard for the 7.7 million domestic and overseas people who attend UK festivals.

From navigating back to your tent to tracking down your lost friends, more and more festivals are using apps to solve problems and help the festival goers survive the event.

One for iPhone owners only, the Find My Friends app pinpoints your companions' locations using information from TomTom, making it easy to find them again once you've been separated. Another app, Periscope allows you to share the festival experience with your friends who were unable to get tickets via livestreaming. You can choose whether to share your livestream with a select few or anyone and everyone, before broadcasting everything from barnstorming headline performances to chatter around the campsite. The third most popular app, Festival Ready, is a basic but fun one-stop-shop for all things camping – including a live weather forecast, packing checklist, and 3D navigation to drop pins along your routes and track down any wayward friends. It also contains an irritating sound flare for attracting attention, and a customisable LED ticker (Williams, 2015 [online]).

The case study below discusses the active use of the mobile phone as a marketing tool.

Case study 1: Lowlands outdoor music festival, the Netherlands

The Lowlands Festival is a three-day, progressive outdoor festival that focuses on alternative music, but offers much more than just that, with a complete programme of stand-up comedy, film, visual arts, literature and (street) theatre. For three days in August, a city rises in the middle of Holland: a township with 55,000 inhabitants, several hundred performances, many bars and global restaurants, a market, hippie hangouts, campsites with showers, radio broadcasts, a daily newspaper, and a unique currency. It's all there, divided over three areas and eight stages. Lowlands is one of the largest festivals in Holland. In 2009 and 2010 tickets were sold even before the final artist line-up was announced.

Over the years MOJO Concerts has developed a multi-channel marketing strategy with a strong focus on the use of new media (website, online community, mobile application for iPhone users and recently a mobile website). The goal of MOJO Concerts is to create the Lowlands Experience. The use of new media supports the creation and sharing of the festival vibe by mainly focusing on providing updated festival information. Another reason for developing mobile applications with cutting edge features is that MOJO Concerts wants to show its innovation capacity in the festival industry. MOJO develops these applications based on a sponsor and partnership program.

Lowlands Mobile Guide

First developed in 2007, this mobile application combines three types of WAP application. Firstly, it provides context text-based information (festival program, news and artist information), whereby users can create their own festival program by selecting artist performances on a favourite list. An RSS news feed also offers information on changes in the program. Updates are available every time the application is restarted; the costs are dependent on the mobile provider. The images in Figure 12.1 are taken from the smart phone apps, and give an indication of the type of information displayed and the level of detail for the consumer.

There are a number of features within the app that allow festival goers to access information about the festival with a degree of immediacy. Information such as scheduling for bands is available and the app has the ability to inform users if changes arise.

Secondly, it is a community-based application that enables users to interact through chat and instant messaging (in self-enabled channels). Thirdly, it is a service-based application based on GPS location that offers an interactive festival map where visitors can find their friends and send SMS messages (Figure 12.2). Users have the opportunity to stimulate friends to download the guide as well by sending an SMS message; they can also make arrangements to meet each other via a private Buddy Finder channel.

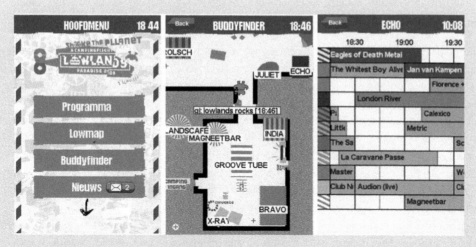

Figure 12.1   Examples from the Lowlands Festival smart phone apps

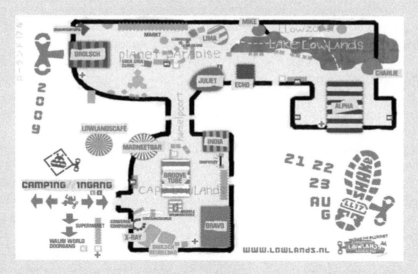

Figure 12.2   Lowland festival site map for smart phone users

Apart from facilitating a platform for social interaction between visitors, the application also offers some 'goodies' from the sponsors. Converse was distributing rain ponchos or sun milk to festival users who could show them the mobile guide at the Converse Compound.

Radio 3FM offered a link to their mobile website (mobiel.3fm.nl) through which visitors could listen to the radio channel, also offering updated festival news. With the Buddy

(Continued)

(Continued)

Finder users can create a channel by giving it a tag and a nickname. Users with the same tag are shown on the festival map, pinpointing their exact location, and their nickname and messages are displayed in a scroll bar. Within the channel they can exchange messages based on instant text messaging (SMS).

Although consumer interaction and brand penetration are their general marketing goals, MOJO Concerts has no hard marketing goals described for the mobile application. The festival organiser is aware of all the possibilities to use consumer data for marketing purposes. At this moment that is not the main target of the Mobile Guide. The main goal is to provide visitors with festival and artist information, to offer a platform for consumers to interact with the festival and each other. By showing its innovativeness MOJO is strengthening the brands of Lowlands and MOJO with festival visitors. The Lowlands Mobile Guide is developed with different partners and is financed through a branded sponsorship with Converse and Radio 3FM. The overall marketing strategy of MOJO for Lowlands is that commercial outings are minimised during the festival. Banners, posters and other promotion tools are not allowed, on site or digitally. MOJO doesn't intend to be a marketing platform for all their partners. The consequence is that sponsors are not allowed to send SMS messages to mobile users. Next to that MOJO is operating very carefully towards SMS marketing, having only sent one text message to previous Mobile Guide users to announce a new updated version just before the festival started. Sponsors were given the opportunity to send messages in the festival news feed, but didn't use that communication channel last year.

In 2009 the Lowlands Mobile Guide was downloaded 15,530 times on 377 different mobile phones. The top five mobile phones were iPhone (37 per cent), Nokia 6300 (3 per cent), Nokia E71 (2 per cent), Nokia N95 8Gb (2 per cent) and Nokia N95 (2 per cent).

The mobile application was distributed across different channels, of which the SMS installations were most popular. In practice it turned out that the SMS download channel experienced quite some installation failures. Due to technical difficulties (both on provider and receiver sides) the number of 'uninstalled' applications went up to one quarter of all requested downloads. Other popular channels were the online application stores (both for iPhone and Android smart phones).

For Lowlands 2010 the organisation intended to build an iPhone native application only, because of the functional opportunities that an iPhone offers, the large share of this smart phone use among the audience and the technical stability of the platform itself. The intention was to make more use of the option to publish festival updates (based on a continuous RSS feed). The updates were to consist of festival news, the festival vibe, and programme changes combined with news from the *Daily Paradise* (a daily printed newspaper for the visitors). In order to monitor consumer experiences the messages in the

Buddy Finder channel were saved and accessible, but only monitored to feel the existing vibe at the festival. It acted as a good thermometer, nothing more. For consumer evaluations during the festival MOJO organised a 'breakfast meeting' with a number of consumers at the festival itself. It was more important to get response on the ongoing festival and on any quick improvements that could be made. During all festival stages MOJO monitored online communities (like FokForum or PartyFlock) to get an insight into consumers' remarks about the festival. MOJO found that festival visitors were more open on third party platforms than on their Lowlands Community site. MOJO's policy was to monitor the content of the exchanged messages, and to intervene only when facts were wrongly communicated. For Marketing Manager Bente Bollmann, it was nice to see Lowlands visitors using the Mobile Guide to find artist information on a totally different pop festival.

Festival visitors were not 'spammed' by marketing outings in the Buddy Finder channels or through direct marketing actions. The Buddy Finder tools were used and experienced as a nice gadget. But the functionality can be improved. MOJO is confronted with technical issues and difficulties with GPS localisation (especially for the indoor facilities) and the speed of processing the sent messages. Overall, this functionality needs time to be working with it. Consumers need to localise themselves and then send a message. For the new iPhone application, MOJO is considering offering and/or integrating functionality from location-based applications like Foursquare or Gowella. In those applications the user localises him- or herself with the use of GPS, then user-generated content like text messages, photos and videos can be combined with a more specific localisation. Another option is to work more closely together with the iPhone applications of Hyves (a Dutch social network community like Facebook), as long as MOJO can find the right balance in using mobile functionality and commercial use or marketing purposes.

Permission and privacy

MOJO has experienced no difficulties with festival users in terms of permission and privacy. Each festival visitor makes a private decision whether or not to download the Lowlands Mobile Guide. By downloading and installing it from the app store or through an SMS service delivery, the consumer gives permission to the mobile provider and the festival organiser. As a festival organisation MOJO has access to particular consumer data (name, phone number, number of updates and so on) but does not use this data for marketing purposes. Phone numbers are not used for event-driven SMS or Bluetooth campaigns.

Privacy is protected by law (national mobile providers and 'anti-spam' policy) and the organisers' policy, that is, not sending commercial messages to the users and not using

(Continued)

(Continued)

consumer data for hard marketing purposes. In our opinion, MOJO is focusing more on a pull marketing strategy, or consumer-demanded approach, which means that the visitor can download updates (that can include sponsor messages) if and whenever he or she needs updated information. With that permission guaranteed, the regulated and edited news feed from the festival organisation respects consumer privacy as well. The future is bright. MOJO envisions a wide range of opportunities for smart phones using native applications and will offer improved functionality to consumers when making good combinations. The overall goal is that the identity and image of the festival should stay the same. That is why developers of future leisure-related applications should have an open option to design and protect these applications for commercial usage by sponsors or partners. On the other hand these applications bring new challenges and options for promoting and publishing leisure or tourism-related information services to consumers.

Source: Screenshots from the Lowlands Mobile Guide app; Festival organiser and rights owner: Mojo/Live Nation and app developed by The Capitals.

SUMMARY

Technological advances have brought us to the point where there is no longer a need for a computer to undertake personal or financial transactions, as all this can be done with a 4G mobile device (Ngai and Gunasekaran, 2007). Extensive research from an international perspective has shown that mobile technology has developed significantly within the last ten years. With that development come a number of challenges for the user in understanding the technology and its capabilities. Mobile operators have attempted to introduce the new service levels to consumers via a number of innovative marketing campaigns. However, research has shown that a large number of users only use a limited number of applications embedded within their phone. Taking pictures and sending a text are the most highly used applications and activities.

What is interesting, and requires further research and development, is the age differential for integrating with consumers. In the younger age range, 18–24 years, users become prolific users of smart phones and have less resistance to any intrusive marketing messages. This sliding scale of acceptance drops off for consumers in the older age range. This could have potential challenges for some events with an older audience profile. The level of privacy becomes an important issue for this target market and care must be taken to have pre-announcements before content is pushed to their smart phones.

The technology at present is robust and can deliver all types of media files to an intended audience. However, timing for content delivery to mobile phones must be taken into consideration, and care must also be taken where alcohol is featured within the event.

The rapid development of different functions in mobile applications (such as mobile payment or integrating augmented reality movies with on-screen action depending on your location) reveals that much will be possible for organisers and consumers in the near future. The question arises as to how these new media tools can be integrated into consumer orientated strategies by the leisure and entertainment industry.

As a marketing medium, third and fourth generation smart phones have broken some of the traditional rules of communicating to a target audience. With that has come legislation to protect the user from intrusive marketers. From a sponsorship/brand positioning perspective, this technology has many long-term advantages for brand recognition and positioning. Used in conjunction with user activity levels, the degree of acceptance can increase exponentially.

On the other hand, new uses of the mobile phone, such as near field communication (NFC) coding for keys and mobile payment, will increase the number of touch points and hence the opportunities to advertise on mobile channels. Mobile advertisers will have to think of new ways to reach users, as services become more direct and more personal. The bottom line is: ads will only get through to the user if they are able to add the right value at the right time. With that knowledge event organisers and marketers have to consider the user of a mobile device as a global citizen who can strengthen brand positioning but also communicate an immediate response in a consumer-led environment.

Discussion questions

Question 1

Describe in detail the technical application of augmented reality as a feature within the Glastonbury festival app.

Question 2

Smart phones have become a common feature for consumers within the UK market, and it is widely known from data gathered that some phone functions have a higher usage rather than the phone itself. Discuss the top five functions used by UK consumers.

Question 3

As recently as 2010, two UK outdoor music festivals launched festival apps. Discuss some of the developmental stages of those apps from initial release to the current date.

Question 4

Since the release of the 4G licences to the UK market, discuss the benefits they have brought for consumers and event organisers.

(Continued)

(Continued)

Question 5

Research has shown that privacy and permission marketing within the smart phone revolution has become a topic of discussion on a global scale. Discuss the merits of considering this aspect when delivering content to consumers via their mobile phones at an event.

Case study 2: Van Gogh augmented reality Netherlands

Layar is a mobile platform for discovering information about the world around you. Using augmented reality (AR) technology, Layar displays digital information called 'layers' into your smart phone's field of vision.

A web browser can be seen as a window into the virtual world. Instead of seeing web pages inside that browser window, you see the environment around you; except with an added layer of data on top of it. Layar's augmented reality operates within that context. Augmented reality is a term for a live direct or indirect view of a physical real-world environment whose elements are augmented by virtual computer-generated imagery. It is also related to a more general concept called mediated reality in which a view of reality is modified. Consumers can install Layar on their mobile phone; this adds an information layer to the camera imaging with which information about locations or objects can be sought. Layar is currently only available on the iPhone and Android phones with GPS and compass.

Walking through the Dutch village of Nuenen, Vincent van Gogh fans can be introduced to the life and work of this world famous artist. With a mobile phone in hand, visitors to Nuenen are able to view Vincent van Gogh's life by watching detailed information, photos, audio and video files which are related to real buildings and places linked to the great artist. Routes to the points of interest are shown on a Google Map, and directions as to how to get there are given too. Customers can step into the route at any point, it is not necessary to walk a planned route. All this is done by building a van Gogh browser (layer) in the mobile AR-application Layar. The van Gogh layer is developed by Vrijetijdshuis Brabant, Ordina and 'Schatten van Brabant', the cultural programme of the state of Noord-Brabant. With the van Gogh layer they try to unlock important places in the life of the great artist for a new generation (Figure 12.3). Digital natives have the future, but now also have access to the past. The layer shows nine points of interest (on (GPS) locations) indicating where van Gogh lived in Nuenen and created his world famous paintings (i.e. Aardappeleters). This layer is one example of what will be developed in the near future.

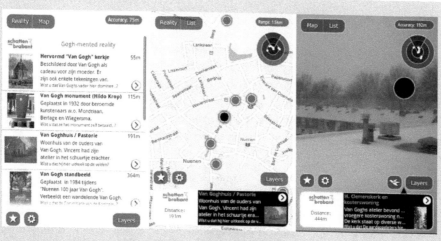

Figure 12.3   Examples from the van Gogh browser in Layar

This innovative demo is not related to specific marketing goals and the story in itself is not complete. More interesting is the question of what the leisure and tourism sector can gain with these new opportunities. For the leisure industry, mobile applications and services create new opportunities in product development and entrepreneurship. The challenge is to develop consumer-oriented services that create added value for their leisure experiences. Another layer already developed is offering the agenda of 'Uit in Brabant', which provides an event calendar of leisure activities for all the cities and places in Noord-Brabant. All of these are of course shown and displayed in terms of those 'nearest to you' based on GPS location and the direction of the Layar sensor. The information offered is related to events per day within a five-kilometre range and links are provided to find detailed information. Layar is built on a two-layer model. The first layer is geographically based on a point of interest and gives summarised information (title, short description, image and link). In the second layer a mobile website can be presented that offers more information or adds multimedia files. Layar is developed for the Android platform, based on an open source software development program.

At the moment Layar is most suited for use in the Netherlands; one reason for this is the availability of and access to broadband (mobile) internet and the increasing market share of smart phones. The current telecommunications network offers the capacity needed and supports GPS location services. This example shows that it is possible to create and deliver rich stories based on local content related to a specific location. Text, photo, video and audio files can be used to create a multimedia package. However, not all

(Continued)

(Continued)

multimedia formats are supported (think of the difficulties in presenting Flash files on an iPhone), but it is likely that these problems will be challenged in the near future. From the marketing and communication perspective, mobile applications like Layar can function as an extra channel to deliver information services to customers. For customers, more interest is created if an extra layer of additional content is offered (like Wikitude or multimedia presentations), or if the application is combined with other mobile services or tools like SMS or Bluetooth marketing.

Permission and privacy

In the Layar example it is the customer who gives permission within the application to show a certain layer of information. Customers can download Layar as an application package and install it. Within Layar you can then 'scan' the surrounding area through the camera and select a certain information layer from the library list. Customers can adjust the settings via which related information is provided.

By installing the application customers must agree to the privacy conditions of Layar. Personal information and mobile numbers of users are available to Layar (as owner of the application) and mobile providers. Both parties have to comply with national and European privacy and spam laws. Personal user details are not shared by Layar with content developers. Developers only receive statistics on the number of downloads, updates and layer requests and the number of users. It is possible for developers to add self-created statistics (like Google Analytics). When it becomes possible to add interactive elements in the second layer, such as contact forms or collecting mobile numbers for SMS alerts, then developers could obtain that information.

Case study 3: Manchester Pride

Manchester Pride is Manchester's annual lesbian, gay, bisexual and transgender (LGBT) festival which is traditionally held over the August bank holiday weekend. The aim of Manchester Pride, themed 'Best of British', is to celebrate LGBT lives and to work towards greater mutual support and co-operation. Manchester Pride attracts participants and spectators from across the UK and around the world.

Manchester Pride has traditionally always been a fundraiser for local HIV and LGBT communities. During recent years and ever increasing in numbers, North West Ambulance Service NHS Trust has participated at Pride through attendance in the parade during the

August Bank holiday and having an Expo stand providing information on the service and gauging user experience. The Pride festival can trace its heritage back to 1990 when the first event was just a jumble sale to raise money for HIV and Aids. The location hasn't changed but the event management team has seen many individuals come and go. The organisation moved from a local team to a City Council collaboration linked to Marketing Manchester and it is now part of the City Tourism destination strategy. The gay village, as the location where the event is held each year is famously known in Manchester, was unfenced in 1998 but a wristband was required to get into the bars and clubs. In 1999, Mardi Gras (as it was then known) was run from an office in Manchester town hall, the gay village was completely fenced off, and £10 entry tickets were introduced.

Under a new corporate name (GayFest), the festival reverted back to being free to enter in 2000 and 2001. In August 2002 the event went back to being called Mardi Gras, but although still free, was cancelled completely with just a few weeks to go. This was due to a dispute between the police and organisers regarding alcohol drinking restrictions on the public highway and crowd safety. In 2003 the event went ahead and was titled Europride; in the same year, Marketing Manchester was collaborating with organisers. Over the years, Manchester's August Bank Holiday gay event has been known as the Carnival of Fun, Mardi Gras, GayFest, Manchester Europride and most recently Manchester Pride.

In 2003, Operation Fundraiser deducted its own running costs (£59,520) from the ticket and collection bucket money it had gathered (£388,946). It handed over £200,000 to Manchester Europride (Marketing Manchester) to cover its running costs and the remainder (£129,426) went to good causes. In 2005 over £115,000 was raised for charity.

Key 103 Manchester radio station and Pride Parade broke all previous records that year, featuring over 78 floats in a huge procession that went through Manchester City Centre, watched by an estimated 50,000 people. The Big Weekend saw another boost in attendance, with ticket sales before and during the Big Weekend up 50 per cent on the previous year. The first ever PrideGames saw teams from across the world participate in a variety of sports and athletic disciplines, promoting equality and diversity in sport.

Source: adapted from www.g7uk.com/manchester-pride-investigation.shtml [accessed 24/10/2016]

FURTHER READING

Balasubramanian, S., Peterson, R.A. and Jarvenpaa, S.L. (2002) 'Exploring the implications of m-commerce for markets and marketing', *Journal of the Academy of Marketing Science*, 30(4): 348–61.

Bauer, H.H. and Barnes, S.J. (2005) 'Driving consumer acceptance of mobile marketing: a theoretical framework and empirical study', *Journal of Electronic Commerce Research*, 6(3): 181–92.

Comscore (2011) 'Mobile'. Available at: www.comscore.com/Industry_Solutions/Mobile [accessed 01/04/2012].

Layar (2012) 'Get more out of AR with Layar Vision'. Available at: www.layar.com [accessed 01/04/2012].

MOJO Concerts, 'MOJO concerts'. Available at: www.mojo.nl [accessed 01/04/2012].

Myles, G., Friday, A. and Davies, N. (2003) 'Preserving privacy in environments with location-based applications', *Pervasive Computing*, January–March: 56–64.

Ngai, E.W.T. and Gunasekaran, A. (2007) 'A review for mobile commerce research and applications', *Decision Support Systems*, 43: 3–15.

Scharl, A., Dickinger, A. and Murphy, J. (2005) 'Diffusion and success factors of mobile marketing', *Electronic Commerce Research and Applications*, 4: 159–73.

UK Music (2015) *Music Tourism: Wish You Were Here 2015*. Available at: www.ukmusic.org/research/music-tourism-wish-you-were-here-2015/ [accessed 07/11/2016].

Vrijetijdshuis Brabant, Vrijetijdshuis. Available at: www.visitbrabant.nl [accessed 16/11/2016].

PART 4

EVENTS PREPARATION
AND OPERATION

13

EVENTS ASSESSING, PLANNING AND MONITORING

In this chapter you will cover

The purpose of this chapter is to explain and discuss the assessing, planning and monitoring of festivals and events. The chapter will present an integrated model for the successful planning of events, based on the authors' approach to planning as a generic subject area. In order to understand the planning of an event we will identify the fundamental elements of the planning process and work through them in a logical order. We will incorporate business planning alongside these main elements in order to develop an integrated approach.

(It is worth noting here that the chapter will focus on event planning and not organisational planning, which is concerned with strategic processes and positioning of the overall organisation and all of its business operations.)

This in-depth integrated analysis will be illustrated with practical examples, presenting different types of events that have a regional, national and international perspective. These case studies will illustrate academic and industrial perspectives on each topic area. This process will be a prelude to the presentation of a successful event plan, constructed around seven key stages – this is a model first suggested by Watt (2001: 6), which allows the event planner to integrate business and event planning approaches. We will develop this according to our own research and thinking, into a more logical structure of seven stages (see Figure 13.1). The chapter will refer to legislation, regulation and guidelines, where they have universal application, and we will also draw upon the relevant industry working documents.

EVENT PLANNING AND MONITORING CONCEPTS

Once an organisation has decided or been asked to plan and deliver an event, it must first consider the reasons for the proposed event, therefore establishing its aims and objectives. Watt has highlighted the need for a feasibility study, in which research into the external and internal environment is conducted. Watt (2001: 6) sets out seven stages within the planning process: idea and proposal, feasibility study, aims and objectives, implementation requirements, implementation plan, monitoring and evaluation, and future practice.

In Watt's model, the feasibility study, then, is followed by an investigation into the aims and objectives of the event, which will necessitate looking at customer demands and the client's plan. Watt (2001: 6) has taken a customer-led and strategic approach to setting aims and objectives, and this is evident in stages 2 and 3 of his model. The next stage of the process is to look at implementation requirements, which covers marketing, budget, resources and availability. Although these areas will have been covered in stages 2 and 3, this stage also looks at the economic effect of these on the business, event and the wider environment. The implementation plan stage develops the logistical relationships and partnerships associated with the event. This part of the plan is integrated in stages 3 and 4. Watt's final two stages involve monitoring and evaluation and future practice.

The planning process, mechanism or system that an organisation employs to realise an event is, in part, embedded in past experience, so before we deconstruct and reinvent suitable integrated planning mechanisms let's have a look at an integrated reinterpretation.

KEY STAGES WITHIN THE PLANNING PROCESS

Figure 13.1 shows the seven stage model which we have developed out of Watt's basic ideas. In our model, stage 1 of the planning process begins with an assessment of the aims and objectives presented by the business, client or key stakeholders. With clear aims and objectives in place, the organisation can set specific benchmarks and build a process for developing an event. This stage is also vital if the event is to be evaluated meaningfully at the end of the process, since the overall success and outcomes can only be determined if it is clear what the event was intended to achieve.

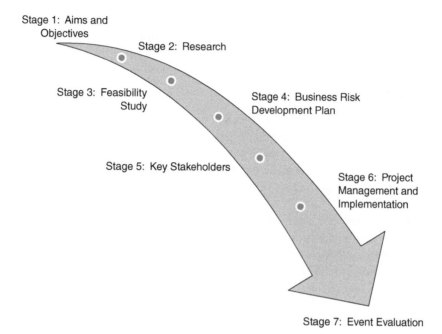

Figure 13.1   Seven stages of the event planning process

Stage 2, the research phase, involves accumulating data on all the key areas that support the event, business and existing sector. Armed with that information, stage 3, the feasibility study, will have a definable focus. The feasibility study should examine and conclude whether the event is viable within the economic climate or business constraints, taking into account internal and external relationships and partnership arrangements. Stage 4, the business risk development plan, will measure all financial risks to and other possible impacts on the business from the event. It should also investigate the likelihood of both positive and negative effects on the external environment.

Stage 5 identifies the key stakeholders and will ascertain in what way and at what level they affect the planning process or event. They may, for example, be linked to the event by sponsorship, partnership arrangements, financial investment or they may be participating directly. Once their level of commitment has been determined, the role of the stakeholders can be integrated within the planning process. At this stage, event planners also need to select the appropriate personnel to head up the process and to ensure the integration of its elements.

Stage 6 is the detailed operational, project management and implementation period. The key concern here is how best to manage the event within the constraints that exist around it, in order to meet its key objectives. Event evaluation, stage 7, is vital if the organisation is to learn, develop and build upon the failures and successes of the event. The evaluation of an event from a business perspective must draw from the aims and objectives, the feasibility study and the key stakeholders. (Customer evaluation would be undertaken at stage 6.)

PLANNING FOR FESTIVALS

We can define a 'festival' as an event that celebrates culture, art or music over a number of hours, days or weeks. Festivals require all emergency services that need access to the event to be represented within the planning process. Apart from the emergency services, a number of agencies should also play a significant role within this process. These may include the Borough Council, Local Authority or associated departments (Scotland has a different legal precedence and process).

Festivals, by definition, are a collection of events, which may be held in outdoor spaces, indoor venues or a combination of both. They are therefore bound by legislation and regulations. These legislative and regulatory frameworks will be presented as a guiding thread as we outline the planning process. The business administration, such as financial marketing, advertising and promotion, can also have a limiting impact on the process if it is not fully integrated within the process.

We will start by considering the planning of a festival. Most outdoor festivals are held on civic-controlled parkland, national heritage grounds or private land. A suitable site or sites should have been identified and researched before embarking on the licence application.

In selecting the site, the organisation will need to determine whether it is likely that a licence can be obtained, and whether the location is appropriate for the audience, facilities and external infrastructure. The selection and design of a site by the event manager must take into consideration all of these components if the event is to be successful. As part of this process, the event team should assess the services and utilities available on the proposed site. This assessment should consider, for example, whether the external lighting on site will be adequate for safety and security, and whether the type of roadway is accessible to emergency vehicles, customers and contractors and is likely to remain so for the duration of the event. This particular aspect must be assessed in all weather conditions and should take account of predicted attendance levels throughout the event.

As part of their assessment, the event team should identify external power conduits to be used by contractors and the event production team. Direct feeds can be connected where external power outlets are operational. An on-site communication network can be established using the landline supply service if a connection is accessible through underground network cabling. This can also be a contingency in the event of a power failure during the event, since communication can be re-established. Such eventualities should be covered by the emergency procedure plan, which is drawn up by the event team in association with other agencies.

Within the planning process, the movement of people within the site boundaries must be clearly defined. To maintain control and safety, it is vital to identify the areas where contractors can obtain access, both prior to, during and after the event. Those attending the festival must be allocated sufficient space for movement at any given time throughout the event, taking into consideration the health and safety issues arising at different times of the day and night and from all possible weather conditions. In planning the site layout, overspill areas for customers should be identified, and where these may impact on the safety of customers, it must be indicated within the emergency plan.

Early consultation with the relevant authorities is vital. The accessibility of the site to emergency vehicles will determine whether the licence agreement is granted and renewed. The event team should therefore consult the local emergency services (fire, police and ambulance) on the choice of site and its layout before applying for a licence.

Where hazards in and around the site have been identified, sufficient measures should be put in place to reduce the risk of harm or injury to contractors, emergency agencies, customers and other personnel working on site. As the planning process develops, so too must the risk assessment document, if the event planners are to ensure that such hazards can be assessed and managed according to health and safety regulations. However, hazards arising from the *construction* of the site need to be assessed before a full licence agreement will be granted for the event. An initial assessment of anticipated hazards must be presented before a full licence is granted. It is also necessary for the event organiser to produce a written document outlining the site rules and regulations. Contractors must be given a copy of this before commencing any work on site.

As part of the licence agreement, and especially where the event site is located within a populated area and/or is likely to have an adverse effect on the local environment, the planning process must consider the potential impact of the event. Under the licence agreement and in accordance with the 2003 Licensing Act, the local community must be informed via a local newspaper and information posted in and around the local environment for a stated duration, prior to the provisional licence being granted. It is therefore prudent to consult the local community before applying for a licence to gauge the degree of support and anticipate any likely opposition that could be presented at the licence hearing.

Investing in consultation with the local community can produce a number of cost benefits for event planners. Such consultation can help to establish a long-term licence agreement with the local authority, which means that the event can be held on a regular basis. Marketing, sponsorship and financial budgeting can thus be planned strategically over time. Securing the support of the local community should also shorten and simplify the application process, thereby reducing the cost of legal representation.

A significant number of outdoor festivals are sponsored by commercial organisations, including V Festival and Carling Festival Leeds. The allocation of sponsorship monies and deals requires long-term planning; however, this type of arrangement guarantees sustainability and longevity.

Before a licence is granted, the event planning team will be required to prepare and present a number of documents, in line with industry guidance, legislation and regulations. For example, when constructing outdoor events, demountable structures will generally be required and the *Temporary Demountable Structures Guidance* will apply. Published by the Institution of Structural Engineers (2007 [online]), this guidance provides a benchmark for procuring, erecting, maintaining and dismantling temporary structures.

The local authority planning and building control department will give guidance and make safety checks on the structure(s) during construction and/or on completion. The fire safety officer from the local fire department operates under the Fire Precaution Act 1971 and *Practical Fire Safety Guidance for Places of Entertainment and Assembly* (Scottish Government, [online]). The Fire Service will issue the event with a fire safety certificate to cover temporary demountable structure(s), where the event requires the structure to be accessed by the general public, contractors or event personnel.

Further documentation will also be required by the local authority. This includes a risk assessment under the Health and Safety at Work Act 1974, which should be presented with the licence. The licence application and the fire safety certificate state that a risk assessment must be undertaken, and an emergency evacuation plan should also be written and presented alongside the fire safety certificate.

In preparing for their planning meetings with the local authority, emergency services and contractors, the event team must acquire and develop an appropriate plan of the site and surrounding areas. This site plan will be an essential tool in designing the site layout and facilities. It is also a requirement of the application process. The plan also gives the event manager/ licensee a clear visual sense of the event and hence enables their strategic control of it.

The scheduling of performers and performances is a key task for all event planners. This must reflect the type of venue, the audience, the theme of the event, the intended impact and the profile of the performer/performance. These factors should be documented alongside the proposed schedule for the event and presented within the licence application.

Once the event team has undertaken adequate consultation with outside agencies, the local community and emergency services, and has obtained a provisional licence for a site under the 2003 Licensing Act, they should consult the *Purple Guide* (Events Industry Forum, 2015 [online]). This is an industry document endorsed by the Health and Safety Executive and used by many local authorities, emergency services, contractors and associated organisations. The *Purple Guide* also has an international reputation as the definitive guide for outdoor festivals and similar events.

The *Purple Guide* provides detailed guidance for on-site services, management and operation, both prior to and during the event. It also describes the regulations that may impact on various aspects of the event, making particular reference to health and safety guidelines. The document gives direction on suitable site design and the layout of amenities and basic services. It directs event planners to the other guidance documents, legislation and regulations that they need in order to manage an outdoor festival.

PLANNING FOR CONFERENCES

A conference has a number of distinct differences within the planning process, as compared to festivals and other events. Although the first, preparatory, stage should be present in all event planning processes, the development of festivals is strongly influenced by the type of licence required. The structuring of a conference, on the other hand, will be greatly influenced by the building or location in which it will be held. The planning of other events may be constrained to varying degrees by licence, location and building factors.

Although there will be similarities to the processes used in festival planning, there are also specific issues to be considered when planning for a conference. Such an event clearly focuses on the key speaker(s) and delegates. A conference may also be described as a 'destination event', since the location is an integral element which can shape the entire planning process.

A conference has many similar characteristics to other events and this section will outline the common characteristics within the planning process. The conference organiser should firstly undertake research and conduct a feasibility study. This process, as highlighted in the previous section, will examine the nature of the business and its ability to hold this particular type of event. An organisation should always undertake this aspect of the planning process before starting to plan all new or existing events. Alongside the feasibility study, a business risk development plan should highlight potential adverse effects for the overall business and assess the level of risk for each.

There are a number of specific factors which must be taken into account when planning a conference. A conference must cater for an agreed number of delegates; it should be housed at a location that is easily accessible to the intended guests; and the event may include an overnight stay tied into the proceedings or offered as an option to delegates. Sufficient research should be carried out and the feasibility study should explore cost, availability and quality. Many conference facilities have developed an all-in-one package for conference organisers. These typically include venue and equipment, hotel, hospitality, labour and external entertainment. Where such a package is offered, it remains the responsibility of the organiser to research every element independently to assess operational levels of service quality.

The financial business risks of the conference are directly associated with the number of delegates, and cost of attending must be factored into the equation to cover all costs to the organisation developing and delivering the event. The overall cost of all external facilities that will contain the event for the given period must be included.

A cost–benefit analysis should be conducted, especially where there is a high financial risk to the organisation of failing to attract sufficient delegates. This analysis should incorporate all costs associated with the event, including the cost of services provided in-house by the organisation and those purchased from external contractors. Where external operators are required, there may be additional costs due to transportation, seasonal cost variations or fluctuations in currency, and these must also be fully investigated, if relevant. Only after these areas have been priced accurately can the charge for delegate places be set. This must, however, also reflect acceptable price levels for this type of conference. The overall cost of the conference cannot be met by the total projected income from delegates' fees.

Many conferences have business-to-business relationships attached to the theme. Therefore most conferences are paid for in full by the company or companies that host them, since they act as a promotional exercise for their business. However, some conferences require publicity to encourage participation. In The City international music conference, which is held annually in Manchester, England, attracts approximately 2,000 international delegates. In 2005, the cost to each delegate was £575 + VAT. For an event of this scale, the planning process must ensure continual marketing, including the production and distribution of promotional information from the previous event. Marketing can influence the number of delegates who attend this type of conference and the marketing strategy should identify and use effective communication platforms to transmit information across international boundaries. Since the conference has a yearly timetable of delivery, researching and targeting both existing and new customers will be a key and continuous part of the strategy.

Commercially driven conferences, apart from relying on delegates who pay to attend, can also get financial assistance with overall costs from sponsors. This is the case for the international music conference mentioned above. In this instance, key stakeholders must play a significant role within the planning process in determining the aims and objectives. This will be more apparent where key stakeholders contribute to the event directly, for example, by supplying free or reduced cost venues and equipment. If a conference is a not-for-profit event, economic assistance may sometimes be allocated from local authorities if the event meets the basic criteria for the area. Where financial assistance is factored into the event planning process, event planners must ensure that the event's aims and objectives are linked to the criteria for assistance and must demonstrate this within their evaluation of the event.

As highlighted previously, delegate registration does not always include accommodation and hospitality; if it does not, then this cost must be borne by the delegates. In developing an overall package, deals should be negotiated with hotels to allocate a block booking for the number of delegates at a reduced cost if possible.

As in the case of festivals, conferences have legislative requirements which can determine the scope of the event. A building in which a conference is to be held must have a licence, though it is the responsibility of the venue operator, rather than the organiser to apply for this. The venue operator and the organiser are, however, jointly liable for fire safety, risk assessment, insurance, and health and safety. The venue or location must always meet the operational requirements of each Act of Parliament. All regulations, be they European or UK, including the health and safety regulations and the British standard on fire retardant materials, must be cross-checked with the insurance risk assessor, as part of venue risk assessment and fire risk assessment. All the documentation pertaining to risk and health and safety must be easily accessible to all organisations and individuals concerned.

If the event is to be successful, the business must allocate adequate resources to the planning process. For example, where the feasibility study and business risk development plan identify tasks such as financial accounting and marketing as significant, the organisation should provide appropriate human and financial resources to support these areas.

The Association for Conference Organisers produces guidance on the planning and delivery of conferences and can direct event planners to other sources of support. The British Association of Conference Destinations plays a major role in the area of venues and locations for conference organisers.

PLANNING FOR EVENTS

All seven stages must carry equal weight when developing and planning the process. Where issues are presented that can affect the business or event, appropriate measures must be instigated to reduce the risk of failure or of a negative impact on the business. Where other organisations, contractors or the emergency services play a major role in the licence application, it is a good idea to involve a representative from each organisation within the planning process.

If a significant level of entertainment and hospitality is included within the event or is required by customers it is necessary to ensure that the facilities can sustain these demands and that the location is accessible for the duration of the event. Again, where sponsors are crucial to the overall event, they should be identified and involved at an early stage in the planning process and their aims and objectives for their sponsorship of the event should be established.

Once the seven key stages have been explored and developed the conference can function as an event. Each step along the process requires continual correlation with the other stages, and the process should be monitored throughout.

Case study 1: In The City – the UK's international music convention and live music festival

This case study will describe an event that has to take a dual approach to planning, in that it is both a conference and a music festival. In addition to the 2,000 international delegates who attend this industry conference on an annual basis, an area within the event is also open to members of the public who wish to attend the unsigned live music acts. The case study will demonstrate how stages within the planning process become an integral integrated business approach.

The 2005 In The City music event (ITC) was supported and sponsored by the North West Development Agency, Radio 1, Lastminute.com, Manchester City Council, Manchester City Music Network, and England Northwest. As part of the event, the city hosted 500 bands in 50 venues over five days. It is estimated that over 100,000 people attended the live music event.

The conference is primarily for industry professionals, who attend various workshops, interviews and discussions presented by specialist panels. These meetings and discussions are scheduled within a one-day programme at the main venue, which for 2005 was the Midland Hotel in the city centre. Due to the number of people attending this event, a selection of hotels within the city offered reduced rates to registered delegates.

In The City could be described as a 'destination event' for Manchester. Manchester City Council, in association with Marketing Manchester and the Tourist Board of Greater Manchester, uses events as a way of furthering the city's key objective to be seen as a culturally diverse and creative environment. The target for this particular objective is to raise Manchester's profile from a regional and national to an international destination location.

(Continued)

(Continued)

In The City music convention is an annual event that was initially launched in Manchester and has subsequently travelled to Liverpool, Dublin, New York and Glasgow. In recent years, it has been held in Manchester City Centre and is usually scheduled for late September.

An event of this magnitude requires a significant amount of planning, logistical operation and control, given the number of artists and venues. The event is a commercially driven venture and is sustained by vital sponsorship. Therefore, the key stakeholders are not just circulating around the sponsors; the 2,000 registered delegates will dictate the style and content of the convention, along with the level of service quality and venues that will support this event.

Integration of the planning process

It is essential for the In The City event to have a distinct commercial aim and objectives at the heart of its planning process (**stage 1**). The event's aims and objectives are shown in Figure 13.2.

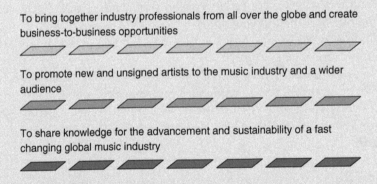

To bring together industry professionals from all over the globe and create business-to-business opportunities

To promote new and unsigned artists to the music industry and a wider audience

To share knowledge for the advancement and sustainability of a fast changing global music industry

Figure 13.2 In The City festival's aims and objectives

Some of the aspects of the event that require a significant amount of research include: venues, hotels, potential or previous sponsors, travel arrangements, panellists/speakers, and interesting and relevant topics for sessions, e.g. new technology for the industry (**stage 2**).

At **stage 3**, the feasibility study should assess all the information accumulated at the research stage. It will look at hotel cost and availability, venue cost, scheduling and contra sponsorship deals, informative and current/explorative areas for workshops, interviews and discussions.

The business risk development plan (**stage 4**) will assess the business, event and the wider environment. The majority of data presented will be financial. The business must determine the overall cost of the event and assess market trends in relation to pricing for delegates. It is vital to identify the break-even point in order to set the correct pricing structure. Where there is a projected shortfall in income the remainder must be acquired by sponsorship/contra deals. The business must also assess the likely financial impact and human resource implications of the event's planning process (**stage 5**). For example, human resources may be required for web development, press and public relations and regional, national and international promotional advertising. When designing the event the facilities needed to support this venture must be considered, as external factors may have a negative impact on the event. Scheduling of the event must take into consideration other events that may reduce hotel availability and participation from the wider audience at selected venues.

Stage 6, project management and implementation, then becomes the litmus test; the success of this stage will depend on how well the first five stages have been carried out. A great deal of logistical and operational management is required throughout the entire event. Therefore, appointed individuals who are fully briefed should deliver the event schedule, with room for flexibility where sudden changes are deemed necessary.

Stage 7 is the evaluation of the event. Quantitative and qualitative feedback can be collected from ITC delegates at the point of contact. Business evaluation will also be necessary due to organisational changes, which may include human resource issues or the acquisition of new business opportunities. This can be carried out with information obtained at stage 4.

This case study has presented the seven key stages of the planning process as they apply to the ITC event. It has shown that planning must be an integral part of any business when undertaking a new or existing venture. It has also set out clear and distinct stages that need to be both understood and realised by the organisation planning the event. A strategic view and effective leadership of the planning process is therefore vital, and all constituent parts and their impact on the process should be monitored continually.

SUMMARY

This chapter has demonstrated that planning for an event is a logical, systematic and yet fluid process. Developing a generic planning process that integrates not just the event, but the business and sector that supports it, should enable the event planner to gain a clearer understanding of the event, the business and the impact of each on the other.

We have also seen how the research and feasibility study is connected to outcome and success. Where a business undertakes a new type of event, the business risk development plan can ascertain the level of financial impact on the business in sustaining the process and delivery of the event. The process has shown the stakeholders' contribution and their relationship to the outcomes highlighted in the aims and objectives.

The chapter has also made reference to recent events that have a national and international profile in order to illustrate the issues pertaining to planning and to give a greater understanding of the organisation supporting the planning process and event. We have also explored this from a financial perspective and looked at the expertise and resources required to sustain delivery. Planning can be a long and arduous task even with all factors taken into consideration.

The chapter has demonstrated the seven key stages within the planning process. This seven stage model can provide a starting point for the planning of festivals, conferences and events. It has been shown that each stage is integral and must be fully integrated with the day-to-day operational business of the organisation. If you are developing a type of event that falls outside of those discussed here, the seven stage model can be used as a template.

Discussion questions

Question 1

Within the event planning process, why should event management clearly identify goals in relation to critical success factors and measures?

Question 2

Within the planning process, outline why it is necessary to undertake a feasibility study.

Question 3

Outline some of the positive cost benefits (to an organisation) that can be derived from community consultation when planning an event.

Question 4

Within the planning process the event manager should look at a method for analysing the event. Explain in detail the Delphi method of evaluation and why this method is an appropriate tool to obtain an understanding of the event from the customer's point of view.

Question 5

Within the planning process a number of stakeholders can determine to a greater or lesser extent the outcome of an event. To ensure that the stakeholder relationship remains positive, what mechanism can an event manager put in place to bring about a stable working environment?

Question 6

As part of the planning process event evaluation can take on two data gathering techniques. Outline how a mixed method approach can be of value when assessing data.

Case study 2: Manchester Histories Festival 2009

In 2009, a selection of public and private institutions came together to celebrate the illustrious history of Manchester. The event was scheduled for March 2009 at the iconic Town Hall building.

The two-day festival orchestrated and planned to occupy several rooms and halls within the Town Hall. Day one (Friday 20 March) had a specific remit to target local school children within Manchester, with the main festival activities taking place all day on Saturday 21 March.

The event had the support of Manchester Metropolitan University, the University of Manchester and Manchester City Council. Furthermore, The Welcome Trust was one of the major financial sponsors for this event. The event also sought further sponsors, who would eventually become part of the evaluation process.

The event was the first of its kind within the city, open to the general public, with a long-term strategy to become an annual or biannual festival. The festival was designed around a number of activities which gave a particular flavour of Manchester history to each target group, including:

1. Lectures (students, general audience).
2. Thematic displays.
3. Displays and exhibits (general audience and family).
4. Performance of drama and music (general audience and children).
5. Archive film and tape recordings (general audience plus 40).
6. 'Ask your question' sessions (general audience).
7. Historical walks (general audience and family).

All the activities that made up the festival from a customer perspective were included within the evaluation strategy. Prior to the event it was crucial to identify how and where respondents could be approached to make certain data could be collected alongside all the activities taking place on Saturday 21 March.

(Continued)

(Continued)

Target audience

The audience profile for this event was multi-faceted and covered various different demographic groups. A comparable distribution of participants between students, general audience and families and school children made up a large part of the audience profile. In a bid to capture all target groups a clear distinction between these was developed in line with the activities throughout the day. Where there were a large number of participants interacting with a particular performance or general exhibits, contact details were sought prior to entering or engaging with an activity. This selection process took into account age, gender and ethnicity. This type of arrangement allowed the team to contact potential responders at a later date without disrupting their overall enjoyment of the festival.

In a bid to support the evaluation strategy, the official website had a page for consumer data collection with a view to becoming part of the evaluation. This was an explicit undertaking through the design of the site prior to, during and post event.

Evaluation strategy

Event evaluation was a significant requirement within the event planning and delivery process. It had a remit to present techniques, ascertain and correlate quantitative and/or qualitative data.

The evaluation paradigm employed a number of methods to acquire the relevant data, with the activities delivered throughout Saturday forming the major part of the evaluation. The Friday evaluation was covered by another team within the organisation who had sufficient knowledge and understanding of the target audience coupled with the activities.

It must be emphasised that the evaluation was not designed around collecting data for an economic impact or environmental study. It was delivered around perception, attitude shift and an understanding of particular artistic and historical interpretations borne out of Manchester's industrial, commercial and artistic history.

Due to the nature of the particular evaluation and the complexity of the event activities, the design required a pre-test and post-test evaluation strategy.

A longitudinal evaluation strategy was adopted to give a complete view from a pre-, during and post-event analysis. Interacting with the customers pre- and post-event also helped to ensure that a significant volume of data could be collated without directly interfering with the respondents' events experience and thereby avoiding the research becoming obtrusive.

The Delphi method was widely used to establish hypotheses about how scenarios/outcomes were likely to develop with intended or eventual outcomes.

In designing the research methodology for the study, it was recognised that the Histories Festival as a particular 'event' with a confined duration, as opposed to a 'season' of opera or ballet, would be an excellent vehicle for employing the long-established Delphi method of evaluation. The Delphi method originated as a post-war movement with the rationale behind the method being to address and overcome the disadvantages of traditional forms of 'consultation by committee', particularly those related to group dynamics. Delphi is primarily used to facilitate the formation of group judgement. It developed in response to problems associated with conventional group opinion assessment techniques, such as focus groups, which can create problems of response bias due to the dominance of powerful opinion-leaders.

To avoid strong-minded respondents dominating the content in a focus group scenario, the study adopted an individual approach to key figures within the event. Each individual was given the opportunity to express their opinion through a structured questionnaire without fear of contaminating the views of others. The Delphi method was conducted in two rounds pre- and post-event. As stated earlier, the evaluation process took a longitudinal approach to capture data to gauge the level of interest, understanding and long-term impact associated with activities connected to the event. It was seen as appropriate, if not essential, to contact respondents at least three months after the event to determine a differential or divergence between early perception and residual impact. The final element of data collection when analysed should feed directly into the future conceptual framework with recommendations for hosting the event again.

As for the major stakeholders, the evaluation strategy looked at a range of attitudinal aspects associated with the brand in order to ascertain whether, and to what degree, the sponsorship of the event could induce attitudinal change in audiences' perception of a brand.

Where the sponsor had key objectives these needed to be measured and the process had to identify and deliver in accordance with the criteria.

An ethical and confidentiality agreement was a crucial part of the strategy for respondents. This was vital to encourage objectivity and participation in the process.

Where a large number of respondents were required as part of the evaluation, a quantitative approach was adopted. This approach was developed in line with the stated aim and objectives. It followed the format of a five-point Likert scale, for example, objective 2, where 1 = not at all, and 5 = extremely well.

The festival set out clear objectives that became a significant part of the event delivery. It also had a requirement to measure the extent to which each objective could be observed, categorised and analysed.

(Continued)

(Continued)

Objectives

1. Bridging the gap plus removing barriers across generations and institutions.
2. Inspire pride in Manchester.
3. Be a celebration.
4. Present Manchester's past, present and future.
5. Highlight the different communities throughout an historical timeframe and how each has changed over time.
6. A mechanism to introduce and bring together communities and institutions.

In the main, the evaluation team consisted of undergraduates from the Events Management course. Overall operational responsibility for each individual to acquire data rested with the Histories Festival organising team and Project Officer.

Through the evaluation process a number of salient issues were presented, therefore, an unbiased and balanced interpretation of information was essential in concluding the final report.

The major stakeholders identified in the event all had individual objectives to achieve through involvement with the Manchester Histories Festival. Any evaluation process therefore needed to encompass these objectives and utilise these as a starting point for developing an applicable evaluation strategy. Prior research has established that longitudinal tests relying on data collected pre-, during and post-event, provide a powerful instrument for assessing behavioural/attitudinal changes in groups of respondents. Due to the quantitative nature of the data collated it facilitates and eases the statistical analysis and comparisons between the individuals and groups identified for this evaluation. Key performance indicators identified in the evaluation process were then fed into future planning and development of the event by providing a crucial benchmark against which to perform. Moreover, decisive opportunities were identified for potential sponsors seeking to associate themselves with this unique festival.

Case study 3: Urban Music Awards

The Urban Music Awards is the premiere R&B, hip-hop, soul and dance music awards ceremony in the world. The Urban Music Awards ceremony had its ninth appearance in 2011, as an annual event which takes place in the USA, France, the Caribbean and Japan with plans to expand to Asia, Dubai and Africa. The Urban Music Awards was born out of the need to build a worldwide awards ceremony to recognise the achievement of urban-based artists, producers, club nights, DJs, radio stations, record labels and artists that are or were previously unrecognised within their country of origin and are a product of the current dance/ R&B, hip-hop, neo soul, jazz, and dance music scene. The event is supported by and in association with British Music Week. British Music Week (BMW) pays homage to the legacy of the UK music industry and is a long-term strategy to promote and safeguard the future of British music.

As one of the premiere entertainment industry events in the United Kingdom, the Urban Music Awards is set to establish itself worldwide and will be the event that the business's top movers and shakers cannot afford to miss.

The Urban Music Awards is the only UK award ceremony to represent 100 per cent British-based urban and underground artists, DJs, musicians, labels and club nights that make up the vibrant underground music scene here in Britain and others who are currently emerging on the urban music scene.

BMW utilize London's most popular music halls and clubs to promote the best British talent. Conferences, seminars and workshops held in venues such as Wembley, Equinox, Hammersmith Palais, 10 Rooms, Rouge, Mean Fiddler, and The Music Rooms will open their doors to the industry and fans for four full days of star entertainment. As a multi-site event with an international profile, this requires a significant amount of planning and logistical operation.

The BMW event has grown considerably from its early introduction to the market in 2001, and had its last showcase event in 2009. British Music Week and the Urban Music Awards combined their resources during that period to promote and highlight urban talent.

The Urban Music Awards has been the showcase for BMW since its creation; its mission is to give recognition to the best of underground dance and urban music and by broadcasting it across the world to enable global appreciation. It aims to reach a diverse worldwide target audience of males and females aged 18–45.

Historically the event had an exclusive 500-person, invitation only, guest list that included a mixture of celebrities, TV stars, sports and entertainment personalities, artists, A&R representatives, artists' managers, film-makers, internet companies, DJ's, booking agents, concert touring companies, distributors, record label presidents, media executives, press, producers and songwriters, etc.

The 2004 Awards were sponsored by Samsung Mobile; other sponsors included Tynant & Alize. Media coverage in 2004 was by ITV, Channel 4, 20 other independent television stations, 53 local radio stations and 42 magazines. In 2005, the event included the launch of the World Online Music Awards, with national coverage by BBC1, newspapers and magazines.

(Continued)

(Continued)

With the digital revolution fully integrated within the consumer market it was only a matter of time before events would realign their objectives to follow consumer trends. The World Online Music Awards is the first of its kind to acknowledge, celebrate and reflect the online revolution, promoting the most popular talent online, independent labels and artists.

Source: www.urbanmusicawards.co/about-uma [accessed 17/04/2016].

FURTHER READING

Greater London Authority (2004) 'Notting Hill Carnival: a strategic review'. Available at: www.london.gov. uk/moderngov/Data/Culture%20Sport%20and%20Tourism%20Committee/20040310/Agenda/5%20 Notting%20Hill%20Carnival%20PDF.pdf [accessed 21/11/2016].

Gursoy, D., Kim, K. and Uysal, M. (2004) 'Perceived impacts of festivals and special events by organizers: an extension and validation', *Tourism Management*, 25: 171–81.

Manchester Histories Festival 2009. Available at: www.manchesterhistoriesfestival.org.uk/.

Watt, D.C. (2001) *Event Management in Leisure and Tourism*. Harlow: Pearson Education.

14

EVENT LOGISTICS

In this chapter you will cover

This chapter introduces the term logistics, and gives a definition of it based on current academic and industry thinking. Using examples and case studies, it explores the relationship between logistics and the event management experience. By using logistics as a business model, we will also be able to demonstrate how it is directly associated with customer satisfaction, and is an integral part of business operations. The chapter will draw upon events across the industry spectrum to create an understanding of the effective application of logistics to achieve efficiency and stabilise cost. Logistics looks at the movement of resources to areas/places where they are required. It is the effective forward and reverse flow and storage of goods and services to meet customer expectations. The chapter will explain these terms, and offer a complete approach to achieving a logistical management framework.

EVENT LOGISTICS

Logistics has a direct historical heritage from a military perspective, which dates back to the Roman Empire. However, this term still has usage and relevance within a modern-day military framework, with the movement of resources and people over large distances and geographical areas. Over time there has been a refinement of the process and adaptation of it within the business world. The process has now influenced the teaching and physical application of event operations management. The notion of logistics may conjure up an image of mega-freight in supertankers travelling to international ports on the far side of the globe. Logistics has come to mean many things but essentially it always comes down to one single quote which defines the process:

> The basic task of a logistics system is to deliver the appropriate supplies, in good condition, in the quantities required, and at the places and time they are needed. (United Nations, 1993: 9 [online])

Event logistics can be considered from a number of areas within the event planning process. The event planning process can include logistical aspects brought in at different stages in the research, development, implementation or delivery of an event. With this in mind a logistical framework is entwined within the event planning process. An organisation should develop logistical requirements for the movement of products, plant/machinery or people to a particular destination/location. This may also require the same identified items to be stored (inventory) or returned to their original place of departure.

In the process of developing a logistical plan it is paramount to bear in mind a number of variables that may have a direct impact on the logistical process. This point will be explained in more detail throughout the chapter. It is impossible to protect the logistical plan from all potential problems or issues born out of unforeseen or completely random circumstances. However, it is possible to manage the logistical plan if sufficient care and attention to detail are implemented consistently throughout, with a review process that allows for continual updating of the plan.

Most organisations will appoint a logistics manager to develop a system, to maintain control of that system, to track progress and to deal with any problems that may arise. The logistics manager must implement a process to obtain information from each relevant department/operational area to allow the development of the plan. Areas such as financial management, marketing and human resources will become a necessary requirement in the management and delivery of the plan.

The logistical plan should never be considered as an independent operational process to the entire event planning process. The interconnected relationship between all areas will determine in a large part the success of the logistical plan.

Within the event management setting it has become essential to implement logistics as a management requirement. This is certainly the case when working on mega events, such as the Olympic Games, or hallmark events, such as the Commonwealth Games. The lessons learned and skills acquired from these events have been well documented within the event management field.

When developing a logistical plan for an event within an organisation, it is essential to differentiate between procurement, purchasing and outsourcing within a supply chain management setting. All these aspects are essential elements within the event management process and will have a direct relationship with the success/failure of the plan. Let's have a look in more detail at each of these three aspects.

Procurement

When an organisation sets out to procure, this process involves obtaining goods or services from one location and moving them to another for the purpose of use at the event. The financial transaction around this process may also include hire purchase or lease agreements. It is essential to remember that this particular activity will be replicated a number of times for different goods or services. In the process, this particular activity will develop into what is commonly known as the 'supply chain'. Where an organisation has a number of companies supplying goods or services to an event over a given period of time, and where each company is connected, this creates a supply chain.

The procurement process has no definite time span; for an event it can be implemented a year or two years in advance. With that in mind, long-term planning is a requirement; it is prudent to negotiate terms well in advance. It is therefore necessary from a financial point of view to establish a method of payment in line with inflation, once the pricing has been agreed between the event management financial controller and the outsourced company. It will become a joint operation to ensure that the goods or services arrive at the event in good time, and also that proper storage is arranged if necessary at the location, so that the goods are ready for their intended use. As indicated earlier, procurement has become a fundamental business requirement for event companies. Therefore it is important to implement systems that ensure the logistical process does not implode on itself because of disconnected levels of internal business communication. The logistics manager must secure from the accounts manager/financial controller the required sum of money to action a process of procurement and payment terms. Service agreements, warranties and insurance, etc., will remain in the domain of the operational manager and within the logistics manager's area of control. Documentation, as mentioned above, if not supplied prior to finalising the procurement deal, may hinder the logistics process. Other departments within the business should also engage with the logistics process. Human resources may be required at various stages within the process of procurement, delivery and use.

Where agency staff are required for setting up a particular product the event company must ensure that the correct levels of staffing have been sourced/requested, and that competent staff are in place to carry out the intended task over a particular staffing period in line with employment and health and safety laws. As the events sector continues to grow, staffing has and will become a bone of contention for many event providers. This is more so when sourcing staff from employment agencies. The availability of trained/competent staff, in particular at peak season, will impact on the event if not considered at a very early stage. Where staff are required to work over a period of more than one day, adequate accommodation should be booked in advance and payment terms for accommodation agreed prior to arrival. This type of forward logistics planning allows the event manager to deliver the event as planned. The human resource issue will have a major impact on any event if not requested and sourced, if required, prior to the roll out of the logistical plan.

Purchasing

Purchasing within logistics has two main areas of concern: items for consumption and resaleable items. The purchasing of goods on behalf of the event relates to the amount of people who may attend the event. This can be calculated by looking at the number of pre-event ticket sales, the capacity of the venue and previous knowledge of similar events. If potential customers are purchasing tickets on arrival, the logistics manager will consult with the marketing team and investigate the strategy for customer awareness. The latter is a less accurate method to calculate purchasing; however, if this is the only method available, a sale or return arrangement for non-perishable goods could be part of the purchasing deal. The operations manager, in association with the logistics manager, could also look at suppliers within the supply chain who are able to provide quick delivery according to fluctuating demand (also known as just-in-time delivery). Demand-based management meets customer needs by changing the staffing requirement throughout various stages of the day and different periods of the event.

The final game for the Cricket World Cup 2007 saw an increase in ticket sales, and a corresponding increase in customers' consumption of perishable goods. It is evidently clear that an increase in staffing procurement is essential to achieve customer satisfaction in this case. The ratio of staff and the number of potential customers for the sale of goods at key demand moments will give a greater return on sales to the organiser and thus customer satisfaction.

Outsourcing

Outsourcing at a logistics level has developed in areas where a deficiency exists within the business/organisation, or where it is cheaper or more efficient to use outside agencies. The International Cricket Council for the West Indies nominated GL Events as their official supplier for temporary structures and all plant and machinery that needed to be erected, decorated and maintained for the period of the event. GL Events is a UK-based company with an international profile in many areas of event management. With specialist knowledge developed over time in delivering corporate hospitality environments through the use of temporary structures, the company has a key market position which helped them to secure a working relationship with the ICC West Indies Cricket World Cup 2007. As part of delivering the event the ICC had to make a number of outsourcing arrangements to meet the project deadline. Each organisation therefore needed to arrange a logistical framework in line with the event planning process.

EXTERNAL AND INTERNAL FACTORS AFFECTING EVENT LOGISTICS

In some areas of the event management field, and in particular outdoor music festivals, logistical issues are based around seasonality factors, competitive pricing for suppliers, high demand across the transportation network, and the need to increase marketing strategies to bring about customer awareness including temporary staff, both qualified and non-qualified.

In the event business, long-term partnership relationships are necessary in order to meet seasonal demand, and so this becomes a strategic function of the event planning process. Contractors are sourced at least a year in advance, or deals can be negotiated on a rolling contractual basis. This allows the main contractor to implement a supply chain if necessary to meet the client's needs. These logistical supply chains are found at many large-scale outdoor events, particularly where one company is over-stretched in the supply of goods or services in high season. The movement of goods and services via the transportation network also becomes an essential logistical issue. Where goods may have been used prior to arrival at the intended site, contractors may be required to undertake an inventory of goods at a designated location before sending them out again. It is important to take a full and complete inventory at the original place of departure. A key representative must be present on behalf of the company to assess the goods before transferring them to another event provider. Time allocated for drivers on the road, maintenance of vehicles to meet industry regulations, and alternative travel routes to ease traffic congestion all become part of the logistics criteria.

Within a highly competitive industry some suppliers operate a fluctuating price strategy in line with demand and seasonality differences. This price is also related to the fixed costs of the business along with replenishing old stock and ongoing maintenance/repairs. Music festivals, by design, function within a high-demand seasonal window. Therefore, higher costs for goods and services become the mainstay of the business relationship. In this type of environment it may be necessary to develop supply partnership arrangements. In the long term this could stabilise costs and achieve continuity throughout.

ON-SITE EVENT LOGISTICS

This section will look at the specific elements that make up event logistics. It will assess the interconnected relationships of each management area for the delivery of a safe and successful outdoor event. Event logistics should be explained as on-the-ground activities in meeting event and customer expectations. In logistical terms, an outdoor facility only differs from a permanent structure in that movement of people, machinery and products are restricted by little else other than weather, space and access. All legal, health and safety requirements must apply in both settings. Restrictions and permitted actions associated with the licence agreement should be followed for both settings.

Communication, emergency planning, fire safety management, crowd management, on-site transportation management, waste management, venue site design, medical facilities/welfare, barriers and fencing are all categories which need to be applied to an outdoor event.

Transportation planning

On the selection of a suitable site for an outdoor event, there are many logistical issues to take into consideration. Site access for all emergency vehicles must be the first priority. If the site is within a residential area consideration should be given to the local community, so that the event does not disrupt local traffic. If necessary, the event provider should apply for a road closure order for roads that are immediately adjacent to the site, with access allowed only for local residents and event traffic. This method needs to be applied and enforced for the pre-set-up, event delivery and de-rig.

The event provider should also look at car parking for customers and staff. Where the event organiser can negotiate deals with public transport suppliers bringing customers to the event, this should be considered in order to reduce carbon emissions, and to reduce car transportation ultimately leading to fewer vehicles on site. National and local bus, rail and coach companies are the preferred option. Car parking on site should be outsourced, if affordable, to an on-site traffic management company. They will have an obligation to liaise with the police, the Highways Agency and the local authority in developing a traffic management system for customers and staff.

Emergency planning

When developing an emergency evacuation plan, the primary importance is the safety of the customers attending the event. The plan should be constructed taking into account all possible scenarios that could have a negative impact on customers. Therefore, adequate evacuation routes must be clearly marked, with stewards/security positioned at those exit points at all times during the event. Those routes must also be kept clear at all times. The emergency evacuation plan will be closely allied with the fire safety management plan, and all site layouts must have fire accessibility around and on the overall site. Remember also that an emergency plan must look at access to the site for all emergency vehicles. An evacuation zone should be located so that customers and staff have a safe place to relocate to.

First aid, welfare and medical provision should have a strategic location on site available on a 24-hour basis. Access to these facilities must take into account emergency vehicle egress and ingress. Customers should also be able to access the facility without too much difficulty. Therefore, all on-the-ground security staff and stewards must have a clear understanding of the exact location.

It is evidently clear that all three emergency services must be given full consideration when developing the logistical movement of people and traffic to and around the site. When applying for a temporary outdoor entertainment licence under the 2003 Licensing Act, the police service must take specific instructions from the event licensee as to the movement of police vehicles on site. The police must also follow vehicle curfews unless they are responding to an emergency situation. This also applies to fire and ambulance services.

Crowd management

Crowd management can be developed from a number of standpoints. Firstly, one should develop crowd management strategies in line with the intended capacity and location. Further development will be consistent with amenities and basic facilities, such as toilets and food concessions. Areas of entertainment which make up the major part of the event must be given serious consideration. Where there is a main stage on site, due attention should be paid to the area immediately in front of the stage, where there should be a considerable viewing area with access for emergency staff and security. Beyond that there must be enough square footage of space for more than 60 per cent of the customers on site. However, this should take into account what other activities are running concurrently with entertainment on the main stage. Therefore, scheduling of activities throughout the site must allow for the movement of large numbers of people from one location to another, without adding to bottlenecks or congestion points. The free flow of people throughout the site will be the test of the scheduled entertainment within the main arena. The location of basic amenities will assist in this process. During the close down of the main arena further announcements should be made by display screens if available, or via strategically placed stewards/security staff who can give customers clear directions to the designated exit point.

On-site transportation

On-site transportation (as opposed to car parking) requires some special measures to avoid potential harm to staff and customers. The first restriction should be an overall speed limit for all vehicles. Where the event runs over more than one day due consideration should be made for the movement of non-essential vehicles at night. If there is a high volume of customers at any given time throughout the event an announcement should be communicated to all personnel who have control over vehicles. A vehicle curfew should be announced and monitored for its duration. Where camping on site is part of the event, specific access should be given to emergency vehicles, with the demarcation of fire lanes throughout the campsite. Each campsite should be identified by large signposts for customers, staff and emergency operatives. Observation towers may also be useful within the campsite; they should have a strategic location to assist in the movement of campers and act as a vantage point for staff and emergency vehicles as they move around the location. To complement this process, fencing around the site and along walkways throughout the campsite will assist in the flow of customers. To ease the movement of traffic and customers throughout the site at night, floodlighting should be placed at all entry and exit points, near food concessions, observation towers and main walkways around the site. If an event has an arena and overnight camping, a clean sweep of the arena is required to remove all customers. At this point the waste management systems can come into operation. All waste vehicles should be allowed into the arena area for the collection of consumable rubbish, and of human waste from sanitation areas. This can only take place once the arena is closed or a section is closed to all customers. The event provider must ensure that all vehicles working at night use hazard warning lights when moving around and keep to the speed limit. All personnel working within that area must also remember to wear high visibility attire at all times.

In managing the movement of all vehicles and personnel associated with each management system around the site, it is best to use a map with grid referencing. Clear communication channels should be in place and an appointed individual charged with the responsibility of delivering communication messages throughout the site. A site map with grid referencing should also be distributed to all emergency services and non-essential services prior to arriving on site.

To assist in the traffic management of vehicles coming to the event site, an accreditation system for all vehicles must be part of the overall management. Vehicles should display at all times a valid vehicle entry pass. Passes should denote areas of access and limited access. If the site is fortunate to have a number of ingress and egress points, these should be earmarked for contractors arriving or leaving the site along with other event traffic. While the event is up and running, specific notification must be made to ensure that designated points of arrival are clearly signposted. Public transport, taxi collection and drop-off points must be kept clear at all times. The effect of the heavy volume of traffic approaching the event should be taken into account, with diversion routes set up on local roads if appropriate. Heavy vehicles have weight restrictions and therefore this must be taken into consideration before procurement and acquisition of goods. In collaboration with the Highways Agency and local police, overhead motorway traffic information boards should warn other road users about the event in advance and while the event is under way. Monitoring of the major road network to the site and around the site is also the domain of the event provider, and this should be done in collaboration with the Highways Agency and police. If traffic accidents occur on the road network and have a significant impact on event traffic, the event provider must have measures in place for communicating information to customers.

Disability access

Disability access, the location of amenities and viewing platforms must also be given sufficient consideration at outdoor events. Where appropriate the location of viewing platforms must take into consideration access for emergency vehicles. Disabled toilets and car parking must also reflect accessibility at all times during the event. Designated staff and on-site vehicles may also be required for transporting disabled and vulnerable adults throughout the event.

TRANSPORTATION LOGISTICS FOR EVENTS

If an organisation is delivering any type of goods there are a number of factors to consider. The first question to ask is, what is the nature of the product that needs distributing? Is it perishable, chemical, expensive, etc.? If your goods are of a chemical nature, there are strict requirements for packaging and labelling the goods, and for the training of drivers. Further advice can be obtained from the Department of Transport Dangerous Goods Office.

There are some items within the logistical framework that may require the service of couriers, hauliers and freight forwarders. A courier service is normally used for small goods. Couriers specialise in speedy and secure delivery nationally and internationally, but will only deliver packages up to a certain weight.

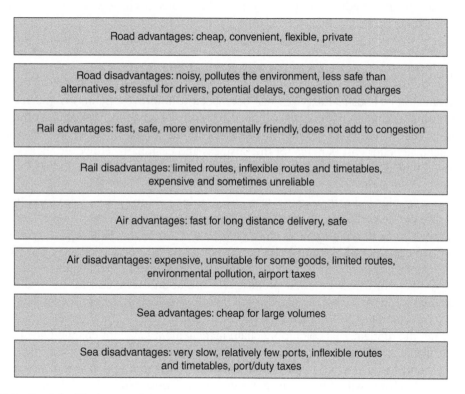

Figure 14.1   Events logistical pros and cons

Hauliers, on the other hand, will collect goods from your premises and deliver them to your chosen destination. This type of arrangement will be done by road and could prove to be expensive if your goods don't fill up the entire vehicle.

Freight forwarders specialise in 'consolidation'. They combine your goods with other consignments in a single container or vehicle, reducing the cost. Due to the nature of their business and international logistical operation, they generally offer related services, e.g.

organising the paperwork for export. They can manage the entire transportation process, tracking goods and providing warehousing and local distribution centres if necessary. For further advice, contact the British International Freight Association (BIFA), who can assist with many of the logistical requirements.

With so many event companies working internationally, an understanding of the available services has become an important part of event logistics. With all these service providers there are ultimately pros and cons for each mode of transportation, depending on distance, destination, volume and type of goods. Figure 14.1 highlights the pros and cons associated with each mode.

Before developing a logistical plan that may require the services of companies that specialise in this sector, sufficient forward planning is essential to develop a mix of services that best meet the requirements of the event profile. As with all event planning processes it is also essential to attach a credible contingency plan that looks at all potential variables including weather-related impacts.

LOGISTICAL CHALLENGES FOR THE FUTURE

The automation of logistical services has been seen to improve operations and reduce costs to the business in most companies where the supply of goods is essential to the business operation. That is not to say that event providers should adopt an expensive automated service to achieve better cost benefits for the business and customers. However, there are aspects that can be highlighted and if appropriate could be deemed a successful addition to meet the challenges of the future.

Many companies today that have a large geographic area to cover set up local distribution centres to meet customer demand. Where appropriate, event providers should actively seek distribution centres or contractors in close proximity to the event. This helps to save travelling time, reduce cost and where perishable goods are required, local produce can be obtained.

Contractors who supply equipment to events can also look at labelling and security tagging of their goods prior to leaving their premises for use at an event, and for their safe return to their original location. A proper inventory is therefore essential at both locations if the company is to meet supply and demand effectively.

Although the fundamentals of supply chain management have not changed greatly over the years, in that it is still based around planning procurement and outsourcing, the scope and control around this aspect of logistics will continue to change and develop. As pointed out earlier, supply chains will continue to grow in length due to demand and at peak season.

An interesting feature of the future is the likely reduction in the use of HGVs, with a corresponding increase in the use of smaller goods vehicles (LGVs). Predictions of transportation congestion, and in particular for urban delivery vehicles, throughout the UK indicate that this is a likely trend.

Other future trends in the industry might include:

- consolidation of transportation, with the polarisation of different supply chain strategies
- better collaboration between event providers and suppliers – where goods and services follow a similar route, cooperation could assist

- procurement delivery to site, as is seen within the construction industry, where construction materials are cut and delivered to order – translating this to the events industry is acceptable in some sectors such as exhibition design and build, and could help to reduce overall cost, human resources and time
- the carbon footprint and possible carbon tax is a challenge – particularly in how to measure it and set the boundaries.

With the Far East becoming a major source for imported goods, traffic at ports will also become congested in the future. Cities outside of London have implemented, and are thinking of implementing, congestion charges for road users. In January 2012 the low emission zone was introduced in London, to reduce PM10 particulates in the atmosphere, which are a direct result from vehicles that consume diesel. The case study below, Green Festival Denmark, provides a model which has been used by Danish festival organisers for managing traffic at festivals and events.

Case study 1: Green Festival Denmark

Denmark is home to a number of well-established outdoor music festivals, one in particular is the Gron Koncert, which translates as the 'Green Festival'. This is the largest touring outdoor music festival in Northern Europe. It dates back to 1983, with an original concept that remains to this day, as a registered charity which raises money for muscular dystrophy.

Logistically this festival travels to eight cities in Denmark over a two-week period. For 2012 the festival ran from 19 to 29 July, concluding the tour in Copenhagen, the capital city of Denmark. Over the years this festival has migrated to a number of cities but remains true to the original concept. Audience figures at each location have fluctuated between 15,000 and 50,000 due to relocating to other outdoor sites. Vejle is a city on the east coast of the peninsula to the west of the country, with a population of 50,000. In 1986 the Green Festival toured to that city and visited again every year until 2002, with an estimated capacity of 15,000 customers each year. In 2003 the festival was cancelled in Vejle because of rain and never returned to that location. The year 2010 saw the highest number for audience figures over the eight locations, with 187,000 people attending. In 2011 the collective audience figure dropped to 135,000; the Green Festival attributed the fall in numbers to bad weather conditions that year. A survey from 2011 of 2,600 festival goers gave the festival a 96 per cent satisfaction rate.

The Green Festival travels to each location where performers play live from 1.30 to 9.30 pm. At the end of each day the festival goes through a complete de-rig and is transported to another location where it goes through a complete rebuild ready for the next day and new set of customers. The distance between Kolding and Randers, the first and second cities on the tour for 2012 is 111 km. The festival then travelled from Randers to Arhus (36 km); from Arhus to Aalborg (101 km); from Aalborg to Esbjerg (198 km); from Esbjerg to Odense

(Continued)

(Continued)

(122 km); from Odense to Naestved (89 km); and the final run from Naestved to Copenhagen was 70 kilometres. Between the eight locations the festival crew, equipment, performers and contractors covered approximately 727 km, which equates to 451 miles.

No other outdoor festival in Northern Europe can claim to have a logistical operation of this nature. This type of logistical arrangement requires substantial planning and contingencies to mitigate any potential road hazard that could inhibit the set schedule. The documenting and inventory of equipment becomes an essential element to maintain operational fluidity between the locations. Equipment stored in boxes will have identification marks or colour coding to ensure they are stored on the correct truck and taken to a specific location at the next site. Secondary equipment, if within the budget, will also be part of the plan along with preferred suppliers at each location if essential equipment is needed at short notice. This event must run similar to a small mechanised army moving from one location to another ready to do battle upon arrival. Each site has a small team of operatives who manage the location before the contractors arrive to set up. As with most major festivals, planning for the Green Festival commences directly after the last performance in the tour date. In 1983 the volunteer force was 40; for 2012 the aim was to have 700 volunteers. The majority of volunteers travel with the festival to each location, collecting more volunteers at other sites as it goes through the tour dates. All volunteers have their food, travel and accommodation taken care of to ensure they are ready to work each day. Accommodation for volunteers is not on the festival site but in local schools at each location.

Volunteers relocate stalls, fences, stages, light and sound equipment from one town to the next overnight. For that purpose the 700 volunteers use a car park for 50 articulated lorries (each of which weighs 15 tons), four vehicles of 5 tons each, 16 buses and several trucks and fork-lift trucks. Volunteers erect the stage and the tents, they sell food and drinks during the concerts, and finally they dismantle all the gear and transport it to the next town on the tour – all this in less than 24 hours. The crew takes down the stage starting at 9.30 pm, just after the music has stopped, and the last truck with equipment leaves the concert site at about 1.30 am.

The crew, which builds the stages in the next town/city, commences work at 4.30 am. They finish building 6 hours later. Cabling for all electricity on the outdoor site amounts to more than 13 km in length.

The title 'Green Festival' is not linked to its sustainable credentials, rather to its main commercial sponsors, Tuborg, who have sponsored the festival from its conception (Figure 14.2). Carlsberg, the owner of the alcohol brand Tuborg, has trademarked any event that promotes the word 'green' in association with an event of any description throughout Denmark. Therefore 'green' is only used as a commercial representation linked to the corporate colour of the brand.

Figure 14.2   The Green Festival, Denmark

SUMMARY

This chapter has highlighted the significant use of logistics within the event management framework. It has shown how the process has been developed into a credible business model. Further development of the process has shown its flexibility in applying the process to on-site event logistics. This process and application has synergy with all types of events and locations. Logistics for event managers is not only a business requirement but has methodologies that apply to pre-event, during the event and close down. Logistics is now a paramount concern when applying for an entertainment licence under the 2003 Licensing Act, where licensees have a duty of care to ensure that customers leaving the event have appropriate access to transportation, without causing harm to themselves or others in the process.

A report was compiled in 2006 by the HSE on Management Standards for Workplace Transport. In this document there are some alarming statistics which relate to transportation injuries and fatalities:

> On average, annually there are around 70 fatalities related to workplace transportation (in 2003/04, 57% were 'struck by a vehicle' and 7% were 'falls from vehicles'). (Health and Safety Executive, 2006a: 1)

These statistics exclude transportation by rail, public highway and water transport.

This has given rise to a whole new conceptual model for managing outdoor events. In this chapter, we have looked at logistics from a wider perspective than just the standard recognisable setting of transportation logistics. The term logistics was presented alongside and partnered with a number of operational management processes, including supply chain management, demand management and inventory management. A case study was presented to show the diverse application of logistics in the overall business of running an event company and event.

We have also seen that fire safety has close links with the emergency evacuation plan, and that all site layouts must have fire accessibility around and on the overall site. The chapter has shown that crowd management can be developed from a number of standpoints, but that crowd management strategies need to be developed in line with the intended capacity and location.

The scheduling of activities was discussed, and the provision of a site plan, which is needed to allow for the movement of a large number of people from one location to another. The location of basic amenities can assist in this process.

Discussion questions

Question 1

Demonstrate your understanding of the business relationship between event logistics and supply chain management. Outline your concept within an event management context.

Question 2

Outline two challenges that will face event organisers in the future when developing their logistical transportation plans.

Question 3

Demonstrate how seasonality issues within the outdoor events sector can have a negative impact on transportation logistics for event providers.

Question 4

Outline and discuss some of the logistical challenges inherent in the 2007 Cricket World Cup in the West Indies.

Question 5

When delivering the Cricket World Cup 2007 in different locations discuss some of the logistical, cultural and human resource issues in acquiring technically competent personnel.

Question 6

Transportation as a logistical operation for spectators attending an event is an aspect that must be addressed by the event planning team. Discuss the type of transportation methods that can be introduced to reduce the impact of traffic on a host community.

Case study 2: Human resources at the 2007 Cricket World Cup in the West Indies

There are many logistical human resource issues in delivering an event of this type on time and to the requirements of the client, event organisers and consumers. This event was held over five islands throughout the West Indies (Figure 14.3). Apart from the overall management team with the core contingent from the five islands, resources for specialist skills in other areas were brought to the event. Security, media and event management, alongside the large contingent of local crew and voluntary workers, were brought together in the pre-event stage to form a sound foundation for the event. Training and adequate management of staff enabled the event to be completed and opened on time. This type of event resourcing would have been undertaken with the assistance of local knowledge by way of employment agencies and previous events held in those islands. This type of forward planning to meet the event schedule for erecting temporary structures primarily for hospitality use was carried out four months in advance.

As outlined earlier, the supply chain is the cornerstone of the logistics process, and in particular where long-term event planning with suppliers is necessary. Therefore, supply chain management, the control process to enable the supply chain to function without too much difficulty, must also be an integral part of logistics. In developing long-term business relationships with suppliers, the current industry trend looks towards supply partnerships. This particular thinking encourages suppliers to have a vested and shared interest with the client's strategic vision for a sustainable working relationship. Within a logistics framework this is an encouraging situation, where the long-term benefits to both parties emerge over time. Procurement deals with third party suppliers will smooth over internal and external

(Continued)

(Continued)

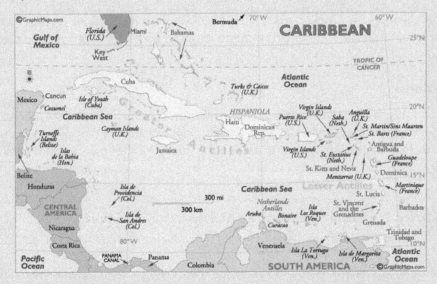

Figure 14.3   Map of the West Indies

Source: www.worldatlas.com used with permission.

factors affecting both organisations. The Confederation of British Industry and the Department of Trade and Industry are working closely to bring about supply partnership as a business philosophy across all industries, large or small.

It was estimated that in excess of US$100 million was invested in construction and infrastructure in Barbados in advance of the Cricket World Cup (CWC).

The country had an expectation of 20,000 visitors during the CWC, and as the event was held during the high season for tourism, the logistical challenge to accommodate all the visitors would ultimately test the Barbados government. Current room stock was estimated at 8,000 rooms, so to alleviate this situation the government of Barbados created a Bed and Breakfast/Home Accommodation Loan Fund. This fund was available to house owners who wished to develop their homes for bed and breakfast accommodation. Saint Lucia was also selected as one of the eight venues to host matches for the CWC 2007. (Initially Saint Lucia submitted a joint bid with Barbados, but eventually the country was able to make a bid on its own.) Within the bid, Saint Lucia made reference to their national stadium for cricket.

The Beausejour Cricket Ground (BCG) is a modern fully serviced cricket stadium, constructed to international standards, with a seating capacity of 12,487 and completed in 2002 at a cost of US$16 million. It will be upgraded to 21,000 seats, 7,878 of which will be covered, for 2007. (The Saint Lucia Bid for Cricket World Cup West Indies – 2007 (2004): 4 [online])

The report also alludes to initiatives to meet the international challenge. To dispel any concern regarding Saint Lucia's ability to have enough staff available and trained to international standards, the government implemented ahead of 2007 an extensive volunteer programme, including special training under a new government initiative.

Transportation within Saint Lucia was developed and documented in the Match Day Transportation Plan (MDTP). A Park and Ride system linked to five dedicated parking areas used 30- and 40-seat shuttle buses to move spectators from one ground to another. Parking at the official cricket ground was designated for VIPs, team vehicles, emergency transportation and shuttle buses.

Case study 3: Lame Horse night club - Russia

In December 2009, a fire at the Lame Horse night club in Russia killed 109 people. Officials from the Urals city of Perm, where the incident took place, investigated why so many people lost their lives. The incident in question has similar characteristics to the Station night club fire in 2003, at West Warwick, Rhode Island, in the USA, when 100 people died when pyrotechnics set off on the stage as part of the performance ignited flammable acoustic foam at the rear of the stage. It was stated that fire engulfed the club in 5 minutes 30 seconds.

Following the incident in Perm, mobile phone footage from the night was broadcast on Russian television, showing a large section of the audience dancing as sparks ignited the ceiling. As with the Station night club, pyrotechnics were set off inside the club hitting the ceiling which was covered in decorative twigs and plastic sheeting. Officials investigating the fire stated:

> Russian authorities say the tinderkeg-dry wooden ceiling, the single narrow exit for a space capable of holding more than 400 people and the indoor use of fireworks, were all strictly against local fire codes and other laws that should have been enforced. (Weir, 2009 [online])

Firefighters who were stationed directly opposite the club arrived on the scene in minutes.

The Lame Horse night club only had one exit point; the Station night club had more than one.

Rules and regulations inherited from the old Soviet Union were reported to have exacerbated the high death rate. Some 18,000 Russians die in fires every year, with safety rules often unenforced and safety precautions ignored. President Dmitri Medvedev ordered new fire alarms to be put into all care homes after the country's previous record disaster, when 67 died in a nursing home blaze in 2007.

(Continued)

(Continued)

Packed night clubs have previously turned into death traps. In 1981, 48 people died when a blaze broke out at the Stardust club in Dublin. The worst ever such disaster happened at the Cocoanut Grove night club, in Boston, in 1942, where 492 people lost their lives and hundreds more were injured.

History can reveal that a significant number of people have died at venues throughout the world due to ineffective monitoring, management, enforcement or regulatory requirements to protect individuals attending places of entertainment. Event managers must therefore take very close account of the legal requirements when deciding to admit members of the public into venues. Management, legislative, design, psychological and enforcement issues should all be taken into consideration when investigating any incidents of this type.

How does one prevent an incident of this type from engulfing a venue again? There are a number of agencies that can assist and enforce legislative requirements from a UK perspective. A cumulative approach to existing legislation and European directives will enable event managers to understand and apply the necessary requirements to minimise the potential fire risk at venues.

Figure 14.4   The Lame Horse night club before the fire

Figure 14.5   Dancers at the Lame Horse night club before the fire

FURTHER READING

The Saint Lucia Bid for Cricket World Cup West Indies – 2007 (2004) 'Media Guide'. Available at: http:// archive.stlucia.gov.lc/gis/nationwide/2004/NationWide21August2004.pdf [accessed 01/03/2016].
United Nations (1993) 'Disaster management training programme'. Available at: http://www.unisdr.org/ files/9866_DisasterRiskReductionintheUnitedNat.pdf [accessed 01/03/2016].

15

EVENT PRODUCTION, DESIGN AND LIGHTING

In this chapter you will cover

The events industry and lighting industry in conjunction with event production have moved forward considerably over the past 10–15 years; this chapter will identify historical and current apparatus along with equipment developed to enhance production and performance within the live event industry and hopefully capture the imagination of the target audience who attend live events throughout the world. The live event industry has incorporated not only sound and lighting equipment to enhance the experience, the industry has seen a significant increase in the use of visual production technology and in particular 3D technology as an application in creating video walls, scenic backdrops and video mapping on the external and internal fabric of buildings. The software and hardware now available within the live event industry has allowed a greater degree of creativity to be deployed across all types of event. Mega events, in particular opening ceremonies attached to the European Football Championship, Rugby Championship, Olympic Games and many more, have seen the introduction of spectacular performances that involve mechanical automation fused with lasers, pyrotechnics, set design and construction, lighting, sound arrays and visual 3D technology encapsulating a live performance from a band or dancers. All this can only be achieved by production managers/event managers who have a good understanding of the different specialisms and production equipment required for the planning, rehearsal and live performance. It therefore means live shows are mapped against computer programs that are sequenced to fall in line with all technical equipment and the live performance. To meet those standards within the live event industry requires individuals who have been trained over many years within an academic/industry setting who can deliver on bespoke technical and industry expectations. This will allow the next generation of live event producers/managers to test their knowledge within a real world environment.

This chapter will cover these areas in terms of legal requirements, contractual responsibilities, regulations, policies and procedures, aligning the discussion to industry standards and best practice. The events industry has seen new regulations as a requirement to meet clear roles and responsibilities and accountability.

We will also look at how event producers select universal equipment when touring internationally. Technical procedures will also be redefined, to allow for changes in regulations. A practical approach to applying lighting at events and venues will be outlined by using current industry practice, underpinned by theoretical understanding. The chapter will also demonstrate the atmospheric and psychological approach to lighting at events to achieve customer satisfaction. Health and safety regulations will be presented along with lighting equipment and technology which can help to achieve management and operational control.

IDENTIFYING EQUIPMENT IN DIFFERENT VENUES

The term 'production' is both a process and a business entity, within the wide spectrum of organised events. In this chapter we will look at production as an outsourced requirement for developing aspects that are generally associated with the finer points of live performance/entertainment. Where static, mechanical or electrical equipment is being used, certified and trained individuals become a requirement. The chapter will provide a minimum working standard and develop a framework that gives event management companies the ability to engage in a business relationship that is mutually beneficial to both parties. The framework is aimed at organisers (who will know what they expect to receive), the production company (who will know what they expect to provide) and associated agencies that are also connected with the production process.

Production within the events industry has many specialist roles and responsibilities. The principal working practices are governed by the Health and Safety at Work Act 1974 and the Management of Health and Safety at Work Regulations 1999, with numerous UK and European regulations attached to this process. Those regulations and legislation have remained as the foundation for event managers and technical freelancers who apply their knowledge within a live performance. Event production and control as a business entity also covers many areas within the event experience and should take into consideration the different types of venues and how they are regulated. Freelancers within the live event management sector have seen a considerable growth year on year. This growth has been recognised by the current government who have set out new requirements for those individuals, such as IR35, part of the Her Majesty Revenue & Customs (HMRC) rules, and a new tax status and inclusion for employers when engaging freelancers.

Firstly, this chapter will outline the different types of events covered by production and identify some of the specific areas within events that are relevant to it. Through this process we will build a clear understanding of the integral role of production as a tool to enhance the quality of the event experience.

In today's global business environment production can be a feature of many events. The corporate sector of event management has remained at the cutting edge of technological advancement through its use of ground-breaking multimedia equipment; especially where a corporate event has a speaker or performer demonstrating a product or a service to an invited audience over a given time span, multimedia is used to engage and focus the attention of the audience and enlarge the physical presence of the presentation. A large video wall, satellite links with live feedback or pre-programme information accompanied by laser, amplified sound and lights can be combined to achieve a memorable and powerful experience. Alternatively, single elements may be selected or further combinations, perhaps including static or mechanical equipment, may be specifically designed to generate a memorable and visual impact.

VENUES FOR LIVE EVENTS

Identifying and selecting the appropriate equipment for a particular event, in association with venue facilities and performers, has become an area that requires training and a degree of knowledge gained through education or industry experience. Venues have been designed and constructed with particular understanding to allow different types of live events to be performed without too much adjustment. To a large degree shows must be designed within the constraints of the venue in which the event will be delivered.

Arenas, which have become a common feature in most cities throughout the UK and Europe, carry similar design features. The O2 Arena in London and New York's Madison Square Garden arena are two of many arenas that have become a common feature of post-industrial cities.

Manchester Arena, opened in 1995, was designed and constructed to host more than one type of live event; this is a standard protocol for all arenas built in or after 1995. Over many years the Manchester Arena has received numerous consecutive awards and is recognised as one of the busiest arenas in the world. Essentially the space can hold about 21,000 people, however, different design configurations will reduce seating. The venue has the ability for articulated trucks to drive on to the arena floor and unload, with a celling rig built into the arena roof that allows visual display walls, sound and light rigs to be suspended from the rig; various types of truss design can be suspended from the rig and lowered and raised on a chain motor. It is possible to walk in the rig but this requires specific health and safety regulations and permits to be in place and adhered to. Other than arenas, one can also find stadiums built primarily for sporting events. The Millennium Stadium in Wales can be considered as a multi-purpose venue, which is also mirrored by the Stade de France stadium in Paris, which has a revenue stream not dependent on football throughout the calendar year. Live events that are commonly scheduled within an indoor arena can be constructed and performed within those stadiums and similar stadiums across the world.

Moving away from stadiums and arenas, event managers and promoters can also consider exhibition and convention venues. Birmingham National Exhibition Centre in the UK is probably the largest and best known venue for live events. Built in the main to host exhibitions and conferences, the venue is widely used by the entertainment arm of the industry to host live events. The exponential economic growth within the events sector within the UK has seen more and more traditional and non-traditional venues used to host live events. Stately homes – of which the UK has many, generally managed by the National Trust – are also used for outdoor festivals and live events normally scheduled for indoor arenas. Venues such as the Birmingham National Exhibition Centre (NEC) are costly to hire and so ticket prices must be high to ensure a sizable profit margin. In the main live music events are scheduled across many venues in different locations, for several reasons: 1) to satisfy the audience in different locations, 2) to increase ticket sales and marketing opportunities for further music sales, 3) to spread the tour over a number of venues to ensure economic success. The Muse live music tour in 2016 was considered one of the most ambitious uses of aerial drones supporting large balloons within an indoor setting. The drones were unmanned and pre-programmed throughout the live event. This production could only be hosted within venues such as an arena or site similar in size. This live music tour went to 11 countries from the 2 to 20 August 2016 and toured to Switzerland twice.

EXHIBITIONS AND PRODUCTION

The exhibition industry has a far-reaching and global appeal with many internationally recognised venues throughout the UK, such as Earls Court, London and Birmingham NEC. Exhibitors are constantly developing ways of competing within a closed environment, on a designated floor space to a trade or consumer audience. Where budgets are sufficient, exhibitors may employ professional production personnel to create an element of excitement and visual presence. There may be logos from the company's corporate colours displayed using lights and gobos (a metal stencil attached to a light fitting that enlarges and illuminates an image over a surface or distance). The exhibition environment may employ moving images projected and displayed strategically on walls surrounding the designated area. Ambient amplified sound may also be used within a semi- or fully enclosed area of the exhibition stand. Exhibition stands are essentially constructed to carry a marketing message so production equipment will usually serve to expand on and amplify the company image. The installation of production equipment at exhibition venues must comply with regulations linked to health and safety in the first instance. As these are venues where all the structures are made of temporary material that could suffer damage when exposed to extreme heat for a long period, all materials must be fire retardant and meet the BSI standard along with the venue safety officer checks that may be carried out on all exhibits prior to allowing customers into the space. The intensity of heat emitted from light fittings within an event production setting can render an environment unsafe if not checked.

COMMERCIAL MUSIC EVENTS AND PRODUCTION

Music events, both in closed venues and outdoors, are among the biggest exponents of light, sound and stage equipment, since these are the core elements that create a powerful, dominating and hopefully memorable atmosphere. There are many possible combinations, generally determined by the budget, performers and creative production team. All of this must be closely monitored in line with fire regulations, health and safety and UK and European regulations. At music events, professional sound engineers have a duty to amplify sound in a way that both meets the artist's/band's requirements while giving the audience audible sound. They are also required to work within the licence agreement on allocated hours for performance and decibel levels. Professional lighting engineers at large outdoor music events can sometimes be working with up to 30–50 individual lighting units arranged on a lighting rig above the stage. Some lighting rigs supported above the stage can be static or mechanically operated. It is the responsibility of the lighting engineer to pre-programme the rig and lights to work in tandem with the music and performance. Technology today allows lighting and sound engineers a greater degree of flexibility in achieving artist and customer satisfaction. Sound and lighting desks at live music performances can be operated manually or can be pre-programmed at source with an option to store the information on a CD, disk or memory stick, thereby enabling pre-programmed information to be transported electronically across international boundaries. Again, we can draw comparisons with many other areas of the events industry and begin to build our knowledge and understanding of the use of production equipment and personnel. In setting up an environment which follows international protocols for live band performance, be that in a stadium, live music arena or outdoor field, the equipment's cost to purchase can run to hundreds of thousands of pounds. A professional sound desk can cost somewhere in the region of £200,000. Therefore adequate insurance liability for production equipment must meet the market cost.

LIVE PUBLIC EVENTS

Events that involve the use of lasers, fireworks, strobe lights and outdoor bonfires are regular features within the UK calendar. When open to the public, these events have additional regulations and guidance for the safe control, use and management of fire. Fireworks must comply with the Fireworks (Safety) Regulations 1997, which have now been updated by the Fireworks Safety (amendment) Regulations 2004, which have principal responsibility for consumer protection. The British Standard 7114 (1989), although not law, is called up in the Fireworks Safety Regulations. Supplementary guidance is provided in the British Pyrotechnists Association (BPA) and Explosive Industry Group (EIG) Fireworks Handbook 2000/01. The enforcement of fireworks law rests with the Health and Safety Executive (or their agents), the Department of Trade and Industry and local authority trading standards. Firework operators at public events must work with the local authority to establish safe storage, a safe fall-out area for projectiles and the amount of explosive intended for use at the event. Certification for personnel handling fireworks should be forwarded to the local authority by the event organiser or contracted agent setting up the firework display. Laser operators who are not fully conversant with their equipment should obtain guidance from the Entertainment Laser Association. Laser operators under the HSE have a duty of care to the public who are exposed to lasers, be they customers or operators. This is also the case for strobe lights, which can induce fits in people with epilepsy. Clear information must therefore be included in pre-event publicity and before entering venues/sites. Information should also be displayed throughout the venue and announced through the use of an amplified sound system if one is available. Such procedures enable the event manager to operate with due diligence under the Health and Safety Act and create a safe environment for employees and customers. With production equipment that has the potential to cause harm or injury to customers or employees, event managers have a responsibility to limit, reduce or remove risk of injury or harm. This can be done through information, public announcements or limiting exposure over a given time span.

ROLE OF THE PRODUCTION COMPANY

So far this chapter has introduced events of different sizes, audience profile, location and content. What is constant and apparent is the use of production personnel and equipment.

Production equipment may include mechanically operated machinery designed for its purpose and assembled on-site; or an integration of special effects such as lasers, fireworks and strobe lights. Multimedia technology is used to enhance customer enjoyment by creating a memorable experience. This is also the case at large-scale music events where amplified sound and light become the driving force behind presenting and promoting a live stage performance.

To gain a greater understanding of the production process and the procedures that support the successful integration of these elements within the event management experience, we must first illustrate the working principles of a production house and personnel. A production company located within the events industry generally operates as a specific and specialist supplier of equipment and trained/qualified personnel. On the whole, event management companies outsource to production companies when required. The working relationship between the event management company and the production company will be critical to achieving a successful outcome.

Production company safety and legal requirements

A reputable production company prides itself in the first instance on key personnel who are able to translate ideas into a working solution on time and within budget. It must also maintain high standards which must be demonstrated through inspections and the production of certification documents. These companies may be affiliated to a UK association recognised by the industry as acceptable. They will also have trained and qualified personnel (if required) who are responsible for the maintenance and use of a particular type of equipment. Depending on the exact nature of the work undertaken by these companies, it may be necessary for them to show permits and certification before work can proceed. The production company, in agreement with the organiser, local authority and suppliers if required, will assess the type of activity and assign a particular type of equipment and personnel to complete a task.

It is the responsibility of an organiser to request, if not presented with, certification and permits for activities/equipment that are to be used both at the pre-build stage or during the event itself. It is necessary to obtain this information as the event insurance liability cover may be invalid if work is carried out without clear supervision, certification or a permit if required. Insurance therefore becomes a significant issue for all production companies and event organisers should request a copy of the insurance cover from the production company before any work commences. Insurance liability cover for equipment and personnel will fluctuate from company to company. Mechanical machinery and flammable substances that are used either to generate power or to install and erect both off-the-shelf and specifically designed equipment should have a premium cover that is commensurate with the type of activity. Individuals who carry out a particular task on behalf of the production company, whether freelance or employed directly by it, may also require significant employee insurance liability cover and a permit to work if the activity or task has been assessed as potentially hazardous to health. This is sometimes the case for people who work at heights. If an event is held within a venue which has the structure to allow working at height, the venue manager should insist that employees wear a harness when working above head height. Again, if this procedure is not adhered to the venue insurance cover could be invalidated, along with the insurance cover held by the production company, including the venue licence, in some cities and venues in the UK.

Within the production company there are a number of operational procedures that require validation and support.

A health and safety policy/statement, risk assessment and method statement are fundamental operational procedures for production companies. If they are to fall in line with the Health and Safety at Work Act and the numerous UK and European regulations while also safeguarding their insurance liability, adherence to these procedures must become the common working practice.

Production company planning of supervision

An order to commence work on a site/venue can resemble a logistical and military operation. The production manager will draw up a checklist and site supervision order. It is the responsibility of the production manager to appoint roles and responsibilities for all personnel and any sub-contractors. The production manager will set up a method for communicating with all production personnel and appointed sub-contractors and will compile an emergency procedure plan if one is not already available. This document must be verbally announced and/or given to all personnel before they commence work. The emergency procedure should conform to the health and safety policy.

The production manager may be required to set up an office on the site/venue if one is not already available. The office is where all documentation and agreements pertaining to the production set-up should be held. If any inspecting organisation, agent or authority (fire officer, local authority operative, etc.) makes an appearance on the site/venue, information should be made available to them. If an inspection is carried out by any expert advisers, agencies or departments from the local authority, a copy of the documentation relating to the inspection should be held with the production manager on site. If erecting a temporary structure outdoors for a commercial or public event under licence, it is advisable for a fire officer to inspect the structure before allowing public admittance. A fire certificate will be presented to the production manager stating the fire regulations for that structure and its readiness for use. Some temporary structures may require a qualified structural engineer to inspect and sign them off before allowing further work to commence within the structure.

It may also be a requirement to have a qualified professional to inspect an area or structure before allowing any personnel to carry out work. This is likely to be the case where a stage/platform or temporary tented structure has been erected. The risk transfer and liability will rest with the professional upon completing an inspection and signing documentation (to show that the site/venue is fit for purpose).

The production manager should also appoint a site supervisor if the type of event requires a considerable number of sub-contractors, personnel and equipment over a lengthy time period. This division of labour allows the site supervisor to deal with site deliveries, construction requirements and on-the-ground health and safety issues. This may include monitoring the working procedures of each contractor on site. Large-scale events like outdoor festivals catering for 40,000–80,000 people will require all of the above production personnel with the possible addition of an appointed health and safety officer. This type of arrangement is common at large-scale air displays (e.g. Farnborough Air Show) where a safety officer is appointed by the event organiser to monitor all contractors on site.

If the production site/venue requires mechanical handling equipment, there is a legal responsibility for each production manager to ensure that contractors provide adequate and proper training in the use of cranes and lifting appliances in accordance with the manufacturer's test certificate and the load test certificate. All this information should be made available for inspection on request.

Security at a production site must be considered a necessity, especially if working outdoors. It is the responsibility of the event organiser to appoint an accredited security firm to monitor security on site. Accredited security guards should wear distinctive markings or uniforms in line with the Private Security Industry Act 2001. Further guidance for the events industry can be obtained from the Security Industry Authority website (www.sia.homeoffice.gov.uk/Pages/home.aspx).

Final handover

A final checklist should be used by the production manager to bring any outstanding issues to the attention of the event organiser, inspecting officer or associated agencies. This part of the production process can act as an official handover once the checklist is completed and the organiser and authorities are satisfied. The official sign-off for the production can then take place and full responsibility for the event reverts back to the organiser.

Production managers have a great deal of documentation to process prior to and during an event. The Event Safety Guide for Pop Concerts and Similar Events (known as *The Purple Guide*) endorsed by the Health and Safety Executive has been designed in part with this process in mind.

ASSOCIATED AGENCIES AND ORGANISATIONS

So far in this chapter we have touched briefly on the relationship of production with associated agencies. There are a number of regulatory agencies and organisations that have an integral part to play within the production process. We will now consider how legislation and information governance sit within the production process and help production managers in delivering an exciting and memorable element to an event.

When developing a production process that has a direct relationship to an entertainment licence (under the 2003 Licensing Act) of some description, a production manager must take considered or specific instructions from that licensing authority. Where an event has a public audience, the onus will be placed on the organiser and production manager to demonstrate that elements of the event that have a risk attached have been investigated adequately and constructed to fit the intended use, without causing harm, injury or disturbance to the audience, workforce or resident community.

A number of stipulations regarding the use of equipment prior to and during the event may thus be inserted into the licence agreement. For example, a road closure order may be required where large vehicles are supporting the set-up process for the event, delivering equipment, and the event is located in a residential or business area that has a high throughput of traffic. Such an order can be obtained from the local police station in advance of the vehicles arriving. The licence agreement may also indicate that machinery that might disturb local residents can only be operated within agreed times. Where an event (be it indoors or outdoors) has amplified music that might cause a disturbance to the local residents, a decibel level could be set in place by the local authority or venue. Checks are sometimes carried out by the licensing authority to ensure that the event does not break any of the conditions set. As an event manager, it is vital that any such conditions are brought to the attention of the production manager and sound engineer.

The testing of sound equipment will be allowed only within permitted hours as in the agreement. Any public entertainment licence obtained from a local authority will have a number of conditions set, which may either be statutory or specific to the location/venue and community. Breaching these conditions may risk the licence being revoked or a fine levied against the organiser. Once the local authority licensing department has granted a licence, the organiser must appoint a licensee approved by the local authority to take full responsibility for the licence.

In addition to the local authority, another key associated agency is the fire service, clearly having a principal responsibility for fire safety. They have the authority to have full access to the venue/site at all times. An appointed officer from the local fire service will be given the authority to check that any electrical equipment, material or environment, temporary or otherwise, meets with fire regulations. They will check that appropriate firefighting equipment is within the venue and in good working order, with clear signs in line with European law. They will also check if any flammable substances are being used at the event and that they are stored and managed as prescribed by regulations.

SOUND AND LIGHTING REQUIREMENTS

Apart from the documentation and legislation accompanying the area of production we also have sound and light. These two particular aspects to the event experience have become a fundamental element in creating a memorable and lasting impact. This section will highlight the benefits of sound and light equipment, and specification and implementation within the production process.

Alongside this it is essential to organise a set-up procedure for sound and lights. This will involve a full list of equipment and personnel, with a production schedule that demonstrates the full implementation process of all equipment to a designated location. This information is crucial as most production managers are working to a finite deadline. Within the production schedule it is also necessary to include rehearsal time for performers.

Sound

When working with amplified sound it is essential to assess the type of venue in relation to overall floor size, internal material finishes, audience capacity, venue proximity to other buildings or adjacent rooms, type of performance and the number of people performing. Apart from the areas mentioned above there may be other areas that could impact on the type of sound system that is required for use within a chosen venue. There may be a restriction on decibel level set by the local authority, particularly if the venue is located in a residential area. Other restrictions may cover aspects such as hours within the day or night that amplified music can be played or the type of performance allowed within any particular venue. To accompany this there are also the HSE Control of Noise at Work Regulations 2005. These regulations do not apply to members of the general public who make an informed choice to enter noisy places, rather they apply to employees who work in a noisy environment.

Under these regulations, employers must undertake a risk assessment, provide hearing protection, look at ways to reduce noise levels, limit the time spent in a noisy area, check that suppliers are aware of their duties and keep records of the decision process to help show that they have met their legal duties.

Within the production process it is essential to delegate to and communicate with a qualified sound engineer, where sound equipment will be brought into a venue to meet the performance and audience requirements. A sound engineer can determine the type of equipment to achieve the set outcomes. Amplified sound operates within a frequency range of high to low frequency. A qualified sound engineer can set the frequency range as required for the performance or venue. As sound propagation can be a very personal experience, it is essential to monitor sound levels throughout the venue and in particular when full audience capacity has been obtained. This can be done by the sound engineer or any member of the event team. The golden rule is, if you can't hear it there is a good possibility that your audience is having the same difficulty.

Therefore, when selecting a sound system it is essential to have a clear idea of the type of performance you are planning. In creating the right type of audible sound, various speaker systems and arrangement of those systems will go far in setting quality sound and atmosphere. The most common type of speaker arrangement is to house them in cabinets; these are designed for all types of sounds. This method is commonly used in home hifi systems. Each cabinet could have a three-band arrangement including low band, mid band and high band; this will be the frequency range emanating from the speaker cabinet. Or all three bands could be separated within individual speaker cabinets.

Figure 15.1   Millennium Square Leeds, sound and lighting equipment, high powered lasers

Figure 15.2   Virgin Festival 2002, main stage speakers

When operating within a closed environment such as a school hall or medium-sized music venue with a capacity of approximately 1,000, with the entertainment positioned at one end of the venue on a stage/platform, speakers should be placed where they can provide a good distribution of sound across the venue. If speakers are placed on a platform/stage or suspended from the ceiling, better distribution of sound will be achieved within the venue. Speakers suspended above head height, positioned to direct sound into the audience, are commonly applied to larger venues such as arenas, sports stadiums and outdoor live music festivals, where sound must travel over a greater distance and maintain its frequency range along with clarity of sound (Figures 15.1 and 15.2). All this should be achieved by a competent sound engineer.

Delay speakers, as the name suggests, allow music to be heard at a greater distance from the stage with the same frequency range and clarity. As sound travels over a greater distance it can be interrupted and become unintelligible. Again these can be of use in larger venues such as arenas, sports stadiums, concert venues and outdoor live music festivals.

To achieve consistency with the music coming from the stage speakers, delay speakers are set with a minimum delay to coincide with the performance on stage. Any member of the audience standing in the locality of the delay speakers should hear an audible and clear sound. The average speed of sound is 340 metres per second. This depends on wind speed, humidity and air temperature. The equation for setting delay time is the distance in metres from the stage divided by 340 and multiplied by 1,000, which equals the time in milliseconds. From the information presented thus far it should become clear why a competent sound engineer is required when selecting and setting up sound systems. So far, we have only just touched upon some of the elements associated with sound systems. Apart from a sound engineer it is essential to have a qualified electrical engineer available at all times. This individual, apart from ensuring the power distribution is commensurate with venue supply, must also give their signature as part of the final handover process. Once the set-up/installation has been achieved to meet the legal standards of health and safety and fire risk assessment, handover to the event manager is the final stage.

For live music performances with individuals performing with musical instruments, it is essential to work with a sound engineer if the final outcome is to achieve quality sound. This individual will have control over what is called a 'sound desk', which allows music to be mixed and distributed appropriately through the speakers within the venue. The sound engineer (generally positioned some distance back, facing the stage) can also mix the music for the performers on the stage. This process enables the band to have an indication of the quality of sound produced, to check if they are playing in time with each other, or to hear only themselves or another member of the band if they wish. To achieve this, each performer on stage must have their own independent mix, via a microphone which in turn is linked back to the sound engineer at the sound desk/front of house desk.

To achieve sound quality that is commensurate with the status of the performers, sound equipment on stage mixes the sound that is produced by the performers (Figure 15.3). Once this has been achieved it is distributed automatically to the front of house sound desk where it is then channelled to the speakers for the audience. The sound desk on stage is called a monitor desk. The monitor operator can mix the sound for all performers on stage. It can be channelled to each performer via a wedge monitor speaker (Figure 15.4) which is located in front of each performer.

Figure 15.3   Millennium Square Leeds, sound equipment on stage with effects rack

Figure 15.4   Millennium Square Leeds, sound equipment – five wedge monitor speakers for each performer

Within the collection of sound equipment, to achieve quality sound, a sound engineer must also work with power amplifiers, graphic equalisers and an arrangement of effect racks enabling him or her to stabilise and deliver quality and audible sound. The effects rack, along with the power amplifiers, has a similar heritage to a quality home hifi system. A stacked home entertainment system comes with an independent amplifier and graphic equaliser. However, the amount of equipment and cables required to set up a quality sound system at an event can fill up an entire truck. Therefore a crew should be made available to unload equipment at the designated location.

Lighting

As touched upon earlier, sound equipment can help to create a memorable experience. To enhance that experience sound engineers also work in partnership with lighting engineers. This joint partnership is also carried forward with the performers who communicate to a large extent the type of lighting arrangement that is required.

A lighting designer, just like a sound engineer, can undertake a number of courses in developing their skills. But on-the-job training is the true test of any lighting designer.

Lighting designers are commonly working within a digital setting; the analogue approach is increasingly becoming obsolete within the sector. Therefore, to design a light show requires an understanding of lighting software and particular visualisation programs such as Green

Hippo, Wysiwyg and Blacktrax along with the hardware to plot and interpret how the show could look before sourcing equipment and installations. Lighting designers have an industry norm for working with digital light desks that can be manually operated or pre-programmed throughout the show. Companies such as Clay Paky, a lighting manufacturer, have been in the market for 40 years and Martin, a Danish lighting company, has a history that dates back to the late 1970s. Martin's major achievement is supporting the Beijing 2008 opening ceremony for the Olympic Games with over 1,000 lights, the largest supplier of luminaires at the opening ceremony. Clay Paky and Martin are two of the most widely used lighting suppliers across the world. Over the past 20 years a new company has arrived innovating on some standard lighting equipment and gaining a significant market share. Robe Lighting design and manufacture all their lights from a large facility in the Czech Republic. In 2003 Robe Lighting opened offices in America, Italy and the UK. This company has introduced and upgraded some of the standard lighting equipment currently on the market with innovative manufacturing techniques to prolong and enhance the durability of the light fittings that now have to work in conditions that go from extreme heat and humidity to extreme cold temperatures. In the world of moving lights which are common across all lighting manufacturers, Robe has introduced the BMFL (Bright Multi-Functional Luminaire), which comes with four fast shutter blades with an electronic motor stabiliser, allowing the light to move and stop faster, as seen in the floor mounted lights in Figure 15.5.

The family of lights from the Parcan range have been around for many decades (Figure 15.6).

Figure 15.5 Situated on the plinth, the 1,000 LED beam and the largest in the range, the BMFL Blade. All lights can be operated via wireless control.

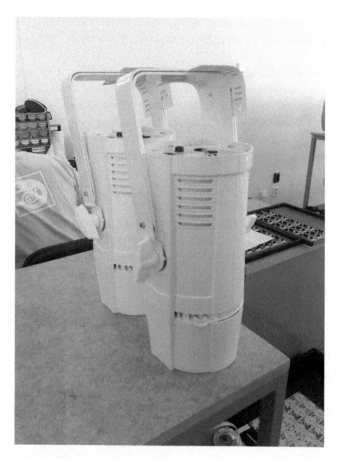

Figure 15.6 The ParFact 100 lightweight moulded composite unit

In today's environment the majority of lighting desks are pre-programmable. This allows the lighting designer to work from a lighting arrangement stored on a disk. It also allows the lighting engineer to have a degree of flexibility with each performance on stage. In association with that process there may be a requirement to interpret a lighting plot. A lighting plot will enable a lighting designer to have a clear idea of the amount of trusses needed, and the cabling required for patching into the dimmer rack.

There are common features that have been translated into the events and entertainment industry from the theatre sector. For example, chalk positions on stage will help the follow spot operators to pinpoint performers effectively, and aids the positioning of performers and stage equipment. Equipment brought in from a truck can also be colour coded according to its eventual location on stage: stage left and right or front of house.

Lighting arrangements on stage come in two basic formats, fixed and moving lights. In addition there is also special effect lighting, such as strobe lights and lasers. Moving lights (Figure 15.7)

can be controlled via the lighting desk as designed by the manufacturer. Fixed lights can also be controlled by the lighting desk adjusting the intensity of the light, which is sometimes covered with a colour filter.

The distance to which each lamp can illuminate an object or area without losing intensity is governed by the inverse square law. If the distance between each light/lamp is doubled, the light intensity is reduced to one fourth the original. Even though you may achieve a greater spread of light over a surface, the optimal range from that light will diminish as the distance increases. Therefore it is necessary to know the optimal working range for each light fitting.

Lighting on stage can have an adverse effect on performers, as the intensity of light is far greater than what is used within the general home or working environment. The average bulb, or lamp as it is called within the trade, could be 1,000W. There is no particular legislation or regulation that determines how many light fittings can be positioned on stage, neither is there any regulation covering the amount of light emitted from each bulb.

Each performance determines the lighting arrangement. There are many different types of light fittings, and the most popular light fitting used across all types of performances, venues and events is the PAR can (parabolic aluminised reflector). They come in a range of sizes with the largest labelled as PAR 64 (the number indicates the diameter of the lamp in eighths of an inch). Working as a lighting engineer requires a good degree of creativity in selection, arrangement and interpretation of the performance to the audience. When setting up a lighting arrangement, venues may have the facility to hang lights from a roof structure. This structure is generally called a lighting truss; it may be fixed to the ceiling or have the capability to be lowered to floor level. The lowering of the truss allows easy access for connecting the light fitting to the structure.

Figure 15.7   Taking Liberties. Vodka fields outdoor event, Bramham Park, Leeds, 2001

Production personnel attach chain supports to a triangular truss before lifting it above the stage. Prior to the truss being fully raised the PAR 64 in a bank of six with colour filters will be attached to the truss. Before lifting commences all lamp connections will be checked. The truss will be checked for tightness and safety. Once the truss has been lifted into position it must be checked that it is level otherwise undue stress on the structure can cause it to fail.

When it comes to connecting light fittings to a structure one should have a rigger who has their own insurance and permit to undertake a job of work.

An outdoor music event that runs into the late evening must look at installing independent general lighting at strategic areas throughout the site. Portable lighting units (as seen in Figure 15.8) are powered independently by an internal generator.

Figure 15.8 Ear to the Ground outdoor live music event (Dpercussion), Castlefield Arena, Manchester, 2006, portable lighting units

As sound and lighting equipment has a tendency to consume a large amount of power, it is essential when selecting a venue to ensure that independent power units are available to run sound and lighting equipment separately. The amount of power for a lighting system depends upon the number of lamps and their wattage. The power for a sound system is calculated from the amplifiers driving the speakers. If too much power is drawn from a venue the result is a blown fuse or blackout. To operate a sound and lighting system for a live music concert in a stadium or arena-type venue three-phase and single-phase independent power units are required.

Apart from having lights fixed to the stage via a lighting rig or trusses, some performers may request a spotlight, commonly known as a follow spot, with an operator who ensures that the light follows the performer on stage as and when the cues dictate. A follow spot is a very powerful light unit and should only be operated by a trained individual. Part of the process of lighting is the amount of cables needed. Cables that are used for lighting at events should never be left tightly wound. The cables have the potential to create an enormous amount of energy/heat and thus can burn the cable's outer casing. Cables should never have restrictions on their route, be strung up above fire exit doorways or run through a duct. The electrical connection process should be made in this order: lamps, dimmer rack, power, with the lighting desk connected to the dimmer rack. The dimmer rack's main purpose is to vary the amount of electricity sent to a lamp, thus controlling the brightness. This process is no different to a common dimmer on a house light. Theoretically, a dimmer does not switch off, therefore keeping efficiency and heat low. To conclude, the operational process requires a level of communication between lighting personnel. The front of house lighting operator will need to communicate with operatives on the stage or riggers attached to the truss. An intercom system not only allows the team to set the lights as required, it also enables continuous communication throughout the performance.

REGULATIONS, LEGISLATION AND STANDARD DOCUMENTS EXPLAINED

As stated earlier in this chapter, the Health and Safety at Work Act 1974 is the overarching legislation, and therefore covers all areas of production within the UK. Many regulations come directly from Europe but not all are embedded into UK law. Compliance by employers and employees is sometimes questionable across various industries. It requires robust monitoring and evaluation from the Health and Safety Executive (HSE) and its regional offices, trade unions and their representatives, to ensure that employers and employees understand and implement regulations throughout. With appropriate reporting of incidents to their regional office, the local authorities can work directly with the HSE and employees to raise working standards.

UK and European regulations have a major impact on production equipment and personnel. Let's have a closer look at these two specific areas. Prior to the European Parliament announcing new regulations for all new member states, it was the domain of the UK government to update working practices by way of regulations. The Work at Height Regulations started life as a UK regulation; it consolidated European Council Directive 2001 and replaced all previous regulations. The Health and Safety Executive has reported that in 2003–4 there were 67 fatal accidents and 4,000 major injuries in the UK workplace. This particular regulation was brought about to prevent deaths and injuries caused each year from working at heights. The implementation of this regulation is crucial within the event production field. Working at height can relate to anyone up a step ladder, suspended from a fixed roof truss, climbing a scaffold structure or operating an extendable mechanical cherry picker – these are just some of the areas associated with this regulation. Within event production, be it exhibitions, conferences or outdoor live music events, there will generally be some aspect of working at height. As stated earlier some venues throughout England do not allow working at height unless a permit has been applied for to the local authority, and the person also has adequate personal insurance including a recent risk assessment. If an individual is employed directly by an organisation or event production company, it becomes the responsibility of that company to ensure that all documentation is completed to support that particular task. The 2005 regulation sets out employers' responsibilities relating to the type of activities undertaken. The general responsibilities as stated in the Work at Height Regulations 2005 are:

> Avoid work at height where they can; use work equipment or other measures to prevent falls where they cannot avoid working at height; and where they cannot eliminate the risk of a fall, use work equipment or other measures to minimise the distance and consequences of a fall, should one occur. (Work at Height Regulations 2005: 3 [online])

It must also be noted that working at height remains a high risk activity, therefore the area underneath where a person is working (known as a sterile area) must be designated a hazardous zone by the health and safety officer or appointed production manager.

As indicated earlier there are numerous regulations covering this area. The Health and Safety Executive website gives a full catalogue of regulations applicable to various types of industries and working conditions.

The 'Six Pack' regulations, introduced in 1993, are aimed primarily at management within the Health and Safety at Work Act 1974. Figure 15.9 outlines six regulations that need to be followed.

When working within the field of production it is essential that whoever has operational/ health and safety responsibilities must understand and implement where necessary the regulations listed in Figure 15.9.

It is very common that regulations 1, 2, 4, 5 and 6 on the list will have universal application to most sites/venues where production equipment and personnel are required to undertake a degree of physical work.

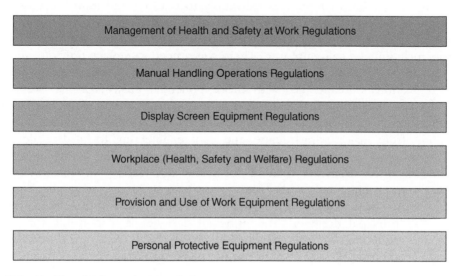

Management of Health and Safety at Work Regulations

Manual Handling Operations Regulations

Display Screen Equipment Regulations

Workplace (Health, Safety and Welfare) Regulations

Provision and Use of Work Equipment Regulations

Personal Protective Equipment Regulations

Figure 15.9   Health and Safety at Work Regulations

Occupational health has become a major and significant area of concern for all industries, including the production industry. The Health and Safety Executive report from 2004, titled *Thirty Years On*, looked forward to the development and future of the health and safety systems in Britain.

One of the trends that has been increasingly evident in our work is the growing emphasis on occupational health matters. (Health and Safety Executive, 2004: 6 [online])

Occupational health assessors are becoming common in many industries and in particular the public sector, with companies assessing the health of new or existing employees before allowing them to undertake a particular task. Such assessments must also become standard practice for production companies, as cases may be subject to industrial tribunals or legal proceedings if companies are found negligent or non-compliant with assessing the health risk associated with employees at work. Therefore, when developing a health and safety policy, occupational health assessments must take centre stage.

PRODUCTION PROCEDURE FOR THE ERECTION OF TEMPORARY STRUCTURES

There are specific roles and responsibilities for an event manager in erecting and maintaining an indoor or outdoor festival/event. In 2015 new legislation was introduced which is now part of UK law: the Construction Design and Management (CDM) Regulation, specific to the events and entertainment industry with a main focus on managing health and safety when constructing infrastructure. This can apply to outdoor and indoor events but will have greater usage for outdoor festivals. The 2015 regulation replaced the CDM 2007 regulation and will be of interest to designers, principal contractors, contractors and sub-contractors including the self-employed. There was a need to replace previous and similar regulations, because the working public was unsure as to their responsibility and found previous regulations bureaucratic. With the exponential growth of the events sector over the past ten years and in particular of outdoor events, it was time the regulation took into account construction on a temporary basis. The 2007 regulation covered all types of constructions, from major infrastructure and civil engineering to small scale work at domestic premises. Part 4 and Schedule 2 of the 2007 regulation remain, which set out the specific technical requirements relating to health and safety on construction sites. Discharging responsibility before the pre-construction stage rests with the business in charge of the pre-construction and the named individual who will have responsibility is known as the 'principal designer'. The principal designer is responsible for planning, managing and monitoring the pre-construction phase of a project in the same way that the principal contractor (PC) is responsible for planning, managing and monitoring the construction phase.

The principal designer is responsible for:

- planning, managing and monitoring the pre-construction phase
- ensuring that where reasonably practicable, risks are eliminated or controlled through design work
- passing information on to the principal contractor
- ensuring co-operation and co-ordination; ensuring designers comply with their duties
- assisting the client in preparing the pre-construction information; and preparing the health and safety file.

The HSE continues to give advice and guidance on all legislation and regulations including new regulations that could ultimately have cross over and potential impact on aspects within the live events industry. Therefore it is essential to register with that organisation to receive information and keep up-to-date.

When implementing a management procedure within the area of production related to a specific task, it is essential to outline the human resources required to carry out the task. This should include all technical, qualified and non-technical individuals. It is also a requirement to ascertain which regulations will relate to a particular working practice or situation.

Any working environment or situation has an overarching legal requirement, the Health and Safety at Work Act 1974. This act governs the working practice and situations common in all working environments under UK law. To accompany the 1974 regulations there are the Management of Health and Safety Regulations 1999.

Establish which company you intend to hire your stage from, then ascertain if the stage will come with competent individuals who are qualified in the erection of the structure. If the stage will be erected by personnel under your control, it is essential that the structure when delivered should be accompanied with an outline method statement.

For erecting an outdoor stage, you will require a technical/qualified team, including:

- a qualified site surveyor
- a trained and licensed forklift operator
- a competent supervisor
- a trained and competent workforce with appropriate working attire under health and safety regulations
- a qualified and licensed structural engineer
- a trained and licensed rigger with personal insurance indemnity.

Legal regulations applicable to this situation include:

- The Health and Safety at Work Act 1974
- The Management of Health and Safety at Work Regulations 1999
- The Lifting Plant and Equipment Regulations
- The Manual Handling Operations Regulations 1992
- The Event Safety Guide, Health and Safety Executive 1999.

When choosing an area on the site to erect an outdoor stage, you will need to check the following:

- Does the ground need draining?
- Does it have sufficient load-bearing capacity?
- Do you require a qualified surveyor to level the ground before erecting the stage?
- Does the area within which the stage will be erected infringe or cause danger to surrounding vegetation?
- Can adequate access be maintained at all times for emergency vehicles and at a good distance from nearby buildings?

If your event is regulated by an occasional entertainment licence, the conditions within the licence will indicate the checks and procedures that your licensee must undertake to manage the event effectively.

Under the authority of a competent production manager/supervisor the build sequence can commence. Mark out the area where the stage will be erected; if on grass you can do this with string and tent pegs. Place the base level so that it is levelled and squared. This can be undertaken with a qualified surveyor and competent workforce. If a method statement is available all directions relating to the structure should be followed to the letter. Any further inquiries should be directed to the supplier. Any recent test certificates should be requested and supplied with the structure; this information is required if requested by the fire officer or any member of the local authority. A 'no unauthorised access' area should be maintained around the build process.

Any machinery employed in the build process of the stage should be accompanied by a trained and licensed individual or competent person. All documentation related to that machinery and individual must also be filed at the site office.

If riggers are employed in the erection of the stage, a designated area below their working environment must be labelled as a 'no unauthorised access' area until work has been completed. The rigger undertaking the job of work must at all times wear a full body harness. Riggers can take the National Rigging Certificate (NRC), a qualification that allows them to demonstrate they have attained a professional standard within their chosen rigging discipline.

Any equipment that is attached to the structure must be within the load-bearing capacity of the structure and a secondary mechanism must be used to support that equipment in the event of failure. A D-shackle is the preferred safety device. This equipment is a steel cable with a calculated hanging and breaking strain.

Once all light, sound and scenery equipment has been hung from the structure, a structural engineer must undertake a full calculation of all equipment on the structure. These figures should be presented prior to the build and checked on completion.

When the structural engineer is satisfied with the fully erected stage and equipment attached, a signed certificate must be presented to the production manager and filed in the site office.

A fire officer will also undertake a final check, for correct fire extinguishers and evacuation procedures along with fire certificates for fire retardant materials.

Information should be available to all performers indicating fire and emergency evacuation from the stage procedures. Continual safety checks must be made throughout the duration of the event. All scenery draped or hung from the erected structure must be fire tested and fire retardant and carry a test certificate to authenticate it. All documentation associated with the temporary structure must be held at the site office.

SUMMARY

In this chapter the production process was identified from a particular point of view, and it has been illustrated with a number of relevant and new regulations and legislation appropriate to achieving successful outcomes within the area of sound, lighting and construction. It is impossible to list and discuss all regulations and legislation that have an impact on production as this must take into account the many types of event and their creative elements that could introduce different operating procedures. Therefore, and as mentioned earlier in this chapter, it is important to monitor the HSE website to make sure you have a full and complete understanding of all regulations associated to this particular area. It is also necessary to make available within an organisation the new *Purple Guide* republished in 2014 with 23 chapters that give a better understanding for managing festivals and outdoor events. A great deal of the focus has hinged upon health and safety as the main driver for successful event producers. This chapter should have given you an insight into the very complicated area of work within this aspect of event management. It has shown how integral the working relationship of various skilled individuals is to achieving a quality production. This chapter outlines the technological skill set required for lighting designers as clients and event producers require ever more creative and complicated performances. Event managers need to have an understanding of the work of sound and lighting engineers and production managers. The chapter aims to facilitate a level of communication and understanding between two parties who are ultimately working towards the same end. Further reading and training are therefore suggested in order to develop your knowledge and understanding in this particular field. There are two well-recognised trade organisations within the UK that represent production personnel: the Production Service Association (PSA), a trade association for companies and individuals involved in the live events production industry; and PLASA, which operates across the live events, entertainment and installation industries representing the leading providers of professional audio, AV, lighting, rigging, staging and related disciplines.

Discussion questions

Question 1

Discuss the reasons why the 2007 CDM Regulation was superseded by the 2015 CDM Regulation and explain how this will benefit the live event industry.

Question 2

Outline your understanding of the term 'rigger' and describe the documentation required by that individual before he/she can commence work, and discuss the necessity for riggers to acquire certification by way of a qualification.

Question 3

Outline your understanding of two visualisation software programs available to lighting designers and explain how they are beneficial within the design and planning phase for a live performance.

Question 4

The music industry has seen significant growth over many years; with that growth venues have become more adaptable to meet production and installation requirements. Discuss which types of venues and attributes are necessary for commercial, operational, production facilities to achieve success and profitability for a major international touring artist or band.

Question 5

Discuss the benefits for live event producers of implementing new legislation and regulations for the build process for outdoor events and who should have principal responsibility.

Question 6

What legislation and general training can event managers/principal designers put in place to reduce injuries and fatalities in the workplace?

Case study 1: Outdoor dance and live music festival

This is a licensed site for 40,000 people, within a location on site that has full operational management of the event under licence. Event Control operates on a 24-hour rolling basis over night and day duties for Saturday and Sunday.

Duties include the management of all multi-agency operatives, licensing authority and environmental issues, with responsibility to the event licensing officer and safety officers. The licensee has full and complete responsibilities for all operational and licensing issues attached to this event. The safety officer's main duties are health and safety and risk management issues reporting directly to Event Control and the licensee. Within the role of event manager one must respond and deal with many issues; most issues are operational or related to production equipment on site. Below are some of the general issues that may fall within the scope of an event manager within Event Control while carrying out their duty.

Operational incidents and actions taken:

1   Firework display not part of the licensing requirement and ignited on Saturday night. Complaints from the local inhabitants and reports given directly to the licensing authority. Final action: firework display cancelled for the duration of the event weekend.
2   Customer related death on site. Location within a dance arena within the licensed site. Action taken: emergency services in attendance, police, ambulance, security and licensing authority. Person pronounced dead on site by medical team. The location of death is now deemed a crime scene. Ordered by the safety officer to commence a show-stop in the designated area. All customers and artists to vacate temporary arena. Security and police to contain location from all non-essential personnel. Artist scheduled within arena given an option to relocate to another arena. Production schedule and timing adjusted to meet new demands across all existing arenas within the licensed site. Initial call for customer related incident came directly to Event Control from the production manager in the arena. The message was then passed on to the medical representative in Event Control including the location and potential situation at hand. Policies and procedures must be followed for all medical vehicle movements within the licensed site, and where a medical vehicle requires access through one of the main gates into the arena, security operatives must be informed prior to arrival to allow access.
3   Closure of one arena. Action taken: extra police personnel were drafted in to the licensed site as a precautionary method to manage crowd behaviour. This precautionary method was not required as no crowd disturbance was reported.
4   Within the licensed site fairground rides closed due to mechanical failure which left one customer trapped. Action taken: safety officer in consultation with fairground operatives and fire services to remove individual and make safe fairground structure. The injured individual was taken off site to a general hospital to be offered a comprehensive medical assessment. Fairground closed for the duration of the night awaiting assessment from the day safety officer issuing a new safety certificate to reopen fairground attractions.
5   Severe weather warning, 15 mm of rain within a four-hour period. Action taken: welfare given the responsibility of issuing space blankets to customers thereby protecting them from excessive heat loss.

(Continued)

(Continued)

6   Customer admitted to local hospital due to excessive intake of alcohol. Action taken: condition monitored over a six-hour period before individual was deemed stable enough to be released.

7   Due to severe weather warning, main stage closed during the day. Stage deemed to be unsafe from a structural perspective. Action taken: artists and headline artists scheduled for main stage cancelled. Offered the option to perform in one of the temporary arena structures.

8   Related to capacity, numbers and production considerations, main stage closed for the duration of the event. Action taken: main stage cordoned off for all customers at a safe distance on safety officers' recommendation.

9   Shut down of all radio communication with all medical operatives on site. Action taken: licensee suggested that all medical operatives be transferred to another free channel on existing radio frequencies.

10 Customer complaints through the customer complaint line of loud music. Action taken: licensing authority sent to check decibel levels in the local area. Decibel levels in excess of the licensing agreement. Information passed directly to all temporary arenas within the licensed site to adjust sound levels in accordance with the licensing agreement. Situation continually monitored and checked throughout the duration of the event.

11 Reports from campsite of excessive rainfall. Action taken: customers provided with facilities for drying clothes.

12 End of the event, tents in campsites checked to determine how many customers were still on site.

13 Communication to customers on site regarding operational changes carried out via Bluetooth application on mobile phones. Security operatives also briefed at key locations throughout the site to disseminate operational changes. Information also posted on official website and communicated to external media representatives.

Case study 2: Amaechi Basketball Tournament

Media coverage and awareness

Manchester played host to the Haris Junior U18s International Tournament, in December 2009 at the Amaechi Basketball Centre (ABC). This type of spectator sport is unable to reach the international heights seen with the sport in the USA. On the whole, international sports receive more free coverage through television, radio and newspapers than any other part of the leisure sector. Evidently this helps to maintain awareness in the minds of the public and keep interest levels high, which subsequently could be capitalised upon to encourage attendance at sports events. However, a superficial scanning of both traditional and online versions of a variety of national and regional newspapers has revealed that as an individual sport, basketball struggles to achieve any prominent coverage and is often completely overshadowed by football, cricket, rugby and boxing. That is, the majority of the reviewed online media do not feature direct links to basketball on their homepages nor the sports section of the websites. For Amaechi Basketball Centre and in particular the 'Manchester Magic' brand this 'glass ceiling' of media attention needs to be broken through within the Manchester area. To achieve this it is paramount to deliver an effective message designed to influence the target audience's perception of Manchester Magic. In addition, the club had to capitalise on building relationships with the media currently covering the sport, such as the *Manchester Evening News*.

The Olympic effect and match attendance

With London being awarded the Olympic Games 2012, subsequently there has been an increased focus on sports in general. Arguably the sports presenting Great Britain with realistic opportunities for winning medals will be at the centre of attention. These sports will not only benefit from increased governmental funding but moreover a rising consumer awareness and interest in live sports, which should be converted into wider match attendance and accordingly increased revenue for the clubs offering live events.

Although Team GB Basketball failed to qualify for the Beijing Olympics 2008, they did qualify for London 2012, so ABC and Manchester Magic should be able to build on the increased general interest in basketball.

FURTHER READING

British Standards Institute (BSI) *Introducing Standards: Raising Standards Worldwide*. Available at: www.bsigroup.com/en-GB/standards/british-standards-online-database/bsol-academic/ [accessed 01/11/2016].

Civil Aviation Authority (2003) *Guide for the Operation of Lasers, Searchlights and Fireworks in United Kingdom Airspace*. Available at: http://webarchive.nationalarchives.gov.uk/20070506120329/http://caa.co.uk/docs/33/CAP736.PDF [accessed 01/11/2016].

Health and Safety Executive (2002) *Use of Contractors – a Joint Responsibility*. Liverpool: HSE.

Health and Safety Executive (2006) *Consulting Employees on Health and Safety: A Guide to the Law*. Liverpool: HSE.

Health and Safety Executive (2006) *Health and Safety Law: What You Should Know*. Liverpool: HSE.

PLASA (Professional Lighting and Sound Association). Available at: www.plasa.org.

PSA (Production Service Association). Available at: www.psa.org.uk.

16
CROWD CONTROL AND CROWD DYNAMICS

In this chapter you will cover

Crowd management and crowd control are two distinct areas that should never be confused. The understanding and correct application of both methods could be the defining aspect of an event's success or failure. Recent crowd management and crowd control failures have been characterised by numerous incidents that ultimately demonstrate a lack of knowledge and understanding of the application of the methods to ensure crowd safety and control, which can have catastrophic results for people who attend those events. This chapter will define and explain the difference between crowd management and crowd control. It will highlight the guidance and regulations that have become the industry norm and standards for the wider events industry. The chapter will also explain how certain venues within the industry have particular legislation and regulations dependent on the type of event held in the venue.

In recent times and as a direct result of major crowd incidents within the UK, the teaching of crowd management and control is now a formal and recognised industry requirement. Across the industry there remain pockets of non-compliance in the training available to ensure that individuals responsible for decision-making are competent in the execution of their duties. The chapter will also make reference to a number of institutions and recognised bodies as well as individuals who have developed, taught and published extensively within this field.

Much can be said and has been written about the 1989 Hillsborough disaster, where 96 people were killed as a result of crowd management decisions made by individuals who had insufficient knowledge and understanding of crowds within a venue, with devastating impact on the audience attending the football match. The government of that time and future governments had to intervene and appoint experts to establish the facts. The Taylor Inquiry was the first of many investigations that would follow over the next 30 years. This reference to the Hillsborough disaster draws attention to the groundswell within the events industry over many years to bring about training, legislation, guidance and regulations that would minimise the possibility of this situation occurring again.

CROWD MANAGEMENT

When developing a crowd management strategy one should also consider 'what if' scenarios to determine what should be the appropriate response to a given situation. Crowd management can best be described according to the guidance of the Emergency Planning College, an institution in the UK dedicated to the teaching of crowd dynamics and public safety at sports grounds and events. With the support of the University of Leeds and the Cabinet Office and Emergency Planning College, a guidance document was published in 2009 to assist anyone working within the area of crowds, including event crowds, crowd management, crowd control and emergency services. A number of prominent individuals who have practitioner and research knowledge within the chosen field of discussion have contributed to the publication.

> There is no single, agreed, detailed definition of 'a crowd'. Given the wide range of different crowd types, it may be more appropriate to devise multiple definitions, relevant to the varying types. (Cabinet Office and Emergency Planning College, 2009: 43 [online])

However, we do have an agreed definition for crowd management and crowd control. In 2014 the Health and Safety Executive published *Managing Crowds Safely: A Guide for Organisers at Events and Venues*. Where crowd management is discussed within this publication it is viewed in the context of a person who has primary responsibility for the safety of crowds:

> The person appointed would need to ensure that there are enough staff with the required skills to carry out crowd management duties during both normal and emergency situations. (Health and Safety Executive, 2014: 12 [online])

It can be stated that crowd management rests with well-trained and responsible individuals who have a clear and unambiguous strategy for managing crowds. Alternatively, crowd control is different from crowd management but both are inextricably linked.

> If safety rules are not visibly enforced, or crowd control is not maintained, the spread of non-compliant behaviour can have a serious impact on crowd safety. (Health and Safety Executive, 2014: 13 [online])

Crowd control has a direct approach in terms of the application of methods by a person who must anticipate and react to crowd control issues throughout the event life cycle. In doing so they must have an understanding of individuals and groups within a crowd to monitor and anticipate the impact of their behaviour.

CROWDS AND THEIR DEMOGRAPHICS

The definition and types of crowd attending an event will change from event to event. Anyone charged with the responsibility to manage and control crowds should make it their duty to develop a competent understanding of the types of crowds attending an event. From this initial standpoint one is able to draft a strategy for crowd management and control. In determining how to control crowds, event organisers have tended to denote their existence and coined the phrase 'mass gathering'. This gives at times a simplistic understanding of the collective and common characteristics of a crowd. They may share a common location and have a similar identity but it does not make them one harmonious group who always move and think the same under all conditions and circumstances. A major factor that should always be considered is the design of the space within which people move, that can and has determined the mass movement of crowds. It has been argued and controlled tests have demonstrated that crowds can have a group mentality but this should never be taken as a constant norm.

Research published by the *Journal of Crowd Safety and Security Management* highlights an attribute within groups that is sometimes overlooked. There are a number of theories that illustrate the type and behaviour of a crowd. Collective thinking, where one or a small group of people behave in a particular way and many follow because they may deem it acceptable, is explained by the 'emergent norm theory', as described in the *Journal of Crowd Safety and Security Management*:

> Questioned in relation to an age group that might be more susceptible to such tactics, Dorris suggests that those over the age of fourteen have a propensity to 'follow suit' more, and that 'seventeen to twenty four' is the age group that would maximise success in influencing a group. (Stuart, 2012: 16)

At this point it can be agreed that any number of people who gather together at the same location to watch a specific event for a period of time have a common identity and display common characteristics: they can be considered as a crowd. We are able to shed some light on the different types of crowds that may commonly show up at certain types of events, described in the list below. However, one must be extremely cautious and remember to address typical behaviours to successfully prepare for crowds at events.

1. A spectator crowd – i.e., a crowd watching an event that they have come to the location to see, or that they happen to discover once there.

2. A demonstrator crowd – i.e., a crowd, often with a recognised leader, organised for a specific reason or event, to picket, demonstrate, march, or chant.

3. A dense or suffocating crowd – i.e., a crowd in which people's physical movement rapidly decreases – to the point of impossibility – due to high crowd density, with people being swept along and compressed, resulting in serious injuries and fatalities from suffocation.

4. A violent crowd – i.e., a crowd attacking, terrorising, or rioting with no consideration for the law or the rights of other people.

5. An escaping crowd – i.e., a crowd attempting to escape from real or perceived danger or life-threatening situations, including people involved in organised evacuations, or chaotic pushing and shoving by a panicking mob. (Cabinet Office and Emergency Planning College, 2009: 44)

This list should never be considered as a universal definition for similar events but can be used as a framework and measurement tool to establish common characteristics. Within the definitions of types of crowds one may find compliant and non-compliant participants. It is those differences that should be monitored closely to determine the appropriate response in dealing with crowds. The same publication also illustrates differences within 'demonstrator crowds'. Terms are used such as:

- Totally compliant protesters – i.e., passionate but do not cause trouble.
- Slightly more difficult protesters – i.e., no disorder but may commit civil disobedience.
- Protesters who are willing to commit disorder if they become caught up with the emotion of the crowd and are pushed by other fellow members.
- Professional/subversive protesters – i.e., intent on causing and provoking disorder.
- Individuals who are not genuine protesters, but will use a protest as a cover to commit disorder. (Cabinet Office and Emergency Planning College, 2009: 44–5)

One is able to deduce from this list that within 'demonstrator crowds' there are further differences that can determine the overall outcome of a situation. It is therefore imperative that event organisers have trained individuals who can spot situations, individuals or groups who may have the propensity to cause crowd disturbance.

BEHAVIOUR OF CROWDS AND CROWD HAZARDS

Crowd behaviour can be explained from a psychological perspective; the study of human behaviour under any given circumstances has been documented by many authorities. As discussed by Helbing et al. (2001), individuals within a crowd prefer not to take detours or move against the crowd even if the route is crowded. Typically people will take the fastest route to a destination where it is allowed and this can be seen when a large number of people move across a festival site. Within a closed environment the sight line may be impeded by the design of, and density of the people within, the location. Each person is reliant on the persons in front or around them to determine the appropriate direction to take. It has been shown that people will normally take the shortest route to a location even when multiple routes are in place. For many people the sight line will determine the direction to take to travel across distances. Even when there is a designed route that has a suitable constructed pathway with adequate lighting, people will find the route of least resistance even if that route does not match with the designated route for people to follow.

When designing an environment for an event or using an existing space, all potential hazards must be removed if possible or correct measures must be put in place to limit access and be monitored as deemed appropriate once a full risk assessment has been drawn up for that potential hazard. When designing a site and locating particular activities for the enjoyment of the audience, it is necessary to remember that during peak times food outlets can become an obstacle and potentially a hazard for the movement of people. The arrival of crowds within an open space will generally fill it unevenly, for example, people gather in clusters near the stage, bar or entrance. Therefore, it is sometimes necessary to usher people into a space to ensure an even distribution and to retain some free flowing areas before the event starts. When large numbers of people who have a close affinity to each other arrive together they tend to move around and leave together. Where this is seen within an event, attention should be paid to those individuals, especially if the space they occupy is sizable within the entire designated venue. They may cause an obstacle for others to manoeuver around or through and if they become excitable, may become a problem for crowd control.

> In order to avoid collisions, people try to keep a certain distance from other people and from environmental borders, such as walls or obstacles. This distance decreases if the individual is in a hurry or if crowd density increases, for instance, around a particularly attractive place, such as a food outlet. (Cabinet Office and Emergency Planning College, 2009: 48)

In determining how crowds move around or through a site, movement can be assisted if the venue/site has sufficient and appropriate signs indicating directions to specific locations that large numbers of people will use while at the location. Where such information is absent it becomes difficult for people to navigate at a location and could ultimately create frustration for groups or individuals. A lack of signs to direct crowd behaviour is ever more problematic when an emergency evacuation is required. In an emergency people have the propensity to respond to persons or information that could hopefully save them from injury.

CROWD SIMULATION AND MODELLING

It is not difficult to understand that a large open space allows people to determine their own route of travel and this can best be viewed when crowd density is low. Once activities and obstacles are placed within the space they increase the risk of injuries and potential hazards.

Fire safety officers calculate the distance it will take for a person to travel a given distance in an emergency when leaving a venue. This is also measured in the crowd space they occupy within the venue and any obstacles that may impede their movement. One person per meter squared is considered the optimal crowd density within a venue. However, in reality it is generally the norm for some events to have more than one person per meter squared. Where high density occurs within a venue and exceeds the fire safety certificate, the venue is in jeopardy and the audience are placed in a risk environment. In the event of an emergency it is difficult for everyone to leave within a given time frame and this increases their chance of an injury.

The modelling for the movement of people within a given space is also calculated on how many exit points are available for the amount of people within that given space. The term 'bottleneck' is sometimes used to explain where people pass through a point that is narrower than where they came from originally, sometimes called a pinch point. For example, a tunnel was the control measure put in place for a large number of people entering and exiting the Love Parade outdoor site in Duisburg, Germany in 2010 where 21 people died due to a crowd crush in the tunnel. If this is avoidable when designing a space it should be deemed unacceptable. Large numbers of people attempting to move through a narrow opening in an emergency can increase the risk of injury.

> According to social facilitation theory, this is because individuals, when in a particular environment and aroused by the presence of other crowd members, are more likely to perform their habitual behaviours, e.g., using a particular entrance and exit route. (Cabinet Office and Emergency Planning College, 2009: 55)

Crowd modelling shows that people in the main tend to leave a location in an emergency from where they originally entered the location, regardless of the many emergency exit points. The Station nightclub fire in the USA in 2003, where 100 people died, is a case in point. The entry point for the venue became the exit point for many and resulted in the large casualty list at that pinch point. Many other factors also contributed to the high death rate, such as a lack of a sprinkler system within the venue.

When crowds cross a festival site in large numbers and come up against another large crowd attempting to reach a music stage in another location, this is problematic at best. Therefore it is essential to carefully locate music stages on a festival site to allow large numbers of people to travel with little impedance and also to schedule artists on music stages at different times to keep the largest gathering of people at one particular location and thus decrease the potential for large crowds trying to cross each other's path.

CROWD DYNAMICS

How one reacts to and treats a crowd will determine the behaviour of that crowd. It should be noted for the preseveration of human life that crowds have crowds within crowds and if abused or ill-treated by people in authority this can result in a negative outcome.

Crowd simulation to determine their flow rate within a given space is a scientific modelling tool now used by individuals charged with the responsibility to undertake an investigation where a crowd incident resulted in injury or death. It is also used to develop a comprehensive crowd management strategy for any given event.

Regression modelling is used extensively at large-scale indoor and outdoor mega events.

> For example, simple spreadsheet models are an incredibly useful means of measuring and predicting flow variables such as ingress and egress rates, flow rate, speed of movement, and density. (Cabinet Office and Emergency Planning College, 2009: 78)

After the Hillsborough disaster and as a result of the first inquiry, new legislation and guidance was imposed for sports stadiums within the UK and in particular stadiums within the top tier of English football. Regression modelling is a common feature that can be used to determine how large numbers of people arrive at and leave a football stadium.

Some academics liken the movement of crowds to the way water moves within a controlled environment. This method can be used to describe the way in which crowds move but one must remember that people are both rational and irrational and such behaviour can be displayed within a crowd.

The social forces model is another measurement tool used to show how long it takes high or low density crowds to travel over a given distance to a specific location, calculating the time as a major factor.

> Each individual is represented by a self-driven particle subject to social and physical forces. Accordingly, individuals – each with a certain mass – like to move in a certain direction at a certain speed, adapting their velocity within a certain time period, whilst keeping their distance from other individuals and obstacles. (Cabinet Office and Emergency Planning College, 2009: 79)

When millions arrive in Saudi Arabia as part of their Holy Pilgrimage to Mecca, known as Hajj, many temporary routes are imposed by the organising committee to allow large numbers of people to move across the city to their destination. In 2015 along one of the controlled temporary routes, it was reported that 2,236 people were killed due to a crowd crush. Social forces modelling can measure how long it will take a high density crowd to travel across a given distance within a controlled route, but it is difficult to measure the amount of people that could lose their life in the event of a crowd crush. When modelling to determine crowd dynamics one must also consider many other variables that will ultimately give different results. Age, gender, size and walking speed are factors within a population sample that should be taken into account to give a near accurate outcome.

SUMMARY

The world is littered with many incidents over a short historical time frame where people have lost their life or been injured due to inadequate planning and preparation for mass gatherings at events. It would seem that a number of countries, too many to list all of them, have witnessed their 'Hillsborough': the USA 2003, Germany 2010, Russia 2009, Denmark 2000 and more recently Romania and Saudi Arabia 2015. Each incident had the same outcome, loss of life with a similar causational factor underpinning all of them: insufficient knowledge and understanding of crowd control and how crowds behave in an emergency situation. Each situation did not factor in the necessity to meet fire codes or regulations as was required within their particular country; did not learn from previous crowd situations that are now well documented in academic papers and industry reports; or exhibited a total disregard for human life where criminal negligence was clearly evident. The small sample listed above has resulted in over 2,500 deaths over a period of 15 years. Looking forward over the next 15 years one should be able to predict a significant decrease in the number of deaths for people who gather together for any particular occasion. It is unwise to predict that no further fatal crowd incidents of a similar nature will occur again, however one should be able to predict that more trained individuals will be in a position of authority and therefore able to alleviate some of the high risk factors that could impact negatively on individuals or groups.

Discussion questions

Question 1

The Emergency Planning College makes reference to the terms 'demonstrator crowd'. Name two attributes that one can find within a demonstrator crowd and give your reasons as to how you would apply crowd control measures to them.

Question 2

Social forces is a scientific modelling tool to measure crowd movement and behaviour. Discuss how the model can be utilised within the events sector to minimise crowd disorder.

Question 3

Discuss the distinction between crowd management and crowd control and illustrate by way of an event example how the two will apply.

Question 4

There is no agreed definition of a crowd but there are many definitions of crowd types. Name three different types and discuss how each can be controlled within an event of your choice.

(Continued)

(Continued)

Question 5

Discuss the importance of the 2014 Health and Safety Executive published guidance for managing crowds safely.

Question 6

Identify and analyse the primary design feature that led to the 21 deaths at the Love Parade in Duisburg Germany.

Case study 1: Gron Koncert, Denmark

Crowd management begins long before any attendees arrive at the event site. All staff associated with the event operation should be well trained in security measures and crowd management techniques. A chain of command should be laid out to ensure who has authority to inform and instruct appropriate operatives to deal with any eventuality. The Gron Koncert, a one-day outdoor music festival located in eight cities in Denmark, follows similar crowd management techniques for the movement of people who enter the festival site at all locations. Before the patrons enter the event, the entrance process should be well defined to ensure smooth entry. It is important to lay out the plan for how attendees will be kept outside of the event before it starts. The space outside the event site for attendees to assemble is just as important as the event site. Attendees in the main tend to arrive early to an outdoor music festival. With that in mind organisers have a duty to manage the assembly area outside the event site as well. In a bid to have better control of attendees when they arrive at the festival site, the V Festival weekend site in Staffordshire has lanes for attendees within the Parkland, which gives a greater degree of control of the festival crowd before they embark upon the weekend of entertainment.

Sites selected by the organising team for the Gron Koncert have in the main a regular rectangular shape, with two stages located at the longest ends of the rectangle and toilet blocks positioned in the corners of the rectangle (Figure 16.1).

The centre of the rectangle has a bar with a 360 degree viewing platform for attendees. This central feature allows people to travel freely around the site in large numbers. Food and other concessions are located on the perimeter of the rectangle and help to denote the overall shape of the licensed site. As discussed in this chapter people tend to arrive at events in large groups and fill up the space in uncontrolled clusters. A site that has a familiar shape with two music stages at opposite ends of the festival site gives the attendees the opportunity to find their designated location within the site where

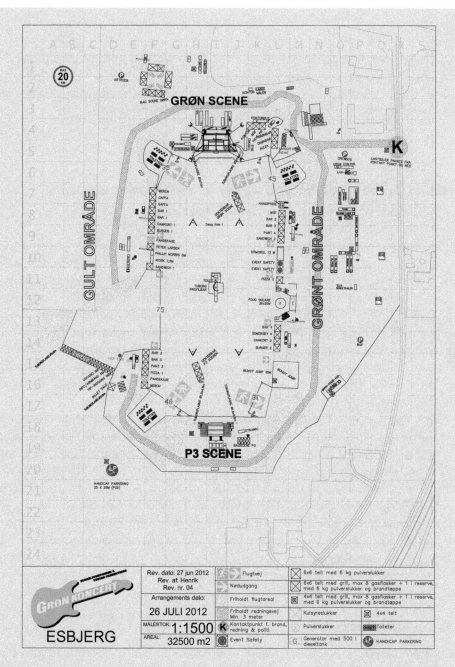

Figure 16.1   Grid map of Gron Koncert (Green Festival), Denmark

(Continued)

(Continued)

they can visibly locate essential items and facilities without too much difficulty. In the event of an emergency evacuation, as already discussed, attendees in the main will gravitate to the point of entry to exit the site. With sufficient space to allow people to exit and space outside the festival site that shouldn't hinder their safety.

Case study 2: How to use and apply crowd management and crowd control during the Brazil World Cup

In order to implement the best security policy, the Brazilian government decided to base its plan on four pillars. Indeed, considering the numerous issues of security in Brazil (drug, violence, thefts), the government had an obligation to assure the security of the event.

First, the government chose to integrate the existing policies of all the police forces to secure the event, the most important being assuring the security of the visitors, the players and also the staff of the events. Second, they planned to use technology to modernise the security tools and to apply the security process outside and inside the stadium, before, during and after the event. Third, human resources training was also critical, so staff were thoroughly trained on the security issues in order to be able to react quickly in case of any incident. The fourth and last pillar was respect for human rights; the government sought to ensure that no person would become a victim of any kind of discrimination or violence.

The crowd management was managed by a special department in charge of the coordination of the event: the Special Security Secretariat. They had to think of, create and implement all the security measures for the events. For instance, in 2011 they decided to use technology robots and went into every stadium to make anti-bomb inspections; they also created a national database of all the workers in order to be able to identify them in case of an accident. The security forces of the government included 14 command and control centres throughout the country. For small events the federal and civil polices would be present and the airforce and the army would guarantee the security for big events. In total there were more than 170,000 personnel in the security contingent in the country.

Was the event well secured?

In 2014 the police wanted to go on strike to protest the limited workforce and the poor salaries that deter police officers from their work. For instance there were only 10,000 police officers to control airports borders and passport procedures whereas more than

600,000 visitors were expected. Moreover the incidence of injured workers building the stadium in Sao Paulo did not reassure people about security issues for the World Cup.

How was the crowd managed around each stadium?

The government had a public security plan to train and to prepare police officers and staff members to manage the crowd. But unfortunately, the plan was not followed, and delays ensued. According to Andriano Pires, director of the Brazilia Centre for Infrastructure, a solution was found to reduce the flow of passengers transported and therefore reduce the risk: declare a holiday on match days, which meant almost a month's vacation.

Many tools were used to guarantee the security of the public. For example, a public policy developed by local authorities assured security in the streets around the stadiums and private security personnel employed by the management assured security in the stadiums during a match, and both policies worked together to reduce risks. Common methods were used: check all the tickets, include maps and directional signs to guide the people to the different exits and subway stations.

Source: adapted from www.copa2014.gov.br/sites/default/files/publicas/12272012_balanco_copa_geral. pdf and www.copa2014.gov.br/en/brasilecopa/sobreacopa/balancos [accessed 10/11/2016]

FURTHER READING

Cabinet Office Emergency and Planning College (2009) *Understanding Crowd Behaviours: Guidance and Lessons Identified.* Available at: www.gov.uk/government/uploads/system/uploads/attachment_data/file/62638/guidancelessons1_0.pdf [accessed 01/11/2016].

17

EXPOS, CONFERENCES AND CONVENTIONS

In this chapter you will cover

This chapter introduces the concept of expos, conferences and conventions. The expos, conferences and conventions market is very multifaceted and disjointed, with many different business stakeholders: event managers, conference venues and centres, museums, hotels, destination management companies, travel agents, events planners, exhibitions and convention organisers, etc. The expos, conferences and conventions industry generates income for stakeholders and develops long-term strategic economic advantages for cities and regions. Expos, conferences and conventions promote the destination and attract international meetings, incentives, conferences and exhibitions that can help expand economic development, jobs and knowledge creation in the host country. The case studies within this chapter explore the expos, conferences and conventions market and the positive contribution that these exhibitions, conventions and meetings play in developing the major regions around the world.

EXPOS, CONFERENCES AND CONVENTIONS

The expos, conferences and conventions industry has grown rapidly over the last two decades and this upward trend continues in a number of countries around the world. The report *Global Exhibition Industry: Trends, Opportunities & Forecasts, 2016–2021* (BusinessWire, 2016 [online]) states that the global exhibition industry is growing very fast in the USA, European Union and Asia Pacific. The growth of the exhibition and convention industry is becoming a major driver for the local economy in many regions around the world. Therefore, local authorities are encouraging the development of convention centres in major cities. A *Global Exhibition Barometer* report states that:

> In all regions, a large majority of companies intend to develop new activities, in either the classic range of exhibition industry activities (venue/organiser/services), other live events or virtual events, or in both: 75% in the Middle East & Africa, 86% in Asia/Pacific, 87% in Europe and 93% in the Americas. (UFI, 2016: 1 [online])

The expos, conferences and conventions industry has helped local economies over the last decade and has helped businesses to grow. As local communities look for new ways to enhance their economic strength, the expos, conferences and conventions industry plays a vital role in developing and supporting the local economy through employment, entertainment, hospitality and increased local tourism. Rogers (2013) states that:

> Meetings, conferences and conventions are at the forefront of modern communications, whether this is for internal communications (sales meetings, training courses, board retreats, major annual congresses, for example) or as a vehicle for communicating with key audiences (such as press briefings, product launches, annual general meetings, some technical conferences). Meetings, conferences and conventions are generic terms to describe a diverse mix of communications events. (2013: 3)

A study by Sung and Lee (2015), stated that in the US market, around 1.87 million meetings took place, generating $280 billion in direct spending, and contributing more than $115 billion to US GDP. The international expos, conferences and conventions industry has increased in size over the last ten years as Table 17.1 highlights. One of the main reasons for the expansion of the expos, conferences and conventions industry is that globalisation has decreased the importance of the traditional meaning of borders between countries and this has resulted in more businesses and people moving to other countries to attend or to organise various types of special events.

Table 17.1   Industry size and growth: USA and Canada

465	Number of convention centres in the USA and Canada
93 million	Total exhibition space supply in the USA and Canada
3.1%	2013 US and Canadian centre revenue growth
3.0%	2013 convention and exhibition net sq. ft. growth
4,500	Major convention and exhibitions in the USA and Canada

Source: adapted from Red 7 Media Research & Consulting; CEIR. Available at: www.visitsandiego. com/sites/default/files/Red7MHughes.pdf [accessed 24/10/2016]

The growth in the GDP of countries, better and improved economic conditions over the last five years and increased demand from business entrepreneurs are other key factors driving the growth of the exhibition industry. Table 17.2 highlights the increase in exhibition venues worldwide.

Table 17.2   Exhibition venues worldwide

	Values
Indoor exhibition space available in Europe	15.6 million m²
Indoor venue exhibition space available in the USA	6.71 million m²
Exhibition space rented in the USA	41.1 million net m²
Exhibition space of Messe Hannover (Germany)	466.1 thousand m²

Source: www.statista.com/topics/1413/exhibitions-convention-and-meetings/ [accessed 24/10/2016]

Tables 17.3 and 17.4 further analyse the economic impact and infrastructure of the US meetings industry. This clearly shows that the meetings industry is growing and contributing to GDP. Given the growing competitiveness among different countries, the convention and meetings industry recognises that service plays a vital role in the industry products and is key for a successful approach to customers.

Table 17.3   US meetings industry: economic impact

	Values
Economic contribution of the US meetings industry	770.38
Direct spending of US meetings industry on meeting planning and production	$106.66 billion
Spending in the US meetings industry on corporate business meetings	$132,127 million

Source: www.statista.com/topics/1413/exhibitions-convention-and-meetings [accessed 24/10/2016]

Table 17.4   US meetings industry: infrastructure

	Values
Size of McCormick Place (Chicago, IL)	2.6 million ft^2
Number of corporate/business meetings in the USA	1,298.31 thousand
Number of domestic conferences/congresses/convention attendees	33,670,000

Source: www.statista.com/topics/1413/exhibitions-convention-and-meetings/ [accessed 24/10/2016]

Convention and exhibition centres generally do not generate profitability for a city. The main reason that local governments build convention and exhibition centres is to enhance the external benefits that are derived for the local community. They support a variety of industries within the tourism sector, which helps local hotels, restaurants, transportation, retail and other stakeholders. The local governments analyse and measure external benefits through the number of new visitors coming to convention and exhibition centres. This commonly used, simple method provides a rough approximation of convention centre related spending.

Convention and exhibition centres are large buildings designed to host a convention, exhibition or tradeshow, as well as other events. These venues are able to host large indoor events and to attract organisers who are looking for core venue services, such as exhibit hall and room rental on a daily basis and for longer periods, as well as expanded hospitality services. In recent years expo, conference and convention organisers are looking for technology infrastructure and services that can provide a fast, reliable wi-fi network that they can depend on, 24/7 during the event. The case study below looks at the Schaumburg Convention Center and Hotel.

Case study 1: The Schaumburg Convention Center and Hotel

The Schaumburg Convention Center and Hotel's purpose is to attract visitors to Schaumburg to support and enhance the local economy. These visitors who might not otherwise come to Schaumburg play an important role as consumers of goods and services sold by local businesses. The estimated annual impact to the business community is approximately $43 million. It is for this reason the village purchased a previously underproductive tract of land, agreed to levy small consumption taxes, and built the convention center and hotel. The facility generates far more economic activity than is collected from these taxes.

Approximately $6.9 million in taxes are dedicated each year for the purpose of paying off a portion of the debt sold to build the facility. These taxes are primarily paid for by visitors. The taxes and their rates are:

(Continued)

(Continued)

- Amusement tax (5%)
- Hotel tax (2%)
- Food and beverage tax (0.45%).

In 2014, the Convention Center hosted 67 events with an estimated 160,000 attendees. These visitors to Schaumburg spend their money in retail centers, restaurants, and entertainment venues. Of the $6.9 million in taxes collected, $2 million was collected directly from users of the convention center and hotel.

Source: www.villageofschaumburg.com/depts/cd/economic/convention.htm [accessed 21/11/2016]

THE DEVELOPMENT AND GROWTH OF THE CONFERENCE INDUSTRY

Over the last decade the development and growth of the conference industry has continued with a number of conference and convention centres being built around the world. The development and recognition of a proper industry dates from the middle part of the twentieth century. This is mainly due to the increasingly widespread use of commercial air travel in the 1950s which led to an increase in the number and frequency of conferences and the subsequent globalisation of the industry. This created a demand for venues and gave rise to the construction of purpose built flagship conference venues to attract the associated economic benefits.

THE UK CONFERENCE AND CONVENTION INDUSTRY

The words 'conference', 'congress', 'convention' and 'meeting' are used interchangeably and with different meanings according to numbers, duration and purpose. For the purpose of this chapter a conference is defined as:

> an event used by an organisation to meet and exchange views, convey a message, open a debate or give publicity to some areas of opinion on a specific issue. (Rogers, 2013: 16)

The UK conference industry appears to be thriving. The International Conference and Convention Association's (ICCA) annual destination reports show the UK regularly positioned among the top three conference destinations worldwide. The UK Conference Market Survey (UKCAMS, 2015) also states that the UK conference and meetings market is successful and provides a significant contribution to the national business economy. The UK conference and convention industry plays a vital role in the UK economy in generating exports. Many conferences, conventions and exhibitions held in the UK have established themselves as a strong base for international trade. For example, UK exhibitions attract over 13 million visitors each year, generating £11.0 billion in spending. The figures below indicate that these events (conferences and meetings, exhibitions and trade fairs, incentive travel and performance improvement, corporate hospitality and corporate events) are creating jobs for the local community and enhancing the local economy.

• conferences and meetings – £19.9 billion
• exhibitions and trade fairs – £11.0 billion
• incentive travel and performance improvement – £1.2 billion.

These figures indicate that conferencing remains a growing and stable industry. This has led to the mass construction of purpose built conference centres, specifically designed to host and facilitate meetings and conferences for hundreds if not thousands of delegates. This current trend in the construction of purpose built conference centres is due to it being well documented that they are capable of providing positive economic impact all year round for towns and cities due to visitors spending an above-average amount. However, it takes more than the provision of a conference centre to attract conferences. Therefore developing a conference centre should not be the direct solution for areas suffering economic problems. Shone (1998) outlines the essential elements for any destination pursuing conferences and business tourism as being:

the availability of attractions, the provision of transport, the availability of accommodation, food and drink, and the provision of infrastructure and support services. (Shone, 1998: 10)

It therefore becomes apparent that the whole package of conference and tourism infrastructure must be in place before this economic development strategy to construct a conference centre is pursued.

In the conference industry cities fiercely compete not only with other cities but also with other countries. Despite this there is a growing popularity for purpose built conference centres and the UK Conference and Meeting Survey (UKCAMS, 2015) points out that conference centres are currently the third most popular choice of venue for the association market, while the most popular choice of venue across sectors remains hotels.

The UKCAMS report, published in June 2015, provided the following figures, which clearly highlight that the conference industry is developing and enhancing the economy and creating employment for local people. The conference market is recognised as the leading sector in the UK's business visits and events (or business tourism) over the last five years.

• In 2014 there was an estimated £21.4 billion of direct expenditure generated by conference and meeting delegates and organisers in venues and wider destination spend, an increase on 2013.

- There were an estimated 1.28 million business events in the UK in 2014, similar to the total for 2013, although the average event size was larger.
- There was an average of 366 events per venue in 2014, this was on a par with 2013 (356 events) and 2012 (373 events).
- The majority (61 per cent) of events were held in hotels, with a further 20 per cent held in unusual/multi-purpose venues.
- The average event duration was 1.6 days. However, most events (64 per cent) lasted a day or less.
- The majority of venues indicated that their business performance was up in 2014 compared with 2013, and venues were optimistic about prospects for 2015. (UKCAMS, 2015)

The conference industry has proved itself to have wide ranging positive impacts on the economy, which is the reason governments are increasingly turning to tourism and in particular business tourism as a growth sector capable of delivering economic benefit and job creation. The main

Table 17.5 Direct spending by commodity

Commodities	Direct spending (in $ millions)	Per cent
Travel and tourism commodities		
Accommodation	39,315	14
Food and beverage	29,832	11
Air transportation	23,761	8
Retail	8,235	3
Gasoline	7,498	3
Recreation and entertainment	7,034	3
Car rental	6,258	2
Travel services and other tourism commodities	3,707	1
Other transportation	2,369	1
Urban transit	1,577	1
Rail and water transportation	600	<1
Subtotal	*130,186*	*46*
Meetings and other commodities		
Meeting planning and production	106,658	38
Venue rental	10,363	4
Other meetings-related commodities	33,195	1
Subtotal	*150,216*	*5*
Total direct spending	**280,402**	**100**

Source: PricewaterhouseCoopers LLP (2012)

economic benefit brought about by a purpose built conference centre is the conference-goers' expenditure in the local community.

The conference delegates create a positive economic impact on the host community. The delegates spend their money on a wide variety of goods and services. They purchase accommodation, food/beverages, entertainment services, goods from retail outlets and tour/travel services. A PricewaterhouseCoopers LLP report, *The Economic Significance of Meetings to the US Economy: Interim Study Update for 2012*, indicates the direct spend by delegates during their visits to expos, conferences and conventions (Table 17.5).

The purpose built conference centres distribute benefits and provide employment to the local community. The UKCAMS (2015) report valued the sector at an estimated £21.4 billion in venue and destination direct spend in 2014. The report also indicated that there has been an increase in the total number of delegates to 104 million compared with 91 million delegates in 2013.

Conferences and expos like any other type of event are capable of attracting significant numbers of foreign visitors to a destination. The overnight visitor invariably brings the highest expenditure per head. Large-scale international corporate and association events subsequently lead to major economic impact as it is the money brought in from outside the immediate region which has the power to stimulate true expansion of the local economy as visitors spend significantly more than local attendees, and stay for more nights. See the case study of the Japan Expo exhibition hosted in Paris each year.

Case study 2: Japan Expo

Launched for the first time in 1999, Japan Expo is an exhibition which wants to highlight and to promote Japanese culture through a lot of activities: meetings, panels and signings, showcases and live performances, workshops, games and activities, video games launches, traditional culture, manga and cosplay exhibitions, martial arts and sports, screenings, fashion shows, exhibitors and vendors from Japan.

Key facts of Japan Expo:

- 4 days
- 600 exhibitors
- more than 250,000 visitors
- turnover: €5,500,000
- profits: €400,000.

Each year, Japan Expo is held at Le Parc des Expositions, a space equivalent to more than 18 soccer fields, all dedicated to Japanese culture and leisure activities.

(Continued)

(Continued)

At present five towns in France are welcoming this four day exhibition and the founding company is planning to extend the event to other regions and countries in Europe. Since 2007, Japan Expo is the biggest Japanese culture and leisure exhibition organised in Europe.

Japan Expo is an attractive and dynamic exhibition, which has benefits as well as drawbacks. Japan Expo has very positive economic impacts. During this exhibition a large number of video game firms (such as Nintendo) or writers of manga (such as Ken Akamatsu, the writer of *Love Hina*) show their products and try to attract consumers, actually more than 90 per cent of the exhibitors have something to sell. It is a place to sell, to promote and to share their values, universes and products. One year Nintendo organised a tournament during these days based on their most famous video games like Mario Kart 8, Pokémon Rubis Omega or Splatoon.

Japan Expo develops business around Villepinte. Hotels, restaurants, clubs are booked especially for this event thanks to its reputation. Moreover for foreigners, going to this exhibition is a way to discover Paris so it also has an impact on the tourist locations in the capital. Expo tourism creates employment and increases income for local hotels, restaurants and transport.

Furthermore, Japan Expo also creates economic impact for Japan: Japan Expo is a way for the country to promote its products. The Japanese government also participates in the exhibition through the tourism office which has a stand. That is why this exhibition contributes to increases in tourism to Japan and by showing an image of a dynamic country.

CONFERENCE AND EVENT BUDGETING

The event budgeting process is a very important and essential part of the conferences and events industry. The budget is the key element of each conference and event. Therefore, conference and event budgeting is one of the key financial documents for event managers to complete, while planning for a conference and event. Conference and event budgeting is a tool which helps to analyse what money will be made from the event and to indicate the actual profit for the event.

The budget provides a formal basis for monitoring the progress of the event as a whole and of its component parts in relation to the targets set by the original objectives and plans. In addition, it is vital for the event organisation to produce a budget as a benchmark to provide a guideline for the client.

Table 17.6 shows how a budget should be developed for a conference and event.

The preparation of a budget is one of the essential elements of the conference and event. It is tool which provides fundamental information to predict the actual net profit or loss.

Table 17.6   Japan Expo, Paris 2015

	Budgeted	Actual
Revenue	£	£
Grant from local government	60,000	60,000
Sponsorship	105,000	105,000
Income from food/cloths stands	56,000	49,500
Total revenue	**221,000**	**214,500**
Payments		
Venue hire	25,000	25,0000
Advertising cost	30,500	32,200
Printing costs	5,700	5,700
Staff cost	69,900	73,200
Artist fees	18,400	18,400
Stage and lighting	17,100	17,100
Security charges	9,200	11,500
Cleaning cost	16,800	16,800
Total expenses	**192,600**	**199,900**
Surplus/deficit	**28,400**	**14,600**

This is achieved by identifying and costing all probable expenditures and by totaling all expected revenues (income).

SUMMARY

This chapter has shown how expos, conferences and conventions are a major force in the events industry and create a very positive economic impact for the host community. The expos, conferences and conventions industry has helped local economies over the last decade and has helped businesses to grow, playing a vital role in developing and supporting local economies through employment, entertainment, hospitality and increased local tourism. The chapter has also illustrated that conference centres are not money-making machines for destinations facing economic hardship, as a conference centre and its tourism infrastructure have a large part to play in the success of a conferencing destination.

This chapter has also examined the conference and event budgeting process and explained how budgeting helps conference and event managers to manage and organise the event. The budgeting process is a vital tool for conference and event organisers, it helps the project director or manager to plan and control the expenditure of the conference and event regardless of its size. The budget helps to analyse each item of the costs and sets the standards for the individual director or manager to plan and control the overall business activities in line with set budgets.

Discussion questions

Question 1

Discuss the difference between an expo, a conference and a convention.

Question 2

Discuss and evaluate the impact of the conference industry in the UK compared to the US market.

Question 3

Investigate the role that expos, conferences and conventions play in the host country economy.

Question 4

Critically discuss the benefits and drawbacks of expos, conferences and conventions.

Question 5

Explain and describe the national frameworks for expos, conferences and conventions.

Question 6

Compare and contrast the relationship between expos, conferences and conventions.

Case study 3: Hong Kong Convention and Exhibition Centre

The Hong Kong Convention and Exhibition Centre (HKCEC) opened in November 1988, after which Hong Kong's exhibition industry experienced a period of rapid growth enabling Hong Kong to establish its position as Asia's trade fair capital and a premier international convention and meeting location.

The HKCEC, located on the magnificent and renowned Victoria Harbour, is owned by the Hong Kong Trade Development Council (TDC) and the Hong Kong Special Administrative Region Government. The TDC is entrusted by government to be responsible for the Centre's development, design and management. The TDC has contracted with Hong Kong Convention and Exhibition Centre (Management) Limited (HML) for management and operation of the Centre. HML is a wholly-owned subsidiary of NWS Holdings Ltd.

The mission of HML, with a staff team of over 850, is to position the HKCEC as the best exhibition and convention centre in Asia, internationally renowned for excellence and hosting the world's greatest events, supported by innovative and creative operating techniques.

Having experienced escalating demand from its time of opening, the HKCEC was expanded in June 1997, more than doubling its prime function space. The expanded venue further strengthened Hong Kong's leading position as Asia's trade fair hub, assuring that Hong Kong could successfully meet the growing demand for space into the 21st century.

Since its opening in 1988, the Hong Kong Convention and Exhibition Centre (HKCEC) is arguably the most iconic building on the island. The HKCEC has been significantly expanded and upgraded since then, and now offers:

- an exhibition space of 89,000 square feet (8,268 square metres)
- rentable multi-use space of 99,000 square feet (8,547 square metres).

The convention hall and two theatres are in high demand. The HKCEC's schedule is regularly booked with meetings, shows, banquets, and special events. The convention hall, while interspersed with larger spaces, has smaller function rooms equipped with video conferencing, teleconferencing, satellite links, and simultaneous interpretation in up to eight languages. Much of the original analogue equipment is used daily and thanks to regular maintenance is still in perfect working order.

The cost of the HKCEC when it first opened in 1988 was approximately HK$1.6 billion (US$207 million), not including land cost. The first expansion completed in 1997 cost HK$4.8 billion (US$620 million), including site reclamation which began in June 1994; and the second expansion completed in 2009 cost HK$1.4 billion (US$180 million).

HKCEC convention facilities

- 5 exhibition halls
- 2 convention halls (total seating)
- 2 theatres (total seating 1,000)
- 52 meeting rooms
- pre-function areas (8,000 m²)
- 7 restaurants (total seating 1,870)

(Continued)

(Continued)

- business centre (150 m²)
- carparking spaces (1,300 cars and 50 vans)
- total available rental space (92,061 m²)
- capacity: 140,000 visitors per day.

Despite the regular maintenance performed on the original analogue AV equipment, a recent infrastructure failure necessitated an urgent installation of a new system. Most importantly, the integrator would have to work around the HKCEC's busy schedule. Y.H. Shum, director of the chosen integrator, China-Tech Engineering Company, explains the situation further: 'The HKCEC cannot simply cancel booked events or turn away business. While we could have closed the building and completed the installation relatively quickly, we chose to work around the HKCEC's packed diary of events allowing them to honour their commitments to their customers. The installation was simplified by not having to run new cabling'.

Sources: adapted from http://c353616.r16.cf1.rackcdn.com/Biamp_Case_Study_Hong_Kong_Convention_Centre.pdf [accessed 24/10/2016] and www.chinaexhibition.com/china_trade_shows_venue_profile/44-Hong_Kong_Convention_and_Exhibition_Centre_(HKCEC).html [accessed 24/10/2016].

Case study 4: Sands Expo and Convention Center

Imagine that you're in the heart of Las Vegas, somewhere between the mountain's highest peaks and the desert warmest winds that the State of Nevada is famous for.

You're in one of the world's most exciting destinations for conventions, nuptials, vacations, gambling, parties, and simple relaxation. There is such a diverse selection of things to see and do, that it's easy to get caught up in the magic of those neon lights.

For decades, Vegas has been home to some of the world's greatest events and business gatherings, spanning the lavish lobbies to the event halls, to the plush and picturesque conference centers throughout the city. Among the largest and most successful venues under the desert sun, is the Sands Expo and Convention Center.

The Sands boasts 2.2 million square feet of flexible exhibition and meeting space connected to the Sands Expo, the Venetian and the Palazzo hotels. It's huge. It's bold. It's one of the most prestigious show floors on the planet – and every inch of it is covered by Wi-Fi.

'We need Wi-Fi we can count on 24/7. We never shut down so neither can our internet connection', says Justin Herrman, IT Manager at the Sands. When it came time to evaluate the Sands' wireless network, Justin and his team know one thing for sure – down time was not an option for the main Sands Expo floor, adjacent meeting rooms and common areas at the Palazzo and Venetian hotels.

The Sands was running smoothly with their recently installed wireless network. It covered the large and small spaces of the show floor, but when it came to ubiquitous roaming, the network was at times, unreliable. What was needed was additional wireless support to complement the network already in place. With no shortage of service providers and multiple vendors clamouring to get through the door at the Sands, it was SignalShare, Extricom's US partner, who were quick to guarantee a Wi-Fi network with low density, instant availability and market-proven wireless communication.

'SignalShare had proven performance in the field. We contracted them for some of our events and they delivered seamless internet each and every time', commented Herrman.

'We were sold on Extricom from the start'. SignalShare set up a complementary, hybrid network alongside the Sands' existing WLAN. With Extricom's patented Channel Blanket™ technology to support the current infrastructure, the Sands' show floor and adjacent spaces were sufficiently covered with uninterrupted, high quality internet connectivity. Uniquely suited for large indoor venues, Channel Blanket architecture allows single channels to blanket entire sections of the show floor, eliminating the need for difficult, virtually impossible to deploy, microcell system designs. Now, the Sands could provide their oftentimes, 100,000 clients, with basic Wi-Fi (data transfer), voice over WLAN, and video streaming services. This translated into clients accessing a mobile concierge and having a viable VPN on their mobile phones and tablets. SignalShare installed Extricom's WLAN throughout the entire show floor.

Source: adapted from www.extricom.com/files/SandsExpoCaseStudy_Final.pdf [accessed 24/10/2016]

FURTHER READING

Mair, J. (2014) *Conferences and Conventions: A Research Perspective*. Oxon: Routledge.

PricewaterhouseCoopers LLP (2012) *The Economic Significance of Meetings to the US Economy: Interim Study Update for 2012*. Available at: www.conventionindustry.org/Files/2012%20ESS/CIC%20Meetings%20ESS%20Update%20EXECUTIVE%20SUMMARY-FINAL.pdf [accessed 01/11/2016].

Rogers, T. (2013) *Conferences and Conventions: A Global Industry*, 3rd edn. Oxon: Routledge.

Rogers, T. and Davidson, R. (2016) *Marketing Destinations and Venues for Conferences, Conventions and Business Events*, 2nd edn. Oxon: Routledge.

UFI (2016) *Global Exhibition Barometer*, 16th edn. Available at: www.ufi.org/wp-content/uploads/2016/07/UFI_Global_Exhibition_Barometer_report17.pdf [accessed 01/11/2016].

PART 5

EVENTS AND BEYOND

18

SUSTAINABLE FESTIVALS AND EVENTS

In this chapter you will cover

This chapter examines and evaluates the subject of sustainability and aims to draw a clear link between the current global benchmark indicators from the United Nations and the European Union. With specific reference to the UK economic, environmental and social landscape, where those three pillars converge on sustainable issues, they will be critically discussed. Where there is legislation, guidance documents and codes of practice to assist organisations in meeting the climate challenge, these will be introduced and explained as to their applicability within a given context.

SUSTAINABILITY FRAMEWORK

Sustainability within a global context starts with one basic premise, CO_2 emissions. From the time of the first international climate conference in 1979, organised by the United Nations, CO_2 levels throughout the world were stated as significantly high, and the impending impact of those levels was said to present a significant negative effect on the world climate. The Intergovernmental Panel on Climate Change (IPCC) released their first document in 1990. The international community at this point made specific reference to the first report and developed policies to bring about change. International discussions among the global community commenced in 1990 and the first international agreement was signed by 154 states and the European Community in 1992.

The United Nations 2010 conference in Copenhagen brought together the international community to look at and discuss the conclusion of the Kyoto Protocol (published in 1997), and to set targets for the future. Climate change, when viewed from a European and UK perspective, has a far broader remit, due to the diverse social, environmental and economic disparities within each member state. Within the UK, climate change is generally included under the broad heading of 'sustainability'. Under this banner a number of government-appointed agencies have a specific remit to communicate strategies and set targets for all business sectors. The Environment Agency has a specific remit to develop a strategy for the disposal of commercial and non-commercial waste in the UK. Another government agency, the Department for Environment, Food and Rural Affairs, published a number of documents on air quality in Britain. This agency has also published guidance documents for a number of business sectors including the events industry.

Clearly, the problems are complex and worldwide problems cannot be solved by a single planning solution and probably not by any single action. Moreover, there is a continuous discourse surrounding the dichotomy of economic and environmental principles, and the suggestion that one principle takes priority over another. Consequently, social considerations are frequently given less attention. Within this book, and within this chapter, equal consideration is given to all three principles, including the implementation of social frameworks as fundamental to the concept of sustainable event management.

As a sector, the events industry is now facing many challenges to fall in line with the current wind of change. This has brought about many opportunities for some organisations, and costly operational changes for other businesses. In maintaining a competitive advantage, organisations must adapt to the impending global issues. There are some formidable barriers when attempts are made to translate the principles of sustainability into action in the context of events, such as lack of reliable information, individual and organisational inertia, employee perceptions and the failure to use planning and performance standards. In essence, events are fragmented – made up of many stages, many suppliers, many performance indicators and many clients. Therefore, any attempt at introducing a sustainable policy should be integral to all elements of the event, in the pre-, live and post-event stages and across the whole life cycle of event management.

The nomenclature of events includes mega, special, social, major, hallmark and community events. Events are categorised according to their size, scope and scale. Moreover, events can be categorised according to their type or sector, such as conferences and exhibitions, arts and entertainment, sports events and charitable events. The Accepted Practices Exchange (APEX) *Industry Glossary* of terms (published by the Convention Industry Council) defines an event as:

> [a]n organised occasion such as a meeting, convention, exhibition, special event, gala dinner, etc. An event is often composed of several different yet related functions. (cited in Bowdin, 2011: 14)

Events are explicitly linked to fundamentals of the human race – social and cultural values, and the more basic ladders of social inclusion, a sense of belonging and a sense of identity. Dwyer et al. (2000) support the view that organising and managing a planned event involves many component parts and many stakeholders. Often the decisions to organise and host events are taken from different stakeholder viewpoints. A good economic rationale is a strong indicator, coupled with the social and cultural benefits to a destination, raising awareness of community/ social issues, enhancing the exchange of ideas, networking and business contacts. The social elements of the three pillars of sustainability are often neglected and often ambiguous. The scope of any framework should encompass those working at, participating in and attending the event and consider social inclusion as a key principle to widening participation and encouraging interest from all aspects of the surrounding community.

Significantly, the move towards the creation of a number of published frameworks for sustainable event management has provided not only a sense of professionalism in light of contemporary concerns, but highlighted best practice within the industry, advice and guidance, practical solutions, and an inward-looking sense of the importance of events in modern society.

THE GLOBAL PERSPECTIVE

Through the United Nations, the international community has published a number of documents, including the Intergovernmental Panel on Climate Change 4th Assessment Report, in 2007. This outlines the global position in relation to environmental impact and in particular the four greenhouse gases: carbon dioxide, methane, nitrous oxide and sulphur hexafluoride. These four should be given due attention when developing long-term policies for each state or member of the European community.

The European Parliament has also published and given clear guidance to the European community. In some aspects it has enacted specific regulations that require uniform acceptance from all member states.

It is those gases that have become the main issue for many environmentalists and policy-makers in determining the short- to long-term integration of change to ensure that as a country the UK meets the international challenge of 'climate change'.

Even though this issue has been debated for over 20 years in the international arena, with clear guidance published to move this agenda forward, it is only over the past ten years that the UK events industry has collectively and actively engaged with specific guidance and understanding to drive the sector forward.

In 2007, the British Standards Institute (BSI) published the BS 8901 specification for a sustainable event management system with guidance for use. This document was updated and re-published in 2009. In 2006, the Department for Environment, Food and Rural Affairs (Defra), a government agency, published Environmental Key Performance Indicators for UK businesses. To accompany that document Defra published the booklet, *Sustainable Development Indicators in Your Pocket* (Defra, 2009 [online]). Again, in the same year for the first time, the Department of Trade and Industry (DTI), another government agency, published *Meeting the Energy Challenge: A White Paper on Energy* (DTI, 2007 [online]). The UK government also introduced the UK Sustainable Development Strategy. This attempts to consolidate and present a way forward for business and the country as a whole. The very first international and highly recognised standard came via the International Organization for Standardization, in 2004 – the ISO 14001: 2004 and the ISO 14004: 2004. As a sector, we now have a considerable number of official documents from established, recognised agencies and organisations that can assist in the integration of environmental policies and standards. In 2008, the UK government brought into law the Climate Change Act, the first EU country to enact legislation of this type. This Act refers to a number of specific remits within the realm of sustainability and environmental impact. It presents a baseline figure for the reduction of carbon dioxide in the atmosphere by 80 per cent in line with 1990 estimates. This reduction is benchmarked and has a direct correlation with the Kyoto Protocol published in 1997 by the United Nations, which referred to CO_2 emissions and the need for reduction by the year 2012 below 1990 figures.

> The Parties included in Annex I shall, individually or jointly, ensure that their aggregate anthropogenic carbon dioxide equivalent emissions of the greenhouse gases listed in Annex A do not exceed their assigned amounts, calculated pursuant to their quantified emission limitation and reduction commitments inscribed in Annex B and in accordance with the provisions of this Article, with a view to reducing their overall emissions of such gases by at least 5 per cent below 1990 levels in the commitment period 2008 to 2012. (United Nations Framework Convention on Climate Change, 1997: 3 [online])

EUROPEAN AND UK PERSPECTIVE

It is clear how the Kyoto Protocol contributed in part to the introduction of the Climate Change Act, as the UK is a signed up member to the agreement. As a European member state at the time of writing a clear strategy is required that allows industry to enact appropriate policies with incentives to bring about a tangible reduction in CO_2 emissions. In accordance with the Act, the European Parliament introduced the Carbon Accounting Regulations in 2009. This regulation is now part of UK law and allows each member state to trade carbon credits and set carbon budgetary levels. The levels set for each country have direct lineage from the Kyoto Protocol 1997. The 2009 regulation works in conjunction with the EU Emission Trading Directive from 2003.

Governance for this type of scheme in relation to trading and setting carbon budgets is controlled by the Environment Agency, a UK government organisation. The Environment Agency has set stringent rules in relation to the Kyoto agreement. Where carbon credits are surplus they will not be carried over but cancelled out. It has also been agreed by the Environment Agency that carbon credits generated outside the UK and used to meet the carbon budget must be cancelled out, and the method of double counting for credits will also be removed. It must also be noted that the UK carbon reduction commitment under this scheme is only 60 per cent of the UK carbon emissions. This scheme in the broadest terms has more relevance to the UK industrial sector and large energy emitters.

In order for small-to-medium-sized businesses to contribute to this environmental initiative, and have a positive influence on the remaining 40 per cent, they must take control of their businesses from a unit level.

Local authorities in the UK, and in other countries worldwide, are building collaborative and integrated schemes, and planning to develop policies and guidance documents to bring about sustainable and long-term change. For example, Shoalhaven City Council (in New South Wales, Australia) is in the process of developing a sustainable events policy statement for the future (see Figure 18.1).

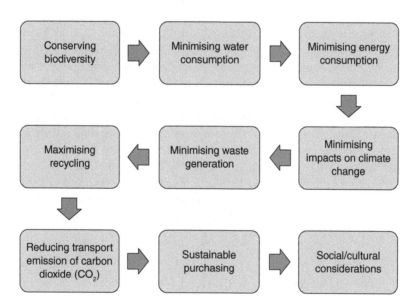

Figure 18.1 Sustainable events strategies

Shoalhaven City Council is planning a detailed policy to implement sustainable events strategies to ensure events held in Shoalhaven are organised and conducted in a sustainable manner. 'Sustainability' will be defined as using fewer natural resources, at the present, so that they are available for future generations. In practice, it means choosing suppliers or procedures or products that have low impact on the planet and ensure the well-being of people and the environment.

Shoalhaven City Council wants all future events to be planned and implemented with the goal of reducing the impact of the event on the environment. The policy is being developed to achieve that outcome through encouraging events organisers to adopt strategies of meaningful collaboration and consultation with the community when planning future events.

There are a number of policies and legislation documents that can assist in the development of a clear and workable strategy. It is inconceivable that an organisation can enact wholesale change across a business operation in the first instance. This process of change should have collective agreement within an organisation, which allows for sustained commitment, and which can then be communicated to suppliers, partners and business associates.

The implementation of the ISO environmental standard calls for a gradual approach to changing business operations, with continued assessment by the ISO on businesses potentially seeking ratification and continued certification under the terms of agreement. A business must clearly demonstrate, through developing policies and guidance for internal use, that employees have a full understanding of their specific remit when operating within the business unit and externally. Where a business has a need to engage with outside organisations to achieve the delivery of their product or service, there is a requirement to implement change through dialogue and agreement. This aspect will become the cornerstone for a cohesive long-term environmental strategy.

The most high-profile event in the UK that achieved ratification by the ISO were the London 2012 Olympic and Paralympic Games. The London Organising Committee Olympic Games (LOCOG) published a number of documents that outlined their commitment to meet the climate challenge strategy, but also to educate the UK population and the international community.

'London 2012: Towards One Planet' makes specific reference to the fact that the Kyoto Protocol (published in 1997) set an expiry date of 2012 for the international agreements signed at Kyoto. Therefore, 2012 was a significant milestone for the international debate on climate change and how international agreements signed at the Kyoto conference can move the agenda forward under a new agreement. The consolidation of the Kyoto agenda came about at the Copenhagen conference held in 2010. The Copenhagen Accord was signed by a number of countries, and also for the first time by China and developing nations. A legally binding agreement was not ratified by each country, however. What was agreed, was an aspirational goal of limiting global temperature increase to 2 degrees Celsius.

LONDON 2012 SUSTAINABLE CHALLENGE

As a mega event the Olympic Games had an impact over five major London boroughs: Greenwich, Hackney, Newham, Tower Hamlets and Waltham Forest.

Figure 18.2 highlights the foundation of London 2012's sustainable strategy. From the five objectives, inclusion in particular requires further investigation to draw a distinction with the social and political remits that needed addressing by the UK government. The aim, according to LOCOG, was:

> To host the most inclusive Games to date by promoting access, celebrating diversity and facilitating the physical, economic and social regeneration of the Lower Lea Valley and surrounding communities. (LOCOG, 2008: 6 [online])

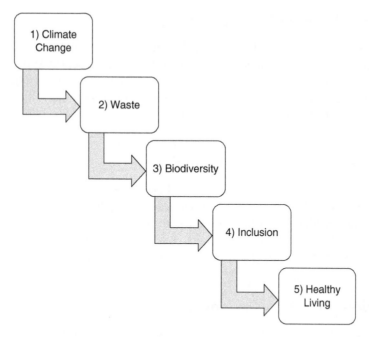

Figure 18.2   London 2012 sustainable strategy

It is generally noted that inhabitants of the five boroughs on which the London Olympic Games were centred are subject to higher levels of inequality. This theory is backed up by data from the Office for National Statistics, which shows that there were significant differences between inner and outer London boroughs in the areas of crime, deprivation and health.

Outer London borough – Newham

1. Violence against persons: 7,003 incidents during the period April 2010–March 2011.
2. Criminal damage including arson: 3,108 incidents during the period April 2010–March 2011.
3. Social services incidents: 1,299 during the period January 2006–December 2006.
4. Total number of county court judgements: 5,361, with an average value of £2,439.49.
5. Coronary heart disease cases for the period April 2007–March 2008: 3,950 admissions.

Inner London borough – Hackney

1. Violence against persons: 5,952 offences during the period April 2010–March 2011.
2. Criminal damage including arson: 2,205 incidents during the period April 2010–March 2011.
3. Social services incidents: 2,460 during the period January 2006–December 2006.
4. Total number of county court judgements: 4,256, with an average value of £2,337.24.
5. Coronary heart disease cases for the period April 2007–March 2008: 2,369 admissions.

Inner London borough – Tower Hamlets

1. Violence against persons: 6,315 offences during the period April 2010–March 2011.
2. Criminal damage including arson: 2,803 incidents during the period April 2010–March 2011.
3. Social services incidents: 3,144 during the period January 2006–December 2006.
4. Total number of county court judgements: 3,155, with an average value of £2,978.56.
5. Coronary heart disease cases for the period April 2007–March 2008: 787 admissions.

Outer London borough – Waltham Forest

1. Violence against persons: 5,456 offences during the period April 2010–March 2011.
2. Criminal damage including arson: 2,585 offences during the period April 2010–March 2011.
3. Social services incidents: 885 during the period January 2006–December 2006.
4. Total number of county court judgements: 3,860, with an average value of £2,252.25.
5. Coronary heart disease cases for the period April 2007–March 2008: 3,206 admissions.

Inner London borough – Greenwich

1. Violence against persons: 5,435 offences during the period April 2010–March 2011.
2. Criminal damage including arson: 3,191 incidents during the period April 2010–March 2011.
3. Social services incidents: 1,482 during the period January 2006–December 2006.
4. Total number of county court judgements: 4,235, with an average value of £2,191.55.
5. Coronary heart disease cases for the period April 2007–March 2008: 3,157 admissions.

When we compare these statistics with another London borough such as Camden, we see a comparable situation.

Inner London borough – Camden

1. Violence against persons: 5,867 offences during the period April 2010–March 2011.
2. Criminal damage including arson: 2,269 incidents during the period April 2010–March 2011.
3. Social services incidents: 2,367 during the period January 2006–December 2006.
4. Total number of county court judgements: 2,469, with an average value of £3,473.53.
5. Coronary heart disease cases for the period April 2007–March 2008: 3,157 admissions.

Outer London borough – Kingston-Upon-Thames

1. Violence against persons: 2,234 offences during the period April 2010–March 2011.
2. Criminal damage including arson: 1,327 incidents during the period April 2010–March 2011.
3. Social services incidents: 480 during the period January 2006–December 2006.

4. Total number of county court judgements: 1,529, with an average value of £2,865.32.
5. Coronary heart disease cases for the period April 2007–March 2008: 2,537 admissions.

Outer London borough – Barnet

1. Violence against persons: 4,438 offences during the period April 2010–March 2011.
2. Criminal damage including arson: 2,686 incidents during the period April 2010–March 2011.
3. Social services incidents: 1,314 during the period January 2006–December 2006.
4. Total number of county court judgements: 4,058, with an average value of £3,392.39.
5. Coronary heart disease cases for the period April 2007–March 2008: 3,491 admissions.

Outer London borough – Merton

1. Crime against persons: 2,874 offences during the period April 2010–March 2011.
2. Criminal damage including arson: 1,838 incidents during the period April 2010–March 2011.
3. Social services incidents: 621 during the period January 2006–December 2006.
4. Total number of county court judgements: 2,550, with an average value of £3,189.85.
5. Coronary heart disease cases for the period April 2007–March 2008: 2,441 admissions.

Outer London borough – Harrow

1. Crime against persons: 3,260 offences during the period April 2010–March 2011.
2. Criminal damage including arson: 1,577 incidents during the period April 2010–March 2011.
3. Social services incidents: 561 during the period January 2006–December 2006.
4. Total number of county court judgements: 2,771, with an average value of £3,047.89.
5. Coronary heart disease cases for the period April 2007–March 2008: 3,433 admissions.

Outer London borough – Bromley

1. Crime against persons: 4,841 offences for the period April 2010–March 2011.
2. Criminal damage including arson: 2,808 incidents for the period April 2010–March 2011.
3. Social services incidents: 933 during the period January 2006–December 2006.
4. Total number of county court judgements: 3,073 with an average value of £2,946.45.
5. Coronary heart disease cases for the period April 2007–March 2008: 5,265 admissions.

There were a total of 32 London boroughs, of which 12 were designated as inner London and 20 as outer London. There were significant differences between inner and outer London boroughs in terms of health, crime and social deprivation. Looking at one particular dataset across all boroughs leads to the conclusion that crime shows a wide and disproportionate impact in relation to particular locations. As for ill health, this is not completely predicated on where you live but on how informed you may be on issues of healthy living. It is also important to bear in mind that clusters of ethnic groups in some inner London boroughs have a high propensity for coronary heart disease.

These statistics can also be linked with an independent study compiled by the Association of Public Health Observatories, which reported that the UK had the highest levels of obesity within the populations of all our European partners. This particular issue needed to be tackled by the government, health professionals, food producers and retailers, and required an immediate response. In 2009, the UK government introduced a campaign titled Change4Life, a campaign that initially targeted children to become more active, although it has since increased its remit to include parents. The UK government also took some lessons from its European partners. In 2003, Denmark was the first country in the world to outlaw food containing transfats, a move which effectively bans partially hydrogenated oils (the limit is 2 per cent of fats and oils destined for human consumption). Switzerland followed Denmark's transfat ban, and implemented its own in 2008. The National Institute for Health and Clinical Excellence (NICE) reported that transfats contribute to 40,000 early deaths a year in the UK. Coincidentally, McDonalds and Coca Cola were global partners of the Olympic Games – by default a host nation must work with and promote those partners.

It is these and other issues that were on the political agenda which indicate why London 2012 included healthy living and inclusion as two of the five objectives for the London Games.

Air quality

There is no direct reference to air quality in the Kyoto Protocol and other United Nation documents linked to climate change. However, health associated with clean air has currency with the Clean Air Act and European regulations.

The Environment Act 1995 has a remit for all local authorities within the UK to assess and monitor their air quality. If the level of pollutants in the air rises above the limits set, the local authority will be designated an Air Quality Management Area and must draw up an action plan to remove the pollutants. There are seven pollutants identified in the Act, which local authorities must monitor; Manchester City, for example, was meeting the standards on six out of the seven pollutants in 2010. However, nitrogen dioxide (NO_2) is predicted to increase within the city, and is likely to be a problem for all major cities within the UK.

Alongside this legislation, the UK government and the European parliament have also drawn attention to the problem of PM10 particles, the main sources of which are road transport, power generation and industry.

> Associated with respiratory problems, e.g. coughs, colds, shortness of breath and bronchitis, PM10 is made up of many substances, some of which may increase the risk of developing cancer. (Manchester City Council, 2006: 7 [online])

All of the five boroughs where the 2012 Games had an impact (Hackney, Newham, Greenwich, Tower Hamlets and Waltham Forest) are under an Air Quality Management Area

(AQMA) for nitrogen dioxide (NO_2) and particulates (PM10), and therefore Air Quality Action Plans are in place.

The Hackney State of the Environment report, published in 2008, concludes that:

> Current levels of air pollution are still predicted to cause just over 1,000 premature deaths and a similar number of extra respiratory hospital admissions each year in London. (London Borough of Hackney, 2008: 14 [online])

London's air quality is among the worst in the UK, according to the report. As in Manchester, Hackney has problems with the pollutants NO_2 and PM10, which have also become a concern for many metropolitan cities in the UK.

The UK government is currently in breach of the 1999 Clean Air Act and European regulations. Since the regulations became legally binding in 2005, the UK has failed to meet these limits every year. The UK government has put measures in place to meet the EU compliance standards for these limits through a UK wide system of over 145 air quality monitoring stations known as the Automatic Urban and Rural Network (AURN), together with a Pollution Climate Mapping (PCM) model. The European Commission issued a final warning to the UK government in 2009, with a potential fine of up to £360 million. To remedy this problem, on 3 January 2012, London introduced the Low Emission Zone, which is in force 24 hours a day and 7 days a week. It targets vehicles of a particular size (from 4x4 cars to articulated trucks) that run on diesel fuel. If vehicles are found to be in breach of the Low Emission Standard, fines can be charged from £250 to £1,000.

The introduction of the Low Emission Zone enabled the London 2012 Olympic and Paralympic Games to meet one of the five objectives and to measure with conclusive data a reduction in PM10 particles in areas of London identified by the European Commission which have been in breach of the regulations.

SUSTAINABLE DEVELOPMENT THROUGH THE OLYMPIC GAMES

The International Olympic Committee (IOC), recognising the importance of sustainable development, now takes into consideration the environment as an integral part of the organisation of the Olympic Games. As a part of the bidding process the IOC ensures that potential host cities for the Olympic Games take into consideration a sustainable environment plan. One of the key requirements for host cities is to collaborate with the relevant public or private authorities to deliver more environmentally friendly games.

The Rio de Janeiro 2016 Olympic Games adopted criteria to deliver standards for sustainable management to positively impact the country and the region. The Rio 2016 Organising Committee's Sustainability Management Plan (SMP) from the outset aimed to build an environmentally friendly Games and to reduce the environmental impact of the 2016 Games, leaving as small as possible an environmental footprint. The Organising Committee took into account sustainable infrastructures by using existing structures for the Olympic Games where possible.

Table 18.1   Rio 2016 Olympic Games structures

	Existing structures	New structures	Temporary structures
Deodoro	3	2	2
Maracana	3	–	–
Copacabana	2	–	2
Barra	2	1	1
TOTAL	10	3	5

For Rio 2016, ten existing structures, three new structures and five temporary structures were used. Table 18.1 outlines the structures used for the 2016 Games.

The 2016 Olympic Games acted as a positive catalyst for Rio's city development and it improved Rio's international recognition all over the world. This was based on economic, financial, tourism and sustainable opportunities.

Secondly, the Games provided financial benefits for local people through employment. There were over 100,000 people directly involved in delivering the Rio 2016 Olympic Games, including 70,000 volunteers, and millions were directly or indirectly involved in the city, around the country and across the continent. The Olympic Games represented a real opportunity for national firms to raise their sales.

Thirdly, the Games created employment. Indeed, this boost happened during the preparation for the Games, with new employment created in the construction sector, in passenger land transport, business services and sports facilities. Besides this, many restaurants, hotels and shops hired additional staff to cope with the huge influx of people during the Games.

Case study 1: Denmark achieves ISO 20121 certification for the 2012 EU Presidency

The Danish Foreign Ministry, responsible for the organisation of the 2012 European Union Presidency, announced the compliance of their event management system against the new ISO 20121 standard for sustainable event management. Externally verified by the global certification company SGS, this is the world's first ISO 20121 certification of a large international government event. The Ministry's event management system covers the logistical organisation of 110 meetings, attracting 15,000 attendees at three venues between January and June, 2012.

'The complexities involved with organizing so many diverse events required a smart, efficient and flexible management system. The ISO 20121 standard helped us align our sustainability goals with practical business processes in a sensible and practical way', reported Andreas Clausen-Boor, Head of Logistics for the Ministry of Foreign Affairs,

Denmark. 'We felt a responsibility to deliver effective events at an efficient cost. Sustainable practices saved us money while protecting the quality for which Danish events are known.'

Guy Bigwood, Sustainability Director of MCI Group and project consultants for the certification and Danish Sustainable Events Initiative commented, 'Due to the scale and complexity of the Presidency, this may be the most ambitious event certification project attempted in the business meetings and events sector. With this announcement, The Danish Foreign Ministry provides the latest example of the business case for sustainable practices and provides evidence that Denmark is a premier destination for innovative, high-quality, low-risk events'.

'The meetings industry has been asking for practical examples of creating better events through sustainability', said Steen Jakobsen, Convention Director at Wonderful Copenhagen. 'With their leadership and direct action to successfully integrate sustainability and use international standards, the Ministry event team is an inspiration for the meetings industry in Denmark and, indeed, the world.'

'Already, the Danish capital has a pioneering status when it comes to sustainable meetings. Today, 65% of all hotel rooms and all the key congress venues in Copenhagen are eco-certified. We are hopeful that the new ISO 20121 standard will encourage meetings businesses in Denmark to advance their sustainability practices and bolster Denmark's position as a leading events destination', noted Markus Diefenbach, International Marketing Manager – Business Tourism at VisitDenmark.

The Danish government is the first member of the European Union to create and certify their sustainable event management system against international standards.

SUMMARY

The creation of a number of published frameworks for sustainable event management has provided not only a sense of professionalism in light of contemporary concerns, but highlighted best practice within the industry, advice and guidance, practical solutions, and an inward-looking sense of the importance of events in modern society.

It is clear that sustainability as a movement, political agenda or a stream of social consciousness, requires political support and strategic direction. Governments and in particular European member states should have a uniform approach to accepting Directives and EU Regulations into their legal statutes. Where we have discrepancies among member states in pushing forward one or all of the issues there will be significant disparity between member states. This will present itself in the health of a nation, its economic strength to provide alternative energy supplies at an affordable cost to meet long-term demand, and increased taxation on goods and services to change consumer attitudes and purchasing decisions. These are just a few of the major issues that now become milestones for small-to-medium-sized businesses.

Biodiversity, waste and climate change cover a multitude of issues including energy, water resources management, infrastructure development, transport, local food production and carbon offsetting. Through their official website, LOCOG released a number of documents which clearly show how they met their objectives. However, healthy living and inclusion are two objectives which are particular to the UK and in need of long-term political intervention post 2012.

Discussion questions

Question 1

Discuss and critically evaluate ISO 20121 and what it means to the events industry in the future.

Question 2

In 2007 the British Standards Institute (BSI) introduced a sustainability guidance document for the events sector. Discuss the perceived difference between the ISO 14001 Environmental Standard and the BSI guidance for sustainable events.

Question 3

Sustainable event management is developed by adopting many practices that can be employed wholly or in part in an effort to reduce the impact of an event on the environment. Discuss and explain sustainable event management with supporting examples from a festival you are familiar with.

Question 4

Discuss the practicalities and benefits for the organisers and host community of sustainable approaches for waste and energy with real life examples from a festival.

Question 5

Critically discuss the real drive that will change behaviour among event organisers and audiences. How can sustainable policies among the event managers and key stakeholders be encouraged?

Question 6

The United Nations has organised a number of conferences on climate change. Discuss whether any of those conferences have been an instrument for international agreement and long-term policy change development for member states.

Case study 2: How green is Glastonbury Festival?

The UK's largest music festival has adopted an environmental policy. Each year more than 175,000 party goers descend on Worthy Farm in Pilton, Somerset, for one of the world's biggest popular music festivals. But what of Glastonbury's green credentials? Glastonbury aims to recycle 60 per cent of all waste and the site features around 15,000 refuse and recycling bins. The 2015 festival used more sustainable loos than ever before. The sanitation company 'Natural Event' provided 1,111 composting toilets to the festival, making up around a fifth of all toilets on site for the more than 175,000 visitors and staff.

Here we take a look at Glastonbury Festival's Top 10 in sustainability:

1   It costs £780,000 to dispose of all the rubbish left over at the festival, which this year expects 175,000 people to attend. To promote recycling and waste disposal, the organisers work by the motto of 'Love the Farm, leave no trace'.
2   Glastonbury aims to recycle 60% of all waste this year and the site features around 15,000 refuse and recycling bins.
3   The festival team features a 1,300 volunteer 'Recycling Crew'. Many of the volunteers receive free tickets in exchange for working shifts over the weekend or helping to clear up afterwards.
4   Organisers estimate that 1 million plastic bottles are used each year during the five days of music. More than 11 million litres of water are consumed each year at the festival.
5   Therefore, in order to reduce plastic waste, this year organisers are distributing reusable steel bottles and have set up 400 drinking water taps around the site.
6   Glastonbury is 'Not For Shale'. On the June 20, Michael and Emily Eavis, who run Worthy Farm where Glastonbury is hosted, released a statement saying that the farm will never be used as a site for fracking:
    'I oppose Fracking on the grounds that Shale gas is not the type of energy that we should be producing in Britain. We should be investing in renewable resources for future generations and for the health of our Planet'.
7   Worthy Farm features the largest privately owned solar photovoltaic array in the UK, with 1,500 square metres of solar panels with a capacity of 200kW. Solar and wind power areas around the site including cafés, stalls and stages.
8   Festival organisers have been using New Holland tractors which are capable of running on 100% biodiesel recycled from used cooking oil. Eleven of the British-built 'green tractors' will be used on the site.

(Continued)

(Continued)

9   Glastonbury donates £1m to international and local charities each year. It is the single biggest regular donor to Greenpeace and also supports its official partners WaterAid and Oxfam.

10 Glastonbury runs a Green Traveller scheme to encourage travel by public transport or bicycle, offering prizes and free food vouchers to those who participate. An estimated 40,000 people, 23% of festival goers, will travel to Glastonbury by coach or train this year.

Source: adapted from www.edie.net/news/5/How-green-is-Glastonbury--Top-10-sustainability-facts----/ [accessed 24/10/2016]

Case study 3: HebCelt Festival

2013 was the 18th annual outing of HebCelt. The festival regularly attracts audiences of over 15,000 over its four day run, many of whom travel to the island specifically for the event. The majority of visitors have local ties choosing this time to visit family and friends. All site facilities have to be brought on to the island and therefore logistics is both challenging and costly with many factors playing a part in the successful staging of the festival. Environment considerations are extremely important for the team behind the festival and improvements have been made over the last 3–5 years particularly in reducing waste to landfill.

Onsite costs are minimal as the festival enjoys in-kind support from key suppliers such as electricity, waste and water companies.

HebCelt sustainability objectives for 2013 included:

- To reduce their carbon emissions targeting transport mileage
- Reducing emissions on site by shifting reliance from generators to mains
- Further reducing waste to landfill by 10%
- Reducing plastic waste onsite
- Positive PR around promoting their sustainability measures and raising the profile of their environmental targets.

Meeting the objectives

Reducing transport mileage was the festival's biggest challenge. However they did manage to source some equipment from different suppliers, and in working with their transport manager to rationalise loads, reduced road mileage for site facilities by 18% which was over the initial target HebCelt set for itself. The festival was able to make a further 10% reduction in waste to landfill. This was a supreme effort by volunteer staff who managed to ensure that 67% of all waste generated onsite was either recycled or processed by the local digester plant.

HebCelt also took part in a government backed pilot initiative through Zero Waste Scotland to place Reverse Vending machines on the main site. This helped to raise awareness of their environmental targets and provided further strong statistics for future measuring.

Overcoming difficulties

The hot weather played a significant part in the increased demand for site water. Two public facing water points were established, installed with cup dispensers. The use of water bottles was promoted by retailing branded bottles, made from recycled materials, to allow festival goers to replenish free of charge.

Supplies of bottled water, although initially halved from the amount purchased in 2012, had to be replenished due to the extremely hot weather. It was therefore difficult to track exactly what, if any, reductions were made in reducing plastic onsite in 2013. There now exists however a more accurate record for future measuring.

Outcomes and achievements

Monitoring of suppliers and the materials that are brought onsite is critical as despite the clear issuing of terms and conditions some will disregard these, particularly in the case of food dispensing. This area will require closer monitoring.

Through the Reverse Vending project and the associated publicity generated HebCelt received excellent feedback from festival goers on the cleanliness of the site throughout the festival. Post event feedback was tremendous and this single project did a huge amount to raise the festival's profile as a 'green' event.

> Thought the recycling was a fantastic idea as we didn't see any discarded rubbish anywhere also it kept the kids busy. (Festival Attendee)

HebCelt's sustainability efforts during 2013 were also recognised by A Greener Festival, where they achieved an Outstanding Award, the only festival in Scotland to have received such a high accolade.

(Continued)

(Continued)

HebCelt sustainability future

2013 was a highly positive year punctuated by the publicity surrounding the Reverse Vending machines and HebCelt are confident that they have made significant inroads in meeting sustainability action plan goals.

Beyond 2013 the festival will need to consider how to replace the Reverse Vending machines and how to fund the clear up in future whether through a cup return scheme or another new project.

HebCelt do feel sure that they can continue to work at reducing waste to landfill although a great deal of volunteer effort is required to continue this excellent progress.

The event perceives that it will be a challenge to make many more inroads on reducing site transportation because of the island nature of the location which will always be subject to availability of the infrastructure required during the busy summer season.

HebCelt will continue to seek ways of reducing its carbon footprint and work with suppliers to do so.

Source: www.eventscotland.org/assets/3607 [accessed 24/10/2016]

FURTHER READING

Climate Wave Enterprises (2012) Available at: www.climatewave.com/green-events/green-events-make-economical-social-environmental-sense/ [accessed 20/02/2016].

HebCelt Festival (2013) Available at: www.eventscotland.org/assets/3607 [accessed 20/02/2016].

LOCOG (London Organising Committee for the Olympic Games) (2007) 'London 2012 Sustainable Plan November: Towards One Planet 2012'. Available at: www.sel.org.uk/uploads/London-2012-Sustainability-Plan.pdf [accessed 12/08/2015].

London Borough of Hackney (2008) 'The Hackney State of the Environment Report'. Available at: www.hackney.gov.uk/Assets/Documents/hackney_state_of_the_environment_report_2008.pdf [accessed 12/08/2015].

Manchester City Council (2006) 'Greater Manchester Air Quality and Action Plan'. Available at: www.greatairmanchester.org.uk/documents/LTP2%20AQ%20Strategy%20and%20Action%20Plan%202006.pdf [accessed 23/08/2015].

Sustainability Management Plan: Rio 2016™ Olympic and Paralympic Games (2013) Available at: www.rio2016.com/sites/default/files/Plano_Gestao_Sustentabilidade_EN.pdf [accessed 20/08/2015].

United Nations Framework Convention on Climate Change (1997) 'Kyoto Protocol'. Available at: http://unfccc.int/resource/docs/convkp/kpeng.pdf [accessed 20/08/2015].

19

LONG-TERM LEGACY
AND IMPACTS

In this chapter you will cover

The aim of this chapter is to critically review the development and implementation of the long-term legacy and impacts of events on host destinations. The chapter will present compelling evidence on the economic and social impact linked to the long-term legacy and impacts within the host location. The chapter will show that bidding for and hosting a mega event is not only predicated on a nation's ability to meet the international criteria, but that strategic alliances with international organisations are required, and the adoption of western political methods of governance can play a major role in achieving the end game. The chapter will discuss the historical development of the long-term legacy and impacts of events on a global platform with special attention to western democratic nations. A number of case studies will also be introduced to illustrate the broader issues from positive and negative perspectives.

IMPACTS OF EVENTS

In the events industry impact studies are undertaken for a variety of purposes. Frequently they consider elements of cost–benefit analysis concerning the event, in comparison to income generation and visitor expenditure. Events give greater economic life to the host city and raise its profile by developing employment through increased tourism potential, additional trade and business development.

It could be argued that a catalytic effect ensues whereby following an increase in investment, additional monies are made available for local infrastructure and long-term promotional benefits are created. Further to this, other tangible benefits are improved tax revenues and increased property prices, with subsequent connections to the community.

However, event managers often put great emphasis on the financial impacts of events, and invariably become myopic concerning other possible impacts occurring during the event. It is important for the event manager to realise this potential situation and to identify and manage both positive and negative impacts resulting from the event.

Events provide the host city with great economic resources, which can leave a lasting legacy to the local community. In addition, local businesses rely on mega events and festivals to boost their income for the year; for many it may well be 'the icing on the cake'. Getz offers a definition of mega events:

> Mega events, by way of their size or significance are those that yield extraordinarily high levels of tourism, media coverage, prestige, or economic impact for the host community, venue or organisation. (2005: 18)

A wide range of events exists, and can involve cultural, environmental and social impacts. Each has its own popularity that helps to categorise the size and type. The Olympic Games is recognised as the world's largest sports mega event allowing substantial economic, social and political benefits for the host nation and local community.

LONG-TERM LEGACY OF EVENTS

> In order for the demands related to the Olympics to be satisfied, resources are required, and some of those resources may be diverted from other uses. To the extent that demands related to the Olympics absorb resources that would not otherwise have been utilised, such as labour resources, they will add to both employment and the total output of the economy. (Office of Financial Management, 1997)

The legacy has caused constant discussion (see Table 19.1).

Table 19.1   Types of legacy (International Olympic Committee, 2013)

Legacy	
Sporting	The introduction of a variety of sports within the area
	Increased participation of women in the Olympic Games improves the percentage of females actively involved in sports activities in the host community
	World class sporting facilities
Political	Potential for improvement in education
	Promote the Olympic Truce as a cultural aid
	Introduction of various cultural considerations to the host community
Economic	Difficult to measure due to constant variables
	Long-term benefits for the community through regeneration projects
Social	Builds upon national pride and traditions
	Long-term recognition as a successful sporting nation
	Used as an historical tool, educating the young community about its social past

Host cities for the Olympic Games

Up until 1968 the IOC awarded the Games to western democratic nations. From 1896 to 1964 the Olympic Games were held 17 times and over that period were subject to many economic and political intrusions. This chapter will examine those intrusions at an international and national level and explore the ways in which they contributed to the social, economic and environmental impact of the Olympic Games for the host cities. The most obvious intrusions were the First and Second World Wars; during those periods the Olympic Games did not take place. However, at the end of each war countries that were on the losing side were excluded from bidding for and participating in the Olympic Games for a short while.

In 1920 the games were awarded to Antwerp, Belgium; they were then given to Paris in 1924. In 1928 Amsterdam, the Netherlands, was seen as a viable option due to its neutral status in the First World War. After the Second World War, London hosted the event in 1948. As the country was economically bankrupt after the war, it received approximately $4 billion in financial assistance from the American government under the Marshall Plan. Without this loan, Britain could never have maintained its balance of payments or world power at the centre of the Commonwealth. With that financial assistance, Britain was able to bid for and host the Olympic Games in 1948. In 1952 Helsinki was host to the Olympic Games, followed by Melbourne, Australia, in 1956, then Rome in 1960. In 1964 Tokyo, Japan, was awarded the rights to host the Olympic Games. The city of Tokyo was devastated by bombing in the Second World War but also followed a western political style of government. By 1956, Japan had joined the United Nations and from that point on was viewed as an economically strong and technological powerhouse of production.

In 1968 the IOC awarded the Olympic Games to Mexico. At that point in history Mexico was under an authoritarian government and with that came a number of political demonstrations by the young student population seeking political and civil freedom from oppression. On 2

October, ten days before the start of the Games, 44 student and civilian protestors were killed by government troops at a demonstration. It could be argued that this episode was one of the worst social impacts to a host nation because of the Olympic Games.

The long-term legacy of the London 2012 Games

Higgins (2008) identified the five main areas in which the London 2012 Games needed to invest in order to develop its long-term legacy (see Figure 19.1).

Figure 19.1   Long-term legacy framework for the London 2012 Games

Costs of staging the Olympics, Beijing 2008

Table 19.2 identifies construction costs of hosting the 2008 Olympic Games and regenerating a city. Table 19.3 shows regeneration expenditure for Olympic and non-Olympic related investments.

This improvement increases the standard of living for the city's residents and is therefore a positive impact for the host community.

ECONOMIC IMPACTS OF EVENTS

Historically, economic impact reports have been published as a prelude to the event and when the event concludes, particularly in the case of mega events. Academics and established independent organisations have consistently been given the responsibility to produce reports, and

Table 19.2   Cost and revenues for the 2008 Beijing Olympic Games

Revenues	US$ million	%
Television rights	709	43.63
The Olympic Partner (TOP) Programme sponsorship	130	8.00
Local sponsorship	130	8.00
Licensing	50	3.08
Official suppliers	20	1.23
Olympic coins programme	8	0.49
Philately	12	0.74
Lotteries	180	11.08
Ticket sales	140	8.62
Donations	20	1.23
Disposal of assets	80	4.92
Subsidies	100	6.15
Others	46	2.83
Total	1625	

Expenditure	US$ million	%
Capital investment	190	11.69
Sports facilities:	102	6.28
Olympic village	40	2.46
Main Press Conference and International Broadcast Centre	45	2.77
Media Venues	3	0.18
Operations	1419	87.32
Sports events:	275	16.92
Olympic village	65	4.00
MPC and IBC	360	22.15
MV	10	0.62
Ceremonies and programmes	100	6.15
Medical services	30	1.85
Catering	51	3.14
Transport	70	4.31
Security	50	3.08
Paralympic games	82	5.05
Advertising and promotion	60	3.69
Administration	125	7.69
Pre-Olympic events and coordination	40	2.46
Other	101	6.22
Surplus	16	0.98
Total	3234	

Source: BOCOG, www.beijing-2008.org

Table 19.3   Regeneration costs, Beijing 2008

Capital investments	Construction cost (US$ million)								
	2001	2002	2003	2004	2005	2006	2007	2008	Total
Planned non-Olympic expenditure									
Environment protection	1000	1000	1500	1500	1500	1300	827	0	8627
Roads and railways	547	592	636	636	636	313	313	0	3673
Airport	12	30	31	12	0	0	0	0	85
Olympic-related expenditure									
Sports venues	213			425	496	283	12	0	1429
Olympic village	111					159	135	38	442
Total	1559	1622	2380	2573	2743	2055	1287	38	14257

Source: BOCOG, www.beijing-2008.org

have made available to the wider public evidence that suggests mega events can bring a significant economic value to a host community, whether through tourism or major infrastructural build programmes. In addition to this, economic studies have also been published by the host nations and official rights holders after each Olympic Games. The spending is reported as providing significant and worthwhile additions to the host locations. In most circumstances that infrastructure in the shape of homes, roads and commercial buildings is a welcome addition to any city. However, the initial spend to acquire those assets to a large degree comes from the local and national taxpayers within the host nation.

In 2004 PricewaterhouseCoopers published a report that analysed the economic impact of the Olympic Games on host countries (PricewaterhouseCoopers, 2004). It made a clear distinction between the overall financial costs of hosting the Games and those costs that can be met by revenue directly generated from the games. The report takes into consideration the size of the host nations, and measures economic effects at a local and national level, for example in the USA and in Greece. The report looks at pre-, during and post-Games impact. Broadcasting revenue is also explored – this is the largest economic revenue driver from the Olympic Games, although the IOC will generally take a significant share of these revenues. In building an economic profile of the Games within a host city the report makes reference to what is known by economists as the 'multiplier effect'. This is an economic indicator applied to test and measure the economic performance via aggregated spend.

The report takes into consideration seven countries that hosted the Games from 1972 to 2000. Of the seven countries analysed within the economic report there was one anomaly that must be recognised: the Los Angeles Olympics, which were able to break the economic cycle of debt to the host nation. The local organising committee was able to secure all the financial outlay by way of sponsorship. No other country before 1984 or after has been able to finance and bring the event in with a surplus.

The economic performance within each country was measured over a period of 8–10 years to see if there was any significant impact on GDP, investment, private and public consumption and consumer expenditure. The report does not take into consideration, but draws to the reader's attention, global economic situations that could have an effect on growth and economic performance for some countries, such as with Greece due to the Iraq war and an increasing security budget. The report clearly shows that economic performance increases in the pre-Games impact stage for nearly all countries. However, in the Games impact and post-Games impact, economic performance related to GDP and the other indicators as mentioned earlier level out, and for some host cities economic performance drops off for a number of years.

The Australian government reported, and the IOC concluded, that the Sydney Olympic Games in 2000 were an economic success. However, the PricewaterhouseCoopers report shows that GDP for the New South Wales economy dropped off and consumer expenditure and public consumption levelled out. In Sydney's bid for the 2000 Olympic Games, the budget was $AUS 3 billion (£1 billion), of which just $AUS 363.5 million would be borne by the public. In 2002 the Auditor-General of New South Wales undertook a further audit, confirming that the Sydney Games had cost $AUS 6.6 billion and the public paid $AUS 1.7–2.4 billion. Such a budget discrepancy can be seen with many bids, including that for London 2012, where the local organising committee decide to negate/exclude capital cost for facilities and infrastructure, which ultimately becomes the most costly aspect of the bid.

In 2005 the Department of Culture Media and Sport, in association with Pricewaterhouse-Coopers, published the Olympic Games Impact Study Final Report for the London 2012 Olympic Games. The report draws a conclusion which detracts from the information contained in the 2004 economic profile of seven Olympic countries.

> It shows, for example, that there is an 84.4% chance that the Olympics will have a positive impact on UK GDP over the period 2005–2016: in London, the comparable probability is 95.3%. (PricewaterhouseCoopers/DCMS, 2005: 5 [online])

Before London won the rights to host the Olympic Games in 2005, the government undertook some extensive research and published a report: House of Commons Culture, Media and Sport Committee (2002-3).

It detailed what the cost would be to host the Olympic Games in 2012. The report took into account factors such as infrastructure cost, inflation, land acquisition, uncertainties and assumptions of a ten-year project, with an investigation of the Athens, Sydney and Manchester Games. The final budget that was put forward was £4.674 million, with public subsidy set at £2,624 million by the Department for Culture, Media and Sport (DCMS). Considering the fact that the security budget alone for Athens 2004 was documented at 1.4 billion Euros, and the Greek government required loans from the IMF to cover the cost of the Games, it is difficult to believe that the government with associated partners put forward such an underestimated cost to host the Games.

The Secretary of State emphasised in oral evidence the risks involved in budgeting for the Games with reference to the experience of Sydney and Athens. She said that both had found their outturn to be double their estimated costs. We asked the DCMS what work had been undertaken to assess and avoid the failure of Sydney and Athens in predicting costs. (House of Commons Culture, Media and Sport Committee, 2002–3: 17)

The security cost for London 2012 was budgeted at £600 million, but the actual cost was over £1 billion. Some media commentators draw a comparison with the Athens 2004 security budget of 1.4 billion Euros. By 2007, the budget for the London Olympics had doubled in cost.

The budget for the London 2012 Games, announced in March 2007 by the Minister for the Olympic and Paralympic Games and Co-Chair of the Olympic Board, was £9,325 million. (Olympic Delivery Authority, 2011: 17 [online])

Taking into consideration the 2004 report, where Olympic cities did not show any significant movement in GDP post-event but in some cases economic performance dropped off, and assimilating this alongside other Olympic cities that were not included within the sample for the 2004 report, the evidence shows a very similar characteristic in terms of economic performance. The London 2012 Games achieved a significant economic impact on the host community.

When charting the economic impact of mega events on western nations we are confronted with a level of inconsistency regarding published data. This is compounded by a continued effort on the part of the IOC to demonstrate that hosting the Olympic Games is seen as a financial success and a status symbol for stable economies, and emerging and developing nations.

URBAN REGENERATION OF CITIES THROUGH MEGA EVENTS

Within western democratic nations and in particular in the UK, bidding for mega events is driven in the main by a policy known as 'urban regeneration', a product of urban neglect in many metropolitan cities. Coupled with that programme of redevelopment we also have social impact, a major addition included within bidding documents for mega events.

The policy of urban redevelopment comes directly from the national government, but urban decline is also on the European agenda, as is evident in the European Commission Objective targets given to underperforming cities or regions. Objectives 1, 2 and 3 are status targets that give a social and economic profile to a city in the broadest terms. Liverpool was granted Objective 1 status by the European Commission for nearly 20 years, as the city had recorded some of the worst economic and social impacts to communities within Europe.

It was not until 2008, when Liverpool was officially European Capital of Culture, that the city began to experience new investment opportunities and was removed from Objective 1 status. This can also be seen with the location of the 2002 Commonwealth Games in Manchester, the 2012 Olympic Games in London and the 2014 Commonwealth Games in Glasgow.

The Manchester 2002 Commonwealth Games were located to the east of Manchester city centre, an area noted for its economic and social problems. Blighted by underinvestment in all areas, East Manchester required significant economic investment to turn around years of decline. Derelict land was earmarked for redevelopment with a sustainable long-term future. Manchester Commonwealth Games post-event analysis by a number of academics and independent organisations has presented significant success stories by way of new homes, jobs, improved transportation and road networks including sporting facilities which have sustained use from the local inhabitants. The London 2012 Games were located on contaminated and derelict land untouched since the Second World War. The event had a social, environmental and economic reach over five boroughs in London which rank as the worst performing in many social aspects in comparison with other boroughs.

The 2014 Commonwealth Games in Glasgow were strategically located to the east end of the city. Again this area is ranked as one of the worst performing areas within the UK from a health perspective, and also manifests a range of other social problems linked to ill health. The European Commission also places it as one of the most deprived locations in Europe. It is no accident therefore that mega events have a strategic role to play when attempting to enhance the lives of the local inhabitants. The methodology applied across the three events gives a clear picture that mega events have the propensity to change the social and economic fabric of a city for the better.

THE ECONOMIC LEGACY OF THE RIO OLYMPIC GAMES

The preparation for such an event would allow Brazil to create 120,000 jobs by 2016. According to the Brazilian Finance Minister, Guido Mantega, the organisation of the Olympic Games would reinforce economic growth of at least 1 per cent through investments in different infrastructure. Acceleration of infrastructure investments (that would not have been made 10, 15 or 20 years earlier without this event) mostly benefited the Olympic region of 'Barra'.

Three major projects were constructed: the Olympic Park, where different sports competitions were held; the Olympic Village, which comprised 31 residential buildings with 3,604 apartments for housing athletes (after the event they were sold); and the City of Rock, a recreation park for the athletes during the Games.

The forecasts estimated that the 7,000,000 ticket entries would bring US$36 billion. This was beneficial for tourism and caused some short-term growth in the local economy: hotels, restaurants, local shops and tourist attractions all benefited from this sport tourism and the money spent by visitors.

However, it is important to note the very high cost of this event for Brazil. The Rio Olympic Games cost at least US$13 billion: 58.52 per cent was financed privately and 41.48 per cent by public funds. The estimated budget in 2009 when Rio was chosen to host the Olympics was 28.9 billion reals, which represents US$9 billion (38.1 billion reals in present value, according to the daily *Folha de Sao Paulo*). But these 38.1 billion are not the final amount; official figures have not so far been released.

In addition, other economic issues have arisen. Not all investments were profitable for the city council after the Olympic Games. Indeed, the citizens do not use all these grandiose infrastructures because the majority cannot afford to, and their maintenance is costly for the city.

Moreover, as *Estado Sao Paulo* pointed out, the massive influx of tourists revealed some shortcomings in capacity and municipal management. The Ministry of Tourism recognised that 'the main challenge' was to train more professionals in this sector, which included new investment in training.

ENVIRONMENTAL AND SOCIAL IMPACTS OF EVENTS

Event organisers are now using historical and cultural themes to develop annual events that attract visitors and create cultural images in the host cities by holding festivals within community settings. Even so, many event organisers do not take into account the social and environmental impacts.

The impacts of events can greatly affect the quality of life of the local residents. It has been argued that strategies need to be adopted to take control of the social and environmental impacts of festivals and analysis is required when looking at the economic impact of each individual event. Event organisers may only take into consideration the economic implications and ignore the residents' perceptions, which provide an important non-economic dimension for gauging how events benefit or impinge on the host community (Hall, 1992).

Therefore, it is important for event managers to address the concerns of the local people and reduce the negative impacts. Event managers should also deliberate on the perceptions of the local residents and show willingness to discuss the initial proposal for the festival with the local community. Many leading authors have suggested that it is important for event organisers to have a clear awareness and understanding of residents' concerns and attitudes. This, Delamere et al. (2001) believe, will encourage a balance between social and economic development forces within the community. The view of the host community may also help to refine the analytical framework used by planners and policy-makers in helping the industry to be sustainable in the long term (Williams and Lawson, 2001; Raj and Musgrave, 2009).

Without the support of the local community the success of any event cannot be ensured so it is a matter of urgency and even commonsense to get the local community on board from the outset. Event organisers who do not take into account local feeling will only store up feelings of animosity and a sense by the local community that they do not belong, that it is no longer their event. This is only one of a number of potential problems with the measurement of event impacts, in that the costs and benefits are unevenly distributed, and may occur in the short or long term.

Environmental impacts of Rio 2016

It is important to establish both *how* and *who* are affected by the costs and the benefits of the Rio Olympic Games. The Organising Committee of the Rio Olympic Games launched its sustainable development plan to look at the environmental impacts of the Games on the host community. The signing of the technical cooperation agreement with the United Nations Environment Programme (UNEP) provided a link between the people of Brazil and Rio 2016. To this end, the organising committee created a sustainability logo, baptised 'Embrace Rio 2016', which was affixed to all products and information materials for the campaign. This brand helped to mobilise the public and encouraged them to take part in events to promote sustainable development.

The organising committee of the Olympic Games announced that the 4,924 gold, silver and bronze medals, which were distributed during the Olympic and Paralympic Games were produced from recycled materials. For this, the committee relied on Brazilian Mint, a state company that specialises in recycling dismantled objects of everyday life to extract the precious metals.

Designed by the Swiss company RAFFA, the Solar City Tower won the architectural competition for the 2016 games. The Solar City Tower has a solar power plant at its base and a tower above a skyscraper, from which flows an artificial waterfall. It supplies energy to part of the city and the Olympic Village. The manufacturer Dow, official carbon partner of Rio 2016, estimated that the Rio Olympic Games would have a half-million tonne CO_2 footprint, but this does not take into account the negative impact that may be caused by the construction of such a work in Brazil: the materials used and emissions from the building site, the logistics difficulties and financial cost of cleaning the bay. A lot of competitors criticised the water quality of the bay and accused the authorities of a lack engagement. The governor proposed a plan to depollute the water with a special treatment. Currently only 49 per cent of work to depollute the bay has been carried out by the local government, which had promised 80 per cent.

Despite many efforts to reduce the environmental footprint of the Rio Olympic Games, they are minimal compared to its ecological consequences. The Games were estimated to produce around 3.6 million metric tonnes of carbon, according to the Federal Government of Brazil (5 August 2016), related to various road and building construction projects, but also emissions including domestic flights connecting the cities, international flights, tourism and shuttles between airports, stadiums and hotels (edie.net, 2016 [online]).

Social impacts of Rio 2016

The Olympic Games were an opportunity for the Brazilian population to share and gather together. Also events such as this kindle the enthusiasm and pride of citizens due to the visibility and prestige of being the centre of the world in the most publicised event in the world.

Despite the public demonstrations in 2014, the organising committee decided to rent or sell the flats in the Olympic village at exorbitant prices to take advantage of the economic climate. The 10,160 rooms have been converted into 3,600 luxury flats. In a country where economic and social disparities are significant (only 16 countries are more unequal), this idea was not accepted by the Brazilian population. Furthermore, the Olympic Village was built on the site of the favelas, so the local population (more than 7,000 families) were forced to relocate against their will. Drug trafficking and availability of drugs increased as drug cartels took the opportunity of the Olympic Games to expand their trade. The underground economy thrived due to the Olympic Games.

Portuguese is the main language in Brazil and the World Cup in 2014 and Olympics Games in 2016 led to a new government programme, 'Crianca Global', which was created to expand educational opportunities for school children, including requiring public schools in Rio de Janeiro to teach English as a second language With 350 new teachers hired and trained in 2014, there was a positive impact for 100,000 primary schoolchildren and students. Also 19 towns received funds from the government programme during 2016.

Case study 1: $350 million hole is biggest Brazil World Cup legacy for hosts

The 22-kilometer (13.7-mile) scar disfiguring the center of Cuiaba is a daily reminder to citizens of this Brazilian city of failed World Cup promises. And matters may be about to get worse. A billion reais ($350 million) of public money has already been spent on a light railway system and construction companies say it will take at least 400 million reais more to complete. The state of Mato Grosso has suspended activities and may scrap the entire project, said Gustavo Oliveira, state secretary for strategic projects. The railway was supposed to be finished three months before the inland city of 550,000 located in western Brazil hosted four World Cup group games in June.

With just one station completed, tracks not laid and other unfinished work lining its route, Cuiaba's rail system is the most visible failure of projects linked to the 2014 World Cup. The city has failed to complete 22 other promised legacy works including a hospital and several transport infrastructure programs.

'The works are suspended for now because the schedule wasn't kept, costs are not as predicted and the estimate for the final bill is not consistent,' Oliveira said in an interview. If the numbers don't add up and local sentiment turns against the rail system, known locally as VLT, the project will be scrapped.

Debris and unfinished work litter the center of Cuiaba, capital of the state of Mato Grosso, where cattle outnumber humans. Half-complete metal structures that would be stations line the route, two electric sub stations are complete, while the 40 wagons that would move passengers are gathering dust near the city's airport. Commuters wait for a local bus at a station built for trains that may never arrive.

Government probe

While officials weigh the future of the VLT, local prosecutors are considering bringing fraud charges … against members of the former Mato Grosso government that suddenly scrapped plans for a cheaper bus system in favor of the VLT.

'What we are talking about now is to identify what is the financial value, and then discuss if this is a priority or not,' Oliveira said.

The future of the transit system isn't the only World Cup-related concern that's taxing local officials. The city doesn't have a team in Brazil's top soccer leagues, making it hard to fill the 41,000-seat, 570 million-reais Arena Pantanal. Cuiaba was chosen as part of former Brazil President Luiz Inacio Lula da Silva's promise to take the tournament to all corners of the country. Officials in the Amazon capital Manaus are also struggling to make their new stadium pay its way.

On a recent morning the perimeter of the Cuiaba stadium attracted a smattering of elderly joggers and a couple of stray dogs. Since hosting the World Cup games, the arena has held 17 matches and one religious event. Local teams rarely attract more than 1,000 fans, while larger numbers attend games involving popular Rio or Sao Paulo-based teams like Corinthians or Flamengo.

Emergency repairs

The stadium was temporarily closed for emergency repairs. The state allows local teams to play there rent free, and isn't close to earning the 15 million to 18 million reais needed annually to ensure it's not another burden for the public coffers, said Oliveira. The Arena Pantanal held World Cup games before construction was complete, and will be shuttered again for further works.

Despite its troubles Paulo Cesar, the stadium's superintendent, says it is a source of pride for locals.

'We've only had one broken seat since it opened so you can see they like it,' he said. Cesar said the World Cup raised the profile of the city and taught the local population about the requirements to host a world class event. Oliveira said Russia, the next World Cup host, should look at what happened in Cuiaba and learn from its experiences.

'You can't think ... just about the event, you have to understand what the costs are going to be and about the next 20 or 30 years,' he said.

Source: Tariq Panja (2015) www.bloomberg.com/news/articles/2015-02-19/-350-million-hole-is-biggest-brazil-world-cup-legacy-for-hosts [accessed 14/11/2016]

SUMMARY

This chapter suggests that the spending by visitors on local goods and services has a direct economic impact on local businesses and also passes the benefits more widely across the economy and the community.

The chapter has debated the validity of economic assessments and shown that there is disagreement regarding the most accurate method of assessing the performance of an event. Substantial attention, however, is still paid by governments and the events industry to the economic dimensions of impacts, as this is often regarded as a measure of the immediate success of the event and associated developments. The event organiser and local government only take into account the economic impacts and ignore the implications of social impacts of the events. As the events industry develops, it is the role of the event manager to catalogue and forecast possible impacts to stakeholders while creating plans to decrease all negative impacts.

Evidence clearly shows that the social and economic impact within the mega event arena is a common issue that must be taken seriously by future governments when deciding to bid for international mega events. The long-term social scars for some inhabitants will remain long after the event is over. The fiscal debt which remains with the host inhabitants has created a great deal of resentment towards mega events in host communities. Official documents produced as a way of explaining the overall legacy and impact of mega events must follow consistent criteria and in particular when presenting financial data. Infrastructure costs must always be included when presenting a pre- and post-event impact report. Long-term financial projections should pay close attention to similar bids where the financial data gives an accurate account of fiscal spend.

Transparency and accountability should not be seen as a cursory comment tagged to a final report but used as a mechanism to address problems and set new standards for the future to nations who intend to bid.

Discussion questions

Question 1

Investigate and explore the challenge of creating a lasting legacy of sustainability through Olympic Games. Discuss how Olympic Games improve the physical and social environment of a host city.

Question 2

Discuss the rationale as to why there is conflicting information published by credible and accredited bodies representing mega events.

Question 3

Urban regeneration is a political and government policy to redevelop areas within a region, city or town that has seen significant decline. Mega events have taken on this political agenda. Explain the difference between impact and legacy.

Question 4

Successful legacies are well planned, well delivered and embedded in existing strategies, policies and programmes. Considering Greece, China and the UK, discuss why events were allocated to those three countries.

Question 5

Discuss and critically evaluate the benefits that mega sporting events have in host cities and analyse how these events are a major boost to the economy.

Question 6

The evidence through research indicates that legacy and sustainability from major sporting events varies in terms of quality and benefits. Discuss and investigate how hosting major events can create a legacy and economic success for key stakeholders.

Case study 2: The Games accelerated the physical transformation of East London

The creation of the Olympic Park and the wider development in its immediate surrounding area has resulted in unprecedented change in this part of East London.

Through a comprehensive programme of land acquisition, remediation and development, the Olympic Park was created on a largely derelict, polluted and inaccessible site, a site that was 'fragmented in terms of urban form and use'.

The transformation process began with the remediation and clean-up of 2.5 square kilometres of brownfield land, including the demolition of more than 200 buildings and the undergrounding of 52 power pylons. It continued through the development of six permanent sporting venues (along with a number of temporary venues), the building of the Athletes' Village, the creation of 80,000 square metres of business space through the International Broadcast Centre and Main Press Centre, the building of more than 30 bridges and connections across the Olympic Park and the creation of 100 hectares of green space.

Following the Games, and with the transfer of responsibility for the transformation of the Olympic Park from the ODA to the London Legacy Development Corporation (LLDC), work continues. The Park is in the process of being transformed from Games-time use to its legacy use as 'one of London's most dynamic urban districts', hosting nearly 10,000 new homes, two primary schools, a secondary school, nine nurseries, three health centres, and a number of multi-purpose community, leisure and cultural spaces.

While plans for this part of East London – including a longer-term vision and proposals for its regeneration – developed prior to the awarding of the Games to London, the Games played a central role in driving forward the transformation of the Olympic Park site and its

(Continued)

(Continued)

immediate surrounding area. For some aspects of the physical change, such as the creation of the permanent sporting venues, the transformation effect and benefits they will bring are wholly attributable to the Games. For others, the Games served as a significant catalyst to regeneration in East London – an acceleration that was, it should be noted, always the intention. In particular, the Games resulted in both:

- A 'more comprehensive and joined up site', as it would have been unviable for the private sector to have brought forward a site of a similar scale which would have been subject to multiple ownerships; as well as

Predominant land uses – Baseline (2005)

- Brownfield
- Old Ford Nature Reserve
- Travellers site
- Rail
- Power lines
- Commercial (around 200, primarily industrial, businesses, e.g. car breakers yards)
- Residential (small numbers, poor quality)
- Open space – scarred by shopping trolleys, car tyres, discarded white goods, with potential habitats suffocated by invasive plant species such as Japanese Knotweed and Floating Pennywort

Predominant land uses – Post Games (2013 onwards)

- Olympic Stadium
- Aquatics Centre
- ArcelorMittal Orbit
- Velo-park
- Copper Box (Multi-Use Arena)
- Tennis and Hockey Centre
- Energy Centre
- Commercial (91,000 sq m created through conversion of Press and Broadcast centre)
- Retail (Westfield Stratford City plus approximately 30,000 sq m of additional retail space)
- Residential (around 10,000 new homes)
- Open space (100 hectares)

Figure 19.2   Predominant land use on the Olympic Park - 2005 and 2013

Source: Olympic Delivery Authority (2011) and London Legacy Development Corporation (2013)

- A more integrated timetable for regeneration. The Games ensured that there was both a firm and immovable deadline for delivery, while also 'protecting' the public and private sector investment in regeneration activities in this part of East London from spending cuts that affected a number of other major regeneration projects across the UK.

The catalytic role of the Games is also apparent in the transformation of public transport in East London. The Games resulted in a number of TfL's plans being brought forward significantly as a result of both the demand provided by the Games and the additional funding from the ODA which helped unlock planned investments. This included a project to double the capacity of Stratford Station, upgrades to the Dockland Light Railway and upgrades to the North London Line. The permanent nature of these enhancements mean that they form a vital part of the wider Games Legacy as they significantly improve transport capacity and reliability across East London, and will do so for many years to come.

This story of the Games acting as a catalyst and accelerator is repeated with regard to the wider transformation of the public realm across East London, as the host boroughs sought to maximise the impact of the Olympic Park development and better integrate the site into the sub-region. While much of the activity delivered was part of larger and longer-term development schemes, the presence of the Games brought forward and increased the scale of a significant proportion of the projects, including improvement to Hackney Wick and Fish Island, Greenwich Riverside and Town Centre and Stratford Town Centre. These improvements have made a positive contribution to the transformation of East London as a place beyond the Olympic Park.

In considering the wider physical regeneration effects of the Games, the evidence available to date suggests that they are limited to Stratford and the immediate vicinity of the Olympic Park. The most notable impact was the role that the Games played in bringing forward the Westfield development at Stratford City – and all the employment and economic benefits associated with it – by between five and seven years. For both the Westfield development and others where it has not been possible to quantify the nature of the role played by the Games, such as Lend Lease's in Stratford's International Quarter and Inter IKEA's in Stratford, it would appear that the impact of the Games is again catalytic. Not least in the context of driving investment in development in a time of economic downturn.

As a result of the Games it can be concluded that parts of East London – particularly the Olympic Park site and the area immediately surrounding it – already look, feel and function differently. These are changes that may have occurred in the absence of the Games, but they would have taken significantly longer and would have been far less

(Continued)

(Continued)

integrated. However, while change is already apparent, the true physical transformation legacy and impact will not be fully realised for a number of years. The challenge will be to ensure that both the existing transformation plans are delivered while also ensuring that positive transformation effects ripple out more widely across East London

Source: Department for Culture, Media & Sport (2013) *Report 5: Post-Games Evaluation. Meta-Evaluation of the Impacts and Legacy of the London 2012 Olympic Games and Paralympic Games.* Available at: www.gov.uk/government/uploads/system/uploads/attachment_data/file/224181/1188-B_Meta_Evaluation.pdf [accessed 18/11/2016]

Case study 3: The impact of the FIFA 2014 World Cup for Brazil

The impact of the World Cup for Brazil should be examined in two ways, positive and negative. The following case study will analyse the impact on the nation and the local people by considering the economic, social, cultural and environmental aspects.

Economic impact

Positive

Brazil built 12 sport stadiums before the World Cup, and many new extensions for the event were built at the same time. These constructions increased employment and provided job opportunities for local people, especially in the construction industry. During the event, there were lots of visitors travelling to Brazil. The visitor expenditure brought money to the local economy through tourism related services, which included travel, accommodation, restaurants and shopping. The expenditure brought revenue to local people. In order to hold a great event, Brazil's government has to invest in infrastructure which provided long-term promotional benefits and tax revenues after the event.

Negative

Negative impacts included increased income creating price inflation on goods and services. If the lower classes did not gain economic benefit, increasing prices created financial pressures, due to higher living costs.

Meanwhile, increased spending by the government during preparation for the event led to tax increases for local people. Tax is one of the most important incomes for governments, and an increasing tax rate can lead to social conflict.

Social and cultural impact

Positive

Increased reporting of the World Cup in the media created a sense of pride and national identity for local people. The event provided an opportunity for local people to develop and share their culture, which created a sense of values and beliefs for the international tourism industry. Meanwhile, it was a chance for local communities and visitors to communicate cross-culturally.

The event attracted media attention around the world, with a focus on the nation during a short period, which was a useful way to improve and change the national image.

Construction projects improved Rio's systems such as transport, which became more efficient and convenient. The city spent US$2 billion upgrading the BRT transport system.

Negative

When the nation was put under the media spotlight, reporting of each small national problem spread through the world, creating a negative image. In order to have enough space to build the event buildings, Brazil relocated the lower classes to outside the city, far away from the centre. This was called 'eviction' by one journalist. Local people were paying the price for all this World Cup development. The government had to compensate the lower classes. A peaceful environment is needed for a World Cup!

Environmental impact

Brazil has rich environmental resources. In order to welcome visitors from around the world, Brazil spent lots of money rebuilding and replanning the city, creating a more suitable space and cleaner more efficient city. These were the positive impacts, but at the same time, the rebuilding process caused some problems, such as construction rubbish, noise and air pollution, and environmental disruption. There is always a balance between development and protection of the local community, which should be considered by the government. The World Cup is important, but the citizens' quality of life should be protected at the same time.

The risks of the FIFA 2014 World Cup Brazil

Pre-event risks

There were some essential problems for the organisation of the 2014 Brazil World Cup in the pre-event period. This section is going to discuss construction problems and marketing risks.

(Continued)

(Continued)

Construction risks

The construction problems mainly concerned the budget for stadium construction, engineering quality, environmental issues, scheduling issues, etc. The Brazilian government projected its construction budget for hosting the World Cup would be about US$13.3 billion, of which US$3.4 billion would be spent on the construction and renovation of the 12 stadiums. Also, the construction of public transport, commercial buildings or other required projects would also need large amounts of money. However, there were difficulties due to lack of financing, meaning that the construction of stadiums in some cities was stopped.

Another significant issue was the quality and safety of construction; accidents like the collapse of the San Paolo Stadium should not happen again. Health and safety should focus attention on protecting workers and supervising the building process. An additional issue was that the organiser and construction teams had to accelerate the construction process to prevent delays in stadium construction.

Marketing risks

The marketing risk here refers to protecting the rights of the big affiliates and sponsors. Main affiliates like adidas, Coca Cola and Emirates, etc., had to be protected from ambush marketing by their competitors, because most of the event's revenue was directly related to advertising and the sale of sponsoring slots. If the benefits for sponsors couldn't be ensured, there would be losses for the whole event in return. Therefore, ambush marketing would reduce income and put the World Cup at risk.

The following are some suggestions for an organisation confronting ambushing problems during a World Cup. The organiser, with the legislation department, should pass specific legislation which forbids and punishes the unauthorised use of FIFA trademarks and potential marketing infringement. All of the host stadiums and cities should implement restricted areas, to prohibit the sales, campaigns or advertising of non-sponsoring companies. Information and suggestions should be given to the affiliates and the public about how to protect their benefits and rights.

Event period risks

During the event period, there are also many risks which organisers must deal with and solve. In this section, some examples are given concerning the risks that occurred during FIFA World Cup 2014.

During a large-scale sports event, the risk that is most likely to occur is personal injury. This could mean crowd damage, fights between players, etc. For example, during the

World Cup South Africa, a crowd accident happened in the warm-up match between North Korea and Nigeria. In this accident, more than 20 people were injured. The reason is that many more fans came to watch the match than the organisers expected and the stadium had only one exit. Football violence is very common during matches, as you will see if you search 'football violence' on YouTube.

In order to reduce or even eliminate the probability of personal injury occurring, there are some recommendations for event organisers. For crowd management, the FIST (force, information, space, time) model is one of the solutions. This model should be followed to manage security, offering information to audiences and managing space and time; an emergency plan and measures should also be prepared.

Another risk that occurs frequently is responsibility risk. It refers to coaches' and players' liability due to the injuries caused by occupational behaviours; and in cases of negligence, the possibility of organisers and government officials denying public liability. For instance, after the crowd accident mentioned above, FIFA said they were not the organiser of that warm-up match, thus FIFA could not take responsibility for the accident. This embarrassed South Africa and led to positive action in reporting accidents in the future. Therefore, contracts that clarify responsibility are very important. The host should contact outside agencies, such as national police and governments, to verify who is responsible for accidents or other incidents that might occur.

Technological problems are another common risk. There was a technological problem during the opening ceremony of the Sochi Olympics. When the five light points became circles, one of the light points did not move, so the Olympic rings appeared as four circles and one point. Technological problems include broadcast issues as well. However, technological problems are easier to prevent than the other risks as long as organisers carefully implement the necessary checks before the event.

Political risks

Different political and religious interest groups may take advantage of large sports events to fight against each other, which can result in boycotts and damage events.

On an international level, for example, in the 1972 Munich Olympic Games, Palestinian militants attacked the Israeli team, resulting in 11 athletes losing their lives. In the 1982 Moscow Olympics, the US team boycotted the event, resulting in the US audience's unwillingness to watch the Games broadcast on television and the network that had purchased broadcast rights suffered huge losses, so the insurance company had to pay hundreds of millions of dollars in compensation. In the 2004 Athens Olympics, the host purchased terrorist attacks insurance. Risk transfer is a recommendation when facing potential risks.

(Continued)

(Continued)

On a domestic level, during the Athens Games, domestic public boycotts of foreign teams impacted events. In Brazil, First Capital Command in Sao Paulo, Brazil's largest criminal organisation, claimed that they would create panic during the 2014 World Cup.

Natural risks

Natural risks are caused by irresistible natural factors, such as earthquakes, storms and epidemics. Natural forces interrupt, delay and even cancel some sports events, resulting in financial losses. For example, the 1995 FIFA U-20 World Cup was planned to be held in Nigeria. But finally, it was held in Qatar due to an epidemic.

There were about seven games held around 13:00 in the Northeast region of Brazil near the equator. FIFA's executive committee announced that the games would be suspended at least once, to allow the players to take a break and drink more water.

FURTHER READING

Daily Mail (2012) 'Armadillo! World Cup mascot for Brazil 2014 unveiled by Ronaldo'. Available at: www.dailymail.co.uk/sport/football/article-2204405/Armadillo-unveiled-mascot-2014-World-Cup-Brazil.html [accessed 12/01/2016].

Davis, J. (2013) London School of Economics Public Policy Group. *2012 London Olympics: The Impact of the Olympics: Making or Breaking Communities in East London*. Published in British Politics and Policy Blog. Available at: http://blogs.lse.ac.uk/politicsandpolicy/files/2013/01/Olympics.pdf [accessed 01/03/2016].

Department for Culture, Media & Sport (2013) *Report 5: Post-Games Evaluation. Meta-Evaluation of the Impacts and Legacy of the London 2012 Olympic Games and Paralympic Games*. Available at: www.gov.uk/government/uploads/system/uploads/attachment_data/file/224181/1188-B_Meta_Evaluation.pdf [accessed 18/11/2016].

House of Commons Culture, Media and Sport Committee (2002–3) *A London Olympic Bid for 2012: Third Report*. London: House of Commons.

Leopkey, B. and Parent, M.M. (2009) 'Risk management issues in large-scale sporting events: a stakeholder perspective', *European Sport Management Quarterly*, 9(2): 187–208, DOI: 10.1080/16184740802571443.

London Legacy Development Corporation (2013) 'Three Year Business Plan 2013/14–2015/16'. Available at: www.queenelizabetholympicpark.co.uk/~/media/qeop/files/public/lldcbusinessplanv42012_132015_161.pdf [accessed 20/11/2016].

Olympic Delivery Authority (2011) 'The ODA plan and budget'. Available at: www.london2012.com/documents/oda-publications/oda-plan-2011.pdf [accessed 16/01/2016].

PricewaterhouseCoopers/DCMS (2005) 'Olympic Games impact study final report'. Available at: www.gamesmonitor.org.uk/files/PWC%20OlympicGamesImpactStudy.pdf [accessed 13/01/2016].

Raj, R. and Simpson, H. (2015) 'Exploitation of Notting Hill Carnival to increase community pride and spirit and act as a catalyst for regeneration'. *Journal of Hospitality and Tourism*, 13(1): 27–47.

Raj, R. and Vignali, C. (2010) 'Creating local experiences of cultural tourism through sustainable festivals', *European Journal of Tourism, Hospitality and Recreation*, 1(1): 51–67.

Tourism Insight (2012) 'Sharing sector expertise, analysis and intelligence'. Available at: www.insights.org. uk/articleitem.aspx?title=Case%20Study:%20The%20Impact%20of%20Sports%20Infrastructure%20 Investment%20on%20Visitor%20Numbers%20to%20Cardiff [accessed 23/01/2016].

20

THE FUTURE OF THE EVENTS INDUSTRY

In this chapter you will cover

The aim of this chapter is to discuss the future of the events industry. The chapter explains how sustainability, globalisation, innovation and technology will impact greatly on the industry. The global events industry has been growing rapidly in the West for the last decade. In particular, the experience and knowledge economy is in the ascendant and therefore business events must be much more experience and knowledge oriented. Furthermore, the use of the internet, mobile technology and virtual applications will considerably affect the events industry. The internet will continue to shape conferences and seminars as delegates may no longer need to attend these events to gather information that is now available via the internet. With these future changes, the event professional will need to be adaptable, and have greater transferable skills.

DRIVERS FOR CHANGE IN THE GLOBAL EVENTS INDUSTRY

With the downturn in the economy, several organisations have cut their budgets and are reducing costs by getting rid of staff, cutting services and limiting business travel. Furthermore, due to climate change and the realisation that our natural resources are in short supply, many organisations are going green and investing in different ways to reduce their carbon footprint. These changes, coupled with cultural shifts, the search for original consumer experiences, the relationship between sports, economics and events, and developments in technology such as mobiles and virtual applications represent some of the challenges facing the events industry professional. In response, organisations have been looking for ways to cut costs and remain environmentally friendly, including looking at whether it is necessary to have face-to-face meetings. The *International Association of Exhibitions and Events* (IAEE) carried out a study in 2013, later updated in 2015, to identify and predict the future trends impacting the exhibition and events industry internationally. The IAEE predicted 13 future trends as summarised in Table 20.1.

Based on the findings of the IAEE (2015) and other research we present the key drivers for future trends in the events industry as represented by Figure 20.1.

Table 20.1 Thirteen future events impacting the exhibition and events industry (2015)

Future trend	Summary
1. Generational issues	Some of the issues facing the industry include the changing generations of employees:
	• How to relate across all generations of employees, customers and clients.
	• How to hire, train and motivate college graduates as employees and to also keep them in the industry.
	• How to reach, engage and teach the younger 'online generation' about attending or exhibiting at trade shows and the value of face-to-face marketing.
	• How to continue to keep current customers from 'aging' out of the industry or leaving the industry because they do not see the value of 'modern', digitally-enhanced trade shows due to long exposure to the historical trade show models (note: this includes exhibitors, attendees and trade show industry veterans). The industry needs to educate 'customers' on how to view a 'modern' trade show or event as integral to advancing their marketing and advocacy agendas.
	• How to recognise that communication tools to reach and influence population segments will continue to include all traditional media plus current and emerging digital and social media formats.
	• How to anticipate the direction and magnitude of disruption in the larger marketing community and our own industry as the technology wave sweeps throughout society.
	• How to customise the exhibition experience for each generation to maximise participation and engagement (e.g. offering digital and printed materials, segmenting and tailoring marketing for each generation, offering a diverse mix of educational offerings, etc.).

(Continued)

Table 20.1   (Continued)

Future trend	Summary
2. Big Data	Big Data is the collection of every bit of information that can be collected relevant to customers, the community and event. Once collected, the data has to be 'mined' with advanced analytical tools to understand issues and trends that may not have been visible or considered with the use of more traditional, analytical methods.
3. Data Capture, Recording and Reporting	With increased data capture capability from all types of sources, exhibition management will be challenged to develop an integrated data plan as part of its ongoing marketing activities. It will be important for show management to learn what data it needs to capture, how to interpret the data it captures, and how to turn that data into action steps as part of its total business operation and marketing plan.
4. Technology	The following developments in technology will have considerable impact on the events industry: • The adoption of mobile devices • Cloud computing • High quality video and video-communications capabilities • Elimination of paper by digital files • Mobile apps.
5. Social Media Marketing	The growth in social media platforms such as Google, Facebook, Twitter, LinkedIn and Pinterest illustrate the acceptance of targeted communication and more importantly – community building. Each of these platforms embodies its own community with its own social structure.
6. Year-round Communities	The growth of social media communities now enables shows and events to participate in communities as active 'members' on a year-round basis. As such, building year-round communities is a growing trend for shows and show management. The competitive need for year-round, exhibition-related communities is driven by social media and its 24/7 competitive interaction with target audiences vs a fixed-date trade show and its narrow interaction with its target audience.
7. Experiential Trade Shows	As the exhibitions and events industry evolves, and as advanced technologies and social media also evolve, the art and science of person-to-person engagement and experience must also evolve. Exhibition organisers will have to recognise that the 'experience' of the trade show has to be included as one of the measurements in assessing a show and its performance for both exhibitors and attendees.
8. Non-Attendee Engagement	By definition, non-attendees are not present at the live event, but this does not necessarily mean they are not interested in what is taking place at the exhibition itself. Engaging the 'non-attendee' can also take place through social media. Google (and others) provides a number of search tools that can enable a show producer to discover and then engage a potential audience member or group. SEO (Search Engine Optimisation) and keyword search tools and techniques are available to assist a show producer in finding a potential audience currently considered non-attendees.
9. Exhibitors	Exhibitor education and booth staff training on how to successfully use face-to-face marketing will present an ongoing challenge and opportunity for the entire industry. This includes not only exhibition organisers, but also meeting/event producers, booth builders, publications, etc. Marketing decision-makers will need to fully understand face-to-face marketing and its benefits, and not leave their marketing decision-making to their own electronic and personal handheld device biases.

Future trend	Summary
10. International Trends	As developing international markets begin to expand, there is a growing trend for new shows to be launched, or existing international shows to expand, into new markets. It is anticipated that this trend will continue as developing countries (e.g. China and India) represent growing markets for US-based exhibiting companies. Economic development leads to increased exhibition development. As a result, global show coordination or competition is expected to continue as an element in show date, venue selection and international visitor/exhibitor considerations
11. Internet Connectivity	The cost of, and access to, the internet at exhibition venues is an important feature of producing a show. The increasing use of 'apps' and wireless programming means show organisers need low-cost/no-cost access to robust high-speed internet services. The trend for successful internet solutions in the future will centre on venues having significant bandwidth access, clear and consistent pricing, reliable service, and vendor trust.
12. Private Events	The private-event trend will continue to 'shape' the strategic options of major exhibitors as they consider marketing investment tradeoffs between their own private events and their buy-in to exhibit in public trade shows.
13. Complexity	The increased competition for customers, changes in marketing approaches and the use of advanced-technology options have significantly increased the complexity of doing business today. Complexity in managing a successful enterprise is only going to increase in the future. Understanding strategy, the differences between strategy and tactics, and how to build strategy to deal with the complexity, will be a future consideration for the industry.

Source: adapted from IAEE (2015) [online]

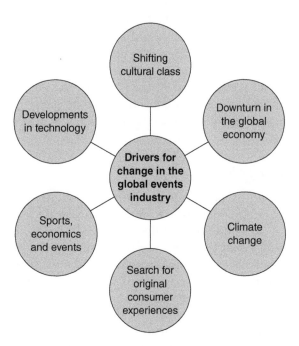

Figure 20.1   Drivers for future changes in the global events industry

Shifting cultural class

Even today as consumers are becoming financially better off, they distinguish themselves by their use of cultural, experiential and social knowledge and individual identity. It is no longer about the wealth you have, but what you do with that wealth and who you know. The cultural capital of events is how communities and tourists talk about their experience of festivals and sporting occasions and their participation in them, hence the cultural consumption of festivals.

Search for original consumer experiences

Event goers are continually searching for original and new experiences rather than the old traditional events. There is an increasing need to seek out experiences and products which are authentic and not contaminated.

Sporting events and the changing economy

Sport contributes considerably to the economy of most countries in terms of mega sporting events, print and digital media, health and well-being and amateur sports. Hosting mega sports events such as the FIFA Football World Cup is highly contested and prized, not least because of the potential positive impacts on the destination.

On the other hand, mega events have had negative impacts on the economy of certain countries, such as Greece, where some have argued that the 2004 Olympic Games was a catalyst to the country's later economic problems. The 2004 Athens Olympics cost nearly twice as much as its initial budget. In 2010, more than half of Athens' Olympic sites were barely used or empty, although the Games did improve the transportation system with a new metro system, a new airport, and a tram and light railway network. However, given the looming fiscal deficits in many countries, arguments about the economic benefits of mega events will diminish.

Sporting events and politics

Sport has always been used by politicians as a means to influence political reform or as a way to bring about change in countries. For instance, during the cold war, some countries (predominantly western) decided to boycott the Moscow Olympics, and during the apartheid era in South Africa several countries refused to play against them. More recently, there has been controversy as to whether the Formula One Grand Prix should have been held in Bahrain in 2012 when the regime there has treated very harshly protestors demanding political reforms motivated by the Arab Spring in the Middle East (AutoSport, 2012). There were also question marks as to whether Russian athletes would be allowed to compete in the Rio 2016 Olympics after allegations of widespread doping. Nevertheless, mega sporting events will continue to be influenced by politics and will also have influence on world politics.

DEVELOPMENTS IN TECHNOLOGY

The internet and mobile technology

There are over three billion mobile phone subscribers globally. The mobile revolution has and will continue to transform the way that we communicate, get information, find our way around, buy things, and the way that event professionals do business.

There is a coming together of technology trends which is driving these changes. For instance, advances in phone hardware have led to mobile phones increasingly being used for far more than just making calls. Increasingly they are becoming mini-computers with functionalities such as advanced web browsing, geo-positioning, video, and contact management capabilities, to name a few. Smart phones will provide more powerful processing capabilities in smaller and more convenient packages.

In addition, advances in web technology have been the main delivery medium for software. Google and other major players are investing in web-based mobile tools, most of them at little or no cost to the user. The use of web technology has been greatly impacted by advances in high-speed broadband internet access through wireless networks. Soon, everywhere you go, broadband internet, the carrier for the mobile web software tools mentioned above, will be available.

GPS (global-positioning technology) is already available in many phones and increasingly this will become a common mobile phone feature over the next few years. Finally, NFC (near field communication) wireless technology (which is widely used in Japan with trials in the United States, Germany, Finland, the Netherlands and a few other countries) will turn mobile phones into secure credit or debit cards. A chip embedded in a phone will allow users to make a payment by using a touch-sensitive interface or by bringing the phone within a few centimetres of an NFC reader. Your credit card account or bank account is then charged accordingly.

These converging trends in mobile technology will affect how some events are organised and managed. For instance, several meetings-related applications, including mobile-based conference agendas, exhibition guides, and networking guides and web-based mobile phone guides, could help conference attendees to explore the conference agenda and enable connection between exhibitors and other conference attendees. Mobile city guides and mapping programs will become increasingly helpful to convention goers in unfamiliar cities. The iPhone and its competitors, with robust web functionality, make the many excellent location-based mapping websites such as Ask City (http://city.ask.com) and Google Maps (http://map.google.com) much more accessible.

Additionally, mobile products such as Google Mobile Maps (www.google.com/gmm) offer directions, real-time traffic and satellite imagery. Geovector (www.geovector.com) is an example of a mobile-phone-based mapping tool allowing users in Japan to search for movies, restaurants, buy tickets, make restaurant reservations and more, and get step-by-step GPS-based guidance on how to get there. Advanced mobile phone GPS capabilities are likely to be able to help attendees find hotels, reception locations, rooms in a convention centre and navigate efficiently while at events.

Furthermore, interactive audience response keypads are excellent tools that engage attendees and can provide very useful data. The challenge is that rental fees for these systems can be expensive, costing up to US$10 per person per day. In the future, when a speaker or event organiser would like to use audience voting capabilities, attendees will be able to pull out their phones and use them as a voting keypad. Already, companies such as Log-On offer text message voting using mobile phones. In the future, using web-based survey products, this will become much easier with the ability to graph the results instantly on the screen. Additionally, companies such as VisionTree (www.visiontree.com) are providing advanced audience polling, surveys and continuing education tracking using any web-enabled mobile device.

There are many excellent web-based as well as proprietary hand-held business networking products which help people with like interests to find each other at events. The challenge is that the standard web-based tools are not very mobile and the hand-held tools can be too expensive for many groups. Better web-browsing functionality in phones will allow the benefits of both – high quality conference networking systems that are mobile and at lower cost.

This will likely be tied to a conference messaging system giving the meeting planner the ability to make broadcast announcements to all attendees or a subset (for example in the event of a major session change), and allow attendees to send messages to other conference goers.

The current system, where exhibitors are charged large sums by registration companies for barcode or magnetic barcode scanning equipment, will likely become outdated in the next few years. Using NFC enabled mobile phones, attendees will be able to easily exchange contact information. This can be between two phones or between a phone and an NFC-enabled badge and will be as simple as tapping the two devices together. Similar technology could be used for access verification (with an embedded ID photo), for electronic tickets, continuing education unit (CEU) tracking, tote bag distribution and more.

There are more than 1,500 technology products in 30 categories available as part of online registration processes designed to assist in the meeting planning process (www.corbinball. com/bookmarks). Many of these tools are web-based. With the increasing functionality of web-based mobile products, these tools will be increasingly accessible via mobile phones.

Online registration is just one example of many. A mobile phone-based registration solution could work as follows:

- Event attendee receives an email on a mobile phone for an upcoming conference.
- The attendee clicks on the link to the registration page.
- Using the functionality of 'auto-fill', the registration form is completed and the authorisation for payment is carried out.
- By return the confirmation email contains a printable receipt and a confirmation barcode (or NFC e-ticket).
- The attendee takes the barcode or e-ticket received on the mobile phone to check-in on site.

These are just some of the ways that mobile phones are possibly going to change the events industry. The next generations of mobile phone will revolutionise meetings management and the business process in general in very significant ways.

While acknowledging that ever-changing technology makes it difficult to tell what might happen next, there will be certain parts of the events industry which are fundamental and will continue to require meetings to take place face-to-face. For example, successful sales teams are built through zeal for a goal that comes from face-to-face meetings.

Microsoft has suggested that in the coming years, 50 per cent of US gross domestic product will be taken up by training and knowledge delivery. Progressive organisations will continue to bring people together to meet. Commentators have argued against the predictors of doom who claim that the meeting business is in a death spiral.

The constant reassessment and the desire for new innovative ideas is a key to staying ahead of the game. In order to achieve this, innovative organisations possess certain characteristics which are presented in Figure 20.2.

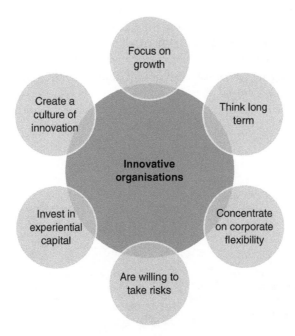

Figure 20.2 Characteristics of world class innovative organisations

VIRTUAL EVENTS

Some organisations and businesses have begun to re-evaluate the necessity of face-to-face meetings and events and, in some cases, choose to hold them virtually. Over 70 per cent of event professionals felt that reduction in budgets would be their biggest challenge in 2010, and 38 per cent were planning to replace live meetings with virtual meetings or conference calls (Scofidio, 2009 [online]).

Consequently, organisations will increasingly use virtual worlds to hold meetings and special events. A study in 2009 found that 40 per cent of corporate brand marketers and 31 per cent of exhibition marketers held virtual events; 71 per cent of respondents used virtual reality to accommodate geographically widespread workforces and customers, with webinars (81 per cent) being the most commonly used (Center for Exhibition Industry Research, 2009).

The virtual events market, consisting of many different products and services, is estimated to increase to around $18.6 billion from 2010 to 2015 (Market Research Media, 2010). Market Research Media (2010) identified a range of services included within the virtual conference and trade show market, which are shown in Figure 20.3.

The scope of virtual reality applications found within the event industry ranges from entertainment, to visualisations, to architecture/design, to education and training.

Virtual reality applications are becoming increasingly more relevant in these times of change; however, most event professionals do not have a clear understanding of what they are and how they may be employed to address business needs.

Virtual events can have benefits for both exhibitors and attendees. For exhibitors, virtual events can create new and lucrative opportunities for the organisation, increasing content delivery options, driving more robust networking, and extending sponsorship options while exceeding customer expectations.

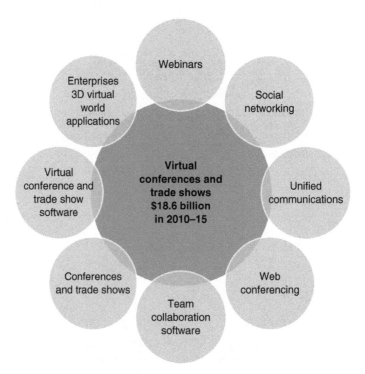

Figure 20.3 Virtual conferences and trade shows spending

Source: Market Research Media (2010)

Furthermore, virtual events can give event organisers the ability to increase revenue and cut costs, to extend the brand, to broaden the brand community, to track attendees, and to permit rapid response. The benefits for attendees include decreased costs and time associated with travel, which may lead to increased education and training participation.

In the face of changing technology and the quest for new products what is needed is continuous education and training for event managers who will need to adapt transferable personal skills to keep up to date with the developments in the industry.

THE TRANSFERABLE PERSONAL SKILLS OF AN EVENT MANAGER

Events are an exceptionally powerful medium of communication. People may not remember exactly what was said or heard, exactly what was done or seen, but they do remember how the event made them feel. This is true whether you are witnessing a major sporting achievement, a musical performance or keynote speaker, or whether you are attending an exciting exhibition, a well-orchestrated new product launch or your own perfect wedding.

If excellent event experiences are to be produced and the 'experiential marketing' of events is thus to be successful, then highly skilled event professionals are required. Such professionals share a set of common skills, whether they are organising concerts or conferences, meetings or matches, fashion shows or film festivals.

So what are the transferable personal skills of event managers? Having examined numerous job advertisements, descriptions and person specifications for event management posts, the following skills are invariably featured:

- organisational and logistical skills
- time management skills – running to a schedule
- leadership skills – a team player/team leader
- motivational skills – self-motivated and able to motivate others
- people skills – with a wide range of people at different levels
- marketing skills – media, sales
- public relations skills – generating interest, copywriting, contacts
- communication skills – to colleagues, clients and authorities
- presentation skills – in several forms and media
- research skills – gathering and interpreting information
- commercial awareness – finance, budgets and break even points
- a positive and adaptable attitude – contributes positively to the achievement of team objectives
- problem solving skills and 'can do' attitude
- innovation and creativity – generating the 'wow' factor.

Many of these skills, especially when combined together, are those expected at graduate level and this explains the increasing number of universities and higher education institutions around the world now offering events management programmes at both undergraduate and postgraduate level.

There are also professional development initiatives within the industry. These often bring together diverse aspects of the industry, for example, the Events Sector Industry Training Organisation (ESITO). ESITO is officially accredited by City & Guilds in the UK as the assessment centre for the Events National Vocational Qualifications (NVQs). Events NVQs are available to virtually everyone in the events industry, particularly those involved in organising events, working at event venues, exhibiting and supplying goods and services for events.

ESITO is supported by 12 leading organisations. They are:

ACE – Association for Conferences and Events

ABPCO – Association of British Professional Conference Organisers

AEO – Association of Exhibition Organisers

BECA – British Exhibition Contractors Association

EVA – Exhibition Venues Association

ITMA – Incentive Travel and Meetings Association

MIA – Meeting Industry Association

MPI (UK) – Meeting Professionals International

MUTA – Made Up Textiles Association

NEA – National Exhibitors Association

NOEA – National Outdoor Events Association

TESA – The Event Services Association.

ESITO is involved in projects seeking to identify the common skills, knowledge and understanding required by international events organisers and managers. They are undertaking this research in the Czech Republic, Germany, Portugal and the UK.

The Association of Conferences and Events (ACE), which was the original founder of ESITO, began the first careers fair aimed purely at the conference and events industry in 2003.

SUSTAINABILITY IN THE EVENTS INDUSTRY

Within the events sector the pace of change varies, with a different focus in each country at present. This is understandable, as the events sector is still developing as a recognised sector, and as a result it is difficult for education and customer service to be standardised in the same way across the globe.

Some parts of the events industry still do not really understand the term sustainability and while some countries show fantastic examples of fair trade, social welfare and heritage considerations these initiatives are not communicated under the label 'sustainability'. An example of the mindset change which may be required in the future is the customer service attitude so integral to the event industry. For example, an event attendee last in line at a buffet lunch picking up the last roll and seeing food portions for one person would not think, 'this event has been well planned with the consideration of food waste'. Instead, the current industry attitude towards customer service would be, 'there is not enough food at this event – I do not feel well looked after'. Practitioners have suggested a change in customer service thinking could take place with the arrival of the next generation in the workplace (Pelham, 2011).

In Brazil, the existence of two large global events (the FIFA World Cup and the Olympic and Paralympic Games) was seen to be forcing the industry to change. The fact that the eyes of the world are on these events and that such large-scale events offer significant business opportunities for the host country means that both the 'carrot' and 'stick' approaches to change are evident. In other words, there are business opportunities and external customer pressures which will influence the implementation of sustainability and change the host country event industry business model.

It is argued by some commentators in the industry that economics is one of the main barriers to the acceptance and widespread implementation of sustainability throughout the event industry. This is due to two reasons: firstly, the perception that becoming sustainable is costly; and secondly, there is a need to factor in the actual cost related to people taking the time and acquiring the knowledge needed. This barrier can be overcome by raising the profile and changing the perception of the event professional. Showing leadership in the field of sustainability, using the international best practice tools created by the industry for the industry (e.g. ISO 20121 and GRI Event Organiser Sector Supplement) is an opportunity for people to notice and recognise the strategic importance of the event practitioner role.

A study carried out by Pelham of events practitioners makes the following recommendations for sustainability in the events industry:

- Industry practitioners should not wait for there to be a definite demand for sustainability before changing their product/service offer. To do this would risk their brand and their client's brand with the event attendees, potentially damaging both beyond repair.
- Governments and corporate clients are likely to lead the way in requesting sustainable events to align with their reputation and economic goals.
- Industry practitioners should research to see if their client currently reports on sustainability, as the growth of corporate reporting on sustainability will result in an increased need for the consideration of sustainability in events.
- Large events, which create international public attention and widespread business opportunities (e.g. the Olympic Games) are likely to focus increasingly on sustainability and this will significantly drive the demand.
- Despite the existence of internationally recognised frameworks for the implementation of and reporting on sustainability (e.g. ISO 20121 and GRI Event Organiser Sector Supplement),

the practitioners felt it likely that regulation on sustainability would compel the event industry in the near future to change the business model more quickly and to a more significant extent.

- Transparency was highlighted as an area where the industry will need to make changes to the current business models. For example, declaring commissions.
- The next generation of the event industry were recognised as passionate about sustainability and likely to bring a level of enthusiasm and even expertise. (Pelham, 2011: 6)

SUMMARY

Reduced budgets combined with increased demands resulting from globalisation, environmental sustainability concerns and developments in IT have forced events practitioners to be innovative in meeting business needs. However, many have argued the events industry has been slow to adapt to its changing environment, including the adoption of IT solutions.

In the future the implementation of internet-based solutions will result in cost savings by presenting the opportunity of increased attendance at events due to lower costs, by expanding the reach to event goers. One such development that will continue to have an impact on the event industry will be the creation of virtual applications.

Several forward-thinking companies have adopted virtual reality applications that meet business needs while also addressing social concerns. Virtual meetings and virtual special events are environmentally friendly, less expensive and provide alternatives to face-to-face meetings. They are innovative and viable methods to effectively and efficiently meet organisational needs. Virtual worlds represent a growing space for collaborative play, learning, work and e-commerce.

Strong competitive forces require the constant reassessment of competencies, and event practitioners must be accustomed to industry needs and wants if they are to be viable players in such a competitive environment. The awareness of such IT applications and the provision of such services may be a point of differentiation for organisations; it is only a matter of time before a business or organisational presence in a virtual world is as commonplace as a website is now for a business.

Discussion questions

Question 1

Discuss the future drivers of change in the events industry.

Question 2

Analyse the role of sustainability in arranging events.

Question 3

Explain how developments in virtual technology will affect the events industry.

Question 4

Evaluate how digital technologies are forcing the events industry to change.

Question 5

In what ways will the event professional need to adapt to the changes in the events industry?

Question 6

Discuss the changing nature of the environment and its influence on the events industry.

Case study 1: EXPO Dubai 2020 – a preview

After winning in 2013 the final battle for being the host city of EXPO 2020 against Turkish, Brazilian and Russian candidates, Dubai is now preparing for the event. Here, we will discover a bit more on the theme, venues and program of the first edition of the world's fair to be hosted in the Arabian Peninsula. EXPO Dubai will run from October 2020 through April 2021.

Main theme and sub-themes

Taking the cue from Dubai's Arabic name *Al Wasl* (الوصل), which means 'the connection', EXPO Dubai 2020 will be based on an ambitious theme entitled 'Connecting Minds, Creating the Future', further articulated into three sub-themes:

Opportunity – Unlocking new possibilities for people and communities to become successful contributors to the future. Focusing on people's and businesses' inter-connection as a factor for the world's social and economic development.

Mobility – Creating smarter and more productive physical and virtual connections. Focusing on people, goods and data mobility strategies, devices, and infrastructures.

(Continued)

(Continued)

Sustainability – Pursuing our hopes of progress without compromising the needs of future generations. Particularly focusing on sustainable production and consumption of energy and water, two points that, though in a different way, influence the economy and the people's everyday life of many Arabian countries.

The site

The main home of the 2020 World's fair will be a 438-hectare site (1,083 acres, more than double the area of EXPO Milan 2015), part of the new Dubai Trade Centre – Jebel Ali urban development, located midway between Dubai and Abu Dhabi; on-site works started in 2015, with completion scheduled for 2019.

The site master plan, conceived by the US (and multinational) design firm HOK together with celebrated London-based engineering group Arup, combines national pavilions, educational spaces, performance venues, and hosting facilities around a central core. The core features three large pavilions, each dedicated to one of the three themes of the EXPO, radiating from the semi-covered *Al Wasl* central plaza, a large event space inspired by the traditional Arabian marketplace, the *souk* (قوس).

Coherent with the sub-theme 'sustainability' the master plan envisages a large use of low-impact solutions, such as photovoltaic-fabric-based canopies covering the main walkways, waste-water recycling, and the use of a relevant portion (about 30%) of recycled content as building material. It is expected to produce on site about 50% of the required energy from renewable sources, especially solar radiation. Furthermore, at least a part of the structures built for EXPO will remain in place and be reused as research and innovation venues.

Early initiatives – Meet the Artists

While four years have to pass before the official opening of EXPO Dubai 2020, the organisers have already started some initiatives related to its themes. An example is the project 'Meet the Artists', which invited artists from all over the world to create a graphic inspired by the three sub-themes of EXPO: Opportunity, Mobility and Sustainability. The designs are exhibited in 21 public spaces across the United Arab Emirates. 21 artists – from the UK, Italy, the UAE, France, Switzerland, the USA, Spain, New Zealand, Jordan, China, Finland, and Iraq – were involved in the project.

Source: www.inexhibit.com/case-studies/expo-dubai-2020-a-preview/ [accessed 21/11/2016]

FURTHER READING

Center for Exhibition Industry Research (2009) *Digital + Exhibiting Marketing Insights*. Chicago: Center for Exhibition Industry Research.

IAEE (2015) *Future Trends Impacting the Exhibitions and Events Industry 2015 Update*. Available at: http://goo.gl/Q3rD1x [accessed 15/03/2016].

Mair, J. and Whitford, M. (2013) 'An exploration of events research: event topics, themes and emerging trends', *International Journal of Event and Festival Management*, 4(1): 6–30.

Market Research Media (2010) 'Premium market analysis'. Available at: www.marketresearchmedia. com/2010/02/07/virtual-conference/ [accessed 01/04/2012].

Pelham, F. (2011) 'Will sustainability change the business model of the event industry?', *Worldwide Hospitality and Tourism Themes*, 3(3): 187–92.

Scofidio, B. (2009) '2010: Looking ahead', *Association Meetings Magazine*. Available at: http://meetings net.com/corporatemeetingsincentives/news/1123-recession-meetings-impact/index.html [accessed 22/04/2012].

BIBLIOGRAPHY

BOOKS

Allen, J., O'Toole, W., McDonnell, I. and Harris, R. (2000) *Festival and Special Event Management*, 2nd edn. Milton Keynes: John Wiley & Sons.

Allen, J., O'Toole, W., McDonnell, I. and Harris, R. (2002) *Festival and Special Event Management*, 3rd edn. Milton Keynes: John Wiley & Sons.

Association of Accounting Technicians (1990) *AAT Study Text: Cost Accounting and Budgeting Paper 10*. London: BPP Publishing.

Atrill, P. and McLaney, E. (2015) *Accounting and Finance for Non-specialists*, 9th edn. Harlow: Pearson.

Barringer, R.B. and Ireland, D. (2015) *Entrepreneurship*. London: Pearson.

Berridge, G. (2006) *Event Design and Experience*. Oxford: Butterworth-Heinemann.

Blyton, P. and Turnbull, P. (1992) *Reassessing Human Resource Management*. London: Sage.

Boella, M. and Goss-Turner, S. (2005) *Human Resource Management in the Hospitality Industry*, 8th edn. Oxford: Elsevier Butterworth-Heinemann.

Bolton, B. and Thompson, J. (2003) *The Entrepreneur in Focus*. London: Thomson.

Bowdin, G., Allen, J., O'Toole, W., Harris, R. and McDonnell, I. (2011) *Events Management*, 4th edn. Oxford: Butterworth-Heinemann.

Brassington, F. and Pettitt, S. (2000) *Principles of Marketing*. London: Prentice Hall.

Brayshaw, R., Samuels, J. and Wilkes, M. (1999) *Financial Management and Decision Making*. London: International Thomson Business Press.

Brearley, R. and Myers, S. (1999) *Principles of Corporate Finance*, 6th edn. Maidenhead: McGraw-Hill.

Brown, S. (2009) '"Please hold, your call is important to us": some thoughts on unspeakable customer experiences', in A. Lindgreen, J. Vanhamme and M.B. Beverland (eds), *Memorable Customer Experiences: A Research Anthology*. Farnham: Gower Publishing, pp. 253–66.

Brown, S., Blackmon, K., Cousins, P. and Maylor, H. (2001) *Operations Management: Policy, Practice and Performance Improvement*. Oxford: Butterworth-Heinemann.

Burke, R. (2006) *Project Management: Planning and Control Techniques*. Chichester: John Wiley & Sons.

Burns, P. (2005) *Corporate Entrepreneurship*. New York: Palgrave Macmillan.

Butler, R., Davies, L., Pike, R. and Shaap, J. (1993) *Strategic Investment Decisions*. London: Routledge.

Carrell, M.R., Elbert, N.F. and Hatfield, R.D. (2000) *Human Resource Management: Global Strategies for Managing a Diverse and Global Workforce*, 6th edn. Dallas, TX: The Dryden Press.

Carter, P. (2009) *The Complete Special Events Handbook*. London: Directory of Social Change.

Center for Exhibition Industry Research (2009) *Digital + Exhibiting Marketing Insights 2009*. Chicago: Center for Exhibition Industry Research.

Chaffey, D., Mayer, R., Johnston, K. and Ellis-Chadwick, F. (2008) *Internet Marketing: Strategy, Implementation and Practice*. Harlow: Prentice Hall.

Davidsson, P. (2003) 'The domain of entrepreneurship research: some suggestions', in J. Katz and D. Shepherd (eds), *Cognitive Approaches to Entrepreneurship*, Vol. 6. Cambridge, MA: Elsevier Science, pp. 315–72.

Derrett, R. (2004) 'Festivals, events and the destination', in I. Yeoman, M. Robertson, J. Ali-Knight, S. Drummond and U. McMahon-Beattie (eds), *Festival and Events Management: An International Arts and Culture Perspective*. Oxford: Elsevier Butterworth-Heinemann, pp. 32–50.

Dessler, G. (2000) *Human Resources Management*, 8th edn. London: Prentice Hall International.

Drury, C. (2015) *Management and Cost Accounting*, 9th edn. London: Thomson Learning.

Dyson, J.R. (2010) *Accounting for Non-Accounting Students*, 8th edn. London: Pitman.

Egan, J. (2011) *Relationship Marketing: Exploring Relational Strategies in Marketing*, 4th edn. Harlow: Financial Times Press/Prentice Hall.

Elliott, B. and Elliott, J. (2011) *Financial Accounting and Reporting*, 14th edn. Harlow: Pearson.

English Heritage (2000) *Tourism Facts 2001*. Swindon: English Heritage.

Fill, C. (2013) *Marketing Communications: Brands Experiences and Participation*, 6th edn. Harlow: Pearson Education.

Fowler, F.J. (2002) *Survey Research Methods*. London: Sage.

Freedman, H.A. and Feldman, K. (1998) *The Business of Special Events: Fundraising Strategies for Changing Times*. Chelsea, MI: BookCrafters.

Getz, D. (1991) *Festivals, Special Events Tourism*. New York: Van Nostrand Reinhold.

Getz, D. (1997) *Event Management and Event Tourism*. New York: Cognizant Communications Corporation.

Getz, D. (2005) *Event Management and Event Tourism*, 2nd edn. New York: Cognizant Communications Corporation.

Getz, D. (2013) *Event Tourism: Concepts, International Case Studies*. New York: Cognizant Communication Corporation.

Glasson, J., Godfrey, K., Goodey, B., Van Der Berg, J. and Absalam, H. (1995) *Towards Visitor Impact Management: Visitor Impacts, Carrying Capacity and Management Responses in Europe's Historic Towns and Cities*. Aldershot: Avebury.

Glautier, M. and Underdown, B. (2001) *Accounting Theory and Practice*, 7th edn. Harlow: Financial Times Press/Prentice Hall.

Goldblatt, J. (2002) *Special Events Best Practices in Modern Event Management*, 3rd edn. New York: International Thomson Publishing Company.

Goss, D. (1994) *Principles of Human Resource Management*. London: Routledge.

Grönroos, C. (2007) *Service Management and Marketing*, 3rd edn. Chichester: John Wiley & Sons.

Hall, C. (1992) *Hallmark Tourist Events: Impacts, Management and Planning*. Chichester: John Wiley & Sons.

Hall, C. (1994) *Tourism and Politics: Policy, Power and Place*. Chichester: John Wiley & Sons.

Hall, C.M. (1997) *Hallmark Tourist Events: Impacts, Management and Planning*. London: Belhaven.

Hall, C.M. and Jenkins, J. (1995) *Tourism and Public Policy*. London: Routledge.

Health and Safety Executive (2002) *Use of Contractors – A Joint Responsibility*. Liverpool: HSE.

Health and Safety Executive (2006a) *Consulting Employees on Health and Safety: A Guide to the Law*. Liverpool: HSE.

Health and Safety Executive (2006b) *Health and Safety Law: What You Should Know*. Liverpool: HSE.

Heinze, A., Rashid, T., Fletcher, T. and Cruz, A. (2016) *Digital and Social Media Marketing*. London: Routledge.

House of Commons Culture, Media and Sport Committee (2002–3) *A London Olympic Bid for 2012: Third Report*. London: House of Commons.

Idowu, S. (2000) *Capital Investment Appraisal: Part 1*. London: Association of Chartered Certified Accountants.

IMA Study Systems (2006) *Management Accounting Fundamentals*. Oxford: Elsevier Butterworth-Heinemann.

Jobber, D. (2010) *Principles of Marketing*, 6th edn. Maidenhead: McGrawHill.

Johnston, R. and Clark, G. (2008) *Service Operations Management*. London: Prentice Hall.

Kandola, R. and Fullerton, J. (1998) *Diversity in Action: Managing the Mosaic*. London: Chartered Institute of Personnel and Development.

Key Leisure Markets (2001) *Tourism in the UK*. London: MarketScape Ltd.

Key Note (2004) *Market Report 2004: Corporate Hospitality*, 4th edn. London: Key Note.

Key Note (2010) *Leisure outside the Home Market Review 2010*. London: Key Note.

Kotas, R. (1999) *Management Accounting for Hospitality and Tourism*, 3rd edn. London: International Thomson Business Press.

Kotler, P. and Armstrong, G. (2014) *Principles of Marketing*, 15th edn. Harlow: Pearson.

Kurdle, A. and Sandler, M. (1995) *Public Relations for Hospitality Managers: Communicating for Greater Profits*. New York: Wiley.

Lanier, C.D. and Hampton, R.D. (2009) 'Experiential marketing: understanding the logic of memorable customer experiences', in A. Lindgreen, J. Vanhamme and M.B. Beverland (eds), *Memorable Customer Experiences. A Research Anthology*. Farnham: Gower Publishing Limited, pp. 9–23.

Law, C.M. (1993) *Urban Tourism: Attracting Visitors to Large Cities*. London and New York: Mansell.

Leslie, D. (2001) 'Urban regeneration and Glasgow's galleries with particular reference to the Burrell Collection', in G. Richards (ed.), *Cultural Attractions and European Tourism*. Oxford: CABI Publishing, pp. 111–34.

Lock, D. (2001) *The Essentials of Project Management*, 2nd edn. Farnham: Gower Publishing Limited.

Locker, K. and Kaczmarek, S. (2013) *Business Communication: Building Critical Skills*, 6th edn. Maidenhead: McGraw-Hill Education.

Luecke, R. (2004) *Managing Projects: Large and Small*. Boston, MA: Harvard Business Press.

Lumby, S. and Jones, C. (2000) *Investment Appraisal and Financing Decisions*, 6th edn. London: Chapman & Hall.

Mabey, C., Salaman, G. and Storey, J. (1998) *Human Resource Management: A Strategic Introduction*. Malden, MA: Blackwell Publishers.

Mair, J. (2014) *Conferences and Conventions: A Research Perspective*. Oxon: Routledge.

McCarthy, E.J. (1978) *Basic Marketing: A Managerial Approach*, 6th edn. Homewood, IL: Richard D. Irwin.

McDonnell, I., Allen, J. and O'Toole, W. (1999) *Festival and Special Event Management*. Brisbane: John Wiley & Sons Australia.

McKendrick, E. (2007) *Contract Law*, 7th edn. Basingstoke: Palgrave Macmillan.

McKoen, S. (1997) *Successful Fundraising and Sponsorship in a Week*. London: Hodder Arnold.

McLaney, E. and Atrill, P. (2014) *Accounting and Finance: An Introduction*, 7th edn. Harlow: Pearson.

Mercer, D. (1996) *Marketing*, 2nd edn. Oxford: Blackwell Business.

Meredith, J.R. and Mantel, S.J. (2009) *Project Management: A Managerial Approach*, 7th edn. Chichester: John Wiley & Sons.

Morgan, M. (1996) *Marketing for Leisure and Tourism*. London: Prentice Hall.

Morris Hargreaves McIntyre (2007) '*The Ascent of Manchester*' – *An Independent Evaluation of the First Manchester International Festival 28 June–15 July 2007: Executive Summary*. Manchester, Morris Hargreaves McIntyre.

Mulligan, J. and Raj, R. (2008) 'Destination marketing', in C. Vignali, T. Vranesevic and D. Vrontis (eds) *Strategic Marketing and Retail Thought*. Zagreb: Accent.

Mullin, R. (1976) *The Fund Raising Handbook*. Oxford: A.R. Mowbray & Co. Limited.

Mullins, L.J. (2007) *Management and Organisational Behaviour*, 8th edn. London: Financial Times/ Pitman Publishing.

Mullins, L.J. (2013) *Management and Organisational Behaviour*, 10th edn. London: Pearson.

Murphy, J. (2007) *Street on Torts*, 12th edn. Oxford: Oxford University Press.

Nanto, D.K. (2009) 'The Global Financial Crisis: Analysis and Policy Implications'. CRS Report for Congress. Congressional Research Service.

National Society of Fund Raising Executives (1996) *The NSFRE Fund-raising Dictionary*. New York: John Wiley.

North West Development Agency (2004) *Commonwealth Games Benefits Study: Final Report*. Warrington: NWDA.

Pembrokeshire Association of Voluntary Services (2005) *Developing a Fundraising Strategy*. Haverfordwest: PAVS, August, pp. 1–2.

Pharoah, C. (2008) *Charity Market Monitor. Volume 1: Fundraisers, Volume 2: Grantmakers and Corporate Donors*. London: CaritasData.

Pike, R. and Neale, B. (2006) *Corporate Finance and Investment: Decisions and Strategy*, 5th edn. Harlow: Pearson Education.

Raj, R. and Morpeth, N.D. (2007) *Religious Tourism and Pilgrimage Management: An International Perspective*. Oxford: CABI Publishing.

Raj, R. and Musgrave, J. (2009) *Event Management and Sustainability*. Oxford: CABI Publishing.

Reisinger, Y. and Turner, L. (2003) *Cross-cultural Behaviour in Tourism: Concepts and Analysis*. Oxford: Butterworth-Heinemann.

Richards, G. (ed.) (2001) *Cultural Attractions and European Tourism*. Oxford: CABI Publishing.

Richards, P. (2007) *Law of Contract*, 8th edn. Harlow: Longman.

Rogers, T. (2013) *Conferences and Conventions: A Global Industry*, 3rd edn. Oxon: Routledge.

Rogers, T. and Davidson, R. (2016) *Marketing Destinations and Venues for Conferences, Conventions and Business Events*, 2nd edn. Oxon: Routledge.

Schmitt, B.H. (1999) *Experiential Marketing*. New York: The Free Press.

Shone, A. and Parry, B. (2010) *Successful Event Management: A Practical Handbook*, 3rd edn. Andover: Cengage Learning.

Shone, R. (1998) *Creative Visualisation*. Rochester, VT: Destiny Books.

Silvers, J. (2008) *Risk Management for Meetings and Events*. Oxford: Butterworth-Heinemann.

Smilansky, S. (2009) *Experiential Marketing: A Practical Guide to Interactive Brand Experience*. London: Kogan Page.

Stone, R.J. (2011) *Human Resource Management*, 7th edn. Brisbane: John Wiley & Sons.

Sundbo, J. and Hagedorn-Ramussen, P. (2008) 'The backstaging of experience production', in J. Sundbo and P. Darmer (eds), *Creating Experiences in the Experience Economy*. Cheltenham: Edward Elgar.

Tarlow, P. (2002) *Event Risk Management and Safety*. New York: Wiley.

Tribe, J. (1999) *The Economics of Leisure and Tourism*, 2nd edn. Oxford: Butterworth-Heinemann.

Tomlinson, J. (1991) *Cultural Imperialism: A Critical Introduction*. Baltimore, MD: The Johns Hopkins University Press.

Turner, S. (2007) *Unlocking Contract Law* (Unlocking the Law), 2nd edn. London: Hodder Arnold.

Watson, D. and Head, A. (2013) *Corporate Finance: Principles and Practice*, 6th edn. Harlow: Pearson.

Watt, D.C. (2001) *Event Management in Leisure and Tourism*. Harlow: Pearson Education.

Webster, I., Leib, J. and Button, J. (2007) *The Concise Guide to Licensing*. Leicester: Matador.

Weetman, P. (2010) *Financial and Management Accounting: An Introduction*, 5th edn. Harlow: Financial Times Press/Prentice Hall.

Wickham, P. (2006) *Strategic Entrepreneurship*. Harlow: Financial Times/Prentice Hall.

Wood, F. (2005) *Business Accounting 1*, 8th edn. London: Pitman.

Wood, F. and Sangster, A. (2008) *Business Accounting 1*, 11th edn. London: FT/Pitman Publishing.

Yehsin, T. (1999) *Integrated Marketing Communications*. Oxford: Butterworth-Heinemann.

Yeoman, I., Robertson, M., Ali-Knight, J., Drummond, S. and McMahon-Beattie, U. (2004) *Festival and Events Management: An International Arts and Culture Perspective*. Oxford: Butterworth-Heinemann.

JOURNALS

Alkaraan, F. and Northcott, D. (2006) 'Strategic capital investment decision-making: a role for emergent analysis tool?', *The British Accounting Review*, 38(2): 149–73.

Balasubramanian, S., Peterson, R.A. and Jarvenpaa, S.L. (2002) 'Exploring the implications of m-commerce for markets and marketing', *Journal of the Academy of Marketing Science*, 30(4): 348–61.

Batty, M., Desyllas, J. and Duxbury, E. (2003) 'Safety in numbers? Modelling crowds and designing control for the Notting Hill Carnival', *Urban Studies*, 40: 1537–90.

Bauer, H.H. and Barnes, S.J. (2005) 'Driving consumer acceptance of mobile marketing: theoretical framework and empirical study', *Journal of Electronic Commerce Research*, 6(3): 181–92.

Borden, N.H. (1964) 'The concept of the marketing mix', *Journal of Advertising Research*, 4: 2–7

Boyle, E. (2007) 'A process model of brand co-creation: brand management and research implications', *Journal of Product & Brand Management*, 16(2): 122–31.

Bramwell, B. (1997) 'Strategic planning before and after a mega-event', *Tourism Management*, 18(3): 167–176.

Buch, T., Milne, S. and Dickson, G. (2011) 'Multiple stakeholder perspectives on cultural events: Auckland's Pasifika Festival', *Journal of Hospitality Marketing & Management*, 20: 311–28.

Delamere, T.A., Wankel, L.M. and Hinch, T.D. (2001) 'Development of a scale to measure resident attitudes toward the social impacts of community festivals, part 1: item generation and purification of the measure', *Event Management*, 7(1): 11–24.

Dickinger, A., Haghirian, P., Murphy, J. and Scharl, A. (2004) 'An investigation and conceptual model of SMS marketing'. *Proceedings of the 37th Hawaii International Conference on System Sciences*. DOI: 10.1109/HICSS.2004.1265096.

Dwyer, L., Mellor, R., Mistillis, N. and Mules, T. (2000) 'A framework for assessing "tangible" and "intangible" impacts of events and conventions', *Event Management*, 6: 175–89.

Erickson, G.S. and Kushner, R.J. (1999) 'Public event networks: an application of marketing theory to sporting events', *European Journal of Marketing*, 33(3/4): 348–64.

Foote, D.A. (2004) 'Temporary workers and managing the problem of unscheduled turnover', *Management Decisions*, 42: 863–74.

Gursoy, D., Kim, K. and Uysal, M. (2004) 'Perceived impacts of festivals and special events by organizers: an extension and validation', *Tourism Management*, 25: 171–81.

Hanlon, C. and Jago, L. (2004) 'The challenge of retaining personnel in major sport event organizations', *Event Management*, 9(1–2): 39–49.

Helbing, D., Molnár, P., Farkas, I.J. and Bolay, K. (2001) 'Self-organizing pedestrian movement', *Environment and Planning B: Planning and Design*, 28: 361–83, DOI: 10.1068/b2697.

Kitchen, P.J. and Schultz, D.E. (2000) 'A response to "Theoretical concept or management fashion"', *Journal of Advertising Research*, 40(5): 17–21.

Kobia, M. and Sikalieh, D. (2010) 'Towards a search for the meaning of entrepreneurship', *Journal of European Industrial Training*, 34(2): 110–27.

Krulis-Randa, J. (1990) 'Strategic human resource management in Europe after 1992', *International Journal of Human Resource Management*, 1(2): 131–9.

Lee, M.-S., Sandler, D.M. and Shani, D. (1997) 'Attitudinal constructs towards sponsorship: scale development using three global sporting events', *International Marketing Review*, 14(3): 159–69.

Leopkey, B. and Parent, M.M. (2009) 'Risk management issues in large-scale sporting events: a stakeholder perspective', *European Sport Management Quarterly*, 9(2): 187–208, DOI: 10.1080/16184740802571443.

Mair, J. and Whitford, M. (2013) 'An exploration of events research: event topics, themes and emerging trends', *International Journal of Event and Festival Management*, 4(1): 6–30.

Maslow, A.H. (1943) 'A theory of human motivation', *Psychological Review*, 50(4): 370–96.

McWilliams, G. (2000) 'Building stronger brands through online communities', *Sloan Management Review*, 41(3): 43–54.

Mohr, K., Backman, K., Gahan, L. and Backman, S. (1993) 'An investigation of festival motivations and event satisfaction by visitor type', *Festival Management and Event Tourism*, 1: 89–97.

Myles, G., Friday, A. and Davies, N. (2003). 'Preserving privacy in environments with location-based applications', *Pervasive Computing*, January–March: 56–64.

Ngai, E.W.T. and Gunasekaran, A. (2007) 'A review for mobile commerce research and applications', *Decision Support Systems*, 43: 3–15.

O'Toole, T. (2003) 'E-relationships: emergence and the small firm', *Market Intelligence and Planning*, 21(2): 115–22.

Papatheodorou, A., Rosselló, J. and Xiao, H. (2010) 'Global economic crisis and tourism: consequences and perspectives', *Journal of Travel Research*, 49: 39–45.

Pelham, F. (2011) 'Will sustainability change the business model of the event industry?', *Worldwide Hospitality and Tourism Themes*, 3(3): 187–92.

Pitta, D.A., Franzak, F.J. and Flower, D. (2006) 'A strategic approach to building online customer loyalty: integrating customer profitability tiers', *Journal of Consumer Marketing*, 23(7): 421–9.

Prahalad, C.K. and Ramaswamy, V. (2004) 'Co-creation experiences: the next practice in value creation', *Journal of Interactive Marketing*, 18(3): 5–14.

Raj, R. (2004) 'The impact of cultural festivals on tourism', *Journal of Tourism Today*, 4: 66–77.

Raj, R. (2008) 'The application of destination management models for religious festivals', *Journal of Tourism Today*, 8: 118–28.

Raj, R. and Simpson, H. (2015) 'Exploitation of Notting Hill Carnival to increase community pride and spirit and act as a catalyst for regeneration'. *Journal of Hospitality and Tourism*, 13(1): 27–47.

Raj, R. and Vignali, C. (2010) 'Creating local experiences of cultural tourism through sustainable festivals', *European Journal of Tourism, Hospitality and Recreation*, 1(1): 51–67.

Rashid, T. (2006) 'Relationship marketing and entrepreneurship: South Asian business in the UK', *International Journal of Entrepreneurship and Small Business*, 3(3/4): 417–26.

Scharl, A., Dickinger, A. and Murphy, J. (2005) 'Diffusion and success factors of mobile marketing', *Electronic Commerce Research and Applications*, 4: 159–73.

Shannon, J.R. (1999) 'Sports marketing: an examination of academic marketing publication', *Journal of Services Marketing*, 13(6): 517–35.

Stiernstrand, J. (1996) 'The Nordic model: a theoretical model for economic impact analysis of event tourism', *Festival Management and Event Tourism*, 3: 165–74.

Stuart, E.S. (2012) 'The effect of high-speed communication on crowd attendance and behaviour at events', *Journal of Crowd Safety and Security Management, an online journal*, 2(2): 14–21. Available at: http://ibit.eu/wp-content/uploads/2013/02/Funk-Sabine-2010-The-impact-of-weather-related-hazards-on-risk-assessment-strategies-for-open-air-events-in-Central-Europe-22-34.pdf [accessed 16/11/2016].

Sung, H. and Lee, W. (2015) 'The effect of basic, performance and excitement service factors of a convention center on attendees' experiential value and satisfaction: a case study of the Phoenix Convention Center', *Journal of Convention & Event Tourism*, 16(3): 175–99.

Uysal, M., Gahan, L. and Martin, B. (1993) 'An examination of event motivations', *Festival Management and Event Tourism*, 1: 5–10.

Williams, J. and Lawson, R. (2001) 'Community issues and resident opinions of tourism', *Annals of Tourism Research*, 28(2): 269–90.

WEBSITES

Alphen-Schrade, M. (2014) *Social Media and Events Report*. Available at https://en.xing-events.com/file admin/user_upload/Infomaterial/XINGEVENTS_SMR_EN_low.pdf. accessed 16/04/2016 [accessed 16/04/2016].

Andranovich, G., Burbank, M.J. and Heying, C.H. (2001) 'Olympic Cities: Lessons Learned from Mega Event Politics'. California State University, Los Angeles. Available at: www.academia.edu/4424109/Olympic_Cities_Lessons_Learned_from_Mega-Event_Politics [accessed 24/07/2017].

Annual Reports website for European, UK and Asian financial reports. Available at: www.annualreports.co.uk [accessed 24/07/2017].

AutoSport (2012) Available at: www.autosport.com/news/report.php/id/99121 [accessed 26/04/2012].

Basel Committee on Banking Supervision (2010) *Principles for Enhancing Corporate Governance*. Available at: www.bis.org/publ/bcbs176.pdf [accessed 15/11/2016].

Benson, S. (2013) 'Co-creation 101: How to Use the Crowd as an Innovation Partner to Add Value to Your Brand'. Available at: www.visioncritical.com/cocreation-101/ [accessed 29/04/2016].

Bradford Mela (2011) Available at: www.bing.com/images/search?q=asian+mela+2016&qpvt=asian+mela +2016&qpvt=asian+mela+2016&qpvt=asian+mela+2016&FORM=IGRE [accessed 24/07/2017].

Bradford Telegraph and Argus (2009) 'Thousands Celebrate Mela's 21st Birthday'. Available at: www.thetelegraphandargus.co.uk/news/campaigns/campaigns_brilliant/campaigns_brilliant_news/4437692.display [accessed 14/04/2011].

Brand Finance (2015) *Football 50 2015: The Annual Report on the World's Most Valuable Football Brands*. Available at: http://brandfinance.com/images/upload/bf_football_50_2015.pdf [accessed 15/11/2016].

British Standards Institute (BSI) 'Introducing Standards: Raising Standards Worldwide'. Available at: www.bsi-global.com [accessed 24/06/2016].

British Tourist Authority (2010) 'The British Conference Market Trends Survey 2010'. Available from The Business Tourism Partnership at: www.tourisminsights.info/ONLINEPUB/BUSINESS/BUSINESS%20 PDFS/BUSINESS%20TOURISM%20PARTNERSHIP%20(2003),%20Business%20Tourism%20Briefing%20 %20An%20Overview%20of%20the%20UK%27s%20Business%20Tourism%20Industry,%20BTP,%20 London.pdf [accessed 24/07/2017].

Bughin, J. (2014) 'Three Ways Companies Can Make Co-creation Pay Off'. Available at: www.mckinsey.com/industries/consumer-packaged-goods/our-insights/three-ways-companies-can-make-co-creation-pay-off [accessed 30/3/2016].

Bury Times (2015) Available at: www.burytimes.co.uk/news/12959201.Parklife_Festival_organisers_go_on_charm_offensive_to_ward_off_problems/ [accessed 13/10/2016].

BusinessWire (2016) *Global Exhibition Industry (by Value, by Rented Space, by Country): Trends, Opportunities & Forecasts, 2016–2021 – Research and Markets*. Available at: www.businesswire.com/news/home/20161004005854/en/Global-Exhibition-Industry-Rented-Space-Country-Trends [accessed 16/11/2016].

BVEP (2014) 'BVEP Launches Events are GREAT Britain Report', press release. Available at: http://goo.gl/CyLzJr [accessed 30/04/2016].

Cabinet Office and Emergency Planning College (2009) *Understanding Crowd Behaviours: Guidance and Lessons Identified.* Available at: www.gov.uk/government/uploads/system/uploads/attachment_data/file/62638/guidancelessons1_0.pdf [accessed 01/11/2016].

Camping Flight to Lowlands Paradise (2012) Available at: www.lowlands.nl [accessed 01/04/2012].

Canadian Coalition of Community-based Employability Training (CCBET) (2004) 'Leadership: Fundraising and Resource Development'. Available at: www.savie.qc.ca/Ccocde/An/AccueilPublique.asp [accessed 12/04/2011].

Chartered Institute of Marketing. Available at: www.cim.co.uk/more/getin2marketing/what-is-marketing/ [accessed 21/10/2016].

China Post. Available at: www.chinapost.com.tw [accessed 26/04/2012].

CIA (1968) 'Students Stage Major Disorder in Mexico'. Available at: www.gwu.edu/~nsarchiv/NSAEBB/NSAEBB10/mex03-01.htm [accessed 01/03/2012].

CIPD (Chartered Institute of Personnel and Development) (2011) 'Reflections on the 2005 Training and Development Survey', CIPD, London. Available at: www.cipd.co.uk [accessed 24/07/2017].

CIPR (Chartered Institute of Public Relations) Available at: www.cipr.co.uk/content/careers-advice/what-pr [accessed 25/10/2016].

Civil Aviation Authority (2003) 'Guide for the Operation of Lasers, Searchlights and Fireworks in United Kingdom Airspace'. Available at: www.caa.co.uk [accessed 11/07/2016].

Climate Wave Enterprises (2012) Available at: www.climatewave.com/green-events/green-events-make-economical-social-environmental-sense/ [accessed 20/02/2016].

Comscore (2011) 'Mobile'. Available at: www.comscore.com/Industry_Solutions/Mobile [accessed 01/04/2012].

Corbinball (2016) Available at: www.corbinball.com/bookmarks [accessed 11/11/2016].

Crabtree Associates Ltd, 'Managing a Sports Event Sponsorship for a National Company', CAL Public Relations. Available at: www.calpr.co.nz/what_we_do.php [accessed 24/07/2017].

Daily Mail (2012) 'Armadillo! World Cup mascot for Brazil 2014 unveiled by Ronaldo'. Available at: www.dailymail.co.uk/sport/football/article-2204405/Armadillo-unveiled-mascot-2014-World-Cup-Brazil.html [accessed 12/01/2016].

Daily Mail (2014) Available at: www.dailymail.co.uk/news/article-2835947/The-Great-British-rake-really-happens-billions-donate-charity-Fat-cat-pay-appalling-waste-hidden-agendas.htm [accessed 30/04/2016]

Davis, J. (2013) London School of Economics Public Policy Group. *2012 London Olympics: The Impact of the Olympics: Making or Breaking communities in East London.* Published in British Politics and Policy Blog. Available at: http://blogs.lse.ac.uk/politicsandpolicy/files/2013/01/Olympics.pdf [accessed 01/03/2016].

DCMS (Department for Culture, Media and Sport) (2015) 'Creative Industries Now Worth £8.8 Million an Hour to UK Economy' (press release). Available at: www.gov.uk/government/news/creative-industries-now-worth-88-million-an-hour-to-uk-economy [accessed 15/11/2016].

Defra (2009) *Sustainable Development Indicators in Your Pocket 2009: An Update of the UK Government Strategy Indicators.* London: Department for Environment, Food and Rural Affairs. Available at: www.gov.uk/government/uploads/system/uploads/attachment_data/file/69414/pb13265-sdiyp-2009-a9-090821.pdf [accessed 16/11/2016].

Deloitte (2016a) 'Global Mobile Consumer Survey 2016: UK Cut'. Available at: www.deloitte.co.uk/mobileUK [accessed 16/11/2016].

Deloitte (2016b) 'Leisure Sector Grows to £117 Billion as UK Consumers Prefer Pleasure to Shopping'. Available at: https://www2.deloitte.com/uk/en/pages/press-releases/articles/leisure-sector-grows-to-117-billion.html [accessed 21/11/2016].

Department for Culture Media and Sport. Available at: www.culture.gov.uk/ [accessed 28/04/2011].

Department for Culture, Media and Sport (2013) *Report 5: Post-Games Evaluation. Meta-Evaluation of the Impacts and Legacy of the London 2012 Olympic Games and Paralympic Games.* Available at: www.gov.uk/government/uploads/system/uploads/attachment_data/file/224181/1188-B_Meta_Evaluation.pdf [accessed 18/11/2016].

DTI (2007) *Meeting the Energy Challenge: A White Paper on Energy.* Available at: www.gov.uk/government/publications/meeting-the-energy-challenge-a-white-paper-on-energy [accessed 16/11/2016].

edie.net (2016) 'Rio 2016 Olympics: How Sustainable is the Greatest Show On Earth?'. Available at: www.edie.net/library/Rio-2016-Olympics-sustainability-carbon-emissions-air-and-water-quality/6719 [accessed 18/11/2016].

Edinburgh International Festival (2002) Available at: www.eif.co.uk [accessed 3 January 2012]. Edinburgh Festival also available at: www.festivalsedinburgh.com/sites/default/files/FestivalsImpactRelease2011FINAL.pdf [accessed 01/03/2012].

Event Industry News (2011) Available at: www.eventbrite.co.uk/blog/6-music-trends-in-2015-ds00 [accessed 24/07/2017].

Eventbrite (2015) Available at: www.eventbrite.co.uk/blog/6-music-trends-in-2015-ds00 [accessed 24/07/2017].

Eventia (2010) 'Britain for Events'. Available at: www.eventia.org.uk [accessed 19/06/2012].

Events Industry Forum (2015) *The Purple Guide to Health, Safety and Welfare at Music and Other Events.* Available at: www.thepurpleguide.co.uk [accessed 16/11/2016].

Flora London Marathon (2006) www.marathonfoto.com/Landing/1980200651/flora-london-marathon-2006 [accessed 24/07/2017].

Football Association Premier League. Available at: www.premierleague.com [accessed 30 November 2007].

GCB (2009) 'The German Convention Bureau (GCB) Celebrates Winning the IMEX/GMIC Green Exhibitor Award at IMEX in Frankfurt 2013'. Available at: www.imex-frankfurt.com/press/news-releases/imex-news-releases/2013/05/the-german-convention-bureau-(gcb)-celebrates-winning-the-imexgmic-green-exhibitor-award-at-imex-in-frankfurt-2013 [accessed 16/11/2016].

Geovector www.geovector.com [accessed 06/04/2012].

Government Olympic Executive (2011) *London 2012 Olympic and Paralympic Games: Annual Report February 2011.* Available at: www.gov.uk/government/uploads/system/uploads/attachment_data/file/77633/DCMS_GOE_annual_report_february_2011.pdf [accessed 21/11/2016].

Greater London Authority (2004) 'Notting Hill Carnival: A Strategic Review'. Available at: www.london.gov.uk/moderngov/Data/Culture%20Sport%20and%20Tourism%20Committee/20040310/Agenda/5%20Notting%20Hill%20Carnival%20PDF.pdf [accessed 21/11/2016].

Guay, M. (1976) 'Legacy of the Olympic Games in Montreal – An Introduction'. Available at: http://montrealolympics.com/mg_legacy.php [accessed 01/04/2012].

Hard, R. (n.d.) 'Special Event Planners Identify Sponsorship Categories For Fundraising Events'. Available at: www.eventplanning.about.com/od/eventplanningbasics/a/event-sponsors.htm [accessed 10/01/2012].

Hard, R. (2016) 'Sponsorship Categories for Fundraising Events'. Available at: www.thebalance.com/sponsorship-categories-for-fundraising-events-1223690 [accessed 15/11/2016].

Health and Safety Executive (2004) *Thirty Years On and Looking Forward.* Available at: www.hse.gov.uk/aboutus/reports/30years.pdf [accessed 30/04/2011].

Health and Safety Executive (2014) *Managing Crowds Safely: A Guide for Organisers at Events and Venues.* Available at: www.hse.gov.uk/pubns/priced/hsg154.pdf [accessed 01/11/2016].

HebCelt Festival (2013) Available at: www.eventscotland.org/assets/3607 [accessed 20/02/2016].

Hibberd, M. (2009) 'UK Mobile Usage Patterns'. Available at: http://telecoms.com/opinion/uk-usage-patterns-regular-service [accessed 30/10/2016].

Higgins, D. (2008) 'London 2012 Can Be the "Regeneration Games"', Olympic Board/London 2012. Cited in 'Where's the Olympic spirit?' Available at: www.spiked-online.com/newsite/article/4945#.WC3B601vhNU [accessed 18/11/2016].

HM Treasury (2011) *The Green Book.* Available at: www.gov.uk/government/uploads/system/uploads/attachment_data/file/220541/green_book_complete.pdf [accessed 09/08/17].

Home Office (2015) 'Revised Guidance Issued Under Section 182 of the Licensing Act 2003'. Available at: www.gov.uk/government/uploads/system/uploads/attachment_data/file/418114/182-Guidance2015.pdf [accessed 15/11/2016].

Houghton, Claire (2014) 'Fundraisers – "Stop Firefighting and See the Fire"'. Available at: www.theguardian.com/voluntary-sector-network/2014/feb/04/10-years-time-local-charity-fundraising [accessed 13/10/2016].

IAEE (2015) *Future Trends Impacting the Exhibitions and Events Industry.* Available at: www.iaee.com/docs/document2.pdf [accessed 21/11/2016].

ICOMOS (1999) 'International Cultural Tourism Charter'. Available at: www.icomos-ictc.org [accessed 24/07/2017].

In The City: the UK's International Music Convention and Live Music Festival. Available at: www.manchesterwide.com/2009/08/10/in-the-city-music-convention-and-live-music-festival-manchester-18th-to-20th-october-2009 [accessed 12/08/2016].

Incentives and Meetings International (I&MI) – the worldwide network for professional buyers and planners of international meetings, incentive travel programmes, congresses and corporate events. Available at: www.i-mi.com/Market review [accessed 20/07/2016].

Institution of Civil Engineers (2003) 'Impact of the Olympic Games as Mega-events'. Available at: www.caledonianblogs.net/mefi/files/2011/03/Malfas.pdf [accessed 24/07/2017].

Institution of Structural Engineers (2007) *Temporary Demountable Structures Guidance*, 3rd edn. Available at: www.juicesound.co.uk/tempstructuresguidance1.pdf [accessed 16/11/2016].

International Olympic Committee (2013) 'Factsheet: Legacies of the Games'. Available at: https://stillmed.olympic.org/media/Document%20Library/OlympicOrg/Factsheets-Reference-Documents/Games/Legacies/Factsheet-Legacies-of-the-Games-December-2013.pdf [accessed 18/11/2016].

Keillor, G. (1995) Available at: www.nasaa-arts.org/Research/Best-Practices/State-Spotlight/Minnesota's-Scenic-Byways-Partnership.php [accessed 20/06/2012].

Kim, K. (2002) 'The Effects of Tourism Impacts upon Quality of Life of Residents in the Community' (DPhil thesis). Virginia Polytechnic Institute and State University. Available at: http://theses.lib.vt.edu/theses/available/etd-12062002-123337/unrestricted/Title_and_Text.pdf (accessed 15/11/2016).

Layar (2012) 'Get More out of AR with Layar Vision'. Available at: www.layar.com [accessed 01/04/2012].

Liverpool Culture Company – Liverpool's Matthew Street Festival. Available at: www.liverpool.gov.uk [accessed 13/11/2011].

LOCOG (London Organising Committee for the Olympic Games) (2007) 'London 2012 Sustainable Plan'. Available at: http://discovery.nationalarchives.gov.uk/details/r/C13388178 [accessed 24/07/2017].

LOCOG (London Organising Committee for the Olympic Games) (2008) 'London 2012: Towards One Planet, 2012 Sustainable Plan Update December'. Available at: http://discovery.nationalarchives.gov.uk/details/r/C13388178 [accessed 24/07/2017].

LOCOG (London Organising Committee for the Olympic Games) (2012) 'London 2012 sustainability Guidelines – Corporate and Public Events', third edition. Available at: http://discovery.nationalarchives.gov.uk/details/r/C13388178 [accessed 24/07/2017].

London Borough of Hackney (2008) 'The Hackney State of the Environment Report'. Available at: www.hackney.gov.uk/Assets/Documents/hackney_state_of_the_environment_report_2008.pdf [accessed 02/11/2011].

London Borough of Lambeth (2015) 'Lambeth Local Plan: Authority's Monitoring Report 2015'. Available at: www.lambeth.gov.uk/sites/default/files/annual-monitoring-report-september-2015.pdf [accessed 16/11/2016].

London Legacy Development Corporation (2013) 'Three Year Business Plan 2013/14–2015/16'. Available at: www.queenelizabetholympicpark.co.uk/~/media/qeop/files/public/lldcbusinessplanv42012_132015_161.pdf [accessed 20/11/2016].

Manchester City Council (2006) 'Greater Manchester Air Quality and Action Plan'. Available at: www.greatairmanchester.org.uk/documents/LTP2%20AQ%20Strategy%20and%20Action%20Plan%202006.pdf [accessed 02/11/2011].

Manchester City Council (2007) 'Executive Meeting: Minutes', 14 February. Available at: www.manchester.gov.uk/meetings/meeting/326/executive/attachment/1468 [accessed 21/11/2016].

Manchester Histories Festival (2009) Available at: www.manchesterhistoriesfestival.org.uk [accessed 11/10/2016].

Market Research Media (2010) 'Premium Market Analysis'. Available at: www.marketresearchmedia.com/2010/02/07/virtual-conference/ [accessed 01/04/2012].

Marketing Power. Available at: www.marketingpower.com [accessed 12/03/2012]

Michigan Business School (2004) 'Fundraising' (FACUM). Available at: www.aactmad.org/ppts/fac_UM_fundraising_slides.ppt#31 [accessed 11/03/2007].

Mintel (2004) 'Music Concerts and Festivals', Mintel Report, August 2004. Available at: www.academic.mintel.com [accessed 23/04/2011].

MOJO Concerts, 'MOJO Concerts'. Available at: www.mojo.nl [accessed 01/04/2012].

My Next Race's marathon (2011) Available at: www.mynextrace.com/2011/09/london-marathon-announces-impressivecharity-fund-raising-figures [accessed 20/08/2016].

Ofcom (2011) 'Ofcom Prepares for 4G Mobile Auction'. Available at: http://media.ofcom.org.uk/2011/03/22/ofcom-prepares-for-4g-mobile-auction/ [accessed 01/04/2012].

Office of Financial Management (1997) *Economic Impact of Sydney Olympic Games: Final Report.* NSW Treasury. Available at www.treasury.nsw.gov.au/__data/assets/pdf_file/0020/6644/TRP97-10_The_Economic_Impact_of_the_Sydney_Olympic_Games.pdf [accessed 11/11/2016].

Olympic Delivery Authority (2011) 'The ODA Plan and Budget'. Available at: www.london2012.com/documents/oda-publications/oda-plan-2011.pdf [accessed 01/04/2012].

Osawemen, M. (1987) 'Britain's Relation with South Africa'. Available at: www.niianet.org/documents/articles%20pdf/Britain%27s%20Relation%20with%20South%20Africa.pdf [accessed 15/03/2012].

Panja, T. (2015) www.bloomberg.com/news/articles/2015-02-19/-350-million-hole-is-biggest-brazil-world-cup-legacy-for-hosts [accessed 14/11/2006].

PanStadia & Arena Management, 'Videotron Secures Naming Rights to New Multifunctional Quebec City Arena'. Available at: www.psam.uk.com/tag/naming-rights [accessed 24/07/2017].

Performing Rights Society for Music (2010) 'Adding up the UK Music Industry'. Available at: www.prsformusic.com [accessed 19/06/2012].

Philanthropy UK (2011) 'Charitable Sector Overview'. Available at: http://docplayer.net/32665142-Philanthropy-uk-newsletter-inspiring-giving.html [accessed 24/07/2017].

PLASA (Professional Lighting and Sound Association). Available at: www.plasa.org [accessed 12/11/2016].

PricewaterhouseCoopers (2004) Available at: www.pages.drexel.edu/~rosenl/sports%20Folder/Economic%20Impact%20of%20Olympics%20PWC.pdf [accessed 2/1/2016].

PricewaterhouseCoopers/DCMS (2005) 'Olympic Games Impact Study Final Report'. Available at: www.gamesmonitor.org.uk/files/PWC%20OlympicGamesImpactStudy.pdf [accessed 11/03/2012].

PricewaterhouseCoopers LLP (2012) *The Economic Significance of Meetings to the US Economy: Interim Study Update for 2012.* Available at: www.conventionindustry.org/Files/2012%20ESS/CIC%20Meetings%20ESS%20Update%20EXECUTIVE%20SUMMARY-FINAL.pdf [accessed 01/11/2016].

PSA (Production Services Association). Available at: www.psa.org.uk [accessed 13/04/2011].

Rogers, T. (2013) *Conferences and Conventions: A Global Industry*, 3rd edn. Oxon: Routledge.

Royal Borough of Kensington and Chelsea (2013) 'Notting Hill Carnival 2013: Environmental Impacts and Community Safety. Regulation and Enforcement Review Committee 27 November 2013'. Available at: www.rbkc.gov.uk [accessed 20/10/2016].

Royal Statistical Society (2014) Available at: www.statslife.org.uk/sports/1713-how-much-is-the-premier-league-worth [accessed 29/04/2016].

Scofidio, B. (2009) '2010: Looking Ahead', *Association Meetings Magazine*. Available at: http://meeting-snet.com/corporatemeetingsincentives/news/1123-recession-meetings-impact/index.html [accessed 24/07/2017].

Scottish Government, *Practical Fire Safety Guidance for Places of Entertainment and Assembly*. Available at: www.gov.scot/Resource/0041/00418076.pdf [accessed 16/11/2016].

SEEDA (2009) *Temporary Structures for Outdoor Cultural Events: A Market Opportunity*. Available at: www.secouncils.gov.uk/wp-content/uploads/pdfs/_publications/332-FEI_outdoorStructuresReport.pdf [accessed 16/11/2016].

Seven Pillars Institute (2016) Available at: http://sevenpillarsinstitute.org/case-studies/financing-ethics-and-the-brazilian-olympics [accessed 18/10/2016].

Sport Business Group (2001) 'How to Develop Effective Naming Rights Strategies'. Available at: www.sportbusiness.com/ [accessed 23/03/2011].

Sport England (2006) www.sportengland.org/news-and-features/news/2014/august/7/sport-england-investment-inspires-record-breaking-games-performance [accessed 24/07/2017].

Statista.com (2016a) 'Number of Monthly Active Facebook Users Worldwide as of 3rd Quarter 2016'. Available at: www.statista.com/statistics/264810/number-of-monthly-active-facebook-users-worldwide/ [accessed 16/11/2016].

Statista.com (2016b) 'Leading Social Networks Worldwide as of April 2016, Ranked by Number of Active Users (in millions)'. Available at: www.statista.com/statistics/272014/global-social-networks-ranked-by-number-of-users/ [accessed 02/05/2016].

The Guardian (2011a) www.guardian.co.uk/commentisfree/2011/aug/07/are-pop-festivals-over debate? INTCMP=SRCH [accessed 09/09/2011].

The Guardian (2011b) Available at: www.theguardian.com/culture/2011/aug/28/notting-hill-carnival-police [09/08/2017].

The Saint Lucia Bid for Cricket World Cup West Indies – 2007 (2004) 'Media Guide'. Available at: http://archive.stlucia.gov.lc/gis/nationwide/2004/NationWide21August2004.pdf [accessed 01/03/2016].

The Saudi Arabia Information Resource, the Saudi Ministry of Culture and Information website and official News Agency of Saudi Arabia. Available at: www.saudinf.com [accessed 10/01/2016].

The Voice (2013) Available at: www.voice-online.co.uk/article/notting-hill-carnival-2013-police-arrest-279 [accessed 09/08/2017].

This Is Money (2011) Available at: www.thisismoney.co.uk/money/news/article-2032122/Are-footballers-good-economy-Premier-League-tax-1bn-UK-season.htm [accessed 29/04/2016].

T in the Park. Available at: www.tinthepark.com [accessed 23/11/2011].

UFI (2016) *Global Exhibition Barometer*, 16th edn. Available at: www.ufi.org/wp-content/uploads/2016/07/UFI_Global_Exhibition_Barometer_report17.pdf [accessed 01/11/2016].

UKCAMS (2015) http://ukcams.org.uk/ [accessed 24/07/2017].

UK Music (2015) *Music Tourism: Wish You Were Here 2015*. Available at: www.ukmusic.org/research/music-tourism-wish-you-were-here-2015/ [accessed 07/11/2016].

UK Music (2016) *Wish You Were Here: The Contribution of Live Music to the UK Economy*. Available at: www.ukmusic.org/assets/general/Wish_You_Were_Here_2016_Final.pdf [accessed 15/11/2016].

UK Sponsorship Awards (2014) 'Sponsorship Trends in 2014'. Available at: www.sponsorship-awards.co.uk/sponsorship-trends-2014 [accessed 15/11/2016].

UNEP (2002) Available at: www.uneptie.org/scp/ [accessed 24/07/2017].

United Nations (1993) 'Disaster Management Training Programme'. Available at: www.un-spider.org/risks-and-disasters/the-un-and-disaster-management [accessed 24/07/2017].

United Nations Framework Convention on Climate Change (1997) 'Kyoto Protocol'. Available at: http://unfccc.int/resource/docs/convkp/kpeng.pdf [accessed 02/11/2011].

US Department of Labor, Bureau of Labor Statistics (2011). Available at: www.bls.gov/ooh/Business-and-Financial/Human-resources-specialists.htm#tab-1 [accessed 06/10/2012].

Virgin London Marathon (2010) 'Media Guide'. Available at: http://static.london-marathon.co.uk/down loads/pdf/Media_Guide.pdf [accessed 07/01/2012].

VisitBritain. Available at: www.visitbritain.org/visitor-economy-facts [accessed 28/04/2006].

Vrijetijdshuis Brabant, Vrijetijdshuis. Available at: www.visitbrabant.nl [accessed 16/11/2016].

Weir, F. (2009) 'Russian Nightclub Fire: Corruption behind Lame Horse tragedy?'. Available at: www.csmonitor.com/World/Global-News/2009/1207/russian-nightclub-fire-corruption-behind-lame-horse-tragedy [accessed 27/10/2016].

White Book (2006) 'White Book Directory' (online database). Available at: www.whitebook.co.uk/about/default.aspx [accessed 12/12/2006].

Williams, R. (2015) 'The 10 Best Festival Apps', *The Telegraph*. Available at: www.telegraph.co.uk/technology/news/11680861/The-10-best-festival-apps.html [accessed 07/11/2016].

Work at Height Regulations 2005. Available at: www.legislation.gov.uk/uksi/2005/735/contents/made [accessed 29/10/2016].

Yorkshire Evening Post (2002) Available at: www.thisisleeds.co.uk/ [accessed 24/12/2011].

INDEX

Page numbers in *italics* refer to figures and tables.